West's Law School
Advisory Board

JESSE H. CHOPER
Professor of Law,
University of California, Berkeley

DAVID P. CURRIE
Professor of Law, University of Chicago

YALE KAMISAR
Professor of Law, University of San Diego
Professor of Law, University of Michigan

MARY KAY KANE
Chancellor, Dean and Distinguished Professor of Law,
University of California,
Hastings College of the Law

LARRY D. KRAMER
Dean and Professor of Law, Stanford Law School

WAYNE R. LaFAVE
Professor of Law, University of Illinois

JONATHAN R. MACEY
Professor of Law, Yale Law School

ARTHUR R. MILLER
Professor of Law, Harvard University

GRANT S. NELSON
Professor of Law,
University of California, Los Angeles

JAMES J. WHITE
Professor of Law, University of Michigan

West's Law School
Advisory Board

JESSE H. CHOPER
Professor of Law,
University of California, Berkeley

DAVID P. CURRIE
Professor of Law, University of Chicago

YALE KAMISAR
Professor of Law, University of San Diego
Professor of Law, University of Michigan

MARY KAY KANE
Chancellor, Dean and Distinguished Professor of Law,
University of California,
Hastings College of the Law

LARRY D. KRAMER
Dean and Professor of Law, Stanford Law School

WAYNE R. LaFAVE
Professor of Law, University of Illinois

JONATHAN R. MACEY
Professor of Law, Yale Law School

ARTHUR R. MILLER
Professor of Law, Harvard University

GRANT S. NELSON
Professor of Law,
University of California, Los Angeles

JAMES J. WHITE
Professor of Law, University of Michigan

THE PRACTICE OF FEDERAL CRIMINAL LAW:

Prosecution and Defense

By

Harry I. Subin
Professor of Law Emeritus
New York University School of Law

Barry H. Berke
Partner
Kramer, Levin, Naftalis and Frankel, LLP

and

Eric A. Tirschwell
Partner
Kramer, Levin, Naftalis and Frankel, LLP

AMERICAN CASEBOOK SERIES®

Mat #40143888

Thomson/West have created this publication to provide you with accurate and authoritative information concerning the subject matter covered. However, this publication was not necessarily prepared by persons licensed to practice law in a particular jurisdiction. Thomson/West are not engaged in rendering legal or other professional advice, and this publication is not a substitute for the advice of an attorney. If you require legal or other expert advice, you should seek the services of a competent attorney or other professional.

American Casebook Series and West Group are trademarks registered in the U.S. Patent and Trademark Office.

© 2006 Thomson/West
    610 Opperman Drive
    P.O. Box 64526
    St. Paul, MN 55164–0526
    1–800–328–9352

Printed in the United States of America

ISBN–13: 978–0–314–14613–7
ISBN–10: 0–314–14613–X

TEXT IS PRINTED ON 10% POST CONSUMER RECYCLED PAPER

About the Authors

HARRY I. SUBIN graduated from Yale Law School in 1960. From 1961–1966 he served as a trial attorney in the Organized Crime and Racketeering Section of the U.S. Department of Justice and then in the Department's Office of Criminal Justice and as a Consultant to the President's Commission on Crime and the Administration of Justice. He was Associate Director of the Vera Institute of Justice in New York City from 1966–1969, when he joined the faculty of New York University School of Law. He has taught criminal law, criminal procedure, professional responsibility in criminal practice, and founded clinical and advocacy programs in criminal defense and prosecution. He is now professor emeritus at the school, where he continues to teach seminars in federal criminal practice and other subjects in the criminal law field.

BARRY H. BERKE graduated *cum laude* from Harvard Law School in 1989 and served as a law clerk to Judge Mary Johnson Lowe of the U.S. District Court for the Southern District of New York. From 1990 through 1995, he served as a trial lawyer with the Federal Defender's office in the Southern District of New York where he defended individuals accused of a wide variety of federal offenses in pretrial, trial and sentencing proceedings. He is now co-chair of the White Collar Defense Practice at Kramer Levin Naftalis & Frankel LLP where he defends individuals and corporations in complex criminal and regulatory matters. Since 1995, he has taught courses on professional responsibility and criminal law at New York University School of Law, and lectured frequently on criminal justice issues in a variety of forums.

ERIC A. TIRSCHWELL graduated *cum laude* from Harvard Law School in 1992 and then served as a law clerk to the Hon. David V. Kenyon of the United States District Court in Los Angeles. From 1997 through 2002, he served as an Assistant United States Attorney in the Eastern District of New York, where he prosecuted the full range of federal crimes, from securities fraud, money laundering and mail fraud to embezzlement, international narcotics trafficking and firearms violations. He also served as a deputy section chief, training and supervising new criminal prosecutors. He is now a partner at Kramer Levin Naftalis and Frankel LLP, where he practices principally in the area of white collar defense. From 2001 through 2003 he served as Adjunct Professor of Legal Writing at Fordham University School of Law.

*

Preface

This book examines the work of prosecutors and defense attorneys in applying the constitutional, statutory, ethical and other rules that govern the federal criminal process, from investigation to the decision to charge and through disposition by trial or plea and sentence.

The book is aimed primarily at law students, beginning prosecutors and defense attorneys, federal law clerks, and others whose exposure to the field has largely been through treatises focused on criminal procedure doctrine and case books focused on treatment of that doctrine on appeal. As essential as such sources are, they are not designed to explain how lawyers implement the law of criminal procedure in practice. We discuss the relevant rules in detail, but our principal aim is to contextualize this body of law, describing the real-world process of prosecuting and defending those accused of crime, proving facts, and the skills involved in applying the law to those facts. To accomplish this goal, we use a hypothetical case involving numerous defendants that provides a basis for examining the critical stages of the criminal process and a variety of scenarios that arise at each stage. In addition, we attempt to provide guidance as to how prosecutors and defense attorneys can perform their functions most effectively.

The book includes a full exploration of the operation and impact of the federal Sentencing Guidelines on the federal criminal process, including the implications of the Supreme Court's landmark decision in 2005 in *Booker v. United States*, which transformed those Guidelines from mandatory to advisory only.

The book is exclusively concerned with the federal process, because of its near uniformity in federal districts throughout the country and because state criminal processes are so heavily modeled on it. To the extent that differences in rules and procedures exist, however, they are rarely pronounced, and thus we believe that the book may be useful to those concerned with state practice as well.

HARRY I. SUBIN
BARRY H. BERKE
ERIC A. TIRSCHWELL

December, 2005
New York, New York

*

Acknowledgements

This book had its origin in a set of teaching materials created by Professors Harry I. Subin and Chester L. Mirsky at New York University School of Law. The materials were designed to be used for a course entitled Criminal Procedure and Practice, an eight credit, year long effort in which students not only read case law, but experienced the way in which criminal procedure doctrine was implemented by prosecutors and defense attorneys. Assigned in pairs to simulated federal cases, they performed the written and oral advocacy and engaged in the decision-making involved at each stage of the process from investigation to indictment through jury trial and sentencing.

The materials were revised and published in 1992, as H. Subin, C. Mirsky and I. Weinstein, "Federal Criminal Practice: Prosecution and Defense" (West's Criminal Practice Series), and reprinted the following year by West's Law School Division as "The Criminal Process: Prosecution and Defense Functions."

The present effort, while retaining some of the material found in the earlier version, is substantially revised and expanded in order to explore more fully certain critical aspects of federal practice—most notably the enormous impact of the Federal Sentencing Guidelines and the recent rulings of the United States Supreme Court relating to them—and to account for changes in that practice over the past 13 years.

We wish to acknowledge our great debt to Chet Mirsky, whose experience and wisdom is reflected throughout this work, but whose health prevented him from participating with us. We wish him well. We also wish to thank Professor Ian Weinstein for his contribution to the book's earlier version.

We thank the many associates and summer associates at the Kramer Levin law firm who made significant contributions to various parts of the book, but most especially express our gratitude to Savvas Diacosavvas for his tremendous contributions in updating and revising the manuscript following the upheaval in federal criminal practice wrought by the Supreme Court's January 2005 decision in *Booker v. United States*.

HARRY I. SUBIN
BARRY H. BERKE
ERIC A. TIRSCHWELL

December, 2005
New York, New York

*

Table of Frequent Citations

The following authorities are frequently cited throughout the text in the manner indicated here:

Susan W. Brenner & Gregory G. Lockhart, Federal Grand Jury: A Guide to Law and Practice (1996 & Supp. 2004), *cited as* Brenner & Lockhart

Wayne R. LaFave, Search and Seizure (4th ed. 2004), *cited as* LaFave, Search

Wayne R. LaFave, Jerold H. Israel & Nancy J. King, Criminal Procedure (2d ed. 1999 & Supp. 2004), *cited as* LaFave et al.

Thomas A. Mauet, Trial Techniques (5th ed. 2000), *cited as* Mauet

James Wm. Moore, Moore's Federal Practice § 605.03 (3d ed. & Supp. 2004), *cited as* Moore

John W. Strong, McCormick on Evidence (5th ed. 1999 & Supp. 2003), *cited as* McCormick

U.S. Department of Justice, U.S. Attorneys' Manual *available at* http://www.usdoj.gov/usao/eousa/foia_reading_room/usam/ (May 16, 2005), *cited as* U.S. Attorneys' Manual

Jack B. Weinstein & Margaret A. Berger, Weinstein's Federal Evidence (Joseph M. McLaughlin, ed., 2d ed. 1997 & Supp. 2005), *cited as* Weinstein & Berger

Charles Alan Wright, Federal Practice and Procedure: Criminal (2d & 3d eds. 1999 & Supp. 2005), *cited as* Wright

*

Summary of Contents

Page

ABOUT THE AUTHORS -- iii
PREFACE -- v
ACKNOWLEDGEMENTS -- vii
TABLE OF FREQUENT CITATIONS -- ix
TABLE OF CASES -- xxvii
TABLE OF STATUTES AND RULES -- xxxv

Chapter

1. Overview of the Federal Criminal Process---------------------------------- 1

PART I. THE DEVELOPMENT OF A POLICE INITIATED FEDERAL CASE

2. U.S. v. Mario Long—The Investigation------------------------------------- 10
3. Proof in the Criminal Process --- 26
4. The Initial Decision to Charge: Commencing a Police–Initiated
      Case by Complaint --- 44
5. Proceedings on the Complaint—The Initial Appearance, Bail
      and Preventive Detention -- 70
6. The Preliminary Hearing --- 105

PART II. THE GUILTY PLEA SYSTEM

7. Assessing the Risk of Trial—The Federal Sentencing Guidelines 122
8. Plea Negotiation and the Cooperating Defendant------------------- 145
9. The Guilty Plea Proceeding --- 179

PART III. THE DEVELOPMENT OF A FEDERAL CRIMINAL CASE INITIATED BY THE PROSECUTOR

10. Pre–Indictment Investigations--- 196
11. The Decision to Indict -- 243
12. Plea Negotiation and the Non–Cooperating Defendant------------ 287

PART IV. THE TRIAL PROCESS

13. Pretrial Discovery--- 316
14. Pretrial Motions -- 351
15. Preparation for Trial-- 392
16. The Trial--- 415

Page

PART V.   SENTENCING
Chapter

17.   Sentencing _____ 484

APPENDIX A.   SELECTED PROVISIONS OF THE UNITED STATES CONSTITUTION   527
APPENDIX B.   SELECTED RULES OF FEDERAL CRIMINAL PROCEDURE _____ 529
APPENDIX C.   CHRONOLOGY OF U.S. v. CHRISTOPHER _____ 589
INDEX _____ 593

Table of Contents

                                                                      Page
ABOUT THE AUTHORS --- iii
PREFACE --- v
ACKNOWLEDGEMENTS -- vii
TABLE OF FREQUENT CITATIONS --- ix
TABLE OF CASES --- xxvii
TABLE OF STATUTES AND RULES -- xxxv

Chapter 1. Overview of the Federal Criminal Process -------- 1
§ 1.0   Introduction --- 1
§ 1.1   The Formal Stages of the Federal Criminal Process -------- 2
         § 1.1(a) The Decision to Charge --------------------------- 2
         § 1.1(b) Proceedings on the Complaint -------------------- 3
         § 1.1(c) Proceedings on the Indictment ------------------- 3
         § 1.1(d) Pretrial Proceedings --------------------------- 4
         § 1.1(e) The Trial -------------------------------------- 4
         § 1.1(f) Sentencing ------------------------------------- 5
         § 1.1(g) Appeal --- 5
§ 1.2   The Guilty Plea Process --------------------------------- 5
§ 1.3   Preliminary Reflections on the Federal System ----------- 6

PART I.   THE DEVELOPMENT OF A POLICE INITIATED FEDERAL CASE

Chapter 2.   U.S. v. Mario Long—The Investigation ----------- 10
§ 2.0   Introduction --- 10
§ 2.1   The Investigation by the Drug Enforcement Administra-
         tion --- 10
§ 2.2   The Search and Arrests --------------------------------- 12
§ 2.3   Booking and Identification Procedures ------------------ 14
§ 2.4   The Post–Arrest Investigation -------------------------- 14
         § 2.4(a) Interrogation ---------------------------------- 14
         § 2.4(b) Consent Tape Recording ------------------------ 16
§ 2.5   Memorializing the Investigation—The DEA Reports -------- 17
§ 2.6   Presenting the Case to the United States Attorney's Office   25

Chapter 3.   Proof in the Criminal Process ----------------- 26
§ 3.0   Introduction --- 26
§ 3.1   The Burden of Proof—An Overview ------------------------ 27
         § 3.1(a) The Quantitative Burden ----------------------- 27
         (1) Probable Cause ------------------------------------- 27
         (2) Preponderance of the Evidence ---------------------- 27

Page

(3) Clear and Convincing Evidence 27

(4) Proof Beyond a Reasonable Doubt 27

§ 3.1(b) The Qualitative Burden 28

§ 3.1(c) Allocation of the Burden of Proof 28

  1. Asserting a Claim—The Burden of Going Forward 29

  2. Prevailing on a Claim—The Burden of Persuasion 29

§ 3.2 Proving Facts—Methods of Proof 30

§ 3.2(a) Written Allegations of Fact 30

(1) Charging a defendant with a crime 30

(2) Pretrial motions 31

§ 3.2(b) Live Witness Testimony 31

§ 3.2(c) Written or Oral Proffers of Evidence 31

§ 3.3 Proving Facts—The Evidentiary Hearing 31

§ 3.3(a) The Hearing Process 32

§ 3.3(b) Proof Through Examination of Witnesses—Who Can Be a Witness 33

(1) Competence 33

(2) Relevance 34

(3) Reliability 34

§ 3.3(c) Types of Witnesses 35

  (1) Occurrence witnesses 35

  (2) Authentication witnesses 35

  (3) Opinion witnesses 36

§ 3.3(d) Forms of Questions 36

  (1) Narrative Questions 36

  (2) Open Questions 37

  (3) Closed Questions 37

  (4) Leading Questions 37

§ 3.3(e) Presenting Witnesses—Direct Examination 37

  1. The Structure of Direct Examination 37

  2. Form of Questions on Direct Examination 38

    (a) Narrative Questions 38

    (b) Open Questions 38

    (c) Closed Questions 39

    (d) Leading Questions 39

§ 3.3(f) Confronting Witnesses—Cross–Examination 39

  1. Types of Cross–Examination 39

    (a) Discovery Cross–Examination 39

    (b) Accrediting Cross–Examination 40

    (c) Discrediting Cross–Examination 40

  2. Structuring Cross–Examination; Forms of Questions 41

§ 3.3(g) Controlling Testimony—Objections 41

§ 3.3(h) Rebuttal Evidence 42

§ 3.3(i) Argument 42

Page

Chapter 4. The Initial Decision to Charge: Commencing a Police–Initiated Case by Complaint **44**
§ 4.0   Introduction 44
§ 4.1   The Role of the Complaint in the Charging Process 46
§ 4.2   The Burden of Proof 46
           § 4.2(a) Allocation of the Burdens of Going Forward and of Persuasion 47
           § 4.2(b) Quantitative and Qualitative Burdens 47
§ 4.3   Jurisdictional Issues 48
§ 4.4   Prosecutorial Policy 48
§ 4.5   Learning the Facts of the Case—Interviewing the Case Agent 49
           (1) Searches and seizures—Fourth Amendment protections 50
           (2) Interrogation—The Fifth Amendment protection against self-incrimination 51
           (3) Identification procedures—Fifth Amendment protection of due process rights 52
§ 4.6   The Superior Warehouse Investigation—The Case Assessment 52
           (1) Jurisdiction, Venue, Timeliness and Legal Issues Related to the Arrest 53
           (2) Sufficiency of the Evidence 53
           (3) Legal Issues Arising From the Investigation 55
§ 4.7   Time Constraints on the Filing of the Complaint 55
§ 4.8   Drafting the Complaint 56
§ 4.9   The Complaint in United States v. Santiago, Long and Murphy 57
           § 4.9(a) Meeting the Quantitative Burden 60
           § 4.9(b) Meeting the Qualitative Burden 60
§ 4.10   Warrants 61
           § 4.10(a) Arrest Warrants 61
           § 4.10(b) Search Warrants 61
           § 4.10(c) The Santiago Arrest Warrant 62
           § 4.10(d) The Search Warrant for Superior Warehouse 63
§ 4.11   Proceedings on Arrest and Search Warrants—United States v. Santiago 68

Chapter 5. Proceedings on the Complaint—The Initial Appearance, Bail and Preventive Detention **70**
§ 5.0   Introduction 71
§ 5.1   The Entry of Defense Counsel 72
           § 5.1(a) The Right to Counsel 72
           § 5.1(b) The Initial Defense Interview 74
§ 5.2   Conflicts of Interest 76
           § 5.2(a) Joint Representation 77
           § 5.2(b) Joint Defense Agreements 78
           § 5.2(c) Conflicts with Other Clients 79

Page

§ 5.3   Commencing the Initial Appearance 80
§ 5.4   Reviewing the Sufficiency of the Complaint 80
§ 5.5   Pretrial Release and Detention Proceedings—General 81
§ 5.6   Pretrial Release 81
         § 5.6(a) Standards for Release 81
         § 5.6(b) The Pretrial Release Hearing 83
         § 5.6(c) Conducting the Pretrial Release Proceeding 83
§ 5.7   Preventive Detention Proceedings—Introduction 84
         § 5.7(a) Who May Be Detained 84
                  (1) Eligibility Based Upon the Offense Charged   85
                  (2) Eligibility Based on a Specific Danger Posed
                      by the Defendant 85
                  (3) Detention Based on Conduct After Pretrial
                      Release 85
         § 5.7(b) Detention Proceedings 86
                  1. The quantitative burden of proof 86
                  2. The qualitative burden of proof 87
         § 5.7(c) Review of Detention Decisions 87
§ 5.8   Time Considerations at the Initial Appearance 88
§ 5.9   Ancillary Proceedings at the Initial Appearance 88
         § 5.9(a) Removal Proceedings 88
         § 5.9(b) Temporary Detention 89
§ 5.10   The Initial Appearances of Mario Long, Arthur Murphy
         and Gilbert Santiago 89
         § 5.10(a) The Initial Appearance in U.S. v. Mario Long 90
         § 5.10(b) The Initial Appearance in U.S. v. Arthur Mur-
                  phy 93
         § 5.10(c) The Initial Appearance in U.S. v. Santiago 98
§ 5.11   Litigating the Preventive Detention Issue—U.S. v. Gilbert
         Santiago 99
         § 5.11(a) The Hearing 99
         § 5.11(b) Motion to Review the Detention Decision 103

Chapter 6. The Preliminary Hearing 105
§ 6.0   Introduction 105
§ 6.1   Burden of Proof 107
§ 6.2   Strategic Considerations 107
         § 6.2(a) The Prosecutor 107
         § 6.2(b) Defense Counsel 108
                  (1) Monitoring the direct case 108
                  (2) Conducting the cross-examination 108
                  (3) Presenting defense witnesses 110
§ 6.3   United States v. Santiago 110
         § 6.3(a) The Government's Case 110
         § 6.3(b) Cross–Examination of the Government's Witness 114

PART II. THE GUILTY PLEA SYSTEM

Chapter 7. Assessing the Risk of Trial—The Federal Sentencing Guidelines ------ **122**
§ 7.0 Introduction ------ 122
§ 7.1 The Substantive Law of Sentencing—Introduction ------ 127
§ 7.2 Computing the Sentence ------ 128
  § 7.2(a) Determining the Base Offense Level ------ 128
  § 7.2(b) Applying Specific Offense Characteristics ------ 128
  § 7.2(c) Relevant Conduct ------ 129
  § 7.2(d) Applying Adjustments ------ 130
      (1) Victim Related Adjustments ------ 131
      (2) Role in the Offense Adjustments ------ 131
      (3) Obstruction of Justice Adjustments ------ 131
      (4) Acceptance of Responsibility Adjustments ------ 131
  § 7.2(e) Special Rules for Convictions on Multiple Counts 132
      (1) Closely Related Offenses ------ 133
      (2) Offenses Not Closely Related ------ 133
  § 7.2(f) Calculating the Adjusted Offense Level ------ 134
  § 7.2(g) Determining the Defendant's Criminal History --- 134
  § 7.2(h) Calculating the Guidelines Range ------ 135
  § 7.2(i) Departures ------ 137
§ 7.3 Non–Guidelines Sentences after *Booker* ------ 141

Chapter 8. Plea Negotiation and the Cooperating Defendant ------ **145**
§ 8.0 Introduction ------ 145
§ 8.1 The Decision to Cooperate ------ 146
§ 8.2 The Cooperation Process—Overview ------ 148
  § 8.2(a) The Proffer Session ------ 148
  § 8.2(b) The Cooperation–Plea Agreement ------ 150
§ 8.3 United States v. Santiago—The Cooperation Process ------ 152
  § 8.3(a) The Defense Position ------ 152
  § 8.3(b) The Government's Position ------ 154
  § 8.3(c) Beginning the Cooperation Process ------ 156
  § 8.3(d) Preparing for The Proffer Session ------ 157
  § 8.3(e) Santiago's Proffer Agreement and Statement ------ 158
  § 8.3(f) Santiago's Cooperation–Plea Agreement ------ 167
§ 8.4 Drafting the Formal Charges—Waiver of Indictment and Information ------ 174
§ 8.5 United States v. Mario Long—The Cooperation–Plea Agreement ------ 176
§ 8.6 United States v. Arthur Murphy ------ 177

Chapter 9. The Guilty Plea Proceeding ------ **179**
§ 9.0 Introduction ------ 179
§ 9.1 Pleading Alternatives Under Rule 11 ------ 180
§ 9.2 The Plea Agreement Process ------ 181

                                                              Page
§ 9.2(a) Negotiations Between the Parties 181
§ 9.2(b) Consideration of the Plea Agreement By the
          Court 182
§ 9.2(c) The Plea Allocution 182
§ 9.3 Counsel in the Guilty Plea Process—Providing Effective
       Assistance 184
§ 9.4 The Entry of the Guilty Plea in United States v. Santiago 185
§ 9.5 The Entry of the Guilty Plea in United States v. Long
       Case 192

PART III.   THE DEVELOPMENT OF A FEDERAL CRIMINAL CASE INITIATED BY THE PROSECUTOR

Chapter 10.   Pre–Indictment Investigations **196**
§ 10.0 Introduction 197
§ 10.1 Follow-Up Investigation by Law Enforcement Agents 197
§ 10.2 Obtaining Court Authorization for Police Investigation 198
§ 10.3 The Grand Jury 199
        § 10.3(a) The Grand Jury's Investigative Powers 199
        § 10.3(b) The Role of the United States Attorney in the
                   Grand Jury Investigation 201
        § 10.3(c) Compelling Attendance Before the Grand
                   Jury—The Subpoena 202
        § 10.3(d) The Attorney as Witness 203
        § 10.3(e) Obtaining Immunity for a Witness 203
        § 10.3(f) Representation of Putative Defendants and Wit-
                   nesses Before the Grand Jury 204
            1. Advising Witnesses During Testimony 204
            2. Raising Legal Challenges to Subpoenas 205
                (a) Subpoenas Ad Testificandum 205
                (b) Subpoenas Duces Tecum 205
        § 10.3(g) Compelling Compliance With Grand Jury Com-
                   mands—Civil and Criminal Contempt 207
            (1) Civil Contempt 207
            (2) Criminal Contempt 208
§ 10.4 Approaching and Defending Witnesses and Targets: Intro-
        duction 208
        § 10.4(a) Approaching and Defending Witnesses and Tar-
                   gets: The Government's Perspective 209
        § 10.4(b) Representing Witnesses and Targets 212
§ 10.5 Pre–Indictment Practice in the Superior Warehouse Inves-
        tigation 213
        § 10.5(a) The Government's Review of the Evidence, Po-
                   tential Defendants and Charges 213
            1. The Case Against Paul Christopher 213
                (a) Narcotics Trafficking: Importation, Pos-
                     session with Intent to Distribute, Dis-
                     tribution and Conspiracy to do the
                     Same 214

Page

(b) Money Laundering and Conspiracy to do the Same 214
(c) Structuring and Conspiracy to do the Same 215
2. The Case Against William Van Ness 216
3. The Case Against Ernest Wagner 217
§ 10.5(b) Devising an Investigative Strategy 217
§ 10.5(c) Preliminary Investigative Steps 219
§ 10.5(d) Court Orders 223
§ 10.5(e) Approaching a Witness in the Christopher Case: Barbara Weiss 228
§ 10.5(f) Representing A Witness: Barbara Weiss 231
§ 10.5(g) The Grand Jury Presentation 235
§ 10.5(h) Approaching a Target/Potential Cooperator: Ernest Wagner 236
§ 10.5(i) Representing Ernest Wagner 238

Chapter 11. The Decision to Indict **243**
§ 11.0 Introduction 244
§ 11.1 Grand Jury Review 244
§ 11.1(a) Overview of the Grand Jury Process 244
§ 11.1(b) Burden of Proof at the Indictment Stage 245
§ 11.1(c) Factors Involved in the Prosecutor's Decision to Seek an Indictment 248
§ 11.1(d) Selecting the Charges 250
§ 11.1(e) Indicting a Corporation 253
§ 11.2 Drafting the Indictment 255
§ 11.2(a) General Rules 255
§ 11.2(b) The Count 256
(1) The Gravamen Paragraph 256
(2) The Means Paragraph 257
§ 11.3 Multi–Count and Multi-Defendant Indictments 258
§ 11.3(a) Joinder of Offenses—Constitutional Limitations on Multiple Prosecutions for the Same Offense 259
§ 11.3(b) Joinder of Offenses—Constitutional Limitations on Multiple Punishment for the Same Offense 259
§ 11.3(c) Permissive Joinder of Offenses—Single Defendant Indictments 261
§ 11.3(d) Permissive Joinder of Defendants 262
§ 11.4 Forfeiture 263
§ 11.5 Proceedings on the Indictment 265
§ 11.5(a) Arrest or Surrender of the Defendant 265
§ 11.5(b) Arraignment on the Indictment 265
§ 11.6 Time Limits on Returning the Indictment 266
§ 11.7 The Christopher Indictment 268
§ 11.7(a) Deciding Who to Charge and What to Charge Them With 268
(1) Christopher 268

Page

(2) William Van Ness ----------------------------- 269
(3) Ernest Wagner ------------------------------- 270
(4) CMS Bank ----------------------------------- 270
§ 11.7(b) The Indictment -------------------------- 271
§ 11.8 Grand Jury Presentation in the Christopher Case ------------ 281
§ 11.9 The Arraignments of Christopher, Van Ness and Wagner -- 284

Chapter 12. Plea Negotiation and the Non–Cooperating Defendant --- **287**
§ 12.0 Introduction --- 287
§ 12.1 Charge Bargaining ------------------------------------ 289
§ 12.2 Sentence Bargaining ----------------------------------- 292
§ 12.3 Plea Bargaining for Judicial Leniency: Departures and Non–Guidelines Sentences ----------------------------------- 297
§ 12.4 Additional Features of Plea Agreements ------------------- 299
§ 12.5 Pleas Without an Agreement ---------------------------- 301
§ 12.6 Counseling and Negotiating a Plea: The Defense Lawyer's Perspective --- 301
§ 12.7 The Wagner Plea Negotiation --------------------------- 303
§ 12.7(a) The Government's Position ----------------------- 303
§ 12.7(b) The Defendant's Position ----------------------- 305
§ 12.7(c) The Negotiation-------------------------------- 307
§ 12.8 The Agreement -------------------------------------- 310
§ 12.9 Wagner's Guilty Plea --------------------------------- 313

PART IV. THE TRIAL PROCESS

Chapter 13. Pretrial Discovery --------------------------------- **316**
§ 13.0 Introduction --- 317
§ 13.1 The Law of Discovery—Policy Considerations ------------- 319
§ 13.2 The Right to Notice ----------------------------------- 319
§ 13.2(a) The Defendant's Right to Notice ----------------- 319
§ 13.2(b) The Government's Right to Notice --------------- 321
§ 13.3 The Defendant's Right to Exculpatory Evidence ------------ 322
§ 13.3(a) What Constitutes *Brady* Material --------------- 322
§ 13.3(b) The Materiality Standard ---------------------- 323
§ 13.3(c) The Timing of Disclosure of *Brady* Material ------ 323
§ 13.4 Discovery of Defendant's Prior Criminal Record and Statements, and Witness Statements ------------------------------ 324
§ 13.4(a) Discovery by the Defense of the Defendant's Prior Criminal Record and Statements --------------- 324
§ 13.4(b) Discovery of Government Witnesses and Their Statements by the Defense ----------------------------- 324
§ 13.4(c) Discovery of the Statements of Defense Witnesses by the Government ----------------------------- 327
§ 13.5 Discovery of Documents, Tangible Objects, Reports of Examinations, and Criminal Records ---------------------------- 327
§ 13.5(a) Discovery by the Defense --------------------- 327
§ 13.5(b) Discovery by the Prosecution ------------------ 328

Page

§ 13.6   The Pretrial Discovery Process ---------------------------------- 329
          § 13.6(a) The Initial Discovery Request ------------------------ 329
          § 13.6(b) The Discovery Conference --------------------------- 330
          § 13.6(c) The Final Discovery Letter ------------------------- 330
§ 13.7   Informal Defense Discovery ----------------------------------- 330
          § 13.7(a) Witness Interviews by Defense Counsel ----------- 332
          § 13.7(b) Informal Discovery From the Government ------- 334
          § 13.7(c) Informal Discovery From Other Sources --------- 335
          § 13.7(d) Rule 17(c) Subpoenas ---------------------------- 335
§ 13.8   United States v. Christopher ---------------------------------- 337
          § 13.8(a) Defense Interviews ------------------------------- 337
                     1. Interview of Paul Christopher --------------- 337
                     2. Interview of William Van Ness -------------- 338
                     3. Joint Defense Meeting ---------------------- 339
          § 13.8(b) The Defense Attorneys' Post–Interview Evalua-
                     tion of the Christopher Case ------------------- 339
                     (1) The Indictment --------------------------- 339
                     (2) The Evidence Against Christopher -------- 339
                     (3) The Evidence Against Van Ness ---------- 340
          § 13.8(c) The Discovery Conference ------------------------ 340
          § 13.8(d) Discovery Letters ------------------------------- 341

Chapter 14. Pretrial Motions ------------------------------------- **351**
§ 14.0   Introduction --- 351
§ 14.1   The Statutory Design --- 352
§ 14.2   Drafting the Motion -- 354
          § 14.2(a) Formal Motion Practice ---------------------------- 354
          § 14.2(b) Motion Practice Variations ----------------------- 355
§ 14.3   Grounds for Motions -- 355
          § 14.3(a) Motions for Discovery --------------------------- 356
          § 14.3(b) Motions to Suppress Evidence ------------------- 356
          § 14.3(c) Defenses and Objections Based on Defects in the
                     Institution of the Prosecution -------------------- 356
          § 14.3(d) Defenses and Objections Based on Defects in
                     the Indictment ---------------------------------- 357
§ 14.4   Strategic Considerations ------------------------------------- 357
§ 14.5   The Christopher Motion Papers ------------------------------- 358
§ 14.6   The Government's Response to the Pretrial Motion --------- 372
§ 14.7   Hearings on Pretrial Motions—Introduction ----------------- 379
§ 14.8   Commencing the Hearing—The Burden of Proof ------------- 380
          § 14.8(a) The Burden of Going Forward -------------------- 380
          § 14.8(b) The Burden of Persuasion --------------------- 380
          § 14.8(c) The Qualitative Burden ------------------------- 381
          § 14.8(d) The Quantitative Burden ---------------------- 381
§ 14.9   Examination of Witnesses—Tactical Considerations --------- 381
§ 14.10   Final Argument --- 383
§ 14.11   The Christopher Hearing ------------------------------------- 383
§ 14.12   Appeal From an Adverse Determination --------------------- 389
§ 14.13   Setting a Trial Date—Time Limitations ---------------------- 389

Page

Chapter 15.   Preparation for Trial **392**

§ 15.0   Introduction 392

§ 15.1   Constructing a Trial Theory 393

§ 15.1(a) The Burden of Proof at Trial 393

§ 15.1(b) Trial Theories 394

1. "Pure" Reasonable Doubt 394

2. Conflicting Evidence 395

3. Justification or Excuse 395

§ 15.2   Articulating the Trial Theory—Formulating the Closing

Argument 395

§ 15.3   Proving the Trial Theory—Marshalling the Evidence 396

§ 15.4   Addressing Legal Issues Prior to Trial 397

§ 15.4(a) *In Limine* Motions 397

§ 15.4(b) Proposed Voir Dire Questions 398

§ 15.4(c) Requests to Charge 399

§ 15.5   Preparation of Evidence for Use at Trial 399

§ 15.5(a) Witness Preparation 400

§ 15.5(b) Preparation of Tangible Evidence and Exhibits .. 401

(1) Retrieving Evidence of Criminality in Police

Custody 401

(2) Producing Prior Statements of Witnesses 401

(3) Premarking Evidence 402

§ 15.5(c) Preparation of Stipulations 402

§ 15.6   United States v. Christopher—Preparation for Trial by the

Prosecution and Defense 402

§ 15.6(a) Trial Theories 402

1. Christopher—Case Theory 403

2. Van Ness—Case Theory 404

§ 15.6(b) Proving the Trial Theory—Marshalling the Evi-

dence 405

§ 15.6(c) Addressing Legal Issues Prior to Trial 405

1. In Limine Motions 405

2. Proposed Voir Dire Questions 409

3. Requests to Charge 411

§ 15.6(d) Preparation of Tangible Evidence, Exhibits and

Stipulations 413

Chapter 16.   The Trial **415**

§ 16.0   Introduction 416

§ 16.1   Jury Selection 416

§ 16.1(a) The Voir Dire 417

§ 16.1(b) Strategic Considerations in Selecting Juries 418

§ 16.1(c) The Selection Process 418

(1) The Struck Panel Method 419

(2) The Twelve in the Box Method 419

§ 16.2   Preliminary Instructions to the Jury 420

§ 16.3   Opening Statements 420

Page

§ 16.3(a) Rules Related to the Opening Statement 421
§ 16.3(b) Strategic Considerations—Prosecution and Defense Openings ---------------------------- 421
§ 16.3(c) United States v. Christopher and Van Ness—Opening Statements ---------------------------- 423
    (1) The Court's Ruling on the Motion in Limine 423
    (2) Knapp's Opening Statement ---------------------------- 424
    (3) The Defense Openings ---------------------------- 427
       (a) Clark's Opening for Christopher ----------- 427
       (b) Rothman's Opening for Van Ness ----------- 427

§ 16.4 The Government's Case-in-Chief—Rules Related to Eliciting Testimony ---------------------------- 428
§ 16.4(a) Establishing Competence—Laying the Foundation for the Witness' Testimony ---------------------------- 429
    (1) Personal Qualifications ---------------------------- 429
    (2) Basis of Knowledge ---------------------------- 429
§ 16.4(b) Establishing the Reliability of the Witness' Testimony ---------------------------- 430
§ 16.4(c) Establishing the Relevance of the Witness' Testimony ---------------------------- 431
§ 16.4(d) The Government's Case-in-Chief—Strategic Considerations ---------------------------- 431
    1. Structuring a Believable Narrative ----------------- 431
    2. Establishing the Credibility of the Witness -------- 432
       (a) Evidence of the Witness' Good Character ---------------------------- 432
       (b) Evidence That the Witness' Testimony Is Consistent With Earlier Accounts Given by the Witness ---------------------------- 433
§ 16.4(e) Eliciting Direct Testimony—Forms of Questions 433
§ 16.4(f) United States v. Christopher—The Government's Case-in-Chief ---------------------------- 434
§ 16.4(g) Conducting a Direct Examination—The Testimony of Gilbert Santiago ---------------------------- 435

§ 16.5 Challenging the Government's Case-in-Chief—Cross-examination ---------------------------- 443
§ 16.5(a) The Scope of Cross-examination --------------------- 443
§ 16.5(b) Types of Cross-examination ---------------------------- 444
    (1) Accrediting Cross-examination ----------------- 444
    (2) Discrediting Cross-examination ----------------- 445
§ 16.5(c) Preparing for Cross-examination --------------------- 445
§ 16.5(d) The Decision Whether to Cross-examine ----------- 446
§ 16.5(e) Eliciting Testimony on Cross-examination—The Structure of the Examination ---------------------------- 447
§ 16.5(f) Eliciting Testimony on Cross-examination -------- 449
§ 16.5(g) United States v. Christopher—The Cross-examination of Gilbert Santiago ---------------------------- 453
    1. Cross-examination on behalf of Van Ness ----------- 454
    2. Cross-examination on behalf of Christopher ------- 460

Page

§ 16.6 Re-examination 469
    § 16.6(a) Re-direct Examination 469
    § 16.6(b) Re-cross Examination 470
§ 16.7 Motion for Judgment of Acquittal 470
§ 16.8 The Defense Case 471
§ 16.9 The Rebuttal Case 473
§ 16.10 Concluding the Trial—Requests to Charge 473
§ 16.11 Closing Argument 474
    § 16.11(a) Rules Regarding Closing Argument 474
    § 16.11(b) The Focus of the Closing—The Primacy of Facts 474
    § 16.11(c) Stylistic Considerations 475
    § 16.11(d) The Prosecution Closing 475
    § 16.11(e) The Defense Closing 476
    § 16.11(f) United States v. Christopher—Closing Arguments 477
        (1) The Government's Closing 477
        (2) Christopher's Closing 478
§ 16.12 Jury Instructions 480
§ 16.13 Jury Deliberations 481
§ 16.14 Verdict 481
§ 16.15 United States v. Christopher—The Verdict 481

PART V. SENTENCING

Chapter 17. Sentencing **484**
§ 17.0 Introduction 484
§ 17.1 Determining Sentencing Facts 485
    § 17.1(a) The Presentence Investigation 485
        (1) Presentence Interview of the Defendant 485
        (2) Interview of the Assistant United States Attorney 487
    § 17.1(b) The Presentence Report 487
§ 17.2 Negotiating Challenges to the Presentence Report 487
§ 17.3 Litigating Disputed Facts in the Presentence Report 488
    § 17.3(a) The Presentence Memorandum 488
    § 17.3(b) The Sentencing Hearing—Burden of Proof 488
§ 17.4 The Sentencing Decision 489
§ 17.5 Strategic and Policy Considerations in Connection with Sentencing 490
    § 17.5(a) The Defense Perspective 490
    § 17.5(b) The Prosecution Perspective 491
§ 17.6 The Sentencing of Paul Christopher 492
    § 17.6(a) Calculating Christopher's Sentence 492
        (1) Determining the Offense Level 492
            (a) Narcotics Importation, Distribution and Possession Conspiracy, Narcotics Distribution and Possession, and Attempted Narcotics Possession 493

Page

(b) Money Laundering -------------------------- 494

(c) Structuring -------------------------------- 494

(d) Determining the Combined Offense Level -- 495

(e) Acceptance of Responsibility ---------------- 495

(2) Determining the Criminal History Category 495

(3) Christopher's Guidelines Range ---------------- 496

§ 17.6(b) The Objections Stage ---------------------------- 496

(1) Defense Objections ----------------------------- 496

(2) The Government's Position ---------------------- 499

(3) The Probation Department Response --------- 500

§ 17.6(c) Resolving Contested Issues --------------------------- 500

§ 17.6(d) The Sentencing Hearing ---------------------------- 501

§ 17.6(e) The Imposition of Christopher's Sentence --------- 504

§ 17.7 The Sentencing of Ernest Wagner ------------------------- 504

§ 17.8 The Sentencing of Gilbert Santiago and Mario Long --------- 513

(1) Gilbert Santiago ------------------------------- 513

(2) Mario Long ------------------------------------- 526

APPENDIX A. SELECTED PROVISIONS OF THE UNITED STATES CONSTITUTION 527

APPENDIX B. SELECTED RULES OF FEDERAL CRIMINAL PROCEDURE --------- 529

APPENDIX C. CHRONOLOGY OF U.S. v. CHRISTOPHER ------------------------- 589

INDEX --- 593

*

Table of Cases

A

Abney v. United States, 431 U.S. 651, 97 S.Ct. 2034, 52 L.Ed.2d 651 (1977)— **§ 14.12, n. 55.**

Acevedo, United States v., 842 F.2d 502 (1st Cir.1988)—**§ 4.6, n. 59.**

Acevedo–Ramos, United States v., 755 F.2d 203 (1st Cir.1985)—**§ 5.7, n. 80.**

Adams, United States v., 434 F.2d 756 (2nd Cir.1970)—**§ 11.3, n. 104.**

Agostino, United States v., 132 F.3d 1183 (7th Cir.1997)—**§ 13.7, n. 76.**

Aguilar v. Texas, 378 U.S. 108, 84 S.Ct. 1509, 12 L.Ed.2d 723 (1964)— **§ 4.2, n. 18.**

Aguilar, United States v., 884 F.Supp. 88 (E.D.N.Y.1995)—**§ 12.2, n. 31.**

Algie, United States v., 667 F.2d 569 (6th Cir.1982)—**§ 13.4, n. 58.**

Almeida, United States v., 341 F.3d 1318 (11th Cir.2003)—**§ 5.2, n. 25.**

Andersen, United States v., 940 F.2d 593 (10th Cir.1991)—**§ 11.1, n. 34.**

Apprendi v. New Jersey, 530 U.S. 466, 120 S.Ct. 2348, 147 L.Ed.2d 435 (2000)— **§ 7.0; § 7.0, n. 4; § 8.3, n. 55; § 11.7, n. 160.**

Armstrong, United States v., 909 F.2d 1238 (9th Cir.1990)—**§ 11.7, n. 162.**

Arthur Andersen LLP v. United States, ___ U.S. ___, 125 S.Ct. 2129, 161 L.Ed.2d 1008 (2005)—**§ 11.1, n. 63.**

Ashe v. Swenson, 397 U.S. 436, 90 S.Ct. 1189, 25 L.Ed.2d 469 (1970)—**§ 11.3, n. 91.**

Austin, United States v., 17 F.3d 27 (2nd Cir.1994)—**§ 17.1, n. 7.**

Automated Medical Laboratories, Inc., United States v., 770 F.2d 399 (4th Cir. 1985)—**§ 11.1, n. 62.**

B

Bagley, United States v., 473 U.S. 667, 105 S.Ct. 3375, 87 L.Ed.2d 481 (1985)— **§ 13.3, n. 39.**

Baker, United States v., 894 F.2d 1083 (9th Cir.1990)—**§ 7.2, n. 34.**

Baker v. United States, 401 F.2d 958, 131 U.S.App.D.C. 7 (D.C.Cir.1968)—**§ 11.3, n. 108.**

Barker v. Wingo, 407 U.S. 514, 92 S.Ct. 2182, 33 L.Ed.2d 101 (1972)—**§ 4.7, n. 63; § 14.13, n. 61.**

Barnes, United States v., 604 F.2d 121 (2nd Cir.1979)—**§ 16.1, n. 16.**

Barrow, United States v., 400 F.3d 109 (2nd Cir.2005)—**§ 8.2, n. 16.**

Batson v. Kentucky, 476 U.S. 79, 106 S.Ct. 1712, 90 L.Ed.2d 69 (1986)—**§ 16.1, n. 11.**

Bell v. United States, 349 U.S. 81, 75 S.Ct. 620, 99 L.Ed. 905 (1955)—**§ 11.3, n. 99.**

Bellamy, United States v., 264 F.3d 448 (4th Cir.2001)—**§ 7.2, n. 81.**

Bellomo, United States v., 176 F.3d 580 (2nd Cir.1999)—**§ 11.4, n. 125.**

Benevento, United States v., 836 F.2d 129 (2nd Cir.1988)—**§ 11.4, n. 130.**

Benevento, United States v., 663 F.Supp. 1115 (S.D.N.Y.1987)—**§ 11.4, n. 130.**

Bermingham, United States v., 855 F.2d 925 (2nd Cir.1988)—**§ 17.4, n. 21.**

Bermudez, United States v., 526 F.2d 89 (2nd Cir.1975)—**§ 11.7, n. 159.**

Bess, United States v., 593 F.2d 749 (6th Cir.1979)—**§ 16.3, n. 27.**

Black, United States v., 767 F.2d 1334 (9th Cir.1985)—**§ 13.7, n. 76.**

Blackledge v. Perry, 417 U.S. 21, 94 S.Ct. 2098, 40 L.Ed.2d 628 (1974)—**§ 4.0, n. 4; § 11.1, n. 35.**

Blair v. United States, 250 U.S. 273, 39 S.Ct. 468, 63 L.Ed. 979 (1919)—**§ 10.3, n. 14.**

Blakely v. Washington, 542 U.S. 296, 124 S.Ct. 2531, 159 L.Ed.2d 403 (2004)— **§ 7.0; § 7.0, n. 5.**

Blockburger v. United States, 284 U.S. 299, 52 S.Ct. 180, 76 L.Ed. 306 (1932)— **§ 11.3, n. 92.**

Blue, United States v., 384 U.S. 251, 86 S.Ct. 1416, 16 L.Ed.2d 510 (1966)— **§ 11.1, n. 17.**

Bollin, United States v., 264 F.3d 391 (4th Cir.2001)—**§ 11.4, n. 131.**

Booker, United States v., ___ U.S. ___, 125 S.Ct. 738, 160 L.Ed.2d 621 (2005)— **§ 1.1; § 1.1, n. 17; § 7.0; § 7.0, n. 6.**

Bordenkircher v. Hayes, 434 U.S. 357, 98 S.Ct. 663, 54 L.Ed.2d 604 (1978)—**§ 9.0; § 9.0, n. 3; § 14.3, n. 24.**

Bourjaily v. United States, 483 U.S. 171, 107 S.Ct. 2775, 97 L.Ed.2d 144 (1987)—§ **16.4, n. 59.**

Bowe, United States v., 698 F.2d 560 (2nd Cir.1983)—§ **14.8, n. 42.**

Brady v. Maryland, 373 U.S. 83, 83 S.Ct. 1194, 10 L.Ed.2d 215 (1963)—§ **12.4, n. 57; § 13.3; § 13.3, n. 31.**

Brady v. United States, 397 U.S. 742, 90 S.Ct. 1463, 25 L.Ed.2d 747 (1970)—§ **9.0; § 9.0, n. 2.**

Branzburg v. Hayes, 408 U.S. 665, 92 S.Ct. 2646, 33 L.Ed.2d 626 (1972)—§ **10.3, n. 16.**

Braswell v. United States, 487 U.S. 99, 108 S.Ct. 2284, 101 L.Ed.2d 98 (1988)—§ **10.3, n. 63.**

Brown v. Ohio, 432 U.S. 161, 97 S.Ct. 2221, 53 L.Ed.2d 187 (1977)—§ **11.3, n. 94.**

Brown v. State of Mississippi, 297 U.S. 278, 56 S.Ct. 461, 80 L.Ed. 682 (1936)—§ **4.5, n. 41.**

Brown, United States v., 2002 WL 31771265 (4th Cir.2002)—§ **17.1, n. 7.**

Bruce, United States v., 976 F.2d 552 (9th Cir.1992)—§ **9.2, n. 16.**

Bruton v. United States, 391 U.S. 123, 88 S.Ct. 1620, 20 L.Ed.2d 476 (1968)—§ **11.3, n. 114.**

Bunn, United States v., 215 F.3d 430 (4th Cir.2000)—§ **8.3, n. 58.**

Burch, United States v., 873 F.2d 765 (5th Cir.1989)—§ **17.4, n. 20.**

Bush, United States v., 896 F.Supp. 424 (E.D.Pa.1995)—§ **8.3, n. 48.**

C

Calandra, United States v., 414 U.S. 338, 94 S.Ct. 613, 38 L.Ed.2d 561 (1974)—§ **10.3, n. 14; § 11.1, n. 14.**

Candelaria–Silva, United States v., 166 F.3d 19 (1st Cir.1999)—§ **11.4, n. 131.**

Caporale, United States v., 806 F.2d 1487 (11th Cir.1986)—§ **11.4, n. 130.**

Carrillo, United States v., 229 F.3d 177 (2nd Cir.2000)—§ **11.7, n. 159.**

Carrozza, United States v., 4 F.3d 70 (1st Cir.1993)—§ **12.2, n. 32.**

Carter v. Kentucky, 450 U.S. 288, 101 S.Ct. 1112, 67 L.Ed.2d 241 (1981)—§ **16.8, n. 78.**

Chacko, United States v., 169 F.3d 140 (2nd Cir.1999)—§ **11.3, n. 93.**

Chaparro, United States v., 181 F.Supp.2d 323 (S.D.N.Y.2002)—§ **8.3, n. 47.**

Chavez–Marquez, United States v., 66 F.3d 259 (10th Cir.1995)—§ **14.7, n. 33.**

Cherry, United States v., 876 F.Supp. 547 (S.D.N.Y.1995)—§ **13.7, n. 90.**

Chimel v. California, 395 U.S. 752, 89 S.Ct. 2034, 23 L.Ed.2d 685 (1969)—§ **4.5, n. 38.**

Chimurenga, United States v., 760 F.2d 400 (2nd Cir.1985)—§ **5.7, n. 75.**

Cieslowski, United States v., 410 F.3d 353 (7th Cir.2005)—§ **12.2, n. 28.**

Cincotta, United States v., 689 F.2d 238 (1st Cir.1982)—§ **11.1, n. 62.**

Contreras, United States v., 776 F.2d 51 (2nd Cir.1985)—§ **5.7, n. 76.**

Cook, United States v., 890 F.2d 672 (4th Cir.1989)—§ **17.4, n. 24.**

Coppa, United States v., 267 F.3d 132 (2nd Cir.2001)—§ **13.3, n. 40.**

Corrado, United States v., 227 F.3d 543 (6th Cir.2000)—§ **11.4, n. 129.**

Costello v. United States, 350 U.S. 359, 76 S.Ct. 406, 100 L.Ed. 397 (1956)—§ **10.3, n. 16; § 11.1, n. 17.**

County of (see name of county)

Cox, United States v., 342 F.2d 167 (5th Cir.1965)—§ **4.0, n. 2.**

Crawford v. Washington, 541 U.S. 36, 124 S.Ct. 1354, 158 L.Ed.2d 177 (2004)—§ **3.3, n. 26; § 6.0, n. 11; § 16.4, n. 37.**

Crisci, United States v., 273 F.3d 235 (2nd Cir.2001)—§ **11.2, n. 81.**

Croft, United States v., 124 F.3d 1109 (9th Cir.1997)—§ **16.3, n. 28.**

Crosby, United States v., 397 F.3d 103 (2nd Cir.2005)—§ **7.3, n. 98; § 12.3, n. 54; § 17.4, n. 21.**

Cross v. United States, 335 F.2d 987, 118 U.S.App.D.C. 324 (D.C.Cir.1964)—§ **11.3, n. 108.**

Cruikshank, United States v., 92 U.S. 542, 23 L.Ed. 588 (1875)—§ **11.2, n. 85.**

Curcio v. United States, 354 U.S. 118, 77 S.Ct. 1145, 1 L.Ed.2d 1225 (1957)—§ **10.3, n. 63.**

D

Darden v. Wainwright, 477 U.S. 168, 106 S.Ct. 2464, 91 L.Ed.2d 144 (1986)—§ **16.11, n. 90.**

Davis v. United States, 367 A.2d 1254 (D.C. 1976)—§ **11.3, n. 112.**

Davis, United States v., 177 F.Supp.2d 470 (E.D.Va.2001)—§ **11.4, n. 125.**

DeFries, United States v., 129 F.3d 1293, 327 U.S.App.D.C. 181 (D.C.Cir.1997)—§ **11.4, n. 120.**

Delker, United States v., 757 F.2d 1390 (3rd Cir.1985)—§ **5.7, n. 84.**

DiBella, In re, 518 F.2d 955 (2nd Cir. 1975)—§ **10.3, n. 70.**

Di Bella v. United States, 369 U.S. 121, 82 S.Ct. 654, 7 L.Ed.2d 614 (1962)—§ **14.12, n. 54.**

Dickerson v. Vaughn, 90 F.3d 87 (3rd Cir. 1996)—§ **9.3, n. 37.**

Dionisio, United States v., 410 U.S. 1, 93 S.Ct. 764, 35 L.Ed.2d 67 (1973)—§ **10.3, n. 17.**

Doe, United States v., 870 F.Supp. 702 (E.D.Va.1994)—§ **8.3, n. 48.**

Doe, United States v., 943 F.2d 132 (1st Cir.1991)—§ **10.3, n. 72.**

Donovan, United States v., 339 F.2d 404 (7th Cir.1964)—§ **11.2, n. 80.**

Downing, United States v., 753 F.2d 1224 (3rd Cir.1985)—§ **15.4, n. 20.**

Downum v. United States, 372 U.S. 734, 83 S.Ct. 1033, 10 L.Ed.2d 100 (1963)— § **14.12, n. 58.**

Draper v. United States, 358 U.S. 307, 79 S.Ct. 329, 3 L.Ed.2d 327 (1959)—§ **4.2, n. 14.**

Drew v. United States, 331 F.2d 85, 118 U.S.App.D.C. 11 (D.C.Cir.1964)—§ **11.3, n. 104.**

Duncan, United States v., 400 F.3d 1297 (11th Cir.2005)—§ **7.2, n. 26.**

E

Ebel, United States v., 299 F.3d 187 (3rd Cir.2002)—§ **9.2, n. 14.**

Echeles, United States v., 352 F.2d 892 (7th Cir.1965)—§ **11.3, n. 115.**

Edwards v. Arizona, 451 U.S. 477, 101 S.Ct. 1880, 68 L.Ed.2d 378 (1981)—§ **4.5, n. 43.**

Ellis, In re, 356 F.3d 1198 (9th Cir.2004)— § **12.2, n. 21.**

Estepa, United States v., 471 F.2d 1132 (2nd Cir.1972)—§ **11.1, n. 21.**

Ewell, United States v., 383 U.S. 116, 86 S.Ct. 773, 15 L.Ed.2d 627 (1966)— § **11.6, n. 146.**

F

Fagge, United States v., 101 F.3d 232 (2nd Cir.1996)—§ **12.2, n. 40.**

Fatico, United States v., 603 F.2d 1053 (2nd Cir.1979)—§ **17.3, n. 15.**

F.D.I.C. v. United States Fire Ins. Co., 50 F.3d 1304 (5th Cir.1995)—§ **13.7, n. 78.**

Fernandez, United States v., 2000 WL 534449 (S.D.N.Y.2000)—§ **8.1, n. 5.**

Fernandez–Alfonso, United States v., 813 F.2d 1571 (9th Cir.1987)—§ **5.7, n. 83.**

Fisher v. United States, 425 U.S. 391, 96 S.Ct. 1569, 48 L.Ed.2d 39 (1976)— § **10.3, n. 61.**

Flattum, United States v., 1992 WL 365334 (D.Or.1992)—§ **11.5, n. 142.**

Fleming, United States v., 239 F.3d 761 (6th Cir.2001)—§ **9.2, n. 17.**

Fortna, United States v., 769 F.2d 243 (5th Cir.1985)—§ **5.7, n. 75.**

Foutz, United States v., 540 F.2d 733 (4th Cir.1976)—§ **11.3, n. 109.**

Franks v. Delaware, 438 U.S. 154, 98 S.Ct. 2674, 57 L.Ed.2d 667 (1978)—§ **4.5, n. 36.**

Fruchter, United States v., 411 F.3d 377 (2nd Cir.2005)—§ **11.4, n. 129.**

G

Gammill, United States v., 421 F.2d 185 (10th Cir.1970)—§ **11.2, n. 84.**

Gary, United States v., 74 F.3d 304 (1st Cir.1996)—§ **11.1, n. 33.**

Gelbard v. United States, 408 U.S. 41, 92 S.Ct. 2357, 33 L.Ed.2d 179 (1972)— § **10.3, n. 23.**

Gentile, United States v., 525 F.2d 252 (2nd Cir.1975)—§ **16.3, n. 26.**

Gerstein v. Pugh, 420 U.S. 103, 95 S.Ct. 854, 43 L.Ed.2d 54 (1975)—§ **4.2, n. 12;** § **5.4, n. 38.**

Giglio v. United States, 405 U.S. 150, 92 S.Ct. 763, 31 L.Ed.2d 104 (1972)—§ **8.3, n. 59;** § **12.4, n. 57;** § **13.3;** § **13.3, n. 33.**

Gil, United States v., 297 F.3d 93 (2nd Cir.2002)—§ **13.3, n. 43.**

Gillette, United States v., 383 F.2d 843 (2nd Cir.1967)—§ **14.5, n. 29.**

Giordenello v. United States, 357 U.S. 480, 78 S.Ct. 1245, 2 L.Ed.2d 1503 (1958)— § **4.2, n. 11.**

Glasser v. United States, 315 U.S. 60, 62 S.Ct. 457, 86 L.Ed. 680 (1942)—§ **5.2, n. 20.**

Goodall, United States v., 236 F.3d 700, 344 U.S.App.D.C. 333 (D.C.Cir.2001)— § **12.2, n. 30.**

Gordils, United States v., 982 F.2d 64 (2nd Cir.1992)—§ **10.5, n. 96.**

Gore v. United States, 357 U.S. 386, 78 S.Ct. 1280, 2 L.Ed.2d 1405 (1958)— § **11.3, n. 97.**

Gracia, United States v., 755 F.2d 984 (2nd Cir.1985)—§ **10.3, n. 79.**

Graham, United States v., 305 F.3d 1094 (10th Cir.2002)—§ **11.3, n. 95.**

Grand Jury Subpoena, In re, 103 F.3d 234 (2nd Cir.1996)—§ **11.1, n. 6.**

Grand Jury Subpoena Served Upon Doe, In re, 781 F.2d 238 (2nd Cir.1986)—§ **10.3, n. 43.**

Gregory v. United States, 369 F.2d 185, 125 U.S.App.D.C. 140 (D.C.Cir.1966)— § **13.7, n. 76.**

Grievance Committee for Southern Dist. of New York v. Simels, 48 F.3d 640 (2nd Cir.1995)—§ **10.4, n. 90.**

Griffin v. California, 380 U.S. 609, 85 S.Ct. 1229, 14 L.Ed.2d 106 (1965)—§ **16.8, n. 77.**

Grumbles, In re, N.J. Crim. No. 722–21 (D.N.J. 1973)—§ **10.3, n. 76.**

Gugino, United States v., 860 F.2d 546 (2nd Cir.1988)—§ **11.3, n. 95.**

H

Hadash, United States v., 408 F.3d 1080 (8th Cir.2005)—§ **7.2, n. 89; § 17.4, n. 26.**

Hagner v. United States, 285 U.S. 427, 52 S.Ct. 417, 76 L.Ed. 861 (1932)—§ **11.2, n. 77.**

Hale v. Henkel, 201 U.S. 43, 26 S.Ct. 370, 50 L.Ed. 652 (1906)—§ **10.3, n. 22.**

Halper, United States v., 590 F.2d 422 (2nd Cir.1978)—§ **11.3, n. 105.**

Hamilton v. Alabama, 368 U.S. 52, 82 S.Ct. 157, 7 L.Ed.2d 114 (1961)—§ **11.5, n. 141.**

Hamling v. United States, 418 U.S. 87, 94 S.Ct. 2887, 41 L.Ed.2d 590 (1974)— § **11.2, n. 69; § 13.2, n. 9.**

Hammad, United States v., 858 F.2d 834 (2nd Cir.1988)—§ **10.4, n. 90.**

Hardy, United States v., 224 F.3d 752 (8th Cir.2000)—§ **13.7, n. 90.**

Harris v. New York, 401 U.S. 222, 91 S.Ct. 643, 28 L.Ed.2d 1 (1971)—§ **16.8, n. 80.**

Havens, United States v., 446 U.S. 620, 100 S.Ct. 1912, 64 L.Ed.2d 559 (1980)— § **16.8, n. 80.**

Hawthorne, United States v., 705 F.2d 258 (7th Cir.1983)—§ **11.6, n. 153.**

Hazime, United States v., 762 F.2d 34 (6th Cir.1985)—§ **5.7, n. 76.**

Hendrickson, United States v., 26 F.3d 321 (2nd Cir.1994)—§ **10.5, n. 97.**

Hernandez, United States v., 299 F.3d 984 (8th Cir.2002)—§ **13.2, n. 20.**

Herrera–Figueroa, United States v., 918 F.2d 1430 (9th Cir.1990)—§ **17.1, n. 5.**

Hill v. Lockhart, 474 U.S. 52, 106 S.Ct. 366, 88 L.Ed.2d 203 (1985)—§ **9.0, n. 6.**

Hogan, United States v., 712 F.2d 757 (2nd Cir.1983)—§ **11.8, n. 164.**

Holby, United States v., 345 F.Supp. 639 (S.D.N.Y.1972)—§ **11.5, n. 142.**

Holland, United States v., 117 F.3d 589, 326 U.S.App.D.C. 35 (D.C.Cir.1997)— § **9.2, n. 32.**

Holland v. United States, 348 U.S. 121, 75 S.Ct. 127, 99 L.Ed. 150 (1954)—§ **3.1, n. 6.**

Holloway v. Arkansas, 435 U.S. 475, 98 S.Ct. 1173, 55 L.Ed.2d 426 (1978)— § **5.2, n. 15.**

Holman, United States v., 168 F.3d 655 (3rd Cir.1999)—§ **9.2, n. 26.**

Howard, United States v., 894 F.2d 1085 (9th Cir.1990)—§ **17.3, n. 13.**

Hubbell, United States v., 530 U.S. 27, 120 S.Ct. 2037, 147 L.Ed.2d 24 (2000)— § **10.3, n. 61.**

Hurley, United States v., 63 F.3d 1 (1st Cir.1995)—§ **11.4, n. 129.**

Hurse, United States v., 453 F.2d 128 (8th Cir.1971)—§ **13.2, n. 20.**

Hutcheson, United States v., 312 U.S. 219, 61 S.Ct. 463, 85 L.Ed. 788 (1941)— § **11.2, n. 76.**

I

Illinois v. Gates, 462 U.S. 213, 103 S.Ct. 2317, 76 L.Ed.2d 527 (1983)—§ **4.2, n. 16; § 6.1, n. 15.**

Illinois v. Rodriguez, 497 U.S. 177, 110 S.Ct. 2793, 111 L.Ed.2d 148 (1990)— § **14.11, n. 52.**

In re (see name of party)

J

Jaber, United States v., 362 F.Supp.2d 365 (D.Mass.2005)—§ **8.0, n. 4.**

Jackson, United States v., 883 F.2d 1007 (11th Cir.1989)—§ **7.2, n. 81.**

Jackson v. Virginia, 443 U.S. 307, 99 S.Ct. 2781, 61 L.Ed.2d 560 (1979)—§ **15.1, n. 1; § 16.7, n. 73.**

J.E.B. v. Alabama ex rel. T.B., 511 U.S. 127, 114 S.Ct. 1419, 128 L.Ed.2d 89 (1994)— § **16.1, n. 11.**

Jencks v. United States, 353 U.S. 657, 77 S.Ct. 1007, 1 L.Ed.2d 1103 (1957)— § **13.4, n. 56.**

Jewell, United States v., 532 F.2d 697 (9th Cir.1976)—§ **4.6, n. 55.**

Johnson v. Baldwin, 114 F.3d 835 (9th Cir. 1997)—§ **13.0, n. 2.**

Johnson, United States v., 89 F.3d 778 (11th Cir.1996)—§ **9.2, n. 14.**

Johnson, United States v., 968 F.2d 768 (8th Cir.1992)—§ **16.3, n. 21.**

Johnson, United States v., 347 F.3d 412 (2nd Cir.2003)—§ **12.4, n. 56.**

Jordan, United States v., 291 F.3d 1091 (9th Cir.2002)—§ **8.3, n. 55.**

K

Karo, United States v., 468 U.S. 705, 104 S.Ct. 3296, 82 L.Ed.2d 530 (1984)— § **4.6, n. 51.**

Kastigar v. United States, 406 U.S. 441, 92 S.Ct. 1653, 32 L.Ed.2d 212 (1972)— § **10.3, n. 47.**

Kaufman, United States v., 858 F.2d 994 (5th Cir.1988)—§ **4.6, n. 59.**

Kelly, United States v., 91 F.Supp.2d 580 (S.D.N.Y.2000)—§ **13.4, n. 52.**

Kitchen, Matter of, 706 F.2d 1266 (2nd Cir.1983)—§ **10.3, n. 74.**

Koon v. United States, 518 U.S. 81, 116 S.Ct. 2035, 135 L.Ed.2d 392 (1996)— § **7.2, n. 77.**

Krilich, United States v., 159 F.3d 1020 (7th Cir.1998)—§ **8.2, n. 16.**

Kyles v. Whitley, 514 U.S. 419, 115 S.Ct. 1555, 131 L.Ed.2d 490 (1995)—§ **13.3, n. 39.**

L

Lakeside v. Oregon, 435 U.S. 333, 98 S.Ct. 1091, 55 L.Ed.2d 319 (1978)—§ **16.8, n. 78.**

Lamborn v. Dittmer, 873 F.2d 522 (2nd Cir.1989)—§ **13.7, n. 78.**

Langford, United States v., 946 F.2d 798 (11th Cir.1991)—§ **11.3, n. 99.**

LaRouche Campaign, United States v., 841 F.2d 1176 (1st Cir.1988)—§ **13.7, n. 90.**

Lauersen, United States v., 2000 WL 1693538 (S.D.N.Y.2000)—§ **8.2, n. 18.**

Lawrence, United States v., 179 F.3d 343 (5th Cir.1999)—§ **4.0, n. 2.**

Le, United States v., 306 F.Supp.2d 589 (E.D.Va.2004)—§ **8.3, n. 59; § 12.4, n. 57.**

Ledbetter v. United States, 170 U.S. 606, 18 S.Ct. 774, 42 L.Ed. 1162 (1898)—§ **11.2, n. 84.**

Leeke v. Timmerman, 454 U.S. 83, 102 S.Ct. 69, 70 L.Ed.2d 65 (1981)—§ **4.0, n. 1.**

Lego v. Twomey, 404 U.S. 477, 92 S.Ct. 619, 30 L.Ed.2d 618 (1972)—§ **14.8, n. 43.**

Leonti, United States v., 326 F.3d 1111 (9th Cir.2003)—§ **8.1, n. 5.**

Lewis, United States v., 35 F.3d 148 (4th Cir.1994)—§ **13.4, n. 58.**

Libretti v. United States, 516 U.S. 29, 116 S.Ct. 356, 133 L.Ed.2d 271 (1995)—§ **11.4, n. 123.**

Lincoln, United States v., 413 F.3d 716 (8th Cir.2005)—§ **7.3, n. 99.**

Longley v. United States, 1992 WL 358062 (E.D.Pa.1992)—§ **9.2, n. 32.**

Lopez, United States v., 4 F.3d 1455 (9th Cir.1993)—§ **10.4, n. 90.**

Lopez, United States v., 871 F.2d 513 (5th Cir.1989)—§ **7.2, n. 81.**

Lovasco, United States v., 431 U.S. 783, 97 S.Ct. 2044, 52 L.Ed.2d 752 (1977)—§ **11.6, n. 149.**

M

Manson v. Brathwaite, 432 U.S. 98, 97 S.Ct. 2243, 53 L.Ed.2d 140 (1977)—§ **4.5, n. 47.**

Mapp v. Ohio, 367 U.S. 643, 81 S.Ct. 1684, 6 L.Ed.2d 1081 (1961)—§ **4.5, n. 30.**

Mares, United States v., 402 F.3d 511 (5th Cir.2005)—§ **7.3, n. 99.**

Marion, United States v., 404 U.S. 307, 92 S.Ct. 455, 30 L.Ed.2d 468 (1971)—§ **4.7, n. 64.**

Markin, United States v., 263 F.3d 491 (6th Cir.2001)—§ **17.2, n. 11.**

Martir, United States v., 782 F.2d 1141 (2nd Cir.1986)—§ **5.6, n. 59; § 5.7, n. 77.**

Maryland v. Garrison, 480 U.S. 79, 107 S.Ct. 1013, 94 L.Ed.2d 72 (1987)—§ **4.10, n. 77.**

Matlock, United States v., 415 U.S. 164, 94 S.Ct. 988, 39 L.Ed.2d 242 (1974)—§ **14.8, n. 39.**

Matter of (see name of party)

Mayes v. United States, 177 F.2d 505 (8th Cir.1949)—§ **11.5, n. 144.**

McCann v. Mangialardi, 337 F.3d 782 (7th Cir.2003)—§ **8.3, n. 59; § 12.4, n. 57.**

McDonald, United States v., 964 F.2d 390 (5th Cir.1992)—§ **7.2, n. 34.**

McDowell, United States v., 888 F.2d 285 (3rd Cir.1989)—§ **17.3, n. 14.**

McMann v. Richardson, 397 U.S. 759, 90 S.Ct. 1441, 25 L.Ed.2d 763 (1970)—§ **9.0, n. 6.**

McPartlin, United States v., 595 F.2d 1321 (7th Cir.1979)—§ **5.2, n. 23.**

Mezzanatto, United States v., 513 U.S. 196, 115 S.Ct. 797, 130 L.Ed.2d 697 (1995)—§ **8.2, n. 15.**

Ming He, United States v., 94 F.3d 782 (2nd Cir.1996)—§ **8.3, n. 57.**

Miranda v. Arizona, 384 U.S. 436, 86 S.Ct. 1602, 16 L.Ed.2d 694 (1966)—§ **2.4, n. 5; § 4.5; § 4.5, n. 42; § 10.1, n. 3; § 14.8, n. 37.**

Missouri v. Hunter, 459 U.S. 359, 103 S.Ct. 673, 74 L.Ed.2d 535 (1983)—§ **11.3, n. 94.**

Montalvo–Murillo, United States v., 495 U.S. 711, 110 S.Ct. 2072, 109 L.Ed.2d 720 (1990)—§ **5.7, n. 73.**

Morgan, United States v., 393 F.3d 192, 364 U.S.App.D.C. 169 (D.C.Cir.2004)—§ **11.2, n. 75.**

Morrison, United States v., 536 F.2d 286 (9th Cir.1976)—§ **11.2, n. 79.**

Morton Salt Co., United States v., 338 U.S. 632, 70 S.Ct. 357, 94 L.Ed. 401 (1950)—§ **10.3, n. 15.**

Motamedi, United States v., 767 F.2d 1403 (9th Cir.1985)—§ **5.7, n. 75.**

Murphy v. Waterfront Com'n of New York Harbor, 378 U.S. 52, 84 S.Ct. 1594, 12 L.Ed.2d 678 (1964)—§ **10.3, n. 22.**

Murray, United States v., 618 F.2d 892 (2nd Cir.1980)—§ **11.3, n. 93.**

Mykytiuk, United States v., 415 F.3d 606 (7th Cir.2005)—§ **7.3, n. 99.**

N

Nixon, United States v., 418 U.S. 683, 94 S.Ct. 3090, 41 L.Ed.2d 1039 (1974)—§ **13.7, n. 88.**

North Carolina v. Alford, 400 U.S. 25, 91 S.Ct. 160, 27 L.Ed.2d 162 (1970)—§ **9.0; § 9.0, n. 8; § 9.2, n. 34.**

North Carolina v. Butler, 441 U.S. 369, 99 S.Ct. 1755, 60 L.Ed.2d 286 (1979)— § **14.8, n. 37.**

O

O'Dell, United States v., 247 F.3d 655 (6th Cir.2001)—§ **11.4, n. 122.**

O'Henry's Film Works, Inc., United States v., 598 F.2d 313 (2nd Cir.1979)—§ **10.3, n. 63.**

Ohio v. Roberts, 448 U.S. 56, 100 S.Ct. 2531, 65 L.Ed.2d 597 (1980)—§ **16.4, n. 37.**

Okai, United States v., 2005 WL 2042301 (D.Neb.2005)—§ **7.3, n. 100.**

Oregon v. Elstad, 470 U.S. 298, 105 S.Ct. 1285, 84 L.Ed.2d 222 (1985)—§ **4.5, n. 44.**

Osborne, United States v., 332 F.3d 1307 (10th Cir.2003)—§ **11.7, n. 161.**

Ouber v. Guarino, 293 F.3d 19 (1st Cir. 2002)—§ **16.3, n. 22.**

Ouimette v. Moran, 942 F.2d 1 (1st Cir. 1991)—§ **13.3, n. 37.**

P

Paguio, United States v., 114 F.3d 928 (9th Cir.1997)—§ **11.1, n. 35.**

Palmieri v. Defaria, 88 F.3d 136 (2nd Cir. 1996)—§ **15.4, n. 20.**

Palta, United States v., 880 F.2d 636 (2nd Cir.1989)—§ **17.3, n. 16.**

Parham, United States v., 16 F.3d 844 (8th Cir.1994)—§ **11.1, n. 36.**

Parker v. North Carolina, 397 U.S. 790, 90 S.Ct. 1458, 25 L.Ed.2d 785 (1970)— § **9.0, n. 4.**

Parsad v. Greiner, 337 F.3d 175 (2nd Cir. 2003)—§ **10.1, n. 3.**

Pedroni, United States v., 958 F.2d 262 (9th Cir.1992)—§ **14.7, n. 33.**

Peek v. Mitchell, 419 F.2d 575 (6th Cir. 1970)—§ **4.0, n. 2;** § **11.1, n. 33.**

Pelullo, United States v., 178 F.3d 196 (3rd Cir.1999)—§ **11.4, n. 126.**

Perez, United States v., 22 U.S. 579, 6 L.Ed. 165 (1824)—§ **16.14, n. 96.**

Perry, United States v., 223 F.3d 431 (7th Cir.2000)—§ **15.1, n. 6.**

Peveler, United States v., 359 F.3d 369 (6th Cir.2004)—§ **12.2, n. 32.**

Pimentel, United States v., 932 F.2d 1029 (2nd Cir.1991)—§ **9.2, n. 33;** § **12.2, n. 21.**

Pinkerton v. United States, 328 U.S. 640, 66 S.Ct. 1180, 90 L.Ed. 1489 (1946)— § **11.7, n. 161.**

Pitt, United States v., 193 F.3d 751 (3rd Cir.1999)—§ **11.4, n. 129.**

Pope, United States v., 189 F.Supp. 12 (S.D.N.Y.1960)—§ **11.2, n. 76.**

Powers v. Ohio, 499 U.S. 400, 111 S.Ct. 1364, 113 L.Ed.2d 411 (1991)—§ **16.1, n. 11.**

Price, United States v., 265 F.3d 1097 (10th Cir.2001)—§ **11.3, n. 104.**

Pugach v. Klein, 193 F.Supp. 630 (S.D.N.Y. 1961)—§ **11.1, n. 42.**

Q

Quartermaine, United States v., 913 F.2d 910 (11th Cir.1990)—§ **5.7, n. 79.**

Quintero v. United States, 33 F.3d 1133 (9th Cir.1994)—§ **10.5, n. 122.**

R

Raddatz, United States v., 447 U.S. 667, 100 S.Ct. 2406, 65 L.Ed.2d 424 (1980)— § **14.1, n. 5.**

Rakas v. Illinois, 439 U.S. 128, 99 S.Ct. 421, 58 L.Ed.2d 387 (1978)—§ **14.5, n. 29.**

Ranum, United States v., 353 F.Supp.2d 984 (E.D.Wis.2005)—§ **7.3, n. 97.**

Rawlings v. Kentucky, 448 U.S. 98, 100 S.Ct. 2556, 65 L.Ed.2d 633 (1980)— § **14.5, n. 29.**

Redondo–Lemos, United States v., 27 F.3d 439 (9th Cir.1994)—§ **11.1, n. 33.**

R. Enterprises, Inc., United States v., 498 U.S. 292, 111 S.Ct. 722, 112 L.Ed.2d 795 (1991)—§ **10.3, n. 20.**

Residence Located at 218 Third Street, New Glarus, Wisconsin, United States v., 805 F.2d 256 (7th Cir.1986)—§ **10.5, n. 104.**

Reynolds, United States v., 345 U.S. 1, 73 S.Ct. 528, 97 L.Ed. 727 (1953)—§ **17.5, n. 29.**

Rice, United States v., 52 F.3d 843 (10th Cir.1995)—§ **17.3, n. 14.**

Rios–Ramirez, United States v., 929 F.2d 563 (10th Cir.1991)—§ **17.3, n. 16.**

Riverside, County of v. McLaughlin, 500 U.S. 44, 111 S.Ct. 1661, 114 L.Ed.2d 49 (1991)—§ **4.7, n. 61;** § **5.0, n. 1.**

Rodriguez, United States v., 896 F.2d 1031 (6th Cir.1990)—§ **17.3, n. 14.**

Rosales–Lopez v. United States, 451 U.S. 182, 101 S.Ct. 1629, 68 L.Ed.2d 22 (1981)—§ **16.1, n. 16.**

Roselli, United States v., 432 F.2d 879 (9th Cir.1970)—§ **11.3, n. 111.**

Roviaro v. United States, 353 U.S. 53, 77 S.Ct. 623, 1 L.Ed.2d 639 (1957)—§ **13.4, n. 51.**

Ruggiero, United States v., 934 F.2d 440 (2nd Cir.1991)—§ **11.8, n. 164.**

Ruiz, United States v., 536 U.S. 622, 122 S.Ct. 2450, 153 L.Ed.2d 586 (2002)— § **8.3, n. 59;** § **12.4, n. 57;** § **13.3, n. 41.**

Russell v. United States, 369 U.S. 749, 82 S.Ct. 1038, 8 L.Ed.2d 240 (1962)— § **11.2, n. 85.**

S

Salvucci, United States v., 448 U.S. 83, 100 S.Ct. 2547, 65 L.Ed.2d 619 (1980)—**§ 14.5, n. 29.**

Sanabria v. United States, 437 U.S. 54, 98 S.Ct. 2170, 57 L.Ed.2d 43 (1978)—**§ 11.2, n. 83.**

Santeramo, United States v., 45 F.3d 622 (2nd Cir.1995)—**§ 11.2, n. 69.**

Santobello v. New York, 404 U.S. 257, 92 S.Ct. 495, 30 L.Ed.2d 427 (1971)—**§ 9.0, n. 5.**

Sappe, United States v., 898 F.2d 878 (2nd Cir.1990)—**§ 7.2, n. 81.**

Schilling, United States v., 142 F.3d 388 (7th Cir.1998)—**§ 12.2, n. 40.**

Schneckloth v. Bustamonte, 412 U.S. 218, 93 S.Ct. 2041, 36 L.Ed.2d 854 (1973)—**§ 4.5, n. 39.**

Schneider, United States v., 289 F.Supp.2d 328 (E.D.N.Y.2003)—**§ 8.3, n. 58.**

Scott, United States v., 437 U.S. 82, 98 S.Ct. 2187, 57 L.Ed.2d 65 (1978)—**§ 16.7, n. 76.**

Selioutsky, United States v., 409 F.3d 114 (2nd Cir.2005)—**§ 7.2, n. 89; § 17.4, n. 26.**

Serfass v. United States, 420 U.S. 377, 95 S.Ct. 1055, 43 L.Ed.2d 265 (1975)—**§ 14.12, n. 58.**

Shabani, United States v., 513 U.S. 10, 115 S.Ct. 382, 130 L.Ed.2d 225 (1994)—**§ 11.7, n. 159.**

Shaw v. Martin, 733 F.2d 304 (4th Cir. 1984)—**§ 11.1, n. 34.**

Shaw, United States v., 260 F.Supp.2d 567 (E.D.N.Y.2003)—**§ 14.5, n. 29.**

Shillitani v. United States, 384 U.S. 364, 86 S.Ct. 1531, 16 L.Ed.2d 622 (1966)—**§ 10.3, n. 68, 81.**

Simkin v. United States, 715 F.2d 34 (2nd Cir.1983)—**§ 10.3, n. 77.**

Simmons v. United States, 390 U.S. 377, 88 S.Ct. 967, 19 L.Ed.2d 1247 (1968)—**§ 14.5, n. 29.**

Simon v. United States, 361 F.Supp.2d 35 (E.D.N.Y.2005)—**§ 7.3, n. 97.**

Smith v. Hooey, 393 U.S. 374, 89 S.Ct. 575, 21 L.Ed.2d 607 (1969)—**§ 14.13, n. 60.**

Smith, United States v., 79 F.3d 1208, 316 U.S.App.D.C. 408 (D.C.Cir.1996)—**§ 5.6, n. 59.**

Spicer v. Roxbury Correctional Institute, 194 F.3d 547 (4th Cir.1999)—**§ 13.3, n. 37.**

Stéed, United States v., 646 F.2d 136 (4th Cir.1981)—**§ 16.7, n. 76.**

Stepney, United States v., 246 F.Supp.2d 1069 (N.D.Cal.2003)—**§ 5.2, n. 26.**

Strain, United States v., 396 F.3d 689 (5th Cir.2005)—**§ 11.2, n. 75.**

Strickland v. Washington, 466 U.S. 668, 104 S.Ct. 2052, 80 L.Ed.2d 674 (1984)—**§ 9.3; § 9.3, n. 36; § 13.0, n. 2.**

Strickler v. Greene, 527 U.S. 263, 119 S.Ct. 1936, 144 L.Ed.2d 286 (1999)—**§ 13.3, n. 39.**

Strunk v. United States, 412 U.S. 434, 93 S.Ct. 2260, 37 L.Ed.2d 56 (1973)—**§ 11.6, n. 154; § 14.13, n. 62.**

Suppa, United States v., 799 F.2d 115 (3rd Cir.1986)—**§ 5.7, n. 79.**

T

Taren–Palma, United States v., 997 F.2d 525 (9th Cir.1993)—**§ 16.3, n. 25.**

Taylor v. Louisiana, 419 U.S. 522, 95 S.Ct. 692, 42 L.Ed.2d 690 (1975)—**§ 16.1, n. 5.**

Terry v. Ohio, 392 U.S. 1, 88 S.Ct. 1868, 20 L.Ed.2d 889 (1968)—**§ 3.1, n. 2.**

Thomas, United States v., 274 F.3d 655 (2nd Cir.2001)—**§ 8.3, n. 55.**

Thornburg v. United States, 164 F.2d 37 (10th Cir.1947)—**§ 11.2, n. 82.**

Tyler, United States v., 281 F.3d 84 (3rd Cir.2002)—**§ 17.1, n. 5.**

U

United States v. _____ (see opposing party)

Upton, United States v., 856 F.Supp. 727 (E.D.N.Y.1994)—**§ 13.4, n. 51.**

Urian, United States v., 858 F.2d 124 (3rd Cir.1988)—**§ 16.1, n. 17.**

V

Valenzuela–Bernal, United States v., 458 U.S. 858, 102 S.Ct. 3440, 73 L.Ed.2d 1193 (1982)—**§ 13.4, n. 55.**

Valladares–Helguera, United States v., 2003 WL 22351299 (4th Cir.2003)—**§ 17.3, n. 14.**

Vargas, United States v., 804 F.2d 157 (1st Cir.1986)—**§ 5.7, n. 76.**

Velez, United States v., 354 F.3d 190 (2nd Cir.2004)—**§ 8.2, n. 16.**

Ventresca, United States v., 380 U.S. 102, 85 S.Ct. 741, 13 L.Ed.2d 684 (1965)—**§ 4.2, n. 14.**

Vinson, United States v., 606 F.2d 149 (6th Cir.1979)—**§ 16.4, n. 59.**

Voigt, United States v., 89 F.3d 1050 (3rd Cir.1996)—**§ 11.4, n. 121.**

W

Wade v. United States, 504 U.S. 181, 112 S.Ct. 1840, 118 L.Ed.2d 524 (1992)—**§ 8.2, n. 21; § 9.2, n. 26.**

Wade, United States v., 388 U.S. 218, 87 S.Ct. 1926, 18 L.Ed.2d 1149 (1967)—**§ 13.2, n. 19; § 14.8, n. 43.**

Wainwright v. Sykes, 433 U.S. 72, 97 S.Ct. 2497, 53 L.Ed.2d 594 (1977)—**§ 14.1, n. 18.**

Watkins v. Sowders, 449 U.S. 341, 101 S.Ct. 654, 66 L.Ed.2d 549 (1981)—**§ 13.2, n. 19.**

Watts, United States v., 519 U.S. 148, 117 S.Ct. 633, 136 L.Ed.2d 554 (1997)—**§ 7.2, n. 26; § 12.2, n. 37.**

Wayte v. United States, 470 U.S. 598, 105 S.Ct. 1524, 84 L.Ed.2d 547 (1985)—**§ 4.0, n. 2; § 14.3, n. 24.**

Weeks v. United States, 232 U.S. 383, 34 S.Ct. 341, 58 L.Ed. 652 (1914)—**§ 4.5, n. 30.**

Welch, United States v., 97 F.3d 142 (6th Cir.1996)—**§ 16.3, n. 20.**

Werner, United States v., 620 F.2d 922 (2nd Cir.1980)—**§ 11.3, n. 107.**

Whalen v. United States, 445 U.S. 684, 100 S.Ct. 1432, 63 L.Ed.2d 715 (1980)—**§ 11.3, n. 95.**

Wheat v. United States, 486 U.S. 153, 108 S.Ct. 1692, 100 L.Ed.2d 140 (1988)—**§ 5.2, n. 19.**

White, United States v., 972 F.2d 16 (2nd Cir.1992)—**§ 11.1, n. 35.**

Willard, United States v., 909 F.2d 780 (4th Cir.1990)—**§ 17.4, n. 21.**

Williams v. United States, 168 U.S. 382, 18 S.Ct. 92, 42 L.Ed. 509 (1897)—**§ 11.2, n. 76; § 11.7, n. 162.**

Williams, United States v., 504 U.S. 36, 112 S.Ct. 1735, 118 L.Ed.2d 352 (1992)—**§ 11.1, n. 22.**

Willis, United States v., 956 F.2d 248 (11th Cir.1992)—**§ 11.1, n. 34.**

Wilson, United States v., 350 F.Supp.2d 910 (D.Utah 2005)—**§ 7.3, n. 96.**

Wilson, United States v., 390 F.3d 1003 (7th Cir.2004)—**§ 8.2, n. 24.**

Winship, In re, 397 U.S. 358, 90 S.Ct. 1068, 25 L.Ed.2d 368 (1970)—**§ 15.1, n. 6.**

Wise, United States v., 976 F.2d 393 (8th Cir.1992)—**§ 17.3, n. 17.**

Wong Sun v. United States, 371 U.S. 471, 83 S.Ct. 407, 9 L.Ed.2d 441 (1963)—**§ 4.5, n. 31.**

Wood v. Georgia, 450 U.S. 261, 101 S.Ct. 1097, 67 L.Ed.2d 220 (1981)—**§ 10.5, n. 122.**

Y

Yates v. United States, 355 U.S. 66, 78 S.Ct. 128, 2 L.Ed.2d 95 (1957)—**§ 10.3, n. 78.**

Yaughn, United States v., 493 F.2d 441 (5th Cir.1974)—**§ 16.11, n. 86.**

Yick Wo v. Hopkins, 118 U.S. 356, 6 S.Ct. 1064, 30 L.Ed. 220 (1886)—**§ 4.0, n. 3.**

Z

Zafiro v. United States, 506 U.S. 534, 113 S.Ct. 933, 122 L.Ed.2d 317 (1993)—**§ 11.3, n. 116.**

Zielie, United States v., 734 F.2d 1447 (11th Cir.1984)—**§ 16.3, n. 23.**

Zuleta–Alvarez, United States v., 922 F.2d 33 (1st Cir.1990)—**§ 17.2, n. 12.**

Table of Statutes and Rules

UNITED STATES

UNITED STATES CONSTITUTION

Art.	This Work Sec.	Note
III	1.1	7
Amend.		
4	4.2	
4	4.2	11
4	4.5	
4	4.6	
4	4.6	54
4	4.10	72
4	10.1	2
4	10.2	
4	10.3	
4	14.8	
5	4.5	
5	5.4	40
5	7.3	100
5	8.4	
5	8.4	62
5	10.3	
5	10.3	29
5	10.3	47
5	10.3	48
5	10.5	
5	11.3	
5	11.3	86
5	14.5	29
5	17.1	7
6	1.1	
6	4.8	66
6	5.2	15
6	7.0	
6	7.0	10
6	9.0	
6	10.3	
6	10.4	89
6	10.5	109
6	11.2	
6	11.2	67
6	14.13	
6	14.13	60
6	16.1	1
6	17.1	5
8	10.3	79

UNITED STATES CODE ANNOTATED

8 U.S.C.A.—Aliens and Nationality

Sec.	This Work Sec.	Note
1182(a)(2)	8.3	53

UNITED STATES CODE ANNOTATED

12 U.S.C.A.—Banks and Banking

Sec.	This Work Sec.	Note
3401 et seq.	10.2	10
3413(i)	10.5	103
3420	10.5	104
3420(a)(1)	10.5	104

18 U.S.C.A.—Crimes and Criminal Procedure

Sec.	This Work Sec.	Note
2	11.7	
2(a)	10.5	95
17(b)	15.1	6
19	16.1	1
371	10.5	99
371	11.7	
371	12.1	6
401(3)	10.3	79
656	7.2	45
656	12.1	18
851(a)(1)	8.3	56
924(c)	5.7	
924(c)	11.1	
981(a)(1)(C)	11.4	133
982	11.4	118
982(a)(1)	11.4	129
982(b)(1)	11.4	118
1001	10.5	116
1701	12.1	5
1703	12.1	5
1956	10.5	
1956	12.7	
1956	17.6	
1956	17.7	
1956(a)	10.5	98
1956(c)(7)	11.4	133
1956(h)	10.5	98
1956(h)	11.7	
1961 et seq.	11.4	118
1963	11.4	118
1963(l)(1)	11.4	127
1963(l)(2)	11.4	126
2113(b)	12.1	18
2113(c)	11.2	
2241—2248	5.7	63
2251—2257	5.7	63
2510 et seq.	10.2	7
2510 et seq.	10.5	105
2515	10.3	23

UNITED STATES CODE ANNOTATED
18 U.S.C.A.—Crimes and Criminal Procedure

Sec.	This Work Sec.	Note
2516	10.2	7
2518	10.2	7
2518(3)	10.5	106
3006 et seq.	5.1	4
3006A	5.1	5
3006A	5.1	7
3006A	8.3	58
3006A	12.4	58
3006A(b)	5.10	98
3013	17.6	53
3013(a)(2)(A)	8.3	60
3121—3127	10.5	107
3141 et seq.	14.12	54
3142 et seq.	5.6	42
3142(b)	5.6	43
3142(c)(1)(B)(i)	5.6	44
3142(c)(1)(B)(ii)	5.6	44
3142(c)(1)(B)(iv)	5.6	45
3142(c)(1)(B)(vi)	5.6	44
3142(c)(1)(B)(vi)	5.10	101
3142(c)(1)(B)(vii)	5.6	46
3142(c)(1)(B)(ix)	5.6	44
3142(c)(1)(B)(xii)	5.6	48
3142(c)(2)	5.6	50
3142(d)	5.9	91
3142(d)—(f)	5.7	60
3142(e)	5.7	
3142(e)	5.7	72
3142(e)	5.10	100
3142(e)	5.10	104
3142(f)	5.7	
3142(f)	5.7	74
3142(f)	5.7	80
3142(f)	5.10	
3142(f)	5.10	100
3142(f)(1)	5.7	
3142(f)(1)	5.7	67
3142(f)(1)	5.9	92
3142(f)(1)(A)	5.7	63
3142(f)(1)(B)	5.7	64
3142(f)(1)(C)	5.7	65
3142(f)(1)(D)	5.7	66
3142(f)(2)	5.7	73
3142(f)(2)	5.9	92
3142(f)(2)(A)	5.7	68
3142(f)(2)(B)	5.7	68
3142(g)	5.6	53
3142(g)	5.6	57
3143(a)(2)	8.3	51
3143(a)(2)	9.4	39
3143(a)(2)	9.5	43
3145	5.7	81
3145(a)	5.7	82
3145(b)	5.7	82
3145(c)	5.7	85
3145(c)	8.3	51
3145(c)	9.4	39
3145(c)	9.5	43
3145(c)	14.12	54

UNITED STATES CODE ANNOTATED
18 U.S.C.A.—Crimes and Criminal Procedure

Sec.	This Work Sec.	Note
3148	5.7	69
3148	5.7	82
3148(b)	5.10	102
3148(b)(1)(A)	5.7	71
3148(b)(1)(B)	5.7	71
3148(b)(2)(A)	5.7	70
3148(b)(2)(B)	5.7	70
3161 et seq.	4.7	64
3161 et seq.	11.6	150
3161 et seq.	14.13	63
3161(b)	4.7	64
3161(c)(1)	14.13	66
3161(h)	11.6	150
3161(h)(1)(F)	14.13	67
3161(h)(1)(J)	14.13	68
3161(h)(8)(A)	14.13	69
3162	11.6	151
3162(a)(1)	5.10	97
3162(a)(2)	11.6	152
3162(a)(2)	14.13	64
3231	4.3	23
3237	11.2	75
3237(a)	4.3	25
3238	4.3	25
3281	4.3	26
3281 et seq.	11.6	146
3282	4.3	26
3283	4.3	26
3284	4.3	26
3285	4.3	26
3286	4.3	26
3287	4.3	26
3292	11.6	147
3500	13.4	
3500	13.4	57
3500	13.7	
3500	15.5	
3500	15.5	30
3500	15.6	
3500	16.5	
3500(a)	13.4	58
3500(e)	13.4	57
3501	4.7	62
3501	15.5	
3533(a)	12.3	
3533(b)	12.3	
3551—3585	1.1	16
3551—3585	Intr.Pt.II	
3551 et seq.	11.7	
3553(a)	7.0	
3553(a)	7.3	
3553(a)	7.3	97
3553(a)	9.2	31
3553(a)	9.2	32
3553(a)	12.2	
3553(a)	12.3	
3553(a)	12.3	51
3553(a)	12.6	
3553(a)	12.7	

UNITED STATES CODE ANNOTATED
18 U.S.C.A.—Crimes and Criminal Procedure

Sec.	This Work Sec.	Note
3553(a)	17.1	9
3553(a)	17.4	
3553(a)	17.5	
3553(a)	17.5	27
3553(a)	17.6	
3553(a)(1)—(a)(7)	7.0	8
3553(b)	7.0	
3553(b)	7.0	9
3553(b)	7.3	
3553(b)	12.2	
3553(b)(1)	7.0	
3553(c)	7.2	90
3553(c)	17.4	23
3553(e)	7.2	67
3553(e)	8.0	1
3553(e)	8.3	44
3553(f)	7.2	20
3553(f)	8.3	39
3561(a)	12.1	18
3731	14.12	56
3731	14.12	57
3742	7.2	72
3742	17.4	25
3742(a)(3)	7.2	91
3742(b)(3)	7.2	91
3742(e)	7.0	13
4241	3.3	35
6002	10.3	46
6002	10.4	92
6002—6003	10.4	92
6003(b)	10.3	48

19 U.S.C.A.—Customs and Duties

Sec.	This Work Sec.	Note
1582	2.1	1

21 U.S.C.A.—Food and Drugs

Sec.	This Work Sec.	Note
801—904	5.7	65
841	4.6	49
841	8.3	
841	10.5	
841	17.6	50
841(a)(1)	7.2	
841(a)(1)	10.5	94
841(a)(1)	11.3	
841(b)	7.2	22
841(b)(1)(A)	8.3	27
841(b)(1)(A)	8.3	42
841(b)(1)(A)	17.6	51
843(b)	12.1	19
844	12.1	19
844(a)	11.3	
846	7.2	
846	7.2	22

UNITED STATES CODE ANNOTATED
21 U.S.C.A.—Food and Drugs

Sec.	This Work Sec.	Note
846	10.5	
846	10.5	94
846	12.1	6
848 et seq.	11.4	118
851	8.3	43
851	11.1	
853	11.4	118
853	11.4	134
853(a)(1)	11.4	129
853(k)	11.4	126
853(n)(1)	11.4	127
853(n)(2)	11.4	126
878	10.1	1
878(a)(2)	10.1	4
951—971	5.7	65
952	10.5	
952(a)	10.5	94
960	2.1	1
960	4.6	49
960	10.5	
960(a)(1)	10.5	94
960(a)(1)	11.7	
960(b)(1)	17.6	51
960(b)(1)(B)(ii)	11.7	
963	10.5	
963	10.5	94
963	11.7	

26 U.S.C.A.—Internal Revenue Code

Sec.	This Work Sec.	Note
6103(i)(1)(B)(i)— (i)(1)(B)(ii)	10.2	10

28 U.S.C.A.—Judiciary and Judicial Procedure

Sec.	This Work Sec.	Note
530B	10.4	89
636	9.5	41
636(b)(1)(C)	9.5	42
1291	14.12	54
1651(a)	10.2	9
1746	14.2	20
1783	10.3	39
1826(a)	10.3	67
1861	16.1	5
1861—1869	16.1	6
1865(b)	16.1	7
2461(c)	11.4	
2461(c)	11.4	118

31 U.S.C.A.—Money and Finance

Sec.	This Work Sec.	Note
5313(a)	10.5	99
5324	12.7	
5324	17.6	39

UNITED STATES CODE ANNOTATED
31 U.S.C.A.—Money and Finance

	This Work	
Sec.	Sec.	Note
5324(a)(3)	10.5	
5324(c)(1)	10.5	

46 U.S.C.A.App.—Shipping

	This Work	
Sec.	Sec.	Note
1901—1903	5.7	65

STATUTES AT LARGE

	This Work	
Year	Sec.	Note
2000, P.L. 106–185	11.4	132
2003, P.L. 108–21	7.2	72
2003, P.L. 108–21	7.2	83

CODE OF FEDERAL REGULATIONS

	This Work	
Tit.	Sec.	Note
19, § 162.6	2.1	1
31, § 103.11(gg)	10.5	101
31, § 103.20	10.5	99
31, § 103.20	10.5	100

RULES

MODEL RULES OF PROFESSIONAL CONDUCT

	This Work	
Rule	Sec.	Note
1.6	5.1	13
1.6(a)	10.5	113
1.6(a)	13.7	83
1.7	5.2	29
1.7–10	5.2	15
1.8(f)	10.5	122
1.9	5.2	29
1.10	5.2	30
1.11(a)	5.2	32
1.11(b)	5.2	33
1.11(c)(1)	5.2	31
3.4(e)	16.3	24
3.7(a)	13.7	78
3.7, cmt. 6	10.3	44
4.2	10.4	89
4.2	10.5	121

MODEL CODE OF PROFESSIONAL RESPONSIBILITY

	This Work	
DR	Sec.	Note
5–102(A)	13.7	78
7–104(A)(1)	10.4	89

MODEL CODE OF PROFESSIONAL RESPONSIBILITY

	This Work	
DR	Sec.	Note
7–104(A)(1)	10.5	121
7–106(C)(4)	16.3	24

FEDERAL RULES OF CRIMINAL PROCEDURE

	This Work	
Rule	Sec.	Note
3	3.2	12
3	4.2	20
3	5.4	38
3—5	3.1	3
4	3.2	12
4	4.7	61
4(a)	4.2	22
4(b)	4.2	17
4(d)	4.10	71
5	5.3	35
5	5.9	87
5(a)	5.0	1
5(a)(1)(A)	4.7	60
5(b)	4.7	61
5(c)	5.1	3
5(c)(1)(B)	4.7	60
5(c)(2)	5.9	87
5(c)(3)(C)	5.9	89
5(c)(3)(D)	5.9	90
5(c)(3)(D)(ii)	5.9	88
5.1	5.8	
5.1	6.0	
5.1	6.0	5
5.1(a)	6.0	2
5.1(a)	6.1	13
5.1(b)	5.9	89
5.1(e)	6.0	1
5.1(e)	6.1	14
5.1(e)	14.8	39
6	11.1	5
6(a)(1)	11.1	4
6(d)(1)	10.3	51
6(e)	13.7	82
6(e)(1)	11.1	7
6(e)(2)	11.1	6
6(e)(2)	13.7	80
6(f)	11.1	3
6(f)	11.5	135
6(f)	11.8	165
6(g)	10.5	120
7	3.2	13
7(a)	8.4	63
7(b)	11.0	1
7(b)—(c)	4.1	8
7(c)(1)	11.2	68
7(c)(1)	11.2	70
7(c)(1)	11.2	71
7(c)(1)	11.2	78
7(d)	14.3	27
7(f)	13.2	11
8	4.8	67
8	11.3	

FEDERAL RULES OF CRIMINAL PROCEDURE

Rule	This Work Sec.	Note
8	11.3	89
8	14.1	9
8(a)	11.3	87
8(a)	11.3	102
8(b)	11.3	88
8(b)	11.3	111
9	4.7	61
9	11.5	136
9	11.8	166
9(a)	11.5	139
10	11.5	140
10	11.5	143
10	11.5	144
10(a)(3)	13.2	25
11	1.2	
11	9.0	
11	9.1	
11	9.2	
11	9.2	14
11	11.5	144
11	12.1	
11	12.2	
11	12.2	21
11	12.2	30
11(a)	9.1	
11(a)(2)	1.1	18
11(a)(2)	9.1	11
11(a)(2)	12.5	61
11(b)(1)(A)—(b)(1)(G)	9.2	28
11(b)(1)(H)—(b)(1)(M)	9.2	31
11(b)(1)(M)	9.2	31
11(b)(2)	9.2	30
11(b)(2)—(b)(3)	9.2	27
11(b)(3)	9.2	
11(c)	9.2	
11(c)(1)	9.2	13
11(c)(1)	12.1	8
11(c)(1)(A)	12.1	7
11(c)(1)(B)	9.2	25
11(c)(1)(B)	12.2	22
11(c)(1)(C)	9.2	24
11(c)(1)(C)	12.2	24
11(c)(3)(A)	9.2	24
11(c)(3)(A)	12.1	9
11(c)(3)(B)	9.2	25
11(c)(5)	12.1	10
11(c)(5)	12.1	12
11(c)(5)	12.2	26
11(e)	9.2	22
11(f)	8.2	13
11(f)	9.2	19
11(f)	9.2	21
11(g)	9.2	29
12	4.10	85
12	14.1	
12	14.1	11
12	14.2	
12	14.3	
12	14.6	30
12	14.7	32
12(b)	14.1	

Rule	This Work Sec.	Note
12(b)(1)	14.2	19
12(b)(2)	11.3	100
12(b)(3)	14.1	3
12(b)(3)(A)	14.1	8
12(b)(3)(A)	14.1	12
12(b)(3)(B)	14.1	7
12(b)(3)(B)	14.1	8
12(b)(3)(B)	14.1	13
12(b)(3)(B)	14.1	17
12(b)(3)(C)	13.2	18
12(b)(3)(C)	14.1	11
12(b)(3)(C)	14.1	14
12(b)(3)(D)	14.1	9
12(b)(3)(D)	14.1	16
12(b)(3)(E)	14.1	10
12(b)(3)(E)	14.1	15
12(b)(4)	14.1	11
12(b)(4)(A)	13.2	16
12(b)(4)(A)	13.2	18
12(b)(4)(B)	13.2	17
12(b)(4)(B)	13.2	18
12(b)(4)(B)	14.1	4
12(c)	14.1	4
12(c)	14.1	6
12(d)	14.10	50
12(e)	14.1	3
12(e)	14.1	17
12.1(a)	13.2	26
12.1(a)	16.9	82
12.2	13.2	27
12.2	13.2	29
12.2(a)	16.9	82
12.2(c)(4)	13.5	66
12.3	13.2	28
14	11.3	87
14	14.1	
14	14.1	9
15	6.0	10
15	6.2	
15	13.4	48
15	13.7	75
15	14.0	1
15(a)(1)	6.0	10
16	13.4	
16	13.4	47
16	13.4	49
16	13.6	74
16	13.8	
16	14.1	
16	14.3	
16	15.5	30
16(a)(1)	13.4	47
16(a)(1)(A)	13.4	47
16(a)(1)(B)(ii)	13.4	47
16(a)(1)(C)	13.5	65
16(a)(1)(D)	13.4	45
16(a)(1)(D)	13.5	65
16(a)(1)(E)	13.4	55
16(a)(1)(E)	13.5	62
16(a)(1)(E)	14.8	40
16(a)(1)(F)	13.4	55

FEDERAL RULES OF CRIMINAL PROCEDURE

Rule	This Work Sec.	Note
16(a)(1)(F)	13.5	62
16(a)(2)	13.4	48
16(b)	14.0	2
16(b)(1)(A)	13.5	64
16(b)(1)(B)	13.5	64
16(b)(1)(B)	13.5	65
16(b)(2)	13.5	65
16(b)(2)	13.5	66
16(b)(2)(B)	13.4	60
17	11.1	5
17	13.7	
17	13.7	75
17	14.8	41
17	15.5	27
17(a)	10.3	
17(b)	13.7	86
17(c)	10.3	55
17(c)	10.3	60
17(c)	13.7	
17(c)	13.7	85
17(c)	13.7	86
17(c)	13.7	90
17(c)(2)	13.7	87
17(e)	10.3	
18	4.3	24
18	11.2	75
21	11.2	75
23(a)	15.1	4
23(a)	16.1	2
23(b)(2)(A)	16.1	3
23(b)(3)	16.1	4
24	16.1	19
24(a)	16.1	14
24(b)	16.1	12
24(c)	16.1	19
26.2	6.0	8
26.2	13.4	56
26.2	13.4	57
26.2	13.4	61
26.2	14.9	47
26.2(g)	14.4	28
29	15.1	2
29	16.7	76
29(a)	16.7	72
29(b)	16.7	74
29(c)	16.7	75
29.1	16.11	85
29.1	16.11	87
30	11.3	101
30(a)	15.4	26
30(a)	16.10	84
30(c)	15.4	24
30(c)	16.12	91
30(d)	16.12	92
31(a)	15.1	3
31(a)	16.14	95
31(c)	11.3	101
32(a)	5.7	63
32(c)	17.1	2
32(d)	17.1	3
32(f)	17.2	11

FEDERAL RULES OF CRIMINAL PROCEDURE

Rule	This Work Sec.	Note
32.2	11.4	
32.2	11.4	119
32.2(a)	11.4	120
32.2(b)(1)	11.4	124
32.2(b)(2)	11.4	126
32.2(c)(1)	11.4	121
32.2(c)(2)	11.4	128
32.2(e)	11.4	121
35	17.6	50
35(a)	17.4	24
35(b)(1)	17.6	50
40	5.9	87
41	4.10	74
41	14.8	39
41(b)	4.10	75
41(c)(1)	4.2	21
41(c)(1)	4.10	79
41(c)(2)	4.10	79
41(d)	4.10	84
41(e)	4.10	85
41(e)(2)(B)	4.10	83
41(f)	4.10	85
42(a)(3)	10.3	80
44	5.1	4
44	5.2	18
44(c)	5.2	18
45	14.6	30
46(f)	5.6	49
47	14.2	19
48(b)	14.13	
48(b)	14.13	65
51	16.1	17
52(b)	16.12	92
58	4.1	7
58	16.1	1
58(a)	16.1	1

FEDERAL RULES OF EVIDENCE

Rule	This Work Sec.	Note
103(a)	15.4	19
401	3.3	24
401	16.4	44
402	16.4	45
403	3.3	24
403	3.3	28
403	16.3	29
403	16.4	45
404	13.4	46
404(a)(1)	16.4	48
404(a)(1)	16.4	49
404(a)(2)	16.4	47
404(b)	8.3	40
404(b)	13.2	21
404(b)	13.2	23
404(b)	13.4	46
404(b)	15.3	18
404(b)	16.5	66
405(a)	3.3	34
410	8.2	13
410	9.2	19
501	10.3	57

FEDERAL RULES OF EVIDENCE

Rule	This Work Sec.	Note
602	3.3	22
602	16.4	36
607	3.3	27
607	13.7	79
607	15.5	29
607—609	15.3	17
608(a)	16.4	46
608(a)	16.4	47
608(b)	16.4	47
609	3.3	27
609(a)	16.5	67
609(a)	16.8	79
611(a)	16.4	59
611(b)	16.5	62
611(b)	16.5	63
611(c)	16.4	54
613	13.7	79
613	16.5	68
701—704	3.3	33
702	15.3	16

FEDERAL RULES OF EVIDENCE

Rule	This Work Sec.	Note
702—706	16.4	42
703	3.3	23
703	3.3	32
703	16.4	35
801	16.4	50
801—803	15.3	14
801—807	16.4	41
801(d)(1)(B)	16.4	51
801(d)(1)(C)	16.4	50
801(d)(2)(E)	16.4	58
802	3.3	25
803(5)	16.4	52
803(6)	15.5	31
804(b)(1)	6.0	11
901	3.3	30
901	15.3	15
901—902	16.4	43
901(b)(1)	3.3	31
902	15.3	15
1101(d)(3)	5.6	58

*

THE PRACTICE OF FEDERAL CRIMINAL LAW:

Prosecution and Defense

*

Chapter 1

OVERVIEW OF THE FEDERAL
CRIMINAL PROCESS

Table of Sections

Sec.
1.0 Introduction.
1.1 The Formal Stages of the Federal Criminal Process.
    1.1(a) The Decision to Charge.
    1.1(b) Proceedings on the Complaint.
    1.1(c) Proceedings on the Indictment.
    1.1(d) Pretrial Proceedings.
    1.1(e) The Trial.
    1.1(f) Sentencing.
    1.1(g) Appeal.
1.2 The Guilty Plea Process.
1.3 Preliminary Reflections on the Federal System.

§ 1.0 Introduction

This book describes the federal criminal process from the perspectives of the prosecutor and defense attorney, analyzing the essential tasks that both must perform in the development and resolution of a criminal case. The book is not intended to be a treatise on the law of criminal procedure,[1] but rather a description of the way in which lawyers apply that law in practice. We discuss, of course, the relevant statutory and case law, but that is not our principal focus. Rather, the goal is to describe what happens at every stage from the investigation to the decision to charge to sentencing, in both the "Due Process Model," in which cases are disposed of by trial, and the "Crime Control Model," in

---

1. We will refer throughout to the most comprehensive of these treatises: WAYNE R. LaFAVE, JEROLD H. ISRAEL & NANCY J. KING, CRIMINAL PROCEDURE (2d ed. 1999 & Supp. 2004).

1

which cases are resolved by guilty plea.[2] Through the vehicle of a hypothetical case, we take the reader through the decision-making processes of counsel and illustrate the written and oral advocacy skills required of them.

While the hypothetical case involves a single overall criminal enterprise, we illustrate within it two distinct ways in which criminal cases are initiated. The first begins with a police investigation, leading to the filing of charges by the prosecutor. This we call the "police-initiated" case, and is typically the way "street crime" prosecutions originate. In the second category, the investigation, even if begun by the police, is ultimately directed by the prosecutor who, after using his or her own investigative tools, obtains an indictment. This we call the "prosecutor-initiated" case. It most commonly occurs in more complex white collar or organized crime prosecutions. We shall see that there are many points in the process at which the two types of cases proceed identically, but they are sufficiently different to make separate analyses useful.

This chapter will provide an overview of the stages of the process described in detail in the balance of the book and introduce some preliminary reflections on important features of the system on which we will comment throughout.

§ 1.1 The Formal Stages of the Federal Criminal Process

§ 1.1(a) The Decision to Charge

The decision whether to charge persons with violations of the federal criminal law is exclusively that of the federal prosecutor who, in almost all cases, operates out of United States Attorney's Offices located in each of 94 federal districts.

The decision to charge can take one of three forms:

(1) A *complaint,* filed before a magistrate judge or in a United States district court.[3] The complaint can serve as the final charge in misdemeanor cases, but it must be superseded by an indictment in felony cases, unless the indictment is waived.[4] "Police-initiated" cases are typically commenced by the filing of a complaint;

(2) An *indictment,* returned by the grand jury, or, where the grand jury right is waived;

(3) An almost identical document called an *information*.

Both indictments and informations filed in district court.[5] "Prosecutor-initiated" cases most often begin with an indictment or information.

---

2. The terminology is Herbert Packer's. *See* Herbert Packer, *Two Models of the Criminal Process,* 113 U. Pa. L. Rev. 1 (1964).

3. *See infra* Chapter 4 (The Initial Decision to Charge).

4. A prosecutor's information then replaces the complaint.

5. *See infra* Chapter 11 (The Decision to Indict).

§ 1.1(b) Proceedings on the Complaint[6]

When a case is initiated by complaint, the defendant is brought before the magistrate judge, advised of his or her rights, and assigned counsel if unable to afford one.[7] The magistrate judge reviews the complaint to determine whether it meets the applicable standard for legal sufficiency, namely, probable cause to believe that the defendant has committed a federal offense.[8] The magistrate judge then sets the terms of pretrial release or orders detention in jail. In misdemeanor cases the case is adjourned for trial. In felony cases the case is adjourned for a preliminary hearing,[9] where testimony is presented by the government to demonstrate that probable cause exists to hold the defendant for further action. If the hearing is held, and probable cause is found, the defendant is "bound over" for the action of the grand jury. Very often, however, the hearing will be mooted either by the defendant waiving the right or by the prosecutor presenting the case to a grand jury prior to the date of the hearing and obtaining an indictment.

§ 1.1(c) Proceedings on the Indictment[10]

In police-initiated cases in which the defendant is bound over for the action of the grand jury, or in typical prosecutor-initiated cases, the evidence will be presented by the prosecutor to the grand jury in an *ex parte* proceeding. If, as is almost invariably the case, the grand jury votes to return an indictment, the defendant will be brought before a district court judge for arraignment. Where the case has been commenced by complaint, counsel appointed by the magistrate judge at the initial appearance will usually continue to represent the defendant unless private counsel is retained. If the case begins with an indictment, counsel will be retained or appointed at this point, unless counsel had been retained during the investigative stage as is common in white collar cases. The defendant will then enter a plea. If the defendant were to plead guilty at this stage, the case would be adjourned for sentencing. If, as is usually the case, the defendant enters a not guilty plea, the case will be adjourned for pretrial and trial proceedings. In either situation, the judge will make a decision with respect to the release status of the

---

6. *See infra* Chapter 5 (Proceedings on the Complaint—The Initial Appearance; Bail and Preventive Detention).

7. Magistrate judges (previously designated commissioners, and later magistrates) are subordinate to "Article III" United States district court judges. They have jurisdiction to dispose of misdemeanor cases, but not felonies. In the latter, they commonly handle the preliminary stages, as described in this section. Magistrate judges also perform a number of other functions in felony cases, conducting evidentiary hear-

ings and making recommendations to district court judges as to how those hearings should be decided.

8. An overview of the subject of proof in the criminal process is provided in Chapter 3.

9. *See infra* Chapter 6 (Preliminary Hearing).

10. *See infra* Chapter 11 (The Decision to Indict).

defendant, i.e., whether the defendant will remain at liberty or be detained in jail pending resolution of the case.

§ 1.1(d) Pretrial Proceedings

The rules require that formal motions be filed and litigated prior to trial. These motions deal with a number of issues, most commonly, motions to compel discovery[11] and motions to suppress evidence alleged to have been illegally obtained.[12]

With the resolution of contested pretrial issues by the court, cases not disposed of by plea or dismissal are ready for trial.

§ 1.1(e) The Trial[13]

The defendant has a constitutional right under the Sixth Amendment to a jury trial in all cases punishable by more than one year in prison.[14] Juror lists are created in accordance with plans adopted by the district courts. Once a panel of jurors is called, the trial begins with a jury selection process in which jurors found by the court not to be able to render a fair and impartial verdict are excused for "cause," and other jurors are excused after the exercise of a limited number of "peremptory" challenges (i.e., not for cause) by the parties.

Once the jury is empanelled, the trial commences with the prosecutor's opening statement, usually followed by an opening statement by the defense. The prosecution then puts on the case-in-chief, calling all of the government's witnesses and introducing all of its tangible evidence. All witnesses are subject to cross-examination by the defense.

After the government has completed its case, it rests. At that point the defendant may move for a judgment of acquittal, arguing that there is insufficient evidence upon which a jury could determine that the government has met its burden of proof (beyond a reasonable doubt). If that motion is granted, the case is concluded. If not, the defendant may then put on witnesses, including the defendant if he or she chooses to testify, examined in the same manner as in the government's case. Alternatively, the defendant may choose not to present any evidence, in which case the defense simply will rest.

Each side's closing argument follows the completion of the evidentiary stage of the trial. After the arguments, the judge will instruct the jury on the law, and the jury will retire to deliberate. The decision of the jury to convict or acquit must be unanimous. If the jury cannot reach a unanimous verdict, it is "hung," and the government may bring the case to trial again.

---

11. *See infra* Chapter 13 (Pretrial Discovery). Pre-indictment investigations conducted by the prosecutor and defense attorney are discussed in Chapter 10.

12. *See infra* Chapter 14 (Pretrial Motions).

13. *See infra* Chapter 15 (Preparation for Trial); Chapter 16 (The Trial).

14. That right can be waived, and the issue of guilt submitted to the judge, although it rarely is.

§ 1.1(f) Sentencing[15]

If the defendant is convicted, a date will be set for sentencing. Prior to that time, a probation officer will conduct a presentence investigation for the court. The parties have the opportunity to litigate disputed factual findings in the presentence report. Historically the judge had a very broad sentencing discretion. However, from the passage of the Sentencing Reform Act of 1984[16] (hereinafter the "Sentencing Reform Act") until 2005, all sentencing in federal cases was governed exclusively by the United States Sentencing Guidelines (hereinafter "Guidelines" or "Sentencing Guidelines"), which imposed significant limitations on the court's discretion in sentencing. The Guidelines are an elaborate compilation of rules and calculations that—with limited exceptions—set narrow ranges of punishment that the judge must impose depending on the facts and circumstances of the particular crime and the history of the particular defendant. In January 2005, the Supreme Court ruled in *United States v. Booker* that while the Guidelines still had to be "considered" in every case, they were advisory only, thus restoring at least some of the judicial discretion lost under the Sentencing Reform Act.[17]

Convicted defendants who are sentenced to prison are incarcerated in federal correction facilities ranging from low security camps, in which inmates live in dormitories, to "super" maximum security prisons providing almost complete isolation of individual prisoners.

§ 1.1(g) Appeal

A defendant convicted at trial has a right to appeal to the United States Circuit Court of Appeals with jurisdiction over the district in which the trial took place.[18] That court is the court of last resort in all but the very small number of cases that reach the United States Supreme Court.

§ 1.2 The Guilty Plea Process

At any stage after the filing of the indictment (and even at times before the filing of the indictment) the case may be resolved by a guilty plea. The guilty plea usually follows a negotiation between the prosecutor and defense attorney. We describe the all-important guilty plea system in three chapters. One deals with negotiations between prosecutors and "cooperating" defendants, i.e., those who become eligible to receive typically substantial sentencing reductions based on the prosecu-

---

15. *See infra* Chapter 7 (Assessing the Risk of Trial—The Sentencing Guidelines); Chapter 17 (Sentencing).

16. 18 U.S.C. §§ 3551–3585.

17. 125 S.Ct. 738 (2005) (discussed in detail in Chapter 7 below).

18. Defendants convicted upon guilty pleas also may have certain rights to appeal, *see* FED. R. CRIM. P. 11(a)(2), although guilty pleas that are the result of negotiation with the government typically require the defendant to waive these rights.

tor's determination that they can and will provide substantial assistance in the prosecution of other persons and/or crimes.[19]

A second chapter deals with negotiations with defendants who are not trading information and cooperation in exchange for a sentence reduction, but who receive sentencing concessions for saving the system's resources by giving up their right to trial.[20] Negotiations in these cases focus on the facts that will (or would) be presented to the court to maneuver the case either into an agreed-upon sentence under the Sentencing Guidelines, or toward a non-Guidelines sentence if the judge is willing to exercise the discretion to impose one. Such negotiations may concern the charges to which the defendant will plead or other sentencing factors that are relevant to the Guidelines range or a non-Guidelines sentence. (The difference between a Guidelines Sentence and a non-Guidelines Sentence is discussed in detail in chapter 7.)

The third chapter dealing with guilty pleas describes the process by which these pleas are entered in court.[21] This process is governed by Rule 11 of the Federal Rules of Criminal Procedure. That rule is designed to make the terms of the agreement part of the record and to assure that the defendant is fully informed of the consequences of his or her action.

§ 1.3   Preliminary Reflections on the Federal System

In 2004, some 82,000 felony defendants' cases were terminated in the federal system. Of these, about 90% resulted in convictions, and about 96% of the convictions were the result of pleas of guilty.[22] Most of these guilty pleas were the result of a bargain struck between the government and the defendant, in which the defendant, in return for sentencing concessions, agreed to waive the right to trial as well as to pretrial discovery and proceedings to determine the admissibility at trial of the government's evidence.

As these statistics suggest, the federal criminal process normally operates in a manner far different from Professor Packer's "Due Process Model" of criminal justice—a kind of "obstacle course" to conviction involving elaborate adversarial testing of the strength of the government's case and of the propriety with which it was made.[23] In that model, the crowning event is trial by jury, at which the government must sustain a heavy burden of proof against a defendant protected by the presumption of innocence. As we have just seen, however, in the system actually in operation, the trial, far from being the crowning event, is in fact responsible for the resolution of a small percentage of all cases in

---

19. *See infra* Chapter 8 (Plea Negotiation and the Cooperating Defendant).

20. *See infra* Chapter 12 (Plea Negotiation and the Non–Cooperating Defendant).

21. *See infra* Chapter 9 (The Guilty Plea Proceeding).

22. Judicial Business of the United States Courts, Table D–4, *available at*

http://www.uscourts.gov/ judbus2004/appendices/d4.pdf (Sept. 30, 2004). Of the 10% of the cases in which the defendant was not convicted, 92% were dismissed, and only 8% were acquitted after a trial. *Id.*

23. *See* Packer, *supra* note 2.

which the government's ability to prove the defendant's guilt is determined.

In the guilty plea system—Packer's "Crime Control Model" of justice—the focus is not on adversarial testing of the strength of the government's case or on protecting against government overreaching, but on the speedy conviction and sentencing of defendants presumed to be factually guilty. Here, the locus of power is not the judge and jury; it is the prosecutor. The prosecutor has virtually total control over whether and what to charge and also will determine the crime to which the defendant may plead guilty. The defendant, moreover, will usually agree to plead guilty because the consequences of being convicted at trial are likely to be far greater punishment.

The primacy of the prosecutor is a feature of the criminal justice system in every jurisdiction in the country. In the past two decades, however, it has been enhanced substantially in the federal system with the passage of the Sentencing Reform Act and implementation of the Sentencing Guidelines. As noted, we will discuss in detail below the Guidelines and the Supreme Court's recent modification of them. Suffice it to say here that the prosecutor's control over the charging decision and substantial influence over the factors that go into the sentencing decision greatly enhance his or her power over the sentence under even an advisory Guidelines system.

The added concentration of power in the prosecutor and the concomitant marginalization of the judicial function call into question the viability of traditional notions of how the criminal justice system can assure fairness and accuracy. The courts have long abdicated any reviewing function over the fairness of charge decisions or whether facts sufficient to support them exist. With the high rate of guilty pleas, the protections afforded defendants by the formal rules of pretrial practice mean very little in the vast majority of cases. Thus relatively few formal challenges are made to the legality of police conduct in obtaining evidence. Pretrial discovery rights, already limited at least in part on the theory that the prosecution must make full disclosure of its evidence at trial, often provide little assurance that the defendant will be fully informed of the government's case before entering a guilty plea. As a practical matter, the historic role of judge and jury in assuring a fair and impartial determination that the charges are proven beyond a reasonable doubt is significantly diminished.

Appellate review of the sufficiency of the evidence on which convictions are based, and on the fairness of the trial and pretrial process, is also an insignificant factor in the guilty plea system in practice. In almost all cases disposed of by plea, the defendant waives his or her right to appeal. In 2003, of the approximately 12,000 criminal appeals filed in the courts of appeals (a year in which there were 75,000 convictions), almost 85% involved at least some sentencing issues; only 15% concerned exclusively non-sentencing issues.[24] The Supreme Court's opinion in *United States v. Booker* has generated a flood of appellate cases, not likely to abate for several years, relating overwhelmingly to sentencing issues. It seems likely, therefore, that sentencing issues will continue to dominate appellate calendars.

What the Crime Control Model assumes, as Packer put it, is that the police and prosecutor can accurately distinguish the guilty from the innocent and can be relied upon to enforce the law fairly. To the extent that there is an institutional check on the prosecutor's power in the guilty plea system, it is the defense attorney. Without de facto access to the courts, however, the check is exercised informally, through the process of negotiating dismissals, guilty pleas, and sentences with the prosecutor. We shall try to demonstrate that resourceful and imaginative defense counsel, while hardly an equal negotiating party, can do much to safeguard the client's rights or at least to soften the inevitable blow.

Having described a system in operation very different from the Due Process Model with which a substantial portion of this book is concerned, a word of explanation is in order as to why we focus so much attention on that model. The justification is that the Due Process Model is a kind of intellectual default on which prosecutors and defense attorneys premise their actions in practice. In a competently operationalized Crime Control system, cases are evaluated by counsel as if they were to go through rigorous adversarial testing, even though the parties know that the odds of that happening are slim. In this sense, a party's stance in negotiation is based upon a prediction of what would happen if the case went through the formal process.

Needless to say, the guilty plea system does not always operate in this way. At its worst—in the overwhelmed state courts—it can be a mindless operation through which cases are processed by attorneys and judges who have little knowledge of the facts and whose principal, if not only, concern is the disposition of the day's calendar.[25] While the pressure to dispose of cases without trial is great even in the less congested federal courts, in our experience the parties there are far more likely to engage in the factual and legal investigation described in this book. Notwithstanding the primacy of the Crime Control Model, a significant number of cases—albeit a small percentage of the overall cases—are resolved by trial at which all of the adversarial testing of the Due Process Model takes place, including the requirement that the government prove its charges beyond a reasonable doubt to the satisfaction of a unanimous jury.

---

24. Judicial Business of the United States Courts, *supra* note 22, at Table S–6.

25. *See* Harry I. Subin, The New York City Criminal Court: The Case for Abolition (1992) (unpublished manuscript, on file with The Center for Research in Crime and Justice, New York University School of Law, Occasional Papers No. XII).

Part I

THE DEVELOPMENT OF A POLICE INITIATED FEDERAL CASE

Chapter 2

U.S. v. MARIO LONG—THE INVESTIGATION

Table of Sections

Sec.
2.0 Introduction.
2.1 The Investigation by the Drug Enforcement Administration.
2.2 The Search and Arrests.
2.3 Booking and Identification Procedures.
2.4 The Post–Arrest Investigation.
     2.4(a) Interrogation.
     2.4(b) Consent Tape Recording.
2.5 Memorializing the Investigation—The DEA Reports.
2.6 Presenting the Case to the United States Attorney's Office.

---

§ 2.0 Introduction

This chapter will describe the investigation, arrest, search and post-arrest processing in our model police-initiated case. It contains considerable factual detail concerning police activities. Some of the facts are included for the purpose of describing police investigative and processing procedures with which the reader may not be familiar. Other facts are included to form a basis for discussion of a number of potential legal issues arising from the police activities in the model case. A chronology of the factual events described in this and subsequent chapters is included as Appendix C.

§ 2.1 The Investigation by the Drug Enforcement Administration

International Food Distributors Incorporated ("IFD") is owned by Paul Christopher. The company imports coffee and other food products from Colombia and other Latin American countries and distributes these products to retailers in the New York City metropolitan area. Imported products are held for distribution at Superior Warehouse, Inc., a wholly-owned subsidiary of IFD located in Queens, New York. The goods IFD imports typically arrive at Kennedy Airport, an international border supervised by the United States Customs and Border Protection ("Customs"). Customs agents are charged with interdicting the importation of controlled substances, illegal currency, weapons, and other contraband.[1]

On January 5, 2005 an agent of the Drug Enforcement Administration ("DEA") received information from a confidential informant (designated by the agency as "CI–4") who stated that crates containing cocaine were being shipped to Superior Warehouse at 149 Grand Street, Queens, New York, hidden in coffee consignments. The DEA agent entered this information into a law enforcement data log shared with Customs, and set up a computerized "lookout" for shipments from Colombia destined for Superior Warehouse.

On January 11, in response to this tip and the "lookout," Customs agents identified a shipment of twelve crates consigned to IFD that were awaiting delivery to Superior Warehouse. DEA Agent Ralph Martinez was notified and went to the airport.[2] A Customs agent then opened the crates. Martinez found 10 cloth packages in one of them. Inside the packages was a white powder, which the agent "field-tested." The substance proved to contain cocaine. A total of 9.8 kilograms of the substance was discovered. Martinez substituted packages containing flour for the cocaine, leaving only a small trace amount of the drug in one of them. Before resealing the crates he placed a homing device inside the crate in which the trace amount of cocaine had been left. The homing device would convey a signal to a beeper carried by the agents, enabling them to monitor the movements of the crate and to locate it when it reached its destination.

On January 12, Agent Martinez and two of his colleagues, Agents William Foster and Gloria Richards, placed Superior Warehouse under surveillance from an unmarked van parked nearby. One of the people observed was Gilbert Santiago, a person whom Agent Martinez identified (after running the license plate of the car he was driving) as having been previously convicted of trafficking in cocaine. The agents observed Santiago enter and exit the warehouse on three different occasions between 9 a.m. and 1 p.m. on January 12. Santiago was driving a 2002 brown Mercedes Benz automobile.

The next step in the DEA operation was to make a "controlled delivery" of the crates containing the cocaine. On January 12, at about 2:00 p.m., DEA Agent Richard Sobel, posing as a truck driver, drove a

---

1. The importation of cocaine is criminalized by 21 U.S.C. § 960. Title 19, United States Code § 1582 and 19 C.F.R. § 162.6 give customs officers broad powers to examine and search persons, baggage and merchandise for violations of United States customs laws.

2. Federal agents typically are designated "special agents." For simplicity we will refer to them as "agents."

truck containing the crates to Superior Warehouse. He parked at the loading dock and entered the warehouse office. There, he was met by a man wearing a work-shirt with the name "Mario" written on it. Sobel asked to see the foreman in order to have the bill of lading signed. "Mario" said that he was the foreman. He signed the documents as "Mario Long" and requested and received a receipt. He then told Sobel that his men would remove the crates from the delivery truck. Agent Sobel then left the office, opened the truck and waited in the cab while a worker removed the crates, including the crate containing the trace amount of cocaine and the homing device. The worker opened an overhead door and brought all of the crates into the warehouse. Agent Sobel noticed the worker looking around nervously during the unloading process.

After the unloading was completed, the door was closed. Agent Sobel noticed that all of the crates were handled in the same way. In all, Sobel's contact with Long lasted 3–4 minutes. He was waiting for the truck to be unloaded for approximately 30 minutes, but was not in visual contact with the worker during this time and did not speak with him.

When he drove away from the warehouse, Agent Sobel radioed a description of Long and the worker to Agents Martinez, Foster and Richards. The description was the same as that which he entered in his account of the transaction in his memo book. He described Long as a male, Caucasian, aged 35–40, 5'10", 165 pounds, with dark brown hair, round glasses, and brown moustache. He described the worker as male, Caucasian, age 20–25, wearing gray overalls.

§ 2.2 The Search and Arrests

Shortly after Sobel's departure, Agents Martinez, Foster and Richards proceeded to the warehouse door. Foster turned on the tracker in order to locate the crate in which the homing device had been placed. Agent Martinez rang the bell by the office door. A person in green work clothes with the name "Mario" inscribed on his right pocket opened the door. Martinez showed Mario his badge and identified himself as a DEA agent. Martinez stated that the agents were "working on a narcotics investigation and wanted to search the warehouse." Mario stated "I'm not sure whether to let you in. I think I should wait for Gil." He said that Gil was the manager of the warehouse. At this point, Agent Martinez told Mario that if the agents were not permitted to search, they would secure the warehouse to assure that nothing was destroyed or moved and that no one was armed, and would wait there until a search warrant was obtained. Mario then said, "Go ahead and look around then. I don't want any trouble." At that point, Agents Martinez, Foster and Richards entered the warehouse.

The agents first noticed that eleven of the twelve crates from the delivery made by Sobel were stacked alongside one of the walls. As Agent Foster approached these crates, the beeper signal became weaker. When

Foster turned toward the opposite wall the signal became stronger. In the center of this wall was a locked metal door. Agent Martinez asked Mario whether anything was behind the locked door. Mario said that some very valuable crates were placed there to protect against theft. Martinez then asked Mario to open the locked door. Mario responded again that he was not sure that he should because Gil was not there. Martinez again told Mario that it was up to him, but that if he refused the agents would get a warrant and then break open the door. Mario asked whether he could return to his office to obtain the key. Agent Martinez responded by stating that he could do so, but that one of the agents would have to go with him. Mario shrugged and started to walk toward a glass-enclosed office, a distance of about 50 feet from the wall where Martinez and Foster stood. Agent Richards went with him. They soon returned and Mario gave the key to Agent Martinez who then opened the door. The twelfth crate was present behind the door and the beeper emitted a loud sound. Martinez opened the crate and determined that it contained the trace of cocaine. The agents arrested Mario. They also arrested a worker named Arthur Murphy who appeared to fit the description given by Agent Sobel of the person who had removed the crates from the truck and had been looking around nervously.

After the agents frisked the men and determined that they were unarmed, Mario and the worker were taken to DEA headquarters. The crate containing the cocaine was taken and vouchered with the DEA property clerk. At DEA headquarters, the agents also inventoried all the personal property of the two men and placed it in bags to accompany them throughout the detention process. During the inventory, Agent Martinez found a date book that Mario was carrying. He read the names, addresses, and phone numbers of various trucking firms listed on various dates. On the January 12 page, he saw the name and telephone number of Van Ness Trucking. Martinez also noted and copied the driver's license, social security number, and credit cards contained in Long's wallet.

Martinez then called the United States Attorney's Office for the Eastern District of New York (where Kennedy Airport and Superior Warehouse are located) and described the facts to Assistant United States Attorney ("AUSA") Laura Knapp, the Deputy Chief of the Narcotics Section, who was on duty. It is not uncommon in cases of this kind that the AUSA will decide at that point whether there is sufficient evidence to justify continuing the case against the individuals who have been detained or, instead, whether those persons should be released.[3] Knapp authorized Martinez to continue to hold Long and Murphy for prosecution by the United States Attorney's Office, and they were lodged

---

3. As in this case, agents may contact the AUSA just after the initial detention of the suspects. It is not, however, required that they do so; the first review of the case by the AUSA may come at the time that the agent appears at the U.S. Attorney's office.

in cells at DEA Headquarters.[4] Martinez then went to the United States district courthouse where AUSA Knapp's office was located.

§ 2.3 Booking and Identification Procedures

While still at DEA headquarters, the men were processed by Agent Foster. Foster also fingerprinted both men to determine whether either of them had a prior criminal record or whether they had used an alias.

As part of the processing, Foster also asked background or "pedigree" questions of each of the men to determine their residence, age, marital status and the like.

Long informed Foster that his name was Mario Long and that he resided with his wife at 110 East 103rd Street in Manhattan. He stated that he was a high school graduate who had taken some business courses at a community college and that he had lived his entire life in New York City. He said that he had been employed at Superior Warehouse for 10 years and for the last five years as the foreman of the warehouse. He said his boss was Gilbert Santiago, the manager of the warehouse. Long said that he received an honorable discharge from the army 15 years ago and had achieved the rank of sergeant. He stated that he had never been arrested before, something that was later confirmed by a fingerprint check conducted by Agent Richards.

Agent Foster asked similar kinds of questions of the other worker, who gave his name as Arthur Murphy. Murphy had been employed at the warehouse for two months prior to the arrest. He had no prior criminal record and was married with children. Murphy volunteered that he had just arrived at work when the agents were making the arrests and that he had no idea that there were any drugs in the crates or in the warehouse.

While both Long and Murphy responded to Agent Foster's booking questions, they sat in a room containing a two-way mirror that enabled Agent Sobel to view them unobserved. After Agent Foster completed the booking questions, he spoke with Agent Sobel in the adjacent room. Sobel identified Long as the foreman who received the shipment and signed the bill of lading. He indicated that Murphy was the worker who had removed the crates from the truck. Upon receiving this information, Agent Foster removed Long to another room, a holding cell, to be interrogated by Agent Martinez.

§ 2.4 The Post–Arrest Investigation

§ 2.4(a) Interrogation

Agent Martinez began by reading Long the so-called "*Miranda* warnings"[5] from a card provided to agents by the DEA. He advised

---

4. Depending upon the time of day and other circumstances, the arrestees might also be taken directly to the United States courthouse, to be lodged in court pens until the case cleared the U.S. Attorney's Office and was presented to the magistrate judge, or to a detention facility (a jail) in which pretrial detainees and inmates serving short sentences are held, if one is available in the district.

5. Miranda v. Arizona, 384 U.S. 436 (1966).

Long: that he had a right to remain silent; that anything he said could be used against him in court; that he had a right to speak to an attorney before answering questions, and to have an attorney with him; and that if he could not afford an attorney one could be appointed to represent him at no expense to him. After each of the warnings, Martinez asked Long if he understood what Martinez had said, and Long responded "yes." Martinez then told Long that he wanted him to cooperate with the DEA and asked him if he would sign a waiver of rights form on which he would affirm in writing that he had been advised of his rights and was voluntarily agreeing to waive them and to answer questions without the assistance of a lawyer. Martinez told him that there was no point in taking responsibility for the cocaine if he was acting under the direction of others. Martinez said that he would inform the Assistant United States Attorney assigned to Long's case of his cooperation. He told Long that it was up to the prosecutor to determine whether to let him cooperate, but that if the prosecutor did, and if Long cooperated fully and helped the government convict others, the prosecutor might recommend that he get a lower sentence. He said, however, that he could not make a specific promise regarding any sentence a judge might impose. Long responded that he was not certain whether to cooperate and that he would think about it for a while. Agent Martinez told him that he had two hours to decide and that if he agreed he would have to tell everything he knew, including what role Gilbert Santiago played in the importation and distribution of cocaine. Martinez also explained that should Long decide to cooperate, he would ask Long to tape a phone conversation with Santiago.

About 30 minutes later, Long asked to speak with Agent Martinez. Long told him that he was willing to tell him everything he knew about the crates and Gilbert Santiago. Agent Martinez then repeated the *Miranda* warnings and asked Long whether he was now willing to sign the waiver form and make a statement in the absence of an attorney. When Long responded "yes," Martinez asked him to read the Advice of Rights and Waiver of Rights form and to sign the form. After signing the form, Long made the following statement, which Martinez transcribed on a DEA Investigation Report.

> I had nothing to do with importing the cocaine and was never told that the crates contained illegal narcotics. All I did was move any crates containing a special mark to a place behind the locked door. Then I would see to it that only Van Ness Trucking Co. would be permitted to take possession of those crates. Santiago said that once a shipment with a specially marked crate was delivered, he would inspect the crate behind the locked door. Today, Van Ness Trucking was scheduled to pick up the specially marked crate once Santiago returned and inspected the crate.

When Martinez finished typing the statement, he handed it to Long and asked Long to read the statement to confirm that it was correct. Long acknowledged the accuracy of the statement and signed his name at the bottom.

Agent Martinez then asked Long about the names found in the date book in Long's possession at the time of his arrest. Long stated that these were the names of all trucking firms that did business with Superior Warehouse along with the phone numbers and dates on which each firm either delivered or received a shipment. When Agent Martinez asked Long how he was paid, Long said that checks were written by a bookkeeper at the direction of Santiago.

§ 2.4(b) Consent Tape Recording

Following the interrogation, Agent Martinez brought Long to a room containing a telephone and tape recording device. He explained to Long that the purpose of the device was to record a conversation between him and Gilbert Santiago. Martinez showed Long how the mechanical device would be attached to the telephone receiver and the tape recorder. Long then said that he did not know what to say to Santiago. Agent Martinez told Long not to tell Santiago that he had been arrested, but, rather, to say that the shipment had arrived and that he was having trouble contacting Van Ness to pick it up. Martinez said that Long should say that he was nervous having the stuff around and that it wasn't worth it to him to take the risk. Martinez told Long to let Santiago do most of the talking and said that he would be there to help if a problem arose.

Long dialed a phone number that Santiago had given him in case of an emergency. The following taped telephone conversation ensued between Long and Gilbert Santiago:

Long: Gil, this is Mario. I got the shipment from Kennedy. Where the hell is Van Ness? I tried to call him and I can't reach him.

Santiago: OK, calm down. There's nothing to worry about. Where's the material?

Long: It's in the back room. Listen, I don't want to be here with this shit. Murphy's freaking out too.

Santiago: You know, we've gone over this before. Everything is cool as long as you just shut up. You don't know nothing. And Murphy don't know nothing either, right?

Long: Yeah. But get Van Ness, will you?

Santiago: OK.

* * *

Once the conversation was complete, the agent played the tape back to Long and asked him whether it was an accurate recording of the conversation. When Long responded that it was, Martinez had Long sign a document to that effect. He then placed the tape in a sealed DEA evidence envelope with the arrest number of the case attached to the envelope and vouchered the envelope with the DEA property clerk.

Agent Martinez then attempted to interview Arthur Murphy, but Murphy requested a lawyer and declined to speak.

§ 2.5 Memorializing the Investigation—The DEA Reports

Throughout the investigation of Superior Warehouse, Agent Martinez memorialized his actions and those of the other agents by preparing investigation reports pursuant to DEA regulations. Relevant information is recorded on a form called a "DEA 6." DEA 6 forms memorializing the developments in our model case appear below.

U.S. Department of Justice
Drug Enforcement Administration

REPORT OF INVESTIGATION

Page 1 of 1

1. Program Code	2. Cross File	Related Files	3. File No. NO-05-053	4. G-DEP Identifier
5. By: Ralph Martinez, S/A At: JFK Airport Office	☐ ☐ ☐ ☐ ☐		6. File Title Superior Warehouse, Inc.	
7. ☐ Closed ☐ Requested Action Completed ☐ Action Requested By.	☐		8. Date Prepared January 11, 2005	
9. Other Officers				
10. Report Re: Case Initiation Report				

DETAILS

DATE OF INITIATION:

1. On January 11, 2005, case file number NR–05–0053 with file title Superior Warehouse, Inc., was assigned to this investigation.

BASIS OF INITIATION:

2. On January 5, 2005, the New York Field Division of the Drug Enforcement Administration ("DEA") was contacted by CI–4. CI–4 advised that crates containing cocaine were being shipped to Superior Warehouse, Inc. ("Superior") and disguised in coffee consignments.

3. On January 11, 2005, Customs Agent Donald Mercado opened the crates consigned to Superior in the presence of S/A Ralph Martinez who seized from 1 of them 10 cloth packages each containing approximately 1 kilogram of a white powdery substance which field tested positive for cocaine. The crate was addressed to International Food Distributors, Inc. c/o Superior Warehouse, 149 Grand St., Queens, New York. Investigation revealed that International Food Distributors, Inc. ("IFD") is owned by Paul Christopher, and that Superior is a wholly owned subsidiary of IFD.

4. The contents of the cloth packages were then removed except for a small amount of cocaine left in 1 of the packages, and the packages were refilled with flour. The packages were then returned to the crate, and a homing device was installed.

5. S/A Richard Sobel was assigned to make a controlled delivery of the crates to Superior on January 12, 2005.

TARGETS OF INVESTIGATION:

    6. The targets of this investigation are the owners and operators of Superior, their sources of supply, as well as any of their associates involved in the cocaine trafficking organization.

OBJECTIVES:

    7. The objective of this investigation is to identify Superior's owners and operators, their sources of supply, associates, and their methods of importation and distribution.

INDEXING

11. Distribution:	12. Signature (Agent)	13. Date
Division	*Ralph Martinez*	January 11, 2005
District		
	14. Approved (Named and Title)	15. Date

U.S. Department of Justice
Drug Enforcement Administration

REPORT OF INVESTIGATION			Page 1 of 1	
1. Program Code	2. Cross File	Related Files	3. File No. NO-05-053	4. G-DEP Identifier
5. By: Ralph Martinez, S/A At: JFK Airport Office	☐ ☐ ☐ ☐ ☐		6. File Title Superior Warehouse, Inc.	
7. ☐ Closed ☐ Requested Action Completed ☐ Action Requested By.			8. Date Prepared January 12, 2005	
9. Other Officers S/As William Foster, Gloria Richards and Richard Sobel				
10. Report Re: Controlled Delivery of Exhibit #1 and Arrests of Mario Long and Arthur Murphy				

DETAILS

    1. Reference is made to DEA–6 dated January 11, 2005 by S/A Ralph Martinez under this case number and file title.

    2. On January 12, 2005, S/A Martinez observed Gilbert Santiago enter and exit Superior Warehouse, Inc. ("Superior"), 149 Grand St., Queens, NY on three occasions. On each occasion Santiago remained for approximately fifteen minutes and then left, driving a 2002 brown Mercedez–Benz 560 SEL. A registration check of this vehicle revealed that it was registered to International Food Distributors, Inc. (249 Queens Blvd., Queens, NY), Paul Christopher, president. Santiago was identified by S/A Martinez as someone who had been convicted of cocaine distribution in the Eastern District in 1998.

    3. On January 12, 2005, at approximately 2:00 pm, S/A Richard Sobel, who was acting in an undercover capacity, delivered twelve crates to Superior at 149 Grand St., Queens, New York. Exhibit N-1 was the crate in which the cocaine referenced in DEA-6 by S/A Martinez on January 11, 2005 had been found at Kennedy Airport.

4. S/A Sobel parked his truck at the loading dock of Superior Warehouse at the above address and entered the warehouse office. He was met by a man wearing a workshirt with the name "Mario." Mario said that he was the foreman and he signed "Mario Long" on the receipt documents, marked as Exhibit N–2. Long directed a worker to remove Exhibit N–1 and the other crates, marked Exhibit N–3 a-k, from Agent Sobel's truck. During the unloading the worker was observed looking around suspiciously. After Exhibits N–1 and N–3, were moved into the warehouse, S/A Sobel left the area while S/A Martinez, Foster, and Richards continued surveillance. At approximately 2:30 pm, the agents rang the bell at the office door of the address. Long opened the door and in response to S/A Martinez's request to enter and search, stated "I am not sure whether to permit you to enter. I think we should wait for Gil." Long identified "Gil" as the manager of the warehouse. S/A Martinez informed Long that if he did not permit the agents to enter, a search warrant would be obtained. Long then said "Go ahead and look around. I don't want any trouble."

5. After the homing device indicated that Exhibit N–1 was located behind a locked door, S/A Martinez asked Long what was behind the door. Long said that valuable crates had been placed there to protect against theft. When S/A Martinez asked Long to open the door, Long again stated that he was not sure that he should open the door without Gil being there. When S/A Martinez again informed Long about obtaining a search warrant, Long went with S/A Richards to obtain a key for the locked door from Long's office.

6. When Long and S/A Richards returned to the locked door, Long gave the key to S/A Martinez who opened the door and observed Exhibit N–1. Thereafter the agents arrested Long and the worker described by S/A Sobel, Arthur Murphy. Those arrested were escorted to DEA offices at JFK Airport.

CUSTODY OF EVIDENCE:

Exhibit N–1, a crate containing a trace amount of cocaine, was seized by S/A Martinez behind a locked door at the address. S/A Martinez maintained custody of Exhibit N–1 until it was transported back to DEA offices at JFK Airport, Queens, New York for safekeeping pending its transfer to the DEA/Northeast Laboratory for analysis and safekeeping via DEA Form 7.

Exhibits N–2 and N–3 were maintained by S/A Martinez at the DEA office at JFK Airport pending their transfer to non-drug evidence custodian at DEA/555 West 57th Street, New York, New York via DEA Form 7a.

INDEXING

11. Distribution: Division District	12. Signature (Agent)	13. Date January 12, 2005
	Ralph Martinez	

	14. Approved (Named and Title)	15. Date

DEA Form   -6
(Jul. 1996)

U.S. Department of Justice
Drug Enforcement Administration

REPORT OF INVESTIGATION   Page 1 of 1

1. Program Code	2. Cross File	Related Files	3. File No. NO-05-053	4. G-DEP Identifier
5. By: Ralph Martinez, S/A At: JFK Airport Office	□ □ □ □ □		6. File Title Superior Warehouse, Inc.	
7. □ Closed □ Requested Action Completed □ Action Requested By.			8. Date Prepared January 12, 2005	

9. Other Officers
S/A William Foster

10. Report Re: Post-Arrest Statements of Mario Long and Arthur Murphy

DETAILS

1. On January 12, 2005, Mario Long was arrested by DEA/Group 13 agents after obtaining custody of a crate containing cocaine. Long was placed under arrest and advised of his constitutional rights from DEA Form 13 by S/A Ralph Martinez, as witnessed by S/A Rich Sobol. Long was asked if he understood his constitutional rights, to which he verbally stated "yes." Long voluntarily made the statement which appears on the attached post-arrest statement form, after reading and signing the Advice of Rights and Waiver of Rights form Exhibit N–5.

2. Long resides at 110 East 103rd Street, New York City, New York. When S/A Martinez asked Long about the names found in the datebook in his possession, Exhibit N–6, Long stated that these were the names of trucking firms that did business with Superior Warehouse, Inc. along with their phone numbers and dates on which they either delivered or received a shipment.

3. Following the post-arrest statement, Long agreed to place a telephone call to Gilbert Santiago and consented to the recording of the conversation, Exhibit N–7. During the conversation which was overheard by S/A Martinez, Long told Santiago that a shipment had arrived from Kennedy. Santiago asked Long where the "material" was, and Long said it was in the back room. Long told Santiago that he did not want to be there with this "shit," and that Murphy was "freaking out." He asked Santiago where Van Ness was. Santiago said that everything would be "cool" if Long shut up, and that "you don't know nothing. And Murphy don't know nothing either, right?"

4. On January 12, 2005 Arthur Murphy was arrested at the time and place of the arrest of Mario Long. While providing pedigree information Murphy volunteered the following statement, without being asked any questions about what happened at the warehouse. Murphy stated: "I just got to work at the time you were arresting Mario. I had no idea there were any drugs there."

CUSTODY OF EVIDENCE:

Exhibits N–5 through 7 were maintained by S/A Martinez at the DEA office in JFK Airport pending their transfer to non-drug evidence custodian at DEA/555 West 57th Street, New York, New York via DEA form 7a.

INDEXING

11. Distribution:	12. Signature (Agent)	13. Date
Division	*Ralph Martinez*	January 12, 2005
District		
	14. Approved (Named and Title)	15. Date

DEA Form   -6
(Jul. 1996)

U.S. Department of Justice
Drug Enforcement Administration

REPORT OF INVESTIGATION			Page 1 of 1	
1. Program Code	2. Cross File	Related Files	3. File No. NO-05-053	4. G-DEP Identifier
5. By: Ralph Martinez, S/A At: JFK Airport Office	☐ ☐ ☐ ☐ ☐		6. File Title Superior Warehouse, Inc.	
7. ☐ Closed ☐ Requested Action Completed ☐ Action Requested By.			8. Date Prepared January 12, 2005	
9. Other Officers				

10. Report Re: Post-Arrest Statement of Mario Long

<u>DETAILS</u>

Having been advised of my constitutional rights by S/A Ralph Martinez, and after having read the Advice of Rights and Waiver of Rights Form, and after having signed the waiver, Exhibit N–7, I hereby make the following statement:

"I understand and know what I am doing. No promises or threats were made to me and no pressure or coercion has been used against me."

"I had nothing to do with importing the cocaine and was never told that the crates contained illegal narcotics. All I did was move any crates containing a special mark to a place behind the locked door. Then I would see to it that only Van Ness Trucking Co. would be permitted to take possession of those crates. Santiago said that once a shipment with a specially marked crate was delivered, he would inspect the crate behind the locked door. Today, Van Ness Trucking was scheduled to pick-up the specially marked crate once Santiago returned and inspected the crate."

I have read this statement and it is true and correct to the best of my knowledge.

Mario Long

Mario Long
January 12, 2005

Ralph Martinez

S/A Ralph Martinez, Witness
January 12, 2005

<u>INDEXING</u>

11. Distribution: Division District	12. Signature (Agent) *Ralph Martinez*	13. Date January 12, 2005
	14. Approved (Named and Title)	15. Date

DEA Form   -6
(Jul. 1996)

DEA Form 13   (Exhibit N-7)

INTERROGATION; ADVICE OF RIGHTS

YOUR RIGHTS

Place: _____DEA JFK Airport Office_____

Date: _____January 12, 2005_____

Time: _____4:00 PM_____

Before we ask you any questions, you must understand your rights:

You have the right to remain silent.

Anything you say can be used against you in court.

You have the right to talk to a lawyer for advice before we ask you any questions and to have a lawyer with you during questioning.

If you cannot afford a lawyer, one will be appointed for you before any questioning if you wish.

WAIVER OF RIGHTS

I have read this statement of my rights and I understand what my rights are. I am willing to make a statement and answer questions. I do not want a lawyer at this time. I understand and know what I am doing. No promises or threats have been made to me and no pressure or coercion of any kind has been used against me.

Signed: _____*Mario Long*_____

Witness: _____*Ralph Martinez*_____

Witness: _____*Rich Sobel*_____

---

§ 2.6 Presenting the Case to the United States Attorney's Office

The case is now ready for formal presentation to the United States Attorney's Office in the district responsible for it—here, the Eastern District of New York, which includes Queens County in New York City, where the cocaine was seized and where Superior Warehouse is located. In most districts, an experienced Assistant United States Attorney is assigned to screen all incoming arrest cases in accordance with guidelines set by the Office.[6] Newer AUSAs are assigned to intake on a rotating basis. They draft complaints as well as applications for arrest and search warrants when necessary.[7] Because this is a narcotics case and AUSA Laura Knapp had already been consulted as Deputy Chief of the Narcotics Section, we will assume for the sake of simplicity that she will continue to handle the case instead of assigning it to another AUSA.

---

6. In the Eastern District of New York, for example, this AUSA holds the position of Chief of Intake; in narcotics cases the Chief or Deputy Chief of Narcotics authorizes arrests and prosecutions.

7. These functions are discussed in Chapter 4.

Chapter 3

PROOF IN THE CRIMINAL PROCESS

Table of Sections

Sec.
3.0 Introduction.
3.1 The Burden of Proof—An Overview.
    3.1(a) The Quantitative Burden.
    3.1(b) The Qualitative Burden.
    3.1(c) Allocation of the Burden of Proof.
3.2 Proving Facts—Methods of Proof.
    3.2(a) Written Allegations of Fact.
    3.2(b) Live Witness Testimony.
    3.2(c) Written or Oral Proffers of Evidence.
3.3 Proving Facts—The Evidentiary Hearing.
    3.3(a) The Hearing Process.
    3.3(b) Proof Through Examination of Witnesses—Who Can Be a Witness.
    3.3(c) Types of Witnesses.
    3.3(d) Forms of Questions.
    3.3(e) Presenting Witnesses—Direct Examination.
    3.3(f) Confronting Witnesses—Cross-Examination.
    3.3(g) Controlling Testimony—Objections.
    3.3(h) Rebuttal Evidence.
    3.3(i) Argument.

§ 3.0 Introduction

We are about to begin our description of the criminal process, from its inception with the decision to charge, through the various pretrial screening stages, plea bargaining, trial and sentencing. Before doing so, however, we must discuss the concept of proof; that is, the various burdens of proof faced by the parties at these stages and the methods by which facts are proven. It is through the proof lens that prosecutors and defense attorneys view their work at every stage, assessing what facts must be established, how they must be established and with what degree of certainty. We will address these questions in detail in subsequent chapters. Here we will introduce the terminology of proof, which we hope will make the later discussions more comprehensible.

§ 3.1 The Burden of Proof—An Overview

The term "burden of proof" is best understood by dividing it into three components. The first is the *quantitative* burden: how much evidence must be produced at a particular stage of the process. The second is the *qualitative* burden: how reliable must the evidence be at that stage. The third relates to the *allocation* of the burden: which party must assert and prove a claim.

§ 3.1(a) The Quantitative Burden

As we shall see, the amount or weight of the evidence necessary to prevail varies with the issues involved. Here are the terms used to define the quantitative burden, from the lightest to the heaviest, accompanied by explanations derived from judicial decisions defining these burdens.[1]

(1) Probable Cause.[2] Probable cause exists where, considering the totality of the facts and circumstances, a person of reasonable caution in light of common experience would believe that a crime has been committed by the defendant.[3]

(2) Preponderance of the Evidence. Proof that convinces the trier of fact that the existence of the contested fact is more probable than its nonexistence.[4]

(3) Clear and Convincing Evidence. Evidence that persuades the trier of fact that the truth of the matter is "highly probable."[5]

(4) Proof Beyond a Reasonable Doubt. Evidence sufficient to overcome in the mind of a juror any doubt to which the juror can ascribe a reason.[6]

---

1. It should be noted that there is no absolute uniformity with respect to the definition of these terms. Courts have used many different formulations to explain them. The practical distinction between those various formulations, however, is small.

2. There is a special circumstance in which a burden lighter than probable cause has been approved, namely "reasonable suspicion," which authorizes police officers to "stop and frisk" a person when, in light of the officer's experience, he or she reasonably believes that criminal activity may be afoot and that the object of the stop may be armed and dangerous. *See* Terry v. Ohio, 392 U.S. 1 (1968). Since the reasonable suspicion standard is not otherwise applicable to criminal proceedings, it is not included in the continuum described here.

3. *See* FED. R. CRIM. P. 3–5; *see also* LaFAVE ET AL., § 3.3.

4. *See* JOHN W. STRONG, McCORMICK ON EVIDENCE § 339 (5th ed. & Supp. 2004). An essential difference between the preponderance and probable cause standards is that the former involves the weighing of evidence on both sides of the issue, while the latter weighs only one side. As we shall explain below, this *qualitative* difference makes the preponderance standard a heavier one. *See* WRIGHT, § 52.

5. *See* McCORMICK, § 340.

6. *See, e.g.,* Holland v. United States, 348 U.S. 121, 140 (1954); *see also* 1 LEONARD SAND ET AL., MODERN FEDERAL JURY INSTRUCTIONS § 4.01, Instruction 4–2 (2004).

One can see that the different quantitative burdens, regardless of the specific words used to denote them, are intended to create a continuum of probability. Since in the legal process proof to a mathematical certainty is rarely possible (and hence never required), the best that can be done is to have the trier of fact determine how probable it is that a particular fact exists. The degree of certainty that is required depends upon the stage of the process and nature of the proceeding. If, for example, the question is whether an officer acted reasonably in arresting and holding an individual for judicial proceedings, all that is required is that the government prove that the officer had probable cause to believe that the defendant committed a crime. On the other hand, an individual cannot be convicted unless there is a very high probability ("beyond a reasonable doubt") of guilt. Even though many other definitions will be encountered, it may help the reader to think of the quantitative burden in terms of comparative degrees of probabilities.

§ 3.1(b) The Qualitative Burden

The qualitative burden, which also varies according to the issue to be proved, refers to how reliable the evidence must be in order to be accepted by the trier of fact. Reliability in the litigation process is measured by two things: first, the extent to which rules of evidence (and particularly the hearsay rule) apply to the proceeding; and second, whether the proceeding is *ex parte* or adversarial. As we shall see, two proceedings in which the quantitative burden is the same can present very different obstacles to successfully proving facts, depending upon the qualitative burden imposed.[7] To take the extreme case, it is considerably easier to prove a matter when the trier of fact is permitted to rely on a second-hand recitation of the facts and when the person reciting them is not subject to cross-examination, than in a proceeding in which a witness must have personal knowledge of the facts and is subject to cross-examination.[8]

§ 3.1(c) Allocation of the Burden of Proof

The question as to which party has the burden of proving a claim must be divided into two components: who must assert the claim; and

---

7. A good example is the difference between factual determinations in a preliminary hearing and a grand jury proceeding, where the quantitative burden is probable cause in both instances. In the former, defense counsel is present and can cross-examine and present witnesses; the latter is an *ex parte* proceeding at which the government alone presents its evidence. *See* discussion *infra* §§ 6.2, 11.1(b).

8. It is for this reason that the term "probable cause" is defined in the preceding section as imposing a lighter burden than "preponderance of the evidence." The former standard is always applied in *ex parte* proceedings, those in which no competing evidence is presented. The latter, by its terms, relates to the weighing of evidence offered on both sides of a proposition.

who must ultimately demonstrate that it is adequately supported by the evidence.

1. Asserting a Claim—The Burden of Going Forward

The party bearing the burden of asserting a claim is said to have the burden of "going forward" (sometimes called the "burden of production"). This term can be defined as the obligation of a party seeking the particular relief to demonstrate to a court that it should consider (or allow a jury to consider) the party's claim. By "claim" we refer both to pleadings (e.g., the complaint or indictment) or motions (e.g., a motion to suppress evidence). The purpose of imposing such a burden on the movant is to protect the court against frivolous claims by requiring the movant to make a preliminary factual showing that sufficient evidence exists to support its position. Claims that on their face do not satisfy the burden of going forward do not require a response, and further litigation is therefore averted.

The obligation imposed by the burden of going forward is frequently described as that of making out a *prima facie* case that the relief should be granted. The phrase itself obviously suggests a facial measurement of the evidence, one which, as we shall use the term, asks this question: without considering any evidence that might be offered to the contrary (or assuming for the moment that there is no such evidence), *could* a reasonable trier of fact, *if* accepting the movant's factual allegations as true, find that the movant's burden of persuasion has been satisfied? Note that when a party is said to have "made out a *prima facie* case" this does not mean that it has produced any particular amount of evidence, as would be so if the party were said to have proven its point by a "preponderance" of the evidence or "proof beyond a reasonable doubt;" those are *quantitative* burdens. Rather, a *prima facie* case is made out when the factual allegations, if accepted as true, would satisfy whatever quantitative standards applied in the proceeding.[9]

2. Prevailing on a Claim—The Burden of Persuasion

How the burden of proof is allocated involves determining which party has the burden of persuasion as well as the burden of going forward. That is, once the burden of going forward is met, the trier of fact must then determine whether the facts alleged have been established to the degree of certainty required at that particular stage of the process. The focus shifts from the question whether, *if* accepted as true, the facts would establish the right to relief, to the question whether the

---

9. Thus, while it is not incorrect to define a *prima facie* case as one in which "the evidence presented, taken in the light most favorable to the prosecution, must be sufficient to allow a reasonable finder of fact to convict the defendant at trial," LaFave et al., § 14.3(a), this definition may be mis- leading in the sense that it suggests that proof beyond a reasonable doubt is necessarily required to make out a *prima facie* case. The term is equally applicable at other stages of the process, where the quantitative burden is different from that at trial.

facts *are* accepted as true. The party that has the burden of convincing the trier of fact that its factual allegations should be accepted has the burden of persuasion.

Generally, the party that has the burden of going forward will also have the burden of persuasion, since it is this party that is seeking relief. There are exceptions to this rule, the most important being: (a) the defendant must assume the burden of going forward, or the burden of persuasion, or both when asserting certain defenses to criminal charges;[10] and (b) the government must assume the burden of persuasion when the defendant has made out a prima facie case of unconstitutional police conduct in obtaining evidence.[11]

§ 3.2 Proving Facts—Methods of Proof

Whether the stage of the process involves charging the defendant with a crime, evaluating the charges that have been brought, resolving pretrial issues concerning the government's right to bring charges or to use certain evidence, or deciding the ultimate question of guilt, a fundamental concern for the attorney is how facts are adduced to support his or her legal theory. Just as the burden of proof varies depending upon the nature of the matter to be proved, so do the methods used to establish the relevant facts. We will refer throughout to three methods of proving facts.

§ 3.2(a) Written Allegations of Fact

This method of proof is used in two situations:

(1) Charging a defendant with a crime. A criminal case can be commenced by a complaint that will be accompanied by an affidavit (or declaration) containing the facts supporting the charge.[12] It will commonly be accompanied by an application for an arrest or search warrant, although these applications may be pursued separately. An indictment is also a form of written allegation although, for reasons explained later, it will often contain a minimal amount of factual support.[13] Unlike a civil complaint, neither a criminal complaint nor an indictment is responded to by written allegations by the defendant.

---

10. Statutory defenses are categorized as "defenses" or "affirmative defenses." In the case of a *defense* (e.g., self-defense under federal law), the defendant has the obligation of placing that defense in issue, but the government then has the burden to disprove it (e.g., prove that the defendant did not act in self-defense). In the case of an *affirmative defense* (e.g., insanity under federal law), the defendant not only has the obligation to go forward with the defense, but also to prove it by clear and convincing evidence. *See* 2 PAUL H. ROBINSON, CRIMINAL LAW DEFENSES §§ 132, 173 (1984).

11. For example, when the defendant demonstrates that a search was conducted without a warrant, the government will have to prove a recognized exception to the warrant requirement. *See* WAYNE R. LaFAVE, SEARCH AND SEIZURE § 11.2(b)(4th ed. 2004).

12. FED. R. CRIM. P. 3, 4.

13. *See* FED. R. CRIM. P. 7, discussed *infra* at § 11.2.

(2) Pretrial motions. When a party brings a pretrial motion, it often will contain one or more affidavits describing the facts in support of the relief requested. If the opponent of the motion disputes the facts alleged by the movant, it will submit affidavits in response.[14]

We shall describe in detail below the role of written allegations in resolving issues. Suffice it to say here that such allegations may be sufficient where no dispute over the facts exists. If there is such a dispute, it will have to be resolved in an evidentiary hearing.

§ 3.2(b) Live Witness Testimony

Live witness testimony can be required by the court at any stage of the process,[15] and will always occur in adversary proceedings, preliminary hearings, hearings on pretrial motions, and at trial.

§ 3.2(c) Written or Oral Proffers of Evidence

A proffer is a representation by a party as to what evidence it has in its possession regarding a fact in issue. In other words, it is a statement of what the party could establish through witnesses if it were to call them. It is regularly used in connection with bail and preventive detention proceedings,[16] as well as in guilty pleas and sentencing proceedings.[17] In all of these situations, proffers serve as substitutes for proof through live witness testimony.

§ 3.3 Proving Facts—The Evidentiary Hearing

Facts asserted in the pleadings or motion papers described above must be sufficient on their face to satisfy the burden of persuasion and therefore to justify the granting of relief if there is no factual dispute. But once a dispute is identified, an evidentiary hearing must be held. There, neither the facts alleged in a complaint or indictment, nor those contained in an affidavit accompanying a motion, have any evidentiary value. All evidence relevant to proving a fact in an evidentiary hearing must be elicited through witnesses testifying at the hearing or, in the case of certain non-trial proceedings, through attorney proffers of the testimony that witnesses would provide. Similarly, all evidence relevant to *disproving* a fact must be elicited through the cross-examination of opposing witnesses or the presentation of the party's own witnesses.

This point may seem simplistic, but it is of great importance to the trial lawyer, who should always proceed in accordance with this working rule: take no fact for granted. Each fact must be *established,* either

---

14. *See infra* § 14.2.

15. Technically, there is a form of live witness testimony even in situations in which an *ex parte* application is made, for instance, at the filing of a complaint or application for a search warrant. It consists of the deponent (agent) swearing to the

truth of the facts alleged in the application. On some occasions, moreover, the court may take additional testimony from the agent. *See infra* § 4.10.

16. *See infra* § 5.6.

17. *See infra* §§ 9.2, 17.3.

through the words of witnesses and/or the introduction through witnesses of "things" (usually tangible objects or documents) carrying evidentiary weight themselves. Our emphasis on the word "establish" is intended to make the point that the attorney must be concerned not only with the words that the witness utters, but also with the credibility of that witness. Techniques for proving (and disproving) the credibility of a witness and the story that witness tells will be discussed later.[18]

We now turn to the hearing process, which includes live witness testimony. The discussion is applicable to all such evidentiary hearings, although we have noted that, depending on the issue, different rules apply regarding the allocation of the burden of proof and its quantitative and qualitative weight. [19]These matters will be discussed in detail at the appropriate stage; the point here is to describe elements of the process common to all live witness evidentiary hearings.

§ 3.3(a) The Hearing Process

The sequence of all proceedings involving the testimony of live witnesses is essentially as follows:

(1) The party with the burden of going forward will present its *case-in-chief*, through the direct examination of witnesses.[20] These witnesses will each be subject to cross-examination at the completion of their direct testimony. Following cross-examination, there may be a re-direct examination by the party offering the witness, but limited solely to addressing issues raised on cross-examination. If a re-direct examination takes place, the opposing party often has the opportunity to conduct a re-cross examination, similarly limited to that which was raised on re-direct. This process can continue in successive rounds of re-examination, after which the witness is excused.[21]

(2) After the movant's case-in-chief has been completed, the court will entertain a motion to dismiss the movant's claim on the grounds that the movant has not sustained its burden of going forward, i.e., has not made out a *prima facie* case of entitlement to the relief requested.

(3) If the court determines that the burden of going forward has been met, the opposing party will have the opportunity to present its case-in-chief. If it chooses not to do so, it will rest, and the case will then go to the trier of fact on the strength of the movant's case and the opponent's cross-examination of that case. Note that this sub-

---

18. *See infra* §§ 16.4, 16.5.

19. Resolution of disputes by proffer involves no formal process, but simply the assertions of opposing counsel.

20. In Chapter 14, we will explain that in pretrial hearings this process may be altered in practice, depending upon what issues are in dispute.

21. In general, once a witness is excused, that witness may not be called again. There are occasions, however, when a party may request to defer examination, or where a witness will be kept available assuming some matter is subsequently raised about which the witness would have relevant testimony.

mission of the case is different from that described in the preceding paragraph. The issue for the trier of fact now is whether the movant has met its burden of persuasion, not its burden of going forward. That is, the issue is whether the facts have been proven, not, as in a *prima facie* case, whether a reasonable trier of fact could find that they have been.

If opposing witnesses are presented, they too will be subject to cross-examination, and re-examination may occur in the manner described above.

(4) When the opposing party's case is completed, there may in certain circumstances be a *rebuttal* case. (But not, of course, when the opposing party has rested without putting on evidence, since there would be nothing to rebut.) This may occur when a matter is raised in the opponent's case that could not have been raised in the movant's case-in-chief, and that must be responded to with additional proof. The rebuttal case may not be used to adduce evidence that should have been raised in the movant's case-in-chief. Witness examination in the rebuttal case proceeds in the same way as has already been described.

(5) Following the completion of testimony, both parties will typically present *oral argument*. They will also commonly submit a memorandum of law in pretrial hearings. These provide both an opportunity to persuade the trier of fact as to what facts it should find and how those facts apply to the relevant law.

§ 3.3(b) Proof Through Examination of Witnesses—Who Can Be a Witness

A "witness" is a person with "competent," "relevant" and "reliable" testimony to offer.

(1) Competence. The basic rule of witness competency is this: a person must have knowledge about the subject of his or her testimony.[22] Note that the knowledge requirement does not necessarily mean that the witness has to be shown to have personal knowledge, i.e., to have been a direct observer of the facts in question. A witness who was told something by someone (a hearsay witness) has knowledge also, but it is knowledge of what they were *told,* not of the underlying fact. If such knowledge is deemed sufficiently relevant and reliable at the hearing in question, it is admissible. Similarly, the law provides that expert witnesses need not have personal knowledge as a basis for their opinions,[23] in deference to their special and particular role in the fact-finding process. Competence, in other words, is directly related to what it is that the witness is to be examined about.

---

22. Fed. R. Evid. 602.   **23.** Fed. R. Evid. 703.

(2) Relevance. The fact that a witness may be competent to testify as a result of knowledge or expertise does not mean that the witness will be permitted to do so. The testimony will be received only if it is relevant. As defined in the Federal Rules of Evidence, relevant evidence is that which has "any tendency to make the existence of any fact that is of consequence to the determination of the action more probable or less probable than it would be without the evidence."[24]

(3) Reliability. The fact that a witness may be competent to testify and may have relevant testimony does not mean that the testimony necessarily will be admitted at the hearing. Competence and relevance are the necessary preconditions to admissibility, but a number of other rules may affect whether the testimony will be heard by the trier of fact. Whether these rules can be invoked in turn usually depends upon the stage of the process and the type of evidentiary hearing that occurs at that stage. Again, the most rigorous rules governing admissibility will be applied only at the trial stage, reinforcing the dual functions of the trial as the system's best guarantee that the results will be accurate and that the rights of the defendant will be protected. In pretrial proceedings, the need to assure these goals is arguably less great, and therefore some types of evidence that would be inadmissible at trial may be permitted.

Assuring reliability is a principal function of the rules of evidence. Rules limiting the use of hearsay,[25] for example, are designed to reinforce the right to challenge testimony through cross-examination, the chief means of assuring reliability in the fact-finding process.[26] Rules relating to impeachment of witnesses exist for the same reason,[27] as do rules preventing the admission of overly prejudicial testimony.[28] Again, the extent to which these rules will be applied at a particular hearing depends upon a balancing of the values at stake at that hearing during that stage of the process. As we noted earlier, where the matter being dealt with is a preliminary one, the interference with individual rights relatively minor, and the state interest significant, the rules limiting admissibility will be more loosely applied, if at all.[29] And even at the trial

---

24. Fed. R. Evid. 401. Rules permitting the introduction of relevant testimony are tempered by rules that vest in the court the power to exclude testimony that is judged more likely to unfairly prejudice the trier of fact than prove the fact in issue, and testimony that is confusing, redundant or otherwise a waste of time. Fed. R. Evid. 403. Rule 403 indicates that such testimony can be excluded even if "relevant."

25. Fed. R. Evid. 802.

26. The Supreme Court has recently imposed substantial new restrictions on the use of hearsay testimony at trial. *See* Crawford v. Washington, 541 U.S. 36, 68 (2004) ("Where testimonial evidence is at issue . . . the Sixth Amendment demands what the

common law required: unavailability and a prior opportunity for cross-examination.").

27. Fed. R. Evid. 607, 609.

28. Fed. R. Evid. 403.

29. Certain policies other than that of assuring reliability also operate to exclude evidence. Thus, illegally obtained evidence may, of course, be very relevant and very reliable. If challenged in a timely manner, however, it will be excluded *at trial,* although not at other hearings, in order to enforce constitutional or statutorily created limits on the investigative powers of law enforcement officers. On the exclusionary rule, see LaFave et al., § 3.1.

Similarly, potentially relevant testimony may be excluded from a hearing on the

stage, the rules will be applied differently if the trial is before a judge and not a jury. Judges, it is assumed, need not protect themselves against irrelevant or prejudicial evidence in the same way that they must protect jurors.

§ 3.3(c) Types of Witnesses

Witnesses serve three different purposes in the proof process: they describe the events involved in a dispute (*occurrence* witnesses); they identify various forms of tangible evidence (*authentication* witnesses); and they interpret evidence (*opinion* witnesses). A single witness can give two, or all three kinds of testimony, but in any case because the nature of each type of testimony is different, the witness must be shown to be qualified to testify about each. A witness who, for example, is competent to testify about an occurrence may not be competent to authenticate a document related to that occurrence.

What follows is a description of the three types of witnesses and a discussion of the prerequisites for demonstrating the competence of each to testify. The reader should again keep in mind that, while all of the types of witnesses may appear in any evidentiary hearing and while all must be qualified as competent, it is at trial that one will most likely find all of the witness types and where the most elaborate form of witness qualification will be undertaken. Less testimony and less rigorous qualification of witnesses will be found at preliminary stages, for reasons noted in the previous section.

(1) Occurrence witnesses

Occurrence testimony includes all testimony about events in issue at the hearing or trial. The competence of an occurrence witness is established by showing that the witness has knowledge of either one of two things: a) an event or object directly perceived through his or her senses; or b) what another person said to the occurrence witness about the event or object, assuming such testimony is otherwise admissible.

(2) Authentication witnesses

When "things," as opposed to a witness' perceptions or opinions, are offered as proof, it is necessary to have a witness testify that the thing is what it purports to be.[30] Such a witness is an authentication witness, testifying not to the contents, meaning or significance of the thing in question, but solely to the fact that it is authentic.

---

grounds of privilege. The testimonial privileges—e.g., attorney-client, spousal, doctor-patient—are designed to reinforce specific interrelational values regardless of the effect on the goal of assuring that facts are accurately determined. Because the divulgence of privileged information at any hearing would defeat the purpose of the privi-

lege, if the privilege is properly asserted such testimony will not be permitted. *See* JACK B. WEINSTEIN & MARGART A. BERGER, WEINSTEIN'S FEDERAL EVIDENCE § 501 (Joseph M. Laughlin, ed., 2d ed. 1997 & Supp. 2005).

30. FED. R. EVID. 901.

Common examples of authentication testimony include handwriting or voice identification, identification of all varieties of fruits or instrumentalities of a crime, photographs and documents, or business records. Again, given the very literal nature of the proof process, the authenticity of such things, while often stipulated to, will not be assumed.

A person is competent to give authentication testimony if he or she either: (a) has personal knowledge of the authenticity of the thing,[31] or (b) is qualified as an expert to give an opinion as to what the thing is.[32]

(3) Opinion witnesses

Opinion testimony includes all testimony in which interpretations are offered as to the meaning of events or actions or the condition of things introduced at the hearing or trial.[33] Opinion witnesses do not testify about occurrences, but are used to shed light on them.[34]

Most opinion witnesses are experts in specific areas, especially the sciences, in which neither judges nor jurors can be expected to be able to interpret facts without assistance. To qualify as an expert, an adequate showing of training and experience must be made. When that is done, the witness can be asked to provide an opinion on the facts in question and to explain the basis for that opinion. Most expert testimony occurs at the trial stage.[35]

§ 3.3(d) Forms of Questions

In this section we discuss four commonly identified types of questions used in the examination of witnesses. We shall see that the way in which a question is posed has a significant effect on the nature of the witness' response: each of the forms of questions described here represents a different point on a continuum of control over the witness' answer. Because this is so, the form of question asked will to a significant degree be a function of the nature of the particular hearing and the role of the questioner in it. The four types of questions are these:

(1) Narrative Questions

A narrative question introduces a very general subject and places on the witness the burden of selecting what information about that subject he or she believes relevant to relate: in effect it invites the witness to define the question and to that extent shifts control of the examination

---

31. Fed. R. Evid. 901(b)(1).

32. Fed. R. Evid. 703.

33. Fed. R. Evid. 701–704.

34. Opinion testimony relating to a person's character may also be adduced, *see* Fed. R. Evid. 405(a), although it rarely is.

35. Experts do testify at some pretrial motions. Examples include situations in which the identity of the defendant is rele-

vant and can be established through scientific means, or when it is relevant to demonstrate that the witness is a law enforcement expert who took certain action based upon that expertise. Others include cases that raise issues of mental competency under 18 U.S.C. § 4241, which may require pretrial testimony by mental health professionals.

from the attorney to the witness. A question that asked "What did you do on July 4, 2000?" would be narrative in form.

(2) Open Questions

An open question is one that seeks to control the response to a greater extent than does the narrative question, but still leaves control of the answer to the witness. It is a sort of focused narrative question. An example would be: "What were you doing at 9 p.m. on July 4, 2000?"

(3) Closed Questions

A closed question further orients the witness as to a specific detail of the matter about which the witness is testifying. Like the narrative and open questions, however, it preserves in the witness the responsibility for providing the facts, as would this question: "Calling your attention to July 4, 2000, at 9 p.m., do you recall whether you were at home?"

(4) Leading Questions

A leading question shifts to the attorney the most control possible over the witness' response. A leading question is one that not only asks a question but also suggests its answer: "At 9 p.m. on July 4, 2000, you were at home watching fireworks on television, correct?"

§ 3.3(e) Presenting Witnesses—Direct Examination

1. The Structure of Direct Examination

The ultimate goal of direct examination is to prove to someone with no personal knowledge of the facts (the judge or jury) that an event occurred in the manner proposed by the direct examiner. In order to accomplish this task, it will be necessary to present witnesses so that they are perceived as believable people, with believable stories. The following guidelines might be considered:

(1) The initial, introductory questions to the witness—those that identify the witness to the trier of fact—should elicit facts about his or her background that show the witness to be a person worthy of belief.

(2) The witness' competence to give either occurrence, authentication or expert testimony should be established before he or she is questioned on the merits of the case. If the witness' basis for knowing (or being able to interpret) facts in issue is established at the outset, it will increase the likelihood that the trier of fact will credit the witness' story when it is heard.

(3) Questions regarding the substance of the witness' testimony should, to the extent possible, follow a chronological order. People are conditioned to hearing stories with a beginning, middle and end, and the impact of the presentation may be lessened if they are presented in another way.

These guidelines apply to all evidentiary hearings. The principal difference between direct examinations at various types of hearings is not in how they are structured, but how elaborate they are. That in turn is largely a function of the quantitative and qualitative burdens of proof—the lighter those burdens, the more skeletal the testimony can be.

2. Form of Questions on Direct Examination

We have indicated that the critical goals of direct examination are to show that a witness is believable and has a believable story to tell. It follows from this that the more one hears from the witness, the better able the trier of fact will be to assess those issues. This in turn suggests the form of the questions that should be used. Let us reconsider the four types of questions discussed earlier.[36]

(a) Narrative Questions

Ideally, the goal just stated could best be accomplished if the attorney simply called the witness to the stand and asked the following question: "Tell the court everything relevant you know about this case, and how you came to know it." The problem with such a question is that it opens a whole universe of possible responses, some of which may be relevant in the sense that the rules use that term and some of which may be relevant only because the witness believes them to be so. Similarly, without guidance as to what legal competence to testify means, the witness could say many things that do not address that point. And, of course, the witness' testimony might be so overinclusive as to waste the court's time or so underinclusive that the critical facts are not presented at all. Finally, during testimony the witness might include statements that are inadmissible under the rules of evidence. For all of these reasons, narrative questions are usually not good vehicles for attaining the goals of direct examination. They are especially problematic at trial, where the consequences of permitting improper testimony are the most dire, not just for the defendant but for the prosecution as well. Somewhat more tolerance for narrative questions might be expected at preliminary evidentiary hearings, where concerns about prejudice are lessened; however, the potential that narrative questions will lead to irrelevant and time-wasting responses cautions against their use even then, except where the witness is fully prepared and experienced at giving testimony.

(b) Open Questions

Open questions, on the other hand, can be a useful vehicle on direct. By guiding the witness to the areas that need to be covered, the vices of the narrative question are avoided, but the witness is still given fairly wide latitude to provide the requested information from his or her own mouth. Nevertheless, open questions will be more prevalent at trial than

36. *See supra* § 3.3(d).

at other hearings because they are less efficient than the more focused alternatives and, with the movant's burden at other hearings being less weighty, it is more appropriate to get to the issue at hand more directly.

(c) Closed Questions

These questions directly bring the witness to the matter at issue. Moreover, even where open questions are used, very frequently the witness will not respond with the degree of detail or specificity that the lawyer needs. It is perfectly appropriate to ask more specific follow-up questions in such instances.

(d) Leading Questions

As a general rule, leading questions are not appropriate on direct examination and may be objected to if asked. The reason is that the purpose of direct examination is to obtain the witness' testimony and to assess the witness' demeanor, and that purpose is best accomplished when the witness provides answers that are not suggested by the attorney. As with the other forms of questions about which we have spoken, these goals are most important at the trial stage, where every element of the crime must be proven beyond a reasonable doubt. At that stage, however, there will be many facts that must be adduced even when there is no dispute between the parties as to those matters. The leading question is the most efficient means for accomplishing this task and therefore might be permitted at trial, at least on preliminary, uncontested matters. It follows, therefore, that the use of leading questions on direct in preliminary evidentiary hearings is also appropriate and commonly more pronounced. Open and closed questions become necessary principally when the examination focuses on the crux of the issue.

§ 3.3(f) Confronting Witnesses—Cross–Examination

1. Types of Cross–Examination

As with direct examination, the purpose of cross-examination will depend greatly on the type of hearing being conducted. The general goal of all cross-examination is to provide factual support for the theory of the case advanced by the party conducting it. Cross-examination contributes to that goal in three ways:

(a) Discovery Cross–Examination

One way in which cross-examination provides factual support is by enabling the cross-examiner to discover facts otherwise unknown. Such cross-examination is not so much designed to *prove* one's theory of the case as it is to obtain the factual basis for developing one. This type of cross-examination is not "confrontational" in any sense. Rather, it is a means used—and tolerated, if not formally legitimized—to compensate for the absence in criminal litigation of the deposition process available in civil litigation. Questioning techniques are therefore similar to those used on direct examination.

Discovery cross-examination can occur at any hearing, including the trial. However, it is far more likely to occur at preliminary proceedings for two reasons. First, discovery is most useful when obtained earlier in the litigation process. Second, at the preliminary stages, the party whose witnesses are being confronted (usually the government) has a comparatively lower burden of proof; the cross-examiner therefore has relatively little to lose by open-ended questioning that might produce damaging responses.

It is apparent that neither of these situations normally exist at the trial stage, where the overriding purpose of cross-examination is to prove something, not to discover evidence. The same may be said about certain pretrial hearings where the result is determinative of the outcome of the prosecution.[37] In these situations, the opponent will be more likely to employ an "accrediting" or "discrediting" cross than to use cross-examination as a discovery device.

(b) Accrediting Cross–Examination

Like discovery cross, this type of cross-examination attempts to elicit information that elaborates on the story told by the witness on direct examination. It is not, however, designed to provide the attorney with additional information, but to enable the attorney to demonstrate that the witness' account is actually consistent with (or at least not inconsistent with) the cross-examiner's theory of the case. As we shall describe in more detail later, an accrediting cross, while employing leading questions, is not conducted in a hostile manner and bears little resemblance to the popularized image of the cross-examiner *qua* executioner. Accrediting cross-examination does not attack the witness or attempt to undermine his or her story. Rather, it attempts to create a "separate reality"—i.e., to put a meaning on the matters at issue in the case different from that which was conveyed on direct and, of course, in a way consistent with the theory of the cross-examiner's case.

(c) Discrediting Cross–Examination

Discrediting cross-examination seeks to demonstrate one or both of the following:

> (1) The witness is not a person whose testimony should be believed because of limitations that affect his or her competence (e.g., the ability to observe the events in question) or because of negative character traits (e.g., prior conduct that demonstrates dishonesty) or because of bias, prejudice or personal interest.

---

37. An example is a prosecution for drug distribution, in which the proof against the defendant is overwhelming but where the case cannot be won if, in a pretrial hearing on a motion to suppress, the drugs are determined to have been illegally seized.

(2) The witness' account should not be believed because it is contrary to fact or because it is internally inconsistent, otherwise illogical or contrary to common experience.

Note that each of these forms of cross-examination—discovery, accrediting and discrediting—can be used in the examination of a single witness. Strategic considerations involved in structuring a cross-examination are described in Chapter 16.[38]

2.   Structuring Cross–Examination; Forms of Questions

The considerations involved in ordering questions in a cross-examination are quite different from those relevant to direct examination. The purpose of cross-examination is not to have the witness restate the direct examination—it is to elicit specific information for discovery, accrediting or discrediting purposes. As a result, the cross-examination may be fragmented; it may begin at any point, and it may ignore the chronology of the events.

The questioning techniques on cross-examination depend entirely on the purpose of the testimony. To the extent that discovery is the goal, the cross-examiner uses questioning techniques similar to those used on direct examination. Narrative questions, if not objected to, may yield the most information, and again it is of no great concern to the cross-examiner if some of it will be prejudicial, at least in pretrial hearings. Open questions are more likely to be permitted by the court and can produce a similar yield. Or, since the direct testimony already exists as a basis for questions, the witness can be focused immediately through closed questions to salient points made on direct. Leading questions are not objectionable, but will be less commonly used in a discovery cross.

When either an accrediting or discrediting cross is appropriate, reliance on leading questions will be much greater. As we have noted, a leading question is one that suggests the answer. Leading questions should be used in both of these types of cross-examinations when the attorney knows the answer and simply wants the witness to confirm it. When searching for an answer anticipated of the witness to further accredit the examiner's theory, or to discredit the witness, closed questions are appropriate. There is one caveat in conducting such a search: the more harmful to the examiner's case it would be were the witness to respond to a question in an unexpected way, the more prudent it is to avoid asking that question. Again, this caveat applies more acutely at the trial stage than at any other.[39]

§ 3.3(g)   Controlling Testimony—Objections

The attorney must closely follow the testimony being elicited by an opponent to assure that it is proper under the rules. Grounds for

---

38. *See infra* § 16.5.

39. It is common to hear this caution expressed as never asking a question to which one does not know the answer. A more accurate formulation might be not to ask a question when the answer could be damaging.

objections to testimony fall into two main categories: *substantive* objections, those on the grounds of competency, relevance or admissibility, as described above; or *objections as to form,* those on the grounds that the type of question is impermissible given the nature of the examination (e.g., leading questions on crucial points in direct examination) or that the question is confusing in one way or the other (e.g., the question is "compound" or asked in the alternative).[40] Whether a question is objectionable, and whether an objection should be made as a tactical matter, are concerns that are so dependent upon the specific proceeding that it seems best to defer discussing them until the various proceedings themselves are described. Thus, we have already noted that a question that might be objected to as leading at trial might be desirable at a pretrial hearing. Similarly, objections on substantive grounds—e.g., hearsay objections—obviously cannot be made in proceedings in which hearsay is admissible.[41]

§ 3.3(h) Rebuttal Evidence

As noted above,[42] rebuttal witnesses may be offered by the party that initiated the testimony in order to meet evidence adduced by the opponent. This will occur when an issue arises in the opponent's case that could not have been raised in the case in chief, as, for example, when a defense witness testifies to some fact that had not been set forth in the prosecution's case and the prosecution wishes to introduce its own witness to counter that testimony. The rebuttal case is limited to such circumstances; the court will be reluctant to allow it if the matter should have been addressed in the case in chief.

§ 3.3(i) Argument

The final stage of the hearing process for the lawyer is the argument to the court on preliminary matters or to the jury at trial. We will discuss argument techniques later. Here we wish to stress certain fundamentals common to all argument.

(1) Argument at the hearing stage is, first and foremost, about facts. We feel the need to emphasize this point because legal education, with its overriding focus on the appellate process, largely overlooks the importance of fact determination in the litigation process. Facts in the appellate process are obviously relevant, but they are given—having been found by the hearing court. Our focus is on the fact-finding court which, before it turns to the application of legal doctrine, must reach a conclusion as to what has been proven.

---

40. A witness' answer may also be objectionable as a matter of form when it does not respond to the question asked.

41. For useful compilations of objections and how to phrase them, see THOMAS A.

MAUET, TRIAL TECHNIQUES, ch. 10 (5th ed. 2000).

42. *See supra* § 3.3(a)(4).

(2) The argument stage is the point in the process at which the lawyer's interpretation of the evidence is relevant. Up to the argument stage, the focus of attention is on the witnesses; how the lawyer views the case is not relevant, and it is not permissible for the lawyer to express his or her views (e.g., by engaging in objectionable argument with a witness). It follows that the argument is the occasion for the lawyer to put the facts together for the judge or jury—to "solve" the case, as it were, by presenting the facts in a way that supports the theory of the case. The argument is therefore not simply a recitation of the testimony of the witnesses. It goes further than that and attempts to draw inferences from that testimony. It is perfectly appropriate, and essential, for the attorney to integrate and construct the story and not simply leave the deductive process to the trier of fact. With the factual predicate thus propounded in the argument, the attorney then can proceed to relate the facts to the relevant legal principles.

This concludes the overview of matters of proof. We will refer to the principles described here as we describe the stages of the criminal process.

Chapter 4

THE INITIAL DECISION TO CHARGE: COMMENCING A POLICE–INITIATED CASE BY COMPLAINT

Table of Sections

Sec.
4.0   Introduction.
4.1   The Role of the Complaint in the Charging Process.
4.2   The Burden of Proof.
   4.2(a) Allocation of the Burdens of Going Forward and of Persuasion.
   4.2(b) Quantitative and Qualitative Burdens.
4.3   Jurisdictional Issues.
4.4   Prosecutorial Policy.
4.5   Learning the Facts of the Case—Interviewing the Case Agent.
4.6   The Superior Warehouse Investigation—The Case Assessment.
4.7   Time Constraints on the Filing of the Complaint.
4.8   Drafting the Complaint.
4.9   The Complaint in United States v. Santiago, Long and Murphy.
   4.9(a) Meeting the Quantitative Burden.
   4.9(b) Meeting the Qualitative Burden.
4.10 Warrants.
   4.10(a) Arrest Warrants.
   4.10(b) Search Warrants.
   4.10(c) The Santiago Arrest Warrant.
   4.10(d) The Search Warrant for Superior Warehouse.
4.11 Proceedings on Arrest and Search Warrants—United States v. Santiago.

§ 4.0   Introduction

In the federal system, the prosecutor's control over the decision to institute formal proceedings is, for practical purposes, total. A case brought to the United States Attorney's Office by law enforcement authorities will end there unless the prosecutor agrees to proceed, regardless of the views of the victim or other private complainant or of the law enforcement agents who investigated the case.[1] Even a court cannot compel a federal prosecutor to proceed with a case.[2] The power of the court to reject the prosecutor's decision to proceed is almost as limited: the defendant faces the nearly insurmountable task of proving that the prosecutor's motive was to discriminate against the defendant in a manner that violates the Equal Protection Clause—a "selective prosecution"[3]—or that the prosecutor brought the charges to punish a person for exercising his or her constitutional rights—a "vindictive prosecution."[4] Such controls as do exist over how this sweeping power is exercised are internal ones, those implemented either by the various United States Attorney's Offices or by generally applicable regulations adopted by the Department of Justice and enforced as the Department sees fit; there is no access to judicial review by one who claims that a prosecution was brought in violation of Office or Department policy.[5] We will discuss these policies below.[6]

This chapter describes the way in which a prosecution is begun by complaint, including when such a document is used and how it is drafted. It also describes arrest and search warrants, often issued in conjunction with the complaint. Finally, the complaints and warrants in the model case are presented. The rules governing the formal commencement of a criminal prosecution are in large part derived from the criminal Bill of Rights and the Federal Rules of Criminal Procedure, the most relevant of which are included in Appendix A and Appendix B, respectively.

1. *See* Leeke v. Timmerman, 454 U.S. 83, 86 (1981) ("[A] private citizen lacks a judicially cognizable interest in the prosecution or nonprosecution of another.") (citation omitted).

2. *See* Peek v. Mitchell, 419 F.2d 575, 577 (6th Cir. 1970) (separation of powers considerations prevented court from interfering with federal attorney's control over criminal prosecutions); United States v. Cox, 342 F.2d 167, 171 (5th Cir.1965) ("[T]he courts are not to interfere with the free exercise of the discretionary powers of the attorneys of the United States in their control over criminal prosecutions."). *See also* Wayte v. United States, 470 U.S. 598, 607 (1985) (the strength of the case, the prosecution's enforcement priorities and the prosecution's relationship to the government's overall enforcement plan are not easily susceptible to judicial analysis); United States v. Lawrence, 179 F.3d 343, 347 (5th Cir. 1999) (the decision to prosecute is "vested with the government"); JOSEPH F. LAWLESS, PROSECUTORIAL MISCONDUCT § 3.03 (3d ed. 2003) ("As an arm of the executive

branch, the courts reason, the prosecutorial exercise of discretion [to charge] should not be subject to strict judicial supervision.").

3. *See, e.g.,* Yick Wo v. Hopkins, 118 U.S. 356 (1886) (discriminatory enforcement of business laws on the basis of race).

4. *See, e.g.,* Blackledge v. Perry, 417 U.S. 21 (1974) (defendant reprosecuted on more serious charges after exercise of right to trial *de novo*).

5. *See* U.S. DEPARTMENT OF JUSTICE, U.S. ATTORNEYS' MANUAL § 1–1.000, *available at* http://www.usdoj.gov/usao/eousa/foia_reading_room/usam/ (May 16, 2005) ("The Manual provides only internal Department of Justice guidance. It is not intended to, does not, and may not be relied upon to create any rights, substantive or procedural, enforceable at law by any party in any matter civil or criminal.").

6. A discussion of policy considerations at the charging stage is found in §§ 4.4 (complaint stage) and 11.1(d) and (e) (indictment stage).

§ 4.1　The Role of the Complaint in the Charging Process

Felony cases can be *commenced* in two ways: with the filing of a complaint; or with the return of an indictment by a grand jury.[7] A felony case cannot reach a *final disposition*, however, until an indictment is returned or waived.[8] The complaint, therefore, is only a preliminary charging instrument. It is typically used in police-initiated cases such as the one described in Chapter 2, where an arrest has been made (as in the case of Mario Long and Arthur Murphy) or where the law enforcement agency seeks the United States Attorney's permission to make an arrest (as in the case of Gilbert Santiago) and/or to conduct a search.[9] In either of these situations, immediate action is called for; the decision to file a complaint is made under considerable time pressure, often before a full investigation of the facts or the applicable law can be completed. The complaint is, in effect, an instrument designed to "freeze the action" by providing a basis to obtain (or retain) custody of a person or to prevent or investigate criminal conduct in which the person is believed to have been involved.

By contrast, the *final* decision whether to proceed with a felony prosecution after a complaint is filed will be made only after the prosecutor has had time to obtain additional evidence, if necessary, and research the law more fully. This more fully digested and investigated case will be presented to a grand jury, just as in the situation in which a case is commenced by indictment following an investigation supervised and/or conducted by the prosecutor.

Because of the provisional nature of the prosecutor's decision whether to file a complaint, a number of the factors that the prosecutor must consider in reaching his or her final decision to prosecute will not be particularly relevant, or relevant at all, at this point in the process. We therefore limit the present discussion to those issues that the prosecutor must consider at the complaint stage: first, whether there is sufficient proof to persuade a judge that a federal law has been violated; second, that the prosecution can be brought in the prosecutor's district; and third, whether, despite the adequacy of the proof, Justice Department policy requires or permits the prosecutor to decline to initiate the prosecution.

§ 4.2　The Burden of Proof

In Chapter 3 we presented the terminology we will employ throughout this book in defining the burden of proof at various stages of the

---

7. This book is concerned exclusively with felony prosecutions. For rules governing the commencement and trial of misdemeanor cases, see FED. R. CRIM. P. 58.

8. When the defendant waives indictment, an "information" is filed by the prosecutor. The information is identical in form to the indictment, except that it is signed by the United States Attorney, not the foreperson of a grand jury. *See* FED. R. CRIM. P. 7(b)-(c), discussed *infra* at § 8.4.

9. Applications for search warrants can, of course, be made independent of an arrest and do not require that a complaint be filed.

criminal process.[10] This section addresses those concepts at the complaint stage.

§ 4.2(a) Allocation of the Burdens of Going Forward and of Persuasion

The government bears the burden of going forward at the complaint stage.

§ 4.2(b) Quantitative and Qualitative Burdens

The Fourth Amendment requires that "seizures," including seizures of a person, be made on probable cause.[11] In cases where a warrantless arrest has already taken place, the complaint must provide the probable cause required to continue the restraint on the defendant's liberty, whether by detention or by imposing conditions on his or her release.[12]

As noted, "probable cause" exists when, considering the totality of the facts and circumstances, a person of reasonable caution in light of common experience would believe that a crime has been committed by the defendant.[13] There must be more than "mere suspicion" that an offense has been committed by the accused. The person making the allegations (the deponent) is almost always either the case agent or another law enforcement agent, and the judge may consider the agent's expertise, reliability and character,[14] as well as the judge's own experience in matters of the sort before the court.[15] These factors along with the historical and ongoing facts recited in the complaint contribute to the "totality of the circumstances" that the judge may consider in determining whether probable cause exists.[16]

As to the qualitative burden, the source of the deponent's information may be either personal knowledge of the facts or hearsay, i.e., information from others with personal knowledge, whom the deponent

---

10. *See supra* § 3.1.

11. U.S. Const. amend. IV. *See* Giordinello v. United States, 357 U.S. 480, 485 (1958) ("The language of the Fourth Amendment, that '. . . no warrants shall issue, but upon probable clause, supported by oath or affirmation, and particularly describing . . . the persons or things to be seized,' of course applies to arrest as well as search warrants.") (citation omitted).

12. The Constitution requires that the probable cause determination, if not made by a judge or grand jury in the first instance, i.e., prior to arrest, be confirmed by a judge promptly after arrest in order to justify the continued restraint. Gerstein v. Pugh, 420 U.S. 103, 114 (1975). Proceedings on the complaint are discussed further in Chapter 5.

13. *See supra* § 3.1(a).

14. The judge may presume the agent's reliability on the basis of the agent's official status as a law enforcement officer without requiring independent corroboration. *See, e.g.,* United States v. Ventresca, 380 U.S. 102, 108–111 (1965). *See also* LaFave et al., § 3.5(a). By contrast, when the deponent is an anonymous or a paid informant, or a cooperating defendant, with either first or second hand knowledge of the facts, corroboration will be required to satisfy the burden of proof. *See* Draper v. United States, 358 U.S. 307, 313 (1959) (substantial corroborative evidence supplied by police officer regarding a paid informant's reliability supported a finding of probable cause).

15. *See Draper,* 358 U.S. at 313.

16. *See* Illinois v. Gates, 462 U.S. 213, 238–39 (1983); LaFave et al., §§ 3.3–3.4.

has reason to believe are reliable.[17] If the deponent relies on other police officers, the court will presume that the statements are reliable.[18]

The government's burden of persuasion at the complaint stage can be met simply by having the deponent appear before the judge[19] and swear to the truthfulness of the complaint's allegations.[20] The proceeding is *ex parte*. Normally, no testimony will be taken, although the judge may question the deponent about any of the allegations contained in the complaint[21] and may consider other affidavits accompanying the complaint.[22]

§ 4.3 Jurisdictional Issues

The evidence offered by the agent must provide probable cause to believe a federal statute has been violated.[23] It must also demonstrate that venue requirements are met. In the usual case, venue is proper if the crime was committed in the district.[24] A case may also be prosecuted in any district where an offense was begun, continued or completed.[25] Finally, the offense must meet the requirements of the statute of limitations. With certain exceptions, a federal indictment or information must be filed within five years of the commission of the offense.[26]

§ 4.4 Prosecutorial Policy

As described in § 4.1, the decision to file a complaint is not a final charge decision and thus will not require the prosecutor to consider all of the factors identified by the Department of Justice as relevant to the final charge.[27] At this point in the process, the prosecutor's inquiry will

---

17. FED. R. CRIM. P. 4(b). *See* CHARLES ALAN WRIGHT, FEDERAL PRACTICE AND PROCEDURE: CRIMINAL, §§ 51–52 (2d & 3d eds. 1999 & Supp. 2005).

18. Where the officer relies upon a private citizen, however, there must be additional proof of the informant's reliability. *See* Aguilar v. Texas, 378 U.S. 108, 113–15 (1964) (affidavit of undisclosed informant was not proof of reliability); WRIGHT, §§ 31–52.

19. We do not distinguish here between a district court judge and a magistrate judge, both of whom have jurisdiction at the complaint stage. Typically, magistrate judges preside at the complaint stage.

20. FED. R. CRIM. P. 3. *See* WRIGHT, §§ 41–42; LaFAVE, SEARCH § 4.3.

21. FED. R. CRIM. P. 41(c)(1). *See* WRIGHT, § 662.

22. FED. R. CRIM. P. 4(a). *See* WRIGHT, §§ 41–52.

23. Federal law provides that the United States district courts shall have original and exclusive jurisdiction over all federal offenses. 18 U.S.C. §§ 3231 ("The district

courts of the United States shall have original jurisdiction, exclusive of the courts of the States, of all offenses against the laws of the United States.").

24. FED. R. CRIM. P. 18.

25. 18 U.S.C. § 3237(a). Venue is also proper in any district through which property or persons committing crimes involving interstate commerce or the mails moves. Crimes not committed in any state or federal district can be prosecuted in the district where the defendant is arrested or first brought or last resided. 18 U.S.C. § 3238.

26. 18 U.S.C. § 3282. The exceptions mostly relate to: capital offenses (18 U.S.C. § 3281.); sexual abuse of children (18 U.S.C § 3283); concealment of bankruptcy assets (18 U.S.C. 3284); criminal contempt (18 U.S.C. § 3285); terrorism (18 U.S.C. § 3286); and certain offenses during wartime (18 U.S.C. § 3287).

27. See *infra* §§ 11.1(d) and (e) for a discussion of policy considerations at the indictment stage.

be relatively limited. A principal concern in many United States Attorney's Offices is controlling the volume of business entering the office; intake guidelines instruct assistants to leave to state prosecutors the decision to proceed on what are considered relatively insignificant cases or cases not involving a particularly federal interest. For example, in a narcotics case such as the one under discussion here, the Office might authorize the filing of a complaint only when the amount of drugs involved exceeds a certain amount. Typically, prosecutors defer consideration of whether other factors might militate in favor of different charges, or against prosecution, until the case is to be presented to the grand jury.

§ 4.5　Learning the Facts of the Case—Interviewing the Case Agent

As described in the model case, the first contact that the prosecutor has with a "police-initiated" case is when it is presented by the case agent, generally the officer in charge of the investigation. This agent may or may not be the arresting officer and may or may not have been directly involved with the investigation. The main interest of the prosecutor is, of course, to determine whether there is sufficient evidence to establish probable cause. However, the prosecutor conducting the interview should attempt to obtain all of the information the agent has about both the case and the defendant that might be relevant to the final disposition of the case. In situations where the case agent was not directly involved with the arrest or in conversations with the defendant, the prosecutor should make contact with any officers who were so involved as soon as possible in order to assure that all details of these events are known.

The following is a checklist of items to be addressed at the interview:

(a) Jurisdiction and venue—As noted in § 4.3, the facts must demonstrate that a federal criminal statute has been violated; that the case is properly brought in the district in question; and that prosecution is not barred by the statute of limitations.

(b) Facts about the crime—A primary goal of the interview is to obtain as clear a description of the crime as possible. There will, of course, be differences among agents in terms of how coherently they present the evidence; but in general, it is probably a good technique to begin by allowing the agent to present an overview of the case and then conduct what can be analogized to a direct examination[28]— questioning that sets the scene, and then takes the witness chronologically through the events culminating in the arrest or other stage of the case in which the prosecutor becomes involved. At each stage of the chronology, the prosecutor should, through the use of specific

---

28. *See supra* § 3.3(e).

"closed" questions, try to learn everything that the agent knows—and to learn who else might know what the agent does not. While the questioning can and should be very specific, leading questions should be avoided, just as they should on direct examination at trial.

(c) Facts about the police investigation—It is theoretically possible that a prosecutor would decide not to proceed with a complaint because crucial evidence was obtained in a manner so clearly violative of the constitutional rights of the defendant that no prosecution could be sustained. It is unlikely, however, that such a judgment would be made at the time of the initial interview, even if the legality of the police action is problematic. Moreover, it is unlikely that the facts surrounding the arrest or search can be accurately determined at this stage. Since a complaint cannot be challenged on the grounds that evidence supporting it was unconstitutionally obtained,[29] any questions relating to this issue will almost always be deferred. However, it is important to gather as much information as possible on these potentially important issues, and therefore a summary of the relevant doctrine is in order here.

When the defendant has been arrested, and any search (of his or her person or otherwise) has been conducted; or when any statements have been made by the defendant; or where he or she has been subjected to an identification procedure conducted by the police, the facts surrounding these events must be obtained in as much detail as possible since the government's ability to use the evidence at trial may be affected. The Supreme Court has ruled that in order to deter unlawful police conduct, evidence that is illegally obtained by the police cannot be admitted into evidence at the defendant's trial.[30] This "exclusionary rule" applies not only to the evidence itself, but in the case of most unlawful police conduct, to the "fruit of the poisonous tree," meaning evidence that is derived from the illegal conduct.[31]

It is beyond the scope of this book to describe in any depth the vast body of law that has been generated in this area. We offer here only a cursory summary of the doctrine with which a prosecutor should be familiar in the interview with the agent.

(1) Searches and seizures—Fourth Amendment protections[32]

A search is an intrusion on a "container"—a building, a package, a person—in which a person has a reasonable expectation of privacy.[33] A seizure occurs when the freedom of movement of a person or thing is

---

29. WRIGHT, § 52

30. Weeks v. United States, 232 U.S. 383, 398 (1914) (illegally seized evidence inadmissible in a trial in federal court); Mapp v. Ohio, 367 U.S. 643, 657 (1961) (exclusionary rule applied to state trials). *See generally* LaFAVE ET AL. §§ 9.1–9.6.

31. Wong Sun v. United States, 371 U.S. 471, 485–86 (1963); LaFAVE ET AL., § 9.3.

32. *See generally* LaFAVE ET AL., §§ 3.1–31.0.

33. *Id.*, § 3.5(e).

restrained in a significant way.[34] The Fourth Amendment does not prohibit all searches and seizures, of course, but only "unreasonable" ones. Fourth Amendment rights are personal: the fact that evidence is offered against a person does not give him or her standing to object to its admission if another person's rights were violated by the police in obtaining it.[35]

A search or seizure is presumptively reasonable if it is based on probable cause found by a neutral magistrate who issues a search or arrest warrant. Only if an officer deliberately misinformed the magistrate can such a warrant be invalidated.[36]

This does not mean, however, that all warrantless searches or seizures are unconstitutional. Intrusions into areas in which a person does not have an objectively reasonable expectation of privacy are valid, e.g., searches conducted at the border.[37] Likewise, warrantless intrusions or seizures under "exigent circumstances," when it would be impractical to obtain a warrant, e.g., arrests when police officers see a crime being committed, or when evidence could be destroyed, are valid.[38]

A person's Fourth Amendment rights can be waived by freely given consent.[39]

(2) Interrogation—The Fifth Amendment protection against self-incrimination[40]

The Fifth Amendment's protection against compulsory self-incrimination applies not only to the right not to be a witness against oneself in court, but to police interrogations as well. There are two ways in which the police can violate the defendant's Fifth Amendment rights.

(a) Actual coercion—Statements obtained by physical or psychological coercion sufficient to overcome a person's will are inadmissible, as is evidence derived from such statements.[41]

(b) Implied coercion—In *Miranda v. Arizona* the Supreme Court held that, because the atmosphere in the police station was "inherently coercive," a person in custody had to be informed of his right to remain silent, that anything said may be used against him, of his right to consult with an attorney before answering questions, and of his right to stop answering questions at any time.[42] The defendant's *Miranda* rights extend not only to custodial interrogation in the precinct, but to any interrogation conducted while in custody. A defendant who refuses to answer questions can be given the warnings again and requestioned,

34. *Id.,* § 3.5.

35. *Id.,* § 9.1.

36. Franks v. Delaware, 438 U.S. 154, 155–56 (1978); LaFave et al., § 3.4(d).

37. LaFave et al., § 3.4(f).

38. Chimel v. California, 395 U.S. 752, 773 (1969).

39. Schneckloth v. Bustamonte, 412 U.S. 218, 227 (1973).

40. *See generally* LaFave et al., §§ 6.1–6.10.

41. Brown v. Mississippi, 297 U.S. 278, 287 (1936).

42. 384 U.S. 436, 467–68 (1966).

unless he or she asks to speak with an attorney in which case all questioning must cease.[43]

Suppression of statements obtained in violation of *Miranda* extend only to the statement itself. Evidence derived from such statements is admissible.[44] A defendant can waive his *Miranda* rights and need not speak to an attorney before doing so.[45]

(3) Identification procedures—Fifth Amendment protection of due process rights[46]

Identification procedures used by the police include: line-ups, in which several persons including the defendant appear before witnesses; show-ups, in which the defendant is viewed alone; and photo arrays and single photo identifications, the pictorial analogs to in-person line-ups and show-ups.

In-court identifications based on pretrial identification procedures deemed overly prejudicial will not be permitted. Whether an identification procedure is unconstitutionally prejudicial depends upon the totality of the circumstances under which it was conducted, measured by five factors: the opportunity of the witness to view the defendant at the time of the crime; the witness' degree of attention; the accuracy of his prior description of the defendant; his level of certainty; and the time between the crime and the confrontation.[47]

(d) Facts about the defendant—It is also important to learn as much as possible about the background of the suspect. This may ultimately be relevant to the policy determination of whether prosecution is warranted, and, more immediately, it will always be relevant to the pretrial release decision assuming that the suspect is charged.[48]

§ 4.6   The Superior Warehouse Investigation—The Case Assessment

On January 13, 2005, Agent Martinez went to the United States Attorney's Office and met with AUSA Laura Knapp, to whom he described the seizure of the drugs and the arrest and processing of Mario Long and Arthur Murphy. After the interview, AUSA Knapp made the following assessment of the case:

---

43. Edwards v. Arizona, 451 U.S. 477, 484–85 (1981).

44. A statement taken in violation of *Miranda* may also be admitted if, after the violation, the warnings are given and the defendant repeats the statement. *See* Oregon v. Elstad, 470 U.S. 298, 314 (1985).

45. LaFave et al., § 6.5(b); *see generally id.* § 6.9(b).

46. *See generally* LaFave et al., § 7.1–7.5.

47. *See* Manson v. Brathwaite, 432 U.S. 98, 114 (1977); LaFave et al., § 7.4 (overview of identification procedures and related issues).

48. Pretrial release is discussed in Chapter 5.

(1) Jurisdiction, Venue, Timeliness and Legal Issues Related to the Arrest

Importation of a controlled substance and possession with the intent to distribute, as well as conspiracy to commit these crimes, are acts that plainly violate federal law.[49] Since all of the acts known to the government at this point took place in the Eastern District of New York, venue is obviously established there. All of the acts in question were also committed within the past five years, meeting statute of limitations requirements. As to the legality of the police activities, no Fourth Amendment issues are raised by opening the crates at the airport, since border searches are an exception to the probable cause and warrant requirements.[50] Similarly, neither placing the homing device in the crate[51] nor surveillance of the warehouse create constitutional issues.[52] A question may arise as to whether Mario Long's consent to the search was valid, but, for reasons noted above, that issue will be deferred.[53] There is no evidence that any statement made by any defendant was coerced, and there is no apparent *Miranda* violation. There are no grounds for an objection by Santiago to the recorded telephone call with Long.[54]

(2) Sufficiency of the Evidence

The sufficiency of evidence available to connect the several possible defendants to the crime is clear with respect to some, but not all of the individuals. Here is how the evidence stacks up against each potential defendant:

Mario Long. Mario Long possessed the kind of information from which a clear inference of knowledge of involvement in the drug operation, or at the very least conscious avoidance of such knowledge,[55] could be drawn. As the foreman of the warehouse, Long had been told by Gilbert Santiago that if one of the crates contained a special mark, it was to be placed behind a locked door. Long also knew that only Van Ness' trucking firm would be permitted to take possession of the specially marked crate and that Santiago would inspect the crate prior to its removal from the warehouse. From these facts, a judge could infer that Long knew or should have known that the crates contained contraband.

---

49. *See* 21 U.S.C. § 960 (importation) and 21 U.S.C. § 841 (possession with intent to distribute).

50. LaFave et al., § 3.9(f) (probable cause not required in border searches).

51. *See* United States v. Karo, 468 U.S. 705, 712 (1984) (insertion of homing device not a "search"); LaFave et al., § 3.2(j).

52. LaFave et al., § 3.2(j) (no expectation of privacy violation from visual surveillance from public street).

53. For a discussion of consent searches, see LaFave et al., §§ 3.10(a)-(e). Challenges to the validity of a search are

not cognizable until a motion to suppress is brought after indictment. *See infra* Chapter 14.

54. Consent of one party to the recorded conversation obviates any Fourth Amendment concern. *See* LaFave et al., § 4.3(c).

55. Proof of conscious avoidance can satisfy the intent element. *See* United States v. Jewell, 532 F.2d 697, 701 (9th Cir. 1976) (construing the term "knowing" as including either positive knowledge or a willful avoidance of such knowledge).

Although it is not necessarily clear that Long knew that the contraband was cocaine or some other controlled substance (and he in fact denied being so told), his knowledge can be inferred from Santiago's conversation with Long that Agent Martinez recorded. In that conversation, Santiago referred to a prior discussion with Long about what to say if questioned about the matter, alluding to "material," a word commonly used in connection with drugs.

Probable cause appears quite certain to be found. However, given the degree to which Mario Long cooperated with Agent Martinez, policy considerations militate in favor of release on bail or his own recognizance[56] and of entering into a cooperation agreement to dispose of the case.[57] Long was clearly following orders given to him by Gilbert Santiago and could, therefore, be a key witness against Santiago and any other individuals with whom he had contact during the distribution scheme.

Arthur Murphy. While Agent Sobel identified Murphy as being directly involved in moving the crates into the warehouse, the other evidence against Murphy is limited to: his statement that he had just arrived at the warehouse at the time of the arrest (which could be offered by the government as a false exculpatory statement to show consciousness of guilt, since he was seen at the warehouse at the time of the controlled delivery);[58] his looking around suspiciously while loading the crates; and Santiago's recorded statement to Long to "remind" Murphy about what he was supposed to say (which provides at least some evidence that Murphy was part of the scheme).

While the evidence against Murphy is clearly thinner than that against Long, it still seems likely that, as with Long, probable cause would be established. Adding Murphy to the complaint would keep the government's options open in case further evidence develops against him. The government would not oppose Murphy's pretrial release and, if nothing further developed, the charges against him would be dismissed.

Gilbert Santiago. Santiago is implicated in the distribution scheme by Mario Long's post-arrest statement to Agent Martinez and by the telephone conversation Martinez recorded between Long and Santiago. In his statement to Martinez, Long stated that Santiago controlled the delivery of the crates and informed him when specially marked crates were to be placed behind the locked door. Thereafter, according to Long, Santiago would inspect the crates before permitting them to be delivered. Long's post-arrest statement regarding Santiago's involvement was corroborated by Agent Martinez's observations of Santiago prior to the controlled delivery of the cocaine and by the telephone conversation Agent Martinez recorded between Long and Santiago. Martinez saw Santiago enter and leave Superior Warehouse and he was able to identify Santiago as an individual who had previously been convicted of traffick-

56. *See infra* §§ 5.6–5.7.
57. *See infra* Chapter 8.
58. *See* WEINSTEIN & BERGER, § 401.08.

ing cocaine. In his telephone conversation with Long, Santiago seemed to confirm his knowledge of the cocaine distribution scheme and directed Long not to reveal anything about the scheme. These facts would establish probable cause.

Paul Christopher and William Van Ness. Christopher was identified as the owner of the warehouse and as such is potentially chargeable with constructive possession of the cocaine if it can be shown that he had the power and intention to exercise dominion over the drugs.[59] Van Ness was identified by Long as the trucker who picked up the crates whenever there was a special shipment. At this point, however, there is not enough direct evidence of either Christopher's or Van Ness's knowing participation in the drug operation involving Superior Warehouse to establish probable cause, because it is just as probable that Christopher and Van Ness were totally ignorant of the illicit activity. Therefore, charges would not be warranted at this time. Further investigation is appropriate to determine whether criminal knowledge and intent in fact existed.

(3) Legal Issues Arising From the Investigation

AUSA Knapp determined that, while there were a few issues to investigate further, there was nothing in the police investigation that precluded going forward with a complaint.

Thus, having decided to proceed against Long, Murphy and Santiago, AUSA Knapp must prepare a complaint.

§ 4.7   Time Constraints on the Filing of the Complaint

Rules designed to assure prompt resolution of cases exist at various stages of the pretrial process and will be noted throughout the text. The first of these rules relates to the filing of the complaint. The Federal Rules provide that following an arrest a defendant must be taken before a magistrate judge[60] "without unnecessary delay," and that unless a complaint and warrant have already been issued, a complaint must be "promptly" filed in the district in which the crime was allegedly committed.[61]

---

59. *See United States v. Acevedo, 842 F.2d 502,* 507 (1st Cir. 1988); United States v. Kaufman, 858 F.2d 994, 1000 (5th Cir. 1988); Jules Epstein, *Narcotics Crimes, in* 1 DEFENSE OF NARCOTICS CASES ch. 1, § 1.04(c) n.4 (David Bernheim ed., 2004) (citing cases where constructive possession equals dominion or control).

60. The rules also permit an arrestee to be brought before a state or local judicial officer if a magistrate judge is not reasonably available. *See* FED. R. CRIM. P. 5(a)(1)(A) and 5(c)(1)(B).

61. FED. R. CRIM. P. 5(b). *See* WRIGHT, §§ 71–75. Where a warrantless arrest is made, the appearance must, absent extraordinary circumstances, be made within 48 hours. *See* County of Riverside v. McLaughlin, 500 U.S. 44, 56 (1991). Where a warrant has been issued either on a complaint (pursuant to FED. R. CRIM. P. 4) or an indictment (pursuant to FED. R. CRIM. P. 9), no new probable cause determination need be made by the magistrate judge, but other important rights of the defendant will be enforced, e.g., appointment of counsel and bail. *See infra* Chapter 5.

Unreasonable delay in bringing an arrested defendant before the magistrate judge may result in the exclusion of statements made by the defendant.[62] The complaint stage is also important in connection with the defendant's constitutional right to a speedy trial.[63] The right "attaches" either at the time of the arrest or the filing of a complaint or indictment, whichever comes first.[64]

§ 4.8 Drafting the Complaint

The criminal complaint performs the function of a complaint in a civil proceeding, namely, to state the cause of action against the defendant. The comparison between pleadings in civil and criminal proceedings ends at this point, however, because in criminal cases the defendant is not—indeed cannot be—called upon to submit responsive pleadings. The presumption of innocence and self-incrimination privilege protect the defendant from having to reply to the allegations of the government, other than to enter a "general" plea of guilty or not guilty after final charges (i.e., an indictment or information) are filed. As explained earlier, the complaint is not a final charge in a felony case, and therefore not even a general plea can be entered at this point.[65] Also unlike civil proceedings, the government can never prevail in a criminal case solely on the basis of facts alleged in the pleadings, unless the defendant concedes those facts by pleading guilty. For constitutional reasons, there can be no summary judgment against a criminal defendant.[66]

The complaint—and the indictment and information, discussed later—is composed of one or more separate sections or "counts," each of which charges one or more defendants with a different crime.[67] It is, of course, drafted by the prosecutor, but the deponent—the one alleging that the defendant committed the crime—is almost always the case agent.

Each count has two components, commonly drafted in separate paragraphs: one stating the "gravamen" of the crime; and the other

---

62. *See* 18 U.S.C. § 3501 (adopting a 6–hour rule between arrest and initial appearance, presumptively excluding any statements taken after a 6–hour delay unless good cause is shown). In cases where the defendant has not been arrested, and therefore has not been subjected to any restraint, the only time limitation in filing a complaint is the statute of limitations.

63. U.S. Const. amend. VI. *See* Barker v. Wingo, 407 U.S. 514 (1972).

64. United States v. Marion, 404 U.S. 307, 313 (1971). Speedy trial rights are also provided by the Speedy Trial Act of 1974, 18 U.S.C. §§ 3161 *et seq.* However, under the statute, the pretrial period is measured from the time at which personal jurisdiction over the defendant is obtained by arrest or summons, regardless of when the complaint is filed. § 3161(b).

65. *See supra* § 4.1. Almost invariably, moreover, complaints are brought before a magistrate judge rather than a district court judge, and only the latter has jurisdiction to dispose of felony cases. *See supra* § 1.1(b).

66. The Sixth Amendment provides every criminal defendant with a right to a trial by jury.

67. Rules related to the "joinder" of defendants and offenses apply only to the indictment or information, not the complaint, and will be discussed in connection with those pleadings. *See infra* § 11.3, and Fed.R.Crim.P.8.

stating the "means" by which the crime was committed. The gravamen paragraph notifies the defendant of the crime being charged, by reciting the literal language of the relevant criminal statute and, in the case of a statute that is vague on its face, by incorporating any language from case law necessary to clarify the definition of statutory terms.[68]

The means paragraph of the complaint provides the facts on which the court makes its probable cause determination.[69] The prosecutor is free to include all of the facts known at the time, or only those sufficient to make out probable cause. In deciding how fully the facts should be stated, it should be kept in mind that if the deponent is subsequently required to testify about the facts asserted in the complaint, he or she can be impeached on the basis of what is said in the complaint if the testimony varies from it. This risk militates against including facts beyond those required to make out probable cause if there is any doubt about them. Similarly, the complaint should not contain a description of investigative techniques that might be the subject of a motion to suppress, unless again those facts are necessary to make out probable cause. It must, that is, be kept in mind that this is an early stage in the process, and the facts may be better understood at a later time.

§ 4.9 The Complaint in United States v. Santiago, Long and Murphy

Here is the complaint drafted by AUSA Knapp and executed by Agent Martinez, charging Gilbert Santiago, Mario Long and Arthur Murphy with possessing with intent to distribute cocaine and conspiracy to do the same. The complaint contains two substantive components. The gravamen paragraph traces the statutory language with respect to both the *mens rea* and *actus reus* requirements. The means paragraphs enumerate the factual allegations upon which the probable cause determination will be made. Note that in addition to providing enough detail to satisfy the quantitative burden of proof, the complaint must, in order to satisfy the qualitative burden, indicate the source of the deponent's allegations.

68. In some cases the statute will state in the disjunctive different acts by which the crime can be committed. If more than one act is relevant in a particular case, they should be charged in the conjunctive so as to give notice to the defendant as to everything he or she will be required to address.

69. This distinguishes the complaint from the indictment; in the latter, there is no need to relate the facts on which the charges are based, but only sufficient facts to provide adequate notice so that the defendant can prepare a defense. *See infra* § 11.2.

Approved: Laura Knapp
        Assistant United States Attorney

Before: Honorable Roger Brown
       United States Magistrate Judge
       Eastern District of New York

UNITED STATES DISTRICT COURT
EASTERN DISTRICT OF NEW YORK

UNITED STATES OF AMERICA

        --against--

GILBERT SANTIAGO, MARIO LONG,
and ARTHUR MURPHY,

             Defendants.

COMPLAINT

Case no. 05 M 0063

(T.21, U.S.C. §§ 841(a)(1) and 846)

EASTERN DISTRICT OF NEW YORK, SS:

RALPH MARTINEZ, being duly sworn, deposes and says that he is a Special Agent with the United States Drug Enforcement Administration assigned to John F. Kennedy International Airport, Group 14, duly appointed according to law and acting as such.

Upon personal knowledge and information and belief, there is probable cause to believe that on or about January 12, 2005, within the Eastern District of New York, the defendants, MARIO LONG, ARTHUR MURPHY, and GILBERT SANTIAGO, together with others, did knowingly and intentionally possess with intent to distribute cocaine in violation of Title 21, U.S.C. §§ 841(a)(1)(a) and conspire to possess with intent to distribute cocaine in violation of Title 21, U.S.C. § 846.

The source of my information and the grounds for my belief are as follows:

1. On January 11, 2005, I was present at Kennedy Airport, Queens, New York when agents of the United States Customs Service opened a shipment of twelve crates containing coffee which had been shipped from Colombia and consigned to International Food Distributors, Incorporated ("IFD") for delivery to Superior Warehouse, Inc. ("Superior"). On opening one of the crates, a Customs Agent discovered 10 cloth packages each containing approximately 1 kilogram of a

powdery substance which your deponent field tested positive for cocaine. Flour was then substituted for all but 1 ounce of the cocaine found in the cloth packages, and the packages were returned to the crate.

2. The crates were addressed to Superior Warehouse, Inc., at 149 Grand Street, Queens, New York.

3. I was informed by Special Agent Richard Sobel that on January 12, 2005 at approximately 2:00 pm, he posed as a truck driver and drove a truck containing the 12 crates to Superior at 149 Grand Street, Queens, New York. The defendant, MARIO LONG, the foreman of the premises, accepted delivery of the crates and signed for them. The defendant, ARTHUR MURPHY, removed the crates from the truck and brought them into the warehouse. While doing so, MURPHY was observed to be looking around nervously and suspiciously.

4. At approximately 2:30 pm, your deponent and other agents entered the warehouse. At the time of the entry, your deponent had in his possession a homing device to identify the crate containing the cocaine. Upon entering the warehouse, your deponent noticed that that crate was not located with the other 11 crates described in Paragraph 1. The homing device indicated that the missing crate may have been placed in another room, the door to which was locked. When your deponent asked the defendant MARIO LONG what was in the room LONG responded, in substance and in part, that valuable crates were placed there, and that he thought he should wait for Gilbert, the manager of the warehouse, before opening the door. The defendant MARIO LONG thereafter obtained a key from a hook on his office and opened the locked door, revealing a single wooden crate. Upon opening the crate, your deponent discovered the packages that had been observed at Kennedy Airport, including the package containing the cocaine.

5. Your deponent observed the defendant GILBERT SANTIAGO enter and exit Superior on January 12, on three (3) occasions prior to the controlled delivery. The defendant GILBERT SANTIAGO is known to your deponent as someone who, in 1998, had been convicted of possession with intent to distribute cocaine in this District.

6. Upon questioning by your deponent, the defendant MARIO LONG stated the crate which was found to contain cocaine had a special mark which enabled him to identify it and to deliver it to a trucking firm specified by the defendant GILBERT SANTIAGO. The defendant MARIO LONG stated that the defendant GILBERT SANTIAGO informed him of all shipments with specially marked crates and stated that once such a crate was delivered, the defendant GILBERT SANTIAGO would inspect the crate behind the locked door.

7. In a subsequent consensually recorded conversation which your deponent overheard, the defendant GILBERT SANTIAGO instructed the defendant MARIO LONG not to reveal anything about his knowledge of the material contained in the shipment which LONG had received. Further, the defendant GILBERT SANTIAGO instructed the defendant MARIO LONG to tell the other person arrested, an apparent reference to the defendant ARTHUR MURPHY, to remember to say that he knew nothing about the material contained in the shipment.

8. At the time of his arrest the defendant ARTHUR MURPHY falsely denied having unloaded crates, including the crate containing cocaine, at the warehouse, stating that he had not been at the warehouse when the crates were unloaded.

9. The defendant ARTHUR MURPHY was identified by S/A Richard Sobel of the Drug Enforcement Administration and by the defendant MARIO LONG as the other person who unloaded the crates at the time and place in question.

WHEREFORE, your deponent respectfully request the defendants MARIO LONG, ARTHUR MURPHY, and GILBERT SANTIAGO be dealt with according to law.

Ralph Martinez

Ralph Martinez
Special Agent
Drug Enforcement Administration

Sworn to before me this 13th day of January, 2005

Roger Brown

Roger Brown
United States Magistrate Judge
Eastern District of New York

---

§ 4.9(a) Meeting the Quantitative Burden

The allegations found in means paragraphs 1 through 9 contain the essence of the information Agent Martinez recounted to AUSA Knapp. The court's first task, further described below, is to determine whether they establish a *prima facie* showing of probable cause that satisfies the government's burden of going forward.

§ 4.9(b) Meeting the Qualitative Burden

Assuming that, if believed, the allegations would establish probable cause, the court must next evaluate the source of the allegations to determine whether the facts are sufficiently reliable to satisfy the government's burden. In the Santiago complaint, the names of the sources of the information, the DEA agents, are given. In many situations, however, the sources will not be personally identified because to do so would jeopardize ongoing investigations or the sources personally. The name of the source is generally irrelevant to a determination of his or her reliability. What the law requires is a description of the source of the information that is sufficiently detailed to enable the magistrate judge to determine his or her probable reliability. Since a presumption of reliability attaches to the observations of the DEA agents, their designation as the source of the allegations—whether named or not—will not require further corroboration to satisfy the qualitative burden. Thus, the designation of Agents Martinez and Sobel as the sources of most of the information in the complaint will be sufficient to meet the qualitative burden without more. By contrast, Mario Long's allegations must be corroborated by evidence that establishes the truthfulness of his assertions. The corroborative allegations are found in the assertions made by Agent Martinez based upon his own observations contained in paragraphs 5 and 7. Martinez observed Santiago enter and exit the warehouse and overheard his conversation with Mario Long in which Santiago revealed his knowledge of the scheme and his desire to conceal the circumstances from the DEA.[70]

§ 4.10   Warrants

§ 4.10(a)   Arrest Warrants

When a complaint is issued prior to the arrest of the defendant, an arrest warrant is drafted by the prosecutor and submitted to the magistrate judge along with the complaint. A finding that the complaint meets the probable cause standard will justify the issuance of the arrest warrant, which is executed in the manner described in the Federal Rules.[71]

The Constitution requires that arrest warrants describe the person to be seized with specificity.[72] The specificity requirement is fulfilled when the caption of the action contains the name of the defendant or, if his or her name is unknown, any name or description by which the defendant can be identified with reasonable certainty.[73] For example, either the name Gilbert Santiago or "John Doe, a male, Latino, age 35–40, 5'10", 175 pounds, with brown hair and glasses, working at Superior Warehouse, 149 Grand Street, Queens, New York," will reasonably assure that the right person will be apprehended.

§ 4.10(b)   Search Warrants[74]

Unlike the arrest warrant, a search warrant will not be authorized simply on a showing of probable cause that a crime has been committed. Since the purpose of the search warrant is to search for and seize evidence, instrumentalities, fruits of a crime, or contraband, the warrant must specifically designate the items to be seized and the whereabouts of these items.[75] For search warrants, the particularity requirement safeguards the individual's privacy interest against a general exploratory rummaging.[76] However, search warrants, like arrest warrants, will be

---

70. Additional indications of reliability will be required in cases where the source is a paid government informant, whose credibility may appear suspect because of the informant's interest in providing information. *See* LaFave et al., § 3.3(c). In such situations, the complaint would include a section entitled *Reliability of the Informant,* which contains facts designed to corroborate the informant's story and/or the informant's past history of providing truthful information. The deponent would relate facts personally known to him or her, including knowledge of the reputation of the source or any other indications of the source's reliability.

71. Fed. R. Crim. P. 4(d). *See* Wright, § 55.

72. U.S.Const. amend. IV.

73. *See* LaFave, Search § 3.1(g).

74. *See generally* Fed. R. Crim. P. 41.

75. *See* Fed. R. Crim. P. 41(b); Wright, § 664.

76. *See* LaFave, Search § 4.6.

judged on their practical accuracy rather than technical sufficiency.[77] Absolute precision is not required in identifying the place to be searched or the things or persons to be seized.[78]

The warrant itself is accompanied by an affidavit, sworn to by the case agent or other officer who will conduct the search.[79] Where the application for a search warrant is made at the time of the filing of a complaint, or after a complaint has been filed, the complaint will be attached and will establish probable cause to believe that a crime has been committed. The complaint might not, however, establish probable cause to believe that the property sought is related to the crime being investigated[80] or that the property is at the place to be searched.[81] In that case, a separate affidavit will be required.

§ 4.10(c)   The Santiago Arrest Warrant

The following is the arrest warrant for Gilbert Santiago. Note that the caption of the action contains both the name of the defendant and a description. Where a name is available, the description is optional, because it is unlikely that there would be more than one person with the same name at one place.[82]

---

77. *See* Maryland v. Garrison, 480 U.S. 79, 88 (1987) (refusing to suppress evidence seized when officers searched two apartments, reasonably believing them to be only one residence).

78. WRIGHT, § 670.

79. FED. R. CRIM. P. 41(c)(1). *See* WRIGHT, § 662. A warrant may, however, be issued on the basis of an oral application, including an application by telephone, if the circumstances are such as to make it reasonable to dispense with a written affidavit. FED. R. CRIM. P. 41(c)(2). *See generally* WRIGHT, § 670.1.

80. *See* WRIGHT, § 670.

81. On the execution of arrest and search warrants, see LaFAVE, SEARCH §§ 4.7–4.12.

82. *Id.* § 4.9(a)–(c).

Approved: Laura Knapp
     Assistant United States Attorney

Before: Honorable Roger Brown
     United States Magistrate Judge
     Eastern District of New York

UNITED STATES OF AMERICA

                                  ARREST WARRANT

       --against--

                                    Case no. 05 M 0063

                                    (T.21, U.S.C. §§ 841(a)(1) and
GILBERT SANTIAGO, male, Latino,   846)
age 35–40, 5'10", 175 pounds, brown
hair and glasses, working at Superior
Warehouse, located 149 Grand Street,
Queens, New York,

                   Defendant.

TO ALL AUTHORIZED LAW ENFORCEMENT OFFICERS:

You are hereby commanded to arrest Gilbert Santiago and bring him forthwith before the Magistrate Judge for the Eastern District of New York in the City of New York to answer a complaint charging him with possession with intent to distribute and conspiracy to possess with intent to distribute cocaine in violation of Title 21 U.S.C. §§ 841(a)(1) and 846.

R Brown

United States Magistrate Judge

Dated: Brooklyn, New York
       January 13, 2005

---

§ 4.10(d)   The Search Warrant for Superior Warehouse

The Superior Warehouse search warrant follows. Note that the caption is different from the arrest warrant. This is because the subject of the search warrant is a specific location rather than a named individual. Note also that all of the items listed in the body of the warrant are generically described, but include, as they must, enough specificity to enable a law enforcement officer to distinguish between what is sought and other items contained in the warehouse for which there is no connection to the crime being investigated. The warrant authorizes a "daytime only" search because the affidavit did not establish reasonable cause to believe that an exigency exists requiring the magistrate judge to approve the execution of the warrant between 10:00 pm and 6:00 am.[83] Finally, the warrant indicates that should any of the property be found on the premises and seized, a written inventory or "return" must be made before the magistrate judge who authorized the issuance of the warrant.[84] This provision guarantees that anyone whose privacy interests have been adversely affected by the warrant will be able to determine whether the items seized exceed the authorizing provisions limiting the scope of the seizure.[85]

---

83. Fed.R.Crim.P. 41(e)(2)(B) requires search warrants to be executed in daytime unless there are circumstances requiring a search at night.

84. This provision is required by Fed. R.Crim.P. 41(d). *See* Wright, § 672.

85. A person aggrieved by an unlawful search may move for the return of any property seized, *see* Fed.R.Crim.P. 41(e), and/or move that it be excluded from use in a prosecution, Fed.R.Crim.P. 12, 41(f). *See generally* Wright, § 74.

UNITED STATES DISTRICT COURT
EASTERN DISTRICT OF NEW YORK

UNITED STATES OF AMERICA

In the Matter of The Search Of   **SEARCH WARRANT**

PREMISES KNOWN AND DESCRIBED AS   Case no. 05 M 0063

                                      T.21 U.S.C. §§ 841(a)(1)
SUPERIOR WAREHOUSE, LOCATED AT   and 846
149 GRAND STREET, QUEENS,
NEW YORK

TO: Any Authorized Officer of the United States:

An Affidavit having been made before me by Special Agent Ralph Martinez who has reason to believe that on the premises known as Superior Warehouse at 149 Grand Street, Queens, New York in the Eastern District of New York there is now concealed a certain person or property, namely

1. Quantities of cocaine; 2. Books and records, including names, addresses and telephone numbers of cocaine distributors and suppliers; 3. Books and records showing cash transactions, prices and quantities of cocaine imported, purchased, and sold; 4. Currency used to purchase cocaine which reflects the proceeds of sales of cocaine; and 5. Cutting agents and drug paraphernalia including bags, scales, and stamps.

I am satisfied that the affidavit establishes probable cause to believe that property so described is now concealed on the premises above-described and establishes grounds for the issuance of this warrant.

YOU ARE HEREBY COMMANDED to search on or before January 22, 2005, the place named above for the property specified, serving this warrant and making the search in the daytime (6:00 am to 10:00 pm), if the property be found there to seize same, leaving a copy of this warrant and receipt for the property taken, and prepare a written inventory of the property seized and promptly return this warrant to ROGER BROWN, U.S. Magistrate Judge, as required by law.

January 13, 2005, 4:00 pm at Brooklyn, New York

_____

Roger Brown
United States Magistrate Judge

UNITED STATES DISTRICT COURT
EASTERN DISTRICT OF NEW YORK

UNITED STATES OF AMERICA

In the Matter of the Search of

PREMISES KNOWN AND DESCRIBED AS

SUPERIOR WAREHOUSE, LOCATED AT
149 GRAND STREET, QUEENS, NEW YORK

**AFFIDAVIT IN
SUPPORT OF A
SEARCH WARRANT**

Case no. 05 M 0063

T. 21 U.S.C. §§ 841
(a)(1), 846

EASTERN DISTRICT OF NEW YORK, SS:

RALPH MARTINEZ, being duly sworn, deposes and says that he is a Special Agent with the United States Drug Enforcement Administration assigned to John F. Kennedy International Airport, Group 14, duly appointed according to law and acting as such.

Upon information and belief, there will be located at the PREMISES KNOWN AND DESCRIBED AS SUPERIOR WAREHOUSE, 149 GRAND STREET, QUEENS, NEW YORK, (the "PREMISES"):

(1) quantities of cocaine, (2) books and records including the names, addresses and telephone numbers of cocaine distributors and suppliers, which books and records would reveal the identities of confederates in cocaine trafficking, (3) books and records showing cash transactions, prices and quantities of cocaine imported, purchased and sold, which books and records would reveal the extent of involvement of confederates in narcotics trafficking, (4) currency used to purchase cocaine which reflects the proceeds of sales of cocaine, and (5) cutting agents and drug paraphernalia including bags, scales, and stamps, all of which constitute evidence, fruits, and instrumentalities of violations of Title 21, United States Code, Sections 841(a)(1), 846, 952 and 963.

The source of my information and the grounds for my beliefs are as follows:

1. On January 12, 2005, at approximately 2:00 pm, I recovered, at the PREMISES, a cloth package containing approximately 1 ounce of cocaine which had been the subject of a controlled delivery.

2. The cocaine was located in a crate concealed behind a locked door. The crate had been shipped to the PREMISES from Colombia, and discovered by agents of the United States Customs Service at Kennedy Airport on or about January 11, 2005. The crate contained approximately 9.8 kilograms of cocaine.

3. Agents of the D.E.A. personally observed Gilbert Santiago enter and exit the premises on three (3) different occasions between 9:00 am and 1:00 pm on January 12, 2005. Santiago has previously been convicted in this District of trafficking in cocaine.

4. After the crate containing cocaine was recovered from the premises, the foreman, Mario Long, informed your deponent that Gilbert Santiago would notify Long when a shipment containing special markings would be made, and had done so with respect to this crate. Long further informed your deponent that Van Ness Trucking was scheduled to pick up this crate.

5. On January 12, 2005, your deponent found a date book in the possession of the foreman, Mario Long. The date book contained names, addresses, and telephone numbers of various trucking firms listed on various dates. On the January 12, 2005 page, your deponent saw the name "Van Ness Trucking".

6. I have been with the Drug Enforcement Administration for approximately four (4) years in narcotics interdiction, and based on my experience in narcotics investigations during that time, it is my belief that in light of the information learned in this investigation, there is probable cause to believe that Superior Warehouse, 149 Grand Street, Queens, New York, is being used as a location to receive, store and distribute cocaine and other controlled substances imported into the United States. It has been my experience that such locations often contain, besides quantities of cocaine and controlled substances, narcotics related records, paraphernalia, as well as large amount of cash that constitute the proceeds of narcotics distribution.

7. Therefore, based on my experience and knowledge of the facts of this case, there is probable cause to believe that inside the PREMISES KNOWN AS SUPERIOR WAREHOUSE, 149 GRAND STREET, QUEENS, NEW YORK, there are quantities of cocaine, narcotics-related records, narcotics paraphernalia, and currency relating to the proceeds of narcotics sales.

WHEREFORE, I respectfully request that a search warrant issue allowing DEA agents, with proper assistance from other law enforcement officers, to search THE PREMISES OF SUPERIOR WAREHOUSE AT 149 GRAND STREET, QUEENS, NEW YORK, and to seize there from the following evidence of a cocaine importation and distribution scheme: (1) quantities of cocaine and other controlled substances, (2) books and records including the names, addresses and telephone numbers of narcotics purchasers and suppliers, which books and records would reveal the identities of confederates in narcotics trafficking, (3) books and records showing cash transactions, prices and quantities of cocaine imported, purchased and sold, which books and records would reveal the extent of involvement of confederates in narcotic trafficking, (4) currency used to purchase cocaine or which reflects the proceeds of sales of cocaine, and (5) bags, scales, stamps, and cutting agents, all constituting drug paraphernalia; all of which constitute evidence, fruits and instrumentalities of violations of Title 21, United States Code, Sections 841(a)(1) and 846.

Ralph Martinez
Special Agent
Drug Enforcement Administration

Sworn to before me this 13th day of January, 2005

Roger Brown
United States Magistrate Judge

§ 4.11   Proceedings on Arrest and Search Warrants—United States v. Santiago

With the complaint and warrant applications drafted, AUSA Knapp and Agent Martinez appeared before Magistrate Judge Brown at the courthouse in the Eastern District of New York.[86] The agent, as the affiant on the complaint and the affidavit in support of the search warrant, swore to their truthfulness. The magistrate judge ruled that probable cause had been established.

Special Agents Foster and Richards then went to Superior Warehouse to conduct the search. When they arrived, they found Gilbert Santiago there and arrested him. Agent Foster took him to DEA headquarters for processing and then to the magistrate judge's court for his initial appearance. In cases such as Santiago's, it is unnecessary for the prosecutor to draft another complaint, since Santiago was jointly charged in the complaint with Mario Long and Murphy; the original complaint upon which Santiago's arrest warrant was based would suffice.

Agent Richards completed the search at Superior Warehouse. She then reported what she found to AUSA Knapp and prepared a "return," or inventory of the items seized. The return was attested to by Richards and thereafter filed with the magistrate judge. The return from the search of Superior Warehouse is presented below.

---

86. For obvious reasons, this appearance will be *ex parte*.

UNITED STATES DISTRICT COURT
EASTERN DISTRICT OF NEW YORK

UNITED STATES OF AMERICA

In The Matter of the Search of   **RETURN**

                                        Case no. 05 M 0063

PREMISES KNOWN AND DESCRIBED AS   T. 21 U.S.C. §§ 841
SUPERIOR WAREHOUSE, LOCATED AT   (a)(1), 846
149 GRAND STREET, QUEENS,
NEW YORK

EASTERN DISTRICT OF NEW YORK, SS:

       GLORIA RICHARDS, being duly sworn deposes and says that she is a Special Agent with the United States Drug Enforcement Administration assigned to John F. Kennedy International Airport, Group 14, duly appointed according to law and acting as such.

       I received the attached search warrant dated January 12, 2005 and have executed it as follows:

       On January 13, 2005 at 5:00 pm, I searched the premises described in the warrant, and I left a copy of the warrant attached to the door of the premises together with a receipt for the items seized.

       The following is an inventory of property taken pursuant to the warrant:

       Invoices for Superior Warehouse from the period from January 1, 2004 through January 12, 2005.

       Bookkeeping records and other books showing transactions for the period between January 1, 2004 and January 12, 2005.

       Superior Warehouse deposit slips with CMS Bank for the period between August 1, 2004 to January 12, 2005.

       This inventory was made in the presence of S/A William Foster, and I swear that this Inventory is a true and detailed account of all property taken by me on the warrant.

Gloria Richards
_____
Gloria Richards
Special Agent
Drug Enforcement Administration

Sworn to before me this 13th day of January, 2005

[signature]
_____
United States Magistrate Judge
Eastern District of New York

Chapter 5

PROCEEDINGS ON THE COMPLAINT—THE INITIAL APPEARANCE, BAIL AND PREVENTIVE DETENTION

Table of Sections

Sec.
5.0 Introduction.
5.1 The Entry of Defense Counsel.
   5.1(a) The Right to Counsel.
   5.1(b) The Initial Defense Interview.
5.2 Conflicts of Interest.
   5.2(a) Joint Representation.
   5.2(b) Joint Defense Agreements.
   5.2(c) Conflicts with Other Clients.
5.3 Commencing the Initial Appearance.
5.4 Reviewing the Sufficiency of the Complaint.
5.5 Pretrial Release and Detention Proceedings—General.
5.6 Pretrial Release.
   5.6(a) Standards for Release.
   5.6(b) The Pretrial Release Hearing.
   5.6(c) Conducting the Pretrial Release Proceeding.
5.7 Preventive Detention Proceedings—Introduction.
   5.7(a) Who May Be Detained.
   5.7(b) Detention Proceedings.
   5.7(c) Review of Detention Decisions.
5.8 Time Considerations at the Initial Appearance.
5.9 Ancillary Proceedings at the Initial Appearance.
   5.9(a) Removal Proceedings.
   5.9(b) Temporary Detention.
5.10 The Initial Appearances of Mario Long, Arthur Murphy and Gilbert Santiago.
   5.10(a) The Initial Appearance in U.S. v. Mario Long.
   5.10(b) The Initial Appearance in U.S. v. Arthur Murphy.
   5.10(c) The Initial Appearance in U.S. v. Santiago.

5.11   Litigating the Preventive Detention Issue—U.S. v. Gilbert Santiago.
     5.11(a)   The Hearing.
     5.11(b)   Motion to Review the Detention Decision.

---

§ 5.0   Introduction

The Federal Rules provide that after arrest the defendant must be brought "without unnecessary delay" before a magistrate judge for his or her initial appearance.[1] After drafting the complaint the Assistant United States Attorney will notify the magistrate judge's chambers that a case is to be presented. The AUSA will also request that the case agent find out from the defendant whether he or she will be represented by private counsel or will require counsel to be appointed. If the defendant does not have an attorney, the magistrate judge will arrange for assigned counsel to meet with the defendant prior to the initial appearance.

Also prior to the appearance, and typically before meeting with defense counsel, the defendant will be interviewed by a representative of the Pretrial Services Agency, who will obtain information relevant to the bail decision. The interview will be concerned with the defendant's roots in the community—family, friends and length of residence, as well as any ties to other countries; mental and physical health, including drug and alcohol dependency; employment and financial condition; and educational background. This information will be included in a report that will also contain a description of the offense, the defendant's prior criminal record and his or her history of appearing in court. On the basis of all of these factors, Pretrial Services will make a recommendation to the court as to whether the defendant should be released (indicating what restrictions are warranted, if any) or detained pending resolution of the case. If enough information cannot be obtained, Pretrial Services will submit the report without a recommendation.[2]

When the case is called before the magistrate judge, counsel will be formally appointed or assigned. The magistrate judge will advise the defendant of his or her rights, rule on the sufficiency of the complaint and determine the defendant's pretrial release status. In this chapter we will describe the rules and practices relevant to these determinations, and we will illustrate these concepts by describing the initial appearances of Mario Long, Arthur Murphy, and Gilbert Santiago.

---

1. FED. R. CRIM. P. 5(a). The initial appearance must normally take place within 48 hours of arrest. *See* County of Riverside v. McLaughlin, 500 U.S. 44, 56 (1991) (defining "without unnecessary delay"); 24 JAMES WM. MOORE, MOORE'S FEDERAL PRACTICE § 605.03 (3d ed. & Supp. 2004).

2. There are some situations in which the defense attorney will attempt to waive the pretrial services interview, such as where the likelihood of detention is great (e.g., where the defendant is a noncitizen drug courier with no ties to the United States and the interview could produce damaging statements or other information without offering any possible advantage to the defendant. There is no right to waive this interview, however, and the magistrate judge may insist that it be held.

§ 5.1   The Entry of Defense Counsel

§ 5.1(a)   The Right to Counsel

The Federal Rules provide that the defendant is entitled to be represented by counsel at the initial appearance.[3] Private counsel, hired by the defendant, may enter an appearance at this stage. If the defendant is financially unable to retain an attorney, one will be assigned in accordance with the Criminal Justice Act of 1964.[4] The Act provides for assignment of counsel according to plans adopted in each judicial district[5] and for compensation with federal funds.[6] There are two types of indigent defense plans: one provides for panels of private attorneys assigned on a more or less rotating basis as cases enter the system. Panels are in place in every federal district, and they are the exclusive means of indigent representation in 20 of the 94 federal districts. The other type of plan consists of Federal Defender Offices, which in turn may be composed of federally employed attorneys or of attorneys associated with a state or local public defender agency. In many districts the responsibility for indigent defense is divided between a defender organization and panel attorneys. For example, in the Eastern District of New York, primary responsibility for these cases is assumed by the Federal Defender Service, and panel attorneys appear in cases in which that office has a conflict of interest.[7]

About one-third of federal defendants are represented by private counsel.[8] However, defendants in police-initiated cases, even if they eventually will be represented by private counsel, generally will not have their own counsel at this early stage of the process. More than likely, the attorney who will be involved at that point will ordinarily represent indigent defendants. Whether that attorney will remain in the case is a function primarily of the financial condition of the defendant. In the initial interview, the attorney will inquire into this matter, and, if the defendant meets indigency standards,[9] the attorney will complete a financial statement to be presented to the magistrate judge at the initial appearance.[10] This statement will include an affidavit from the defendant detailing information about his financial circumstances, a copy of which follows. Since a substantial percentage of all defendants in these cases are unable to afford attorneys, there is a good likelihood that, barring a conflict of interest, the attorney who conducts the initial interview will represent the defendant for the duration of the case.

---

3. FED. R. CRIM. P. 5(c).

4. 18 U.S.C. §§ 3006 *et seq.*; *see also* FED. R. CRIM. P. 44; WRIGHT, §§ 731–740. Attorneys assigned under the statute to represent indigents may also represent non-indigents for arraignment purposes only, in recognition of the fact that many otherwise financially ineligible defendants may not have had time in the period between arrest and the initial appearance to retain counsel.

5. 18 U.S.C. § 3006A.

6. *See* Caroline Wolf Harnow, *Defense Counsel in Criminal Cases,* U.S. Dep't. of Justice Bureau of Justice Statistics, *available at* http://www.ojp.usdoj. gov/bjs/pub/pdf/dccc.pdf (special report Nov. 2000).

7. *See* § 3006A.

8. Harnow, *supra* note 6.

9. *See id.*

10. *See infra* § 5.3.

FINANCIAL AFFIDAVIT

IN SUPPORT OF REQUEST FOR ATTORNEY, EXPERT OR OTHER COURT SERVICES WITHOUT PAYMENT OF FEE

IN UNITED STATES	☐ MAGISTRATE	☐ DISTRICT	☐ APPEALS COURT or	☐ OTHER PANEL (Specify below)

IN THE CASE OF

_____ VS _____	FOR
	AT

LOCATION NUMBER

PERSON REPRESENTED (Show your full name)

DOCKET NUMBERS
Magistrate
District Court
Court of Appeals

CHARGE/OFFENSE (describe if applicable & check box →) ☐ Felony ☐ Misdemeanor

1 ☐ Defendant – Adult
2 ☐ Defendant – Juvenile
3 ☐ Appellant
4 ☐ Probation Violator
5 ☐ Parole Violator
6 ☐ Habeas Petitioner
7 ☐ 2255 Petitioner
8 ☐ Material Witness
9 ☐ Other (Specify) _____

EMPLOY-MENT

Are you now employed? ☐ Yes   ☐ No   ☐ Am Self Employed

Name and address of employer: _____

IF YES, how much do you earn per month? $ _____
IF NO, give month and year of last employment
How much did you earn per month? $ _____

If married is your Spouse employed? ☐ Yes   ☐ No
IF YES, how much does your Spouse earn per month? $ _____
If a minor under age 21, what is your Parents or Guardian's approximate monthly income? $ _____

ASSETS

OTHER INCOME

Have you received within the past 12 months any income from a business, profession or other form of self-employment, or in the form of rent payments, interest, dividends, retirement or annuity payments, or other sources? ☐ Yes ☐ No

IF YES, GIVE THE AMOUNT RECEIVED & IDENTIFY THE SOURCES

RECEIVED _____ SOURCES _____

CASH

Have you any cash on hand or money in savings or checking account ☐ Yes ☐ No   IF YES, state total amount $ _____

PROP-ERTY

Do you own any real estate, stocks, bonds, notes, automobiles, or other valuable property (excluding ordinary household furnishings and clothing)? ☐ Yes ☐ No

IF YES, GIVE THE VALUE AND DESCRIBE IT

VALUE _____ DESCRIPTION _____

OBLIGATIONS & DEBTS

DEPENDENTS

MARITAL STATUS
☐ SINGLE
☐ MARRIED
☐ WIDOWED
☐ SEPARATED OR DIVORCED

Total No. of Dependents _____

List persons you actually support and your relationship to them _____

DEBTS & MONTHLY BILLS

(LIST ALL CREDITORS, INCLUDING BANKS, LOAN COMPANIES, CHARGE ACCOUNTS, ETC.)

APARTMENT OR HOME	Creditors	Total Debt	Monthly Pay't
		$	$
		$	$
		$	$
		$	$

I certify under penalty of perjury that the foregoing is true and correct. Executed on (date) _____

SIGNATURE OF DEFENDANT (OR PERSON REPRESENTED) ▶ _____

§ 5.1(b) The Initial Defense Interview[11]

What occurs at the initial defense interview can have an important effect upon the case, both in terms of the immediate problems facing the defendant as well as the ongoing interpersonal relationship between the attorney and the client. As to the immediate situation, the attorney's most pressing task is usually to attempt to secure the defendant's release from detention prior to trial. While there may be occasions when the initial appearance results in the dismissal of all charges, that is extremely rare in the federal system.[12] As to the long term relationship, if a level of trust and rapport is established at the outset, it will be easier in the long run for the attorney to provide effective and useful counsel.

The task of establishing rapport is, however, a difficult one. In most cases, the defendant will be traumatized by the impact of being arrested and held in custody for many hours, perhaps as long as a day or so, without having contact with friends, relatives or indeed anyone who seems to have his or her interests at heart. Even persons who have been through the process before cannot be unaffected by the isolation of this experience. Then, when the defense attorney does arrive, he or she will in most cases be unknown to the defendant. Adding to the difficulty, the interview will take place in a guarded detention area rather than a calm attorney's office or other more private space. And it will have to proceed quickly since the magistrate judge likely will be waiting to call the case.

Under these conditions, the attorney's very first task is to make certain that the defendant knows who the attorney is and understands his or her role. It may seem evident, but it is useful to communicate this information clearly—the defense attorney is the first person to meet the defendant in the process who is unequivocally on the defendant's side, and that fact should be emphasized. Moreover, counsel should tell the defendant that the information the defendant imparts during the attorney-client relationship is privileged.[13] To the extent that the defendant believes in the promise of confidentiality, he or she may be encouraged to speak freely regarding the issues that could be useful for the bail argument.

Assertions of loyalty by the attorney, however, may not be sufficient to overcome the defendant's apprehensions. It is much more effective for the attorney to actually demonstrate concern. One useful way of doing so is by ensuring at the outset that the defendant understands his present

---

11. *See generally* THOMAS L. SCHAFFER & JAMES R. ELKINS, LEGAL INTERVIEWING & COUNSELING (3d ed. 1997); MARILYN J. BERGER, JOHN B. MITCHELL, & RONALD H. CLARK, PRETRIAL ADVOCACY ch. 5 (1988).

12. Moving to dismiss the complaint at the initial appearance is illustrated in § 5.10(b). In almost every case, as in the example, the burden of proof on the government is too low for such a motion to succeed at this stage.

13. MODEL RULES OF PROF'L CONDUCT R. 1.6 (1983, as amended 2003) (hereinafter "MODEL RULE").

situation, what the charges are, what is about to happen and what the attorney's role will be. The client should be made to understand that the case will not be resolved at the initial appearance and that the most important matter that will be determined at that point is the defendant's pretrial release status. If the defendant understands this limited focus, it should be easier to explain why the attorney will need to ask questions that seem to relate more to the defendant's background than to the facts of the case. An effective bail argument is important to the defendant for the obvious reason that his or her most immediate concern is to obtain release from custody. It is important to the attorney-client relationship as well, because it is undoubtedly one of the most powerful ways to build trust under the circumstances. Even if the bail argument on behalf of the defendant is unsuccessful, if it is vigorously made, it will convey a positive message. Asking background questions is also advisable because it will enable the client to interact with the attorney on the least volatile issues first.[14]

Aside from information relevant to the bail decision, it is important at the initial interview for counsel to obtain as much detail as possible concerning the events that occurred since the time of the arrest because this information will be fresh in the defendant's memory. These questions should be very specific to gather as much information as possible regarding what evidence the government has and whether the police obtained it legally. The goal of this aspect of the interview is to obtain a step-by-step account from the moment of the encounter with the agents onward, addressing any conversations that occurred, statements that were taken, searches performed or identification procedures conducted.

After addressing the bail and post-arrest issues, the defense attorney can preliminarily discuss the facts of the case. This inquiry is a delicate matter. There most likely will be substantial evidence alleged in the complaint against the defendant, but it is not particularly useful for the attorney to point that out at the outset of the discussion or to demand an explanation. Such an approach may lead the client to associate the attorney with the prosecution, and as a result the client may not be as forthcoming about the details of his situation and instead may relay a version of the events designed to convince the lawyer of his innocence. The lawyer should therefore remain non-judgmental and should not go into the facts in great detail at this time. However, since at the initial appearance the magistrate judge will ask the defendant whether he or she has had an opportunity to read the complaint and is familiar with the charges, it will be necessary for the attorney to read the complaint to the client (or read it with the client) and thus to deal superficially with

---

14. For a discussion of the considerations relevant to the bail determination see *infra* § 5.7(a)-(b).

the allegations. When doing so, however, we stress again that it is advisable not to be confrontational. One useful approach in reviewing the complaint with the defendant is to explain that these are the agent's allegations, that they are not necessarily true, and that the defendant will have the opportunity to challenge these allegations at a hearing and at trial. The defendant may wish to explain, and it may be effective for the lawyer to demonstrate interest in the defendant's version. If the responses given seem confused or dubious, it is probably best to move away from the matter for the time being and to explain that there will be time in the future to go over the facts thoroughly and that the limited time at hand must be spent on other more pressing matters, namely, pretrial release and the post-arrest facts.

At the conclusion of the interview, the attorney should attempt to ensure that the defendant knows what is about to happen in court and what is likely to occur thereafter. It is always inappropriate at this stage for the attorney to initiate a conversation about either a guilty plea or the likely result of a trial or other proceeding, or about the likely sentence in the case. Despite the fact that the defendant may understandably wish to know these things, the chances are great that the advice that the attorney gives at this point will be uninformed and may well be wrong, with potentially disastrous effects on the attorney-client relationship. Only practitioners with very extensive experience should risk such predictions, and even they will be unlikely to do so in cases of any complexity. To understand why this tentative attitude should be taken, one need only consider the fact that all of the evidence against the defendant may not by any means be included in the complaint and that the information the attorney learns from the defendant at the initial interview likewise may be incomplete or inaccurate.

§ 5.2 Conflicts of Interest

Once a lawyer decides to undertake a representation, counsel must consider the body of rules designed to assure that loyalty to the client is not compromised by competing interests or obligations.[15] A detailed discussion of conflict of interest rules is beyond the scope of this book,[16] but it seems appropriate to comment on three important aspects of the conflicts issue. The first involves cases in which an attorney considers representing co-defendants. The second concerns joint defense agreements which may be useful when multiple defendants are prosecuted within the same case. The third involves situations in which an attor-

---

15. The Sixth Amendment right to effective assistance of counsel includes the right to counsel unburdened by conflicts of interest. Holloway v. Arkansas, 435 U.S. 475, 482 (1978). *See* 21A Am. Jur. 2d *Crimi-* *nal Law* § 1229 (1998 & Supp. 2003); Mod-el Rule 1.7–10.

16. *See* Charles W. Wolfram, Modern Legal Ethics § 8.2 (West Publishing Co. 1986); LaFave et al., § 11.9.

ney's present or past relationship with another client may create a conflict with the representation under consideration.

§ 5.2(a) Joint Representation

Joint representation in criminal cases is not necessarily prohibited by law or by ethical rules, unless the co-defendants actually have conflicting defenses.[17] However, joint representation is viewed with suspicion. The Federal Rules require the court to inquire into the propriety of the representation whenever two or more defendants are jointly represented and to take "appropriate measures" to protect the right to effective assistance of counsel unless there is "good cause" to believe that no conflict is likely to arise.[18] It is good practice for the attorney to raise the potential conflict issue, though it may be raised in the first instance by the government in a motion to disqualify or by the court *sua sponte*. The court has broad latitude to disqualify counsel if it appears that there is a potential for conflict. The defendant may be permitted to waive a conflict, but has no right to do so, because the need to assure the integrity of the justice system supersedes the defendant's right to any particular lawyer.[19]

Even if an attorney is permitted by the court to represent co-defendants, sufficient hazards remain so as to make it unwise in almost every case to do so. It is true that additional expense might be avoided when two defendants have the same attorney. It is also true that a single attorney may have a better overall perspective on the case and be better able to present a consistent defense theory. But the potential difficulties are considerable and, very often, not predictable. Positions that appear harmonious based on early assertions by the parties may turn out less so as the facts develop. Co-defendants frequently have different degrees of involvement in the events in question, and that difference may become blurred if both are represented by the same attorney. All of the evidence in the possession of the government may not be known at the outset of the representation and may soon require a change of strategy for one defendant and not the other. One defendant may at some future date

---

17. *See Holloway*, 435 U.S. at 482; LaFave et al., § 11.9.

18. Fed. R. Crim. P. 44(c). The advisory committee notes indicate that while the rule does not specify the steps that a court might take, those steps would include obtaining a knowing and intelligent waiver, ordering a severance, or requiring that separate counsel be appointed. *See* Fed. R. Crim. P. 44 advisory committee's note.

19. *See* Wheat v. United States, 486 U.S. 153, 159 (1988); LaFave et al., § 11.9(c).

believe it prudent to plead guilty and cooperate with the government against the other, and the attorney, because of confidentiality rules, might, among other things, not be able effectively to cross-examine such a cooperator.[20] In all of these scenarios, the attorney representing two or more defendants is placed in the untenable position of having to prefer the interests of one client over the other. Should any of these situations arise during the representation, the attorney would have to withdraw.[21]

§ 5.2(b) Joint Defense Agreements

One technique to reconcile these potential conflicts while preserving the benefits of joint representation is to execute a joint defense agreement, pursuant to which co-defendants agree to share information and strategy. Under normal rules governing the attorney-client privilege, the only protected communications are those between the client and attorney made outside the presence of third parties.[22] The joint defense privilege is an exception to this rule, preserving the privilege when the defendants and their counsel share confidences among each other.[23] While the privilege can be asserted even in the absence of a written joint defense agreement, the better practice is to execute the agreement in writing.[24]

While the joint defense agreement can be a useful tool for defense counsel, potential hazards require that it be used with care. The agreement cannot prevent a party to it from deciding to cooperate with the government and testify against the other defendants. If that were to occur, the cooperator may be deemed to have waived the privilege with respect to statements he made pursuant to the joint defense agreement and may be subject to cross-examination about them by other defen-

---

20. Glasser v. United States, 315 U.S. 60, 72–76 (1942).

21. A special conflict situation may arise where co-defendants are brought before the magistrate judge and the only counsel present is a representative of a defender organization, either because a defendant's private attorney has not been contacted in time or because no members of the Criminal Justice Act panel are available. To avoid potential conflicts, the magistrate judge should delay the initial appearance of one (or more) of the co-defendants until separate counsel is present. At times, however, the magistrate judge will order the defender to represent the co-defendant "for bail purposes only." This in turn re-

quires the attorney to advise the temporary client to say nothing about the facts of the case, notwithstanding that such facts are relevant to the bail decision. Counsel should attempt to resist such an assignment. If the magistrate judge is not persuaded, however, there is no ready answer to the dilemma.

22. See McCORMICK, § 91.

23. United States v. McPartlin, 595 F.2d 1321, 1336 (7th Cir. 1979); WEINSTEIN & BERGER, § 503.21.

24. For a model agreement, see *Joint Defense Agreement*, TRIAL EVIDENCE IN THE FEDERAL COURTS: PROBLEMS AND SOLUTIONS (ALI–ABA Course of Study) Apr. 8, 1999 at 31.

dants.[25] Moreover, counsel for non-cooperating defendants who have learned confidential information from the cooperator (or from other defendants who testify in their own defense) may face a disqualification motion based on an argument that the lawyer's duty to the cooperating defendant may limit the extent to which they could cross-examine that cooperating defendant.[26]

For these reasons, attorneys should be very cautious both about entering into joint defense agreements and about the disclosures that they and their clients make in joint sessions.[27]

§ 5.2(c) Conflicts with Other Clients

When considering a representation, the defense lawyer also must examine rules regarding possible conflicts between the proposed defendant's interests and those of past or existing clients. Again, a full discussion of this subject is beyond the scope of this book and is mentioned here simply to alert the reader to undertake the appropriate investigation.[28] The rules in substance preclude the lawyer from representing a proposed client if another client has an interest that is materially adverse to the proposed client or if the representation would require the use of privileged information gained from the other client.[29] Such conflicts may be waived if the other client gives informed consent. If there is no waiver, neither the attorney nor her colleagues can undertake the representation.[30]

While the principal focus of the conflicts rules is on defense counsel, prosecutors also face potential conflicts. These conflicts relate to the so-called "revolving door" problem, that is, the attorney who leaves private practice to become a prosecutor or who leaves the prosecutor's office to enter private practice. In addition to the general rules regarding conflicts discussed above, these special rules prohibit a government lawyer from participating in a matter in which he or she was substantially involved while in private practice and require government consent[31] before a former prosecutor can participate in a matter in which he or she was substantially involved as a government lawyer.[32] Former government

---

25. United States v. Almeida, 341 F.3d 1318 (11th Cir. 2003).

26. *Id.* at 1323. This problem can be avoided, however, if the joint defense agreement contains a waiver of the conflict. United States v. Stepney, 246 F.Supp.2d 1069 (N.D. Cal. 2003).

27. For a comprehensive discussion of the issues related to joint defense agreements, see WEINSTEIN & BERGER, § 503.21.

28. *See generally* WOLFRAM, *supra* note 16, at chs. 7 & 8.

29. MODEL RULES 1.7 (present clients), 1.9 (former clients).

30. MODEL RULE 1.10.

31. MODEL RULE 1.11(c)(1).

32. MODEL RULE 1.11(a).

lawyers are also prohibited from representing a person who has interests adverse to a person about whom the lawyer obtained confidential information while serving as a government lawyer.[33]

§ 5.3   Commencing the Initial Appearance

When the defendant's case is called, the magistrate judge first must inform the defendant of the nature of the charges. The defendant will also be advised of the privilege against self-incrimination, the right to counsel,[34] and the right to a preliminary examination.[35] The court will explain that a decision about pretrial release will be made. In felony cases the defendant will not be asked to enter a plea, since the magistrate judge does not have jurisdiction to finally dispose of felony cases.[36]

The initial appearance may also involve defendants who are arrested in one district but who have been charged in another. In such cases the defendant must be "removed" to the other district. Removal proceedings will be discussed below.[37]

§ 5.4   Reviewing the Sufficiency of the Complaint

We shall not repeat here the legal requirements for a proper complaint, except to note that it must contain "essential facts" to support a probable cause determination.[38] If the defense attorney believes that it does not, he or she may move to dismiss the complaint on the grounds that the government has failed to sustain its burden of proof. Recall, however, that the sworn complaint alone may satisfy the government's burden of persuasion at this stage of the proceedings, and the magistrate judge may make the probable cause determination on the basis of that document without conducting an adversary hearing.[39] Testimony will rarely be taken, and a motion to dismiss will be considered only on the grounds that the complaint is insufficient on its face.

Because the quantitative and qualitative burdens are so low, it is extremely rare that such a motion will be successful. In the event a complaint is dismissed, moreover, there is no bar to rearresting the

---

33. Model Rule 1.11(b).

34. See supra § 5.1.

35. Fed. R. Crim. P. 5.

36. As noted in § 4.1, a felony case can only be disposed of after the grand jury has voted an indictment or indictment has been waived, and for that reason as well no plea is entered before the magistrate judge. But because the magistrate judge does not have jurisdiction in these cases, no plea can be entered even if the initial appearance before the magistrate judge occurs after indictment.

37. See infra § 5.9(a).

38. Fed. R. Crim. P. 3. See Wright, §§ 42, 52. As we have noted, the complaint will only be reviewed at the initial appearance if the defendant was arrested without a warrant. In such a case, the constitution requires a judicial determination of probable cause to continue the detention or impose other restraints on freedom. Gerstein v. Pugh, 420 U.S. 103, 114 (1975).

39. See supra § 4.2(b).

defendant and filing a new complaint or to presenting the case to a grand jury, which can supersede any action previously taken on the complaint by returning an indictment.[40]

§ 5.5   Pretrial Release and Detention Proceedings—General

The most significant action that will occur at the initial appearance will be determining the pretrial release status of the defendant. Whether the defendant is incarcerated or released prior to trial is a matter of immediate and quite obviously major personal concern and can have a substantial long-term impact on the case as well.

Federal law provides for three types of pretrial status: unconditional release; release on one or more conditions; and pretrial detention. There is also a separate provision for temporary pretrial detention of defendants who may be wanted by other jurisdictions or agencies, which will be discussed below.[41]

Note that the law and, in turn, the following discussion, distinguish between hearings and procedures that address *what* conditions, if any, to impose on pretrial release and hearings and procedures addressing *whether* the defendant should be released pretrial. We refer to the former as "pretrial release hearings" and the latter as "preventive detention hearings."

§ 5.6   Pretrial Release

§ 5.6(a)   Standards for Release

The Bail Reform Act of 1984[42] expresses a preference for pretrial release on a defendant's own recognizance (i.e., without the imposition of financial or other conditions) or after executing an unsecured appearance bond, both conditioned on the defendant not engaging in any additional criminal activity pending trial.[43] If, however, the magistrate judge determines that such unrestricted release will not reasonably assure the reappearance of the defendant or the safety of others in the community, a range of conditions on release can be imposed. The law prefers the least restrictive means feasible to reasonably assure the defendant's future appearance and the public's safety. Conditions may include requirements that the defendant become or stay employed,

---

40. The defendant is protected against reprosecution under the Double Jeopardy Clause of the Fifth Amendment only if jeopardy has "attached" in a prior proceeding, i.e., after the jury is sworn or, in a bench trial, after the first trial witness is called. *See* LaFave et al., § 25.1(d).

41. *See infra* § 5.9(b).

42. 18 U.S.C. §§ 3142 *et seq.*

43. *See* § 3142(b).

refrain from use of drugs, undergo treatment, report to police or other agencies, or submit to third party custody.[44] Restrictions on travel[45] and curfews[46] also may be imposed. An example of an appearance bond and conditional release is found below in § 5.10(b).[47]

The statute also permits the court to require the defendant to post a secured bond, requiring either collateral or solvent sureties.[48] If financial conditions are imposed, failure to appear will result in forfeiture proceedings.[49] However, there is an extremely important caveat to the power of the court to impose such a bond, or any other financial condition, in lieu of pretrial release. The statute mandates that financial conditions may not be imposed (or must be modified) if they result in the pretrial detention of the defendant.[50] This provision attempts to end the practice of using excessive money bail *sub rosa* to detain a defendant.[51] It does not mean that pretrial detention is prohibited; it simply requires that the pretrial detention issue be addressed honestly in a preventive detention proceeding.[52]

The Bail Reform Act enumerates the traditional factors that the magistrate judge should consider in determining the release status of the defendant. These factors include: the nature and circumstances of the offense; the weight of the evidence; the character of the defendant, including mental condition, prior criminal record, and the like; and any evidence of a specific danger, including the risk of flight, that the defendant poses.[53]

Recent experience under the Bail Reform Act indicates that about 38% of all defendants are released prior to trial, either at their initial appearance or soon thereafter.[54] Most of these defendants (almost 77%)

---

44. § 3142(c)(1)(B)(i), (ii), (vi), & (ix).

45. § 3142(c)(1)(B)(iv).

46. § 3142(c)(1)(B)(vii).

47. See § 5.10, infra.

48. § 3142(c)(1)(B)(xii). It does not appear necessary for the sureties to demonstrate that they have sufficient assets to cover the face amount of the bond that is set. The statute says only that the sureties must agree to forfeit an amount reasonably necessary to assure the defendant's reappearance. In practice, courts are satisfied if the sureties will incur a substantial financial loss if the defendant does not appear.

49. FED. R. CRIM. P. 46(f). The rule provides, however, that the court may set aside the forfeiture if the surety later surrenders the defendant or if justice does not require the forfeiture.

50. § 3142(c)(2).

51. *See* MOORE, § 646.21(5)(b)(i). A court can, however, insist on a financial condition greater than the defendant can meet, so long as it justifies its action in a manner consistent with the preventive detention provisions of the statute, providing written findings of fact and conclusions of law. *Id.*

52. *See infra* § 5.7.

53. *See* § 3142(g).

54. Judicial Business of the United States Courts, Table H–9, *available at* http://www.uscourts.gov/judbus2004/ appendices/h9.pdf (Sept. 30, 2004).

are released either on their personal recognizance or on an unsecured appearance bond.[55]

§ 5.6(b) The Pretrial Release Hearing

The Bail Reform Act is silent about the nature of the hearing that is to be held to determine what conditions of release, if any, to impose on the defendant.[56] All that is required is that the court "take into account the available information" concerning the enumerated factors.[57] An evidentiary hearing is not precluded under the statute, although the statute gives no guidance regarding standards of evidence or burdens of proof at such a hearing. There is a presumption in favor of unconditional release, but it is not clear that the government has the burden of going forward at a release hearing. Nor is the burden of persuasion expressed, other than the ill-explained authority to impose conditions if there is no "reasonable assurance" that the defendant can be otherwise released with confidence. As to the qualitative burden, the Federal Rules of Evidence do not apply to bail hearings,[58] and the courts have adopted a lenient and flexible standard. Typically, the parties will be permitted to rely on proffers rather than produce witnesses.[59] Evidentiary hearings on conditions of pretrial release are extremely rare. With the elimination of money bail as a detention device, imposing conditions on pretrial release seems to be viewed as a tolerable infringement on the defendant's liberty that is not so serious as to require a more extensive evidentiary hearing.

§ 5.6(c) Conducting the Pretrial Release Proceeding

If the prosecutor does not object to a release on recognizance, it will almost invariably be granted, although the magistrate judge can, of course, impose such conditions as he or she may see fit. If the prosecution believes that conditions on release are appropriate, it will likely stress the nature and seriousness of the offense, the defendant's prior record, any ties to foreign countries, and, of course, any record of failing to appear in other criminal cases.

The defense attorney's argument, in response, will emphasize the statutory presumption and will attempt to establish that the defendant's roots in the community and lack of prior criminal activity demonstrate that the defendant is not a flight risk or a danger to the community. In support of this argument, defense counsel should try to arrange for relatives, employers or others who can attest to the defendant's reliabili-

---

55. *Id.*, Table H–6, *available at* http://www.uscourts.gov/judbus2004/appendices/h6.pdf (Sept. 30, 2004). Another 9% posted cash, 7% posted collateral, and 6% were released after securing bail bonds. *Id.*

56. More detailed procedural rules apply to the statute's preventive detention provisions. *See infra* § 5.7.

57. § 3142(g).

58. FED. R. EVID. 1101(d)(3).

59. United States v. Smith, 79 F.3d 1208, 1210 (D.C. Cir. 1996); United States v. Martir, 782 F.2d 1141, 1145 (2d Cir. 1986); LAFAVE ET AL., § 12.1(d). Proffers are discussed in § 3.2(c).

ty and reputation for peacefulness to be present for the hearing. If that is not possible, the attorney may make a proffer by alleging facts based upon telephone contact with such persons.

Defense counsel also should think creatively about proposing (and arranging for) conditions of release that might ease the magistrate judge's concerns about the risk posed by the defendant. For example, the defendant could be required to be placed in the custody of a third party; to undergo substance abuse testing and treatment; to submit to house arrest, electronic monitoring, or curfews; or to be supervised by the Pretrial Services Agency. In addition, restrictions can be proposed on travel and personal associations. However restrictive any of these conditions may appear, they are substantially less onerous than pretrial detention.

If it is likely that money bail will be set as a condition of pretrial release, it is critically important that the defense attorney advise the magistrate judge as to what amount of bail the defendant can post. Should the defendant be unable to post the amount requested, he or she is entitled to return to court to require either that the bail be reduced to an amount that can be posted or that the government proceed to a preventive detention hearing.

§ 5.7 Preventive Detention Proceedings—Introduction

The preventive detention provisions of the Bail Reform Act[60] should be considered in the context of its overall pretrial release scheme. That is, the court must first consider the statute's presumption of release on the least restrictive conditions consistent with the defendant's risk of flight or dangerousness. It is only when the court determines that no conditions will reasonably assure against these possibilities that it can consider pretrial detention. Even then, as we shall see, detention can be ordered only in certain cases and after following certain procedures. Still, preventive detention is a very significant part of the federal bail system as over half of all defendants are detained.[61] The data do not reveal the reasons for these detentions, but it seems likely that a substantial percentage of those defendants were charged with narcotics offenses, which make up a significant portion of the federal caseload, and in which the bail statute creates a rebuttable presumption of risk of flight and dangerousness in most cases.[62]

§ 5.7(a) Who May Be Detained

Defendants subject to detention fall into the following three categories:

60. § 3142(d)–(f).

61. Judicial Business of the United States Courts, Table H–9, *supra* note 54; *id.*, Table H–5, *available at* http://www.uscourts.gov/judbus2004/appendices/h5.pdf (Sept. 30, 2004).

62. *See infra* § 5.7(b)(1). Table H–5, *supra* note 61, indicates that 27% of the detention orders relied on presumptions.

(1) Eligibility Based Upon the Offense Charged

Defendants charged with the following crimes can be considered for preventive detention:

(a) a "crime of violence,"[63]

(b) an offense punishable by life imprisonment or death,[64]

(c) a narcotics offense under Title 21 punishable by a maximum sentence of 10 years or more,[65] or

(d) any felony, if the defendant had twice before been convicted in state or federal court of any of the types of felonies enumerated in (a)–(c), above.[66]

Detention under any of these categories can only be considered on motion of the government and not by the court *sua sponte*.[67]

(2) Eligibility Based on a Specific Danger Posed by the Defendant

Regardless of the crime with which the defendant is charged, he or she may be detained if there is either a serious risk that the defendant will flee or a serious risk that the defendant will obstruct justice or pose a threat to a prospective witness or juror.[68]

Detention hearings for defendants who fall into these categories can be ordered either on the government's motion or on the court's own motion.

(3) Detention Based on Conduct After Pretrial Release

The statute also authorizes detention in the case of a defendant who has been granted pretrial release and who violates a condition of that release.[69] Once again, the government must demonstrate either that no additional conditions on release will reasonably assure against flight or danger or that the defendant is unlikely to abide by any condition or combination of conditions of release.[70] In addition, the government must demonstrate either probable cause to believe that the defendant has committed another offense while on release or clear and convincing

---

63. § 3142(f)(1)(A). A crime of violence is defined as "a crime that involves the use, attempted use, or threatened use of physical force against another's person or property" and also includes crimes codified at 18 U.S.C. §§ 2241–2248 and 2251–2257. FED. R. CRIM. P. 32(a).

64. § 3142(f)(1)(B).

65. § 3142(f)(1)(C). These offenses are prescribed in: the Controlled Substances Act, 21 U.S.C. §§ 801–904; the Controlled Substances Import and Export Act, 21 U.S.C. §§ 951–971; and the Maritime Drug Law Enforcement Act, 46 U.S.C. app.

§§ 1901–1903. Virtually all felonies under these statutes qualify.

66. § 3142(f)(1)(D).

67. § 3142(f)(1).

68. § 3142(f)(2)(A) and (B).

69. 18 U.S.C. § 3148. Where there is probable cause to believe that the defendant committed a felony while on release, there is a rebuttable presumption that the defendant poses a danger to the community. *Id.*

70. § 3148(b)(2)(A) and (B).

evidence that the defendant has violated any other condition set forth in the release order.[71]

§ 5.7(b) Detention Proceedings

Pretrial detention cannot be ordered without providing the defendant the opportunity for a hearing.[72] The hearing must be held at the time of the defendant's initial appearance, but continuances can be granted and are regularly. Except for good cause, however, a request for continuance by the defendant cannot exceed 5 days, and a request by the government may not exceed 3 days.[73]

1. The quantitative burden of proof

Section 3142(f), which sets forth detention hearing procedures and rules designed to determine both dangerousness and risk of flight, only specifies a quantitative burden of proof with respect to dangerousness: the determination that no release conditions can be imposed to reasonably assure public safety "shall be supported by clear and convincing evidence."[74] The statute is silent as to the burden of proof when the concern is risk of flight. However, courts have uniformly held that the court can order detention on that ground by finding that a preponderance of the evidence supports it.[75] Whether the issue is flight or dangerousness, the government is aided in meeting its quantitative burden by two presumptions included within the statute:

(a) Section 3142(e) imposes a rebuttable presumption of dangerousness in cases involving defendants charged with crimes enumerated in § 3142(f)(1), namely, crimes of violence, capital crimes, or narcotics offenses, *provided* that the defendant has previously been convicted of such a crime; *and* that the offense for which the defendant had been convicted was committed while that defendant was on release pending trial for an offense; *and* that the conviction (or release from prison) for the prior offense is not more than 5 years old.

(b) Section 3142(e) also imposes a rebuttable presumption of both a risk of flight and dangerousness regardless of prior convictions where a court finds that there is probable cause to believe that the defendant has committed certain specified crimes, most importantly the following:

(1) a narcotics offense punishable by more than 10 years in prison (which includes most federal narcotics offenses), or

---

71. § 3148(b)(1)(A) and (B).

72. § 3142(e).

73. § 3142(f)(2). Failure to comply with this provision, however, will not defeat the government's detention application. *See* United States v. Montalvo–Murillo, 495 U.S. 711, 717 (1990); Moore, § 646.20.

74. § 3142(f).

75. United States v. Chimurenga, 760 F.2d 400, 405 (2d Cir. 1985); United States v. Fortna, 769 F.2d 243, 250 (5th Cir. 1985); United States v. Motamedi, 767 F.2d 1403, 1406 (9th Cir. 1985). *See* LaFave et al., § 12.3.

(2) a violation of 18 U.S.C. § 924(c), which provides for enhanced punishment for the use of a firearm during the commission of a drug offense or crimes of violence.[76]

In the case of both of these presumptions, courts have held that the statute imposes on the defendant the burden of going forward with rebuttal evidence, but that, having done so, the burden of persuasion is on the government.[77]

2. The qualitative burden of proof

The statute is silent as to the quality of the evidence that the government must present. Courts have held that the government may proceed by proffer,[78] and this has become common practice, particularly when the government can take advantage of one of the presumptions of flight or dangerousness contained in the statute.[79] Where the presumptions are not applicable, the government is somewhat more likely to elicit testimony. Since the rules of evidence do not apply to the detention hearing, however, that testimony is commonly in the form of hearsay.[80]

§ 5.7(c) Review of Detention Decisions

Federal law gives both the government and the defendant the right to seek review of release or detention decisions.[81] The review procedure provides that if the initial release or detention decision was made by a magistrate judge, the party seeking review must file a motion for revocation or amendment of the order with the district court.[82] The

---

76. The rebuttable presumption arising from a finding of probable cause is normally sustained when the government proffers either a complaint approved by a magistrate judge or an indictment returned by a grand jury. *See* United States v. Vargas, 804 F.2d 157, 163 (1st Cir. 1986); United States v. Contreras, 776 F.2d 51, 54 (2d Cir. 1985); United States v. Hazime, 762 F.2d 34, 37 (6th Cir. 1985); U.S. Attorneys' Manual § 9–6.145.

77. United States v. Martir, 782 F.2d 1141, 1144 (2d Cir. 1986). *See also* Weinstein & Berger, § 301.28.

78. *Smith*, 79 F.3d at 1210; *Martir*, 782 F.2d at 1144.

79. Where the presumption is triggered by a finding of probable cause to believe that the defendant has committed the offense, as is the case with a narcotics or firearm offense, the government can meet its qualitative burden simply by submitting the indictment. If the presumption is not rebutted, the indictment alone can satisfy the government's burden of persuasion. *See* United States v. Quartermaine, 913 F.2d

910, 916 (11th Cir. 1990); United States v. Suppa, 799 F.2d 115, 118–19 (3d Cir. 1986).

80. § 3142(f). The use of hearsay in a detention hearing was upheld in United States v. Acevedo–Ramos, 755 F.2d 203, 206–207 (1st Cir. 1985); Moore, § 646.20. However, the court did stress the discretion of the hearing court to test the reliability of the hearsay. *Acevedo–Ramos*, 755 F.2d at 207–208; *see also* LaFave et al., § 12.3. *See also* U.S. Attorneys' Manual § 9–6, 192(B) ("[T]he only government witness at the hearing should be the law enforcement officer who is to give hearsay testimony to allow the court to evaluate the weight of the evidence.").

81. 18 U.S.C. § 3145.

82. § 3145(a), (b). Grounds for revocation are enumerated in 18 U.S.C. § 3148, which also contains a rebuttable presumption that the defendant poses a danger to the community if there is probable cause to believe that he or she committed a felony in violation of federal or state law while on release. 18 U.S.C. § 3148.

statute requires that the motion be determined "promptly."[83] Review in the district court is *de novo*,[84] which means that the court must consider anew the evidence and arguments of the parties and may conduct a hearing in which testimony is taken.

Where the initial release or detention decision was made by the district court, or where a district court judge reviews a magistrate judge's determination and renders a decision, both the defendant and the government may appeal to the court of appeals.[85]

§ 5.8 Time Considerations at the Initial Appearance

Rule 5.1 provides that at the close of the initial appearance the case will be adjourned for a preliminary hearing. The rules require that the preliminary hearing be held within 10 days of the initial appearance if the defendant is detained or within 20 days if the defendant is released. As discussed in the next chapter, however, in many districts preliminary hearings are rarely held, either because an indictment or information is returned prior to the 10 or 20 day time limit or because the defense waives its right to the hearing at the initial appearance.

Time constraints related to preventive detention proceedings were noted in § 5.7(b) above.

§ 5.9 Ancillary Proceedings at the Initial Appearance

In addition to matters concerning the initial processing of defendants in cases pending in the district of arrest, the magistrate judge will frequently address issues concerning defendants who are involved in matters elsewhere. One of these situations involves defendants who have been charged in another district and who will be subject to "removal" to that district. The other involves defendants who are sought for matters other than a pending prosecution and who are subject to temporary detention pending notification of other authorities.[86]

§ 5.9(a) Removal Proceedings

It is not uncommon for a defendant who has been charged in one district to be arrested in a different one. In such situations, a proceeding must be held by the magistrate judge in the district of arrest before the

---

83. *See* LAFAVE ET AL., § 12.3. *See e.g.,* United States v. Fernandez–Alfonso, 813 F.2d 1571, 1572 (9th Cir. 1987) (delay of 30 days violated the requirement that the motion be dealt with "promptly").

84. United States v. Delker, 757 F.2d 1390, 1394 (3d Cir. 1985). *See* LAFAVE ET AL., § 12.3.

85. § 3145(c). This appeal is also to be determined "promptly."

86. A third involves circumstances in which the arrested person faces charges in the federal district of arrest and contemporaneously faces charges pending in one of the various states. For discussion of the custodial concerns and potential jurisdictional conflicts at issue in these situations, see Savvas S. Diacosavvas, Note, *Vertical Conflicts in Sentencing Practices: Custody, Credit, and Concurrency,* 57 N.Y.U. ANN. SURV. AM. L. 207 (2000).

defendant is taken to the district in which the complaint was filed.[87] The defendant is entitled to a hearing to determine that he or she is truly the same person who has been charged in the district of the offense.[88] He or she also may be entitled to a preliminary hearing in the district of arrest to determine whether the complaint establishes probable cause to believe a federal offense has been committed.[89] The defendant may waive both the identity inquiry and the preliminary hearing. In that case, or if the court finds against the defendant, the defendant will be transferred to the district in which charges are pending upon receipt of a warrant from that district.[90]

§ 5.9(b) Temporary Detention

The Bail Reform Act authorizes the court to order persons detained for up to 10 days for the purpose of notifying other federal or state officials who have an interest in obtaining jurisdiction over the person.[91] The defendants who are subject to this provision are those who were on release pending trial for a felony, sentencing or appeal; or who were on probation or parole for any offense in another jurisdiction; or who are not citizens or lawful permanent residents. In these cases, detention can be ordered if the judge finds that the person may flee or pose a danger to the community.[92] If detention is ordered, the government is required to notify the relevant agency. If the agency does not take the defendant into custody, the court will then make a pretrial release decision on the basis of the charges on which the instant complaint is based.[93]

§ 5.10 The Initial Appearances of Mario Long, Arthur Murphy and Gilbert Santiago

On January 13, 2005 Mario Long, Arthur Murphy and Gilbert Santiago were taken to the United States Courthouse in Brooklyn for their initial appearances. All were lodged in holding cells and interviewed by a representative of the Pretrial Services Agency, who obtained information relevant to the bail decision.[94] Shortly before their cases were to be called, Inga Porter, an attorney with the Federal Defender

---

87. FED. R. CRIM. P. 5(c)(2) (the initial appearance can instead be in a district adjacent to the district of arrest if it can occur more promptly there, or if the offense was allegedly committed there and the initial appearance will be on the day of the arrest). Until the rules were amended in 2002, "removal" was governed by FED. R. CRIM. P. 40. That rule is now limited to cases in which a defendant is arrested in another district for failure to appear, and Rule 5 does not contain the term "removal."

88. FED. R. CRIM. P. 5(c)(3)(D)(ii).

89. FED. R. CRIM. P. 5(c)(3)(C). As discussed in Chapter 6, if the defendant is indicted prior to the date set for the prelim-

inary hearing, the hearing will be superseded and will not be held. Assuming that there has been no indictment, the defendant may also opt for a preliminary hearing in the district of the offense. FED. R. CRIM. P. 5.1(b).

90. FED. R. CRIM. P. 5(c)(3)(D).

91. § 3142(d).

92. In determining whether there is a risk of flight or dangerousness, the standards set forth in § 3142(f)(1) and (2) apply.

93. *Id.*

94. *See supra* § 5.0.

Service, entered the detention area and was directed to Long's cell. At the same time, Stephen Colletti, an attorney in private practice who is a member of the Criminal Justice Act panel, introduced himself to Murphy.[95] Santiago was represented by Charles Berman, a private attorney who was called by Santiago's family.

The following colloquy occurred at these initial appearances.

_____

§ 5.10(a) The Initial Appearance in U.S. v. Mario Long

Clerk:	United States of America v. Mario Long
Court:	When were the defendants arrested?
Agent Martinez:	At two thirty this afternoon, Your Honor.
Court:	Are you Mario Long?
Long:	Yes.
Court:	I am a United States Magistrate Judge for the Eastern District of New York. The purpose of this proceeding is to advise you as to what you have been charged with and what your rights are. In this case the government charges you with the crime of possession with intent to distribute cocaine and conspiracy to do the same. The complaint is sworn to by Agent Ralph Martinez of the Drug Enforcement Administration. He states that an agent of the DEA delivered cocaine to you at Superior Warehouse and that you later placed the cocaine behind a locked door to be distributed to a third party. Do you understand the charges?
Long:	Yes.
Court:	I will now advise you of your rights. You have a right to remain silent. Anything that you say may be used against you in court. You have a right to an attorney. If you cannot afford an attorney one will be assigned to represent you at no cost to you. Do you understand this?
Long:	Yes.
Court:	You have indicated that you cannot afford counsel and have signed a statement indicating what your

95. As noted, the two co-defendants would, if possible, be represented at the initial appearance by different attorneys because of conflict of interest concerns. *See supra* § 5.2.

90

	financial condition is. Do you swear that this information is true?
Long:	Yes.
Court:	Very well. Ms. Porter, who is with you here, is appointed to represent you. Now you have the right to a preliminary hearing, within 10 days if you are not released and within 20 days if you are. The purpose of the hearing is to examine the evidence to determine whether there is probable cause to believe that the charges against you are true. At your next appearance on this case the preliminary hearing will be held, unless the government obtains an indictment from the grand jury. If an indictment should occur, you will be notified as to when to appear next. Do you understand?
Long:	Yes.
Court:	I find that the complaint makes out probable cause that the defendant committed the crime charged. We will next consider the question of bail. I have the report of the Pretrial Services Agency which indicates that you live at 110 East 103rd Street in Manhattan, that you were employed at Superior Warehouse, and that you have no previous criminal record.
Court:	Does the government wish to be heard?
AUSA Knapp:	Yes, Your Honor. The defendant was the foreman of the warehouse. He accepted shipment of several crates that, before the government intercepted them, contained nearly 10 kilograms of cocaine. He supervised the other defendants in the movement of the cocaine to a safe location. Prior to his arrest he consented to a search of the warehouse and later consented to a recording of a conversation with the co-defendant, Gilbert Santiago. Accordingly, we have no objection to the defendant being released on condition that he execute a bond in the amount of $100,000, secured by two responsible sureties.
Porter:	Your Honor, we have no objection to the government's request for a surety bond, but we submit that there is no need for sureties to secure the bond in light of Mr. Long's substantial ties to the community and the fact that he has no criminal record.

Court: I will set a surety bond in the amount of $100,000. Mr. Long, that means that you will have to sign a note in the amount of $100,000, and produce two people who will guarantee that note.[96] If you sign the note and do not return to court as required, you and your sureties will forfeit that amount of money. In addition, you may be prosecuted for bail jumping and subjected to a penalty of up to five years in prison or to a $5,000 fine or both. Do you understand?

Long: Yes.

Court: All right, anything else, counsel?

Porter: Judge, I've discussed the issue of a preliminary hearing with Mr. Long, and in light of his post-arrest activities, Mr. Long is going to waive his right to such hearing.

Court: Mr. Long, is that correct?

Long: Yes.

Court: All right, the record will reflect that the defendant has waived his right to a preliminary hearing. Call the next matter.

———————

Note that the magistrate judge's probable cause decision and the government's bail recommendation were not vigorously contested by defense counsel. The magistrate judge, as the rules permit, decided the issue of probable cause without input from either party. As to bail, defense counsel was satisfied with the government's recommendation for a bond, and therefore limited her response to challenging whether sureties were also required. Finally, no later court appearance is set—if the defendant is not indicted within 30 days, the complaint must be dismissed or dropped.[97]

96. It may not be necessary for the sureties to have assets sufficient to cover the face amount of the bond. See *supra* note 49. The court may be satisfied if the sureties are employed and financially responsible or are close to the defendant personally. In a situation like the one in our model case, moreover, if the defendant could not find solvent sureties, the court, with the prosecution's consent, might well impose a personal recognizance bond cosigned by persons with close relations to the defendant.

97. § 3162(a)(1). Dismissal of the complaint in these circumstances can be with or without prejudice to bringing a new complaint, in the court's discretion. *Id.*

§ 5.10(b) The Initial Appearance in U.S. v. Arthur Murphy

With the completion of Long's initial appearance, the magistrate judge turned to Arthur Murphy's case. Stephen Colletti was assigned pursuant to the Criminal Justice Act to represent Murphy.[98] Because on its face the complaint contained little evidence against Murphy, Colletti first addressed its sufficiency. If he could obtain a dismissal, Murphy would be released outright, and it would not be necessary to reach the question of bail:[99]

Colletti: Your Honor, the complaint is legally insufficient as to the defendant, Arthur Murphy. All that is alleged is that the defendant removed the crates from the delivery truck and placed them inside the warehouse, he looked around "suspiciously," whatever that means, and that he is alleged to have lied as to when he arrived at the warehouse on the day of the arrest. Later, the crate containing cocaine was discovered behind the locked door. No other evidence exists to suggest that the defendant knew of the contents of the container or that he intended to participate in the distribution of any controlled substances. Your Honor will note that Arthur Murphy had been employed at Superior Warehouse for a short time prior to the arrest, and that his actions on the day in question were totally consistent with the terms of his employment. The culpable parties are the people who set up the delivery, not the working man who was simply asked to remove the crates from the truck, if indeed Murphy was that person. As the government concedes, eleven of the twelve crates found in the warehouse contained coffee and it is this commodity that Superior Warehouse represented to the public and to its employees as the product it imported.

AUSA Knapp: As Your Honor will note from reading the facts in the complaint, the arrest occurred after a controlled delivery was made by the DEA to Superior Warehouse. The earlier inspection of the crate revealed that it was consigned to International Food Distributors, Inc. to be held for distribution at Superior Warehouse. Once the cocaine was discovered, a homing device was placed within the crate so that the DEA agents could later identify and locate it.

98. § 3006A(b).

99. Where a question exists as to the sufficiency of facts alleged on the face of the complaint, magistrate judges may invite argument on the issue. A legally insufficient complaint will be dismissed, and the defendant will be released. However, the government is free to file a new complaint or to present the case to the grand jury and obtain an indictment. Either action will renew jurisdiction over the defendant. *See supra* § 5.4.

When the agents arrived at the warehouse, the crate had already been segregated from the other crates containing coffee and placed in a safe location. Before that, as he was unloading the crates, Murphy was observed looking around nervously and suspiciously. The segregating of the crates evidenced knowledge on the part of Arthur Murphy that the contents contained contraband. The amount of the cocaine evidences their intent to distribute. Furthermore, Murphy lied about his role in unloading the crate when he told Agent Martinez that he wasn't present at the time the crates were delivered. This statement dovetails with the statement made by Gilbert Santiago during the subsequent conversation with Mario Long, in which Santiago told Long to tell Murphy to remember what he was supposed to say, obviously referring to what Murphy should do if he were questioned. Under the circumstances, Your Honor, Murphy's lie indicates a clear consciousness of guilt and Santiago's conversation with Long indicates Murphy's knowledge of the contents of the container.

Magistrate Judge: I agree with defense counsel that at best the government can show that Mr. Murphy played a minimal role in the transaction, but I think that the complaint makes out probable cause. The court accepts the fact that Arthur Murphy moved the crates into the warehouse and acted suspiciously when doing so. While he may have done so under the direction of Mario Long, when he was later questioned about his actions he denied being present. His denial mirrored the instruction given by Gilbert Santiago that Murphy was to keep quiet. I can draw a clear inference of knowledge from these facts, despite the fact that the crate was unopened at the time it was discovered.

Accordingly, I deny the defense motion to dismiss the complaint, but I will hear defense counsel on the question of bail.

Colletti: Arthur Murphy is 42 years old, and has lived in New York his whole life. He graduated from DeWitt Clinton High School. He has lived with his wife and their two children at 216 88th Street in Bay Ridge, Brooklyn, for the last eight years. Mr. Murphy has a steady work history. After high school he enlisted in the United States Navy and served three years. He received an emergency honorable discharge on the grounds of illness. He then worked for a cousin at a candy store in Flatbush. After working there for 11 years, his cousin sold the store and Mr. Long became a salesman for Simon's Furniture Company. He worked for Simon's for two years and left for a higher paying job with Brown Trucking Company in Brooklyn. He worked at Brown for eight years and went to Superior Warehouse in December of 2004. This incident occurred in the course of his current employment. Your Honor, Mr. Murphy has no prior criminal record. He has strong roots in the community. As you have stated, his role in this case, if any, was minimal. I ask that he be released on his own recognizance.

Knapp: Your Honor, in view of the fact that the government consented to a $100,000 unsecured personal recognizance bond for Long, we would make the same request here. In addition, we ask that Pretrial Services supervise Mr. Murphy's release status.

Magistrate Judge: I will set an unsecured personal recognizance bond in the amount of $100,000 on condition that the defendant's release status be supervised by the Pretrial Services Agency, and that he report to them on at least a once weekly basis and comply with any other conditions which the agency deems necessary.[100]

All right, this case is also adjourned until January 23, unless counsel have anything further.

---

100. While the Bail Reform Act authorizes the detention of any individual charged with a narcotics offense under Title 21 punishable by a sentence of 10 years or more, *see* § 3142(e) and (f), under the circumstances here it is unlikely that the government would invoke these provisions because of Murphy's minimal role in the criminal activity, his strong roots in the community, and the inequity which would follow if he were detained while Long were released.

The reader should note that the principal focus of the defense attorney's remarks was on Arthur Murphy's roots in the community, the traditional criterion for determining pretrial release status. The conditions the judge imposed are specifically authorized under the Bail Reform Act[101] and serve to ensure that the defendant's whereabouts will be monitored and that the court will be alerted should the defendant fail to cooperate and appear as required. In the event that the defendant fails to cooperate, the statute provides for revocation of the conditions of release and a reconsideration of the decision whether to release or detain.[102] A sample conditional release order and bond reflecting the terms of Murphy's release follows:

101.　§ 3142(c)(1)(B)(vi).
102.　§ 3148(b).

United States District Court
EASTERN DISTRICT OF NEW YORK

UNITED STATES OF AMERICA   **ORDER SETTING CONDITIONS**
                           OF RELEASE AND BOND

          V.   Case No: 05 M 0063

      ARTHUR MURPHY
           Defendant

RELEASE ORDER

It is hereby ORDERED that the above-named defendant be released as follows, subject to the Standard Conditions of Bond on the reverse and:

[ ] Upon **Personal Recognizance Bond** on his/her promise to appear at all scheduled proceedings as required, or

[X] Upon **Unsecured Bond** executed by defendant in the amount of $ 100,000 or

[ ] Upon **Secured Appearance Bond** as provided herein.

Additional Conditions of Release

Upon finding that release under the standard conditions detailed on the reverse will not by themselves reasonably assure the appearance of the defendant and the safety of other persons and the community, IT IS FURTHER ORDERED that the defendant is subject to the following additional conditions of release:

[ ] 1.   The defendant must remain in and may not leave the following areas without Court permission:_____

[ ] 2.   The defendant shall avoid all contact and not associate with any of the following persons or entities:_____

[ ] 3.   The defendant shall avoid and not go to any of the following locations:_____

[ ] 4.   The defendant shall surrender any and all passports to the U.S. Pretrial Services Agency by _____ and shall not apply for any other passport.

[X] 5.   Defendant is placed under the express supervision of the Pretrial Services Agency, subject to the Special Conditions on the reverse, if applicable, and

      [ ] is subject to random visits by a Pretrial Services officer at defendant's home and/or place of work;

      [X] must report to that agency (X) in person 1 times per week and/or ( ) by telephone_____ times per _____;

      [ ] is subject to home detention with electronic monitoring with the following conditions:_____

      [ ] must undergo [ ] random drug testing [ ] evaluation and/or [ ] treatment for: [ ] substance abuse [ ] alcoholism [ ] mental health problems. [ ] must pay the cost of treatment and/or electronic monitoring by/with personal funds and/or insurance.

[ ] 6.   Other Conditions:_____

APPEARANCE BOND

The undersigned defendant and sureties jointly and severally acknowledge that I/we and my/our personal representatives, jointly and severally, are bound to pay to the United States of America the sum of $ 100,000.   The undersigned agree(s) that this obligation is secured with his/her/their interest in the following property ("Collateral") which he/she/they represent is/are free and clear of liens except as otherwise indicated:

   [ ]   cash deposited in the Registry of the Court the sum of $ _____

   [ ]   premises located at: _____ owned by _____

   [ ]   I/We also agree to execute a confession of judgment in forth approved by the U.S. Attorney _____ which shall be duly filed with the proper local and state authorities on or before _____

   [ ]   Other Conditions _____

_____   Address   _____
    Surety

_____   Address   _____
    Surety

_____   Address   _____
    Surety

The Court has advised the defendant of the conditions of release-per 18:3142(h)(l) and (h)(2). This bond is conditioned, upon the appearance of the defendant and is subject to the Standard Conditions of Bond set forth on the reverse. If the defendant fails to appear as ordered or notified, or any other condition of this bond is not met, this bond shall be due forthwith.

I acknowledge that I am the defendant in this case and that I am aware of the conditions of release. I promise to obey all conditions of release, to appear as directed, and to surrender for service of any sentence imposed. I am aware of the penalties and sanctions set forth on the reverse of this form.

_____
               Signature of Defendant

Release of the Defendant is hereby ordered on January 13 2005

_____ , USMJ

KL3:2415917.9

Standard Conditions of Release

In all cases, IT IS ORDERED that the release of the defendant is subject to the following conditions:

1.   Defendant shall immediately advise the court, defense counsel, and the U.S. Attorney in writing of any change in address and/or telephone number.

2.   Defendant shall appear at all proceedings as required and shall surrender for service of any sentence imposed as directed.

3.   Defendant shall not commit any federal, state, or local crime.

The conditions of this bond are that the defendant named on the obverse is to appear before the Court and at such other places as the defendant may be required to appear, in accordance with any and all orders and directions relating to the defendant's appearance in this case, including appearance for violation of a condition of defendant's release as may be ordered or notified by this court or any other United States District Court to which the defendant may be held to answer or the cause transferred. The defendant is to abide by any judgment entered in such matter by surrendering to serve any sentence imposed and obeying any order or direction in connection with such judgment.

It is agreed and understood that this is a continuing bond (including any proceeding on appeal or review) which shall continue until such time as the undersigned are exonerated.

If the defendant appears as ordered or notified and otherwise obeys and performs the preceding conditions of this bond, then this bond is to be void, but if the defendant fails to obey or perform any of these conditions, payment of the amount of this bond shall be due forthwith. Forfeiture of this bond for any breach of its conditions may be declared by any United States District Court having cognizance of the entitled matter on the obverse at the time of such breach and if the bond is forfeited and if the forfeiture is not set aside or remitted, judgment may be entered upon motion in such United States District Court against each debtor jointly and severally or the amount above stated, together with interest and costs, and execution may be issued and payment secured as provided by the Federal Rules of Criminal Procedure and any other laws of the United States.

Special Conditions of Release

1.   If defendant is subject to home detention, defendant may not leave his/her residence without the approval of the Pretrial Services Agency, except for court appearances and visits with defense counsel in this pending criminal case and for medical emergencies. In all instances, however, the defendant must notify the Pretrial Services Agency of his or her departure from the residence.

2.   If the defendant fails to report as required to the Pretrial Services Agency or to appear for any specified treatment or evaluation, defendant may be subject to such random visits at his/her residence or work by a Pretrial Services Officer as may be necessary to verify his/her residence or place of employment in order to secure compliance with the order of release.

Advice of Penalties and Sanctions

TO THE DEFENDANT: _____Arthur Murphy_____

YOU ARE ADVISED OF THE FOLLOWING PENALTIES AND SANCTIONS:

A violation of any of the foregoing conditions of release may result in the immediate issuance of a warrant for your arrest, a revocation of release, an order of detention, and a prosecution for contempt of court and could result in a term of imprisonment, a fine, or both.

The commission of a Federal offense while on pretrial release will result in an additional sentence of a term of imprisonment of not more than ten years, if the offense is a felony; or a term of imprisonment of not more than one year, if the offense is a misdemeanor. This sentence shall be in addition to any other sentence.

Federal law makes it a crime punishable by up to 10 years of imprisonment, and a $250,000 fine or both to obstruct a criminal investigation. It is a crime punishable by up to ten years of imprisonment, and a $250,000 fine or both to tamper with a witness, victim or informant; to retaliate or attempt to retaliate against a witness, victim or informant; or to intimidate or attempt to intimidate a witness, victim, juror, informant, or officer of the court. The penalties for tampering, retaliation, or intimidation are significantly more serious if they involve a killing or attempted killing.

If after release, you knowingly fail to appear as required by the conditions of release, or to surrender for the service of sentence,

you may be prosecuted for failing to appear or surrender and additional punishment may be imposed. If you are convicted of:

(1) an offense punishable by death, life imprisonment, or imprisonment for a term of fifteen years or more, you shall be fined not more than $250,000 or imprisoned for not more than 10 years, or both;

(2) an offense punishable by imprisonment for a term of five years or more, but less than fifteen years, you shall be fined not more than $250,000 or imprisoned for not more than five years, or both;

(3) any other felony, you shall be fined not more than $250,000 or imprisoned not more than two years, or both;

(4) a misdemeanor, you shall be fined not more than $100,000 or imprisoned not more than one year, or both.

A term of imprisonment imposed for failure to appear or surrender shall be in addition to the sentence for any other offense.

In addition, a failure to appear or surrender may result in the forfeiture of any bond posted.

Acknowledgment of Defendant

I acknowledge that I am the defendant in this case and that I am aware of the conditions of release. I promise to obey all conditions of release, to appear as directed, and to surrender for service of any sentence imposed. I am aware of the penalties and sanctions set forth above.

_____
Signature of Defendant

216 88th St.
_____
Address

Bay Ridge, NY   (718) 123-4567
_____   _____
City and State   Telephone

---

§ 5.10(c) The Initial Appearance in U.S. v. Santiago

We noted in Chapter 4 that Gilbert Santiago had been arrested at the time the agents went to Superior Warehouse on January 13, 2005 to conduct the search.[103] He was subsequently processed and taken to the magistrate judge's court for his initial appearance.

Charles Berman, Santiago's lawyer, was aware of the fact that the magistrate judge had already ruled on the adequacy of the complaint that charged Santiago along with Long and Murphy and decided not to argue that there was no probable cause in Santiago's case. When the magistrate judge asked the government's position on bail, AUSA Knapp moved, pursuant to 18 U.S.C. § 3142(f), for a hearing to determine whether the defendant should be preventively detained. She stated that since the offense with which Santiago was charged was a narcotics offense punishable by 10 years or more in prison, there was a presumption in favor of detention.[104] Defense counsel then asked for an adjournment of two days in order to prepare and, again pursuant to this section, the continuance was granted and Santiago was ordered temporarily detained.

§ 5.11 Litigating the Preventive Detention Issue—U.S. v. Gilbert Santiago

§ 5.11(a) The Hearing

On January 15, 2005, the following occurred before Magistrate Judge Roger Brown in the case of Gilbert Santiago:

AUSA Knapp: The government is requesting the detention of this defendant and is prepared to proceed if information can be presented by a proffer.

The Court: Let me ask defense counsel whether he has any objection to the government's proceeding by way of proffer.

Berman: Your Honor, I would ask the government if it would first state what the nature of the proffer is in order for me to determine whether I would consent to this method of proceeding.

The Court: Ms. Knapp, what is the nature of the proffer?

---

103. *See supra* § 4.11.   **104.** § 3142(e); *see supra* § 5.7(a).

Knapp:	The government will rely on this court's finding of probable cause in the complaint dated January 12, 2005 and filed with the court on that date, and which served as the basis for the arrest warrant that Your Honor issued on that day. Second, the government would rely on the fact that at the time of the commission of the instant offense, the defendant was on supervised release arising out of a previous conviction in the Eastern District for possession with intent to distribute cocaine in violation of 21 U.S.C. section 841.
Berman:	Since the government is willing to restrict itself to the complaint and the defendant's prior conviction and supervised release status, the defendant has no objection to proceeding in this fashion.
The Court:	I will hear the government.
Knapp:	Your Honor, under section 3142(e) there is a presumption that no conditions of release will reasonably assure the defendant's appearance when there is probable cause to believe that the defendant committed a narcotics offense for which a maximum term of imprisonment of 10 years or more is prescribed, as is the case with 21 U.S.C. 841. As Your Honor can see from the complaint, the defendant was the manager of Superior Warehouse, a location at which a controlled delivery of what would have been nearly 10 kilograms of cocaine was made on January 12, 2005. Subsequent to the delivery, the crate containing cocaine was recovered behind a locked door in the warehouse. Thereafter, the foreman of the warehouse had a conversation with the defendant, a conversation that the government taped, in which the defendant indicated knowledge of the cocaine and his intent to conceal the true nature of the operation from the government. Given that the amount of cocaine is nearly 10 kilograms, and that the defendant had been previously convicted in the Eastern District for possession with intent to distribute cocaine in 1998, the defendant is facing a mandatory minimum of 20 years. The government believes that the defendant presents both a risk of flight and a danger to the community.

Berman: This is a case that involves, as has been confirmed by the Pretrial Services Agency, a person who has been married for about seven years, has two children, a stable resident history in Queens for over six years, regular employment since his release from federal custody to supervised release, and a perfect record since that time with the exception of this arrest. Mr. Santiago was raised in Philadelphia and has resided in New York City for approximately 10 years. Mr. Santiago's probation officer, Mr. Rogers, has submitted a letter to this court, a copy of which has been forwarded by me to Ms. Knapp. Mr. Rogers' letter indicates that the defendant has made every one of his scheduled appointments since he was released from federal custody in 2003, after having served a five year federal sentence. Mr. Santiago was first required to report on a weekly basis, and thereafter on a bi-weekly basis; he is currently reporting on a monthly basis. Throughout this period he has been tested for drug use and found not to have used any controlled substances. In addition, Mr. Rogers investigated the defendant's employment at Superior Warehouse and found that it was bona fide, and that as of Mr. Rogers' visit earlier this month, Mr. Santiago was not observed engaging in any illegal activities when acting as the manager of the warehouse. Mr. Rogers verified that Superior Warehouse imports coffee and other food products from Colombia and acts as a distributor for these products in the metropolitan area. His report indicates that Mr. Santiago has performed well in his job. But for the seizure of cocaine, I think that Mr. Santiago's release on either recognizance or a minimum personal recognizance bond would be entirely appropriate. Under the circumstances, the defendant asks the court to allow him to post a personal recognizance bond and the deed to his house. The defendant has no objection to Pretrial Services Agency monitoring his whereabouts during the period of pretrial release and is willing to comply with any other condition of release that this court might reasonably impose upon him to secure his continued presence in court and the safety of the community.

I should point out to the court that the proffer that I have made regarding the defendant's background and circumstances, his residence, marital status and supervised release record, has been independently verified by the Pretrial Services Agency, and they believe that the defendant does not pose a risk of flight. The deed to the defendant's house is here in court in possession of his wife, and a check by Kings County Title Insurance Co. reveals that there are no outstanding liens or mortgages on the house and that the property is valued in excess of $250,000. In addition, Mr. Santiago's wife is willing to co-sign the personal recognizance bond, post $5,000 in cash as additional security and, as the co-owner of the home, execute any documents necessary for the government to perfect its lien against the property.

The Court: Having reviewed the Pretrial Services report, and after having considered the arguments of counsel for the government and the defense, this court finds that the defendant has rebutted the presumption of flight or dangerousness and that the defendant has provided reasonable assurance that he is not a risk of flight and not a danger to the community. Accordingly, this court orders that the defendant be released upon execution of a $100,000 personal recognizance bond co-signed by his wife and secured by the posting of $5,000 cash and the deed to his house. The defendant and his wife are directed to sign all documents necessary to effect a lien against the property, in the event that the defendant should either flee or violate the conditions of this court's release order. It is further part of this order that defendant be supervised during the period of pretrial release by the Pretrial Services Agency and that he be in daily contact with the Agency that will take whatever steps necessary to monitor his activities. The defendant is directed to comply with any conditions set forth by that agency.

Knapp: The government requests that the court stay its release order to permit the government to seek review in district court. The government is prepared to proceed immediately to the district court.

The Court: Very well, the stay is granted. The case is adjourned to January 23.

Note that in the hearing just presented the defense attorney consented to the government's proceeding by proffer, instead of attempting to convince the magistrate judge to require testimony. Often, that approach might be tactically unwise given the possibilities for discovery and impeachment that would be present if the defense could cross-examine the government's witnesses. However, the decision by the defense counsel here is also a reasonable one. By agreeing to restrict the government's presentation to a proffer limited to the facts alleged in the complaint and the defendant's prior criminal record, the prosecutor is precluded from discussing facts which are not in the complaint and that may tend to augment the proof of the defendant's risk of flight or dangerousness. Moreover, the use of the proffer by the government permits a similar use by the defense attorney, who is able to respond by presenting facts learned through the Pretrial Services Agency report and conversations with the probation officer and others, without having to expose such testimony to adversarial testing.

§ 5.11(b) Motion to Review the Detention Decision[105]

Following Magistrate Judge Brown's decision to release Gilbert Santiago, AUSA Knapp and Charles Berman, Santiago's attorney, proceeded directly to district court for *de novo* review of the magistrate judge's decision. Upon hearing a proffer similar to that which occurred before Magistrate Judge Brown, the district court judge reached a contrary conclusion, and entered the following order:

---

105. We describe here how a *de novo* review by the district court would take place. It should be noted, however, that such review is not routinely sought by ei- ther side. It is also rare in practice for either side to appeal a district court's detention decision to the court of appeals.

UNITED STATES DISTRICT COURT
EASTERN DISTRICT OF NEW YORK

UNITED STATES OF AMERICA

      --against--

GILBERT SANTIAGO,

            Defendant.

**ORDER OF DETENTION
PENDING TRIAL**

Case No. 05 M 0063

In accordance with the Bail Reform Act, 18 U.S.C. § 3142(f), a detention hearing has been held. I conclude that the following facts are established by clear and convincing evidence and require the detention of the above-named defendant pending trial in this case.

Factual Findings

(1) There is probable cause to believe that the defendant has committed an offense for which a maximum term of imprisonment of 10 years or more is prescribed in the Controlled Substances Act (21 U.S.C. § 401 *et seq.*).

(2) The defendant has not rebutted the presumption that no condition or combination of conditions will reasonably assure the appearance of the defendant as required and the safety of the community.

(3) The following factors specified in 18 U.S.C. § 3142(g) are present and taken into account by this court:

The defendant was charged with possessing nearly 10 kilograms of cocaine which, if he is convicted, involves extremely harsh penalties with a mandatory minimum of at least 10 and possibly 20 years. Further, at the time it is alleged the defendant committed the instant offense, he was on supervised release in this District for a previous conviction arising out of a violation of 21 U.S.C. § 841. As a result, should the defendant be convicted of the charges, he would have violated the conditions of his release and demonstrated a disregard for the interests of society thereby exemplifying his potential danger to the community.

Conclusions of Law

(1) I find that the credible information submitted at the hearing establishes by a preponderance of the evidence that no condition or combination of conditions will reasonably assure the appearance of the defendant as required, 18 U.S.C. § 3142(e).

(2) The defendant is committed to the custody of the Attorney General or his designated representative for confinement in a corrections facility separate, to the extent practicable, from persons awaiting or serving sentences or being held in custody pending appeal. The defendant shall be afforded a reasonable opportunity for private consultation with defense counsel. On order of a court of the United States or on request of an attorney for the Government, the person in charge of the corrections facility shall deliver the defendant to the United States marshal for the purpose of an appearance in connection with a court proceeding.

Dated: January 17, 2005
       Brooklyn, New York

                                      Walter Sheridan
                                     Walter Sheridan
                                     United States District Judge

Chapter 6

THE PRELIMINARY HEARING

Table of Sections

Sec.
6.0 Introduction.
6.1 Burden of Proof.
6.2 Strategic Considerations.
    6.2(a) The Prosecutor.
    6.2(b) Defense Counsel.
6.3 United States v. Santiago.
    6.3(a) The Government's Case.
    6.3(b) Cross–Examination of the Government's Witness.

§ 6.0 Introduction

In theory, the preliminary hearing is designed to provide a review of the magistrate judge's decision to hold the defendant on the strength of the allegations made in the complaint. While the quantitative burden of proof at the preliminary hearing is the same as that at the complaint stage—probable cause—the qualitative burden is considerably higher. Here, the government must put on testimony rather than rely on a written complaint, and here the proceeding will be adversarial, not *ex parte*, with defense counsel permitted to cross-examine government witnesses and put on defense witnesses as well.[1]

Whatever additional protection the preliminary hearing theoretically may give to the defendant, however, has largely been eliminated by a provision of Rule 5.1 stating that the hearing will not be held if the government obtains an indictment prior to the date on which the hearing is scheduled.[2] As we shall see, the function of the grand jury is the same as that of the court at a preliminary hearing, namely, to determine probable cause. And while the government must adduce

---

1. Fed. R. Crim. P. 5.1(e).

2. Fed. R. Crim. P. 5.1(a).

testimony before the grand jury just as it must at a preliminary hearing, the grand jury proceeding is both secret and *ex parte* and hence both less time-consuming and more protective of the government's evidence from early disclosure to the defense. As a result, if a grand jury is available in the district (as is always the case in major urban areas), prosecutors will invariably procure an indictment prior to the date set for the preliminary hearing.[3]

In districts where a grand jury is not regularly in session, the preliminary hearing will be required unless the defendant waives the right.[4] Even then, however, the determination made at the hearing is of little ultimate consequence to the government. If probable cause is found, the matter will still have to be presented to the grand jury to obtain an indictment. If probable cause is not found, while the defendant must be released, the case can still be presented to the grand jury, which as an arm of the district court has the power in effect to overrule the decision of the magistrate judge and indict the defendant on precisely the same evidence.[5] The defendant would then be rearrested. For these reasons, and because the government rarely will be forced to reveal much about its case beyond what is in the complaint, defense counsel will at times waive the hearing.[6]

Nevertheless, preliminary hearings do sometimes occur in the federal system, even in places where the grand jury is readily available. It is at least arguable that defense counsel should not waive the opportunity in most cases because, given the restrictive criminal discovery rules under federal law,[7] any discovery opportunity may be enough reason to pursue the hearing. While it is likely if such a hearing is held that the prosecution will offer only the testimony of the case agent, the rules require that prior written statements of witnesses be provided to the defense for use in cross-examination.[8] In this way, the agent's written report, otherwise unavailable at this point in the process, may be obtained.

There may be additional advantages to defense counsel in demanding a preliminary hearing in so-called "removal" proceedings,[9] i.e., those that occur in a district other than that in which charges are pending. It may be difficult for the prosecution in that district to obtain an indictment before the hearing date. In that case, either the hearing would have to be held, thereby providing an opportunity for the defense to obtain discovery through the examination of the case agent, or the

---

3. It is common practice for prosecutors to request the last possible adjourned date for the preliminary hearing to give them the most time to present the case to the grand jury.

4. *See* LaFave et al., § 14.2(b).

5. Fed. R. Crim. P. 5.1. *See* Wright § 86.

6. They may also do so in cases likely to be resolved by plea bargaining as a way of carrying favor with the prosecutor.

7. *See infra* Chapter 13.

8. Fed. R. Crim. P. 26.2.

9. *See supra* § 5.9(a).

complaint would have to be dismissed, possibly even on motion by the government.

The prosecution itself may seek a preliminary hearing in certain situations. As an alternative to the limited right to depose witnesses, the hearing can serve to preserve the witness' testimony for use at trial.[10] This opportunity may arise in cases in which the witness is very old, or in poor health, or may leave the country or otherwise not be available at trial. A full presentation of the testimony at a preliminary hearing, with a concomitant right to cross-examine, would assure compliance with the defendant's right to confrontation at trial should the witness become unavailable.[11]

§ 6.1 Burden of Proof

While the probable cause finding must be based upon testimony adduced by the government in an adversary proceeding, the applicable evidentiary standards are clearly intended to provide less than full adversarial testing of the government's case.[12] The rules of evidence applicable at trial are not applicable at a preliminary hearing, and hearsay testimony is specifically authorized.[13] While defense objections based upon competence and relevance may be sustained, the defense is not permitted to object to the government's evidence on the grounds that it was illegally obtained.[14] Most questions concerning the credibility of witnesses are not entertained by the magistrate judge either. For example, while the track record and basis of knowledge of an informant upon whom probable cause is based may be relevant,[15] questioning about the witnesses' prior bad acts or inconsistent statements typically will not be permitted.

§ 6.2 Strategic Considerations

§ 6.2(a) The Prosecutor

In presenting witnesses at the preliminary hearing, the government's chief concern, other than satisfying the probable cause standard, is to limit cross-examination that would lead to discovery of the government's evidence and, in turn, to the possibility that that information may be used to impeach government witnesses at trial.[16] To avoid these

---

10. Depositions in criminal cases are rare. Rule 15 provides that a court can order a deposition under "exceptional circumstances and in the interest of justice." FED. R. CRIM. P. 15(a)(1).

11. *See* Crawford v. Washington, 541 U.S. 36, 61–62 (2004). *See also* LAFAVE ET AL., § 14.1(c)–(d). Rule 804(b)(1) of the Federal Rules of Evidence excepts from exclusion by the hearsay rule former testimony given at a preliminary hearing at which there was opportunity to develop the testi-

mony by direct, cross, or redirect examination.

12. *See* MOORE § 605.1.11. *See also* LA-FAVE ET AL., § 14.4(a).

13. FED. R. CRIM. P. 5.1(a).

14. FED. R. CRIM. P. 5.1(e).

15. *See* Illinois v. Gates, 462 U.S. 213 (1983). *See also* MOORE, § 604.02.

16. Of course the strategy will be different if the government is using the hearing to preserve testimony.

pitfalls, the government will normally only call the case agent, since he or she will be able to provide an overview of the events leading to the arrest of the defendant. The agent may have personal knowledge of only some of the events, but since hearsay is admissible at this hearing, the agent may also testify to statements made by others. To limit the scope of the direct examination, and thereby limit the scope of the cross-examination, the prosecution will direct the witness' attention at the outset to the specific acts from which the magistrate judge may find probable cause. Questions about the witness' background and credibility-enhancing testimony (such as the witness' opportunity to observe) will be limited in order to avoid defense discovery. The prosecutor should properly prepare the agent by explaining this approach in advance of the hearing.

The form of questions used by the prosecutor also will be somewhat different from that used at trial.[17] Here, leading questions will be tolerated because they save time and a judge will not be improperly influenced by them as might a jury. Open questions will be limited to those instances in which the prosecutor is certain that the agent understands the need to limit his or her response to the issues relevant to probable cause and to avoid raising other matters that can be useful to the defendant for discovery purposes—e.g., statements about how the search of Superior Warehouse in our model case was conducted, as opposed to what was found. Defense attorneys, of course, would not object to open questions in this context because the responses likely would broaden the scope of direct examination and, in turn, cross-examination.

§ 6.2(b) Defense Counsel

(1) Monitoring the direct case

We have noted that to the extent defense counsel is primarily interested in the discovery potential of the preliminary hearing, he or she should not object to questions that might in fact be objectionable,[18] e.g., those that call for a narrative or that might be irrelevant to the probable cause issue. On the other hand, the defense attorney should object to leading questions on all important matters because suggestive questions limit discovery of the witness' testimony. Similarly, the defense attorney should object to questions that are confusing, e.g., compound questions, so that the recorded responses are clear and unequivocal.

(2) Conducting the cross-examination

The same considerations that dictate strategy in monitoring the direct case should govern cross-examination. Where defense counsel's

---

17. See § 3.3(d) for an overview of questioning techniques.

18. For discussion of objections, see Chapter 16.

purpose is to obtain a dismissal of the charges for legal insufficiency, the cross-examination would be of the kind conducted at trial, that is, with the use of leading questions to have the witness verify the facts the attorney is positing. Where, however, the government has made out a legally sufficient case and the purpose of cross-examination is to obtain detailed information and to make a record that could serve as a basis for impeachment of government witnesses at trial, the defense attorney should conduct a discovery cross-examination,[19] using a mixture of open and closed questions similar to the kind of detailed questioning of one's own witness that the attorney would use on *direct* examination at trial.

One of the purposes of discovery cross-examination is to elicit damaging information at a stage at which the impact of the information is relatively contained yet where the information itself informs the defendant's future options, particularly whether to pursue the matter to trial or to negotiate a guilty plea or other non-trial disposition. Thus, while cross-examination at trial never attempts to elicit damaging testimony,[20] the same concerns do not govern testimony at a preliminary hearing, which is a safe occasion to obtain any and all information whether favorable or damaging.

As for the kind of information that the cross-examiner seeks, it includes not only the details about the facts adduced on direct examination, but whatever other information the agent might have about the police investigation. The defense attorney should press the inquiry as far as the court will permit, recognizing that the government may object and argue that questions relating to issues other than probable cause are beyond the scope of the proceedings. The response the defense would make is that while probable cause may be found from listening to the government's direct examination, the rules give the defendant the right to cross-examine and, *a fortiori,* the right to explore in detail anything raised by the prosecutor.

One final consideration regarding cross-examinations during preliminary hearings is in order. We noted above that there may be occasions where the government's purpose at the preliminary hearing is to perpetuate a witness's testimony for use at trial. In such situations, the defense attorney should treat the examination as if it were taking place at trial. Moreover, if the testimony of the witness is important to the government, and there is sufficient doubt that he or she will be available at trial, it might be prudent for the defendant to waive the preliminary hearing altogether. The government would then have to move under Rule 15 to depose the witness and to demonstrate to the court that the deposition is required by "exceptional circumstances and in the interest of justice."

19. *See supra* § 3.3(f).   **20.** *See infra* § 16.5.

(3) Presenting defense witnesses

As to the right of the defense to call witnesses, in practice it is of little consequence. In view of the fact that it is highly likely that probable cause will be found (and that in any case the magistrate judge's decision can, in effect, be overruled by the grand jury), calling exculpatory witnesses makes little strategic sense, since it will probably accomplish no more than previewing the defense case for the government and subjecting potential defense witnesses to unwanted cross-examination by the government. Moreover, there is no discovery-related benefit to the defense calling its own witnesses to testify.[21]

§ 6.3 United States v. Santiago

On January 23, 2005, the date set for preliminary hearings in the cases against Arthur Murphy and Gilbert Santiago,[22] Stephen Colletti, representing Murphy, concluded that Murphy would best be served by keeping a low profile, thereby increasing the likelihood that charges against him would eventually be dismissed. Colletti therefore waived the hearing.

As for Santiago, were it a real case in the Eastern District of New York, an Assistant United States Attorney would unquestionably have presented the matter to a grand jury prior to the date set for the hearing. However, we set forth the hearing here, both to demonstrate how one is conducted and to illustrate techniques of eliciting testimony that are relevant to subsequent evidentiary hearings, e.g., the grand jury presentation (particularly, direct examinations at that stage), hearings on pretrial motions and trial.

§ 6.3(a) The Government's Case

As with all formal stages of the process, the first step is the calling of the case and the identification of the parties. Unlike the trial, however, there would be no opening statements. The judge would have the complaint, which will explain what the hearing is about.

Here, in its entirety, is the testimony that the government would elicit.

The Court: The next case is *United States v. Gilbert Santiago*, No. 05M0063, on for a preliminary hearing. Counsel, will you note your appearances?

Laura Knapp, Assistant United States Attorney, for the government.

Charles Berman, 3 South Street, New York City, for the defendant.

---

21. *See* LaFave, et al, § 14.4(d)

22. Mario Long waived his right to a preliminary hearing at his initial appearance.

The Court:	Are both parties ready to proceed?
Knapp:	Yes, Your Honor.
Berman:	Yes.
The Court:	Very well. The government may call its first witness.
Knapp:	The government calls Special Agent Ralph Martinez.
The Court:	Sir, please raise your right hand. Do you swear to tell the truth and nothing but the truth, so help you God?
Martinez:	I do.
Knapp:	Agent Martinez, what is your occupation?
Martinez:	I'm an agent with the DEA.
Knapp:	I direct your attention to January 11, 2005, at about 2:00 pm at the JFK Airport office of United States Customs and Border Protection, and I ask you if you were present at that time and place.
Martinez:	Yes.
Knapp:	Now sir, what, if anything, occurred at that time and place?
Martinez:	A Customs agent opened crates consigned to Superior Warehouse, Inc. Queens, New York in my presence at which time I observed a large quantity of white powder contained in 10 bags in one of the crates. I field tested the powder positive for cocaine. I removed the bags, and replaced the white powder with flour, leaving a small amount of cocaine in one of the bags, and put the bags back into the crate. I also placed a tracking beeper in the crate that had the cocaine in it.
Knapp:	Now Agent Martinez, I direct your attention to January 12, 2005 at approximately 2:00 pm and ask you if you were in the area of Superior Warehouse at that time?
Martinez:	Yes.

Knapp:	Briefly, sir, tell the court what happened.
Martinez:	On January 12, Agent Richard Sobel, posing as a truck driver, delivered the crates that we had found at the airport to Superior Warehouse, 149 Grand Street, Queens, New York.
Knapp:	All right, agent, did Sobel tell you what occurred when he arrived at the warehouse?
Martinez:	Yes. He said he delivered the crates to the foreman of the warehouse, Mario Long, who signed the receipt and who directed a workman, Arthur Murphy, to remove the crates from Sobel's truck.
Knapp:	Now Agent Martinez, did you at any time on January 12 see the defendant Gilbert Santiago at the warehouse?
Martinez:	Yes. Prior to Agent Sobel's delivery of the crates, I had observed the defendant, Gilbert Santiago, enter and exit Superior Warehouse on three occasions.
Knapp:	Did there come a time when Agent Sobel left the area of Superior Warehouse?
Martinez:	Yes, at approximately 2:30 pm.
Knapp:	Did you enter Superior Warehouse at that time?
Martinez:	Yes.
Knapp:	What if anything did you observe inside Superior Warehouse?
Martinez:	Through the use of a homing device, I found that the crate containing cocaine had been placed behind a locked door. I asked the foreman, Mario Long, to open the locked door.
Knapp:	Did he respond?
Martinez:	The foreman stated that he was not sure he should open the door without Gil being there.
Knapp:	Did there come a time when the door was opened?
Martinez:	Yes.
Knapp:	What, if anything, did you discover?

Martinez:	I discovered the crate containing the cocaine behind the locked door.
Knapp:	Agent Martinez, I want to direct your attention to about 4:00 on January 12, 2005 and ask you if you were present at DEA headquarters when a phone call was placed by Mario Long.
Martinez:	Yes.
Knapp:	Were you in a position to overhear that conversation?
Martinez:	Yes.
Knapp:	What did you hear?
Martinez:	I heard Mario Long speak to someone whom he identified as Gilbert.
Knapp:	Do you now recognize the voice of the person to whom Mario Long was speaking?
Martinez:	Yes. It was the voice of Gilbert Santiago.
Knapp:	Agent Martinez, please relate in substance the conversation that you heard between Long and Santiago.
Martinez:	Long said that he had received the shipment, and that he could not find Van Ness. Santiago asked Long where the material was, and Long said it was in the back room. Long said he was nervous about having the material there, and that Murphy was also. Santiago said that everything would be all right if Long and Murphy shut up. He said to Long something like, "You don't know anything and Murphy doesn't know anything."
Knapp:	I have no further questions, Your Honor.
The Court:	Mr. Berman, you may cross-examine.

This would conclude the government's case. It is obviously far short of what would be necessary to convict Santiago at trial because his link to the cocaine is based solely on his presence at the warehouse on the day in question, his supervisory role there and a statement that suggested knowledge of the cocaine but not necessarily involvement with its possession. Similarly, the examination leaves completely unresolved questions concerning the legality of the agents' conduct during the searches, a subject beyond the scope of this hearing. Nevertheless, the testimony would undoubtedly be sufficient to support a finding of probable cause that Santiago had committed the crime of possession with intent to distribute the seized drugs and conspiracy to do the same. Because the testimony is sufficient to meet the probable cause standard, it is, as we shall explain below, comparable to if not the same as that which Knapp would offer in the grand jury.

§ 6.3(b) Cross–Examination of the Government's Witness

With no likelihood of avoiding a ruling that probable cause exists, Charles Berman would conduct a discovery cross-examination. Berman will, in part, be seeking verification (for better or worse) of specific facts—for example, whether more cocaine than that charged in the complaint was found at the time of the airport search and whether Santiago had any direct involvement with the receipt of the crate containing the drugs. In part, however, he will ask questions simply in hopes of obtaining a lead that might be productive. An example might be identifying some confusion in the interdiction of the drugs, which might later help to undermine the government's proof that the drugs it has are the ones seized (chain of custody and authentication concerns). Another example might be uncovering factual details that raise questions about the legality of the search. Note again that Berman will conduct this examination as he would a direct examination at trial, proceeding from topic to topic chronologically and eliciting as many details as possible.

Berman:	Agent Martinez, when you arrived at Kennedy Airport, did you notice one or more than one crate addressed to Superior Warehouse, Queens, New York.
Agent Martinez:	There were 12 crates addressed to Superior Warehouse.
Berman:	Agent, did you open all of the crates?
Agent Martinez:	Yes.
Berman:	In how many of the crates did you find cocaine?
Agent Martinez:	One.
Berman:	Can you say whether there was anything else in the crate containing the cocaine other than the cocaine itself?

Agent Martinez: Yes. The crate contained coffee and the cocaine was buried in the coffee in closed cloth containers.

Berman: Do you know what was inside the other crates?

Agent Martinez: Yes, coffee.

Berman: Was the coffee packaged in the other crates in the same manner as it was packaged in the crate containing the cocaine?

Agent Martinez: Yes. All the crates looked the same on the inside and the outside. It was only upon the examination of the crates that we were able to determine that one had cloth containers containing cocaine.

Berman: Now Agent Martinez did there come a time when you placed Superior Warehouse under surveillance?

Agent Martinez: Yes.

Berman: When was that?

Agent Martinez: About noontime on January 12th.

Berman: You testified on direct examination that you observed Gilbert Santiago enter and exit the warehouse.

Agent Martinez: Yes.

Berman: At the time you observed Mr. Santiago did you know what his business was with the warehouse?

Agent Martinez: No.

Berman: You testified that you saw Mr. Santiago exit and leave on three occasions.

Agent Martinez: Yes.

Berman: Was he alone or with other individuals on each of these occasions?

Agent Martinez: Alone.

115

Berman:	How far were you from Mr. Santiago at the time you say you saw him?
Agent Martinez:	About 200 to 250 feet.
Berman:	Did you observe Mr. Santiago with the naked eye, or was your vision enhanced in some manner?
Agent Martinez:	I was using 15 by 30 binoculars.
Berman:	Could you tell us how long Mr. Santiago remained in Superior Warehouse on each of the occasions you saw him enter and leave?
Agent Martinez:	He would enter and remain for about five minutes and then leave and drive away. He would return about 15 minutes later, enter the warehouse for about five minutes and leave again. This pattern was repeated on three occasions.
Berman:	At what time did Agent Sobel arrive at Superior Warehouse?
Agent Martinez:	At about 2:00 PM.
Berman:	Can you tell us whether Mr. Santiago was present at the time Agent Sobel arrived?
Agent Martinez:	Mr. Santiago had left about 10 minutes earlier.
Berman:	At any time on January 12 after Agent Sobel arrived did you or any of the other agents see Mr. Santiago at the warehouse?
Agent Martinez:	No.
Berman:	When Agent Sobel delivered the crate containing cocaine to Superior Warehouse, did he also deliver the other crates containing coffee?
Agent Martinez:	All twelve crates were delivered at the same time.
Berman:	At the time of the delivery, did the crate containing cocaine appear, from the outside, to be any different from any other crates?
Agent Martinez:	The crates appeared to be identical.
Berman:	Had you altered the interior contents of the crate containing cocaine?

Agent Martinez:	Yes. We removed most of the cocaine. And a homing device was placed inside the crate containing cocaine so that we would be able to later locate the crate.
Berman:	Did Agent Sobel tell you whom he spoke with at the time he delivered the crates to Superior Warehouse?
Agent Martinez:	He said he spoke with the foreman, Mario Long.
Berman:	Did Sobel say that Long signed for the crates?
Agent Martinez:	Yes.
Berman:	Did Agent Sobel tell you whether there was any mention of Mr. Santiago's name at the time the crates were delivered.
Agent Martinez:	According to Agent Sobel, neither he nor Mr. Long discussed Gilbert Santiago at that time.

Berman:	Now, did there come a time, Agent Martinez, in the afternoon of January 12, that you entered Superior Warehouse?
Agent Martinez:	Yes.
Berman:	At about what time was that?
Agent Martinez:	At about 3:00 p.m.
Berman:	How did you obtain entry to the warehouse?
Agent Martinez:	I identified myself to the foreman, Mario Long, and asked whether we could search the warehouse.
Berman:	What did Long say?
Agent Martinez:	He said I am not sure whether to permit you to enter. I think we should wait for Gil, someone he identified as the manager of the warehouse.
Berman:	What was your response?
Agent Martinez:	I informed Long that if he did not permit us to enter, we would obtain a search warrant and secure the premises anyway.

Berman: How did Long respond?

Agent Martinez: He then said we could go ahead and look around.

Berman: Did there come a time when you discovered the crates which Agent Sobel had delivered to Superior Warehouse?

Agent Martinez: Yes.

Berman: Where were the crates located?

Agent Martinez: Eleven of the crates were placed against the south wall of the warehouse, with the crate containing cocaine missing.

Berman: How were you able to determine that the crate containing cocaine was missing?

Agent Martinez: The homing device captured the beeper signal which was emitted from the crate and indicated that the crate was at some location at or near the west wall of the warehouse.

Berman: What did you do at that time?

Agent Martinez: I walked in the direction of the signal and came upon a locked door.

Berman: When you came upon the door, what did you do?

Agent Martinez: I asked Mario Long to open the locked door.

Berman: Did Long comply?

Agent Martinez: Long stated that he was not sure whether to open the door without Gil being there.

Berman: How did you respond?

Agent Martinez: I told Long that if he refused we would obtain a search warrant, and that, pending that, no one would be permitted to enter the locked area.

Berman: What occurred thereafter?

Agent Martinez: Long went with Special Agent Richards to get a key to open the door.

Berman: Did there come a time when Long returned and opened the door?

Agent Martinez: Yes.

Berman: What occurred then?

Agent Martinez: We discovered the crate from which the signal was emitted, opened the crate, and discovered that it contained the cocaine which had been earlier discovered at Kennedy Airport.

Berman: From the time you entered Superior Warehouse until the time you discovered the cocaine and thereafter left, was Gilbert Santiago on the premises?

Agent Martinez: No.

———

After the cross-examination of Martinez, Berman would rest. There would be no strategic advantage to calling defense witnesses, for reasons explained above. Specifically, probable cause is sure to be found, and direct examination testimony would expose a defense witness—especially the defendant—to cross-examination by the government.

As expected, immediately after the evidentiary portion of the hearing was concluded, the magistrate judge announced that probable cause had been established and that the defendant would therefore be bound over for the action of the grand jury.

*

Part II

THE GUILTY PLEA SYSTEM

We must interrupt our description of the progression of a case through the formal stages of the "due process" model of the criminal process to discuss in detail the complex and critically important "crime control" model, in which cases are disposed of by guilty pleas.[1] It is not an exaggeration to say that the *de facto* rule in federal criminal practice is that most cases will be disposed of by such a plea, and only the exceptional case will go through formal pretrial proceedings and trial.

Our description of the guilty plea system begins in Chapter 7 with an overview of the federal law of sentencing, which was changed dramatically—and made considerably more complex—in 1984 with the passage of the Sentencing Reform Act.[2] Since in the case of nearly all negotiated pleas the sentence is what is being negotiated, this seems an appropriate starting point. In Chapter 8 we describe one aspect of the negotiation process, situations involving a defendant who has decided to cooperate with the government. We focus on cooperation at that point because it is a very common phenomenon in "police-initiated" cases of the kind that we have been describing thus far, where the government believes that the defendant can provide information useful in the prosecution of more important cases. In Chapter 9 we discuss the rules that Congress has enacted to regulate the guilty plea process. Then, in Chapter 10, we introduce the "prosecutor-initiated" case, and after describing how it is developed, we proceed to the indictment process in Chapter 11 and then return to the guilty plea system in Chapter 12. There we deal with plea negotiation for non-cooperating defendants, including bargaining over the charges to be brought and the sentencing factors to be considered.

While we believe the kind of sentence-related negotiated plea just described generally reflects current practice in the federal system, there are many variations. Thus, defendants may plead guilty without negotiating at all or may do so for reasons other than the sentence they are offered. Likewise, defendants in police-initiated cases may not be willing or able to cooperate, while seemingly major targets may nonetheless be rewarded for cooperating. The basic rules we are about to describe nonetheless generally operate throughout the guilty plea system.

---

1. *See supra* Chapter 1.   **2.** 18 U.S.C. §§ 3551–3585.

Chapter 7

ASSESSING THE RISK OF TRIAL— THE FEDERAL SENTENCING GUIDELINES

Table of Sections

Sec.
7.0   Introduction.
7.1   The Substantive Law of Sentencing—Introduction.
7.2   Computing the Sentence.
    7.2(a) Determining the Base Offense Level.
    7.2(b) Applying Specific Offense Characteristics.
    7.2(c) Relevant Conduct.
    7.2(d) Applying Adjustments.
    7.2(e) Special Rules for Convictions on Multiple Counts.
    7.2(f) Calculating the Adjusted Offense Level.
    7.2(g) Determining the Defendant's Criminal History.
    7.2(h) Calculating the Guidelines Range.
    7.2(i) Departures.
7.3   Non–Guidelines Sentences after *Booker*.

§ 7.0 Introduction

Historically, sentencing decisions in the federal system were largely within the discretion of the sentencing judge. Congress limited itself in most instances to setting a maximum punishment for each crime. While mandatory minimum sentences were not unknown, not many criminal statutes required a judge to impose a minimum term. A crime such as armed bank robbery, for example, had (and has) a maximum penalty of 25 years in prison and no prescribed minimum. Thus, a judge could grant probation or a suspended sentence or impose any prison term up to the maximum, basing his or her decision on facts brought to the court's attention at the time of sentencing by either party or in the presentence report of a probation officer, but not necessarily determined, or even presented, at trial. Although the defendant had a right to a hearing to determine contested facts, the judge need not have found these facts beyond a reasonable doubt—a preponderance of the evidence was sufficient, and he or she could consider hearsay or other evidence that would have been inadmissible at trial. Appellate review of sentences was very limited. As long as the sentence was legally imposed, the appellate courts would rarely overturn the sentencing judge.

This system produced considerable disparity in sentences among federal districts and among judges in the same district for conduct and offenders that were essentially the same.[3] Moreover, because almost all persons sentenced to prison were eligible for parole, the parole board's decisions also increased the likelihood of disparity, and the time actually served was generally much less than that to which the defendant was sentenced.

This situation changed dramatically with the passage of the Sentencing Reform Act of 1984. Congress sought both to reduce disparity and to assure that defendants would serve the amount of time that the judge imposed. The Act sought to accomplish the first goal by establishing the United States Sentencing Commission, whose mandate was to produce guidelines that courts would be required to follow in arriving at a sentence. It accomplished the second goal by abolishing parole.

Because of recent decisions by the Supreme Court, first in 2000 in *Apprendi v. New Jersey*,[4] then in 2004 in *Blakely v. Washington*,[5] and finally, in 2005, in *United States v. Booker*,[6] the federal sentencing system has undergone another significant change. A brief summary of the relevant provisions of the Sentencing Reform Act and of these decisions is therefore necessary in order to set a foundation for the more detailed description of sentencing in the federal system that follows in this chapter and thereafter.[7]

Section 3553(a) of the Sentencing Reform Act provides that the court shall impose a sentence "sufficient, but not greater" than necessary to comply with enumerated sentencing goals. After considering the "nature and circumstances of the offense and the history and characteristics of the defendant," the court is thus instructed to sentence in accordance with the need for the sentence imposed: (A) to reflect the seriousness of the offense, to promote respect for the law, and to provide just punishment; (B) to afford adequate deterrence to criminal conduct;

---

3. For a leading critique of pre-Guidelines sentencing disparities, including an early call for a commission on sentencing, see MARVIN E. FRANKEL, CRIMINAL SENTENCES: LAW WITHOUT ORDER (1972).

4. 530 U.S. 466 (2000).

5. 542 U.S. 296, 124 S.Ct. 2531 (2004).

6. 125 S.Ct. 738 (2005).

7. Understanding the manner in which sentences are calculated is of central importance to the resolution of cases by guilty plea, which is addressed in Chapters 8 and 12, and to the determination of facts on which the sentence is based, which is addressed in Chapter 17.

(C) to protect the public from the defendant; and (D) to provide the defendant with needed educational or vocational training, medical care or other correctional treatment in the most effective manner. The sentencing court is also directed to consider "the kinds of sentences available"; the kinds of sentences and the sentencing ranges established by the Sentencing Commission as well as any applicable policy statements; "the need to avoid unwarranted sentence disparities among defendants with similar records who have been found guilty of similar conduct"; and "the need to provide restitution to any victims of the offense."[8]

In the next sub-section, 18 U.S.C. § 3553(b), the courts are then instructed, in effect, to defer to the determinations of the Sentencing Commission as to how these factors should be weighed. Thus, § 3553(b) directs that courts "shall impose a sentence" within the range as calculated pursuant to the Sentencing Commission's guidelines, unless there exist aggravating or mitigating circumstances "of a kind or to a degree not adequately taken into consideration by the Commission in formulating the guidelines." Only in such cases could courts "depart" upwards or downwards from the sentence dictated by the guidelines that the Commission would fashion.[9]

For three years following its creation, the Sentencing Commission studied sentencing patterns in order to determine what kinds of sentences judges were imposing and what factors they considered in making their determinations. In 1987 it published the United States Sentencing Guidelines, which were designed to incorporate the factors it deemed relevant to the sentencing decision for each federal crime—in effect, to apply to specific crimes and offenders its interpretation of the just described factors enumerated in § 3553(a). The Guidelines, as will be more fully described below, directed the judge to impose a sentence within a relatively narrow range—in most cases a difference of 25% between the lower and upper end of the applicable range of imprisonment, the latter in virtually every case being considerably lower than the statutory maximum term of imprisonment. Moreover, the appellate courts were to review the sentencing decisions *de novo* in order to assure that the Guidelines were followed.

The system operated in accordance with this design until 2005, with the Commission revising its guidelines from time to time. It also "considered" an increasing number of factors, assuring that the power of the courts to depart on grounds that the Commission had not adequately considered some factor could rarely be exercised. For its part, Congress superseded some of the Commission's decisions, imposed further restrictions on downward departures, and added mandatory minimum sentences primarily in an effort to reduce what it believed to be excessive leniency on the part of sentencing judges.

8. § 3553(a)(1)-(a)(7).   **9.** § 3553(b).

The state of the law of sentencing changed significantly, however, when in January of 2005 the Supreme Court decided *United States v. Booker*, where it held that *mandating* the sentencing judge to impose a sentence within the range prescribed by the Sentencing Guidelines was unconstitutional and that the Guidelines could (and should) be used by the courts only to guide the exercise of their discretion.

To understand the significance of the Court's decision in *Booker* it is necessary to first discuss its earlier decisions in *Apprendi v. New Jersey* and *Blakely v. Washington*. *Apprendi* involved a statute that permitted a judge to impose a sentence higher than the statutory maximum for the offense (possession of a firearm) after finding that the defendant's conduct constituted a "hate crime." Specifically, if the judge (not the jury) determined that the offense was a "hate crime," the judge was authorized to increase the maximum penalty from 10 years to 20 years in prison. The Supreme Court ruled that this statute violated the defendant's constitutional right to have guilt as to a fact that resulted in an enhanced sentence determined beyond a reasonable doubt by a jury. *Apprendi* thus dealt only with the power of the judge to find sentencing facts that would enhance the sentence beyond the statutory maximum. The Court did not consider the question whether the sentencing judge could find facts that increased a sentence in the traditional manner so long as the sentence was no greater than the statutory maximum.

Next came *Blakely v. Washington*, dealing with one state's guideline system. In *Blakely*, the State of Washington's sentencing scheme mandated a "standard" sentence not greater than the top of the guideline range, absent a judicial finding of aggravating facts justifying an "exceptional sentence." The "standard sentence" in the case, based on the facts admitted in connection with a guilty plea for kidnapping, was 49 to 53 months in prison (a range that the government recommended to the court). However, based on a judicial finding that the defendant acted with "deliberate cruelty," the trial judge sentenced the defendant to a term of imprisonment almost twice as long—90 months. The Supreme Court applied the reasoning of *Apprendi* and ruled that the defendant's Sixth Amendment right to a jury trial was violated when the judge (as opposed to the jury) made a finding of "deliberate cruelty" that increased the sentence above the "standard" guideline range, even though it was still less than the statutory maximum (which was 10 years or 120 months).

Finally, in *Booker,* the Court took the widely anticipated step of applying the rationale of *Blakely* to the federal Sentencing Guidelines. In *Booker* the jury found the defendant guilty of possessing with intent to distribute at least 50 grams of cocaine base (crack). Based upon this drug quantity (and the defendant's criminal history), the Guidelines mandated a sentence between 210 and 262 months in prison. At sentencing, the judge found by a preponderance of the evidence that Booker had possessed an additional 566 grams of crack and also that he was guilty of obstructing justice. These findings increased Booker's Guidelines range to a sentence between 360 months and life in prison. Although Booker was sentenced to the 360 month "low end" of this enhanced range, his Sixth Amendment rights as developed in *Apprendi* and *Blakely* were violated, the Court concluded, because, instead of a sentence as low as 21 years and 10 months that the judge could have imposed based upon the facts actually proved to a jury beyond a reasonable doubt, Booker's 30–year sentence was based on facts found only by the judge and only by a preponderance of the evidence.

It would seem to have followed from this part of the majority decision in *Booker* that all facts that would enhance the sentence under the Guidelines would have to have been alleged in the indictment and found by the jury beyond a reasonable doubt.[10] However, in a second part of the majority opinion authored by a different 5–4 majority,[11] the Court ruled that the Sentencing Reform Act, and with it the Guidelines, could be saved from this Sixth Amendment predicament; the Court thus struck 18 U.S.C. § 3553(b)(1), the provision that made the Guidelines mandatory, concluding that as long as the sentencing court had discretion to decide whether to follow them, the defendant's constitutional rights were not violated.[12] The Court stated that the sentencing judge had an obligation to "consider" the punishment range prescribed by the Guidelines and that any variance had to be "reasonable," but it did not provide any guidance as to what either term might mean, leaving that to be developed by the District Courts and Courts of Appeals.[13]

While the result in the remedial part of *Booker* is consistent with traditional sentencing practices prior to the passage of the Sentencing Reform Act—the sentencing judge could base a sentence up to the statutory maximum upon facts found by a preponderance of the evidence—it is difficult to understand how the remedial part is consistent with its substantive part reflecting the rationale of *Apprendi* and *Blakely,* namely, that the Sixth Amendment guarantees the right to have a jury determine beyond a reasonable doubt facts that enhance the sen-

---

10. The exception would be cases in which the defendant waives his Sixth Amendment rights by admitting the relevant facts as part of a negotiated plea. *See Booker,* 125 S.Ct. at 774 (Stevens, J., dissenting) (quoting *Blakely,* 124 S.Ct. at 2541).

11. Only Justice Ginsburg was in the majority in both parts of this decision. She did not author either part.

12. The decision dealt with the right to have a jury determine the existence of factors that enhanced the sentence under the Guidelines even when the final sentence was below the statutory maximum for the defendant's crime. *Booker* does not require a jury determination concerning factors that require the judge to reduce the sen-

tence, e.g., whether the defendant accepted responsibility for the crime. However, since *Booker* made the Guidelines calculus as a whole advisory, it seems clear that adjustments that reduce the sentencing range are advisory also.

13. The Court's reasoning also led it to strike 18 U.S.C. § 3742(e), which governed standards of review on appeals of Guidelines sentences and included a requirement (as of 2003) of *de novo* review of decisions to depart. *Booker* set out a new and more deferential standard of review, holding that sentences would be reviewed on appeal only for "unreasonableness." *Booker,* 125 S. Ct. at 755–56. The appellate review standard is discussed further in § 7.3, *infra.*

tence.[14] As we will discuss below, in the first months following *Booker,* the lower courts have struggled to resolve how to reconcile the two parts of the decision, as well as the crucial question of the meaning to be given to the mandate to "consider" the Guidelines in a system in which the sentencing judge's discretion has been restored.[15]

§ 7.1 The Substantive Law of Sentencing—Introduction

The United States Sentencing Commission published the first set of Guidelines in 1987. It has revised the Guidelines periodically, including most recently in the November 1, 2004 amendments.[16] Before turning to the method by which sentences are calculated under the Guidelines, the basic principles underlying the scheme should be understood.

1. The Guidelines operate within the parameters set by Congress for violation of particular statutes. Thus, the maximum sentence of imprisonment provided for by the statute for the crime of conviction cannot be exceeded, even if the calculation of a sentence under the Guidelines would produce a greater punishment. Similarly, the Guidelines cannot generally result in a sentence lower than any mandatory minimum sentence dictated by the statute, although there are important exceptions to this rule.

2. The Guidelines are based upon a "real offense" theory. Sentences are calculated not on the basis of the elements of the crime for which the defendant was convicted, but rather on the totality of the defendant's "relevant conduct," even if the defendant was not charged with, or indeed was acquitted of, that conduct. This is an extremely important feature of the Guidelines, with a major impact on plea negotiations.

3. The description that follows is designed to explain the mechanics of sentencing under the Guidelines. It is important to note, however, that the actual process has not been as mechanical as this description might suggest. While the pre-*Booker* sentencing discretion of judges was substantially decreased, flexibility remained. Moreover, the constraints imposed on judges by the Guidelines prior to *Booker* did not signal the end of sentencing discretion, but rather an enhancement of the discretionary powers of the prosecutor, at the expense of those of the court, over what sentence will be imposed. The effect of the Court's decision in *Booker* would appear to be to shift some of that power back to the courts. How extensively the judge's new-found (or, perhaps more accurately, newly reacquired) discretion will be exercised remains to be seen. It is clear, however, that given the Supreme Court's mandate that the Guide-

---

14. Thus, the dissenters in the remedial part of *Booker* argued that the enhancing factors either had to be charged in the indictment or be the subject of a jury trial at the sentencing stage.

15. *See infra* § 7.3.

16. All references in this book are to the most recent version of the Guidelines to date, presented in the 2004 edition of the Federal Sentencing Guidelines Manual, which includes the November 1, 2004 amendments.

lines be "considered," they will continue to play a central role in sentencing. Hence, a detailed description of how sentences are computed under the Guidelines is in order.

§ 7.2   Computing the Sentence

Recall that in our model case Mario Long was charged with a conspiracy to possess slightly less than 10 kilograms of cocaine (the amount intercepted at the airport leading to the controlled delivery to Superior Warehouse), in violation of 21 U.S.C. §§ 846 and 841(a)(1). We will assume for purposes of the following analysis that he pled guilty to that charge. We will use this case to illustrate the steps that must be taken to determine his sentence under the Guidelines. It will be easier to understand the process if the reader refers to the Federal Sentencing Guidelines Manual when reading the following.

Below are the steps in the process by which Long's sentence would be computed. (An outline of the calculation process is found in § 1B1.1 of the Guidelines Manual.)

§ 7.2(a)   Determining the Base Offense Level

In the Statutory Index (Appendix A) of the Guidelines Manual each federal criminal statute is listed, with a cross-reference to specific sections of Chapter 2 of the Guidelines. The sections of Chapter 2 govern all federal criminal offenses and must be referred to in order to determine the appropriate *Base Offense Level,* expressed in numbers ranging from 1 to 43, with the latter being the most serious. These sections are categorized generically and broadly by the type of offense.

The section of the Guidelines applicable to Long's offense is § 2D1.1. It provides that in a case such as Long's, one must refer to a "Drug Quantity Table,"[17] in which the base offense level is made a function of the quantity and type of drug involved. In Long's case, since the amount of cocaine was slightly less than 10 kilograms, the base offense level (for 5 to 15 kilograms of cocaine) is 32.

§ 7.2(b)   Applying Specific Offense Characteristics

Each subsection in Chapter 2 also includes a list of *Specific Offense Characteristics* designed to account for various means by which the crime was committed. For example, under § 2D1.1, if a dangerous weapon was used in the commission of the crime, the base offense is increased by 2 levels. (Other specific offense characteristics reduce the offense level.) [18]

---

17. *See* USSG § 2D1.1(c).

18. A separate calculation is involved in determining the base offense level of "career offenders." *See* USSG § 4B1.1. The calculation applies in cases where the offense of conviction is a narcotics offense or a crime of violence and the defendant has two prior convictions for these kinds of offenses. The offense level in these cases will always result in a sentencing range at or near the maximum for the statute of conviction regardless of other factors. An

One such specific offense characteristic should be mentioned because of its relevance to our illustrative case. Congress has provided relief from statutory mandatory minimum sentences otherwise applicable in narcotics cases—the so-called "safety valve" provision—when the court finds that the defendant does not have more than one criminal history point;[19] no violence was involved in the offense; the defendant was not a leader or organizer; and the defendant provides to the government all of the information he or she had about the offense.[20] If the defendant qualifies for this adjustment, he or she is sentenced in accordance with the relevant Guidelines (including a 2 level reduction) and the mandatory minimum provision is disregarded.[21]

Applied to the Long case, qualifying for the "safety valve" would be of great significance to Long because he is facing a mandatory 10 year minimum.[22] That required minimum would be eliminated. Moreover, his base offense level of 32 would be reduced by 2 levels to 30.

§ 7.2(c) Relevant Conduct

As noted, the Guidelines are designed to take into account the "real offense" committed by the defendant.[23] Therefore, they provide that in addition to the specific offense characteristics applicable to the crime for which the defendant was convicted at trial, or to which he pleaded guilty, all *Relevant Conduct* must also be considered in determining the base offense level. Relevant conduct includes: (a) all acts committed or aided and abetted by the defendant in preparation for, in furtherance of, or in avoiding detection of the offense of which the defendant was convicted; (b) all "aggregable" offenses that were part of the same criminal scheme as the offense of conviction; and (c) all harm that resulted from the acts covered in (a) and (b) above.[24] Relevant conduct may also include crimes by others if such crimes were part of the same scheme and were "reasonably foreseeable" by the defendant.[25] Even charges dismissed by the government or of which the defendant was acquitted can fall into the category of relevant conduct and thus be the basis for calculating the

---

"armed" career offender will also face a mandatory minimum sentence of 15 years. *Id.* § 4B1.4. The Guidelines also set forth a minimum offense level for defendants who derive substantial income from a pattern of offenses of which the offense of conviction is a part and who have little legitimate income. *See id.* § 4B1.3.

19. On calculating criminal history points, see *infra* § 7.2(g); USSG Ch. 4.

20. § 3553(f). This provision applies whether or not the defendant has provided substantial assistance in the prosecution of others which, as we shall describe, is the only other ground for avoiding the mandatory minimum under the Guidelines calculus. *See infra* § 7.2(i).

21. § 2D1.1(b)(7). While the court even after *Booker* has no authority to depart below a statutory mandatory minimum, it does appear that once the safety valve provisions are met, the court is not bound to follow the Guidelines provision calling for a 2 level reduction, and could depart further.

22. 21 U.S.C. § 841(b). 21 U.S.C. § 846, the conspiracy statute applicable here, provides for the same penalty as the substantive crime.

23. *See supra* § 7.1.

24. USSG § 1B1.3 (Relevant Conduct).

25. *Id.* § 1B1.3, comment. (n.1–n.3).

defendant's offense level. If the acts are found by a court to be proven by a preponderance of the evidence, they must be considered in determining the defendant's sentence.[26]

The maximum sentence that a defendant can receive will never be more than the maximum allowed by statute for the crime or crimes of which the defendant was convicted—even if consideration of relevant conduct would increase the Guidelines sentence above that maximum. Nevertheless, relevant conduct can have a major effect on the defendant's sentence in three ways. First, it can affect the offense level. For example, relevant conduct includes the total amount of drugs—the aggregable offense—involved in all the dealings that were part of the course of conduct, not just the drugs included in the count or counts on which the defendant was convicted. The total amount of drugs would constitute a single "fungible harm." Thus, if it were found that the conspiracy in which Long participated involved additional shipments of cocaine totaling between 15 and 50 kilograms of cocaine, then the Drug Quantity Table would yield a base offense level of 34, rather than the 32 that would have applied had the conspiracy involved only the 9.8 kilograms that the DEA recovered in January of 2005. This would be the case even though Long was charged only with a conspiracy involving the 9.8 kilograms or more.[27]

Second, relevant conduct can be used to justify an upward departure, i.e., a sentence greater than the calculated Guidelines range.[28] For example, if it were determined at the time of Long's sentence that weapons were involved in the importation conspiracy, an upward departure would be authorized.[29]

Finally, relevant conduct can affect where within the Guidelines range the sentence will be set.[30]

§ 7.2(d) Applying Adjustments

After adding the levels designated for the offense of conviction and any specific offense characteristics and relevant conduct, any applicable *Adjustments* must be calculated. Adjustments relate to certain aggrava-

---

26. United States v. Watts, 519 U.S. 148 (1997); United States v. Duncan, 400 F.3d 1297, 1304–05 (11th Cir. 2005). This seemingly anomalous situation arises because the burden of proof at sentencing is by a preponderance of the evidence, not beyond a reasonable doubt. Thus, while a jury may have acquitted the defendant of a given charge, a sentencing judge may find that the defendant probably committed the criminal act by this lower burden, and the sentence will thus reflect the offense. In this way, the defendant's "real offense" conduct surrounding the criminal transac-

tion is ultimately factored into the sentence.

27. We will explain below the relationship between offense level and sentence. Suffice it to say here that assuming that Long had no prior record, and no other sentencing factors were relevant, a 34 base offense level would result in at least a 30 month increase in the length of the sentence.

28. Departures are discussed *infra* at § 7.2(i).

29. *See* USSG § 5K2.6, p.s.

30. *See infra* § 7.2(h).

ting or mitigating factors that may be involved in the offense, and they appear in Chapter 3 of the Guidelines Manual. There are four categories of adjustments:

(1) Victim Related Adjustments

The defendant's offense level may be raised by a specific number of level because of the vulnerability or status of the victim.[31]

(2) Role in the Offense Adjustments

These adjustments apply in cases in which the defendant acted with one or more others in committing a crime. If the defendant was a leader of the group, his offense level may be raised.[32] Where the defendant played a minor role, his offense level may be reduced.[33] If the defendant played an average role, no adjustment is made.

(3) Obstruction of Justice Adjustments

An upward adjustment may occur when the defendant has engaged in acts that unlawfully impede the investigation or prosecution of the case or the administration of justice, whether before or after the initiation of the prosecution.[34]

(4) Acceptance of Responsibility Adjustments

A downward adjustment may occur when the defendant has demonstrated a recognition of the wrongfulness of his or her act and affirmatively accepts blame for the criminal conduct.[35] The Guidelines Manual

---

31. *See* USSG Ch. 3, Pt. A (Victim Related Adjustments). These adjustments apply in cases in which there was a particularly vulnerable victim, a victim who was a public official, or a victim who had been restrained. Where an act underlying the victim-related adjustment constitutes a specific offense characteristic included within the offense level score, however, it will not be counted again as an adjustment. *See, e.g., id.* § 3A1.3, comment. (n.2.).

32. *Id.* § 3B1.1 (Aggravating Role). Pertinent facts would include whether the defendant had decision-making authority, whether he recruited accomplices, whether he claimed a larger share of the fruits of the crime than others, and whether he was involved in planning the offense and the number of people under his or her control. The Guidelines make a distinction between a leadership role in a group of more than 5 criminally culpable participants (4–level increase) and a managerial role (3–level increase). The Guidelines call for only a 2–level increase for either a leadership or managerial role in a group of less than 5. *Id.*

33. *Id.* § 3B1.2 (Mitigating Role). The reduction can be 2, 3 or 4 levels depending on the defendant's actions, knowledge of the scope of the enterprise and the actions of others in the group.

34. *Id.* § 3C1.1 (Obstruction of Justice). Obstructive conduct includes destroying or concealing evidence, suborning or providing untruthful testimony, threatening witnesses, or lying to a probation officer in the course of the presentence investigation. *See, e.g.,* United States v. Baker, 894 F.2d 1083, 1084 (9th Cir. 1990) (furnishing material falsehoods to a probation officer during presentence investigation may serve as basis for an upward adjustment); United States v. McDonald, 964 F.2d 390, 392–93 (5th Cir. 1992) (use of alias to law enforcement and magistrate judge resulted in increased sentence).

35. USSG § 3E1.1 (Acceptance of Responsibility). The commentary to this guideline notes that a demonstration of acceptance could include, among other things, voluntary surrender and admission of the crime, assistance to authorities, and payment of restitution. *Id.*, comment. (n.1).

states that a downward adjustment for acceptance of responsibility may be available even to defendants who are convicted after trial (although this is quite rare),[36] and that a defendant who enters a guilty plea is not entitled to a sentence reduction as a matter of right (although such a defendant almost always benefits from such a reduction).[37] In practice, however, the adjustment is the Guidelines' formalization of the incentive to plead guilty. Our experience is that a guilty plea almost always earns the adjustment and a trial verdict almost always forecloses it. Where the offense level is lower than 15, a 2-level decrease is authorized. If the offense level is 16 or over, an additional one level decrease can be given on motion of the government that it had been timely notified that the defendant intended to plead guilty and thereby avoided unnecessary preparation for trial.[38]

In the Long case, the only applicable adjustments would be for his particular role in the offense and for acceptance of responsibility. Section 3B1.2 provides for a 4–level reduction if the defendant was a "minimal" participant and a 2–level reduction if he was a "minor" participant. The commentary to this section suggests that Long would be considered a minor participant,[39] and therefore his base offense level would be reduced from 30 to 28.[40]

As to acceptance of responsibility, we have posited that Long pled guilty and therefore would be eligible for at least a 2-level reduction. Since he did this in a timely manner and his offense level is over 16, the government would no doubt move that an additional level reduction be given. This would bring his adjusted offense level from 28 to 25.

§ 7.2(e) Special Rules for Convictions on Multiple Counts

We have posited that Long pleaded guilty to a single count of conspiracy. In cases where the defendant is convicted of more than one count, an additional calculation must be made. The Sentencing Commission explained that it attempted to produce a formula that imposed greater punishment when a defendant is convicted of multiple crimes and at the same time protected against unjustified increases in sentences by "an arbitrary casting of a single transaction into several counts [to] produce a longer sentence."[41]

The calculation of the sentencing range for a defendant convicted of more than one count requires the application of a multiple count adjustment. This process is set forth in Part D of Chapter 3 of the

---

36. *Id.*, comment. (n.2).

37. *Id.*, comment. (n.3).

38. *See generally id.*, comment. (n.2).

39. The application notes accompanying § 3B1.2 describe a minimal participant as one who lacked understanding or knowledge of the scope of the enterprise. It is conceivable that Long could fit that defini-

tion, though there is evidence that he knew of the ongoing nature of the scheme.

40. This calculation assumes that Long would qualify for the "safety valve" provision, discussed *supra* at § 7.2(b), which reduced the base offense level from 32 to 30.

41. USSG § 1A1.1, comment, historical text (§ 1A1.4(e)).

Guidelines Manual. The underlying principle is that all offenses involving the same harm should receive a score reflecting the seriousness of the total harm. For this purpose, the Guidelines distinguish between certain offenses that are "closely related" and others that are not.

(1) Closely Related Offenses

Offenses that involve the same harm are grouped together and are assigned a combined score reflecting the seriousness of the harm.[42] The offense level applicable to a group of closely related offenses is either that of the most serious offense,[43] or, in the case of quantifiably "aggregable" offenses, that of the guideline relevant to the total quantity involved.[44] For example, if the defendant were convicted of embezzling $15,000 from a bank, the base offense level would be 7, and 4 levels would be added for the $15,000 loss amount.[45] If as part of the scheme he were convicted on another count of paying a $1,000 bribe to an internal bank examiner, the base offense level for that crime would be 9.[46] The applicable base offense level would therefore be 11, corresponding to the higher or more "serious" embezzlement count, and the bribery count would be disregarded for this purpose. Using the same example to illustrate how aggregable offenses are treated, if the defendant were convicted on six counts of embezzlement of $10,000 (each one occurring, say, on a different day, and therefore prosecutable as separate crimes), the applicable offense level would be determined in accordance with the Guidelines formula for increasing the punishment on the basis of the amount of money involved—here $60,000—which would produce an offense level of 13.[47] Consistent with the Sentencing Commission's goal of not permitting the multiplication of counts to determine the sentence, the result is the same as if the defendant had been convicted of one count of embezzling $60,000.[48]

(2) Offenses Not Closely Related

When the defendant has been convicted of offenses (or groups of offenses) that are not closely related, a different method of calculation

---

42. *See id.* § 3D1.2 (Groups of Closely Related Counts). Offenses reflect the same harm: (i) when they involve the same victim and act or course of conduct, *id.* § 3D1.2(a), (b); (ii) when the guideline applicable to one count includes the conduct of another count as a specific offense characteristic, *id.* § 3D1.2(c); and (iii), the most common situation, when the offense level is based principally on the amount of harm, e.g., quantity of drugs carried, pollution released or dollars lost, *id.* § 3D1.2(d).

43. USSG § 3D1.3(a).

44. *Id.* § 3D1.3.(b).

45. *Id.* § 2B1.1(a) (base offense level of 7 for crimes carrying 20 or more years imprisonment as the maximum); 18 U.S.C. § 656 (providing 30 year statutory maximum for bank embezzlement); USSG § 2B1.1(b)(1)(C) (adding 4 levels for losses between $10,000 and $30,000).

46. *Id.* § 2C1.2.

47. *Id.* § 2B1.1(b)(1)(D).

48. The result would also be the same if the defendant had been convicted of one count involving $10,000 and, additionally, there was sufficient evidence presented in connection with sentencing to establish embezzlement of the other $50,000, which would then be "relevant conduct" producing the same offense level.

must be used. This requires assigning "units" to each of the offenses, and these units are subsequently totaled and reconverted into offense levels. In essence, the resulting offense level will be keyed to the most serious offense and adjusted upward for offenses with scores relatively close to that of the most serious offense. Offenses with much lower scores are disregarded altogether.[49] For example, suppose a defendant were convicted of two bank robberies,[50] one in which he possessed a gun and stole $11,000 (offense level 28),[51] and the other in which he was unarmed and stole $12,000 (offense level 23).[52] With a 5-level difference between the two offenses, the offense level of the more serious offense is increased by 1 level to 29.[53]

A final note about the Guidelines' treatment of convictions on multiple counts is in order. The provisions of Part D of Chapter 3 are perhaps the most arcane in a scheme that is already complex in many respects. As a practical matter, however, the grouping rules do not come into play in most cases. This is because almost every case is disposed of by guilty plea, and typically that plea will be to one count of the indictment. Since the grouping rules only apply to convictions on multiple counts, they will not apply in these situations. This does not mean, of course, that the charges dismissed in return for the plea will not have an impact on the defendant. That impact, however, will be the result of the application of rules regarding relevant conduct.

§ 7.2(f) Calculating the Adjusted Offense Level

The total accumulated score from the calculations discussed above is the *Adjusted Offense Level,* which determines where the case falls on the vertical axis of a sentencing grid included in the Guidelines.[54] There are 43 offense levels.

As noted in § 7.2(d), Mario Long's adjusted offense level would be 25.

§ 7.2(g) Determining the Defendant's Criminal History

The next calculation concerns the defendant's *Criminal History Category*, the rules for which are found in Chapter 4 of the Guidelines.

49. In cases involving more than one group of counts (each group consisting of one or more related offenses), the combined offense level is determined by calculating the number of "units," a technical term concerning multiple count calculations. The group having the highest offense level is assigned one unit, and each group having an offense level equal to, or within 4 levels of the highest group is assigned one unit. Any other groups that are 5 to 8 levels less serious than the level for the highest group are assigned one-half unit, while any group 9 or more levels less serious is disregarded. USSG § 3D1.4(a)-(c). The total number of units is translated into points by which the offense level for the highest group will be increased.

50. The Guidelines expressly provide that these offenses are not to be considered closely related counts, even if they could be considered part of the same scheme. USSG § 3D1.2(d).

51. *Id.*   §§ 2B3.1(a),   2B3.1(b)(1), 2B3.1(b)(2)(c), 2B3.1(b)(7)(B).

52. *Id.*   §§ 2B3.1(a),   2B3.1(b)(1), 2B3.1(b)(7)(B).

53. *Id.* § 3D1.4(a) and (b).

54. *See* USSG Ch. 5, Pt. A (Sentencing Table), reprinted *infra* at § 7.2(h).

The defendant's criminal history is determined based on points accumulated by the number, seriousness and proximity of past convictions (in any jurisdiction), and it is based on whether the present crime was committed while the defendant was on probation or any type of release status or supervision for another offense.[55] The Criminal History guideline assigns 3 points for each sentence of more than 13 months, 2 points for each sentence between 60 days and 13 months, and 1 point for all other jail sentences.[56] Additional points are added if the defendant was recently released from or is still under some form of supervision, such as parole.[57] The total number of points in a given case will place the defendant in one of the six criminal history categories, from Category I (0–1 points) to Category VI (13 or more points). These categories form the horizontal axis of the sentencing grid.

§ 7.2(h) Calculating the Guidelines Range

The intersection on the sentencing grid of the Offense Level and Criminal History Category identifies the applicable sentencing range. The range is expressed in terms of a minimum and maximum number of months in prison.[58] The groups of ranges in the Sentencing Table are subdivided into four "zones" that dictate different degrees of access to non-prison sentences.[59]

In the Long case, we have posited that Long had no prior criminal record and therefore would fall within Category I. The intersection of an adjusted offense level of 25 and a Category I criminal history level yields a Guidelines range of 57–71 months.

---

55. *See id.* § 4A1.1 (Criminal History Category).

56. USSG § 4A1.1(a)-(c).

57. *Id.* § 4A1.1(d), (e).

58. The lowest range is 0–6 months. The highest range with a minimum sentence is 360 months to life, and there is a final category that provides for a life sentence with no minimum. Death sentences are not included in the Sentencing Table.

59. There are four "zones," based upon the minimum term for the particular range. Defendants in Zone A (no minimum prison term) may receive a sentence of probation. USSG § 5C1.1(b). Those in Zone B (1 to 6 months in prison) may receive probation in conjunction with a form of confinement. *Id.* § 5C1.1(c). Those in Zone C (8 to 10 months) must serve at least half of the minimum term in prison and may be sentenced to another form of confinement for the remainder of the sentence. *Id.* § 5C.1.1(d). All other sentences fall within Zone D (minimum of 12 months) and must include at least the full minimum term for the range in prison. *Id.* § 5C1.1(f).

SENTENCING TABLE
(in months of imprisonment)

Offense Level	Criminal History Category (Criminal History Points)					
	I (0 or 1)	II (2 or 3)	III (4, 5, 6)	IV (7, 8, 9)	V (10, 11, 12)	VI (13 or more)
1	0-6	0-6	0-6	0-6	0-6	0-6
2	0-6	0-6	0-6	0-6	0-6	1-7
3	0-6	0-6	0-6	0-6	2-8	3-9
4	0-6	0-6	0-6	2-8	4-10	6-12
5	0-6	0-6	1-7	4-10	6-12	9-15
6	0-6	1-7	2-8	6-12	9-15	12-18
7	0-6	2-8	4-10	8-14	12-18	15-21
8	0-6	4-10	6-12	10-16	15-21	18-24
9	4-10	6-12	8-14	12-18	18-24	21-27
10	6-12	8-14	10-16	15-21	21-27	24-30
11	8-14	10-16	12-18	18-24	24-30	27-33
12	10-16	12-18	15-21	21-27	27-33	30-37
13	12-18	15-21	18-24	24-30	30-37	33-41
14	15-21	18-24	21-27	27-33	33-41	37-46
15	18-24	21-27	24-30	30-37	37-46	41-51
16	21-27	24-30	27-33	33-41	41-51	46-57
17	24-30	27-33	30-37	37-46	46-57	51-63
18	27-33	30-37	33-41	41-51	51-63	57-71
19	30-37	33-41	37-46	46-57	57-71	63-78
20	33-41	37-46	41-51	51-63	63-78	70-87
21	37-46	41-51	46-57	57-71	70-87	77-96
22	41-51	46-57	51-63	63-78	77-96	84-105
23	46-57	51-63	57-71	70-87	84-105	92-115
24	51-63	57-71	63-78	77-96	92-115	100-125
25	57-71	63-78	70-87	84-105	100-125	110-137
26	63-78	70-87	78-97	92-115	110-137	120-150
27	70-87	78-97	87-108	100-125	120-150	130-162
28	78-97	87-108	97-121	110-137	130-162	140-175
29	87-108	97-121	108-135	121-151	140-175	151-188
30	97-121	108-135	121-151	135-168	151-188	168-210
31	108-135	121-151	135-168	151-188	168-210	188-235
32	121-151	135-168	151-188	168-210	188-235	210-262
33	135-168	151-188	168-210	188-235	210-262	235-293
34	151-188	168-210	188-235	210-262	235-293	262-327
35	168-210	188-235	210-262	235-293	262-327	292-365
36	188-235	210-262	235-293	262-327	292-365	324-405
37	210-262	235-293	262-327	292-365	324-405	360-life
38	235-293	262-327	292-365	324-405	360-life	360-life
39	262-327	292-365	324-405	360-life	360-life	360-life
40	292-365	324-405	360-life	360-life	360-life	360-life
41	324-405	360-life	360-life	360-life	360-life	360-life
42	360-life	360-life	360-life	360-life	360-life	360-life
43	life	life	life	life	life	life

Zone A: levels 1–8
Zone B: levels 9–10 (col. I region)
Zone C: levels 10–12
Zone D

7-15

In a typical case in which the judge decides to impose a Guidelines sentence, the judge must select a specific sentence within the Guidelines range.[60] In doing so, the Guidelines state that the judge should consider

---

60. Minimum jail sentences are the greater of 6 months or 25% less than maximum sentences within any offense level.

factors related to the person of the defendant, called *Specific Offender Characteristics*. The Guidelines list twelve such factors. Among these are: the defendant's age, education, mental condition, employment history, drug dependence and socio-economic background.[61] Note that these offender characteristics are relevant here to determine a specific sentence within the Guidelines range. These characteristics may also be relevant to departures from a particular range, which we discuss in the next section.

§ 7.2(i) Departures

The Guidelines also permit *Departures* from the applicable sentencing ranges.[62] Rules concerning departures are contained in two sections of Part K of Chapter 5 of the Guidelines. Although the rules permit both upward departures when "aggravating" circumstances are found and downward departures when there are "mitigating" circumstances, virtually all departures under the Guidelines have in fact been downward: in 2003, only 0.8% of all sentences included upward departures, as compared to 29.7% that included downward departures.[63]

The rules regarding departures are divided into two categories:

(1) <u>Departures Based Upon Substantial Assistance to Authorities by the Defendant</u>[64]

The Guidelines provide that the court may impose a sentence below the relevant Guidelines range when the government makes a motion notifying the court that the defendant has "cooperated," i.e., provided substantial assistance in the prosecution or investigation of other persons and/or crimes.[65] The court has discretion (rarely exercised) to refuse a downward departure in this situation, but it cannot grant a departure for substantial assistance absent a motion by the government.[66] Not only can substantial assistance departures result in sentences lower than the minimum Guidelines range, but they can also bypass mandatory minimum sentences provided for in various statutes.[67]

Downward departures for substantial assistance have been a significant component of federal sentencing under the Guidelines; in 2003, for

---

61. USSG §§ 5H1.1, p.s.—5H1.12, p.s. (Specific Offender Characteristics).

62. *See id.* Ch. 5, Pt. K (Departures).

63. U.S. Sentencing Commission 2003 Annual Report, Ch. 5, *available at* http://www.ussc.gov/ANNRPT/2003/Ch5–2003.-PDF (2003).

64. USSG § 5K1.

65. In the wake of *Booker*, there is an open question as to whether sentencing courts may—or will—consider granting leniency to defendants who cooperate or attempt to cooperate but do not receive a § 5K1.1 motion from the government. *See infra* § 8.0 n.4.

66. *Id.* § 5K1.1, p.s.

67. § 3553(e). Virtually all mandatory minimum sentences relate to drug and weapons violations. *See* Ian Weinstein, *Fifteen Years After the Federal Sentencing Revolution: How Mandatory Minimums Have Undermined Effective and Just Narcotics Sentencing*, 40 AMER. CRIM. L. REV. 87 (2003).

example, they accounted for approximately 15.9% of all sentences.[68] Substantial assistance departures also typically confer a significant sentence reduction, with a median 49.9% decrease from the Guidelines minimum term of imprisonment.[69]

Although not included in the substantial assistance section of the Guidelines, there exists another category of government-initiated departures: the so-called "fast track" departures, in which the prosecutor recommends sentences below the applicable Guidelines range for defendants who plead guilty and waive all trial and appellate rights.[70] Prior to 2003, this practice was an informal one, designed to speed up the disposition of routine drug and immigration cases, principally in districts on the Mexican border.[71] With the passage of the PROTECT Act[72] in 2003, Congress expressly incorporated the program and ordered the Sentencing Commission to promulgate a policy statement authorizing a downward departure of not more than 4 levels pursuant to a plan in any district approved by the Attorney General.[73] The Attorney General has in turn established guidelines for such plans, limiting fast track departures to non-violent crimes and in circumstances where the volume of these cases is interfering with the work of the office.[74]

"Fast track" departures in a typical year accounted for some 7.8% of all sentences, with the vast majority occurring in the Southern District of California.[75]

(2) "Other Grounds" for Departure

Section 5K2.0 of the Guidelines contains a general provision permitting courts to depart on the basis of "circumstances of a kind or to a degree not adequately taken into consideration by the Sentencing Commission."[76] Prior to *Booker,* where the Commission had explicitly considered a given factor, courts were bound by its determination as to

68. U.S. Sentencing Commission's 2003 Sourcebook of Federal Sentencing Statistics, Fig. G, *available at* http://www.ussc.gov/ANNRPT/2003/fig-g.pdf (2003); *id.,* Table 26A, *available at* http://www.ussc.gov/ANNRPT/2003/table26a.pdf (2003). Government initiated downward departures for reasons other than substantial assistance occurred in 6.3% of all cases. *Id.,* Table 26A.

69. *Id.,* Table 30, *available at* http://www.ussc.gov/ANNRPT/2003/table30.pdf (2003).

70. These departures in the past misleadingly had been subsumed within the "Other Grounds for Departure" category of the Sentencing Commission's statistical reports, which is discussed below.

71. *See* United States Sentencing Commission, Downward Departures from the Federal Sentencing Guidelines, pp.

iv-v, *available at* http://www.ussc.gov/departrpt03/departrpt03.pdf (Oct. 2003).

72. PROTECT Act, Pub. L. No. 108–21, § 401(m)(2)(B), 117 Stat. 650, 675 (2003) (codified at 18 U.S.C. § 3742).

73. *Id.*

74. Attorney General John Ashcroft, Department Principles for Implementing an Expedited Disposition or "Fast–Track" Prosecution Program in a District, *available at* http://www.fpdnj.org/RecentLegal/ashcroft.fasttrack.memo.pdf (Sept. 22, 2003).

75. Downward Departures from the Federal Sentencing Guidelines, *supra* note 71, at 44. This data represents information from the year 2001.

76. USSG § 5K2.0(a)(1)-(4), p.s.

whether such factor could serve as a basis for a departure.[77] For example, the Commission has provided in Part H of Section 5 that certain "specific offender characteristics," such as age, educational and vocational skills, mental and emotional conditions, physical condition, employment record, and family ties, are "not ordinarily relevant" in determining whether a departure should be granted and that other characteristics, including race, national origin and socioeconomic status, may never be considered.[78] The Commission also has specifically enumerated a number of aggravating and mitigating factors related to the commission of the offense or to the mental condition of the offender that may provide a basis for a departure. For example, there may be grounds for an upward departure if the offense was committed in an egregious manner,[79] and a downward departure may be granted if there were certain imperfect legal excuses for the crime.[80] A court may depart upward or downward when the defendant's criminal history category does not adequately reflect either the severity of the defendant's past criminal conduct or the likelihood that the defendant will commit other crimes.[81]

Departures in the "other grounds" category—judicially-initiated departures—have in a typical year accounted for about 7.5% of all cases under the Guidelines.[82] However, judicial discretion to grant such departures was limited significantly as a result of the passage of the 2003 PROTECT Act containing the so-called Feeney Amendment.[83] Among other things, the new law required: (a) the Sentencing Commission to amend the Guidelines so as to "ensure that the incidence of downward

---

77. Koon v. United States, 518 U.S. 81, 95–96 (1996).

78. USSG §§ 5H1.1, p.s.—5H1.12, p.s.

79. USSG § 5K2.0, p.s. (Grounds for Departure). The examples include loss of life during the commission of the offense, physical injury to the victims, extreme psychological injury, abduction during the crime, property damage or loss, use of a weapon, and disruption of a governmental function. These factors are available as grounds for departure when they are not specific offense characteristics or where the applicable guideline does not adequately account for some unusual or extreme fact that they reflect.

80. Examples include the victim's contributory wrongful conduct, avoidance of a greater harm, coercion and duress, and diminished capacity (for non-violent offenses). The Guidelines envision that these factors can be considered at sentencing even if the defendant failed to raise them at trial or failed to persuade a jury with respect to those which would otherwise constitute a legal defense to the crime. *See* USSG § 5K2.0, p.s. & comment. (backg'd.).

81. USSG § 4A1.3. *See, e.g.,* United States v. Sappe, 898 F.2d 878, 882 (2d Cir. 1990) (upward departure warranted because of under-representative criminal history); United States v. Bellamy, 264 F.3d 448, 456 (4th Cir. 2001) (court properly departed upward 3 levels for under-representative criminal history). When the court departs on this ground, it must determine the appropriate criminal history category and then recalculate the defendant's Guidelines range incorporating the new category. USSG § 4A1.3; United States v. Jackson, 883 F.2d 1007, 1009 (11th Cir. 1989); United States v. Lopez, 871 F.2d 513, 514 (5th Cir. 1989). Lack of a criminal record cannot justify a downward departure because Category I accounts for defendants with no prior record.

82. U.S. Sentencing Commission's 2003 Sourcebook of Federal Sentencing Statistics, Table 26A, *supra* note 68.

83. PROTECT ACT, *supra* note 72, § 401(m).

departures is substantially reduced;" and (b) that the scope of appellate review of departure decisions be changed from the highly deferential "abuse of discretion" standard adopted by the Supreme Court[84] to one of *de novo* review.[85] In response, the Sentencing Commission rewrote § 5K2.0 to reflect Congress' policy with respect to downward departures, emphasizing that they are to be granted only in "exceptional" cases[86] and specifically curtailing the power of sentencing judges to depart downwardly in a number of respects.[87]

These Congressional efforts to circumscribe and limit downward departures were undermined less than two years later, if not rendered largely academic, by the Supreme Court's 2005 decision in *Booker*. *Booker* specifically excised the recently mandated requirement of *de novo* appellate review of departures, replacing it with the more deferential standard that the sentencing decision as a whole must be "reasonable,"[88] and some post-*Booker* decisions suggest that departure decisions in particular—as one component of the overall sentencing decision—may now be reviewed under an "abuse of discretion" standard.[89] As we discuss in the next section, *Booker* also specifically authorized "reasonable" non-Guidelines sentences, according judges greater freedom to deviate in appropriate cases from the Guidelines' prior mandates.

Whenever a court departs from the Guidelines range, it must state its reasons in open court at the time of sentencing and, with limited exceptions, must also specifically state its reasons in the written judgment and commitment order.[90] The defendant has an automatic right to

---

84. Downward Departures from the Federal Sentencing Guidelines, *supra* note 71, at ii.

85. A useful analysis of the statute and the Commission's response to it appears in David M. Zlotnick, *The War Within the War on Crime: The Congressional Assault on Judicial Sentencing Discretion*, 57 SMU L. Rᴇᴠ. 211 (2004).

86. "[C]ircumstances warranting departures should be rare. Departures were never intended to permit sentencing courts to substitute their policy judgments for those of Congress and the Sentencing Commission." U.S. Sentencing Commission, Amendments to the Sentencing Guidelines, p. 9, *available at* http://www.ussc.gov/2002suppc/OCT03CON.pdf (Oct. 27, 2003); USSG § 5K2.0, p.s., comment. (backg'd).

87. The rules now prohibit departures based on the defendant's acceptance of responsibility, mitigating role, decision to plead guilty without more, or fulfilling res-

titution obligations. New restrictions were adopted on the availability of other grounds for departure, including those related to diminished mental capacity and family ties and responsibilities. *See* USSG § 5K2.0(d), p.s. *But see infra* § 7.3 & Chapter 17.

88. *See supra* note 13.

89. *See* United States v. Selioutsky, 409 F.3d 114, 119 (2d Cir. 2005) ("Since the sentencing judge has discretion with respect to departures, *see* U.S.S.G. § 5K2.0 (court 'may depart'), we consider whether the District Court abused (or exceeded) its discretion in using a family circumstances departure to select the Defendant's Guidelines sentence."). *Cf.* United States v. Hadash, 408 F.3d 1080 (8th Cir. 2005) (holding that while "challenges to the applicability of the Guidelines" will still be reviewed *de novo*, the ultimate sentence is reviewed for "unreasonableness," and thus errors in the application of the Guidelines (including an error in a decision to depart) may be harmless).

90. § 3553(c); USSG § 5K2.0(e), p.s.

appeal any upward departure, and the government has the same appeal right with respect to any downward departure.[91]

(3) Application of departure rules to the Long case

We have noted that Mario Long may be able to avoid the 10 year mandatory minimum sentence that he faces if he qualifies for the "safety valve" provision. He could also avoid this minimum sentence if he is able to provide sufficient information about the drug operation at Superior Warehouse and thus persuade the government to move for a substantial assistance departure under § 5K1.1. And, depending on his personal circumstances, he may have grounds to move for a downward departure or to argue under *Booker* for a non-Guidelines sentence, to which we now turn.

§ 7.3 Non–Guidelines Sentences after *Booker*

Prior to the *Booker* decision in 2005, once the sentencing court had calculated the Guidelines and considered departures, as outlined in §§ 7.2(a) through 7.2(i), the process of arriving at a sentence was finished. Absent a departure, the judge was required to impose a sentence within the Guidelines range of imprisonment found to be applicable. If a departure was granted, the sentence could be reduced (or increased) at the judge's discretion to a point outside the Guidelines range, but still could not be less than any statutory mandatory minimum or greater than any statutory maximum penalty.

By excising the mandatory directive of § 3553(b) and thus rendering the Guidelines only "advisory," *Booker* added an additional and more individualized layer of analysis to every sentencing. Specifically, while the sentencing court must "consider" what a sentence in conformity with the Guidelines would be, the court also must consider the additional § 3553(a) sentencing considerations—listed in § 7.0, supra, and including, *inter alia*, the "nature and circumstances of the offense," "the history and characteristics of the defendant," the need for the sentence to "reflect the seriousness of the offense," deter future criminality, protect the public, and provide the defendant with needed training, medical care, or other correctional treatment, and the need to avoid unwarranted sentence disparities among similarly situated defendants— to arrive at a "reasonable" sentence.[92]

Notwithstanding the additional measure of sentencing freedom and flexibility afforded by the *Booker* decision, at the time of this writing it appears that the Guidelines remain the central feature of the federal sentencing system. The data collected by the Sentencing Commission

---

91. 18 U.S.C. § 3742(a)(3) and (b)(3). After *Booker*, it would also seem that, if a non-Guidelines sentence is imposed, the adversely impacted party will have an automatic right to appeal under these provisions.

92. It should be emphasized that *Booker* did not in any way affect a judge's inability to sentence below a statutory mandatory minimum or above a statutory maximum punishment.

indicate that judges have continued to impose Guidelines sentences in the vast majority of cases. The United States Sentencing Commission reports that as of July, 2005 61.3% of all sentences were within the Guidelines range, and another 24.1% were government sponsored departures below the applicable range, mostly in the cases of cooperating defendants.[93] Moreover, in cases disposed of by negotiated plea, to the extent that the parties agree to a sentence calculated under the Guidelines, as they frequently do, it is likely that that sentence will be imposed.[94]

Be that as it may, at the time of this writing some eight months after the *Booker* decision, courts are grappling with the question of how much discretion the decision gives them to sentence outside of the Guidelines—in other words, how free they are to disagree with the Commission's determinations of how the factors enumerated in § 3553(a) of the Sentencing Reform Act[95] should be applied. From the first post-*Booker* sentencings to the present the district courts have gone in two directions: some have ruled that the Guidelines should be followed except in extraordinary cases, arguing, in effect, that control over sentencing is vested in Congress and that, by accepting the determination of the Sentencing Commission as to how sentencing factors should be balanced, Congress has exercised that control.[96] Other courts have deemed the Guidelines just one factor among all of those enumerated in § 3553(a), arguing that the Supreme Court in *Booker* sought to restore some of the traditional power of the courts to individualize sentencing decisions.[97]

The courts of appeal have thus far been slow to address this issue, although to the extent that they have it appears that they view *Booker* as having retained a predominant role for the Guidelines. It seems clear that at the very least that the sentencing judge will continue to be required to perform the Guidelines calculations before deciding whether to impose a Guidelines or non-Guidelines sentence and to provide reasons why a Guidelines sentence would not be reasonable.[98] Two

---

93. U.S. Sentencing Commission, Special Post–Booker Coding Project, available at http://www.ussc.gov/Blakely/PostBooker_080805.pdf (August 3, 2005). Of the remaining 14.6%, 14% were upward departures and 13.2% downward departures. The data are not clear as to exactly how many of the downward departures were non-Guidelines departures based upon *Booker*.

94. This matter will be discussed in Chapters 8 and 12 dealing with negotiated pleas.

95. *See supra* note 2.

96. *See, e.g.,* United States v. Wilson, 350 F.Supp.2d 910, 925 (D. Utah 2005)(court will depart only in "unusual cases for clearly identified and persuasive reasons").

97. *See, e.g.* United States v. Ranum, 353 F.Supp.2d 984, 987 (E.D. Wis. 2005) (Guidelines are a starting point in arriving at a just sentence); Simon v. United States, 361 F.Supp.2d 35, 40 (S.D.N.Y. 2005)(Guidelines deserve equal but not greater weight than other factors in § 3553(a)).

98. *See, e.g.,* United States v. Crosby, 397 F.3d 103, 111–12 (2d Cir. 2005).

Courts of Appeal have gone further, ruling that a sentence within the Guidelines range is presumptively reasonable.[99]

The courts have also confronted the question of what burden of proof applies after *Booker* in determining sentencing facts (including relevant conduct). It appears that the traditional standard, i.e., that the judge may base a sentencing decision on facts found by him or her by only a preponderance of the evidence, will be applied.[100]

Finally, it remains to be seen what action if any Congress will take in response to the *Booker* decision, in light of the fact that the Guidelines can no longer be treated as mandatory. It has been suggested that *Booker's* impact could be neutralized by making the upper range of each guideline the same as the maximum statutory penalty for the offense. Then no sentence would be unconstitutionally enhanced by a judicial finding of fact, the specific vice identified by the Court. This "solution," however, would risk greatly increasing disparity in sentencing because there would be such a wide gap between the upper and lower Guidelines ranges.[101] Congress could also move toward a determinate sentencing system, in which a specific sentence is mandated in all cases. That, however, would undermine the goal of individualizing sentences. To the extent that Congress is concerned with judges being too lenient, it could impose mandatory minimum sentences for more crimes, since the *Booker* court stated that its decision did not affect Congress' power to dictate such minimums. One proposal along these lines, at the time of this writing, has been introduced in the House of Representatives.[102] Or, Congress could dictate—as Attorney General Alberto Gonzales suggested in June 2005—that the low end of the Guidelines range in each case be considered a "mandatory minimum" sentence.[103]

We will return to the potentially far-reaching impact of *Booker* on the federal criminal process in Chapters 8, 9 and 12 (dealing with plea

99. United States v. Mykytiuk, 415 F.3d 606 (7th Cir. 2005)(sentence correctly calculated under the Guidelines is entitled to a rebuttable presumption of reasonableness); United States v. Lincoln, 413 F.3d 716 (8th Cir. 2005)(sentence within the Guidelines range is presumptively reasonable). *See also* United States v. Mares, 402 F.3d 511 (5th Cir. 2005)(explaining that it will be rare for a reviewing court to find that a sentence calculated consistent with the Guidelines is unreasonable)

100. *See* United States v. Mares, 402 F.3d at 519; United States v. Crosby, 397 F.3d at 109 (traditional authority of sentencing judge to find facts does not violate the Sixth Amendment). *But see* United States v. Okai, 2005 WL 2042301 (D. Neb. 2005) (holding that Fifth Amendment requires that facts such as amount of loss that significantly enhance a sentence be found by the judge beyond a reasonable doubt).

101. If the lower limit were increased by a commensurate amount to keep the size of the range constant, the length of federal sentences would grow dramatically.

102. *See, e.g.,* Defending America's Most Vulnerable: Safe Access to Drug Treatment and Child Protection Act of 2005, H.R. 1528, 109th Cong. (2005).

103. Attorney General Alberto Gonzales, Speech Before the National Center for Victims of Crime, *text of remarks available at* http://sentencing.typepad.com/sentencing_law_and_policy/files/gonzales_remarks_sentencing_guidelines_as_prepared.doc (June 21, 2005).

negotiation and guilty pleas) and, finally, in Chapter 17 (dealing with the sentencing process).

Chapter 8

PLEA NEGOTIATION AND THE COOPERATING DEFENDANT

Table of Sections

Sec.
8.0 Introduction.
8.1 The Decision to Cooperate.
8.2 The Cooperation Process—Overview.
    8.2(a) The Proffer Session.
    8.2(b) The Cooperation–Plea Agreement.
8.3 United States v. Santiago—The Cooperation Process.
    8.3(a) The Defense Position.
    8.3(b) The Government's Position.
    8.3(c) Beginning the Cooperation Process.
    8.3(d) Preparing for The Proffer Session.
    8.3(e) Santiago's Proffer Agreement and Statement.
    8.3(f) Santiago's Cooperation–Plea Agreement.
8.4 Drafting the Formal Charges—Waiver of Indictment and Information.
8.5 United States v. Mario Long—The Cooperation–Plea Agreement.
8.6 United States v. Arthur Murphy.

§ 8.0 Introduction

Unless a prosecutor can be persuaded to discontinue the prosecution, there are essentially three options open to someone who, like Gilbert Santiago or Mario Long, has been arrested and charged with violations of the federal criminal law: (1) take the case to trial; (2) plead guilty; or (3) plead guilty and cooperate with the government. We focus in this chapter on the third option, cooperation, since the question of whether to cooperate typically must be addressed early in a case, and in subsequent chapters take up the other two.

As we have indicated, the Sentencing Reform Act allows a defendant who chooses cooperation to escape the imposition of a statutory mandatory minimum term of imprisonment.[1] The Sentencing Guidelines afford similar relief: cooperation is the principal means by which a defendant can obtain a downward departure, i.e., move to an offense level lower than that otherwise prescribed by the Guidelines.

The Guidelines provide that a downward departure in return for cooperation with the government can only be granted upon motion of the prosecutor.[2] This motion is often known by defendants as a "5K1.1 letter," referring to the particular Guidelines section that authorizes such motions. Theoretically, the court may deny a 5K1.1 motion, but in practice it will invariably grant it rather than second-guess the government's sentencing policies for cooperating defendants. Thus, while the sentencing judge makes the ultimate decision as to how much a cooperator's sentence should be reduced (if at all), the prosecutor alone decides whether to file the motion. Consequently, the cooperation rules plainly give the prosecutor a powerful negotiating tool.[3]

Following the Supreme Court's *Booker* decision, described in Chapter 7, it now may be possible for a sentencing judge to grant leniency on the basis of cooperation even absent a government 5K1.1 motion. Still, such a "non-Guidelines sentence" could not go below any applicable statutory mandatory minimum term of imprisonment. And the prosecutor is still the only one who can allow a defendant to cooperate in the first place. For these reasons, it is unlikely that *Booker* will have a material impact on the balance of power in the cooperation process.[4]

§ 8.1   The Decision to Cooperate

The defense attorney has a responsibility in connection with exploring and facilitating a client's cooperation. In fact, at least one court has gone so far as to say that in the era of the Sentencing Guidelines, a defense lawyer's ability to persuade the prosecutor that the lawyer's client should be allowed to cooperate and "earn" the opportunity to receive a potentially dramatically reduced sentence is now as important as his or her ability to persuade a judge or jury.[5]

---

1. 18 U.S.C. § 3553(e).

2. USSG § 5K1.1, p.s. *See* LaFave et al., §§ 21.2(d), (h).

3. *See, e.g.,* Lisa Egitto, *Substantial Assistance Departures: Threat to Sentencing Goals or Necessary Evil,* 17 St. John's J. Legal Comment. 585, 588 & nn.18–19 (2003) (discussing different positions commentators have taken on prosecutorial discretion in deciding whether a substantial assistance departure is warranted); Elkan Abramowitz, *Prosecutorial Input on Downward Departures for Assistance,* N.Y.L.J., Jan. 5, 1999, at 3 (describing the deference accorded prosecutorial decisions to withhold downward departure motions in the Second Circuit).

4. *Booker* may, however, open up a new option for leniency for some of the class of defendants who in fact cooperate but, through no fault of their own, do not receive a 5K1.1 letter (typically because their cooperation has not yielded any concrete "substantial assistance" to law enforcement). *See, e.g.,* United States v. Jaber, 362 F.Supp.2d 365, 380 (D. Mass. 2005) (defendant's efforts show "extraordinary acceptance of responsibility").

5. United States v. Fernandez, 2000 WL 534449, at *1 (S.D.N.Y. 2000). *See also* United States v. Leonti, 326 F.3d 1111, 1117–18 (9th Cir. 2003) (discussing the importance of effective assistance of counsel in a defendant's attempt and decision to coop-

Counseling a defendant with respect to cooperation, however, is one of the most sensitive tasks performed by the defense attorney. Because cooperation must usually be discussed early in the case, before much of an attorney-client relationship has developed, defendants anticipating a trial may react negatively to their attorney raising the possibility of pleading guilty and cooperating. Some defendants, whether because of loyalty, stigma, or fear for their own safety or that of their family, resist informing on their accomplices. Others are morally, philosophically and/or psychologically opposed to assisting the government in its investigation and prosecution of others despite the obvious potential benefits.[6]

However difficult or futile broaching the subject may be, it would seem that defense counsel has an obligation to raise the possibility of cooperation, and raise it early, particularly in cases in which lengthy mandatory minimum sentences or severe Sentencing Guidelines ranges are involved.[7] Judges virtually always reward cooperation with significantly lower sentences than they otherwise would have imposed—on average, according to one recent report, 50% lower than what the Guidelines would dictate.[8] A cooperation agreement also can lead to the release of the defendant from pretrial detention in certain types of cases, a consideration that is of extreme importance to most defendants. These substantial benefits explain why past statistics indicate that approximately 20% of all federal defendants and 30% of federal narcotics defendants receive cooperation-based downward departures.[9]

While the benefits of cooperation must be explained to the defendant, it is also critical that the attorney explain to the client the dangers involved in entering into discussions with the prosecutor. If the defendant participates in an initial interview with the government (known as a "proffer session"), but does not enter into a cooperation agreement— whether because the defendant changes his mind, the government is not interested in the defendant's cooperation, or the government believes the defendant has been less than candid—it is extremely difficult for the

---

erate; holding the cooperation period to be a "critical stage" of the criminal process).

6. *See generally* Daniel C. Richman, *Cooperating Clients,* 56 OHIO ST. L. J. 69, 77 (1995) (describing the "tug of loyalty, the fear of retaliation, and the shame of snitching").

7. *See, e.g., Fernandez,* 2000 WL 534449, at *1 (noting how critical it is that defense counsel advise their clients of the cooperation option early on in the case, and suggesting that failing to do so may be legal malpractice); Ellen Yaroshefsky, *Cooperation with Federal Prosecutors: Experiences of Truth–Telling and Embellishment,* 68 FORDHAM L. REV. 917, 929 (1999) (explaining that "[c]ompetent defense lawyers must discuss the option of cooperation with clients early on in the representation").

8. U.S. Sentencing Commission's 2003 Sourcebook of Federal Sentencing Statistics, Table.30, *available at* http://www.ussc.gov/ANNRPT/2003/SBTOC 03.htm (2003).

9. *See* Michael A. Simons, *Retribution for Rats: Cooperation, Punishment, and Atonement,* 56 VAND. L. REV. 1, 14 & nn.58–60 (2003). In the Second Circuit, the percentage of defendants receiving substantial assistance departures was 17.5% in 2003. U.S. Sentencing Commission's 2003 Sourcebook of Federal Sentencing Statistics, Table 26A, *available at* http://www.ussc.gov/JUD-PACK/2002/ny02.pdf (2003). *See also* Robert G. Morvillo & Robert J. Anello, *Sentencing Guidelines in 2003: Too Easily Abused?,* N.Y.L.J., Feb. 4, 2003, at 3.

defendant to go to trial and contest the charges, particularly where he or she has acknowledged guilt.[10] Similarly, if the defendant enters into a cooperation agreement but the defendant's cooperation efforts are unsuccessful (e.g. because the defendant's information did not lead to an arrest or prosecution or because the government concluded that the defendant had not been fully truthful or cooperative), the defendant will almost always be in a much worse position than if he or she had simply pled guilty without attempting to cooperate. For these reasons, the decision of whether or not to attempt to cooperate with the government is an extraordinarily important one, and it is incumbent upon the attorney to ensure that his or her client understands both the significant potential benefits as well as the substantial risks.

§ 8.2 The Cooperation Process—Overview

The cooperation process normally consists of several stages, to be described in detail below. The first is the "proffer session," in which the defendant indicates what information he or she has, in order to determine whether the government is at least potentially interested in the defendant's cooperation. Prior to making a statement, the defendant will execute a "proffer agreement." If after hearing the defendant's proffer the prosecutor is interested in having him or her cooperate, the parties enter a "cooperation-plea agreement," which supersedes the proffer agreement.

§ 8.2(a) The Proffer Session

To evaluate whether a given defendant can provide useful information, the prosecutor must, of course, learn what the defendant knows about the case or about other criminal activities. Because revealing the defendant's knowledge to the government may be incriminating, negotiations over cooperation often begin with an "attorney proffer," in which the attorney will give the prosecutor a general version of what the defendant hypothetically would say. In rare cases, an attorney proffer may be sufficient to negotiate a cooperation agreement; but, more commonly, the prosecutor will require an interview of the defendant.

This interview is known as a "proffer session." Present are the defendant and defense counsel, the prosecutor, and agents involved in the investigation of the case. As noted, the parties usually sign a proffer agreement,[11] which spells out the conditions under which the defendant will speak. These agreements can take different forms, depending upon the practices in the district and, less frequently, the results of negotia-

---

10. The uses to which the defendant's statements made in a proffer session can be put are discussed *infra* at § 8.2(a).

11. These are sometimes referred to as a "Queen for a Day" agreement. On the origin of the term "Queen for a Day," *see*

Benjamin A. Naftalis, *"Queen for a Day" Agreements and the Proper Scope of Permissible Waiver of the Federal Plea–Statement Rules*, 37 Colum. J.L. & Soc. Probs. 1, 2 n.4 (2003).

tions between the prosecutor and defense attorney in a particular case.[12] They normally contain a waiver of the broad protections that otherwise would preclude the government from using admissions made by a defendant during plea negotiations,[13] offering instead a limited form of use immunity. Specifically, the prosecutor will agree that the defendant's statements at the session will not be used in the government's case-in-chief or at sentencing in the event that no cooperation agreement is reached and the defendant proceeds to trial.[14] However, the agreement also normally provides that if the defendant were to testify at any such trial and contradict what was said in the proffer, the proffer statements may be used to impeach the defendant's testimony.[15] In other words, a defendant who has admitted his or her guilt at a proffer session but fails to reach a cooperation agreement will not later be able to deny the crime when testifying at trial without being confronted with the prior admission. More recently, and more controversially, many proffer agreements provide that proffer statements may be used not only to impeach a testifying defendant, but also to rebut evidence or arguments offered by the defense even if the defendant does not testify.[16]

The proffer agreement also typically provides that the government may make derivative use of the information proffered by the defendant to pursue leads to further its own investigation. The agreement also allows the use of proffer statements in prosecutions for perjury, false

---

12. *See generally* FEDERAL BAR COUNCIL, COMMITTEE ON SECOND CIRCUIT COURTS, PROFFER, PLEA AND COOPERATION AGREEMENTS IN THE SECOND CIRCUIT (2003) (demonstrating the differences between the plea, proffer, and cooperation agreements utilized by United States Attorney's Offices in the Second Circuit); Naftalis, *supra* note 11. *See also* Joel Cohen, *Has the Federal Government Made it Harder for One's Client to Cooperate?*, N.Y.L.J., Feb. 2, 1998, at 1 (discussing the proffer agreements in use at the U.S. Attorney's Offices in the Eastern and Southern Districts of New York).

13. FED. R. EVID. 410 (precluding admission of evidence of "any statement made in the course of plea negotiations with an attorney for the government which do not result in a plea of guilty . . .''); FED. R. CRIM. P. 11(f).

14. If and when a cooperation-plea agreement is executed by the defendant and the government, that agreement supersedes the proffer agreement, including the promise in the proffer agreement that the defendant's proffer statements will not be used at sentencing (or at a trial) should the defendant violate the cooperation-plea agreement.

15. The Supreme Court has upheld proffer agreement waivers that allow the

government to use a defendant's proffer statements for impeachment. *See* United States v. Mezzanatto, 513 U.S. 196, 210 (1995).

16. In *Mezzanatto*, 513 U.S. at 211, the Supreme Court left open the question of the enforceability of waivers that would allow proffer statements to be used for more than just impeachment. In the lower courts, defendants' challenges to the relatively new and more sweeping exceptions for the use of proffer admissions have met with little success. *See, e.g.*, United States v. Velez, 354 F.3d 190, 192 (2d Cir. 2004) (upholding a waiver provision that allowed the government to use defendant's proffer statement "to rebut any evidence or arguments" offered by the defendant "at any stage of the criminal prosecution" despite the fact that defendant did not testify); United States v. Barrow, 400 F.3d 109, 117–120 (2d Cir. 2005) (upholding waiver similar to *Velez* and applying contract law principles to waiver in discerning "expansive" definitions for "rebut" and "any evidence."); United States v. Krilich, 159 F.3d 1020, 1024–26 (7th Cir. 1998) (upholding waiver that allowed proffer statements to be used for more than just impeachment purposes).

statements or obstruction of justice based on statements or actions that occur during or after the proffer session.[17]

In short, by giving the government potential impeachment and rebuttal material, and by disclosing potential investigatory leads, an initial proffer session that does not mature into a cooperation-plea agreement can leave the defendant in a significantly worse position—and with significantly fewer options for mounting a defense at trial—than if the defendant had simply exercised his or her right to remain silent. Indeed, prosecutors have argued that a defendant who admits to criminal conduct in a proffer session effectively bars his or her attorney from later arguing affirmatively to a jury that their client is innocent.[18] The defendant and the defense counsel therefore must make a careful decision as to the appropriate course of action.[19]

§ 8.2(b) The Cooperation–Plea Agreement

Following the proffer session (or multiple sessions, which are often required), if the prosecutor is interested in the defendant's cooperation, plea negotiations will begin. If the parties arrive at an agreement, it will be formalized in a cooperation-plea agreement. These agreements vary in form. In some districts, formal agreements are executed, while in others, the agreements are in letter form. The agreements differ in substance as well, depending upon the negotiation, but a number of central points will be covered in all of them.

(1) Charge and sentence. The parties will agree on the charge to which the defendant will plead guilty. The statutory maximum (and any minimum) sentence will be noted. In many, if not most, districts the parties will also enter into an agreement about their understanding of the Guidelines calculation, possibly including a stipulation as to certain

---

17. The proffer agreement, or, later, the cooperation-plea agreement, may also preclude the government from using a defendant's statements to increase his or her sentencing exposure under the Guidelines. USSG § 1B1.8. However, the prosecution typically insists that the defendant agree to forego the protections of § 1B1.8, worrying that if the jury learns, for example, that the cooperator sold 100 kilograms of cocaine, but will only be sentenced on the basis of 10 kilograms because of a deal with the government, his or her credibility, and the government's credibility, will be too severely damaged.

18. *See* United States v. Lauersen, 2000 WL 1693538, at *8 (S.D.N.Y. 2000) (holding that even if proffer agreement is not enforceable, ethical rules preclude defense counsel who was present for proffer admissions from eliciting "substantive (non-impeachment) testimony, either on

cross-examination of witnesses called by the Government or from witnesses called to testify on her behalf, or to present arguments to the jury at any stage of the proceeding, including opening statements, that directly contradict specific factual statements made by" the defendant during her proffer).

19. *See, e.g.,* Robert G. Morvillo & Robert J. Anello, *Cooperation: The Pitfalls and Obligations for Defense Attorneys,* N.Y.L.J., Dec. 5, 2000, at 3 (suggesting, among other things, that prosecutors "may be seeking to make more aggressive use of proffer statements—using them not merely as tools for collecting information, but to hem in the defense and foreclose the full panoply of defense theories" and that "the prevailing process for seeking a cooperation agreement from federal prosecutors effectively may cripple a defendant who later chooses to exercise his trial option").

facts relevant to that calculation.[20] Such stipulations are obviously desirable from a defendant's point of view, as they provide much more predictability and control over the ultimate Guidelines calculation (although they almost never bind the court). In cases involving financial crimes, with substantial issues of restitution and/or forfeiture, the parties also may enter into stipulations about the precise amounts of money that the defendant will have to return to the victim(s) and/or pay to the government. (In Chapter 12, we discuss Guidelines stipulations in more detail in the context of non-cooperation plea agreements.)

(2) Defendant's obligations. The defendant will be obligated in very broad terms to tell the truth, to provide all information requested by the government, to meet with the government as requested, to testify in court if necessary, and to agree to postpone his or her sentencing until the cooperation is completed. Under the typical cooperation plea agreement, however, the defendant cannot withdraw his or her guilty plea once it has been entered.

(3) Government's obligations. If the government determines that the defendant has fulfilled his or her obligations under the agreement and provided "substantial assistance," its principal obligation is to make a 5K1.1 motion, advising the court of the nature and scope of the defendant's cooperation and triggering the court's legal authority to depart downward from both any statutory mandatory minimum prison term and the applicable Guidelines range. The government also agrees not to bring any additional charges related to any of the criminal activity that the defendant disclosed during the proffer session(s). On the other hand, if the government determines that the defendant has violated any provision of the agreement or has not provided "substantial assistance," the government is released from all of its obligations.

In determining whether to file the 5K1.1 motion, the prosecutor must act in good faith. As the Supreme Court has defined that test, the refusal to make the 5K1.1 motion on behalf of a defendant who has provided substantial assistance cannot be based on an unconstitutional motive, such as race or religion, or on "factors that are not rationally related to a legitimate Government end."[21] To obtain a hearing on the matter, the defendant must make a "substantial threshold showing" of bad faith.[22] It is necessary but not sufficient to demonstrate that assistance was provided. In response, all that the government need show is that it made a rational assessment of the cost and benefit that would flow from making the motion.[23] It is, therefore, unlikely that the defendant deprived of a 5K1.1 motion will prevail in the attempt to obtain judicial intervention.[24]

* * *

20. USSG § 6B1.4, p.s.

21. Wade v. United States, 504 U.S. 181, 186 (1992).

22. *Id*.

23. *Id*.

24. *But see, e.g.,* United States v. Wilson, 390 F.3d 1003, 1010–11 (7th Cir. 2004) (refusal to make 5K1.1 motion in order to

Once the "deal" is finalized between the parties, the defendant will appear in court and enter a plea of guilty to the agreed-upon charges. Only after the plea is entered do the cooperation agreement and relationship become formalized and enforceable. From that point forward, the defendant will assume all of his or her obligations as a cooperating defendant.[25]

§ 8.3   United States v. Santiago—The Cooperation Process

We turn now to the case of Gilbert Santiago who, having been arrested and charged with serious violations of the federal narcotics laws, faces perhaps the most important decision of all in his criminal case: whether, assuming the prosecutor cannot be talked out of bringing charges against him,[26] he should take the case to trial, plead guilty, or plead guilty and cooperate with the government. After exploring in detail the path that Santiago will have to follow here if he wishes to plead guilty and cooperate, we will return briefly to the case of Mario Long. Long, it will be recalled, began cooperating immediately upon his arrest, including making a recorded phone call to Santiago. For Long, then, while the same three options in theory remain, the decision to cooperate is a much more obvious and straight forward one.

§ 8.3(a)   The Defense Position

At this stage, Charles Berman, Santiago's lawyer, reviewed the complaint, interviewed his client, and had a discussion with AUSA Knapp about the case. Berman knew that just under 10 kilograms of cocaine had been seized. Santiago admitted to Berman his involvement with the intercepted shipment as well as his past involvement in moving and safeguarding close to 40 additional kilograms of cocaine in connection with shipments earlier in the year. Berman also was certain that Mario Long was cooperating with the government. Long would therefore be available to testify that Santiago had instructed him about handling the cocaine shipments. AUSA Knapp had told Berman about the taped telephone conversation between Santiago and Long, which provided further evidence of Santiago's involvement. Berman also knew that Santiago had a prior narcotics conviction, which could be used to prove his knowledge and intent if it were put in issue. Berman therefore concluded that if adequate sentencing concessions could be obtained, a guilty plea would be wise, since he believed it likely that Santiago would be convicted at trial.

avoid civil suit for unlawful imprisonment not rationally related to legitimate government interest).

25. It is an interesting and open question whether cooperating defendants' obligations under their cooperation-plea agreement survive past the time when they are ultimately sentenced. As a practical matter, this issue turns on an interpretation of the terms of the particular agreement, because in most cases they are written rather ambiguously on this point.

26. We discuss pre-charge and pre-indictment practice, including the crucial role of defense counsel in attempting to dissuade the prosecutor from bringing charges against his or client, in § 10.4(b).

Berman analyzed Santiago's sentence posture following a conviction as follows: a conviction for conspiracy to possess with intent to distribute more than 5 kilograms of cocaine would carry a 10 year mandatory minimum term of imprisonment with the possibility of an enhancement for being a second-time offender, which would raise the mandatory minimum sentence to 20 years.[27] The offense charged fell under the generic guideline dealing with possession and trafficking in narcotics.[28] The minimum quantity that would be used to calculate the base offense level under the Drug Quantity Table would be the nearly 10 kilograms that were seized. There was also a good chance that the prosecution already knew or eventually would learn that the total quantity of cocaine imported during Santiago's involvement in the conspiracy was just under 50 kilograms. These quantities of cocaine correspond to a base offense level of either 32 or 34, depending on whether the smaller or the larger amount is used as the basis for the calculation.

None of the specific offense characteristics under that offense were applicable in this case.[29] However, Santiago might be subject to an adjustment based upon how his "role in the offense" was evaluated.[30] Thus, he might seek a reduction of anywhere from 2 to 4 levels if he could establish that he played a minor or minimal role, but realistically Berman thought a 2 level adjustment for minor role would be the best he could do.[31] Although the government might seek to increase his Guidelines calculation by anywhere from 2 to 4 levels by arguing that he played the role of leader or organizer, Berman thought any such argument was unlikely to succeed.[32] Finally, if a plea agreement was reached sufficiently in advance of any trial, Santiago would get a 3 level reduction for acceptance of responsibility.[33] Santiago's likely total offense level with a straight plea was therefore between 27 and 31, depending on the quantity of drugs for which he was ultimately held responsible and whether and by how much his Guidelines calculation were adjusted for his role in the offense.[34]

Because Santiago had one prior narcotics conviction, for which he served more than one year in prison, he would receive 3 criminal history points.[35] Because he was still on supervised release from that sentence at the time of this new crime, 2 more points would be added to his criminal

---

27. 21 U.S.C. § 841(b)(1)(A).

28. USSG § 2D1.1.

29. Under USSG § 2D1.1, such factors include death or serious injury resulting from the offense, possession of a dangerous weapon during the commission of the offense, the use of an aircraft other than a regularly scheduled carrier and whether the defendant was a pilot of or otherwise operated any aircraft or vessel carrying a controlled substance.

30. USSG Ch. 3, Pt. B.

31. USSG § 3B1.2.

32. USSG § 3B1.1.

33. USSG § 3E1.1.

34. The total offense levels of 27 and 31 reflect Berman's calculations of best and worst case scenarios as follows: (1) Best—base offense level 32, less 2 levels for minor role, less 3 levels for acceptance of responsibility = 27; (2) Worst—base offense level 34, no reduction for role, less 3 levels for acceptance of responsibility = 31.

35. USSG § 4A1.1(a).

history score.[36] An additional one point would be added because he was released from prison less than 2 years before this new offense occurred.[37] With 6 criminal history points, he would fall into Criminal History Category III.

The sentencing table[38] therefore produced a range of 87–108 months in prison (or approximately 7 to 9 years) assuming an offense level of 27 or 135–168 months (approximately 11 to 14 years) assuming an offense level of 31, both in Criminal History Category III. There were three possible intermediate ranges between those high and low ranges, depending upon how the other issues noted above are resolved.

There is, however, a further complication in this case. As noted, the offenses with which Santiago was likely to be charged carry statutory mandatory minimum sentences, which supersede the Guidelines. Thus, even if the government did not seek an enhancement, the minimum statutory sentence of imprisonment would be 10 years, or 120 months, whereas the least severe Guidelines range sentence would be between 87–108 months. Since the statutory mandatory minimum sentence would exceed the minimum Guidelines range, the possibility of a lower minimum Guidelines range would be of no value. The sentence would simply be 120 months with, at best, a 15% reduction in his jail time for "good behavior."

Berman concluded that unless he could learn facts contradicting the government's evidence or giving rise to an affirmative defense such as entrapment or coercion, Santiago would be best advised to at least consider cooperation, since this was the only way in which he could avoid a lengthy mandatory minimum sentence.[39]

§ 8.3(b) The Government's Position

AUSA Knapp believed that she could readily prove Santiago's involvement in a cocaine importation and distribution conspiracy. Long, who had agreed to cooperate when he was first arrested, would offer testimony linking Santiago with the seized drugs, and that testimony would be corroborated by the taped telephone conversation between Long and Santiago. Santiago's prior narcotics conviction might also be used to prove knowledge and intent.[40] On the other hand, AUSA Knapp believed that Santiago was not the most culpable member of this conspiracy and that he could provide information implicating parties

---

36. USSG § 4A1.1(d).

37. USSG § 4A1.1(e).

38. *See supra* § 7.2(h).

39. Unfortunately for Santiago, because of his prior felony drug conviction, he would be ineligible for the so-called "safety valve," *see* § 3553(f) and USSG §§ 2D1.1(b)(7) & 5C1.2, which effectively removes the statutory mandatory minimum sentences and reduces the Guidelines by 2 levels for first-

time drug offenders who meet certain other conditions (including truthfully disclosing to the government all information and evidence concerning their offense and any closely related conduct). The safety valve is discussed further *infra* at § 8.5 in connection with Mario Long's guilty plea.

40. FED. R. EVID. 404(b). *See also* McCORMICK, § 190.

who were higher up in the chain in the importation scheme, facts that most prosecutors believed counseled strongly in favor of pursuing Santiago's cooperation.[41]

Knapp had leverage against Santiago because his conduct could be prosecuted under several provisions with varying sentencing implications. Her analysis was similar to Berman's. For example, she knew that because the case involved more than 5 kilograms of cocaine, Santiago could be charged under a subsection of 21 U.S.C. § 841 that prescribes a 10 year mandatory minimum sentence, with a statutory maximum sentence of up to life in prison.[42] Moreover, because Santiago had already been convicted of a felony narcotics offense, she also could charge him under the statute's enhancement provision for prior drug offenders, which carries a mandatory minimum sentence of 20 years.[43]

To encourage cooperation, Knapp decided to tell Santiago's lawyer that she was considering proceeding under the enhancement provision, with its 20 year minimum. She would indicate, however, that if Santiago gave accurate and useful information that she could use in pursuing cases against others, she would be prepared to forego the enhancement charge and would sign Santiago up to a cooperation-plea agreement. Under that agreement, he would be eligible for a government motion, or 5K1.1 letter, to allow his cooperation to be considered by the court as a basis for a downward departure at the time of his sentencing.[44] This would give the judge the power to go below both the statutory 10 year mandatory minimum prison term and to depart below the applicable range under the Guidelines. Knapp's personal evaluation was that Santiago's successful cooperation could turn a potential 20 year mandatory minimum prison sentence into a sentence of 5 years or less in jail.

Even if Santiago refused to cooperate, Knapp decided that she would forego the enhancement charge in return for Santiago's guilty plea. The plea would save the government the time and expense of a trial and Knapp felt that a mandatory minimum sentence of 10 years was adequate punishment given Santiago's relatively modest role in the cocaine importation scheme.[45] Of course, to maximize the chances that Santiago would cooperate, Knapp kept this thinking to herself for the time being.

---

41. Simons, *supra* note 9, at 15–16 (describing prosecutorial considerations regarding potential cooperating defendants).

42. § 841(b)(1)(A).

43. *Id.*; 21 U.S.C. § 851 (requiring the filing of a so-called "prior felony information" as a pre-condition to the imposition of enhanced penalties for prior felony drug offenders).

44. *See* § 3553(e); USSG § 5K1.1, p.s.

45. *See* John Ashcroft, Department Policy Concerning Charging Criminal Offenses,

Disposition of Charges, and Sentencing, 1B(5), *available at* http://news.findlaw. comhdocs/docs/doj/ashcroft92203chrgmem. pdf (Sept. 23, 2003) (authorizing federal prosecutors to "forego the filing of a statutory enhancement, but *only* in the context of a negotiated plea agreement," and "only after giving particular consideration to the nature, dates, and circumstances of the prior convictions, and the extent to which they are probative of criminal propensity").

§ 8.3(c) Beginning the Cooperation Process

Following a meeting with AUSA Knapp on January 24, 2005, and mindful of the importance of exploring the cooperation option early, Berman met with Santiago at the jail and counseled him regarding the available options. He discussed the evidence that he believed the government would present at trial. Berman told Santiago that in his view the risk of conviction at trial was substantial, that a 10 year mandatory minimum sentence was virtually certain to be imposed, and that a 20 year mandatory minimum sentence was a very real possibility. Even with a guilty plea, Berman explained, it was unlikely that Santiago could escape at least a 10 year mandatory minimum term of imprisonment. He added that the only way that the mandatory minimum could be avoided was acquittal at trial or if Santiago cooperated to the government's satisfaction.

Berman then told Santiago what the prosecution had offered. He explained that Santiago could cooperate, provide information, and possibly testify against others with whom he was involved in the drug trade. Assuming his cooperation was successful, the government would write a 5K1.1 letter to the sentencing judge explaining the cooperation, and that letter would allow the judge to reduce Santiago's sentence.

Berman cautioned Santiago that once he started down the path of cooperation, and admitted his guilt to the government, it would be very difficult to back out and take his case to trial.[46] Berman explained, while there were no guarantees, and while it would depend heavily on the particular judge assigned to handle Santiago's case, he believed there was a very good chance that, with successful cooperation, Santiago could serve 5 or even fewer years in jail.

By thus laying out the options without seeming to be endorsing cooperation, Berman is more likely to retain the trust of the defendant. Moreover, he is not usurping the defendant's decision as to whether or not to pursue a cooperation agreement. If a defendant is open to cooperation, the sentence reduction itself will usually do all the persuading that is necessary.

Berman's discussion of the risks also included the warnings that the government might conclude that Santiago was being untruthful or that the cooperation could fall apart for other reasons. Aside from the possibility of additional charges, Berman explained that Santiago surely would be in a far worse situation if he became a failed cooperator than if he had simply pled guilty without agreeing to cooperate. The government would be aware of additional crimes he committed and his statements at the proffer session could be used to impeach a contradictory position he may take at sentencing. This is an important part of the discussion because fully informed defendants are far better able than their lawyers to assess whether they will be able to successfully embrace

46. *See supra* § 8.1.

the truth and cooperate after what can be a lifetime of falling short of that standard. For this reason, the risk that even the most enthusiastic cooperator will far short is not insubstantial, and the consequences of such failure are great even for a defendant who has resigned to pleading guilty.

After listening to his options, Santiago told Berman he could not do 10 or 20 years in jail and said that he wanted to cooperate. Berman responded that he thought this was a sensible decision and asked Santiago to tell him about whom he might provide information, explaining that it would not be enough for Santiago simply to tell the government everything he knew. Instead, Berman explained, Santiago's information or testimony would actually have to help the government arrest or convict someone in order to maximize the chances that he would receive the full benefits of cooperation.[47] Santiago told Berman not to worry—that he had solid information about Christopher and, much to Berman's surprise, about a banker who had helped launder the proceeds of the cocaine importation scheme. Santiago said he would be willing to provide information and, if necessary, testify against both of these individuals.[48]

§ 8.3(d) Preparing for The Proffer Session

Satisfied that cooperation was both a prudent and viable path for Santiago, Berman called AUSA Knapp, told her Santiago wanted to cooperate, and scheduled a proffer session for later that week.

Prior to the proffer session, Berman went to the jail and met with Santiago a number of times to prepare. Berman explained to Santiago that he needed to persuade the government that they should allow him to cooperate. To do that Santiago had to be prepared to talk honestly and openly about a number of things. First, the government would require him to disclose the full extent of his own involvement in the cocaine importation scheme that the government was investigating. Berman emphasized that the government would assess Santiago's version of his

---

47. *See* United States v. Chaparro, 181 F.Supp.2d 323, 332 (S.D.N.Y. 2002) (explaining two principal requirements for receipt of a cooperation agreement: "1) truthful disclosure of your own criminal activity and that known to you in which others have engaged, and 2) a sufficient likelihood of being able to provide substantial assistance in the prosecution of others"); Simons, *supra* note 9, at 19–20 & nn.81–86 (explaining that "[w]hether cooperation will be considered 'substantial' varies from district to district and even from prosecutor to prosecutor," and noting that typically, merely providing information or "intelligence" is considered insufficient and "whether a cooperator's assistance is considered 'substantial' will often turn on whether the cooperation yields concrete results" (i.e., arrests, indictments and/or seizures)).

48. In extremely rare cases, prosecutors will enter into cooperation agreements with defendants who themselves cannot provide substantial assistance but who know someone (usually a relative or close friend) who can. So-called "third-party cooperation" can lead to a "substantial assistance" downward departure, but such departures are controversial, and the courts have limited their use. *Compare* United States v. Doe, 870 F.Supp. 702, 708 (E.D. Va. 1994), *with* United States v. Bush, 896 F.Supp. 424, 428 (E.D. Pa. 1995).

own role against what the government knew from its own sources and its own investigation. He advised Santiago to assume the government knew everything and that the reason for their questions was simply to determine if Santiago was prepared to truthfully admit what they already knew to be the case. He also warned Santiago not to make the mistake that he had seen many would-be cooperators make by attempting to minimize his own involvement or knowledge. He assured Santiago that such an approach likely would end with the prosecutor terminating the proffer session and refusing to offer a cooperation-plea agreement.

Berman also explained that the government would want to know not just about the almost 10 kilograms of cocaine they had intercepted, but about all other drug shipments that Santiago had been involved in or was aware of. He told Santiago he would have to speak openly and frankly about the involvement of other people, even close and trusted friends and business associates. And he explained that the government would want to know about any other crimes in Santiago's past, whether or not he had been arrested or charged, whether or not they were drug-related, and whether or not he viewed them as serious.[49]

Berman told Santiago that he had to overcome his reluctance to tell the government about things he thought they might not know or ever find out, explaining that in all likelihood they did know or would find out, and it was critical that they hear it from him first if he was to be a successful cooperator. He told Santiago that if he had concerns about his own safety or his family's safety, he should raise them during the proffer session.

Lastly, Berman questioned Santiago much in the way he anticipated AUSA Knapp would do so at the proffer session until he was satisfied that Santiago was prepared for his crucially important first proffer with the government.

§ 8.3(e) Santiago's Proffer Agreement and Statement

In the afternoon of January 25, 2005, Santiago was produced in AUSA Knapp's office, where he and Berman met with Knapp and Agent Martinez. Santiago was advised by the prosecutor of his right to remain silent and to be represented by counsel, and he also was reminded of the specific provisions of the proffer agreement, including in particular the circumstances under which his statements *could* be used if no cooperation agreement was reached.[50] Knapp advised Santiago that if he lied, she would terminate the proffer session and in all likelihood would refuse to speak to him again. On the other hand, she told Santiago, if she was

---

49. *See* John Gleeson, *Supervising Criminal Investigations: The Proper Scope of the Supervisory Power of Federal Judges,* 5 J.L. & Pol'y 423, 447–50 (1997) (explaining what prosecutors need and expect to get out of a proffer session and the critical role played by the defense attorney).

50. An inadequate explanation by the prosecutor of the uses to which proffer statements may be put has been held to preclude the government from later offering such statements. *See Lauersen,* 2000 WL 1693538 at *6–7.

satisfied that he had been forthcoming, and that the information provided by him was of the type that could help the government investigate and prosecute others, the government would enter into a cooperation-plea agreement.

Santiago and Berman were asked to sign the proffer agreement, acknowledging their agreement to all its terms and limitations. AUSA Knapp then began the interview, telling Santiago she expected him to provide all information he knew about the facts and circumstances surrounding the crimes charged, including both his own involvement and the involvement of others, and to explain any other facts raised by her or the case agents. Agent Martinez took notes and would later draft a report summarizing Santiago's remarks. The proffer agreement and report of Santiago's statement are reprinted below, followed by a brief description of a common type of problem that arises during proffers and how it was resolved.

_____

PROFFER AGREEMENT

With respect to the meeting of Gilbert Santiago ("Client") and his attorney, Charles Berman, Esq., with Laura Knapp of the United States Attorney's Office for the Eastern District of New York ("the Office"), and agents of the Drug Enforcement Administration, held at the offices of the United States Attorney for the Eastern District of New York on January 25, 2005 ("the meeting"), the following understandings exist:

(1)   **THIS IS NOT A COOPERATION AGREEMENT.** Client agrees to provide the Office with information, and to respond to questions, so that the Office may evaluate Client's information and responses in making prosecutorial decisions. By receiving Client's proffer, the Office does not agree to confer immunity, make a motion on Client's behalf, or enter into a cooperation agreement, plea agreement or non-prosecution agreement. The Office makes no representations about the likelihood that any such agreement will be reached in connection with this proffer.

(2)   In any prosecution brought against Client by the Office, except a prosecution for false statements, obstruction of justice, or perjury with respect to acts committed or statements made at or after the meeting, the Office will not offer in evidence any statements made by Client at the meeting (A) in its case-in-chief or (B) at sentencing. The Office may, to the extent it believes it is required by law, notify the Probation Department and the Court in connection with sentencing of any statements made by Client at the meeting. If such notification is made, the Office also will notify the Probation Department and the Court of the Office's agreement not to offer in evidence any such statements at sentencing.

(3)   Notwithstanding paragraph (2) above, the Office may use any statements made by Client: (A) to obtain leads to other evidence, which evidence may be used by the Office in any stage of a criminal prosecution (including but not limited to detention hearing, trial or sentencing), civil or administrative proceeding; (B) as substantive evidence to cross-examine Client, should Client testify; and (C) as substantive evidence to rebut, directly or indirectly, any evidence offered or elicited, or factual assertions made, by or on behalf of Client at any stage of a criminal prosecution (including but not limited to detention hearing, trial or sentencing).

(4)   It is further understood that this agreement is limited to the statements made by Client at the meeting and does not apply to any oral, written or recorded statements made by Client at any other time or to any other information provided at the meeting. Moreover, the provisions of Fed. R. Crim. P. 11(f) and Fed. R. Evid. 410 do not apply to any statements made by Client at the meeting, and Client shall not assert any claim under these or any other provisions of law that such statements or any leads therefrom should be suppressed.

(5) No understandings, promises, or agreements have been entered into with respect to the meeting other than those set forth in this agreement, and none will be entered into unless memorialized in writing and signed by all parties.

Dated: Brooklyn, New York
       January 25, 2005

KEVIN O'REILLY
United States Attorney
Eastern District of New York

By: _____
      Laura Knapp
      Assistant U.S. Attorney

I have read the entire agreement and discussed it with my attorney. I understand all of its terms and am entering into it knowingly and voluntarily.

_____
Gilbert Santiago
Client

_____
Charles Berman, Esq.
Attorney for Client

_____

U.S. Department of Justice
Drug Enforcement Administration

REPORT OF INVESTIGATION   Page 1 of 1

1. Program Code	2. Cross File	Related Files	3. File No.	4. G-DEP Identifier
5. By: Ralph Martinez At: Brooklyn DEA Office	☐ ☐ ☐ ☐ ☐		6. File Title Santiago Investigation	
7. ☐ Closed ☐ Requested Action Completed ☐ Action Requested By.			8. Date Prepared 1/25/05	
9. Other Officers Stuart Marth				

10. Report Re: Meeting with Gilbert Santiago

<u>DETAILS</u>

On January 25, 2005, myself and S/A Stuart Marth met with AUSA Laura Knapp, defendant Gilbert Santiago, and attorney Charles Berman at the offices of the United States Attorney for the Eastern District of New York in Brooklyn.

At the outset of the meeting, AUSA Knapp explained the proffer agreement in detail to Santiago, including the circumstances under which the government could and could not use any statements made during the proffer. Santiago indicated that he understood, he had discussed the agreement with his attorney, and he was ready to go forward. All the parties then signed the agreement.

Santiago stated that he was born in 1975 in Mexico and moved to the United States when he was 7 years old. He became a U.S. citizen in 1986. He grew up in Texas and moved to New York in 1997. In 1998 he was convicted on federal drug charges, sentenced to 5 years in prison and 3 years supervised release, and he finished serving his prison time in September, 2003.

Santiago first met William Van Ness about a month after he was released from prison. In the fall of 2003, he was looking for work and he applied for a job at Van Ness Trucking Company because he had heard that the owner was willing to take a chance on ex-cons. Van Ness hired him as a part time warehouse worker, but eventually he became the foreman.

Sometime in May 2004, Van Ness called Santiago into his office. He introduced him to Paul Christopher, who Van Ness said was his brother-in-law. Van Ness then left the office.

Christopher told Santiago that he understood that he had been in prison for cocaine trafficking. He said that he ran a company called International Food Distributors ("IFD"), which imported coffee and other foods from South America. He said that he had experienced serious financial problems and needed a loan. The banks had turned him down, and he thought that Santiago might be able to help him borrow money from some drug dealer. Christopher said that he knew that these dealers had cash which they could not deposit in a bank, and that he could work out a way to repay the loan with legitimate money. Christopher asked Santiago to put him in touch with the right people. Santiago said he would think about it.

Santiago thought about Christopher's request and decided to try to help him make a contact. Later that week he saw an old acquaintance named Frankie. He mentioned to Frankie that he knew a man who might be able to launder some money and Frankie told him that he thought it was crazy for a man on supervised release to get involved. Frankie offered to take care of Santiago's friend without involving Santiago, and said he knew a man who might be interested in this situation. Santiago said he knew Frankie was trying to take over whatever he might have going, but he saw the sense in Frankie's observation about his being on supervised release. Santiago only wanted to help Christopher out to stay on Van Ness' good side. So he told Christopher how to contact Frankie. He did not see Christopher for several months after that.

In early August, 2004, Christopher called and asked Santiago to come to his office. Christopher told him that he had received a loan of $50,000, and that the deal he had worked out was that he would accept delivery of 3 shipments of cocaine from Colombia, which Christopher would then deliver as instructed. The deliveries would be a month apart and, if successful, would satisfy the debt.

Christopher said that the August shipment, which had already been received, was the last of these three. However, he said that the lender had recently contacted him and told him that he wanted to enter an ongoing relationship with Christopher. He offered Christopher a percentage of the proceeds for each new shipment. Christopher told Santiago that he did not want to continue, but that the man had sounded very insistent, and Christopher was afraid to say no. He therefore decided to accept more shipments, if he could get some help figuring out how to run the operation and what to do with the cash it would generate. Christopher did not mention the name of the lender, and it was clear from the conversation that his identity was to remain secret.

They first talked about how much cash would be involved. Christopher told Santiago that each shipment contained between 9 and 10 kilos of cocaine, packed in a specially marked box that was otherwise indistinguishable from the rest of the shipment of coffee. The lender said that he would pay him $37,500 in cash per shipment. Christopher knew that any single cash bank deposit over $10,000 was governed by special reporting rules. He said that it would be necessary to set up several new business bank accounts and split each payment up among the accounts so that no single deposit equaled more than $10,000. Christopher also said that the deposits could be attributed to food sales on phony invoices which he would prepare.

Christopher asked Santiago to run this operation for him, setting up the bank accounts and making deposits, and supervising the receipt and distribution of the drugs. He said that he would put Santiago on the payroll of International Food Distributors, and pay him one-third of the proceeds from the drug operation. Santiago agreed.

A few days after that meeting, Santiago met Christopher at the Superior Warehouse, which Christopher owned. He was introduced to some of the workers as a new IFD vice-president. Christopher told the workers that they were to follow Santiago's instructions.

On about August 15, 2004, Santiago went to the Coney Island branch of CMS Bank. He met with a vice-president named Ernest Wagner, whom Christopher said had helped him with some business the year before. Santiago told Wagner that Christopher had sent him and that he wanted to open 5 new accounts, for 5 different businesses, all with the same two authorized signatures (his and Christopher's). Wagner asked him what those businesses would be involved with, and Santiago told him that they would be importing things from South America. Wagner asked if Santiago could be more specific, and Santiago said something like "You don't want to know anything more than that." Wagner indicated that he would be willing to provide personal service of the accounts, which Santiago took to be a hint that he wanted to receive extra money. Santiago said that he was certain something agreeable could be arranged.

Wagner then helped open the 5 accounts. Other than the name, all the information for each business account was exactly the same (address, officers, etc.). When they had finished all the paperwork, Santiago told Wagner that the businesses would be all cash, and that Christopher expects in total about $25,000 in cash profits per month (i.e., after deducting his own cut of $12,500 per shipment). Santiago also told him that he would bring about $25,000 in cash to be deposited into the accounts at the end of each month.

Santiago then explained that Christopher was eager to keep government regulators off his back, and asked if Wagner could help with that. Wagner said that any cash deposit greater than $10,000 would trigger a requirement that the bank file a report with the IRS disclosing, among other things, who deposited the money and on behalf of what business entity. Santiago asked if there was any way to avoid this; Wagner said that as long as the amount of profit earned by any single company was less than $10,000, and thus no single deposit was more $10,000, the reporting requirement would not be triggered. But, he added, it's illegal to "structure" or break up deposits into smaller amounts to avoid this reporting requirement. Santiago said great, and told him that because all the businesses were wholly owned by Christopher, he wouldn't care how much was deposited in each account.

In the beginning of September, Christopher told Santiago that another shipment was coming in. Santiago told him that neither of them should risk accepting delivery personally and asked if there was anyone Christopher really trusted among his employees. Christopher said that Mario Long, the warehouse foreman, was very loyal and trustworthy. Santiago suggested to Christopher that they not tell Long what was in the crates, but only how to handle them. Christopher subsequently told Long that he and Santiago had made a special deal for a very high priced shipment and that Long had to take very special care with some specially marked crates.

Christopher, Long and Santiago discussed how to handle the shipment and decided that Long would lock the crates in the security area of the warehouse and hold them there until Santiago had checked them and supervised their loading for delivery. Christopher had told Santiago that he had always used his brother-in-law's trucking company, Van Ness Trucking, and would do so for these shipments.

The September delivery went according to plan. After calling Long and learning that the shipment was in, Santiago went to the warehouse and personally inspected the crate in the security area. Santiago saw 10 sealed packages, wrapped in burlap. He poked a hole in 1 of the packages and tasted the powder, which he recognized as cocaine. He then taped the hole over and called Van Ness Trucking. He stayed at the warehouse until the Van Ness truck arrived. He loaded the crate onto the truck himself. After the truck drove off, he left the warehouse.

The next day he returned to the warehouse and saw Christopher. Christopher took him to his office, where he showed him a briefcase with $25,000 in cash to be deposited and $12,500 in cash in a bag for Santiago to keep for himself.

Each of the remaining deliveries—in October, November and December, 2004—went the same way, until the government intercepted the January, 2005, shipment.

Sometime during the fall, Santiago had called Christopher's cell phone and discussed something to do with one of the cocaine shipments. Santiago had written the cell phone number in his address book, which agents obtained from him at the time of his arrest.

Shortly after each of the 4 deliveries in September, October, November and December, Santiago would bring $25,000 in cash to Wagner at the bank. Wagner was always happy to see Santiago and told him he would "take care" of depositing the money. Each time Santiago saw him, he would smile and say something to the effect of: "No single business made more than $10,000, right?" Santiago always answered yes. In total, Santiago brought Wagner $100,000 in cash before the arrests in January. After the third delivery, at the end of November, Santiago gave Wagner an envelope containing a thank you card and $1,000 in cash, a gift from Christopher.

Santiago was asked about Barbara Weiss, a teller at CMS Bank whose card was found in his wallet at the time of his arrest. Santiago stated that Weiss once assisted him in depositing cash on a day that Wagner was unexpectedly absent from work. He said that he gave Weiss $100 for helping him.

Santiago stated that he did not at first discuss with Long the fact that the shipments contained cocaine, but eventually he did. After the first or second shipment that he was involved in, Long told him that he knew that they had to contain drugs, and that he wanted to be protected in case anything went wrong. Long and Santiago then discussed ways to assure that Long could safely deny any knowledge of the drug operation. Santiago did not pay anything to Long for his involvement, and he is not aware that Christopher did either.

Santiago did not discuss the cocaine shipments with anyone else at the warehouse. He does not know if anyone else knew of them. However, Long seemed to be close to one of the workers, Arthur Murphy, and when Santiago came to the warehouse to check on a shipment, Long and Murphy were always there, but the other workers were different each time. Santiago thought Murphy might have known about the cocaine, but he doubts that anyone else would have even become suspicious.

Santiago does not know where the shipments were delivered from the warehouse, nor the identity of the source of the cocaine. Christopher took care of that part of the business. They split things up that way because Christopher said that the source had told Christopher that if he ever saw anyone else, at any time, in any deal, he would immediately kill Christopher and whoever was with him. Santiago took the threat seriously enough not to ask any questions about who might be paying them.

Santiago stated that he never discussed cocaine or money laundering with Van Ness either prior to or after his first meeting with Christopher. He assumed that Van Ness knew what was being discussed, but Van Ness never told him that. Santiago never told Van Ness about the contact which he had made for Christopher.

11. Distribution:
    Division
 	
    District
	12. Signature (Agent)
	
	Ralph Martinez
		13. Date 1/25/05

	14. Approved (Named and Title)	15. Date 1/25/05

DEA Form   -6
(Jul. 1996)

DEA SENSITIVE
Drug Enforcement Administration

While the DEA agent's report reads quite smoothly, in fact the typical first proffer session is not uncommonly interrupted as the two sides confer. In Santiago's case, there was a point toward the end of the interview, after Santiago had explained what he knew (and didn't know) about Van Ness' role, when Knapp and Agent Martinez stopped the discussion and excused themselves. After conferring outside of Santiago's presence, they returned to the interview room and pressed Santiago about whether he might be concealing something with respect to Van Ness. At that point Santiago's attorney, Berman, asked to speak to Santiago alone, and did so. He told Santiago that Knapp and Martinez were obviously concerned about Van Ness' involvement in the conspiracy, and that if Santiago was withholding information in an effort to protect Van Ness, it was not in his interest to do so. Santiago said he was telling the truth and that he was not in a position to further implicate Van Ness. When the parties reconvened, Santiago said he guessed Christopher would have told his brother-in-law what was going on, but Christopher and Van Ness never talked about the contents of the shipments in his presence, and to Santiago's knowledge Van Ness never saw what was concealed inside of the crates.

Following the interview, Knapp and Martinez discussed what they had learned and what they thought of Santiago. Ultimately, they shared the view that Santiago was being truthful, would make a good witness against Christopher and possibly Wagner, and had given the government some leads to follow on Van Ness. They agreed that the government wanted his cooperation.

Knapp then advised Berman and Santiago that the government would accept a plea to a charge of conspiracy to possess more than 5 kilograms of cocaine with the intent to distribute—with a statutory mandatory minimum jail term of 10 years—and would forego the sentencing enhancement provision. Knapp also explained to Berman that while Santiago had admitted to acts involving a bank that made him guilty of other crimes (such as money laundering), the government would not require him to plead guilty to any additional crimes, since they had only learned about them through Santiago's candid admissions. AUSA Knapp told Berman that assuming the cooperation amounted to substantial assistance in the prosecution of others, as they expected the government would file a 5K1.1 downward departure motion, allowing the judge to sentence Santiago below the 10 year mandatory minimum and also to depart downward from the Sentencing Guidelines range. The agreement would be formalized in a standard cooperation-plea agreement.

Berman then met again privately with Santiago and presented the government's proposal, which he said he believed was the best deal the government would offer under the circumstances and provided the best hope of a sentence below the statutory mandatory minimums. Santiago told Berman that he had given it a lot of thought, and that while he never imagined "giving up" his friends, he felt he had no choice but to go forward with the cooperation by pleading guilty. Santiago requested that Berman ask the government to consent to his being released on bail until he was sentenced. Berman said he would make the request but told Santiago he thought the government was unlikely to agree. Santiago and Berman agreed that Santiago would go forward with the cooperation regardless of whether the government consented to bail.

Berman then informed AUSA Knapp of Santiago's decision, and they agreed that she would draft a cooperation-plea agreement and a charging instrument and they would then schedule Santiago's guilty plea. Berman raised the issue of bail, and Knapp replied that, because of the nature of the case, the relevant law required that Santiago be kept in custody once he entered his plea of guilty, unless there were "exceptional reasons" not to do so.[51] Knapp explained that because Santiago's information was almost entirely about historical facts (i.e., drug shipments and bank transactions that already had taken place), there was no need for Santiago to be out on bail to cooperate. Moreover, because even with successful cooperation he would almost surely be sentenced to some term of imprisonment, she could not think of any reason that made this case an "exceptional" one. Berman said he understood and that Santiago was prepared to plead guilty and cooperate whether he could be released on bail or not.

§ 8.3(f) Santiago's Cooperation–Plea Agreement

It will be seen that in the attached agreement care is taken to protect the government's case. Thus, the agreement is worded in a way best suited to withstand the expected cross-examination of the cooperating defendant at trial suggesting that he or she has a reason to falsely incriminate others in order to earn the coveted 5K1.1 letter and a

---

51. *See* 18 U.S.C. § 3143(a)(2) (requiring detention upon entry of a plea of guilty or a jury finding of guilt in certain categories of cases, including narcotics cases carrying a statutory maximum penalty of 10 years or more, except where, *inter alia*, there is a "substantial likelihood" the conviction will not stand or where the government has recommended that no term of imprisonment be imposed); 18 U.S.C. § 3145(c) (setting forth "exceptional reasons" exception to mandatory remand under § 3143(a)(2)).

downward departure. The agreement emphasizes that the defendant must "at all times give truthful, complete and accurate information and testimony" and not commit any further crimes. If and only if the defendant meets these and the other requirements of the agreement, the government promises to make a 5K1.1 motion, recounting the defendant's cooperation and allowing the court to reduce the sentence. And the agreement explicitly notes that the government will not recommend a specific sentence to the court and cannot promise what the ultimate sentence will be.

But the agreement also states that if the defendant fails to fulfill any of his obligations—e.g., if the defendant lies or testifies falsely—the government will be released from its obligation to file the 5K1.1 letter (and thus the defendant will lose his best chance for a lower sentence). In addition, in the event he violates the agreement, the defendant can be prosecuted for any offenses he may have committed, including crimes he may have admitted during the course of his proffer session or cooperation, and the government would be free to use against him any statements he may have made along the way. In short, what the government hopes by the terms of the agreement to convey to the cooperating defendant (and to a jury hearing the cooperator's testimony) is that the only way to earn a lower sentence is to tell the truth.

Consistent with practice in the Eastern District of New York, there is no Guidelines stipulation accompanying this agreement. (Such stipulations will be discussed in Chapter 12, concerning negotiations in non-cooperator cases.[52]) However, from his discussions with Knapp, Berman understood that the base offense level would be 34, based on Santiago's disclosure of the additional shipments of cocaine, and that he (Berman) could argue, although the government would not agree, that Santiago was entitled to 2 levels off for "minor role." The parties thus understood that, with 3 levels off for acceptance of responsibility, Santiago was facing a Guidelines sentencing range of imprisonment of either 108 to 135 months or 135 to 168 months, depending on whether Berman prevailed on the "minor role" argument. This range was, of course, subject to reduction in the event of successful cooperation and a 5K1.1 motion by the government.

52. *See infra* § 12.2.

UNITED STATES DISTRICT COURT
EASTERN DISTRICT OF NEW YORK

- -

UNITED STATES OF AMERICA)	<u>COOPERATION AGREEMENT</u>
)	
)	
- against -)	CR-05M-0063 (WS)
)	
GILBERT SANTIAGO,)	
)	
Defendant.)	
)	

- -

Pursuant to Rule 11 of the Federal Rules of Criminal Procedure, the United States Attorney's Office for the Eastern District of New York (the "Office") and GILBERT SANTIAGO (the "defendant") agree to the following:

1.   The defendant will waive indictment and plead guilty to a one count criminal information, charging a violation of 21 U.S.C. § 846. The count carries the following statutory penalties:

    1.   Maximum term of imprisonment: life
           (21 U.S.C. § 841(b)(1)(A)(ii)(II)).

    2.   Minimum term of imprisonment: 10 years
           (21 U.S.C. § 841(b)(1)(A)(ii)(II)).

    3.   Minimum supervised release term: 5 years, to follow any term of imprisonment; maximum supervised release term: life, to follow any term of imprisonment; if a condition of release is violated, the defendant may be sentenced to up to 4 years without credit for pre-release imprisonment or time previously served on post-release supervision.
           (18 U.S.C. § 3583(e); 21 U.S.C. § 841(b)(1)(A)(ii)(II)).

    4.   Maximum fine: $4,000,000
           (21 U.S.C. § 841(b)(1)(A)(ii)(II)).

    5.   Restitution: N/A
           (18 U.S.C. § 3663).

    6. $100 special assessment.
           (18 U.S.C. § 3013).

7.   Other penalties: n/a[53]

2.   The defendant understands that although imposition of a sentence in accordance with the United States Sentencing Guidelines (the "Guidelines") is not mandatory, the Guidelines are advisory and the Court is required to consider any applicable Guidelines provisions as well as other factors enumerated in 18 U.S.C. § 3553(a) to arrive at an appropriate sentence in this case.[54]   The Office will advise the Court and the Probation Department of information relevant to sentencing, including all criminal activity engaged in by the defendant, and such information may be used by the Court in determining the defendant's sentence.   Based on information known to it now, the Office will not oppose a downward adjustment of 3 levels for acceptance of responsibility under U.S.S.G. §3E1.1.   The defendant stipulates that his sentence should be calculated based on a drug type and quantity of at least 5 kilograms of cocaine and waives any right to a jury trial in connection with such issue.[55]

3.   The defendant will provide truthful, complete and accurate information and will cooperate fully with the Office.   This cooperation will include, but is not limited to, the following:

a.   The defendant agrees to be fully debriefed and to attend all meetings at which his presence is requested, concerning his participation in and knowledge of all criminal activities.

b.   The defendant agrees to furnish to the Office all documents and other material that may be relevant to the investigation and that are in the defendant's possession or control and to participate in undercover activities pursuant to the specific instructions of law enforcement agents or this Office.

c.   The defendant agrees not to reveal his cooperation, or any information derived therefrom, to any third party without prior consent of the Office.

---

[53] The most common "other penalty" is deportation, in the case of a defendant who, unlike Gilbert Santiago, is not a U.S. citizen. *See* 8 U.S.C. § 1182(a)(2).

[54] This lanuage reflects the Supreme Court's decision in *Booker*, which rendered the Guidelines advisory.

[55] The quantity of 5 kilograms is the minimum required to trigger the 10 year statutory mandatory minimum term of imprisonment.   Under the Supreme Court's decision in *Apprendi v. New Jersey,* 530 U.S. 466 (2000), and its progeny, *e.g.,* United States v. Thomas, 274 F.3d 655, 660 (2d Cir. 2001), drug quantity is considered an element of the offense to the extent that it increases the statutory maximum penalty, and it therefore must be charged in the indictment and submitted to the jury.   *See also* United States v. Jordan, 291 F.3d 1091, 1095 (9th Cir. 2002).

    d.   The defendant agrees to testify at any proceeding in the Eastern District of New York or elsewhere as requested by the Office.

    e.   The defendant consents to adjournments of his sentence as requested by the Office.

4.   The Office agrees that:

    a.   Except as provided in paragraphs 1, 8, and 9, no criminal charges will be brought against the defendant for his heretofore disclosed participation in criminal activity involving (i) possession with intent to distribute, distribution and importation of narcotics, and conspiracy to do the same, and (ii) laundering of the proceeds of narcotics trafficking, all from the period May 1, 2004 through January 13, 2005.[56]

    b.   No statements made by the defendant during the course of this cooperation will be used against him except as provided in paragraphs 2, 8, and 9.

5.   The defendant agrees that the Office may meet with and debrief him without the presence of counsel, unless the defendant specifically requests counsel's presence at such debriefings and meetings. [57]

6.   If the Office determines that the defendant has cooperated fully, provided substantial assistance to law enforcement authorities and otherwise complied with the terms of this agreement, the Office will file a motion pursuant to U.S.S.G. § 5K1.1 and 18 U.S.C. § 3553(e) with the sentencing Court setting forth the nature and extent of his cooperation. Such a motion will permit the Court, in its discretion, to impose a sentence below any applicable mandatory minimum sentence and also to depart downward below the applicable Sentencing Guidelines range. In this connection, it is understood that a good faith determination by the Office as to whether the defendant has

---

[56] Although Santiago is agreeing to plead guilty to only one charge, conspiracy to possess with intent to distribute cocaine, this "coverage" portion of his cooperation-plea agreement is drafted broadly to cover all charges that could conceivably be brought against him based on the full scope of conduct to which he admitted during his proffer. Without such broad coverage, Santiago theoretically could later be prosecuted for different crimes based on his same admitted conduct even if his cooperation was successful. Note also that the document does not address the government's agreement to forego the filing of a "prior felony information" —which, as noted above, would double Santiago's statutory mandatory minimum sentence— as no such filing can be effective unless completed prior to the entry of the guilty plea. *See* 18 U.S.C. § 851(a)(1).

[57] *See* United States v. Ming He, 94 F.3d 782, 792-93 (2d Cir. 1996) (asserting that "cooperating witnesses are entitled to have counsel present at debriefings, unless they explicitly waive such assistance"). *See also* Gleeson, *supra* note 49, at 456-458 (discussing how the right created in *Ming He* has been undermined by a practice in the Second Circuit of incorporating a blanket waiver provision into the cooperation agreement).

cooperated fully and provided substantial assistance and has otherwise complied with the terms of this agreement, and the Office's good faith assessment of the value, truthfulness, completeness and accuracy of the cooperation, shall be binding upon him. The defendant agrees that, in making this determination, the Office may consider facts known to it at this time. The Office will not recommend to the Court a specific sentence to be imposed. Further, the Office cannot and does not make a promise or representation as to what sentence will be imposed by the Court.

7.   The defendant agrees that with respect to all charges referred to in paragraphs 1 and 4(a) he is not a "prevailing party" within the meaning of the "Hyde Amendment," Section 617, P.L. 105-119 (Nov. 26, 1997), and will not file any claim under that law.[58] The defendant waives any right to additional disclosure from the government in connection with the guilty plea.[59] The defendant agrees to pay the special assessment by check payable to the Clerk of the Court at or before sentencing.[60]

8.   The defendant must at all times give complete, truthful, and accurate information and testimony, and must not commit, or attempt to commit, any further crimes. Should it be judged by the Office that the defendant has failed to cooperate fully, has intentionally given false, misleading or incomplete information or testimony, has committed or attempted to commit any further crimes, or has otherwise violated any provision of this agreement, the defendant will not be released from his plea of guilty but this Office will be released from its obligations under this agreement, including (a) not to oppose a downward adjustment of 3 levels for acceptance of responsibility described in paragraph 2 above, and (b) to file the motion described in paragraph 6 above. Moreover, this Office may withdraw the motion described in paragraph 6 above, if such motion has been filed prior to sentencing. The defendant will also be subject to prosecution for any federal criminal violation of which the Office has knowledge, including, but not limited to, the criminal activity described in paragraph 4 above, perjury and obstruction of justice.

---

[58] *See* 18 U.S.C. § 3006A. The Hyde Amendment allows a criminal defendant who prevails against the government's charges to recover attorney's fees where the government's conduct has been "vexatious, frivolous, or in bad faith." *See, e.g.,* United States v. Bunn, 215 F.3d 430, 436 (4th Cir. 2000); United States v. Schneider, 289 F. Supp. 2d 328, 331 (E.D.N.Y. Nov. 3, 2003).

[59] Until 2002 it was assumed that the defendant's right to exculpatory evidence under *Brady v. Maryland,* 373 U.S. 83 (1963), and its progeny discussed *infra* at § 13.3, applied to the decision to plead guilty. However, in *United States. v. Ruiz,* 536 U.S. 622, 633 (2002), the Supreme Court held that the *Brady* rule is designed to assure a fair trial, a right that is waived by the defendant's decision to plead guilty. *Ruiz* involved the failure of the government to provide impeachment material, a category of favorable evidence within the *Brady* rule, *see* Giglio v. United States, 405 U.S. 150 (1972). Cases following *Ruiz,* however, make clear that the principle underlying *Ruiz* is not limited to impeachment material. *See, e.g.,* United States v. Le, 306 F. Supp. 2d 589, 591-92 (E.D. Va. 2004). *But see* McCann v. Mangialardi, 337 F.3d 782, 787-88 (7th Cir. 2003) (*Ruiz* does not permit government to withhold evidence of actual innocence).

[60] 18 U.S.C. § 3013(a)(2)(A) imposes a $100 special assessment for each felony count of conviction.

9.   Any prosecution resulting from the defendant's failure to comply with the terms of this agreement may be premised upon, among other things: (a) any statements made by the defendant to the Office or to other law enforcement agents on or after January 25, 2005; (b) any testimony given by him before any grand jury or other tribunal, whether before or after the date this agreement is signed by the defendant; and (c) any leads derived from such statements or testimony. . . . Furthermore, the defendant waives all claims under the United States Constitution, Rule 11(f) of the Federal Rules of Criminal Procedure, Rule 410 of the Federal Rules of Evidence, or any other federal statute or rule, that statements made by him on or after January 25, 2005, or any leads derived therefrom, should be suppressed.

10.   This agreement does not bind any federal, state, or local prosecuting authority other than the Office, and does not prohibit the Office from initiating or prosecuting any civil or administrative proceedings directly or indirectly involving the defendant.

11.   No promises, agreements or conditions have been entered into other than those set forth in this agreement, and none will be entered into unless memorialized in writing and signed by all parties. This agreement supersedes any prior promises, agreements or conditions between the parties. To become effective, this agreement must be signed by all signatories listed below.

Dated: Brooklyn, New York
        January 30, 2005

                        KEVIN O'REILLY
                        United States Attorney
                        Eastern District of New York

By: _Laura Knapp_
                        Laura Knapp
                        Assistant United States Attorney

Approved by:
                        Nisha Bandhi
                        Supervising Assistant U.S. Attorney

I have read the entire agreement and discussed it with my attorney. I understand all of its terms and am entering into it knowingly and voluntarily.

                        Gilbert Santiago
                        Gilbert Santiago
                        Defendant

Approved by:

                        Charles Berman
                        Charles Berman, Esq.
                        Counsel to Defendant

§ 8.4   Drafting the Formal Charges—Waiver of Indictment and Information

The Fifth Amendment requires that any felony charge be presented to and approved by a grand jury,[62] a process that culminates in an indictment.[63] This process is described in detail in Chapter 11.

As Gilbert Santiago's cooperation-plea agreement makes clear, however, Santiago waived his constitutional right to have his case presented to a grand jury, agreeing instead to plead guilty to a one count "information" reproduced below. The information, or "prosecutor's information," is a charging instrument indistinguishable in form from an indictment, except that it alleges charges by the United States Attorney rather than the grand jury. The information in this case charges Santiago with conspiracy to possess 5 kilograms or more of cocaine with intent to distribute, as agreed by the parties. The waiver executed by Santiago and the information prepared by the United States Attorney's Office follow.

UNITED STATES DISTRICT COURT
EASTERN DISTRICT OF NEW YORK

- -

UNITED STATES OF AMERICA)	**WAIVER OF INDICTMENT**
)	
)	
v.)	05 Cr. 735(WS)
)	
GILBERT SANTIAGO ,)	
)	
Defendant.)	
)	

- -

Having been duly informed of my right to a grand jury indictment, and having been informed of the charges against me in open court, I hereby waive my right to grand jury review and indictment and agree to proceed by way of a prosecutor's information.

Gilbert Santiago
Gilbert Santiago

Brooklyn, New York
February 25, 2005

---

62.   U.S.Const. amend. V.

63.   Fed.R.Crim.P. 7(a).

174

UNITED STATES DISTRICT COURT
EASTERN DISTRICT OF NEW YORK

- -

UNITED STATES OF AMERICA)	**INFORMATION**
)	
v.)	05 Cr. 735 (WS)
)	
GILBERT SANTIAGO,)	
)	
Defendant.)	
)	

- -

The United States Attorney Charges:

In or about and between May 2004 and January 13, 2005, both dates being approximate and inclusive, within the Eastern District of New York, Gilbert Santiago, together with others, did knowingly and intentionally conspire to possess with intent to distribute 5 kilograms or more of cocaine, a Schedule I controlled substance, in violation of Title 21, United States Code, Section 841(a).

(Title 21, United States Code, Sections 846 and 841(b)(1)(A); Title 18, United States Code, Sections 3551 *et. seq.*[64])

Kevin O'Reilly
Kevin O'Reilly
United States Attorney

---

64. The citations are to the Title 21 statutory provisions that make conspiracy to possess with intent to distribute cocaine a felony, and to the Title 18 statutory provisions governing the sentencing for such a felony.

It can be seen that the language of the single count is similar to that of the gravamen paragraph of the complaint—essentially, it tracks the elements of the offense. There are also certain basic facts recited, including in what district and approximately when the crime is alleged to have occurred and the nature and amount of the drugs. Totally absent, however, are details as to how the government knows of these allegations, specifically when and where the criminal activity occurred, and the reliability of the information that supports the allegations. The information, like an indictment, will be measured only on the basis of whether a crime is charged and whether the defendant has adequate notice of the acts alleged to have been committed.[65]

§ 8.5   United States v. Mario Long—The Cooperation–Plea Agreement

Mario Long began to assist the government in the hours after his arrest, as we saw in Chapter 2. By the time counsel was appointed at the initial appearance, AUSA Knapp was already prepared to offer a cooperation-plea to Long, whom she evaluated to be a minor player whose testimony would be valuable to the government. After Long's release on bail, his cooperation developed in the same manner as Gilbert Santiago's. A proffer session was conducted on January 27, 2005, in a manner similar to the Santiago proffer session. Long's factual proffer was consistent with Santiago's version of events. However, based on her review of Long's somewhat equivocal admissions to the agents at the time of his arrest, Knapp wanted to make sure he was clearly admitting he knew there was cocaine or some illegal narcotic in the crates before she agreed to let him cooperate. When she pushed him on this during the proffer, Long confessed that he in fact knew it was cocaine. However, Long insisted that he never told Arthur Murphy about the nature of the shipments. Long said that as far as he knew, Murphy neither knew nor had reason to know that any illegal narcotics were being distributed through the warehouse. By the end of the proffer, Knapp found Long to be a credible witness whose version of the events was consistent with other information she knew about the case.

---

65. This is the simplest form of charging instrument. In many instances, the instrument will be far more descriptive of the facts and circumstances of the crime. A complex indictment is illustrated in Chapter 11.

Long's counsel and AUSA Knapp negotiated a cooperation-p[ ]
agreement similar to Santiago's, with two important differences. First,
because Long played such a small or "minor" role in the shipments,
Knapp agreed that he was entitled to a 2–level reduction in his Guidelines calculation.[66] In addition, because Long had no criminal history
other than this arrest, and because Knapp believed he had truthfully
disclosed all that he knew about the cocaine importation scheme, Knapp
also agreed that Long was entitled to an additional 2–level reduction of
his Guidelines under the so-called "safety valve" provision.[67] By qualifying for the "safety valve," Long also would escape any statutory mandatory minimums, which in his case meant the 10 year mandatory minimum that otherwise would have been required under his plea of guilty.
Indeed, by qualifying for the "safety valve" Long was guaranteed that
the 10–year statutory minimum would not apply to him irrespective of
whether his cooperation ultimately was successful and irrespective of
whether he received a 5K1.1 letter. In sum, the government's estimate of
Long's Guidelines calculation was a level 27 (base offense level of 34, 2
levels off for minor role, 3 levels off for acceptance of responsibility, and
2 levels off for safety valve), carrying a suggested prison term of between
70 and 87 months (in Criminal History Category I), significantly shorter
than the government's estimate of the sentence faced by Santiago. And
of course, if Long successfully cooperated and received a 5K1.1 letter
from the government, his sentence almost certainly would be even
shorter.

As part of his cooperation-plea agreement, Long agreed to plead
guilty to a one-count information identical to Santiago's.

Having agreed to enter into these cooperation-plea agreements,
Santiago and Long were ready to appear in court to formally enter their
pleas of guilty, a subject to which we turn in the next chapter.

§ 8.6 United States v. Arthur Murphy

AUSA Knapp decided that she would move to dismiss the charges
against Arthur Murphy, against whom the evidence was weak, especially
in view of the fact that neither Long nor Santiago would testify that
Murphy knew about the narcotics. There was other evidence that Murphy did know (e.g., Santiago's statement on the recorded telephone
conversation with Long that Murphy should be reminded to say nothing), but it was fairly weak and could only be adduced by challenging the
testimony of the two cooperating witnesses whom the government gener-

---

66. USSG § 3B1.2(b).   **67.** *See supra* note 39.

ally thought were being truthful. In any case, Knapp did not believe that Murphy's testimony would add anything to her case against Christopher or Van Ness. Accordingly, Knapp filed a motion seeking the court's approval for dismissing the criminal complaint against Murphy without prejudice to refiling at a later date. The motion was granted and Murphy and his counsel were notified that the criminal charges had been dismissed and that his bail bond and conditions of release were no longer in effect.

Chapter 9

THE GUILTY PLEA PROCEEDING

Table of Sections

Sec.
9.0   Introduction.
9.1   Pleading Alternatives Under Rule 11.
9.2   The Plea Agreement Process.
      9.2(a) Negotiations Between the Parties.
      9.2(b) Consideration of the Plea Agreement By the Court.
      9.2(c) The Plea Allocution.
9.3   Counsel in the Guilty Plea Process—Providing Effective Assistance.
9.4   The Entry of the Guilty Plea in United States v. Santiago.
9.5   The Entry of the Guilty Plea in United States v. Long Case.

_____

§ 9.0 Introduction

Resolution of criminal cases by a negotiated plea of guilty has been a prominent and increasingly significant feature of American criminal justice since the middle of the 19th Century.[1] Throughout much of this period, the practice was not openly acknowledged, largely because of concern that offering defendants inducements to give up their Sixth Amendment rights was constitutionally suspect. In a series of cases beginning in 1970 with *Brady v. United States*,[2] the Supreme Court laid that concern to rest. There, the Court held that a defendant who accepted the promise of a sentence less than he might receive after conviction at trial was not "compelled" to give up his right to trial. Later, in *Bordenkircher v. Hayes*,[3] the Court made it clear that such an inducement, no matter how extreme, would almost never be considered coercive.[4] Negotiated pleas were, in fact, to be encouraged,[5] so long as the

_____

1. Mike McConville and Chester L. Mirsky, Jury Trials and Plea Bargaining (Hart Publishing 2005).

2. 397 U.S. 742 (1970). *See also* MOORE, § 611.06.

3. 434 U.S. 357 (1978).

4. The defendant was told that if he did not plead guilty in return for a 5 year sentence he would be reindicted under the Habitual Criminal Statute, and sentenced

defendant was adequately represented;[6] steps were taken to assure that the plea was a knowing and intelligent decision; and the promised benefit was delivered.[7] And in *North Carolina v. Alford*,[8] the court approved of the practice of allowing a defendant to plead guilty even if he denied his guilt, so long as there was a factual basis for the plea.[9]

As the constitutional parameters of the guilty plea process became clear, the Federal Rules of Criminal Procedure were periodically amended, most recently in 2002. Rule 11 provides detailed regulation of the guilty plea process, adding a considerable number of provisions that go beyond that which the courts have required. But it has not been amended following *Booker*, and thus the application of certain of its provisions is less clear, as we note in the sections that follow.

§ 9.1   Pleading Alternatives Under Rule 11

Rule 11(a) states that the available pleas are not guilty; guilty; or *nolo contendere*.[10] Rule 11(a) also permits a conditional plea. With the consent of the court and the government, a defendant may enter such a plea in cases in which there has been a decision adverse to the defendant on a pretrial motion—commonly a motion to suppress evidence—that the defendant wishes to appeal. If the adverse decision is reversed, the defendant is then permitted to withdraw the guilty plea, and would do so if the reversal significantly affected the strength of the government's case at trial. The purpose of the rule is to avoid the necessity of holding a

---

to life in prison. The defendant refused to plead, and the prosecutor carried out his threat, admitting that he did so solely because the defendant had insisted on going to trial. The Court characterized these events as the "give and take negotiation . . . between the prosecution and defense, which arguably possess relatively equal bargaining power." *Bordenkircher*, 434 U.S. at 362 (quoting Parker v. North Carolina, 397 U.S. 790, 809 (1970)). *See also* Moore, § 611.07.

5. Santobello v. New York, 404 U.S. 257, 260 (1971). *See also* James Cissell, 1 Federal Criminal Trials § 6–2 (6th ed. 2003).

6. McMann v. Richardson, 397 U.S. 759, 770 (1970). The defendant must show that counsel's assistance is not "within the range of competence demanded of attorneys in criminal cases." *Id.* at 771; *accord* Hill v. Lockhart, 474 U.S. 52, 56, 59 (1985) (same, and examining whether there was a reasonable probability that without the error, defendant would not have pleaded guilty). *See* 1 Mark. J. Kadish et al., Criminal Law Advocacy § 15.04 (2004).

7. *Santobello*, 257 U.S. at 261–62; Kadish et al., *supra note 6*, § 5.05.

8. 400 U.S. 25 (1970).

9. For a general discussion of the law of plea negotiation, see LaFave et al., ch. 21.

10. *Nolo contendere* is the equivalent of admitting guilt while also allowing for denial of guilt in other contexts. It is a rarely exercised plea, a result of a strong Justice Department policy opposing *nolo contendere* pleas, except in extraordinary cases. U.S. Attorneys' Manual § 9–16.010. A *nolo* plea has all of the implications of a guilty plea in terms of punishment, but avoids some of the civil consequences. It is most commonly used in criminal antitrust cases. Since treble damages can be imposed only after a plea of guilty, the defendant entering a *nolo contendere* plea would still have the opportunity to contest the imposition of treble damages in a civil action. *See* LaFave et al., § 21.4(a). The *nolo contendere* plea should be distinguished from the so-called *Alford* plea, which involves a defendant pleading guilty without admitting guilt.

trial for the primary purpose of giving the defendant standing to appeal the decision on the pretrial motion.[11]

§ 9.2 The Plea Agreement Process[12]

Rule 11 envisions a three stage process leading up to the court's acceptance of a guilty plea: (1) negotiation between the parties; (2) consideration of the plea agreement by the court; and (3) allocution of the defendant prior to the entry of the plea.

§ 9.2(a) Negotiations Between the Parties

Rule 11 provides that plea negotiations take place exclusively between the prosecution and defense; the court is not permitted to be involved.[13] This is because a question of fundamental fairness is raised by the prospect of pitting the negotiating power of the judge against that of the defendant, a situation that is viewed as inherently coercive.[14] Violations of this rule have been found where the judge discusses the penal consequences of pleading guilty;[15] when the judge urges the defendant to plead guilty, even if objectively it appears to be the wisest choice;[16] and when the judge attempts to amend a plea agreement reached by the parties.[17] When a violation is found, the defendant is permitted to withdraw the guilty plea.[18]

In order to encourage defendants to engage in plea negotiations, Rule 11 prohibits the use in any proceeding of a defendant's statements made in the course of plea negotiations (including a defendant's attorney's statements) and of the fact that a guilty plea was entered and later withdrawn.[19]

Rule 11(c) permits both charge and sentence bargaining. Charge bargaining occurs when the government binds itself either to move to

11. FED. R. CRIM. P. 11(a)(2), advisory committee's note; WRIGHT, § 175.

12. The discussion that follows is based on the assumption that there will be some kind of negotiation between the prosecution and the defense prior to the defendant's decision to plead guilty. Of course, there is no legal requirement for such negotiation; a defendant is free to plead guilty to all of the charges against him or her, without obtaining any assurance from the prosecution or the court that the decision will be beneficial. While guilty pleas of this sort no doubt occur, they are so rare that no further discussion of them is warranted.

13. FED. R. CRIM. P. 11(c)(1). See WRIGHT, § 175.1.

14. United States v. Ebel, 299 F.3d 187, 191 (3d Cir. 2002); FED. R. CRIM. P. 11 advisory committee's note. See also United States v. Johnson, 89 F.3d 778, 782–83 (11th Cir. 1996) (prohibiting judicial involvement in plea negotiation upholds the

integrity of the judicial process and assures judicial impartiality).

15. Johnson, 89 F.3d at 783.

16. United States v. Bruce, 976 F.2d 552, 558 (9th Cir. 1992).

17. United States v. Fleming, 239 F.3d 761, 764–65 (6th Cir. 2001).

18. Johnson, 89 F.3d at 782–83; MOORE, § 611.07.

19. FED.R.CRIM.P. 11(f), which incorporates the provisions of FED. R. EVID. 410. The protection afforded by Rule 410 is qualified: if the defendant introduces statements made during plea negotiations, other statements made then are admissible if in fairness they should be considered; and a defendant can be prosecuted for making a false statement during the plea allocution if made under oath. As discussed in Chapter 8, the protection of Rule 11(f) can also be waived by the defendant as a condition of a cooperation agreement.

dismiss or not to bring additional charges against the defendant in return for a guilty plea. In sentence bargaining, while the government cannot bind the court, it may recommend a specific sentence, agree not to oppose the defendant's request for such a sentence, or agree as to the applicability of specified provisions of the Sentencing Guidelines.[20] The rule is silent as to what obligations the defendant may undertake other than pleading guilty, but it is common for the government to insist that the defendant waive rights otherwise available under the rule. The most important of these are the waiver of the right to preclude the use of any statement made by the defendant during plea discussions[21] and the right to appeal.[22]

§ 9.2(b) Consideration of the Plea Agreement By the Court

Whatever agreement the parties reach, the ultimate power to accept a plea and impose a sentence rests with the court.[23] The parties may, however, present their agreement to the court in different forms, with different consequences to the defendant in terms of the court's decision about the agreement. Thus, the defendant may withdraw his or her plea if the judge rejects an agreement between the parties that a specific sentence be imposed or a specific interpretation of the Sentencing Guidelines be adopted.[24] On the other hand, when the defendant agrees to plead guilty simply on the understanding that the prosecution will recommend a specific sentence or Guidelines application or will not oppose the defendant's request for such a sentence or application—the most common form of plea agreement—the plea may not be withdrawn even if the court decides not to follow the recommendation.[25] Nor under this latter version can the plea be withdrawn if, in the case of cooperation, the government refuses to make the 5K1.1 downward departure motion.[26]

§ 9.2(c) The Plea Allocution

Rule 11 requires the court to conduct a hearing designed to ensure that before a plea is accepted the court is satisfied that the defendant's

---

20. Further discussion of charge and sentencing bargaining can be found *infra* at § 12.2.

21. FED. R. CRIM. P. 11(f).

22. FED. R. CRIM. P. 11(e).

23. Only a district court judge is empowered to accept a plea and impose a sentence in a felony case. However, it is common practice for a magistrate judge to make the initial evaluation of these matters and then make recommendations to the district court judge. *See infra* § 9.5.

24. FED. R. CRIM. P. 11(c)(1)(C), (c)(3)(A).

25. FED. R. CRIM. P. 11(c)(1)(B), (c)(3)(B).

26. The government's refusal to make a 5K1.1 downward departure motion for a cooperating defendant is reviewable by a court only if the defendant can show the government acted in bad faith or for an unconstitutional reason, such as one based on the defendant's race. Wade v. United States, 504 U.S. 181, 185–86 (1992); United States. v. Holman, 168 F.3d 655, 661 (3d Cir. 1999).

decision is both knowing and voluntary and that there is an adequate factual basis upon which to base a judgment of guilt.[27]

To assure that the defendant understands the consequences of pleading guilty, the rule requires that the judge explain that the defendant is waiving all trial related rights and describe the nature of the charges to which the defendant is pleading.[28] The terms of any plea agreement must be put on the record,[29] and an inquiry must be made as to whether the defendant is pleading guilty voluntarily, in the absence of any threats or promises (other than those contained in a plea agreement).[30]

On the all-important matter of sentencing, Rule 11 requires the judge to inform the defendant of the statutory maximum sentence that can be imposed and of any statutory mandatory minimum sentence that applies, but it does not require that the defendant be advised as to what sentence will in fact be imposed under the Sentencing Guidelines or otherwise. It states simply that the court inform the defendant that it will be obligated to consider the Guidelines and that under certain circumstances it will have the discretion to depart downward or upward from the prescribed range or that it may choose to impose a non-Guidelines Sentence.[31]

While it is not a condition of a knowing and voluntary plea that the defendant specifically understand the Sentencing Guidelines range into which his or her case is likely to fall (in part because counsel at best can only make predictions),[32] the most common practice is for the prosecutor and the defense attorney to calculate the likely range, for the parties to attempt to reach an agreement and stipulate to a common calculation, and for defense counsel to advise the defendant of any such agreement. If no agreement can be reached, defense counsel should advise the

---

27. Fed. R. Crim. P. 11(b)(2)-(3).

28. Fed. R. Crim. P. 11(b)(1)(A)-(G).

29. Fed. R. Crim. P. 11(g).

30. Fed. R. Crim. P. 11(b)(2).

31. Fed. R. Crim. P. 11(b)(1)(H)-(M). Rule 11(b)(1)(M), written before *Booker* was decided in 2005, speaks of "the Court's obligation to *apply* the Sentencing Guidelines." (emphasis added). Post-*Booker*, as noted previously, the obligation is only to "*consider*" the Sentencing Guidelines. In addition, in the post-*Booker* world, the judge taking a plea also will make clear that the ultimate sentence will be determined based on a consideration of all the factors set forth in 18 U.S.C. § 3553(a).

32. *Cf.* United States v. Holland, 117 F.3d 589, 595 (D.C. Cir. 1997) (rejecting ineffective assistance of counsel challenge based on an anticipated Guidelines calculation that ended up differing from the calculation actually adopted and imposed by the

court); Longley v. United States, 1992 WL 358062 at *4 (E.D.Pa. Nov. 23, 1992) (same).

Booker and its progeny raise an interesting related question as to whether, prior to accepting a guilty plea, a judge will or should advise a defendant as to how much weight and deference the judge typically accords the Guidelines in determining the ultimate sentence. Recall that in § 7.3, we described a split of opinion amongst the district courts, with some judges applying the Guidelines as presumptively correct in almost all cases and others considering the Guidelines as only one among a number of equally important factors listed in § 3553(a). Unless and until this split is resolved by the higher courts, a defendant pleading guilty surely will be interested to know how much weight the sentencing judge is likely to accord the Guidelines; that such knowledge will be deemed necessary for a "knowing and voluntary" plea seems much less likely.

defendant of his or her own estimate as well as the government's (presumably higher) estimate. Courts commonly will require both prosecutors and defense attorneys to place their Guidelines estimates on the record during the plea allocution hearing.[33]

Finally, the judge must ensure that there is a factual basis for the plea. Rule 11(b)(3) requires that an independent determination must be made by the judge, notwithstanding the fact that the defendant admits guilt. In this "allocution" the judge will normally ask the defendant what acts he or she committed and with what intent.[34] The court may also inquire into the facts with the prosecutor and defense attorney. This may occur even when the defendant provides a factual basis for the entry of the plea. Such an inquiry guards against later claims of ineffective assistance of counsel by helping to assure that the defense attorney has considered the relevant facts and law and has advised the defendant competently. There is no requirement in the rules that the court inquire directly into the defense attorney's preparation, but it is common for judges to ask defense attorneys whether they know of any defense that could have been successfully asserted or of any reason why a guilty plea is not provident.

§ 9.3   Counsel in the Guilty Plea Process—Providing Effective Assistance

Guiding the defendant through the guilty plea process is one of the most important functions performed by defense counsel. As a "critical stage" of the process, the defendant has a right to counsel and to effective assistance.[35] Having made clear that these rights exist, however, the Supreme Court has not provided much useful guidance as to what it is that an effective attorney should do. The "cause and prejudice" test for effective assistance announced in *Strickland v. Washington*[36] has been applied in the guilty plea setting. Counsel is ineffective if there is a reasonable probability that, but for his or her incompetent performance, the defendant would have gone to trial rather than pleaded guilty. The Supreme Court has held that "in many cases" this in turn requires a

---

33. *See* United States. v. Pimentel, 932 F.2d 1029, 1034 (2d Cir. 1991) (advising district courts and prosecutors to put information on the record in order to avoid confusion and unnecessary appeals). *See also* 2 KADISH ET AL., *supra note 6*, § 11.02.

34. In certain situations the defendant may wish to enter a plea of guilty but may, because of a failure of memory, fear of collateral consequences, or some other reason be unable or unwilling to allocute to a sufficient factual basis to support the plea. As noted above, in *North Carolina v. Alford*, 400 U.S. 25 (1970), the Court held that a

defendant can plead guilty while denying guilt, so long as there is a factual basis for the plea. *See supra* § 9.0; *see also* MOORE, § 611.03. In these situations the parties should first determine whether the court is willing to accept such a plea, since acceptance of an *Alford* plea is completely within the discretion of the trial court and many judges refuse to do so. If the judge agrees, the government will be required to proffer facts sufficient to provide a basis to convict the defendant.

35. *See supra* § 9.0.

36. 466 U.S. 668 (1984).

reviewing court to determine whether, having gone to trial, there was a reasonable probability that the defendant would have been acquitted.[37]

Whatever the wisdom of a rule as speculative as this, it is clear that a finding of ineffectiveness at the guilty plea stage will rarely be made. If anything, this would seem to increase the burden on defense counsel to assure that the plea is in the best interests of the defendant and that the defendant, who ordinarily will be relying heavily on the recommendation of counsel, understands and agrees with the decision.

§ 9.4   The Entry of the Guilty Plea in United States v. Santiago

At the parties' request, Judge Sheridan ordered that Santiago's case be put on the calendar for pleading on February 25, 2005. Before that date, Santiago met with his attorney, Charles Berman, to prepare for the entry of his plea. Berman explained the terms of the cooperation-plea agreement and outlined the questions the judge would ask Santiago. They discussed Santiago's factual allocution, the part of the plea in which he would provide the factual basis for the court's acceptance of the guilty plea.

Berman had discussed the allocution with AUSA Knapp and the two agreed that it would be sufficient if Santiago admitted, in a general fashion, to agreeing with others to possess cocaine with intent to distribute. Santiago would admit that he helped the others by handling the shipments at the warehouse and making the bank deposits.

On February 25, Santiago, Berman and Knapp appeared before Judge Sheridan. Berman informed the court that Santiago wished to enter a plea of guilty to the one count felony information that AUSA Knapp had prepared and was ready to file.

Judge Sheridan then placed Santiago under oath. The following colloquy subsequently took place:

The Court:	Now, as we proceed, you should keep in mind that you are under oath. That means your answers must be truthful. If they are not, the government could later charge you with the offense of perjury, which is lying under oath. Do you understand this?
Santiago:	Yes, Your Honor.
The Court:	Mr. Santiago, do you have any physical problems at this time?

---

37. *Hill,* 474 U.S. at 57; Moore, § 611.03. *But see* Dickerson v. Vaughn, 90 F.3d 87, 92 (3d Cir. 1996) (court granted habeas petition on ground that counsel in- correctly advised defendant that he could appeal after entering a plea of *nolo conten- dere,* no discussion of likelihood of success at trial).

Santiago: No.

The Court: Are you being treated, or have you been treated for any mental illness or condition?

Santiago: No I haven't.

The Court: Have you any history of drug or alcohol abuse?

Santiago: No.

The Court: Are you currently taking any medication?

Santiago: No, Your Honor.

The Court: Are you now, or have you within the past 24 hours been, under the influence of any drug, medication, or alcohol?

Santiago: No.

The Court: What level of schooling have you completed?

Santiago: High school, Your Honor.

The Court: Mr. Berman, have you at any time had difficulty communicating with your client, or do you have any reason to question whether he understands what is about to happen at this proceeding?

Berman: No, Your Honor.

The Court: Mr. Santiago, are you satisfied with the performance of your attorney so far?

Santiago: Yes.

The Court: Would you like for him to continue to represent you as your attorney today?

Santiago: Yes, Your Honor.

The Court: Very well, I find that the defendant is competent to enter a plea of guilty.

The Court: Mr. Santiago, you have the right to have this case presented to a grand jury, and to have the grand jury vote whether to indict you, do you understand that right?

Santiago: Yes, Your Honor.

Berman:	Your Honor, I have explained that to Mr. Santiago, and advised him that he could waive the right to an indictment and proceed by prosecutor's information. Mr. Santiago has signed a waiver of indictment form.
The Court:	All right, the information will be accepted for filing.
The Court:	Mr. Santiago, do you understand that the government charges you with conspiring with others to possess with intent to distribute 5 kilograms of cocaine, and that the penalty for this offense is a minimum term of 10 years and a maximum term of life in prison, followed by a term of supervised release to last a minimum of 5 years up to a maximum of life?
Santiago:	Yes, I do.
The Court:	You should also be aware that this offense carries with it a maximum fine of $4,000,000. Apart from the potential fine, I am required by statute to impose on you a special assessment of $100. Do you understand these penalties?
Santiago:	Yes, Your Honor.
The Court:	Mr. Santiago, before we go any further, I want to make sure that you understand all of your rights, OK?
Santiago:	OK.
The Court:	Even if you are actually guilty, you have the right to persist in your plea of not guilty. Do you understand that?
Santiago:	Yes, Your Honor.
The Court:	And do you understand that if you were to persist in that plea of not guilty, you would be entitled to a speedy and public trial by jury with the full assistance of counsel at every step of the way?
Santiago:	Yes, Your Honor.
The Court:	At a trial, you would have the right to confront and cross-examine the witnesses that the government called to testify against you. Do you understand?
Santiago:	Yes

The Court: At trial you would be able to present evidence. And to do so you would have the ability to compel the appearance of witnesses and the production of possible evidence through the use of a court order. Do you understand?

Santiago: Yes

The Court: Do you understand that at trial you would be able to testify on your own behalf?

Santiago: Yes

The Court: And do you understand also that you could not be forced to testify, or even to present any kind of evidence at all if you did not want to?

Santiago: Yes.

The Court: And if you chose not to testify, I would instruct the jury that under the Constitution your decision not to testify could not be used or held against you in any way. Do you understand?

Santiago: Yes.

The Court: Now, Mr. Santiago, let me review the nature of the charge against you. The government charges that in or about May 2004 through in or about January 2005, in this district, you, together with others, knowingly and intentionally conspired to possess with intent to distribute 5 kilograms or more of cocaine in violation of Title 21, Section 841(a) of the United States Code. Do you understand that this is what the government alleges you to have done?

Santiago: Yes.

The Court: Have any agreements been made in this case?

AUSA Knapp: Yes, Your Honor, this is the cooperation-plea agreement.

The Court: Mr. Santiago, have you reviewed this agreement with Mr. Berman?

Santiago: Yes.

The Court: Do you understand what it provides?

Santiago: Yes, Your Honor.

The Court: Let me generally review certain parts of that agreement with you. The agreement explains the maximum penalties that you face by pleading guilty here today, as I have explained them to you a moment ago. Do you understand those maximum possible penalties?

Santiago: Yes, Your Honor.

The Court: The agreement states that you will assist the government in various ways to investigate and prosecute other individuals. Do you understand those portions of the agreement?

Santiago: Yes.

The Court: And the agreement also states that if satisfied with your assistance, the government may ask me to depart from the federal Sentencing Guidelines and impose a lower sentence. The government is not, however, obligated to make such a request if it is not satisfied with your assistance. Do you understand that portion?

Santiago: Yes.

The Court: Do you have any questions about the plea agreement with the government?

Santiago: No.

The Court: Do you understand that by going through with this agreement you are waiving all of the trial rights I just explained to you?

Santiago: Yes, Your Honor.

The Court: Aside from this agreement, have any other promises been made to you, or any threats of any kind in order to induce or coerce you into pleading guilty?

Santiago: No.

The Court: Counsel, have you made an estimate of the likely sentencing range?

AUSA Knapp: Your Honor, the government believes that the offense level is 31, and the defendant is in the third

Criminal History category,[38] which produces a Guidelines range of 135–168 months in prison, before any possible downward departure resulting from Santiago's cooperation.

Berman: Your Honor, we believe that Mr. Santiago is eligible for at least a 2–level minor role adjustment, which would decrease his total offense level to 29, which would make the range 108–135 months. However, I have explained to Mr. Santiago that the Court might accept the government's estimate and not ours.

The Court: Mr. Santiago, I want to advise you that both the government's and Mr. Berman's calculations are just estimates and that neither the government nor defense counsel could guarantee what the ultimate sentence would be. Do you understand that?

Santiago: Yes.

The Court: Additionally, you should know that the Guidelines that we have just been talking about are not binding. Rather, the law says that those Guidelines are something that the Court must consider when determining the sentence. Do you understand that?

Santiago: Yes.

The Court: And so in addition to the calculations and considerations that are contained within the Guidelines, I will be free to consider a variety of additional things, including the nature and circumstances of the offense as well as the circumstances of your own background and behavior. Do you understand that?

Santiago: Yes.

The Court: That means that come sentencing time, you may be sentenced to a term of imprisonment within either of the estimated ranges, or above or below them. Is that clear to you, Mr. Santiago?

Santiago: Yes, Your Honor.

The Court: And has anyone promised you that a specific sentence would be imposed?

Santiago: No.

---

38. Santiago's Criminal History calculation is explained *supra* at § 8.3(a).

The Court:	Mr. Santiago, state the facts that you believe constitute your involvement in a conspiracy to possess cocaine with intent to distribute it.
Santiago:	From May 2004 to January 2005, I helped other people to distribute more than five kilograms of cocaine by accepting deliveries of cocaine at Superior Warehouse in Queens and loading the cocaine onto trucks for delivery. I also deposited large amounts of cash in several bank accounts.
The Court:	Did you know the deliveries with the marked crates contained cocaine?
Santiago:	Yes.
The Court:	Was the cash that you deposited in those accounts the proceeds of narcotics sales?
Santiago:	Yes.
The Court:	Counsel, are there any other facts that should be elicited?
AUSA Knapp:	No, Your Honor.
Berman:	No, sir.
The Court:	Ms. Knapp, does the government have sufficient evidence to prove a prima facie case against the defendant?
AUSA Knapp:	Yes, Your Honor.
The Court:	Counsel, is there any reason why this plea should not be accepted?
AUSA Knapp:	No, Your Honor.
Berman:	No, Your Honor
The Court:	Mr. Santiago, what is your plea to count one of the information, 05–CR 735, guilty or not guilty?
Santiago:	Guilty.
The Court:	Very well, the plea of guilty is accepted. Is the defendant in custody?
AUSA Knapp:	Yes, Your Honor.

Berman: We have no application at this time for a change in Mr. Santiago's bail status.[39]

The Court: The case will be adjourned to April 25 for sentencing.[40]

---

§ 9.5 The Entry of the Guilty Plea in United States v. Long Case

Shortly after Mario Long's proffer session on January 27, 2005, his attorney Inga Porter and AUSA Knapp phoned Judge Sheridan's courtroom deputy to schedule his guilty plea. Because Judge Sheridan was set to be presiding over a criminal trial in another case during the week that the lawyers were both free to appear for Long's plea, the deputy asked whether Long would be willing to have his guilty plea allocution heard before a United States magistrate judge instead of District Judge Sheridan. Jones said her client would agree to that, and the deputy told the lawyers he would have a waiver form prepared and sent to Magistrate Judge Roger Brown.[41]

The lawyers then called Magistrate Judge Brown's chambers and scheduled Long's plea for February 26. On that day, Long, his attorney

39. 18 U.S.C. § 3143(a)(2) provides that the court shall remand defendants convicted of narcotics offenses carrying a maximum sentence of 10 years or more, unless it finds either that there is substantial likelihood that a motion for acquittal or new trial will be granted, or the government recommends that there be no prison sentence imposed, or that there is clear and convincing evidence that the person will not flee or pose a danger. Release can also be ordered if "it is clearly shown that there are exceptional reasons." 18 U.S.C. § 3145(c).

40. When a defendant pleads guilty, the court typically will schedule sentencing approximately 60–90 days following the plea conference to allow the Probation Department to prepare a Presentence Investigation Report, which provides the sentencing judge with contextual and background information about the offense and the defendant to inform the court's sentencing decision. In cases where a defendant has agreed to cooperate with the government, the sentencing conference will be scheduled following the usual 60–90 day period and will be adjourned as necessary to permit the defendant to conclude his cooperation before sentencing actually occurs. Delaying sentencing in this way has at least a twofold benefit to the government and defendant. It enables the sentencing court to be apprised of the full extent of the defen-

dant's assistance, thus increasing the likelihood and extent of a downward departure. It also allows the government, in cases where the cooperating defendant's assistance includes trial testimony against others, to better resist attacks that the cooperating defendant is self-interested and unreliable. Where no specific sentence has been granted in exchange for the cooperating defendant's testimony, the government can argue that the cooperator's reward of a lower sentence remains contingent on his truthful testimony.

41. 28 U.S.C. § 636 authorizes magistrate judges to conduct hearings and make recommendations on matters pending before district court judges. Some district judges hear all guilty pleas in their own criminal cases; others refer all guilty pleas to the magistrate judges unless a defendant objects; still others do a combination of both. In most cases there tends to be no tangible detriment to the defendant who consents to have the guilty plea taken before the magistrate judge. There are, however, situations—such as an extremely vulnerable or sympathetic defendant—where a defense lawyer may decide that it is strategically important to have the district judge who will be imposing sentence see and hear from the defendant as soon and as often as possible, to make the strongest possible record for a downward departure or other sentencing motion or request.

and Knapp appeared before Magistrate Judge Brown, who first confirmed that Long was willing to give up his right to have his plea taken by Judge Sheridan and was prepared to have the magistrate judge hear his allocution. After Long confirmed his willingness to proceed, all of the parties and the magistrate judge signed a consent order to that effect. Long then waived his right to an indictment and agreed to plead guilty to an information. The magistrate judge proceeded to question Long much as Judge Sheridan had questioned Santiago. At the end of the questioning, the magistrate judge entered a recommendation that Judge Sheridan accept Long's plea of guilty pursuant to his cooperation-plea agreement.[42]

Magistrate Judge Brown then turned to the question of bail. He noted that because Long had just pleaded guilty to a narcotics offense with a statutory maximum term of imprisonment of 10 years or more, remand was basically mandatory, absent "exceptional reasons."[43] Long's attorney advised the court that Long was recently married and his wife—who was present in court that day—was expecting their first child in 8 weeks. Porter further explained that the government had agreed, subject to the court's approval, to allow Long to remain out on bail, but under house arrest, until he was sentenced, so that he could help his wife prepare for and then care for their expected newborn child. AUSA Knapp confirmed that the government had no opposition to Long remaining out on bail. Magistrate Judge Brown then ordered that Long's bail status remain unchanged, finding that these unusual circumstances qualified as "exceptional reasons" to forego the statutory mandatory remand provisions. The appearance was then concluded.

---

42. At the time of sentencing, Judge Sheridan will review the transcription or "minutes" of the guilty plea proceeding before the magistrate judge and decide whether to accept Long's allocution. If there are disputes over findings made by the magistrate judge, they must be determined *de novo* by the district court judge. § 636(b)(1)(C).

43. *See* §§ 3143(a)(2), 3145(c), discussed *supra* note 39.

*

Part III

THE DEVELOPMENT OF A FEDERAL CRIMINAL CASE INITIATED BY THE PROSECUTOR

Chapter 10

PRE–INDICTMENT INVESTIGATIONS

Table of Sections

Sec.
10.0 Introduction.
10.1 Follow-Up Investigation by Law Enforcement Agents.
10.2 Obtaining Court Authorization for Police Investigation.
10.3 The Grand Jury.
    10.3(a) The Grand Jury's Investigative Powers.
    10.3(b) The Role of the United States Attorney in the Grand Jury Investigation.
    10.3(c) Compelling Attendance Before the Grand Jury—The Subpoena.
    10.3(d) The Attorney as Witness.
    10.3(e) Obtaining Immunity for a Witness.
    10.3(f) Representation of Putative Defendants and Witnesses Before the Grand Jury.
    10.3(g) Compelling Compliance With Grand Jury Commands—Civil and Criminal Contempt.
10.4 Approaching and Defending Witnesses and Targets: Introduction.
    10.4(a) Approaching and Defending Witnesses and Targets: The Government's Perspective.
    10.4(b) Representing Witnesses and Targets.
10.5 Pre–Indictment Practice in the Superior Warehouse Investigation.
    10.5(a) The Government's Review of the Evidence, Potential Defendants and Charges.
    10.5(b) Devising an Investigative Strategy.
    10.5(c) Preliminary Investigative Steps.
    10.5(d) Court Orders.
    10.5(e) Approaching a Witness in the Christopher Case: Barbara Weiss.
    10.5(f) Representing A Witness: Barbara Weiss.
    10.5(g) The Grand Jury Presentation.
    10.5(h) Approaching a Target/Potential Cooperator: Ernest Wagner.
    10.5(i) Representing Ernest Wagner.

§ 10.0 Introduction

In Part III, we begin our discussion of the prosecutor-initiated case, which we have defined as one in which the prosecutor plays a central investigatory role, either directing the work of investigative agencies or using the prosecutor's own investigative powers. Prosecutor-initiated cases most commonly involve organized crime, international narcotics trafficking white collar (business) crime and political corruption. As in our illustrative case, they will often grow out of "police initiated" cases, in which defendants are induced to cooperate in identifying other, more significant actors.

In this Chapter, we turn first to the general legal principles that govern the three main investigative tools at the prosecutor's disposal: (1) enlisting law enforcement agents to take investigative steps that the agents are expressly authorized to undertake without the need for prosecutorial or judicial intervention; (2) invoking statutorily granted powers to apply to the court to obtain judicial orders authorizing the collection of certain kinds of evidence; and, most importantly, (3) utilizing the grand jury process to compel the testimony of witnesses as well as the production of documents and other tangible evidence. At each relevant point we discuss the responsibilities of defense counsel in representing clients who are the subject of these investigative techniques. We then return to the illustrative case, starting with AUSA Knapp's review of the cases against Paul Christopher, William Van Ness and Ernest Wagner following Gilbert Santiago's proffer, including consideration of the strength of the government's case against each defendant. We then consider the government's formulation of an investigative plan to gather additional evidence, the investigation that followed, and the defense lawyer's important role in certain aspects of this preindictment practice.

§ 10.1 Follow-Up Investigation by Law Enforcement Agents

Certain investigative steps that AUSA Knapp and Agent Martinez may decide to take involve the kinds of activities that are within the general statutory mandate of a law enforcement agency like the DEA and therefore require no special judicial authorization.[1] These include surveillance by agents,[2] consensual non-custodial interviews,[3] and the

---

1. 21 U.S.C. § 878.

2. Visual surveillance of persons, or photographing, videotaping, or recording them, is not a cognizable Fourth Amendment concern unless at the time the activity occurs the person has a reasonable expectation of privacy in their whereabouts, ap-

pearance, or conversations. *See generally* LaFave et al., § 3.2(a), (j).

3. Note that the police interview can be conducted without concern for *Miranda* warnings so long as the interviewee is not in custody. *See* Miranda v. Arizona, 384 U.S. 436, 467 (1966). *See also* LaFave et al.,

issuance of administrative subpoenas for certain kinds of basic records, like phone records.[4]

§ 10.2　Obtaining Court Authorization for Police Investigation

The government also has available to it investigative tools that are more invasive than basic interrogation and surveillance activities of the sort discussed in the preceding section. Because the use of such tools impinges significantly on privacy rights that have been recognized either by the courts or Congress, the prosecutor must obtain prior judicial approval.[5] A search of some protected space (such as a home or office) for tangible evidence is an obvious example of such an investigative technique and requires (absent some special circumstance) an application to a judge or magistrate for a search warrant and an accompanying affidavit establishing probable cause to believe that a crime has been committed and that evidence or fruits of that crime can be found in a specified place.[6] Similarly, before the government can engage in surreptitious electronic surveillance—such as wiretapping a phone line or monitoring a person's e-mail account—it must obtain consent of one of the parties to the telephonic or e-mail interaction or judicial approval in accordance with rules informed not only by the Fourth Amendment, but also those designed by Congress to provide special protection against this form of intrusion.[7] We will discuss the form that electronic eavesdropping orders take below, as AUSA Knapp considers whether she can tap Christopher's cell phone.[8]

§ 6.6(a)–(f). It should be noted, however, that the question of whether somebody is "in custody" is a fact-sensitive inquiry in its own right. *See, e.g.,* Parsad v. Greiner, 337 F.3d 175, 181–82 (2d Cir. 2003). Another complicated question may arise if the witness is represented by counsel, as ethical rules may prohibit the attorney for the government from initiating contact with a represented person or party.

4. *See* § 878(a)(2) (authorizing DEA or "any State or local law enforcement officer designated by the Attorney General" to, *inter alia*, issue subpoenas).

5. We refer here to the obligation of the prosecutor rather than the investigative agency that in fact will employ the investigative technique in question, because even when the investigation is police-initiated, the agency will almost never have independent access to the courts. Applications will first be approved and then presented to the court by the United States Attorney's Office.

In situations where judicial approval for use of an investigative technique is re-

quired, it is also possible that either the relevant statute or regulations promulgated by the Department of Justice will also require the Department's approval prior to making the application to the court. We will describe one example of this later, in our discussion of a possible wiretap of Christopher's cell phone.

6. *See supra* § 4.10(b).

7. *See* 18 U.S.C. §§ 2510 *et seq.*, which governs requests for eavesdropping warrants. The statute requires approval from a designated official of the Department of Justice before application to a court can be made. *See* 18 U.S.C. § 2516. An affidavit making out probable cause to believe that a crime has been or is being committed and that other investigative means are inadequate to obtain the needed information is required. The affidavit must also indicate the identity of the persons whose communications are to be intercepted, the location, the nature of the conversations, and the time for which the interception is to continue. *See* 18 U.S.C. § 2518.

8. *See infra* § 10.5(d).

Court orders also can be sought to obtain many kinds of more traditional records,[9] and are specifically mandated in a number of statutes, such as those regulating government access to tax and banking records.[10] However, as we shall see, in most of these situations the prosecutor would be more likely to use the subpoena power of the grand jury to obtain the information. If a court order is requested, however, it will take the form of an *ex parte* application,[11] albeit with specific wording requirements tailored to the particular type of intrusion regulated by the statute.[12]

§ 10.3 The Grand Jury

§ 10.3(a) The Grand Jury's Investigative Powers

The most powerful investigative tool available to the prosecutor is the federal grand jury. The grand jury has sweeping powers to compel both testimony (through the subpoena *ad testificandum*) and the production of documents, computer records, and other physical evidence (through the subpoena *duces tecum*). The grand jury's power to issue subpoenas derives from Rule 17(a) of the Federal Rules of Criminal Procedure, which controls the issuance of subpoenas in criminal cases generally.[13]

The grand jury has been described as a "grand inquest" whose power of inquiry is "not to be limited narrowly by questions of propriety or forecasts of the probable result of the investigation, or by doubts whether any particular individual will be found properly subject to an accusation of crime."[14] The proceedings are conducted *ex parte,* in secret,

9. *See* The All Writs Act, 28 U.S.C. § 1651(a) ("The Supreme Court and all courts established by Act of Congress may issue all writs necessary or appropriate in aid of their respective jurisdictions and agreeable to the usages and principles of law.").

10. Access to tax information is regulated by 26 U.S.C. § 6103(i)(1)(B)(i)-(ii) (United States Attorney must show "reasonable cause" to believe that the tax return information is relevant to a criminal investigation and cannot be obtained from another source). Access to bank records is regulated by the The Right to Financial Privacy Act of 1978, 12 U.S.C. §§ 3401 *et seq. See also* U.S. Attorneys' Manual §§ 9–11.142 & 9–13.800 (discussing Department of Justice policies and procedures for following The Right to Financial Privacy Act).

11. An *ex parte* application is made in two situations: (a) when authority to engage in certain types of investigation is sought, such as an application for a search warrant; and (b) where the production of certain evidence is sought from individuals,

e.g., a voice exemplar, in which case the application takes the form of an order to show cause. In both situations the application will be accompanied by an affidavit, which is a sworn statement describing the facts relevant to the relief requested, and by a proposed order.

12. Since these applications are *ex parte*, they obviously cannot be resisted by the person whose privacy rights are at stake. In the case of an order authorizing investigative activities, the defendant's remedy is to move for suppression of the evidence obtained, if it was obtained in violation of constitutional or statutory provisions. In the case of orders to show cause, a person can file an answering affidavit at the time compliance is demanded.

13. *See* Wright, § 271.

14. United States v. Calandra, 414 U.S. 338, 343 (1974) (*citing* Blair v. United States, 250 U.S. 273, 282 (1919)). *See generally Thirty–Second Annual Review of Criminal Procedure: Preliminary Proceedings, Grand Jury*, 91 Geo. L.J. 201 (2003).

and without a judge presiding over them. The grand jury need not justify its investigative activities by meeting any burden of proof that a crime has occurred. Rather, it is empowered to investigate on the mere suspicion that a violation of the law has occurred or simply to ensure that a crime has *not* been committed.[15] It may act on "tips, rumors, evidence proffered by the prosecutor, or the personal knowledge of the grand jurors."[16]

In conducting its investigations, the grand jury is similarly unencumbered by most evidentiary rules, which the Supreme Court has said would burden it with "minitrials and preliminary showings" that delay investigation.[17] Thus hearsay evidence is admissible.[18] A witness cannot resist a grand jury subpoena on the grounds that the grand jury lacks jurisdiction to investigate,[19] or, with very limited qualification, that the information sought is not relevant to the inquiry.[20] Similarly, the Supreme Court has held that Fourth Amendment objections are, for the most part, not cognizable at the grand jury stage. The Court has rejected the argument that a grand jury subpoena is a "seizure" within the meaning of the amendment,[21] which would seem to eliminate all Fourth Amendment challenges, although the Court has long adhered to the view that a subpoena *duces tecum* can be unreasonable if overly broad.[22] The Court has also held that the exclusionary rule is not applicable at the grand jury stage, and thus a witness cannot resist testifying or producing evidence on the grounds that the subpoena was the fruit of illegal police conduct.[23]

15. *See* United States v. Morton Salt Co., 338 U.S. 632, 642–43 (1950).

16. Branzburg v. Hayes, 408 U.S. 665, 701 (1972) (*citing* Costello v. United States, 350 U.S. 359, 362 (1956)).

17. United States v. Dionisio, 410 U.S. 1, 17–18 (1973); LaFave et al., § 15.2(d).

18. *See* Costello, 350 U.S. at 363; LaFave et al., § 15.5(a).

19. *See* Blair, 250 U.S. at 282–83; LaFave et al., § 8.8(a).

20. *See* United States v. R. Enterprises, Inc., 498 U.S. 292, 301 (1991) (person seeking to quash subpoena must show that "compliance would be unreasonable," as where "there is no reasonable possibility that the category of materials the Government seeks will produce information relevant to the general subject of the grand jury's investigation"); LaFave et al., § 8.8(b).

21. *See* Dionisio, 410 U.S. at 9; LaFave & et al., § 8.7(a).

22. *See* Hale v. Henkel, 201 U.S. 43, 76 (1906), *overruled in part on other grounds,*

Murphy v. Waterfront Comm'n of New York Harbor, 378 U.S. 52 (1964); LaFave et al., § 8.7(a),(b).

23. *See* Calandra, 414 U.S. at 349. Although the *Calandra* decision effectively prevents a witness from raising the issue of an illegal search, Justice Department policy recognizes the practical rationale behind the rule and therefore opposes the use of unconstitutionally obtained evidence before a grand jury. It notes: "A prosecutor should not present to the grand jury for use against a person whose constitutional rights clearly have been violated evidence which the prosecutor personally knows was obtained as a direct result of the constitutional violation." U.S. Attorneys' Manual § 9–11.231. Congress has imposed one qualification on the *Calandra* rule: a witness can resist a grand jury subpoena on the grounds that it was issued as a result of evidence obtained through illegal electronic surveillance. *See* 18 U.S.C. § 2515 (preventing introduction before grand jury of illegally intercepted wire communications or evidence derived therefrom); Gelbard v. United States, 408 U.S. 41, 47 (1972) (allowing witness before grand jury to invoke § 2515

There are, however, some limits on the grand jury's investigative powers. As just noted, a subpoena *duces tecum* issued pursuant to Rule 17(a) can be challenged for "overbreadth."[24] Theoretically, at least, lack of relevance could be shown.[25] A grand jury subpoena can also be challenged on the grounds that it was issued merely to harass the witness.[26] It has been held to be an abuse of the grand jury power to issue subpoenas for the purpose of post-indictment criminal discovery[27] or to coerce witnesses into speaking with or providing tangible evidence to the prosecution or police for matters not the subject of a grand jury inquiry.[28]

Proving that any of these abuses has occurred is, however, very difficult. As a result, the most likely way by which a grand jury subpoena can be resisted is through the successful assertion of a testimonial privilege. Of these there are two types: any common law privilege recognized in the federal law; and the constitutional privilege against self-incrimination. Extended discussion of either type of privilege is beyond the scope of this text.[29] Suffice it to say that successful assertion of a common law privilege, such as the attorney-client privilege, precludes the inquiry. A Fifth Amendment assertion will do so as well, unless the witness is immunized in accordance with the process described below.

Grand jury subpoenas—whether for documents, testimony or both—can also be resisted by defense lawyers in informal ways, such as negotiating limitations or a narrowing of the scope of requests for documents or agreeing to a limited interview with the prosecutor in lieu of testifying before the grand jury.

§ 10.3(b) The Role of the United States Attorney in the Grand Jury Investigation

The independence of the grand jury has long been proclaimed as a fundamental principle of the criminal process.[30] The prosecutor's formal role before this tribunal is to act as its legal advisor and to present

---

as defense to production). *See also* LaFave et al., § 8.9 (a), (b).

24. *See Hale*, 201 U.S. at 76; LaFave et al., § 8.7(a), (b).

25. *See R. Enterprises, Inc.*, 498 U.S. at 301; LaFave et al., § 8.8 (b).

26. *See* LaFave et al., § 8.8(h).

27. *Id.*, § 8.8(f). There are, however, major exceptions to this post-indictment criminal discovery "rule." A prosecutor may continue to use the grand jury process to gather evidence post-indictment so long as he or she is investigating in good-faith the possibility of adding more charges or new defendants to the indicted case. *See*

LaFave et al., § 8.8(f). In practice, these exceptions tend to swallow the "rule."

28. *Id.*, § 8.8(e).

29. On the common law privileges, see Edward J. Imwinkelried, The New Wigmore: Evidentiary Privileges, §§ 1–3 (2002). On the Fifth Amendment privilege, see LaFave et al., §§ 8.10–8.12.

30. The U.S. Attorneys' Manual states: "The prosecutor must recognize that the grand jury is an independent body, whose functions include not only the investigation of crime and the initiation of criminal prosecution but also the protection of the citizenry from unfounded criminal charges."

evidence for its consideration.[31] As a practical matter, however, the grand jury is under the prosecutor's virtually complete control,[32] and in effect operates as an investigative arm of the United States Attorney's Office.[33] The prosecutor almost always selects the matters to be investigated and the witnesses to be subpoenaed. The prosecutor issues subpoenas and reviews documents produced in response to subpoenas. The prosecutor routinely interviews witnesses prior to their appearances before the grand jury and conducts virtually all of the formal questioning during grand jury proceedings.[34] For the most part, therefore, the investigation and indictment process is regulated by the Justice Department and the good faith of individual prosecutors.[35] (We discuss the prosecutor's role in presenting evidence and charges to the grand jury and the rules governing that process in Chapter 11.)

§ 10.3(c) Compelling Attendance Before the Grand Jury— The Subpoena[36]

To invoke the grand jury's sweeping investigative powers, the Assistant United States Attorney simply obtains blank subpoenas issued and endorsed by the court and has the witnesses served, usually by an investigative agent,[37] without prior authorization from the grand jury.[38] Rule 17(e) provides for nationwide service.[39] Justice Department practice is to provide witnesses with reasonable advance notice of their obligation to appear before a grand jury. "Forthwith" subpoenas, which require a

U.S. ATTORNEYS' MANUAL § 9–11.010. *See also* LAFAVE ET AL., §§ 8.2(a) & 8.6(a).

31. On this point, the U.S. Attorneys' Manual notes: "The prosecutor's responsibility is to advise the grand jury on the law and to present evidence for its consideration. In discharging these responsibilities, the prosecutor must be scrupulously fair to all witnesses and must do nothing to inflame or otherwise improperly influence the grand jurors." U.S. ATTORNEYS' MANUAL § 9–11.010.

32. *See generally* LAFAVE ET AL., §§ 8.4(b); 13.2(a); 13.3(d). Grand jurors can theoretically proceed in defiance of the United States Attorneys' Office, but such events are notable for their rarity. Even if the grand jury votes an indictment, the prosecutor has the final veto power and cannot be forced to prosecute the case. For an example of a grand jury which was very active and involved in the process, see, Milo Geyelin, *Grand Jury Asks for Unsealing of Its Findings on Weapons Plant*, WALL ST. J., Aug. 2, 1996, at B2.

33. LAFAVE ET AL., § 8.4 (b).

34. *Id.*

35. *See generally* National Association of Criminal Defense Lawyers, Federal Grand Jury Report & "Bill of Rights," *available at* http://www.nacdl.org/public.nsf/freeform/grandjuryreform?opendocument (2000).

36. *See generally* WRIGHT, §§ 271–279.

37. For a discussion on service of grand jury subpoenas, see SUSAN W. BRENNER & GREGORY G. LOCKHART, FEDERAL GRAND JURY: A GUIDE TO LAW AND PRACTICE, §§ 12.1, 12.3 (1996 & Supp. 2004).

38. *See generally* LAFAVE ET AL, §§ 8.1, 8.2, 8.8(g). *See also* Daniel Richman, *Prosecutors and Their Agents, Agents and Their Prosecutors*, 103 COLUM. L. REV. 749, 779–80 (2003) (observing that while, strictly speaking, only grand juries can issue subpoenas, "prosecutors can freely invoke [this power] in the grand jury's name").

39. Service of a subpoena may be made outside the United States if the requirements of the Walsh Act are met. *See* 28 U.S.C. § 1783 (the person named must be a United States national or resident and the testimony is necessary in the interest of justice). *See also* WRIGHT, § 271.

witness' immediate compliance, require special approval and are rarely issued.[40]

Justice Department policy also provides that an Advice of Rights form be appended to all grand jury subpoenas served on a target (a putative defendant) or a subject (a person whose conduct is within the scope of the investigation).[41] In addition, Justice Department policy provides for the use of target warnings informing target-witnesses that they are under investigation.[42]

§ 10.3(d) The Attorney as Witness

An attorney may on occasion receive a subpoena to provide testimony or evidence growing out of his or her representation of a witness or target. Barring a successful claim of privilege, such evidence can be compelled despite its adverse impact on the attorney-client relationship.[43] Ethical rules require that an attorney withdraw as counsel if compelled to give testimony prejudicial to a client.[44] Because of the potential ramifications for the attorney-client relationship, Justice Department guidelines require the approval of the Assistant Attorney General of the Criminal Division before issuance of a subpoena to an attorney for information relating to the client.[45]

§ 10.3(e) Obtaining Immunity for a Witness

A witness who receives either a subpoena *ad testificandum* or a subpoena *duces tecum* may have valid grounds to assert the privilege against self-incrimination. In order to compel testimony from a witness who invokes the constitutional right to remain silent, the government must obtain an immunity order from the court. The immunity statute[46] provides for use and derivative use immunity, meaning neither the testimony compelled under an immunity order nor any information directly or indirectly derived from it can be used against a witness in a criminal case.[47]

---

40. U.S. ATTORNEYS' MANUAL § 9–11.140. *See also* LaFAVE ET AL., § 8.7(e).

41. U.S. ATTORNEYS' MANUAL § 9–11.151. See *infra* § 10.5(e), for an example of such a notice. The definitions of "target" and "subject" are discussed in further detail below.

42. *Id. See also* LaFAVE ET AL., § 8.10(d). An example of a target letter can be found *infra* at § 10.5(h).

43. *See* LaFAVE ET AL., § 8.8(d). *See also* In re Grand Jury Subpoena Served Upon John Doe, Esq. (Roe v. United States), 781 F.2d 238, 249 (2d Cir. 1985) (en banc) (rejecting defendant's claim that "his attorney's appearance before the grand jury will chill his *potential* Sixth Amendment rights").

44. *See* MODEL RULES OF PROF'L CONDUCT R. 3.7 & cmt. 6 (1983, as amended 2003) (hereinafter "MODEL RULE").

45. *See* U.S. ATTORNEYS' MANUAL § 9–13.410. Factors that the Assistant Attorney General must consider include the feasibility of obtaining the information from alternative sources, the existence of reasonable grounds for believing that a crime has been committed, and a determination that the need for the information outweighs the adverse effects on the attorney-client relationship, including the possibility of the attorney's disqualification if compelled to testify. *Id.* Moreover, the subpoena must be "narrowly drawn." *Id.*

46. *See* 18 U.S.C. § 6002.

47. Use immunity, as contrasted with "transactional immunity," does not pre-

The statute requires that the United States Attorney, after obtaining the approval of the Justice Department, assert in a written application to the court that in his or her judgment the witness' testimony may be necessary in the public interest and that the witness has refused or is likely to refuse to testify on the basis of the privilege against self-incrimination.[48] A proposed order granting immunity is attached to the application.

In practice, the prosecutor will commonly know or at least suspect that the witness will assert the privilege against self-incrimination prior to the time the witness testifies. In such situations, Departmental authorization to obtain an immunity order usually is obtained prior to the appearance date. The district court judge will sign the order in advance of the witness' appearance, on the affirmation of the prosecutor that the witness is likely to or has expressed an intention to assert the Fifth Amendment privilege. If an immunity hearing is held, it is perfunctory. The court routinely grants the application for immunity provided that the prosecutor has complied with the statute in obtaining proper authorization.[49]

§ 10.3(f) Representation of Putative Defendants and Witnesses Before the Grand Jury

1. Advising Witnesses During Testimony

The Sixth Amendment right to counsel does not apply to grand jury proceedings,[50] and federal law does not authorize counsel to be present while the witness is being questioned.[51] Most federal courts, however, allow the witness to leave the grand jury room in order to consult with counsel.[52] The attorney will generally assist the witness in answering the specific questions asked or in formulating suitable statements for refusing to testify.

---

clude prosecution for the matters about which the witness testified. The Supreme Court upheld the use immunity statute against a challenge that it did not afford protection commensurate with the Fifth Amendment in *Kastigar v. United States,* 406 U.S. 441, 453 (1972). On immunity law generally, see LaFave et al., § 8.11.

48. *See* 18 U.S.C. § 6003(b). For the Departmental procedures for obtaining authorization for a grant of immunity, see U.S. Attorneys' Manual § 9–23.130. While a witness's invocation or anticipated invocation of their Fifth Amendment privilege theoretically may be challenged on the ground that it is frivolous, *see, e.g.,* Brenner

& Lockhart, §§ 13.21.3 (e), 14.20 (e), in practice this is rarely done. In most cases the validity of the assertion is assumed, and the prosecutor then decides whether to grant immunity.

49. *See* LaFave et al., § 8.11(d) (discussing procedures for granting immunity).

50. *Id.*, § 8.15(a).

51. *See* Fed. R. Crim. P. 6(d)(1) (limiting those permitted in the grand jury room to the grand jurors, the prosecutor, the witness, the stenographer and an interpreter if needed); Wright, § 105.

52. *See* LaFave et al., § 8.15(c).

2. Raising Legal Challenges to Subpoenas[53]

With one exception, the grounds and procedures for challenging grand jury subpoenas are different for a subpoena *ad testificandum* and a subpoena *duces tecum,* and these matters will be discussed separately below. The one ground common to both is that there is a somewhat vaguely expressed right to challenge any subpoena that is "unreasonable" or "oppressive." Such challenges are rarely successful because a presumption of regularity attaches to all grand jury subpoenas.[54] An individual seeking to quash a subpoena has the burden of production, that is, of introducing evidence to rebut the presumption of regularity, and a heavy burden of persuasion in proving that it is unreasonable or oppressive.[55]

(a) Subpoenas *Ad Testificandum*. Legal objection to an *ad testificandum* subpoena can only be made after the subpoenaed person has appeared and been asked a question. Prior to that time, a challenge is not ripe since witnesses are not informed in advance of what questions will be asked and therefore are not in a position to assert whether they will answer or not.[56] Once inside the grand jury room, the witness' refusal either takes the form of announcing his or her unwillingness to testify or asserting the privilege against self-incrimination or a common law privilege valid under federal law.[57] If the prosecutor believes that the witness does not have a valid claim of privilege, he or she can seek judicial intervention to resolve whether the privilege applies or initiate contempt proceedings in the manner described below.[58]

(b) Subpoenas *Duces Tecum*. Unlike a subpoena *ad testificandum,* a subpoena *duces tecum* specifies in advance what material the grand jury is demanding. Because compliance with such a subpoena would forfeit the right to resist, a pre-appearance challenge is appropriate.[59] Such a challenge is made by bringing a motion to quash the subpoena or to modify it.[60]

A witness may generally raise the same challenges in a motion to quash a subpoena *duces tecum* that are raised when a witness appears in response to a subpoena *ad testificandum* and refuses to answer a question. But there are several important limitations on the right to

---

53. We say "legal challenges" because there a number of informal ways in which defense lawyers can and do resist grand jury subpoenas, which we discuss below.

54. *See* LaFave et al., §§ 8.8(b) n. 37, 8.8(e) n. 119.

55. *See* Fed. R. Crim. P. 17(c); Wright, § 275.

56. *See generally* Brenner & Lockhart, §§ 13.19 (on challenging grand jury subpoenas *ad testificandum)* and 13.19.1 (discussing whether such challenges are properly

made by pre-appearance motions). *See also* Wright, § 273.

57. *See* Fed. R. Evid. 501. The most common of these privileges is the attorney-client privilege.

58. *See supra* § 10.3(g).

59. For a discussion on challenging subpoenas *duces tecum,* see Brenner and Lockhart, §§ 14.19–14.21.

60. *See* Fed. R. Crim. P. 17(c). *See also* Wright, § 275.

resist subpoenas for documents. First, the Fifth Amendment privilege against self-incrimination applies only to situations in which the act of producing the documents itself is incriminating. The Supreme Court has held that being compelled to produce pre-existing documents that were not originally generated by any government compulsion does not raise any Fifth Amendment issue, even though the contents of those documents may be incriminating.[61] However, if the government does not otherwise know about the existence of such documents, the act of producing the documents can be incriminating and thereby implicates the Fifth Amendment privilege. Second, a subpoena *duces tecum* is always directed to the person in custody of the material demanded and not necessarily either to the owner of the material or some other person who would be incriminated by its disclosure. (An example would be a grand jury subpoena to CMS Bank calling for IFD's banking records. *See infra,* § 10.5(c).) Since it is the custodian and not the party in interest who is being compelled to act, the party that may be incriminated most likely will have no standing to object to the subpoena.[62] Of course, the custodian is free to assert any personally held privilege. Finally, it should be noted that a corporation has no Fifth Amendment privilege, and thus a document subpoena directed to a corporation—even if it calls for documents incriminating particular individuals employed by or associated with the corporation—cannot be quashed on grounds that production would violate a Fifth Amendment privilege.[63]

An order denying a witness' motion to quash a subpoena *duces tecum* is interlocutory and not appealable. As a general rule, a grand jury witness can appeal the order denying the motion to quash only by refusing to comply with the subpoena, being held in contempt, and then appealing the contempt order.[64] The prosecutor, however, may appeal an order to quash since it is considered final as to the government.[65]

---

61. Fisher v. United States, 425 U.S. 391 (1976); *see also* United States v. Hubbell, 530 U.S. 27 (2000); LaFave et al., §§ 8.12, 8.13. For a discussion of the practical effects of *United States v. Hubbell,* see Lance Cole, *The Fifth Amendment and Compelled Production of Personal Documents After United States v. Hubbell—New Protection For Private Papers?*, 20 Am. J. Crim. L. 123 (2002).

62. *See generally* LaFave et al., §§ 8.12 (e).

63. *Id.* § 8.12(b). *See generally* Braswell v. United States, 487 U.S. 99, 108 (1988) ("It is well settled that no privilege can be claimed by the custodian of corporate records, regardless of how small the corporation may be."). There are some very narrow limitations to this general rule. *See, e.g.,* Curcio v. United States, 354 U.S. 118, 123–24 (1957) ("[A] custodian, by assuming the

duties of his office, undertakes the obligation to produce the books of which he is custodian in response to a rightful exercise of the State's visitorial powers. But he cannot lawfully be compelled, in the absence of a grant of adequate immunity from prosecution, to condemn himself by his own oral testimony."); United States v. O'Henry's Film Works, 598 F.2d 313, 316, 318 (2d Cir. 1979) (while "it is also well settled that an agent of an organization retains a personal privilege against self-incrimination," a corporate custodian may be called upon to identify the documents he does possess "because testimony auxiliary to the production is as unprivileged as are the documents themselves").

64. *See* LaFave et al., § 27.2(e).

65. For a general discussion of prosecution appeals, see LaFave et al., § 27.3.

§ 10.3(g) Compelling Compliance With Grand Jury Commands—Civil and Criminal Contempt

(1) Civil Contempt. A person who without just cause fails to obey a subpoena may be held in contempt of court.[66] The procedure followed in such cases is governed by the federal civil contempt statute,[67] which expressly applies to grand jury witnesses. It authorizes confinement either until the witness complies[68] or until the grand jury's term expires, but in no event longer than 18 months.[69] There is no right to a jury trial, but the witness has a constitutional right to counsel at a contempt hearing since he or she faces imprisonment.[70]

To initiate a civil contempt proceeding, the prosecutor serves the witness with an order to show cause why the witness should not be held in contempt. At the hearing, the government presents evidence that the witness was subpoenaed and refused to comply.[71] Because there is a presumption of legality regarding the justification for a grand jury subpoena, the witness has the burden of going forward to show a right to refuse to comply. If the witness asserts a colorable claim of a right to refuse, the government must prove by clear and convincing evidence that there was no such right.[72] In attempting to rebut the presumption, the witness is entitled to a full adversarial hearing,[73] including the right to cross-examine the government witnesses[74] and to present witnesses and evidence.[75] If the court rules against all of the witness' challenges, it will order the witness to answer the questions or submit the demanded material. The court may ask the witness whether he or she intends to

---

66. WRIGHT, § 279; LaFAVE ET AL., § 8.3(a). For a general discussion, see, Jennifer Fleishcher, *In Defense of Civil Contempt Sanctions*, 36 COLUM. J.L. & SOC. PROBS. 35 (2002) (describing and comparing features of criminal and civil contempt).

67. *See* 28 U.S.C. § 1826(a). *See also* BRENNER & LOCKHART, § 13.15.1.

68. Because a civil contempt commitment is coercive and not punitive, a witness held in contempt can be released at any time by complying with the court order. *See* Shillitani v. United States, 384 U.S. 364, 370–71 (1966); LaFAVE ET AL. § 8.3(a). A witness may also gain release by demonstrating that further confinement will not coerce him or her to testify, as discussed below.

69. A court has discretion to impose a non-punitive fine in addition to or in lieu of imprisonment. *See* BRENNER & LOCKHART, § 13.15.1.

70. *See* In re Di Bella, 518 F.2d 955, 959 (2d Cir.1975) (noting that, because "the burden of imprisonment is just as great" in such a context, it "fosters the need for procedural protection").

71. If the issue is the witness' refusal to answer questions, the government calls the court reporter who transcribed the testimony in the grand jury and elicits the relevant questions and answers. If the issue is the witness' refusal to appear, or to produce material demanded in a subpoena *duces tecum*, the government simply proffers the facts related to the witness' failure to reply.

72. *See generally* BRENNER & LOCKHART, § 13.15.1. *See also* United States v. Doe, 943 F.2d 132, 134–35 (1st Cir. 1991) (holding that "the government bears the ultimate burden of proving that the [individual] was in contempt and the standard of proof is clear and convincing").

73. *Id.*

74. *See* Matter of Kitchen, 706 F.2d 1266, 1272–73 (2d Cir. 1983) (requiring that defendant be allowed to conduct cross-examination, unless "particular and compelling reasons peculiar to the grand jury function require some curtailment of the latter right").

75. *Id.* at 1273.

comply or may send the witness to the grand jury room to testify. If the witness states that he or she will not comply, or returns to the grand jury room and refuses to testify, the court will then hold the witness in contempt.

As we have just noted, civil contempt rules limit the length of time during which a witness can be confined. A witness can also be released prior to that time by demonstrating that the confinement will fail to coerce him or her into testifying and is therefore simply punitive.[76] The witness has the burden of demonstrating that there is no realistic possibility that continued confinement will cause him to testify.[77] Nevertheless, because both a civil commitment and a criminal contempt sentence can be imposed on a witness for the same refusal to testify, upon release the prosecutor can initiate criminal contempt proceedings.[78]

(2) Criminal Contempt. Disobedience of a lawful court order is also a criminal offense, punishable by fine or imprisonment.[79] If the government proceeds criminally, the defendant is entitled to grand jury review, and the same panoply of rights, including the right to a jury trial available to any person charged with a felony under federal law, apply.[80]

Despite the availability of the criminal sanction, grand jury witnesses are generally held in civil rather than criminal contempt. The Supreme Court has strongly advised district courts to first consider the practicability of coercing compliance with compulsion orders through the imposition of civil contempt and to resort to the criminal contempt sanction only if good reason deems the civil remedy unsuitable.[81] Such a case might arise in situations in which the civil commitment has failed to secure compliance before it must be terminated.

§ 10.4 Approaching and Defending Witnesses and Targets: Introduction

In this section we discuss separately the rules involved in approaching "witnesses" and "targets." While the distinction between the two is

---

76. The motion is commonly called a *Grumbles* motion derived from one of the first cases in which it succeeded. *See* In re Grumbles, N.J. Crim. No. 722–21 (D.N.J. Feb. 26, 1973).

77. *See* Simkin v. United States, 715 F.2d 34, 37 (2d Cir. 1983). Factors considered include the time served and the time remaining to be served, the reasons for the witness' noncompliance, and the feasibility of obtaining the evidence from an alternative source. *See generally* BRENNER & LOCKHART, § 13.15.1.

78. *See* Yates v. United States, 355 U.S. 66, 74 (1957) (finding that double jeopardy protections were not implicated). For a gen-

eral discussion of criminal contempt, see WRIGHT, §§ 701 *et seq.*

79. *See* 18 U.S.C. § 401(3). Unique among federal laws, there are no prescribed limits on either the amount of the fine or the length of imprisonment. United States v. Gracia, 755 F.2d 984, 988–89 (2d Cir. 1985) (observing that the only limit in this area is that of "judicial discretion"). However, Eighth Amendment restrictions on cruel and unusual punishment no doubt apply. *See generally* LaFAVE ET AL., § 8.3(a).

80. *See* FED. R. CRIM. P. 42(a)(3); WRIGHT, § 712.

81. *See* Shillitani v. United States, 384 U.S. 364, 371 & n. 9 (1966). *See also* LaFAVE ET AL., § 8.3(a).

sometimes not especially clear, the designation is important to keep in mind. The United States Attorneys' Manual defines a "target" as "a person as to whom the prosecutor or the grand jury has substantial evidence linking him or her to the commission of a crime and who, in the judgment of the prosecutor, is a putative defendant."[82] A "witness," in this context, is essentially the opposite of a "target": someone as to whom the prosecutor does not have substantial evidence, or any evidence at all, suggesting that the person has committed any criminal act, but a person who may have information concerning the commission of criminal acts by others and/or who may have participated, unwittingly, in the criminal acts of others. The Manual contains another category—a "subject"—defined as "a person whose conduct is within the scope of the grand jury's investigation."[83] Based on this definition, a "subject" falls somewhere in between a "target" and a mere "witness", and covers a broad range of individuals with varying degrees of exposure to criminal prosecution." For present illustrative purposes we have divided our discussion according to the two most relevant and analytically distinct categories: "target" and "witness."

§ 10.4(a) Approaching and Defending Witnesses and Targets: The Government's Perspective

With respect to approaching witnesses, the government has several options. One is to see if a potential witness will agree to a voluntary interview, either with the agent alone (perhaps at the witness's home) or with both the prosecutor and the agent (more likely at the prosecutor's office), without invoking the formal grand jury process (and without any need for court authorization). Alternatively, the prosecutor can issue a grand jury subpoena *ad testificandum,* which the agent would then serve on the witness requiring an appearance before the grand jury on a specified date to answer questions under oath. Under this latter approach, Department of Justice guidelines require that a form entitled "Advice of Rights" be attached to the grand jury subpoena, advising the witness of the general nature of the investigation and his or her rights in connection with the subpoena, including the right to consult with counsel and to remain silent if the witness believes answers to any questions might tend to incriminate him or her. As is illustrated below, the prosecutor's decision as to how to approach a particular witness in a particular case is in the end a strategic one, depending on, among other things, the progress of the investigation, information known about the particular witness, and educated guesses about how the witness is likely to react.

A prosecutor's approach to interviewing individuals who are targets or potential targets of their investigation is somewhat different. While

---

82. U.S. ATTORNEYS' MANUAL § 9–11.151.   **83.** *Id.*

legally permissible,[84] subpoenaing a "target" of an investigation to testify before the grand jury is explicitly discouraged under Department of Justice guidelines,[85] and in practice is rarely if ever done.

As to interviewing targets—especially where the person is aware of their status as such—it is unlikely that this will result in a confession or any kind of useful statement. At the same time, and depending on the type of case and the particular target being investigated, any action that would have the effect of notifying a target otherwise unaware that they are being investigated carries significant risks that the target might flee, destroy evidence, or tamper with witnesses. Accordingly, in many routine cases, including most commonly those involving narcotics trafficking and/or violence, the presumption of most prosecutors is against any form of pre-indictment approach.[86]

There are, however, some situations in which a prosecutor may decide to approach a target prior to indictment. One is where the government hopes to "flip" the target, that is, persuade them to cooperate against other (usually more culpable) defendants. Another occurs in complex cases involving white-collar crime, such as securities fraud. In this type of matter, the prosecution may have an interest in testing out its own theory of the case by attempting to hear, in advance of any final charging decision, what the defendant, typically through an attorney, will say in his or her defense.

Whatever the reason, in those situations where the prosecutor chooses to initiate contact with a target prior to any formal charges being brought, there are a number of informal approaches available,

---

84. LaFave et al., § 8.10(c).

85. The United States Attorneys' Manual states that: "before a known 'target' is subpoenaed to testify before the grand jury about his or her involvement in the crime under investigation, an effort should be made to secure the target's voluntary appearance." U.S. Attorneys' Manual § 9–11.150. The United States Attorneys' Manual goes on to require approval by the United States Attorney before a "target" is subpoenaed and sets forth several considerations that should inform the decision of whether to issue such a subpoena. *Id.* These factors include: "the importance to the successful conduct of the grand jury's investigation of the testimony or other information sought;" "[w]hether the substance of the testimony or other information sought could be provided by other witnesses;" and "[w]hether the questions the prosecutor and the grand jurors intend to ask or the other information sought would be protected by a valid claim of privilege." *Id.*

86. The United States Attorneys' Manual is generally consistent with this approach. It states that: "[w]hen a target is not called to testify ... and does not request to testify on his or her own motion, the prosecutor, in appropriate cases, is encouraged to notify such person a reasonable time before seeking an indictment in order to afford him or her an opportunity to testify before the grand jury." U.S. Attorneys' Manual § 9–11.153. However, the United States Attorneys' Manual also sets out several exceptions where such notification "would not be appropriate," including "routine clear cases or where such action might jeopardize the investigation or prosecution because of the likelihood of flight, destruction or fabrication of evidence, endangerment of other witnesses, [or] undue delay." *Id.* In practice, as noted above, the category of identified exceptions tends to sweep in far more cases than those described as "appropriate" for pre-indictment notification.

including agent interviews and the use of "target letters," illustrated below.[87]

Note should be made of restrictions on the right of prosecutors to approach witnesses and targets when either are represented by counsel. Ethical rules governing the conduct of lawyers prohibit attorneys—including government lawyers—from communicating or causing others to communicate with a represented "party" (or "person," depending on the jurisdiction's ethical rules[88]) unless the lawyer is "authorized by law" to do so.[89] The scope of this ethical limitation is controversial in the context of criminal investigations,[90] and the Department of Justice has not issued clear guidelines in the wake of relatively recent changes in the law. Nevertheless, as a practical matter, federal prosecutors typically will not themselves directly communicate, or cause agents to overtly and directly communicate, with either witnesses or targets whom they know to be represented by counsel.[91] Instead, overt communications with such represented individuals most often will occur through their attorneys, with the practical effect of reducing the chances of eliciting incriminating admissions from such persons.

If simply questioning the witness or target is not feasible, or is not likely to produce the desired results, prosecutors have several other means at their disposal to induce cooperation from, or otherwise resolve concerns about, individuals whose conduct may straddle the line between

---

87. See infra § 10.5(h).

88. Federal prosecutors are governed by the ethical code of the state in which the district is located.

89. See MODEL CODE OF PROF'L RESPONSIBILITY DR 7–104(A)(1) (1983 ed.) (hereinafter "MODEL CODE") (prohibiting such contacts with represented "parties"); MODEL RULE 4.2 (prohibiting such contacts with represented "persons"). In the past the Department of Justice took the position that these rules did not apply to federal prosecutors, but Congress overruled that view with passage of the McDade Amendment in 1998. See 28 U.S.C. § 530B (providing that government attorneys are subject to state rules governing attorney conduct).

The term "represented" in this context means that the individual has taken the step of retaining a lawyer to represent him in connection with the particular matter under investigation. It is entirely distinct from the question of when, as the process continues, their Sixth Amendment right to counsel may attach.

In addition, it should be noted that when there is uncertainty as to whether the person is "represented," communication is permissible for the purpose of clarifying that point.

90. See, e.g., Grievance Comm. v. Simels, 48 F.3d 640, 644 (2d Cir. 1995) (narrowly interpreting "party" and "matter" to avoid chilling criminal investigations); United States v. Lopez, 4 F.3d 1455, 1461 (9th Cir. 1993) (holding that a prosecuting attorney has a duty to refrain from communicating with represented defendants at the latest upon the moment of indictment); United States v. Hammad, 858 F.2d 834, 840 (2d Cir. 1988) (condemning use of sham grand jury subpoena to elicit incriminating statements from represented person). See generally MEHLER ET AL., ch. 9 ("Contact with Represented Persons").

91. We use the term "overtly" to refer to situations where the law enforcement person doing the communicating is openly identified as a law enforcement person, and in contrast to "covert" communications by undercover agents or government informants, which the courts generally have held do not run afoul of the ethical rules. See, e.g., Hammad, 858 F.2d at 840 (holding that "the use of informants by government prosecutors in a preindictment, non-custodial situation ... will generally fall within the 'authorized by law' exception").

a non-culpable witness and a culpable target deserving of prosecution. These options include: (1) a so-called non-prosecution cooperation agreement, which grants total immunity from prosecution (known as "transactional immunity") for certain conduct that a person is prepared to admit, in exchange for testimony against others; (2) granting statutory immunity, known as "use and derivative use immunity," which as applied provides virtually the same complete protection as "transactional immunity";[92] or, (3) entering a "deferred prosecution" agreement, under which a target typically admits their guilt and (if applicable) agrees to make restitution in exchange for the prosecutor agreeing to forego prosecution so long as the individual stays out of further trouble for a set period of time. We will discuss these various options further as the investigation in our illustrative case unfolds.

§ 10.4(b) Representing Witnesses and Targets

Effective pre-indictment advocacy may be among the most important services a defense attorney can provide in the type of prosecutor-initiated case under discussion here. The attorney may be able to convince the prosecutor that his or her client has no useful information and should not be called as a witness. Similarly, it may be possible to persuade the prosecutor that the client is merely a witness and should not be considered a target of the investigation. Even if the client is guilty of something (or at least if the prosecution is convinced of that), the defense lawyer may be able to convince the prosecutor that some form of immunity or deferred prosecution is appropriate because of some mitigating facts about the nature of the client's involvement or his or her personal circumstances. Failing any of these non-prosecution options, pre-indictment discussions may at least lead to some reduction in the client's punishment exposure, in the manner which we discussed in Chapter 8—a proffer session leading to more limited charges, or to a cooperation agreement allowing for a downward departure from the Sentencing Guidelines range. Even if none of these avenues is available, a preindictment conference with the prosecutor may at least result in the attorney obtaining useful information regarding what the government knows about activities in which the client might have been engaged and, concomitantly, what it does not know.[93]

When counsel is involved, the initial discussions typically will occur between the attorney and the prosecutor, without the client. Here, there may be an exchange of factual information, or at least an exchange of views about the matter under investigation. Arrangements may then be made for the client to appear, depending upon the circumstances and outcome of the discussions.

92. *See* 18 U.SC. §§ 6002–6003. *See* Mehler et al., § 20A–2 (discussing the substantial amount of protection afforded by § 6002).

93. For an excellent description of this process, see Kenneth Mann, Defending White Collar Crime: A Portrait of Attorneys at Work (1985).

In the case of a client who has been identified as a "target," where the client is interested in cooperating in exchange for a promise not to charge him or her with a crime, the defense attorney and prosecutor may arrange a proffer session. If the attorney takes the position that the target is in fact innocent of a crime or that, although guilty, he or she is not a proper subject for prosecution under the circumstances, the prosecutor will no doubt insist upon hearing the facts from the target and subjecting the target to questioning and further investigation. Such an interview would also take the form of a proffer session with the ancillary agreements described in Chapter 8.

If, on the other hand, the defense attorney views the prosecution's case as weak and/or thinks there is a strong defense, and wishes to preserve the target's ability to defend the case at trial, or if the defense attorney concludes that the prosecutor is not making a reasonable plea offer, or believes the prosecutor's mind is made up and thus no proffer, however compelling, is likely to dissuade the AUSA from bringing charges, the defense attorney may advise the target not to agree to make any proffer statement and to wait and see if he is indicted.

Deciding which approach to pursue in representing a "target" in the pre-indictment setting is often the single most critical decision the defense lawyer will make. We illustrate some of the complexities of this decision-making process in our model case.

§ 10.5   Pre–Indictment Practice in the Superior Warehouse Investigation

Having now reviewed the various legal mechanisms available to the government to carry out an investigation, we move to AUSA Knapp's review of the evidence and potential charges, followed by an investigative strategy meeting between AUSA Knapp and Agent Martinez. Following that meeting, we turn to a description of the activities undertaken and the results obtained in the investigation of Paul Christopher, William Van Ness and Ernest Wagner in connection with the Superior Warehouse drug operation. We also consider the role and responsibilities of the defense lawyer at various critical junctures.

§ 10.5(a)   The Government's Review of the Evidence, Potential Defendants and Charges

1.   The Case Against Paul Christopher

Shortly after the cooperation agreement with Gilbert Santiago was concluded, AUSA Knapp reviewed Santiago's proffer statement and the evidence that had been seized at the warehouse. Based on this review, she concluded that the following charges could be brought against Paul Christopher.

(a) Narcotics Trafficking: Importation, Possession with Intent to Distribute, Distribution and Conspiracy to do the Same[94]

The government has direct evidence of importation of just under 10 kilograms of cocaine on January 11, 2005—the drugs seized at the airport. Santiago can testify about Christopher's role in this shipment as well as Christopher's role in the four previous shipments in which he and Christopher were involved, and he can explain the phony invoices that were used to disguise these shipments. There is also direct evidence of Christopher's knowledge and intent, in the form of Santiago's testimony regarding conversations he had with Christopher about setting up the drug importation scheme.

While Christopher did not himself transport the drugs into the country, possess them, or distribute them, he still could be prosecuted as a principal because he aided and abetted in the importation, possession and distribution.[95] Additionally, it would not be necessary to prove that Christopher personally was in physical possession of the narcotics to charge him as a principal, but only that they were under his control, with the requisite knowledge and intent.[96]

Christopher also can be charged with conspiracy to commit each of the substantive crimes enumerated above. A conspiracy is punishable in addition to the substantive crime.[97] (As will be discussed later, a defendant's sentence upon conviction of a narcotics trafficking offense will be the same whether the defendant is convicted of the underlying substantive offense, the conspiracy, or both.)

(b) Money Laundering and Conspiracy to do the Same[98]

The offense of money laundering also could be charged. The money laundering statute prohibits, among other things, financial transactions,

---

94. *See* 21 U.S.C. §§ 952(a), 960(a)(1) (intentional or knowing importation of a controlled substance); 21 U.S.C. § 963 (attempt or conspiracy to do the same); 21 U.S.C. § 841(a)(1) (possession with intent to distribute and distribution of a controlled substance); 21 U.S.C. § 846 (attempt or conspiracy to do the same).

95. *See* 18 U.S.C. § 2(a) (punishes as a principal one who "aids, abets, counsels, commands, induces or procures" the commission of an offense against the United States).

96. *See* United States v. Gordils, 982 F.2d 64, 71–72 (2d Cir. 1992) (finding that "[c]onstructive possession exists when a person knowingly has the power and the intention at a given time to exercise dominion and control over an object, either directly or through others" and that evidence as to the presence of large quantities of heroin in defendant's apartment was sufficient to meet this standard).

97. In drug-related conspiracies, unlike those involving other criminal activities, the government is not required to prove that the defendant committed an overt act, because "the conspirators agreement to produce narcotics, not the actual possession, sale or delivery of the drugs, is the essence of the crime." United States v. Hendrickson, 26 F.3d 321, 333 (2d Cir. 1994). However, the defendant's *ability* to perform the act in question is significant. As one court noted, "ability often transforms the desire to produce narcotics into intent sufficient to form an agreement to do so; indeed, ability operates much like the overt act required for conspiracies other than drug conspiracies, in that it provides additional proof that an agreement existed." *Id.* at 337.

98. *See* 18 U.S.C. § 1956(a) (liability for money laundering), 1956(h) (conspiracy to commit the same).

including bank deposits of any amount, involving the proceeds of illegal activities such as narcotics trafficking. In addition to proving the illicit source of the funds, the government must prove that the defendant conducting the transaction knew that the money came from some unlawful activity, although not necessarily the particular unlawful activity. Moreover, the government must prove that the defendant either (a) knew that the transaction was designed to conceal the nature or ownership of the proceeds *or* (b) intended to promote the carrying on of the unlawful activity.

Again, Santiago's testimony about Christopher having instructed him to open the accounts in order to launder the drug proceeds constitutes proof of Christopher's knowledge and intent. In addition, Agent Martinez had been able to corroborate a significant point made by Santiago during his proffer—that Christopher made up phony invoices to show payments by a company called "Specialty Products" to cover the $25,000 in monthly cash deposits. In order to confirm Santiago's statement, Agent Martinez had reviewed the invoices seized during the search of Superior Warehouse and located three suspicious-looking "Specialty Products" invoices that were dated January 12, 2005 and totaled exactly $25,000. He then did some internet searches and confirmed that the Queens, New York address for this alleged company did not exist, the phone number listed was not in service, and there was no record of any such company anywhere in Queens or the greater New York area.

(c) Structuring and Conspiracy to do the Same[99]

Federal law requires that banks and other financial institutions file a Currency Transaction Report ("CTR") with the Internal Revenue Service ("IRS") for each transaction in currency (i.e., cash), such as a deposit or withdrawal, in excess of $10,000. CTRs are filed with the IRS on forms that require, among other things, disclosure of the identity of the individual who conducted the transaction and the individual or organization for whom the transaction was completed. The CTR filing requirement assists the United States in criminal, tax and regulatory investigations and proceedings.[100]

Under federal law it is a crime to "structure" transactions such as bank deposits for the purpose of evading the requirement that a financial institution file a CTR with the IRS. Such illegal "structuring" is defined to include subdividing an amount of currency in excess of $10,000 into amounts of $10,000 or less prior to depositing the money with a bank and then making separate deposits of those smaller

99. *See* 31 U.S.C. § 5313(a) (requiring financial institutions to report monetary transactions); 31 C.F.R. § 103.20 (specifying requirements for reporting "suspicious transactions"); 18 U.S.C. § 371 (conspiracy to commit offense against or defraud United States).

100. *See* 31 C.F.R. § 103.20.

amounts, in an attempt to evade the above-described currency reporting requirements.[101]

Proof of the structuring charge would include all of the evidence against Christopher just described, including in particular Santiago's testimony about: (a) how Christopher instructed him to open several separate accounts; (b) how he (Santiago) was instructed to tell Wagner that Christopher was eager to keep government regulators off his back; (c) how he (Santiago) in fact saw to it that the money was divided into amounts under $10,000, thereby avoiding the reporting requirement; and (d) the phony invoices.

AUSA Knapp concluded that the evidence against Christopher would be legally sufficient to convict him of all of these crimes. It was also clear, however, that the case would rest on the credibility of Santiago, who provides most of the significant direct evidence of guilt, and that accordingly Knapp's case was hardly on solid ground. By his own admission, Santiago was the most active participant in the present narcotics smuggling operation, and he also had on his record a relatively recent additional narcotics conviction for cocaine. As a two-time drug offender facing a mandatory minimum prison sentence of 20 years if he did not cooperate, Santiago had a strong incentive to provide the government with information incriminating Christopher, whether or not it was true. The key for Knapp was to find ways to corroborate Santiago's testimony, ideally through unimpeachable sources.

2. The Case Against William Van Ness

The direct evidence against Van Ness with respect to any of the drug charges that might be brought against Christopher was a good deal less substantial. Van Ness could clearly be shown to have in fact transported the cocaine: both Santiago and Long would testify that he did so, and the January 12 "Van Ness" entry in Long's date book—which was surrendered at the time of Long's arrest—would corroborate their testimony. However, evidence of Van Ness' knowledge that he was moving cocaine and his intent to do so was circumstantial and at best equivocal. Santiago could testify that it was Van Ness who introduced him to Christopher, knowing Santiago to be a convicted drug trafficker. Van Ness' family and business relation to Christopher might create some inference that he must have known what Christopher and Santiago were doing. However, Santiago consistently asserted that he had not discussed the cocaine operation with Van Ness and was not otherwise aware that Van Ness knew about or was involved in it.

Knapp nevertheless believed that Van Ness was in fact culpably involved and that there was sufficient direct evidence of his acts—the actual deliveries—to suggest that he was a participant in the importation and distribution of the drugs. The missing proof was that of the mental

---

101. *See* 31 C.F.R. § 103.11(gg).

element, i.e., knowledge and intent, and Knapp's investigation would have to focus on that issue.

3. The Case Against Ernest Wagner

As with Christopher, the question of whether charges could and should be brought against the banker, Ernest Wagner, turned largely on the credibility of Santiago. At this point the only information Knapp had to implicate Wagner was Santiago's version of the conversations that transpired between him and Wagner. If believed, those conversations might be sufficient to convict Wagner on charges of participating in and/or conspiring to commit money laundering and structuring. But Knapp knew that, particularly with respect to someone in Wagner's position—a senior bank employee with no known criminal history—a jury would be unlikely to find him guilty of these crimes based solely on the testimony of a two-time convicted narcotics trafficker. Clearly, Knapp would need hard corroboration of Wagner's knowing participation in structuring the transactions if any charges successfully were to be brought against him. Accordingly, and as with Van Ness, Knapp's investigation of Wagner's involvement would have to focus on his knowledge and intent.

Having reviewed the relative strengths and weaknesses of the evidence against Christopher, Van Ness, and Wagner, AUSA Knapp was ready to consider investigative strategies for strengthening the government's case against each potential defendant.

§ 10.5(b) Devising an Investigative Strategy

As mentioned, on January 25, 2005 Gilbert Santiago and his lawyer, Charles Berman, met with AUSA Knapp and Agent Martinez at the proffer session. A few days later, having decided to cooperate Santiago and after reviewing the evidence gathered so far, AUSA Knapp met with Agent Martinez at her office. Before we turn to discuss the investigative strategy that they crafted, we pause to raise one important consideration in the relationship between prosecutors and law enforcement agencies. Superficially, the line of authority between the United States Attorney's Office and the various federal law enforcement agencies is clear: the ultimate decision as to what evidence is needed, and what cases will be brought, is the prosecutor's.[102] In terms of technical expertise, it is assumed that the prosecutor possesses the knowledge of the law that must guide the investigative process. However, the degree of energy and

---

102. *See, e.g.,* U.S. ATTORNEYS' MANUAL § 1–2.303 ("Information obtained through an FBI investigation is presented to the appropriate United States Attorney or DOJ official, who decides if prosecution, or other action, is warranted."); Federal Bureau of Investigation, Frequently Asked Questions *available at* http://www.fbi.gov/aboutus/faqs/faqsone.htm#anchor463575 (noting,

"Although the FBI is responsible for investigating possible violations of federal law, the FBI does not give an opinion or decide if an individual will be prosecuted. The federal prosecutors employed by the Department of Justice or the U.S. Attorneys' offices are responsible for making this decision and for conducting the prosecution of the case.") (last visited June 6, 2005).

competence that is brought to bear by the agents involved can often be critical to the outcome. The prosecutor generally gives careful consideration to the needs of the law enforcement agency and the agent.

Knapp began the meeting by telling the agent that the first thing she wanted to do was to issue a grand jury subpoena to CMS Bank to obtain all of the records the bank had on file for IFD and all of its accounts, including monthly account statements, deposit slips, cancelled checks, etc. While certain CMS Bank deposit slips had been seized when agents executed their search warrant at Superior Warehouse, these records, Knapp believed, were likely to provide crucial corroboration of Santiago's story concerning the bank accounts he opened at Christopher's behest, the structured deposits that were intended to evade the reporting requirements, and Wagner's role in both. AUSA Knapp was also focused on a few additional facts that had come up during Santiago's proffer session. First, Santiago reported that over the past summer he had once called Christopher's cell phone and briefly discussed with Christopher something about one of the cocaine shipments. Santiago had written the cell phone number in his address book, which he still had when he was arrested, and he provided the number to the agents. Knapp thought that as a first step Agent Martinez should serve a DEA administrative subpoena on the cell phone company to confirm that in fact Christopher was the subscriber to that number and, assuming he was, obtain the calling (or "toll") records for that phone for the past year.

In addition, Knapp recalled that Santiago had mentioned that he believed Van Ness had charged and was paid substantially in excess of the going rates to transport the shipments that contained the drugs. Certain invoices had been seized during the search of Superior Warehouse, but Knapp knew that both IFD and Van Ness Trucking should have additional and more complete records that could be used to corroborate Santiago's assertion. Knapp decided to issue a grand jury document subpoena to Van Ness Trucking. By requiring Van Ness to produce all of its invoices for goods that it transported between January 2004 and January 2005, Knapp hoped to confirm both how much had been charged for the shipments from Superior Warehouse and that certain of those shipments had been billed at noticeably higher rates. (Recall that corporations enjoy no Fifth Amendment privilege as to their corporate records.) She also believed that by issuing a subpoena that was sufficiently general, she would not be giving away too much about her investigation to either Van Ness or Christopher (whom she assumed would find out about it from Van Ness).

Finally, Santiago was asked during his proffer about Barbara Weiss, a CMS Bank teller whose business card Santiago had in his wallet when he was arrested. Santiago had explained that Weiss once assisted him in depositing cash on a day when Wagner was unexpectedly unavailable, and she accepted a $100 bill as a "thank you." Santiago had mentioned that he did not believe Weiss worked at the bank anymore because he had not seen her there for several months. Knapp thought that Weiss was a good person to attempt to interview early in the investigation, and that because she no longer worked at the bank she was much more likely to speak with Agent Martinez without first checking with her former employer and/or a lawyer. But Knapp and Martinez agreed that any interview of Weiss should await their receipt and careful review of all the CMS Bank records relating to IFD, which very well might confirm Weiss' limited role or at least put them in a much better position to ask her informed and probing questions.

Agent Martinez suggested that he arrange for a team of agents to conduct several days of surveillance of Christopher's movements, to see whether he made contact with Van Ness or any other person who might be implicated. Martinez felt that evidence of frequent contacts or regular meetings might help to justify a wiretap, which might lead to direct evidence of Christopher's knowledge of and/or participation in the narcotics conspiracy.

Agent Martinez also wanted to go to the bank and attempt to interview Wagner, but Knapp explained that Wagner would almost certainly defer to the bank's lawyers and refuse to talk. Knapp explained that any approach to Wagner should come at the very end of the investigation, after they had otherwise gathered as much evidence as possible.

Knapp and Martinez also agreed that it did not make sense to approach either Christopher or Van Ness directly at this early stage, because any such actions would simply confirm what these two probably already suspected—that in fact they were now the subjects if not the targets of the government's investigation—and almost certainly would not prompt any incriminating statement or confession.

§ 10.5(c) Preliminary Investigative Steps

Following his meeting with AUSA Knapp, Agent Martinez directed a team of DEA agents to conduct a physical surveillance of Christopher for three days. Through this surveillance, it was learned that Christopher, was driven to his office each day at approximately 9:00 a.m. by William Van Ness. Both men entered the office together, and Van Ness left within 30 minutes. Christopher stayed until approximately 4:00 p.m. on each day, leaving only to make telephone calls from a cell phone and from a public telephone booth on the street outside of the office entrance. During the period of surveillance (January 31–February 2), four such calls were made, two on the cell phone and two on the payphone.

Agent Martinez reported the results of the surveillance to AUSA Knapp, who agreed to start issuing grand jury subpoenas for telephone and bank records. Thus, on February 4, 2005, AUSA Knapp issued subpoenas *duces tecum* to CMS Bank and Verizon, ordering the former to produce copies of IFD bank account records[103] and the latter to produce records of the two calls made from the public telephone booth outside of IFD during the period in which Christopher was under surveillance. She also issued a subpoena to Van Ness Trucking, seeking the documents previously described.

The bank records subpoena is set forth below as an illustration. It would be accompanied by a letter, a sample of which follows, instructing the bank that because of the nature of the charges being investigated (here, narcotics trafficking and money laundering), the law forbids the bank from notifying the customer (here, IFD) that its account records have been subpoenaed. This statutory mandate is of great benefit to prosecutors investigating defendants who, if notified of such an investigation in advance of charges being brought, might flee the jurisdiction or attempt to destroy or alter evidence or tamper with witnesses. The telephone company subpoena would be identical in form, except that, because it involves a pay phone, there is no similar concern about premature disclosure of the investigation. The Van Ness Trucking subpoena would be in the same form as the telephone company subpoena. Note that the same form of subpoena can be used either for the production of documents, for testimony, or for both, by checking the appropriate boxes.

All of the subpoenas would contain language advising the recipient that they could comply by producing the requested documents directly to the investigating agent, as opposed to physically appearing before the grand jury with the documents in hand. This standard procedure demonstrates the reality of the prosecutor-driven nature of the grand jury investigation. Indeed, the courts have upheld this procedure even with respect to records that enjoy special statutory protection appearing to mandate production directly to the grand jury, such as bank records, so long as some report of the content of the records ultimately is presented to the grand jury.[104]

---

103. *See* 12 U.S.C. § 3413(i) (excepting grand jury subpoenas from Right to Financial Privacy Act).

104. The Financial Privacy Act requires that records obtained from banks and other financial institutions actually be presented to the grand jury for its review "unless the volume of such records makes such return and actual presentation impractical in which case the grand jury shall be provided with a description of the contents of the records." 12 U.S.C. § 3420(a)(1). *See, e.g.,* BRENNER & LOCKHART, § 14.6.1(c); U.S. ATTORNEYS' MANUAL § 9–11.142; LAFAVE ET AL., § 8.8(g), n.149 (collecting cases). *See also* United States v. Residence Located at 218 Third Street, N. Glarus, Wis., 805 F.2d 256, 260 (7th Cir. 1986) (interpreting § 3420).

F#2005_____
g.i..sub (Rev. EDNY 11/96)

UNITED STATES DISTRICT COURT

<u>EASTERN</u>   DISTRICT OF   <u>NEW YORK</u>

TO: **CMS Bank**
     1 MacArthur Blvd.
     Brooklyn, **NY 10003**

SUBPOENA TO TESTIFY
BEFORE GRAND JURY

SUBPOENA FOR:
☐ PERSON   ☒ DOCUMENTS OR OBJECT(S)

YOU ARE HEREBY COMMANDED to appear and testify before the Grand Jury of the United States District Court at the place, date and time specified below:

Place	ROOM
United States District Court **Eastern District of New York** **225 Cadman Plaza East** **Brooklyn, New York 11201**	**475**
	DATE AND TIME February 18, 2005 10:00 am

YOU ARE ALSO COMMANDED to bring with you the following document(s) or object(s):

All documents concerning International Food Distributors, Inc., located at Grand Street, Queens, New York, including signature cards, monthly statements, copies of canceled checks, copies of deposit slips, safe deposit box records of access.

YOU MAY COMPLY WITH THIS SUBPOENA BY PROVIDING THE REQUESTED DOCUMENTS TO SPECIAL AGENT RALPH MARTINEZ, WHO CAN BE REACHED AT THE DRUG ENFORCEMENT ADMINISTRATION, 1256 QUEENS BLVD., QUEENS, N.Y., 11213, (718) 454-4789.

   This subpoena shall remain in effect until you are granted leave to depart by the court or by an officer acting on behalf of the court.

CLERK **ROBERT YOUNG**	DATE
(by) DEPUTY CLERK *Levin Nish,*	February 4, 2005

	Name, Address and Phone number of Assistant U.S. Attorney
This subpoena is issued upon **application of the** **United States of America**	Laura Knapp Assistant U.S. Attorney 225 Cadman Plaza East Brooklyn, NY 11201 718-254-7000

U.S. Department of Justice
United States Attorney
Eastern District of New York

February 4, 2005

Legal Department
CMS Bank
1 MacArthur Blvd.
Brooklyn, New York 10003

<u>Re:</u>   Subpoena of Records

To Whom It May Concern:

     As you know, under Title 12, United States Code, Section 3420(b)(1)(A), financial institutions and their employees are precluded from notifying possible suspects of the existence of a grand jury subpoena for records in money laundering and controlled substance investigations. I hereby advise you that the attached subpoena concerns an investigation of possible violations of the money laundering and controlled substance laws, and thus you are precluded from notifying the account holder of the existence of this subpoena.

     I appreciate your prompt assistance in this matter.

                 KEVIN O'REILLY
                 United States Attorney
                 Eastern District of New York

       By: *Laura Knapp*
                Laura Knapp
                Assistant U.S. Attorney

     Agent Martinez served the *duces tecum* subpoenas and obtained copies of the records from all three sources. After reviewing the bank records, Agent Martinez learned several important corroborative facts. First, as Gilbert Santiago had reported, the five IFD bank accounts had been opened in August, 2004, by Ernest Wagner, and the signature cards included the signatures of both Santiago and Paul Christopher. Second, the applications for each of the five accounts were identical, except that each one contained the name of a different IFD subsidiary. Third, copies of the deposit slips showed consistent cash deposits in amounts under $10,000.00. Fourth, all but one of these deposit slips had been initialed with the letters "EW," which Agent Martinez believed to be Ernest Wagner. Fifth, the one remaining deposit slip bore the initials "BW," which Agent Martinez believed corresponded to the one occasion that Santiago had mentioned when Wagner was not present at the bank and a teller named Barbara Weiss had assisted him.

     Agent Martinez also reviewed the records of the two telephone calls that Christopher had made from the payphone outside his office and learned that on both occasions he called the following number in Colombia: 011–63–482–5749.

In response to the subpoena to Van Ness Trucking, Agent Martinez received two boxes of shipping invoices that were produced by a lawyer whom Van Ness Trucking had retained. Although it took a considerable number of hours, Agent Martinez was able to isolate the invoices for the Superior Warehouse pick-ups, and he saw that there was one shipment per month between June 2004 and January 2005 that was billed at double the per-pound rate that Van Ness charged all of its other customers.

Finally, Agent Martinez's administrative subpoena to Sprint PCS confirmed that the cell phone number that Santiago had provided during his proffer session was subscribed to by Paul Christopher. In addition, toll records for this cell phone showed a consistent pattern over the past year of calls to the same number in Colombia that Christopher more recently had been calling from the pay phone outside his office. And the latest toll records showed that in fact Christopher still was using this same cell phone to make calls from outside his office to the same number in Colombia that he sometimes called from the pay phone (as observed by the surveillance agents).

§ 10.5(d) Court Orders

Several days after the surveillance of Christopher and his review of the evidence gathered so far, Agent Martinez again met with AUSA Knapp to discuss whether they could now apply for court authorization under the federal wiretapping statute to listen in on and record Christopher's cell phone conversations.[105]

Knapp had worked on wiretap applications before and knew that the requirements were quite stringent. She would have to demonstrate to a district court judge that, among other things, there was probable cause to believe that Christopher was committing one of a list of enumerated federal offenses (including narcotics trafficking and money laundering) and that there was probable cause to believe that intercepting calls over the specified phone would provide evidence of those crimes.[106] And before any such application to the court, she first would have to convince her superiors in the Department of Justice in Washington D.C. that a wiretap was warranted in this case, and she knew that the Department typically requires, among other things, evidence of at least a few recent "dirty calls" over the "target" cell phone—meaning calls in which there was either overt or coded discussion of one of the listed federal offenses.

After discussing the issue with Agent Martinez, AUSA Knapp met with the chief of her section at the United States Attorney's Office. The section chief pointed out a few problems in making a wiretap application at this point: first, many months had passed since Santiago allegedly

---

105. *See* 18 U.S.C. § 2510 *et seq. See also* U.S. Attorneys' Manual § 9–7.110 (setting forth the rules related to obtaining

Department approval before making an application).

106. *See* § 2518(3).

communicated with Christopher over the "target" cell phone, and they had no direct proof of any recent "dirty calls;" and second, because Christopher no doubt knew of Santiago's arrest, chances were that he either would stop using the same cell phone or would be extremely unlikely to discuss his suspected illegal activities over that phone.

However, as an alternative, Knapp's supervisor proposed that Knapp and Agent Martinez apply to the court for authorization to install a "pen register" on the "target" phone.[107] A pen register would tell them two things, on a real-time basis going forward: (1) what numbers Christopher was calling on his cell phone and what numbers were calling him (assuming the phone was still in use); and (2) the location of the "cell sites" to which Christopher's phone could be traced, which could help the agents find and follow him at any given time. AUSA Knapp thought this was a good idea because the burden of proof for a pen register was much lower than for a wiretap. All that was required was the AUSA's certification to the Court that it was "likely" that information obtained by the pen register would be "relevant to" an ongoing criminal investigation. Moreover, no Department of Justice approval would be required, and federal magistrate judges are authorized to sign pen register applications (as opposed to wiretap applications, which require approval from a district court judge) and do so rather routinely. Agent Martinez agreed that this was a reasonable first step and might help them move toward developing further evidence that later could be used to apply for a wiretap.

Accordingly, on February 22, 2005, AUSA Knapp drafted and then submitted to Magistrate Judge Brown an application for authorization to install a pen register on Christopher's cell phone. The pen register application included a recitation of the basic facts by AUSA Knapp and two proposed orders: one approving the pen register application and the other to be delivered to the cell phone provider—in this case, Sprint PCS—directing Sprint to assist the DEA in installing the pen register device and forbidding them from disclosing the existence of the pen register to their customer, Paul Christopher. AUSA Knapp's application and the basic approval order, both tracking the statutory language, appear below.

107. *See* 18 U.S.C. §§ 3121–3127.

UNITED STATES DISTRICT COURT
EASTERN DISTRICT OF NEW YORK
- x
IN THE MATTER OF AN APPLICATION   :   SEALED APPLICATION
OF THE UNITED STATES OF AMERICA   :
FOR AN ORDER AUTHORIZING THE   :
USE OF A PEN REGISTER WITH CELL   :
SITE LOCATION AUTHORITY   :
ON A CELLULAR TELEPHONE.   :
                                         :
- x

LAURA KNAPP affirms as follows:

1.   I am an Assistant United States Attorney in the office of Kevin O'Reilly, United States Attorney for the Eastern District of New York, and, as such, I am familiar with this matter.

2.   The Government is seeking (a) an order pursuant to Title 18, United States Code, §§ 3121-26 authorizing the use of a pen register in this jurisdiction for a period of 60 days on CELLULAR TELEPHONE NUMBER (917) 123-4567, ESN NO. 3341647829103, A SPRINT CELLULAR PHONE SUBSCRIBED TO BY PAUL CHRISTOPHER, 2312 ROXY STREET, CRANBERRY, NEW JERSEY, 07393-1824 (THE "SUBJECT TELEPHONE"),[108] in connection with a criminal investigation being conducted by the Drug Enforcement Administration ("DEA") of PAUL CHRISTOPHER, WILLIAM VAN NESS, ERNEST WAGNER, and others as yet unknown (the "SUBJECT INDIVIDUALS") regarding conspiracy to import and distribute cocaine in violation of 21 U.S.C. §§ 846 and 963 and conspiracy to launder the proceeds of narcotics trafficking, in violation of 18 U.S.C. § 1956, among other federal criminal offenses.

3.   This Court has jurisdiction pursuant to 18 U.S.C. § 3123 because, as I have been informed by the law enforcement agency involved, the pen register requested herein will be installed and used within the Eastern District of New York.

4.   Pursuant to Section 3121(c) of Title 18, United States Code, I have consulted with the agency in charge of this investigation and have determined that there is no technology reasonably available to the agency that restricts the recording or decoding of electronic impulses to the dialing and signaling information used in call processing.

5.   I have discussed the matter fully with the agents involved in the investigation. Based upon those discussions, I believe and hereby certify that the information likely to be

---

[108]   To confirm that the cell phone number provided by Santiago in fact belonged to Christopher and that the account was still active, Agent Martinez had issued a DEA administrative subpoena to Sprint. See § 10.5 (c), supra.

obtained by the use of a pen register on the subject cellular telephone number is relevant to an ongoing criminal investigation as required by 18 U.S.C. § 3123(a). Specifically, for the last several weeks, the DEA has been engaged in an investigation of a cocaine importation ring operating through a business called International Food Distributors ("IFD"), which is located in Queens, New York. On or about January 12, 2005, DEA Agents intercepted a shipment of coffee addressed to IFD at a warehouse in Queens, New York. In an interview with an IFD employee involved in the cocaine importation scheme, DEA agents learned that SUBJECT INDIVIDUAL Paul Christopher was the owner of IFD and was responsible for receiving multiple shipments of cocaine on behalf of a large-scale international cocaine distribution organization. The cooperating defendant further advised DEA agents that, over the summer, he had spoken to Christopher about the cocaine importation scheme over the SUBJECT TELEPHONE. Within the past few days, DEA agents conducting surveillance have seen Christopher suspiciously exiting the IFD offices and making calls out on the street from both a cell phone and a payphone. Toll records for the SUBJECT TELEPHONE confirm that it has been used over the past year and continues to be used to make calls to a particular number in Colombia.

6.　　　Additionally, I believe there exist specific and articulable facts showing that there are reasonable grounds to believe that the cell site location information also sought herein is relevant and material to an on-going criminal investigation as required by 18 U.S.C. § 2703(d). Specifically, as noted above, the SUBJECT TELEPHONE has been in the possession of an individual who appears to be involved in a conspiracy to import and distribute large shipments of narcotics. Originating and terminating cell site information will provide important information about the location of this individual and/or any other members of the conspiracy who may make use of the SUBJECT TELEPHONE or who may meet with or assist the user of the SUBJECT TELEPHONE. Such information is also valuable because it is probative of the geographic scope of the business and can provide leads to the locations of suppliers and customers.

7.　　　The Government also requests that SPRINT PCS be ordered, pursuant to 18 U.S.C. §§ 2705(b) and 3123(d), not to disclose the existence of this order or the pen register and cell site location authorization to the listed subscriber of the SUBJECT TELEPHONE, or to any other person, unless and until otherwise ordered by the Court. Pursuant to Section 2705(b), such disclosure would severely jeopardize this investigation because disclosure of a pen register on the SUBJECT TELEPHONE would alert the SUBJECT INDIVIDUALS to the existence of the investigation and likely lead to the cessation of operations of the conspiracy at the current locations, the destruction and concealment of evidence, and/or the flight of members of the conspiracy.

8.　　　No prior request for the relief set forth herein has been made. The foregoing is affirmed under the penalties of perjury, 28 U.S.C. § 1746.

Dated: Brooklyn, New York
　　　　February 22, 2005

　　　　　　　　　　　　　　　　Laura Knapp
　　　　　　　　　　　　　　　　LAURA KNAPP
　　　　　　　　　　　　　　　　Assistant United States Attorney

UNITED STATES DISTRICT COURT
EASTERN DISTRICT OF NEW YORK

- x

IN THE MATTER OF AN APPLICATION   :   SEALED AUTHORIZATION
OF THE UNITED STATES OF AMERICA   :
FOR AN ORDER AUTHORIZING THE   :
USE OF A PEN REGISTER WITH CELL   :
SITE LOCATION AUTHORITY   :
ON A CELLULAR TELEPHONE.   :
                                                               :

- x

WHEREAS an application has been made by LAURA KNAPP, an Assistant United States Attorney for the United States of America, pursuant to Title 18, United States Code, §§ 3121-26 and § 2703(d), for an order authorizing the use of a pen register with cell site location authority on a cellular telephone to be monitored in this jurisdiction, and the applicant has certified that the information likely to be obtained by such pen register is relevant to an ongoing criminal investigation being conducted by the Drug Enforcement Administration ("DEA") and the applicant has shown that there exist specific and articulable facts showing that there are reasonable grounds to believe that the cell site location information sought is relevant and material to an ongoing criminal investigation,

IT IS HEREBY ORDERED that pursuant to 18 U.S.C. §§ 3121-26 and § 2703(d), this Court authorizes the use of a pen register with cell site location authority for CELLULAR TELEPHONE NUMBER (917) 123-4567 (THE "SUBJECT TELEPHONE"), for a period of 60 days from the date of this order in connection with a criminal investigation being conducted by the DEA regarding, inter alia, conspiracy to distribute cocaine in violation of 21 U.S.C. § 846; and

IT IS FURTHER ORDERED that the person(s) owning or leasing the lines on which the pen register is authorized, or who have been ordered by this Court to provide assistance to the applicant, not disclose the existence of the investigation to the listed subscribers, or to any other person, unless or until otherwise ordered by this Court; and

IT IS FURTHER ORDERED that this Order shall be sealed until otherwise ordered by this Court, except that copies may be retained by the United States Attorney's Office and the DEA.

Dated: Brooklyn, New York
          February 22, 2005

_____
ROGER BROWN
UNITED STATES MAGISTRATE JUDGE
EASTERN DISTRICT OF NEW YORK

_____

After the magistrate judge signed the orders, AUSA Knapp delivered them to Agent Martinez, who then faxed the appropriate paperwork to Sprint PCS. Later that same night, February 22, DEA agents began receiving a real-time print-out of every phone number that was dialed by Christopher's cell phone and every phone number that called into Christopher's cell phone. In addition, the agents received real-time cell-site information, telling them the general location where the phone was being used.

The agents were then able to verify that Christopher was still using the phone. Over the next two days they were able to match the cell-site locations being provided by the pen register with Christopher's actual physical location at the time calls were being made. The agents discovered an interesting calling pattern: on several occasions, Christopher called the same number in Colombia that he had called from the payphone outside IFD's offices. The calls lasted several minutes, and then each time he immediately called another cell phone number, again for several minutes. The agents were able to determine, through issuance of another DEA administrative subpoena, that this second cell phone number belonged to William Van Ness. When the agents looked back at the toll records on Christopher's cell phone over the past year, they were able to see the same pattern of calls from Christopher's phone to the number in Colombia followed by a call to Van Ness' cell phone. After eight days, Christopher stopped using his cell phone and nothing further was ever recorded by the pen register.

§ 10.5(e) Approaching a Witness in the Christopher Case: Barbara Weiss

Armed with about as much documentary evidence as they could reasonably expect to obtain (short of subpoenaing IFD, which they will consider at the very end of their investigation), AUSA Knapp and Agent Martinez re-convened to discuss the next step in their investigation: attempting to talk to witnesses, in particular, Barbara Weiss, the teller whom Santiago had mentioned during his proffer.

Like many prosecutors, AUSA Knapp's general approach was that once she was involved in an investigation, she preferred to take the lead in interviewing potential witnesses and/or targets. Typically, she would issue grand jury subpoenas *ad testificandum* to any potential witnesses, which an agent would serve on them with an "Advice of Rights" form attached. But she would instruct the agent that, after serving the subpoena, the witness should be told that, if she so desired she could first make an appointment to come down to the United States Attorney's Office for an interview with the agent and the prosecutor. The witness also would be told that they could (but were not required to) bring an attorney along to represent them during such an interview.[109] The agent would further explain that it was completely up to the witness whether or not to agree to the interview, but that if the interview went smoothly, the witness might not have to make a formal appearance before the grand jury.[110] In Knapp's experience, this approach often led witnesses to

---

109. The Sixth Amendment right to counsel does not attach to a pre-indictment, non-custodial interview of a witness, even a prospective defendant. LaFave et al., § 6.4. As a matter of law, if the person does appear, the appearance is non-custodial, and thus *Miranda* warnings are not required. *Id.*, § 6.6.

110. This would be a truthful statement, because federal prosecutors often decide not to have witnesses testify before the grand jury, opting instead to simply have an agent summarize the witness' testimony for

agree to such pre-appearance interviews, sometimes with counsel and sometimes without, giving her the opportunity to assess the credibility and importance of the witness' story before deciding whether to have him or her actually testify before the grand jury. And Knapp knew that, so long as the grand jury subpoena was not used by her and the agents as a ploy to force the witness to appear at her office for an interview, such an approach was legally permissible.[111]

Agent Martinez had a different view. He suspected that if presented with a grand jury subpoena, Weiss would be likely to call her former employer, CMS Bank; CMS Bank no doubt would arrange for her to be represented by counsel; and all of this would significantly slow down the government's investigation. He therefore suggested that in the first instance he simply attempt to interview Weiss without serving any grand jury subpoena.

While Knapp agreed that Martinez's concerns were valid ones, she ultimately persuaded him to follow her standard procedure. Knapp's view was that Weiss might come in alone for an interview anyway, and if, alternatively, she was concerned enough to hire a lawyer or call CMS Bank, it would not necessarily be a bad thing for the investigation. Knapp nevertheless told Martinez that if Weiss volunteered a statement at the time he served her with the subpoena (as many recipients of grand jury subpoenas did), he could feel free to let her talk.

Agent Martinez drove out to Weiss' home in the evening of March 2nd, served Weiss with the subpoena and explained the option of coming down to the United States Attorney's Office for a pre-appearance interview. He also gave Weiss the attached Advice of Rights form, which stated as follows:

NOTICE OF RIGHTS OF GRAND JURY WITNESSES

1. The grand jury is conducting an investigation into possible violations of federal criminal law involving importation and distribution of narcotics, money laundering, and structuring, in violation of Title 21, United States Code, Sections 841, 846, 952, 960 and 963, Title 18, United States

---

the grand jury. In so doing the prosecutor saves the witness from an experience the witness is likely to view as an unpleasant, inconvenient and intimidating prospect, and also obtains a strategic advantage by not creating a sworn prior statement with which the witness might be impeached down the road.

111. SARA S. BEALE ET AL., GRAND JURY PRACTICE AND LAW § 6.2 (1991 & Supp. 2003) ("[T]he courts have generally permitted prosecutors to meet with prospective witnesses in advance of their appearances before the grand jury, as long as the inter-

views with the prosecutors are optional, and as long as the witnesses are given the choice to appear before the grand jury rather than submit to an interview."); LAFAVE ET AL., § 8.8(g) & n.150 (noting that it "is not uncommon for prosecutors to use the occasion of the witness' grand jury appearance to conduct a preliminary interview" and that "[t]he witness will often prefer the interview option, apart from the likelihood of not being required to testify before the grand jury, because the witness' lawyer can accompany the witness at the interview").

Code, Section 1956, and Title 31, United States Code, Sections 5324(a)(3) and 5324(c)(1).

2. You may refuse to answer any question if a truthful answer to the question would tend to incriminate you.

3. Anything that you do say may be used against you by the grand jury or in a subsequent legal proceeding.

4. If you have retained counsel, the grand jury will permit you a reasonable opportunity to step outside the grand jury room to consult with counsel if you so desire.

After reviewing these warnings, Weiss asked the agents what the prosecutor could possibly want to talk to her about. Martinez explained that they wanted to ask her about an incident with Ernest Wagner and the deposit of approximately $25,000 in cash by a CMS Bank customer.

Weiss hesitated, and Agent Martinez told her that she was free to talk to them now or to wait until she appeared before the grand jury— the choice was hers. Weiss, apparently feeling reassured by this, said she would like to tell them what she knew. She began by explaining that she was laid off from CMS Bank a few months ago and was now a salesperson at a department store. She said that she recalled the incident at CMS Bank with Mr. Wagner's customer. The customer was extremely agitated and said that Wagner had promised he would be there to handle the deposit. Weiss said she didn't quite understand why depositing the cash was such a big deal, but agreed to call Wagner on his cell phone. When she reached Wagner, he told her to divide the cash equally between IFD's five accounts, fill out the slips and make the deposits. The customer remained agitated but agreed to allow her to complete the transactions. She never saw the customer again, never gave the incident a second thought, and said this was the only time anything like this had ever happened during her several years as a teller.

Agent Martinez, aware of Santiago's claim that he had given Weiss a $100 "tip," but reluctant to reveal his knowledge to Weiss, asked one general follow-up question: was there anything else he should know about the incident. Weiss hesitated, but said no. Agent Martinez then decided that he should not ask any further questions, as he felt Weiss was likely to lie if asked directly about the $100 payment, and he wanted to give her some time (including time to talk to a lawyer) to consider the consequences before he allowed her to go on record in a way that would surely hurt her credibility—and thus her usefulness to the government— down the road.

Agent Martinez therefore ended the interview, explaining that the prosecutor would need to hear this story for herself, either in an interview at the United States Attorney's Office or in front of the grand jury. Weiss said she would think about the two options and get back to him.

§ 10.5(f) Representing A Witness: Barbara Weiss

For obvious reasons, a person who is served with a grand jury subpoena *ad testificandum* and/or is asked to sit for an interview at the United States Attorney's Office generally would be well advised to consult with counsel before appearing.[112] Weiss did that, was referred by a relative to defense attorney Alex Wells, and on March 4th met with Wells at his law offices. She told Wells the same story she had told Agent Martinez. He asked her if she had left anything out. She answered "no," but appeared nervous. Wells explained to her that she could speak in confidence to him[113] and that he could best help her only if he knew all of the facts.[114] Weiss then stated that she neglected to tell the agent that Santiago had given her $100 in cash as a "thank you" for her help on this particular occasion. She said she had been afraid to admit that because she had not reported the gift to the bank and thought it might have been some sort of violation. Wells asked if the agent had specifically questioned her about receiving anything in return for her actions that day, and she said she was so nervous that she just could not recall if she specifically was asked this.

Wells then obtained background information from Weiss, including any prior involvement with the criminal law, questions that he typically asked all clients who were going to be interviewed as part of a criminal investigation. Based on his experience, he thought that it was probable that the prosecutor would ask these same questions during any interview. After receiving her answers Wells felt reassured that, in considering whether to bring Weiss in for a proffer with the government, he need only focus on her current interactions with Wagner and Santiago and, later, with Agent Martinez.

Wells next considered whether to contact CMS Bank's lawyers and/or Ernest Wagner (or any attorney Wagner may have retained). On the one hand, Wells thought, it would be helpful to learn as much about the government's investigation, and who the real targets were, before having any further discussions with the prosecutor. Wells knew that lawyers representing CMS Bank or Wagner very well might have such information and might be interested in sharing whatever they knew in exchange for learning what Wells knew about the investigation and what his client had said or was going to say to the government. Wells also believed that CMS Bank might be obligated to pay for Weiss' attorneys'

---

112. *See* William L. Osterhoudt, *Representing a Grand Jury Witness*, 16 No. 2 Litig., Winter 1990, at 6.

113. *See, e.g.,* Model Rule 1.6(a) (requiring that "[a] lawyer shall not reveal information relating to the representation of a client").

114. *See, e.g.,* ABA Criminal Justice Standards: The Defense Function 4–3.2, *available at* http://www.abanet.org/crim-

just/standards/ (1991) (instructing that "defense counsel should seek to determine all relevant facts known to the accused" and "should not instruct the client or intimate to the client in any way that the client should not be candid in revealing facts so as to afford defense counsel free rein to take action which would be precluded by counsel's knowing of such facts").

fees, and even if not obligated, the bank would probably offer to pay them, both to ensure she had high quality representation and to maintain, as much as possible, an open line of communication concerning the government's investigation and its implications for the bank.[115] On the other hand, because Wells believed that the government was in the early stages of its investigation and that Weiss would be providing information that was likely to hurt Wagner and, by implication, the bank, he was concerned that contact with either such party at this juncture might complicate things for his client. Wells accordingly decided to defer any communication until it became clear that such contacts would be in his client's best interest.

Wells' next step was to contact the prosecutor and find out where his client stood. He thought it unlikely that Weiss was a target of the government's investigation, but he wanted to confirm that she was simply a witness. He did not know if the government was aware from other sources of the $100 "gift" she had accepted or that she had omitted that fact during her statement to Agent Martinez. He was reasonably confident the government would not want to prosecute Weiss for failing to mention the $100, and he did not think her acceptance of the money itself constituted a crime, much less a federal crime. But he was concerned that if she were to reveal the $100 payment, a zealous prosecutor and/or a perturbed agent might attempt to extract some kind of guilty plea for making a false or misleading statement to a federal agent.[116]

Wells decided that his ultimate goal was to obtain immunity for Weiss. That way, she could appear either for an interview or before the grand jury, admit the $100 payment, and not be concerned that her own statements might be used against her in any later prosecution for making a false statement. Wells also knew that prosecutors were reluctant to apply for immunity for witnesses unless they understood what it was that the witness might have done wrong that required immunity. He was therefore prepared, if pressed, to offer the prosecutor an attorney's proffer of what his client hypothetically might have done, as a way of explaining why he was insisting on immunity.

Wells placed the call to Knapp on March 7, 2005. He told her he had been retained by Weiss, he had reviewed the grand jury subpoena, and wanted to get a sense of what the prosecutor's interest was in speaking to Weiss. Knapp explained that Weiss' name had come up in their investigation of a narcotics smuggling and money laundering investigation but that, based on what the government knew at the time, and based on Weiss' own statement to Agent Martinez, Weiss was not a target of the investigation. But, Knapp explained, they did have one concern about whether Weiss had been completely truthful about wheth-

---

115. For a discussion of the issues that arise when a third-party pays a potential target's legal fees, see *infra* note 123.

116. *See* 18 U.S.C. § 1001.

er she had received anything in return for her assistance to Wagner and the bank customer. Knapp emphasized to Wells that her only interest was in using Weiss as a witness but that in order to do so, she would have to come completely clean.

Wells said he was happy to hear that Weiss was not a target, and he told Knapp that Weiss very much wanted to cooperate. He acknowledged that it was possible that because of nervousness Weiss may have left something out of what she told the agent. He asked Knapp whether, hypothetically speaking, if Weiss admitted to receiving a small "tip" for her help, the government still would be prepared to immunize her.

Knapp had anticipated this request, and she had discussed it with her supervisor. Together they determined that Weiss' testimony would be a great asset to any case brought against Wagner, that her failure to reveal the $100 payment was not worthy of any sort of criminal sanction, and that, if she was willing to be completely truthful with them, including admitting the $100 payment, they would be prepared to immunize her.

Knapp accordingly spelled out for Wells the conditions under which the government would be prepared to apply for and obtain an order of immunity for Weiss. The first step would be for Weiss to be interviewed by Knapp and Martinez. Assuming Weiss convinced them that she was being completely truthful about the incident with Wagner and Santiago, which of course would include admitting the $100 payment, Knapp would request Department of Justice permission to apply for a court order of immunity.

Two days later, after speaking with Weiss, Wells called Knapp and confirmed that Weiss was prepared to make the proffer, to be followed shortly thereafter by an appearance before the grand jury. The proffer session was held the next day, on March 10, 2005, and at the end of the proffer, Knapp and Martinez were satisfied that Weiss was now telling the whole truth, including about her receipt of the $100 payment.

Knapp then applied to the Department of Justice for approval to seek immunity for Weiss, explaining in the request form that without it she would invoke her Fifth Amendment privilege and that her testimony might prove to be a critical piece of evidence in the prosecution of Wagner and others on money laundering and structuring charges. The Department of Justice granted its approval two weeks later, on March 24, 2005. Knapp then submitted an immunity application and proposed order to the on-duty district judge, who signed the order the same day. The order reads as follows:

UNITED STATES DISTRICT COURT
EASTERN DISTRICT OF NEW YORK

- X

IN RE GRAND JURY PROCEEDING   <u>O R D E R</u>

- X

On motion of KEVIN O'REILLY, United States Attorney for the Eastern District of New York, filed in this matter on March 24, 2005;

And it appearing to the satisfaction of the Court:

1.   That Barbara Weiss has been called to testify or provide other information before a Grand Jury;

2.   That in the judgment of the United States Attorney Barbara Weiss is likely to refuse to testify or provide other information on the basis of her privilege against self-incrimination;

3.   That in the judgment of the United States Attorney the testimony or other information from Barbara Weiss may be necessary to the public interest; and

4.   That the aforesaid motion filed herein has been made with the approval of Lou Dembitz, Assistant Attorney General in charge of the Criminal Division of the United States Department of Justice, pursuant to the authority vested in him by Title 18, United States Code, Section 6003(b), and 28 C.F.R., Section 0.175(a).

NOW, THEREFORE, IT IS ORDERED pursuant to Title 18, United States Code, Sections 6002-6003, that said Barbara Weiss give testimony or provide other information which she refuses to give or to provide on the basis of her privilege against self-incrimination as to all matters about which she may be interrogated before the Grand Jury, and in any further proceedings resulting therefrom or ancillary thereto.

IT IS FURTHER ORDERED THAT, pursuant to Title 18, United States Code, Sections 6002 and 6003, no testimony or other information compelled under this Order, or any information directly or indirectly derived from such testimony or other information, may be used against Barbara Weiss in any criminal case, except in a prosecution for perjury, giving a false statement, obstruction of justice, or otherwise failing to comply with this Order.

This Order shall become effective only if after the execution of this Order the said Barbara Weiss refuses to testify or provide other information on the basis of her privilege against self-incrimination.

Dated: Brooklyn, New York
       March 24, 2005

Manny Decos
UNITED STATES DISTRICT JUDGE

Knapp, who was eager to lock in Weiss' testimony before the grand jury, scheduled her appearance for March 27, 2005.[117]

§ 10.5(g) The Grand Jury Presentation

On March 27, AUSA Knapp appeared before the grand jury and began her presentation in the investigation of Christopher, Van Ness and Wagner. She first gave a brief overview of the case to the grand jurors, summarizing the basic facts that the government had learned to date and the elements of the various potential charges against the potential defendants. She reminded the grand jury that what she was saying to them was not evidence and that the only evidence they could consider in ultimately making their decision about whether and whom to indict would come from witnesses who would testify in front of them and documents and other physical evidence that such witnesses might present.

She then explained that on this particular day the grand jury would hear from just one witness—a bank employee—who would offer testimony about one particular incident that they could later consider after they had heard all of the other evidence in the case. At that point AUSA Knapp called in Barbara Weiss, who entered the grand jury room alone (recall that the witness' lawyer is not allowed inside the federal grand jury room) and was sworn in by the grand jury foreperson.

---

117. An alternative approach the government might have pursued could have been to offer Weiss what is sometimes referred to as a "non-prosecution cooperation agreement." Under such an agreement, Weiss would admit to receiving the $100 "tip" and to failing to disclose it to Agent Martinez, and she also would agree to cooperate with the government's investigation and testify truthfully at any grand jury proceeding or trial. In exchange, the government would promise not to prosecute Weiss for either her role in assisting Wagner and Santiago (including accepting the $100) or her failure to disclose the fact of the $100 payment in making her statement to Agent Martinez. The advantage of such a non-prosecution cooperation agreement for Weiss is that it would provide her with an iron-clad promise of non-prosecution, compared to an immunity order, which, as a matter of law, only precludes the government from using her own testimony or evidence derived from it in prosecuting her. The principal disadvantage of such a non-prosecution cooperation agreement is that it would tend to suggest more strongly that Weiss actually committed prosecutable offenses as to which she needed, and the government granted her, immunity, when in fact it was debatable whether she actually committed any chargeable crime. As such, a non-prosecution cooperation agreement is often viewed by prosecutors as making a witness look worse in the eyes of a jury than the witness would if he or she had simply insisted on and received immunity, and it is therefore typically reserved for witnesses who are much more clearly guilty of some federal criminal offense but as to whom the government has decided that prosecution is not necessary or appropriate.

Knapp began by reminding Weiss of her rights, as previously set forth on the form attached to her grand jury subpoena.[118] In response to the first substantive question asked of her, Weiss asserted her privilege against self-incrimination, which she understood to be a required formality. Knapp then asked whether Weiss intended to invoke her Fifth Amendment privilege with respect to all questions concerning the incident with Ernest Wagner and Gilbert Santiago, and Weiss answered yes. Knapp then explained to Weiss that a judge had signed an order of immunity compelling her to testify, and that, having now invoked her privilege, that order required her to testify. Weiss said she understood and would be willing to answer the prosecutor's questions. Knapp resumed her questioning, in response to which Weiss relayed to the grand jury the story of her interactions with Santiago and Wagner. After satisfying herself that Weiss had provided all of the information relevant to the grand jury's inquiry,[119] Knapp excused Weiss from the room and explained to the grand jury that she would return in the next several weeks to present the rest of the evidence the government had gathered in its investigation. The grand jury session then ended.[120]

§ 10.5(h) Approaching a Target/Potential Cooperator: Ernest Wagner

Following this first grand jury session, and before proceeding to the next stage—i.e., deciding whom to charge and with what crimes—Knapp and Martinez decided to try one more thing. While the cases against Van Ness and Christopher had been strengthened by the investigation, the evidence against Van Ness in particular was still far from overwhelming. Knapp thought that if she could get Wagner—as to whom the evidence of structuring, if not money laundering, was quite strong—to "flip" or cooperate against Christopher and possibly provide information about Van Ness, the case against each of them would be on much more solid footing. Knapp viewed Christopher and Van Ness as the more significant defendants, as she believed they were directly involved in the narcotics importation and distribution scheme. She therefore thought it appropriate to attempt to secure against them the cooperation of Wagner, whom she viewed as a less culpable defendant because of the lack of any evidence of his direct involvement in the narcotics importation aspect of the case.

118. U.S. ATTORNEYS' MANUAL § 9–11.151 (providing that "these 'warnings' should be given by the prosecutor on the record before the grand jury and the witness should be asked to affirm that the witness understands them").

119. As explained and illustrated in § 11.8, infra, when the prosecutor finishes his or her questioning of a witness before the grand jury, the grand jurors themselves are given the opportunity to raise any questions they may have.

120. Federal grand juries sit for up to 18 months. FED. R. CRIM. P. 6(g). Larger districts, such as the Eastern District of New York, typically have a different grand jury for each day of the week, so that each separate grand jury sits one day a week for up to 18 months. Thus, AUSA Knapp would know that she could come back any number of weeks later (on the same day of the week) to present the remainder (indeed the bulk) of her evidence to the same grand jury that heard from Ms. Weiss.

Knapp, aware of the policy against subpoenaing a "target" of an investigation like Wagner to testify before the grand jury, decided to send Agent Martinez out to CMS Bank, without a subpoena, to see if Wagner would make a voluntary statement. If he refused, Martinez would give Wagner a "target letter," signed by Knapp, which would be intended to prompt Wagner to hire a lawyer with whom Knapp might then engage in discussions aimed at persuading Wagner to plead guilty and cooperate.[121]

Special Agent Martinez visited Wagner at the CMS Bank Coney Island branch on March 29, 2005. He told Wagner that he wanted to ask him some questions about IFD and some bank accounts he had opened on the company's behalf. Wagner responded by telling Martinez he had nothing to say and that Martinez should speak to the bank's lawyers. At that point, Martinez explained that he had a letter from the prosecutor involved in the case, and he handed Wagner an envelope containing the following "target letter:"

121. Had AUSA Knapp known that Wagner was already represented by counsel, ethical restrictions would have prevented sending the agent to make direct and overt contact with Wagner. *See* MODEL CODE DR 7–104(A)(1); MODEL RULE 4.2. *See also supra* note 89. In that situation, the AUSA in all likelihood simply would have picked up the phone, called Wagner's lawyer, and informed him or her that Wagner was a target. Such a call would trigger the kinds of discussions between the AUSA and the target's attorney that we now describe.

U.S. Department of Justice
United States Attorney
Eastern District of New York

March 29, 2005

Mr. Ernest Wagner
CMS Bank
Brooklyn, New York

Dear Mr. Wagner:

This letter is to advise you that you are now one of the targets of a federal grand jury investigation in this District into the importation and distribution of narcotics, money laundering, structuring, and other matters, in possible violation of federal criminal laws.

The government believes it is appropriate to notify you of the status of this matter before deciding whether to seek an indictment against you. This notice will allow you an opportunity, through legal counsel, to discuss the status and possible disposition of this matter with our office prior to any final grand jury proceedings.

Very truly yours,

Kevin O'Reilly
United States Attorney

By: *Laura Knapp*

Laura Knapp
Assistant United States Attorney
(718) 254-7000

---

§ 10.5(i) Representing Ernest Wagner

Even more so than a "witness" served with a grand jury subpoena, a person who receives a "target" letter is well-advised to consult with an attorney immediately. As soon as Agent Martinez left the branch, Wagner contacted CMS Bank's legal counsel's office and explained what had happened. Within a few hours, after hearing Wagner's version of what the government seemed to be interested in, CMS Bank's in-house attorneys arranged for Wagner to be represented by an attorney with whom they often worked, Isabel Johnson. Although in such a situation the employer would typically pay the employee's attorney's fees, and CMS Bank agreed to pay the fees here, governing standards of professional conduct make it clear that the attorney is to represent and answer to the employee and advance his interests alone, irrespective of whether those interests are aligned or at odds with the paying employer's interests.[122]

122. The controlling ethical rules allow attorneys to accept third-party payments of fees so long as the client consents after "full disclosure." MODEL RULE 1.8(f). Never-

Following a meeting between attorney Johnson and Wagner that would follow the general outline described above with respect to the first meeting between Weiss and her lawyer, Johnson phoned AUSA Knapp, indicated that she represented Ernest Wagner, and said she was calling to discuss the "target letter" that Wagner had received. Knapp told attorney Johnson that Wagner had opened several accounts for IFD and that the government believed that Wagner was aware that the money deposited into those accounts was the proceeds of narcotics sales. Knapp further indicated that it was almost certain that Wagner would be charged with participating in a money laundering and structuring scheme. Knapp also told Johnson that the government might be interested in Wagner's cooperation, and she said they were particularly interested in learning about the relationship between Wagner and Paul Christopher and William Van Ness, who ran IFD and Van Ness Trucking, respectively.

Johnson said that she had spent a good deal of time speaking to Wagner and that Wagner insisted that he had no idea that the IFD accounts were used for laundering drug money or to evade currency reporting requirements. Johnson asked if she could meet with Knapp to further discuss the case. Knapp agreed.

When Johnson and Knapp met the next day, Johnson explained that she hoped to learn as much as possible about the government's evidence against Wagner, so she could go back to her client and have a more informed discussion about how he ought to proceed. Knapp replied that she was not going to spell out the government's case in detail, but she was prepared to tell Johnson that: (1) they knew that Wagner was the bank officer who opened the multiple IFD accounts on the same day; (2) more than one witness had implicated Wagner in taking an active role in structuring the transactions to avoid the currency reporting requirements; and (3) Wagner's initials appeared on several of the deposit slips for amounts under $10,000.00. Johnson asked whether these cooperating witnesses would testify that Wagner knew the money being deposited was drug money and how exactly Wagner played an "active role" in the structuring, and Knapp said she was not going to get into those details. Knapp reiterated that they were interested in knowing what Wagner could tell them about Christopher and Van Ness and that she would be happy to listen to Wagner's story at a proffer session to see if she believed he was in fact innocent. Johnson told Knapp that she would speak again with her client and get back to her.

theless, in somewhat different circumstances "[c]ourts and commentators have recognized the inherent dangers that arise when a criminal defendant is represented by a lawyer hired and paid by a third party, particularly when the third party is the operator of the alleged criminal enterprise." Wood v. Georgia, 450 U.S. 261, 268–69 (1981). "One risk is that the lawyer will prevent his client from obtaining leniency by preventing the client from offering testimony against his former employer or from taking other actions contrary to the employer's interest." *Id. See, e.g.,* Quintero v. United States, 33 F.3d 1133, 1134 (9th Cir. 1994).

Johnson met with Wagner later that week and went through Wagner's story again, this time in even more detail. Wagner described his relationship with Santiago, for whom he admitted setting up the accounts. He stated that he had some suspicions about the transactions, because of the fact that separate accounts were set up within a short period of time and in different business names, and that he suspected that their purpose might be to avoid Internal Revenue Service reporting requirements. But he said he did not think that it was his business to make any specific inquiry of Santiago about this. He told Johnson that he recalled specifically advising Santiago about the laws against "structuring" transactions, a warning he says he gives all customers who inquire about the type of paperwork that needs to be filled out on cash transactions. He denied being involved in the subsequent deposits, except to the extent he may have initialed some deposit slips that Santiago gave him after the amounts already had been filled out. He said he did not pay attention to whether the deposits were in amounts less than $10,000, as he did not view that as his responsibility. And he emphasized the point that he never would have affixed his signature or initials to the deposit slips had be believed the transactions in any way involved or constituted illegal activity.

Wagner told Johnson he did not know Christopher personally, but knew from the account applications filled out by Santiago that Christopher was the president of IFD. He said he had never heard of Van Ness. He indicated that he was very frightened when Agent Martinez visited him and that after the visit he immediately called Christopher and told him that he had been contacted by a DEA agent. He said that Christopher told him that he would call him back and did so within a minute or two. Wagner said he then described to Christopher his brief interview with Martinez. He said that Christopher did not respond, but merely thanked him for calling. The next day, someone from IFD delivered a letter from Christopher directing the bank to close the five accounts. Wagner adamantly denied ever receiving any payments or gifts from Santiago or Christopher in exchange for his assistance.

Johnson explained to Wagner that he had several options. He could proffer the facts to the prosecutors, telling them the same story he had told Johnson, and hope to persuade them of his innocence. Alternatively, Johnson explained, Wagner could do nothing, wait and see if the prosecutor indicted him, and fight the case all the way through trial. A third option was to try to work out some kind of deal now, whereby Wagner would plead guilty to some lesser charge that would carry a lighter sentence under the Guidelines, such as illegal structuring. If he chose to plead guilty, he could also agree to cooperate, although Johnson explained to Wagner that, unless he had incriminating information about Van Ness or Christopher, which did not appear to be the case, the prosecutor was unlikely to be interested in "signing him up" as a government witness.

Wagner said he was absolutely *not* interested in the third option—pleading guilty—because he had done nothing wrong. He asked Johnson whether she thought it would be better to try to convince the government of his innocence now, at a proffer, or instead wait to see if he was indicted and, if he was, take the case to trial and hope to persuade a jury of his innocence. Johnson explained that there was no clear answer to this question. While a successful "innocence" proffer would of course be the best possible outcome, since as it would avoid any charges ever being brought, she told Wagner that, based on her discussions with the prosecutor, she thought it would be difficult for Wagner to persuade the AUSA of his innocence. At the same time, Johnson explained, she suspected that the government's case against him would turn largely on the testimony of cooperating witnesses who were likely to be admitted narcotics traffickers, and for that reason, there was some chance that the government would not go forward in seeking an indictment against Wagner or, if they did, that the government case would be vulnerable at trial.

Johnson also explained that there were significant disadvantages to an unsuccessful "innocence proffer:" Wagner's statement would provide the government with a preview of his defense, it would lock him into a story before his lawyer had a chance to better understand the government's evidence, and it would provide the government with a significant advantage in cross-examining Wagner if, as seemed likely, he later chose to testify in his own defense.

Johnson recommended a preliminary step before Wagner decided what to do. Johnson explained that she could make another appointment to see the prosecutor to present an "attorney proffer." Johnson said that this would give her a chance to let the prosecutor know that Wagner had a viable defense, fill in some of the details of that defense without completely giving it away, and show that Wagner intended to take the case to trial and testify in his own defense. Equally important, this attorney proffer would give Johnson another chance to gauge the prosecutor's confidence in her case. If, after listening to Johnson's attorney proffer, the prosecutor suggested either that she had some doubts about her case or was open to the possibility that Wagner's story might be true, Wagner could seriously consider going in for an innocence proffer. On the other hand, if, after the proffer, the prosecutor made it clear that she believed her own witnesses and their contrary accounts and she still seemed intent on going forward with a case against Wagner, Johnson would recommend against Wagner making any proffer statements. When Johnson was finished explaining this strategy, Wagner agreed to allow Johnson to attempt an attorney proffer.

Johnson phoned AUSA Knapp the next day. She told her she had spoken to her client again at great length and remained convinced that her client is innocent. She asked to meet with Knapp again to present an attorney proffer, during which she promised to explain in some more detail her client's version of events. Knapp said she would agree, but reluctantly, because in her view the only way she could imagine being persuaded not to bring charges against Wagner would be to hear his innocence proffer first-hand from Wagner's own mouth, in a setting where she would have the opportunity to challenge his story and gauge his credibility as he answered her questions. Although Johnson was somewhat discouraged, she set up the meeting for the next day.

When Johnson arrived at Knapp's office, she began by providing a little background about her client. She explained that Wagner had put himself through college, had a wife and three young children, had worked in the banking industry his whole life, had an unblemished disciplinary record with his employers and had never been in trouble with the law. Johnson emphasized that her client was shocked when he received the target letter and was absolutely convinced that Gilbert Santiago—who obviously had lied to him about the nature of IFD's business—was now telling lies to the government, falsely implicating him in an effort to save his own hide.

Johnson had decided that she would not lay out all of the details of Wagner's version of events, and she told AUSA Knapp as much. She said he was prepared to proffer the following facts: (1) Santiago never told Wagner, and Wagner did not believe, that the accounts would be used to deposit the proceeds of illegal activity; (2) Wagner had actually explained to Santiago the prohibitions on structuring, following his standard practice in cases where individuals inquired about paperwork in connection with cash transactions; and (3) while his signature or initials may appear on certain deposit slips, common sense would tell any jury that Wagner never would have put his name on such documents had he known they were part of an illegal scheme.

At the end of Johnson's attorney proffer, AUSA Knapp told Johnson that she had made some interesting points, but that the only way she could assess Wagner's story was to hear it herself first-hand, from Wagner's own mouth. She told Johnson that her witnesses and other information told her a very different story and that while she would have an open mind if Wagner were to come in and proffer, her current intention remained to pursue charges against him. Johnson told Knapp she would discuss Knapp's views with Wagner and get back to her.

Johnson met the next day with Wagner and explained what had occurred. They again discussed Wagner's options and, at the end of the meeting, Wagner asked for some time to think about it. A few days later, Wagner called Johnson and said he did not want to do a proffer. Johnson then called AUSA Knapp and told her that the only way Wagner would make a proffer or testify before the grand jury was with a grant of immunity. Knapp said she was disappointed, thought this was the wrong decision, but understood it was Wagner's to make. Johnson requested that she be notified and be given a chance to meet with Knapp, and possibly appeal to her superiors in the United States Attorney's Office, before any final decision to charge Wagner was made. Knapp agreed.

Chapter 11

THE DECISION TO INDICT

Table of Sections

Sec.
11.0 Introduction.
11.1 Grand Jury Review.
    11.1(a) Overview of the Grand Jury Process.
    11.1(b) Burden of Proof at the Indictment Stage.
    11.1(c) Factors Involved in the Prosecutor's Decision to Seek an Indictment.
    11.1(d) Selecting the Charges.
    11.1(e) Indicting a Corporation.
11.2 Drafting the Indictment.
    11.2(a) General Rules.
    11.2(b) The Count.
11.3 Multi–Count and Multi–Defendant Indictments.
    11.3(a) Joinder of Offenses—Constitutional Limitations on Multiple Prose-
            cutions for the Same Offense.
    11.3(b) Joinder of Offenses—Constitutional Limitations on Multiple Punish-
            ment for the Same Offense.
    11.3(c) Permissive Joinder of Offenses—Single Defendant Indictments.
    11.3(d) Permissive Joinder of Defendants.
11.4 Forfeiture.
11.5 Proceedings on the Indictment.
    11.5(a) Arrest or Surrender of the Defendant.
    11.5(b) Arraignment on the Indictment.
11.6 Time Limits on Returning the Indictment.
11.7 The Christopher Indictment.
    11.7(a) Deciding Who to Charge and What to Charge Them With.
    11.7(b) The Indictment.
11.8 Grand Jury Presentation in the Christopher Case.
11.9 The Arraignments of Christopher, Van Ness and Wagner.

§ 11.0 Introduction

The Constitution requires that a felony case be prosecuted by an indictment returned by a grand jury.[1] Cases may be commenced by the filing of a complaint, but, unless dismissed by the prosecutor, cannot be disposed of until the grand jury has acted. We begin this chapter with a discussion of the indictment process. We then discuss the legal standards for obtaining an indictment, followed by a description of the components of the instrument itself. The chapter concludes with the indictment in our illustrative case.

§ 11.1 Grand Jury Review

§ 11.1(a) Overview of the Grand Jury Process[2]

The grand jury is composed of 23 persons. Sixteen are required for a quorum, and 12 votes are needed for a "true bill," regardless how many jurors are present.[3] Grand jurors are selected from a pool of prospective jurors; members of the same panel will also serve on petit, or trial, juries.[4] Grand jurors sit for a term of the court, typically 18 months, and usually for one day each week. In busy federal districts there will be one or more grand juries in session at all times, and special grand juries may be empanelled as well to hear evidence in a single, lengthy investigation. In less busy districts, the grand jury will meet less frequently.

As we have described earlier, the grand jury has the power to subpoena witnesses and evidence.[5] It meets in secret, and the proceeding is *ex parte*. Grand jurors, prosecutors or other government personnel are not permitted to disclose the contents of the testimony, tangible evidence, or other matters occurring before the grand jury.[6] All matters, however, are recorded, except the deliberations and voting, which are conducted outside of the presence of everyone other than the grand jurors.[7]

A comment on the role of the prosecutor in the indictment process is in order. We noted in the last chapter that the prosecutor is for all practical purposes in complete control of the grand jury as an investigative body.[8] To a somewhat lesser degree that is also true with respect to the grand jury's charging function. While there are occasional instances of grand juries acting contrary to the prosecutor's wishes, they are for

---

1. *See supra* § 1.1(a). An offense may be prosecuted by information rather than indictment if a defendant has waived the right to an indictment in court, after being advised of the nature of the charge and of his or her rights. FED. R. CRIM. P. 7(b); WRIGHT, § 122.

2. Grand jury process is discussed in LaFAVE ET AL., § 8.

3. FED. R. CRIM. P. 6(f).

4. FED. R. CRIM. P. 6(a)(1); WRIGHT, § 102.

5. *See supra* § 10.3; FED. R. CRIM. P. 6 & 17. *See also* WRIGHT, §§ 94, 271.

6. FED. R CRIM. P. 6(e)(2). *See* WRIGHT, § 106. However, no obligation of secrecy can be imposed on anyone other than those individuals enumerated in the rule. Hence, grand jury witnesses are free to disclose such matters should they so choose. In re Grand Jury Subpoena, 103 F.3d 234, 240 n.7 (2d Cir. 1996). Grand jury testimony is also subject to disclosure under the discovery rules, discussed *infra* at § 13.4(b).

7. FED. R. CRIM. P. 6(e)(1); WRIGHT, § 103.1.

8. *See supra* § 10.3(b).

the most part the prosecutor's creature.[9] The prosecutor serves as the grand jury's legal advisor, explaining the law, determining which witnesses to call, and drafting the indictment upon which the grand jury will vote. Grand jurors may at times participate in the proceedings by asking questions and demanding additional evidence,[10] but the result of the proceeding is in the overwhelming majority of cases that which the prosecutor desires.[11] Moreover, if a grand jury refuses to indict, there is no legal bar to the prosecutor presenting the case to another grand jury (although this rarely happens in practice). Conversely, if a grand jury should vote an indictment that the prosecutor later decides he or she does not wish to (or cannot) press forward, the prosecutor can refuse to proceed and the indictment can be dismissed.[12]

As a practical matter, therefore, in most cases the indictment process would be no different if conducted by the prosecutor alone. That said, many federal prosecutors have had the experience at some point in their prosecutorial career of a grand jury challenging and rejecting at least some part of their case, and in this sense an argument can be made that the grand jury does exert some modest policing function on the exercise of the prosecutor's charging power.[13]

§ 11.1(b)   Burden of Proof at the Indictment Stage

The *quantitative* burden of proof at the grand jury stage is low: all that is legally required for a grand jury to return an indictment is probable cause to believe that the defendant committed a crime.[14] Governing ethical rules require no more.[15] This minimal threshold limits the effectiveness of the grand jury as a screening device.

That effectiveness is further eroded when one considers the *qualitative* burden of proof. Evidentiary rules designed to assure reliability at

---

9. For a discussion of the grand jury, see THE GRAND JURY PROJECT OF THE NEW YORK COURT OF APPEALS (1999); MARVIN E. FRANKEL & GARY P. NAFTALIS, THE GRAND JURY: AN INSTITUTION ON TRIAL (1977). *See also* Andrew D. Leipold, *Why Grand Juries Do Not (And Cannot) Protect the Accused*, 80 CORNELL L. REV. 260 (1995).

10. *See* LaFAVE ET AL., §§ 8.4(b),15.2(b).

11. *But see* Judith M. Beall, *What Do You Do With A Runaway Grand Jury?: A Discussion of the Problems and Possibilities Opened Up By the Rocky Flats Grand Jury Investigation*, 71 S. CAL. L. REV. 617 (1998) (examining the positive and negative aspects of encouraging grand jury independence).

12. *See supra* § 10.3(b).

13. A practical benefit that the grand jury offers is worth mentioning. Given the fact that the grand jury is drawn from the same pool as the petit jurors, where the prosecutor presents witnesses who also will testify at trial, the prosecutor can gain a preliminary sense of the petit jurors' likely impressions of that testimony based on the grand jury's reaction.

14. WRIGHT, §§ 101, 110. *See also* United States v. Calandra, 414 U.S. 338, 343 (1974) (noting that one of the grand jury's two main responsibilities is to determine whether there is probable cause to believe a crime has been committed).

15. *See, e.g.,* NEW YORK CODE OF PROF'L RESPONSIBILITY DR 7–103, *available at* http://www.nysba.org/ Content/ Navigation_Menu/Attorney_Sources/ Ethics_Opinions/ Lawyers_Code_of_Professional Responsibility/ CodeofResponsibility.pdf (1970, as amended 2002) (hereinafter "NY CODE") (forbidding a public prosecutor from instituting criminal charges when he or she "knows or it is obvious that the charges are not supported by probable cause").

trial are not applicable at the grand jury stage.[16] Thus, a grand jury can base its vote to indict upon evidence which is legally incompetent or inadmissible—most notably, hearsay evidence—as well as evidence taken in violation of the accused's constitutional rights.[17] An indictment, more-over, is not open to challenge based upon the fact that the evidence presented to the grand jury was inadequate.[18] The defendant's right to demand legally sufficient evidence is considered to be adequately protect-ed by a jury trial. In short, "[a]n indictment returned by a legally constituted and unbiased grand jury, . . . if valid on its face, is enough to call for trial of the charge on the merits."[19]

As noted, grand jury proceedings are conducted exclusively by the prosecutor, who serves as the grand jury's legal advisor. Defense counsel are not permitted to enter the grand jury room, and no judge is present to instruct the jurors on the law.[20] While the prosecutor may not mislead the grand jury as to the nature or the significance of the testimony presented,[21] there is no legal obligation on the prosecutor to present evidence tending to exculpate the defendant[22] or to show weaknesses in the government's case.[23]

While both the quantitative and qualitative burdens of proof before the grand jury are very low as a matter of law, the Department of Justice has adopted internal rules that increase both. The United States Attor-neys' Manual dictates that evidence clearly obtained in violation of a defendant's constitutional rights should not be offered;[24] that hearsay evidence should not be presented to grand jurors in a manner that misleads them into believing the witness is giving his or her own personal account;[25] and that substantial evidence that directly negates guilt should be made known to the grand jury.[26] As with all of the Department's policy statements, however, the Department advises that these provisions cannot be enforced in court.[27]

---

16. LaFave et al., § 15.2(d). The only exception is rules of evidence concerning testimonial privileges, which do in fact ap-ply to grand jury proceedings.

17. *Calandra,* 414 U.S. at 354–55; Unit-ed States v. Blue, 384 U.S. 251, 255 (1966); Costello v. United States, 350 U.S. 359, 363, (1956); LaFave et al., § 15.5(a), (b).

18. *Costello,* 350 U.S. at 363. However, where the prosecutor presents evidence known to him or her to be perjurious, the indictment may be dismissed. *See* LaFave et al., § 15.5(b).

19. *See* Wright, § 102; LaFave et al., §§ 15.4(g), 15.5(b).

20. A judge will impanel the grand jury at the beginning of its term and at that time provide general instructions about its function.

21. LaFave et al., § 15.7(e); United States v. Estepa, 471 F.2d 1132, 1136 (2d Cir. 1972).

22. LaFave et al., §§ 15.6(b), 15.7(f); United States v. Williams, 504 U.S. 36, 55 (1992).

23. *See* LaFave et al., § 15.6(b).

24. U.S. Attorneys' Manual § 9–11.231.

25. *Id.* § 9–11.232.

26. *Id.* § 9–11.233. *Accord* ABA Crimi-nal Justice Standards: Prosecution Function 3–3.6(b), *available at* http://www.aban-et.org/crimjust/standards/ (1991) (hereinaf-ter "ABA Standard") (requiring prosecutors to disclose to the grand jury "evidence which will tend to negate guilt").

27. U.S. Attorneys' Manual § 9–27.150.

Perhaps most importantly, while as a matter of law an indictment properly may be pursued if there is sufficient evidence—legally admissible or not—constituting "probable cause" to believe that the defendant has violated a federal law,[28] the Department of Justice has adopted a higher and more nuanced standard. It provides that charges should be pursued only if the *admissible* evidence in the government's possession, or admissible evidence that the prosecutor reasonably believes will be available and admissible at the time of trial, will *probably* be sufficient to obtain and sustain a conviction.[29] Stated differently, Department policy provides that "no prosecution should be initiated against any person unless the government believes that the person probably will be found guilty [beyond a reasonable doubt] by an unbiased trier of fact."[30]

While these standards are in some ways more restrictive than the law requires, they obviously leave much to the discretion of the individual prosecutors. If asked, many prosecutors will say that they will not seek the indictment of a defendant unless they personally are persuaded of the defendant's guilt beyond a reasonable doubt. Some have suggested that this kind of high threshold—or an arguably even higher standard of "moral certainty"—should be applied universally to the prosecutor's charging decision.[31] In practice, however, if the government believes that the crime or the defendant is particularly deserving of prosecution, the decision may be made to go forward even though the likelihood of conviction is less sure.[32]

28. The ethical standard is the same. *See* n.15, supra; ABA STANDARD 3–3.9 ("Charges should not be brought or maintained when the prosecutor knows that the charges are not supported by probable cause, or in the absence of admissible evidence to support a conviction.").

29. U.S. ATTORNEYS' MANUAL § 9–27.220 (A), (B) & comment.

30. *Id.*

31. *See* Kenneth J. Melilli, *Prosecutorial Discretion in an Adversary System*, 1992 B.Y.U. L. REV. 669, 700 (1992) ("If the beyond a reasonable doubt standard is a necessary cushion against erroneous convictions by the trier of fact, then how can prosecutors, in pursuit of their obligation to 'seek justice,' impose any lower standard upon themselves?"); Bennett Gershman, *A Moral Standard for the Prosecutor's Exercise of the Charging Discretion*, 20 FORDHAM URB. L.J. 513, 515 (1993) (arguing that a prosecutor should "engage in a moral struggle over charging decisions" and then "assure herself that she is morally certain that the defendant is both factually and legally guilty and that criminal prosecution is morally just").

32. There also are categories of cases where the prosecutor may often have difficulty determining (or may even be unable to decide) precisely where the truth lies, yet for institutional reasons the decision is made that the cases must be prosecuted. One example is the recurring problem of "drug mules," who carry illegal narcotics into the country through covert means such as a suitcase with a secret sewn compartment. Defendants in such cases routinely offer stories—suggesting they were unaware that drugs had been placed in the suitcase—that cannot easily be confirmed or disputed. Notwithstanding the difficulties of proof in this category of cases, they are routinely prosecuted, and there are arguments that support the decision to allow juries to be the ultimate arbiters as to whether the defendant knew what he or she was carrying. *See generally* Richard Uviller, *The Virtuous Prosecutor in Search of an Ethical Standard*, 71 MICH. L. REV. 1145 (1973) ("When [the prosecutor] is honestly unable to judge where the truth of the matter lies, I see no flaw in the conduct of the prosecutor who fairly lays the matter before the judge or jury. He need not vouch for his cause implicitly, as he may not ex-

§ 11.1(c) Factors Involved in the Prosecutor's Decision to Seek an Indictment

A prosecutor's reasons for bringing charges against an individual are virtually unchallengeable in the courts.[33] While a prosecutor may neither selectively charge individuals based on improper considerations such as race, religion, or other constitutionally protected classifications[34] nor charge individuals to penalize their exercise of constitutional or statutory rights,[35] courts presume that criminal prosecutions are undertaken in good faith and in a non-discriminatory manner.[36]

When this broad discretion is considered along with the relatively low burden of proof at the indictment stage (even considering the Justice Department's somewhat heightened threshold), as well as the prosecutor's nearly complete control over the process, it seems fair to say that the individual's principal protection against an unwarranted prosecution is the prosecutor, who decides largely as a matter of policy what evidence will be presented to the grand jury and whether the evidence resulting from the law enforcement investigation warrants proceeding further against the defendant.

Since the return of the indictment marks the final decision to charge, it is at this stage of the process that the prosecutor typically confronts and rigorously considers a wide range of legal and policy considerations.[37] The Department of Justice has attempted to provide at least some standards for the exercise of the prosecutor's charging decisions.

As noted, the Department's threshold requirement for prosecution is that the prosecutor "believes that the person's conduct constitutes a

---

plicitly. Nor should he lose sleep over his reliance upon the device the system has constructed for the task of truth-seeking, inexact though he knows it to be.").

33. *See, e.g.,* United States v. Gary, 74 F.3d 304, 313 (1st Cir. 1996); United States v. Redondo–Lemos, 27 F.3d 439, 444 (9th Cir. 1994) (reiterating "extreme deference courts must give to prosecutorial charging decisions"). *See also* Peek v. Mitchell, 419 F.2d 575, 577–79 (6th Cir. 1970) (finding that separation of powers considerations prevented court from interfering with federal attorney's control over criminal prosecutions, and state officials were immune from injunctive sanctions in the absence of arbitrary or discriminatory actions). *See also* LaFave et al., § 13.4.

34. *See* LaFave et al., § 13.4(e). *See, e.g.,* United States v. Willis, 956 F.2d 248, 250 (11th Cir. 1992) (per curiam); United States v. Andersen, 940 F.2d 593, 596 (10th Cir. 1991); Shaw v. Martin, 733 F.2d 304, 311–12 (4th Cir. 1984).

35. *See* Blackledge v. Perry, 417 U.S. 21, 28–29 (1974); United States v. White, 972 F.2d 16, 19 (2d Cir. 1992). An ulterior motive does not necessarily constitute a vindictive prosecution. *See also* United States v. Paguio, 114 F.3d 928, 930 (9th Cir. 1997); LaFave et al., § 13.5(a).

36. *See Gary,* 74 F.3d at 313; United States v. Parham, 16 F.3d 844, 846 (8th Cir. 1994).

37. The considerations that we now discuss are not likely to have been fully addressed, or addressed at all, at the time a complaint may have been filed. See Chapter 4 on the initial decision to charge, in which we noted that the need for a prompt decision to "stop the action," commonly made before the prosecutor had the opportunity to gather and/or assess all of the evidence, typically led to deferral of consideration of many of the factors now reviewed.

federal offense and that the admissible evidence will probably be sufficient to obtain and sustain a conviction."[38] Even if these conditions are met, the prosecutor may decline to prosecute if he or she determines that no "substantial federal interest" would be served by the prosecution, if the person is subject to "effective prosecution" in another jurisdiction, or if there is an "adequate" non-criminal alternative to prosecution.[39]

Among the list of considerations in making the prosecution decision are: (1) federal law enforcement priorities; (2) the nature and seriousness of the offense (including the economic harm to community interests and/or the impact of the offense on the victim); (3) the deterrent effect of prosecution; (4) the person's culpability (including their extent of involvement and motivations for committing the crime); (5) the person's criminal history; (6) the person's willingness to cooperate; (7) the person's personal circumstances; and, (8) the probable sentence (and whether it justifies devoting prosecutorial resources).[40] Prohibited considerations include: (1) the person's race, religion, sex, national origin, or political association, activities or beliefs; (2) the prosecutor's own personal feeling concerning the person, the person's associates, or the victim; (3) the possible effect of the decision on the attorney's own professional or personal circumstances; and (4) the unpopularity of the prosecution or the popularity of the defendant.[41]

Courts that have issued non-binding declarations discussing the considerations that appropriately should guide the decision whether to bring charges recite similar factors:

> Paramount among them is a determination that a prosecution will promote the ends of justice, instill respect for the law, and advance the cause of ordered liberty....

> Other considerations are the likelihood of conviction, turning on choice of a strong case to test uncertain law, the degree of criminality, the weight of the evidence, the credibility of witnesses, precedent, policy, the climate of public opinion, timing, and the relative gravity of the offense. In weighing these factors, the prosecutor must apply responsible standards, based, not on loose assumptions, but, on solid evidence balanced in a scale demanding proof beyond a reasonable doubt to overcome the presumption of innocence....

> Still other factors are the relative importance of the offense compared with the competing demands on the time and resources of investigation, prosecution and trial. All of these and numerous other intangible and imponderable factors must be carefully weighed and considered by the conscientious United States Attorney in deciding whether or not to prosecute.[42]

38. U.S. ATTORNEYS' MANUAL § 9–27.220(A).

39. *Id.*

40. *Id.* at § 9–27.230(A), (B).

41. *Id.* at §§ 9–27.230 & 9–27.220.

42. Pugach v. Klein, 193 F.Supp. 630, 634–35 (S.D.N.Y. 1961).

In day-to-day operation in the United States Attorney's Offices, the charging standard is considerably higher at the indictment stage than at the complaint stage, notwithstanding the fact that the legal threshold— probable cause—is identical. One reason is that there is a much more rigorous approval process for an indictment, which will require at least in some offices review by a section chief and a division chief and in all districts the ultimate approval of the United States Attorney. Also, a complaint can be readily dismissed with little if any fanfare or consequence. The dismissal of an indictment typically requires an elaborate write-up, the approval of supervisors including the United States Attorney, and court approval (although this is virtually automatic). Having to dismiss an indictment may, moreover, be viewed as a reflection of a mistake or bad judgment by the prosecutor who obtained it, unless it is clear that something beyond the government's control occurred after the indictment was filed (such as the unexpected unavailability of an essential witness). Finally, there is a deeply ingrained view among many prosecutors that an indictment should not be pursued unless and until the prosecutor has collected evidence sufficient to prove his or her case at trial, beyond a reasonable doubt, and within a matter of weeks (as might occur in a case where a defendant or a judge presses for a particularly speedy trial).

§ 11.1(d) Selecting the Charges

In 2003, then Attorney General John Ashcroft issued a memorandum for the purpose of stating "with greater clarity" the Department of Justice's policy with respect to deciding "what charges to bring and how cases should be disposed."[43] The Memorandum sought to establish "fair and reasonably consistent policies" to ensure that the charges a defendant faces did "not depend on the particular prosecutor assigned to handle the case."

The Memorandum thus states that, having made the decision to pursue charges, federal prosecutors "*must* charge and pursue the most serious, readily provable offense or offenses that are supported by the facts of the case."[44] "Readily provable" is defined only in the negative: "[a] charge is not 'readily provable' if the prosecutor has a good faith doubt, for legal or evidentiary reasons, as to the Government's ability

43. John Ashcroft, Departmental Policy Concerning Charging Criminal Offenses, Disposition of Charges, and Sentencing, pp. 3–5, *available at* http://www.fd.org/TXW/ pdf_lib/memoagcds.pdf (Sept. 23, 2003) (hereinafter "Ashcroft Memorandum" or the "Memorandum"). Interestingly, news reports attribute the origin of the Memorandum not to Attorney General Ashcroft but rather to an advisory committee of United States Attorneys who "found inconsistencies in the [prior iterations of DOJ] charging policy." David Hechler, *Some See Little Change, Others a Mired System: Ash-*

croft Echoes Thornburgh, Circa 1989, NAT'L L. J., Vol. 26 No. 5, Sept. 29, 2003.

44. Ashcroft Memorandum at IA (emphasis added). For many years before Attorney General Ashcroft's 2003 Memorandum, the U.S. Attorneys' Manual had a more flexible standard, stating that federal prosecutors "should charge . . . the most serious offense that is consistent with the nature of the defendant's conduct, and that is likely to result in a sustainable conviction." U.S. ATTORNEYS' MANUAL § 9–27.300(A).

readily to prove a charge at trial."[45] The "most serious" offense is the one that yields the highest sentencing range under the Sentencing Guidelines.[46] If two crimes have the same statutory maximum penalty and Guidelines range, the one with the higher mandatory minimum jail term is preferred.[47]

The 2003 Ashcroft Memorandum—which was reaffirmed in 2005 following the Supreme Court's *Booker* decision[48]—appears to have been aimed at eliminating a broader version of prosecutorial charging discretion authorized by the previous Attorney General, Janet Reno, and restoring a more restrictive policy similar to that in effect under Reno's predecessor, Attorney General Richard Thornburgh.[49] In a 1993 Memorandum, Attorney General Reno issued a policy stating that "once the decision to prosecute has been made, the attorney for the government *should* charge, or *should* recommend that the grand jury charge, the [1] most serious offense [2] *that is consistent with the nature of the defendant's conduct*, and [3] that is likely to result in a sustainable conviction."[50] While clauses 1 and 3 remain essentially unchanged under the Ashcroft Memorandum (save for the substitution of "must" for "should"), clause 2 was effectively eliminated. And, it was under this clause 2 that DOJ policy as articulated by Attorney General Reno explicitly stated that it was "appropriate," in deciding what charges to bring:

> that the attorney for the government consider, inter alia, such factors as the Sentencing Guideline range yielded by the charge, whether the penalty yielded by such sentencing range (or potential mandatory minimum charge, if applicable) is proportional to the seriousness of the defendant's conduct, and whether the charge achieves such purposes of the criminal law as punishment, protection of the public, specific and general deterrence, and rehabilitation.[51]

The discretion of federal prosecutors to inform their charging decisions by consideration of these types of factors—particularly the likely

---

45. Ashcroft Memorandum at IA.

46. *Id.*

47. U.S. ATTORNEYS' MANUAL § 9–27.300. The rationale for choosing the offense with the higher mandatory minimum is to ensure "equal justice." "It guarantees that every defendant will start from the same position, charged with the most serious criminal act committed." *Id.*

48. *See* James B. Comey, Department Policies and Procedures Concerning Sentencing, p. 2, *available at* http://sentencing.typepad.com/sentencing_law_and_

policy/files/dag_jan_28_comey_memo_on_booker.pdf (June 10, 2005).

49. The language under Attorney General Thornburgh was very close to the Ashcroft language. Thornburgh's memorandum stated that "a federal prosecutor should initially charge the most serious, readily provable offense or offenses consistent with the defendant's conduct." Memorandum from Richard Thornburgh, U.S. Attorney General, to All Federal Prosecutors (Mar. 13, 1989) (on file with authors).

50. U.S. ATTORNEYS' MANUAL § 9–27.300 (emphasis added).

51. *Id.*

sentence—appears to have been largely eliminated by the Ashcroft Memorandum.[52] Less clear is whether this newly articulated policy will have the effect of significantly reining in the exercise of prosecutorial discretion at the charging (or plea bargaining) stage, or instead whether the highly elastic concept of whether a charge is "readily provable," as well as other articulated exceptions that we now discuss, will continue to provide prosecutors with enough "wiggle room" to make the kind of individualized assessment outlined in the Reno Memorandum.

The 2003 Ashcroft Memorandum sets out certain "limited circumstances" in which the "most serious readily provable" offense need not be charged or, having been charged, may be dismissed. One is where the ultimate sentence would not be affected. A second is where a particular United States Attorney's Office has established, with Department of Justice approval, a so-called "fast-track" program whereby certain classes of similar offenders (such as drug "mules" importing illegal narcotics by swallowing them or smuggling them in their luggage or on their person) are offered reduced charges (or downward departures) if they agree to an early guilty plea and waive other rights (such as the right to bring pre-trial motions or to appeal a sentence).[53] A third is where a post-indictment change in the evidence (such as the unavailability of a witness) "causes a prosecutor to determine that the most serious offense is not readily provable." A fourth, applicable only in "rare circumstances," is where declining to charge or pursue a readily provable offense is "necessary to obtain substantial assistance in an important investigation or prosecution." A final catch-all exception is reserved for "rare" and "exceptional circumstances," such as where a United States Attorney's Office is "particularly overburdened," "the duration of the trial would be exceptionally long, and proceeding to trial would significantly reduce the total number of cases disposed of by the office."[54]

The Ashcroft Memorandum also sets forth fairly strict guidelines for charging statutory enhancements.[55] The two most common such enhancements are the filing of a prior felony information under 21 U.S.C. § 851, which doubles the statutory mandatory minimum prison terms for second-time felony narcotics offenders, and the filing of a charge under 18 U.S.C. § 924(c), which adds a mandatory additional five years in prison, consecutive to any sentence under the Guidelines for the underlying crime, if, during the course of a "crime of violence or drug trafficking crime," a defendant "uses or carries a firearm." The Memorandum states that "[t]he use of [such] statutory enhancements is

52. Under pre-Ashcroft Memorandum DOJ policy, factors such as the "probable sentence" also could "be considered by the attorney for the government when entering into plea agreements." *Id.* Oddly, it appears that prosecutors remain free to consider the "probable sentence" in deciding whether to charge a defendant at all (as noted above), but no longer may consider the probable sentence in selecting charges or offering a plea.

53. The fast track program is discussed *supra* at § 7.2(i).

54. Ashcroft Memorandum at IB(6).

55. *Id.* at IB(5).

strongly encouraged" and requires federal prosecutors to take "affirmative steps so that the increased penalties ... are sought in all appropriate cases."[56] More importantly, the Memorandum authorizes prosecutors to "forego the filing of a statutory enhancement ... *only* in the context of a negotiated plea agreement."[57]

The Ashcroft Memorandum reaffirmed long-standing Department policy concerning when additional charges beyond the "most serious readily provable offense" should be brought: (1) when necessary to ensure that the indictment adequately reflects the nature and extent of the criminal conduct involved and provides the basis for an appropriate sentence; or (2) where such charges will significantly enhance the strength of the government's case against the defendant or a codefendant.[58] But the Department also cautions that "[i]t is important to the fair and efficient administration of justice in the Federal system that the government bring as few charges as are necessary to ensure that justice is done" and that "[t]he bringing of unnecessary charges not only complicates and prolongs trials, it constitutes an excessive—and potentially unfair—exercise of power."[59] The Memorandum also reaffirms long-standing DOJ policy that "charges should not be filed simply to exert leverage to induce a plea."[60] And it allows prosecutors to forego charges that would not affect the ultimate Sentencing Guidelines range within which a sentence would be imposed.[61]

§ 11.1(e) Indicting a Corporation

Although the topic is in most respects beyond the scope of this book, we pause here to note the similarities—and a few differences—between Department of Justice policies governing the decision to charge corporations as opposed to persons. As corporations can only act through their employees or agents, the typical basis for corporate criminal liability is vicarious, i.e., the corporation may be held criminally responsible for the acts of an employee or agent if those actions (i) were within the scope of the employee's or agent's duties and (ii) were intended, at least in part, to benefit the corporation.[62] Indicting a corporation is of course unlike indicting an individual in one very obvious sense: the corporation cannot be sent to prison. Similar to an individual charged with a business-related crime, however, it is fair to say that a corporation convicted of federal criminal charges relating to its business activities will face

---

56. *Id.*

57. *Id.*

58. U.S. ATTORNEYS' MANUAL § 9–27.320 (noting, among other things, that "[i]f the evidence is available, it is proper to consider the tactical advantages of bringing certain charges").

59. *Id.*

60. Ashcroft Memorandum at IA; U.S. ATTORNEYS' MANUAL § 9–27.300.

61. Ashcroft Memorandum at IIC.

62. *See, e.g.,* United States v. Automated Med. Labs., Inc., 770 F.2d 399, 406 (4th Cir.1985); United States v. Cincotta, 689 F.2d 238, 241–42 (1st Cir. 1982).

substantial—and sometimes insurmountable—obstacles in continuing in that business on a going forward basis.[63]

Prosecutions of corporations make up only a tiny fraction of all federal criminal cases. Department of Justice guidelines make it clear that prosecuting a corporation should not be viewed as a substitute for, or reason to forego, bringing charges against the criminally culpable individuals within the corporation. Rather, prosecutors are encouraged to consider pursuing charges against corporations in certain cases to further broader regulatory goals, such as prompting remedial steps throughout an industry where an illegal practice may have been prevalent, changing the corporate culture of an organization where misconduct may have been widespread, or deterring particular crimes that carry substantial risks of great public harms and that are, by their nature, most likely to be committed by businesses.[64]

Under a Department of Justice Memorandum issued in 2003 in the wake of massive accounting fraud scandals at companies like Enron and WorldCom, federal prosecutors are directed to consider the following factors, in addition to the traditional considerations such as the likelihood of success at trial and the probable deterrent benefits of a conviction, when deciding whether to criminally charge a corporation:

1. the nature and seriousness of the offense, including the risk of harm to the public, and applicable policies and priorities, if any, governing the prosecution of corporations for particular categories of crime;

2. the pervasiveness of wrongdoing within the corporation, including the complicity in, or condonation of, the wrongdoing by corporate management;

3. the corporation's history of similar conduct, including prior criminal, civil, and regulatory enforcement actions against it;

4. the corporation's timely and voluntary disclosure of wrongdoing and its willingness to cooperate in the investigation of its agents, including, if necessary, the waiver of corporate attorney-client and work product protection;

5. the existence and adequacy of the corporation's compliance program;

---

63. The 2002 federal criminal indictment and conviction of the Arthur Andersen accounting firm on obstruction of justice charges in connection with the Enron investigation stands as one of the most obvious examples of the kind of corporate entity that simply could not survive the taint of first being indicted and then being convicted. Delroy Alexander et al., *Repeat Offender Gets Stiff Justice,* CHI. TRIB. Sept. 4, 2002, § 1; Ken Brown, *Andersen Called to Account: Many Change Their Auditors With Ease,* WALL ST. JOURNAL, June 17, 2002,

at C13. The conviction of Arthur Anderson was later overturned by a unanimous Supreme Court because of errors in the jury instructions. *See* United States v. Arthur Andersen LLP, 125 S.Ct. 2129 (2005).

64. Memorandum from Larry D. Thompson, Deputy Attorney General, to Heads of Department Components & United States Attorneys, I(B), *available at* http://www.usdoj.gov/dag/cftf/business_organizations.pdf (Jan. 20, 2003).

6. the corporation's remedial actions, including any efforts to implement an effective corporate compliance program or to improve an existing one, to replace responsible management, to discipline or terminate wrongdoers, to pay restitution, and to cooperate with the relevant government agencies;

7. collateral consequences, including disproportionate harm to shareholders, pension holders and employees not proven personally culpable and impact on the public arising from the prosecution;

8. the adequacy of the prosecution of individuals responsible for the corporation's malfeasance; and

9. the adequacy of remedies such as civil or regulatory enforcement actions.[65]

Defending corporations that are the subject or target of a federal criminal investigation bears certain similarities to, and reflects a number of critical differences from, the defense of an individual who is the subject or target of such a criminal probe. Issues particularly important in the corporate context include ensuring that relevant evidence is preserved, deciding whether to conduct an "internal investigation," potential conflicts of interest in simultaneously representing employees as well as the corporation, deciding which if any employees to discipline or fire and whether and to what degree to cooperate with the government's investigation (including waiving privilege with respect to the work product generated in connection with any internal investigation).

One final point with respect to the federal prosecution of corporations: sentencing for corporations, which consists mainly of restitution, fines and various forms of government monitored remedial action, is governed by an entirely separate (and confusing) chapter of the Sentencing Guidelines.[66]

§ 11.2 Drafting the Indictment

§ 11.2(a) General Rules

The Sixth Amendment requires that an accused "be informed of the nature and cause of the accusation."[67] This requirement has been incorporated in the Federal Rules by the requirement that the indictment contain a "plain, concise and definite written statement of the essential facts constituting the offense charged."[68] Each charge must be contained in a separate "count." Each count must contain not only all of the statutory elements of the offense charged but also enough descriptive language to provide the defendant with notice of the nature of the offense. The protection afforded by these rules is three-fold: (i) to apprise the defendant of what he or she must be prepared to defend against at

---

65. *Id.* at II(A).

66. USSG Ch. 8 (Sentencing of Organizations).

67. U.S. Const. Amend. VI.

68. Fed. R. Crim. P. 7(c)(1). *See* Wright, § 123.

trial (notice); (ii) to permit the defendant to plead a prior acquittal or conviction in bar of future prosecutions (double jeopardy); and (iii) to ensure that a defendant is tried upon charges found by a grand jury.[69]

The requirements for an indictment are perhaps best explained by comparing them to those required for a complaint. Like the complaint, the indictment must specify the crime or crimes with which the defendant is charged.[70] This is accomplished in the indictment in the same way that it is in the complaint: with a gravemen paragraph reciting the elements of the crime. Unlike the complaint, however, the indictment need not contain means paragraphs which make out probable cause that the defendant committed the offense.[71] It need only contain such facts as are necessary to meet the notice requirements discussed in the preceding paragraph: date, time, and place of the offense and perhaps some description of the means or instrumentalities employed. This is sufficient because the indictment need not *establish* the facts on which the grand jury relies; it is merely an assertion that the grand jury has found them.[72]

§ 11.2(b) The Count[73]

An indictment contains one or more charges. Each charge must appear in a separate "count." Inclusion of two charges in a single count renders the count defectively "duplicitous."[74] Each count must also demonstrate that the court has venue as to the particular charge.[75]

(1) The Gravamen Paragraph

The defendant can only be prosecuted for violation of the statutes specifically cited in the indictment.[76] Each count of the indictment must

---

69. Hamling v. United States, 418 U.S. 87, 117–18 (1974). *See also* United States v. Santeramo, 45 F.3d 622, 624 (2d Cir. 1995); LaFave et al., § 19.2.

70. Fed. R. Crim. P. 7(c)(1). *See* Wright, §§ 123, 124.

71. Fed. R. Crim. P. 7(c)(1). *See* Wright, § 123.

72. *See* Wright, § 111; LaFave et al., § 15.4(a).

73. *See generally* Wright, §§ 123–126.

74. Mehler et al., § 21–7.

75. Venue is a concept similar to but distinct from jurisdiction. In brief, jurisdiction refers to the sovereign's power to proscribe and punish behavior within its territorial reach and largely turns on the situs of the criminal offense. *See* LaFave et al., § 16.4(b). Venue is proper if the case is brought in the district where the crime was committed and may lie in more than one district. *See* Fed. R. Crim. P. 18; 18 U.S.C. § 3237; Wright, § 302. The government

need only prove venue by a preponderance of the evidence. United States v. Strain, 396 F.3d 689, 692 (5th Cir. 2005); United States v. Morgan, 393 F.3d 192, 195 (D.C. Cir. 2004). Motions based on the failure to allege that any act occurred in the district in which the indictment is filed are rare. More common are motions pursuant to Rule 21 of the Federal Rules which permits a defendant to move for a change of venue on grounds of prejudice (usually associated with the particular venire) or convenience or in the interests of justice. The rule also prohibits a change of venue absent the defendant's consent. In this way, Rule 21 serves as a check on the government's ability to choose an inconvenient forum when venue properly lies in more than one district.

76. United States v. Hutcheson, 312 U.S. 219, 229 (1941); Williams v. United States, 168 U.S. 382, 389 (1897); United States v. Pope, 189 F.Supp. 12, 26 (S.D.N.Y. 1960).

contain either a recitation of the language of the statute (as it may have been supplemented by case law) or a paraphrase of that language which touches on every element,[77] and the statutory citation.[78] An overly vague statement of the offense being charged constitutes an impermissible delegation of authority to the prosecutor, because it could permit proof of facts supporting the charge that are at variance from those found by the grand jury.[79]

Uncertainty in the gravamen paragraph may also be a problem when the statute enumerates several alternative means by which the crime can be committed. For example, 18 U.S.C. § 2113(c) punishes a person who "receives, possesses, conceals, stores, barters, sells, or disposes of any property or money or other thing of value" taken from a bank. Pleading those acts in the disjunctive will not adequately notify the defendant of the nature of the charge.[80] The problem is solved by specifying the various ways in which the offense is committed in the conjunctive. By charging all the statutory means by which the offense may be committed, the defendant is adequately notified, since he or she need not guess which theory the government will argue.[81] In the alternative, the indictment can charge one of the means by which the offense may be committed without referring to the others.[82] The double jeopardy clause will protect the defendant from a subsequent trial of any of the alternative means specified in the statute.[83]

(2) The Means Paragraph

The means paragraph is optional, and when used it may simply provide what could be included for notice purposes in the gravamen paragraph: the date, place and venue of the crime, as well as the essential means by which it was committed (e.g., the nature of the contraband possessed or sold or the kind of property stolen).[84] None of the other evidence relied upon by the grand jury need be included.[85]

---

77. Hagner v. United States, 285 U.S. 427, 433 (1932).

78. FED. R. CRIM. P. 7(c)(1); WRIGHT, § 124.

79. *Pope*, 189 F.Supp. at 26. While tracking the language of the statute ordinarily ensures against this problem, there are circumstances in which additional language will be necessary. If the statutory language describes any of the elements in overly general terms, the gravamen paragraph must be more specific in order to assure adequate notice. The most common example of this problem is in statutes that originated in the common law, and which in some instances do not indicate the requisite *mens rea*. Except in rare strict liability offenses, the statute's silence cannot be taken to mean that *mens rea* has been eliminated, and therefore it must be added to the statu-

tory language. *See* United States v. Morrison, 536 F.2d 286, 288 (9th Cir. 1976).

80. *See generally* United States v. Donovan, 339 F.2d 404, 407–08 (7th Cir. 1964).

81. *See, e.g.,* United States v. Crisci, 273 F.3d 235, 239 (2d Cir. 2001).

82. Thornburg v. United States, 164 F.2d 37, 39 (10th Cir. 1947).

83. Sanabria v. United States, 437 U.S. 54, 69–70 (1978).

84. It will, however, be necessary for the government to prove the date of the offense at least sufficiently to satisfy the statute of limitations. Ledbetter v. United States, 170 U.S. 606, 612 (1898); United States v. Gammill, 421 F.2d 185, 186 (10th Cir. 1970).

85. Although this rather limited pleading requirement is the rule, there are some

Prosecutors, however, often include in the indictment a very detailed description of the facts underlying the government's case. There is no limitation on the right of the government to allege all of the facts that it in good faith intends to prove, and there may be strategic reasons to include an expansive factual statement. The indictment typically is read to the jury before the government's opening statement at trial, and it is taken into the jury room at the time of the jury's deliberations. It can, therefore, serve as a useful way of explaining the government's theory to the jury, particularly in cases in which the facts are complex.

§ 11.3   Multi–Count and Multi–Defendant Indictments

Special pleading problems arise in situations in which a defendant may be charged with the violation of more than one statute, or of multiple violations of the same statute, and in situations in which the government seeks to prosecute more than one defendant in the same indictment. In any such case, the essential question is how to balance the promotion of judicial efficiency achieved through joining charges and/or defendants in a single proceeding, against the danger that the proceeding will be unfair to any one particular defendant. The constitutional and statutory rules discussed here reflect the law's attempt to accommodate these interests.

In the multiple charge situation, this balance is struck in the first instance by the double jeopardy clause of the Fifth Amendment, which precludes placing the defendant "twice in jeopardy for the same offense."[86] This requires related charges, as defined below, to be brought in a single indictment. Beyond the constitutional rules, the Federal Rules also govern "joinder" of offenses.[87] In single defendant indictments, Rule 8 liberally permits joinder of offenses of similar character or those that are transactionally related, subject to severance on a showing of prejudice. In multiple defendant indictments, Rule 8 precludes joinder of offenses of similar character,[88] unless all of the defendants were involved

situations in which elaboration of the facts may be necessary. One is where the statutory language itself is very vague. It has been held that "[i]t is not sufficient that the indictment shall charge the offense in the same generic terms as in the (statutory) definition; but it must ... descend to particulars." United States v. Cruikshank, 92 U.S. 542, 558 (1875). For example, if an individual is charged in the gravamen paragraph with contempt for failing to respond to questions "pertinent to the question then under inquiry," the indictment must descend to particulars before it adequately apprises the defendant of facts. Russell v. United States, 369 U.S. 749, 752 (1962).

86.   U.S. Const. Amend. V. The discussion that follows centers on the issue of when an act or series of acts committed by the defendant constitutes the "same" or separate offense(s) for double jeopardy purposes. We are not concerned with the double jeopardy implications of reprosecution of a case after a conviction, acquittal or mistrial. *See generally* LaFave et al., § 25. The issue of reprosecution is beyond the scope of this book. It is well established that a defendant is placed in jeopardy (jeopardy "attaches") when either of the following events occur: the jury is sworn or, in a bench trial, the first witness is sworn. LaFave et al., § 25.1(d).

87.   Fed. R. Crim. P. 8(a) & 14. *See* Wright, §§ 143 & 222.

88.   Fed. R. Crim. P. 8(b); Wright, § 144.

in the same acts or transactions, again subject to severance if prejudice is shown.[89]

In the sections that follow we will discuss the rules of joinder and severance of offenses and defendants separately. It should be recognized, however, that in practice a single indictment may encompass both kinds of joinder.

§ 11.3(a) Joinder of Offenses—Constitutional Limitations on Multiple Prosecutions for the Same Offense

There are many circumstances in which a defendant may commit a single act or engage in a single transaction and yet violate several statutes.[90] There is no constitutional prohibition limiting Congress' power to create such statutes. The double jeopardy clause, however, has been interpreted by the Supreme Court to limit the number of separate prosecutions that can be brought under them.[91] In summary, these rulings state the following: statutes that are the "same" for constitutional purposes must be prosecuted in the same indictment, in order to avoid multiple trials. Statutes are the "same" when each statute requires proof of the same elements, i.e., facts enumerated in the statute defining the offense, *and* when only one of the statutes contains an additional element not found in the other.[92] An example in the Christopher case of two statutes that would constitute the same offense under this so-called *Blockburger* rule would be knowing possession of a controlled substance (21 U.S.C. § 844(a)) and possession of a controlled substance with intent to distribute (21 U.S.C. § 841(a)(1)). All of the elements of the former are included in the latter, which alone has an additional element (intent to distribute). The former is known as a "lesser included offense" of the latter, and it cannot be prosecuted separately.

§ 11.3(b) Joinder of Offenses—Constitutional Limitations on Multiple Punishment for the Same Offense

The double jeopardy hazard of multiple trials can, of course, be avoided by including in one indictment all charges that are the "same" for double jeopardy purposes. Doing so, however, may raise a different

---

89. FED. R. CRIM. P. 8; WRIGHT, § 144. *See* Barry H. Berke & Lauren Freeman–Bosworth, *Severance of Counts in Federal Criminal Proceedings,* 228 N.Y.L.J. 4, Oct. 7, 2002.

90. Our model case provides an example, as we shall see in the indictment set out below, in which the defendants' financial activities violate both the money laundering and structuring laws.

91. *See* LaFAVE ET AL., § 17.4(a) & (b). The principle of collateral estoppel has also been used to preclude reprosecution, where

it can be shown that the jury has determined an "issue of ultimate fact" in a prior prosecution. *See* Ashe v. Swenson, 397 U.S. 436, 444 (1970). Since jury verdicts in criminal cases are general, however, it is usually impossible to conclude that a particular issue of fact has been determined. *See* LaFAVE ET AL., § 17.4(a).

92. If each statute contains an element not found in the other, the offenses are different. Blockburger v. United States, 284 U.S. 299, 305 (1932).

double jeopardy issue, that of "multiplicity."[93] The double jeopardy clause not only protects against multiple trials for the "same offense," but multiple punishments as well. This means that while a person may be charged in a single indictment with violating either separate statutory provisions or continuing to violate the same statutory provision over time, there may be limitations on whether the person may be *punished* for each separate violation.

The Supreme Court has ruled that whether multiple punishments for the "same" offense can be imposed depends in the first instance on the intent of Congress. If it is clear that multiple punishments were intended, there is no double jeopardy bar to their imposition.[94] If, however, it is clear that multiple punishment was not intended for violation of separate statutory provisions, or if congressional intent is not clear, then multiple punishments for these "same" offenses will not be permitted. In these instances the Supreme Court has applied the previously described *Blockburger* "elements" test to the multiple punishment situation.[95]

Multiplicity problems can arise in two kinds of cases. The first is where more than one statute condemns similar conduct although one statute punishes an aggravated form of that conduct.[96] Since it would be impossible to commit the more aggravated form without committing the "lesser included offense," double punishment would violate the *Block-burger* rule since only the greater offense requires proof of an additional fact.[97] In the second type of case, a defendant's continuing conduct may result in multiple violations of a single statutory provision.[98] The question for multiplicity purposes would be whether the defendant has thereby committed only a single offense or is guilty of separate offenses over different intervals of time. The answer to the question is dependent upon the "unit of prosecution" that Congress intended.[99]

A multiplicitous indictment is not fatally defective. A defendant can move to require the government to elect the count on which it will

---

93. United States v. Chacko, 169 F.3d 140, 145 (2d Cir. 1999); United States v. Murray, 618 F.2d 892, 897 (2d Cir. 1980).

94. *See* Missouri v. Hunter, 459 U.S. 359, 368–69 (1983); *Sanabria*, 437 U.S. at 69–70; Brown v. Ohio, 432 U.S. 161, 165 (1977).

95. *See* Whalen v. United States, 445 U.S. 684, 691–92 (1980); United States v. Graham, 305 F.3d 1094, 1101 (10th Cir. 2002); United States v. Gugino, 860 F.2d 546, 549–50 (2d Cir. 1988).

96. *E.g.,* possession of drugs, and possession of drugs with intent to distribute.

97. *Cf.* Gore v. United States, 357 U.S. 386, 391–92 (1958) (upholding a conviction

for a violation of three different sections of federal law by a single sale of narcotics).

98. *Graham*, 305 F.3d at 1099 (explaining that three convictions for explosives transactions were multiplicitous because the statute at issue punished continuing conduct rather than separate offenses; therefore, defendant could only be punished once).

99. Bell v. United States, 349 U.S. 81, 82 (1955). *See also* United States v. Langford, 946 F.2d 798, 802–04 (11th Cir. 1991) (stating that each mailing in an ongoing scheme to defraud is not a separate offense).

proceed and to dismiss the multiplicitous count.[100] A court may, however, reserve ruling on such a motion, but instruct the jury in the alternative—that it can only convict on one of the counts. This is often done in the common case in which lesser included offenses are charged.[101]

§ 11.3(c) Permissive Joinder of Offenses—Single Defendant Indictments

We now turn to a discussion of the rules regarding the joinder of what are concededly separate offenses and therefore could be charged and punished separately in the same indictment without offending the double jeopardy clause. In the case of a single defendant indictment, the Federal Rules allow separate offenses to be joined if they are "of the same or similar character, or are based on the same act or transaction, or on two or more acts or transactions connected together, or constituting parts of a common scheme or plan."[102]

When offenses that are not of the same character or do not result from the same transaction or common scheme are joined in a single indictment, they are "misjoined" within the meaning of the Federal Rules, and the defendant's motion to sever must be granted.[103] Otherwise, the success of a motion to sever will depend upon a showing by the defendant that joinder prejudices his or her opportunity to obtain a fair trial and outweighs the goal of efficient disposition of cases. This balance is more clearly struck in favor of efficiency when the offenses are part of a common scheme or transaction[104] than when the offenses are joined due to their "same or similar character." In the latter situation, because the proof rarely includes the same set of facts, the only time actually saved is that spent selecting a jury.[105] At the same time, there are several ways in which the defendant's case may be prejudiced: the defendant may be unable to present separate defenses to each of the offenses charged; or the jury may conclude that multiple charges indicate that the defendant had a criminal disposition to commit each offense charged and assess guilt accordingly.[106]

Despite this propensity for prejudice, however, many courts have been reluctant to sever offenses of similar character, particularly if they are sufficiently separate and distinct that the "jury would readily exam-

---

100. FED. R. CRIM. P. 12(b)(2); WRIGHT, § 145.

101. FED. R. CRIM. P. 30 & 31(c); WRIGHT, § 498 & 515.

102. FED. R. CRIM. P. 8(a); WRIGHT, § 143 n. 8.

103. See LaFAVE ET AL., § 17.3(b).

104. United States v. Price, 265 F.3d 1097, 1105 (10th Cir. 2001); United States v. Adams, 434 F.2d 756, 758–59 (2d Cir. 1970). Where, however, the joinder of offenses results from the offenses being part

of a common scheme or transaction, prejudice may also occur to the extent that a jury will not be able to consider the evidence admitted to prove each offense separately and distinctly. Drew v. United States, 331 F.2d 85, 88 (D.C. Cir. 1964).

105. United States v. Halper, 590 F.2d 422, 430 (2d Cir. 1978).

106. See generally LaFAVE ET AL., § 17.1(c)–(f).

ine the defendant's conduct on two different occasions separately."[107] To obtain relief from such a prejudicial joinder, a defendant would have to prove that he or she would have testified in his or her own defense on one of the charges, but not on the other,[108] or that evidence of one offense would be inadmissible at a trial of the other offense.[109]

§ 11.3(d) Permissive Joinder of Defendants[110]

Joinder of defendants is only proper in two circumstances: (a) when they are alleged to have participated as principals or accomplices in the same criminal acts; and (b) when they are charged with different crimes, in cases in which they are alleged to have participated in the same "series of acts or transactions" with which the charges are concerned.[111] In such cases, the offenses must be connected or "interrelated in such a manner that proof of charges against one defendant would necessarily have to be introduced in proving the jointly-charged offenses, or that the government otherwise will benefit without further prejudicing the defendant."[112] Offenses of similar character by one defendant may not be joined if they are not part of a common scheme or plan involving the other defendants.

As with misjoinder of offenses, the defendant has a right to severance when he or she has been misjoined with another defendant.[113] If the joinder is proper under the Federal Rules, a severance will be granted only if prejudice is shown. Common grounds for demonstrating prejudice include: (a) cases in which the admission of a statement of one defendant would violate another defendant's confrontation clause rights;[114] (b) cases in which a non-testifying co-defendant would tend to exonerate a defendant;[115] (c) cases in which co-defendants have irreconcilably conflicting defenses;[116] and (d) cases in which the evidence against one defendant would be so prejudicial as to deny another defendant a fair trial.[117]

---

107. United States v. Werner, 620 F.2d 922, 929 (2d Cir. 1980).

108. *Compare* Baker v. United States, 401 F.2d 958, 974–76 (D.C. Cir. 1968) *with* Cross v. United States, 335 F.2d 987, 989–90 (D.C. Cir. 1964).

109. *See* United States v. Foutz, 540 F.2d 733, 738 (4th Cir.1976) (emphasizing the danger for potential prejudice when two offenses are joined together in a situation in which neither would be admissible in a separate trial on the other).

110. Unlike the situation regarding offense joinder, there is no requirement that two or more defendants ever be charged in the same indictment, or tried together, despite the closeness of their connection to the crime charged. Whether to join defendants is within the discretion of the prosecution, subject to the limitations indicated in this section.

111. FED. R. CRIM. P. 8(b); WRIGHT, § 144; United States v. Roselli, 432 F.2d

879, 898 (9th Cir. 1970). *See also* LaFAVE ET AL., § 17.2.

112. Davis v. United States, 367 A.2d 1254, 1263 (D.C. App. 1976), citing *Roselli*, 432 F.2d at 901.

113. LaFAVE ET AL., § 17.3(b).

114. Bruton v. United States, 391 U.S. 123, 128 (1968). *Bruton* and its progeny, which severely limit the applicability of the *Bruton* rule, are fully discussed in LaFAVE ET AL., § 17.2(b). To remedy this problem without having to grant a severance, courts commonly redact the name of the defendant mentioned in the co-defendant's statement.

115. United States v. Echeles, 352 F.2d 892, 897 (7th Cir. 1965). *See* LaFAVE ET AL., § 17.2(c).

116. LaFAVE ET AL., § 17.2(d). Severances on this ground are permitted, but not required. Zafiro v. United States, 506 U.S. 534, 538 (1993).

117. *Id.*, § 17.2(e) & (f).

§ 11.4 Forfeiture

Federal law permits the forfeiture of property involved in, or constituting the proceeds of certain criminal activities for which a defendant is convicted.[118] Forfeiture proceedings are governed by Rule 32.2 of the Federal Rules.[119] The rule provides that a court may not order a forfeiture unless notice of forfeiture is given to the defendant in the indictment.[120] The notice may, but need not, specify particular property. If it does, it is common to provide that if that property cannot be made subject to the court's jurisdiction, forfeiture of substitute property can be ordered.[121] However, only the defendant's share of the jointly owned property can be forfeited in a criminal case.[122]

The Supreme Court has held that criminal forfeiture is part of the defendant's sentence and as such, requires a conviction on the offense giving rise to the forfeiture.[123] Federal Rule 32.2 provides for a bifurcated trial where the forfeiture proceeding must take place "as soon as practicable" after a guilty verdict is entered.[124] If the conviction is by jury, both the government and the defendant have a right to a jury determination whether the government has proven by a preponderance of the evidence that the property in question has the "requisite nexus" to the offense. Otherwise, the determination will be made by the court.[125]

This phase of criminal forfeiture involves only the defendant; third parties are not permitted to contest the forfeiture until both the criminal

---

118. The criminal forfeiture provisions are found in § 1963 of 18 U.S.C. §§ 1961 *et seq.*, the Racketeer Influenced and Corrupt Organizations Act ("RICO"), § 853 of 21 U.S.C. §§ 848 *et seq.*, the Continuing Criminal Enterprise ("CCE") provisions of the narcotics laws, and 18 U.S.C. § 982, the criminal forfeiture provision amended by CAFRA (as discussed below), which authorizes criminal forfeiture for federal offenses related to money laundering, fraud affecting a financial institution, counterfeiting, motor vehicle theft, immigration, health care, and fraud involving telemarketing. All criminal forfeitures other than RICO criminal forfeitures are governed by the procedures set forth in 21 U.S.C. § 853, *see* 28 U.S.C. § 2461(c); 982(b)(1), which are virtually identical to those found in the RICO statute.

119. Fed. R. Crim. P. 32.2.

120. Fed. R. Crim. P. 32.2(a). *See, e.g.,* United States v. DeFries, 129 F.3d 1293 (D.C. Cir. 1997).

121. The court may amend an order of forfeiture at any time to include substitute assets. Fed. R. Crim. P. 32.2(e). The substitute asset provision comes into play, however, only when forfeitable property cannot be identified as directly involved in or traceable to the criminal activity. United States v. Voigt, 89 F.3d 1050, 1086–88 (3d Cir. 1996). The rule also provides rights for third parties who claim an interest in property (other than money) to assert their claims to it. Fed. R. Crim. P. 32.2(c)(1).

122. *See, e.g.,* United States v. O'Dell, 247 F.3d 655, 680 (6th Cir. 2001) (criminal forfeiture "entitles the Government to forfeiture of a convicted defendant's interests and nothing more").

123. Libretti v. United States, 516 U.S. 29 (1995).

124. Fed. R. Crim. P. 32.2(b)(1).

125. *See* United States v. Davis, 177 F.Supp.2d 470 (E.D. Va. 2001). *See also* United States v. Bellomo, 176 F.3d 580, 595 (2d Cir. 1999) (applying preponderance standard to criminal forfeiture).

case and order of forfeiture are completed.[126] An ancillary proceeding is then held where all potential third party claimants are given the opportunity to contest the forfeiture by asserting a superior interest in the property.[127] If no claim is filed in the ancillary proceeding and the ownership of the property is not being litigated by any party, the court must satisfy itself that at least one defendant had an interest in the property.[128]

Federal law permitting forfeiture has been interpreted by courts to impose a rule of joint and several liability for reasonably foreseeable proceeds in the case of a conspiracy or other situation where there is more than one defendant convicted.[129] Property subject to forfeiture is not limited to property acquired solely by the defendant but encompasses property derived by the defendant indirectly from those who acted with him in promoting the criminal enterprise and property acquired by those who acted in concert with him.[130] This rule has even been applied to minor participants in a scheme, and such individuals have been held liable for the full judgment even though they did not play a major role in the commission of the offense.[131]

It should also be noted that the government's ability to seek forfeiture in connection with federal criminal cases was significantly broadened with the enactment of the Civil Asset Forfeiture Reform Act of 2000 ("CAFRA").[132] Congress not only expanded civil forfeiture authority to cover the proceeds of virtually all serious federal crimes,[133] it also made those proceeds subject to criminal forfeiture upon conviction.

---

126. *See* Fed. R. Crim. P. 32.2(b)(2); § 853(k) & (n)(2); § 1963(*l*)(2). *See also* United States v. Pelullo, 178 F.3d 196, 202 (3d Cir. 1999).

127. Wright, § 574. Note that the government is required to provide notice of the criminal order of forfeiture to interested third parties. *See.* § 1963(*l*)(1); § 853(n)(1).

128. F. R. Crim. P. 32.2(c)(2).

129. *See* United States v. Fruchter, 411 F.3d 377 (2d Cir. 2005) (RICO forfeiture imposes joint and several liability); United States v. Corrado, 227 F.3d 543, 558 (6th Cir. 2000) (same); United States v. Pitt, 193 F.3d 751, 765–66 (3d Cir. 1999) (§§ 982(a)(1) & § 853(a)(1) impose joint and several liability with respect to forfeiture); United States v. Hurley, 63 F.3d 1, 22 (1st Cir. 1995) (defendant liable for "so much of [the illegally obtained amount] as was foreseeable" to that defendant under theory that member of conspiracy is responsible for foreseeable acts of other members taken in furtherance of conspiracy).

130. United States v. Benevento, 836 F.2d 129 (2d Cir. 1988) (per curiam). Courts have reasoned that imposing joint and sev-

eral liability is appropriate where precise attribution is difficult because to do otherwise would impair the effectiveness of the remedy by allowing the defendant to conceal or transfer assets to those who also profited from the criminal behavior. *See* United States v. Caporale, 806 F.2d 1487, 1507–08 (11th Cir. 1986); United States v. Benevento, 663 F.Supp. 1115, 1118–19 (S.D.N.Y. 1987). *See also* 31A Am. Jur. 2d § 160 (May 2004) ("Where the government is unable to prove how the illegal proceeds of racketeering activity have been allocated among multiple defendants, a District Court may properly impose joint and several liability on the defendants in its forfeiture order.")

131. *E.g.,* United States v. Bollin, 264 F.3d 391 (4th Cir. 2001); United States v. Candelaria–Silva, 166 F.3d 19 (1st Cir. 1999).

132. Pub. L. 106–185 .

133. *See* 18 U.S.C. § 981(a)(1)(C) (authorizing civil forfeiture of the proceeds of any offense defined as "specified unlawful activity" in 18 U.S.C. § 1956(c)(7)).

Thus, pursuant to 28 U.S.C. § 2461(c), "[i]f a forfeiture of property is authorized in connection with a violation of an Act of Congress, and . . . no specific statutory provision is made for criminal forfeiture . . . upon conviction, the court shall order the forfeiture of the property" in accordance with otherwise established forfeiture procedures.[134] This provision effectively authorizes criminal forfeiture of all property that is subject to civil forfeiture based on the commission of a federal crime unless there is already a specific criminal forfeiture provision for that crime.

§ 11.5 Proceedings on the Indictment

§ 11.5(a) Arrest or Surrender of the Defendant

When an indictment is voted by the grand jury, it is first "returned" in open court to a magistrate judge[135] and then filed with the district court, where a district judge typically will be randomly assigned to preside over the case. The indictment, like the complaint, will serve as authority for the magistrate judge to issue an arrest warrant.[136] The arrest warrant issued after indictment is essentially the same in form as that issued after a complaint is filed.[137] An arrest warrant upon an indictment requires that the defendant be brought before a district court judge for arraignment, rather than a magistrate judge, since the latter does not have jurisdiction over felony cases. However, while district court judges have the ultimate authority to arraign, they routinely assign the arraignment responsibility in indicted cases to the magistrate judge on duty on the day of the arrest.[138]

Of course, in cases that were initiated by complaint, the defendant will almost always already have been arrested and will either be in custody or on pretrial release; rearrest is unnecessary. The defendant will simply be notified by the assigned district court judge of the date for the arraignment on the indictment.

There are, also, alternatives to arrest of an indicted defendant. With the consent of the government, the defendant may arrange to surrender voluntarily.[139] Or, the prosecutor has the option to issue a summons and thereby avoid the need to take the defendant into custody prior to the arraignment.

§ 11.5(b) Arraignment on the Indictment

The arraignment is the first occasion on which the arrested individual appears before a court with jurisdiction to dispose of a felony charge and therefore to enter a plea of guilty or not guilty to it—the primary

---

134. Specifically, 21 U.S.C. § 853.

135. Fed. R. Crim. P. 6(f).

136. Fed. R. Crim. P. 9.

137. *See supra* § 4.10.

138. Wright, § 153.

139. Fed. R. Crim. P. 9(a) states that an arrest warrant only need be issued upon the request of the attorney for the government. Wright, § 151.

purpose of the proceeding.[140] The significance of the plea is that it "formulat[es] the issue to be tried."[141] A not guilty plea places at issue each and every allegation contained in the indictment[142] and is all that is required of the defendant before putting the government to the burden of proving guilt at a trial. However, prior to requiring that the defendant enter a plea, he or she must be provided with a copy of the indictment.[143] In addition, prior to taking the plea, the court must inform the defendant of the nature of the charge by either reading the indictment, stating the substance of the accusations, or asking the defendant whether he or she is familiar with the charges and waives the reading of the indictment.[144]

Bail also will be determined at the arraignment. If the defendant has already appeared before a magistrate judge after the filing of a complaint, or after arrest on an indictment, the bail issue will have been addressed, and that determination generally will be "continued" by the district judge, i.e., kept as the magistrate judge ordered. If the arraignment is the first proceeding, bail will be set precisely as in the manner described in Chapter 5.

The arraignment on the indictment is, of course, a "critical stage" of the proceedings because it may be outcome determinative, and if the defendant does not have counsel, counsel will be appointed at that time.[145]

§ 11.6   Time Limits on Returning the Indictment

Statutes of limitations safeguard against preaccusation delay by the prosecution, creating a time limit for the commencement of criminal proceedings.[146] There are also a number of statutory tolling provisions. For example, where the prosecution can establish that evidence is overseas, the government can make an *ex parte* application to extend a limitations period.[147] In this area, there are often disputes regarding when the subject criminal act has been completed, which is when the

---

140. FED. R. CRIM. P. 10; WRIGHT, § 161.

141. Hamilton v. Alabama, 368 U.S. 52, 55 n. 4 (1961).

142. United States v. Flattum, 1992 WL 365334 (D.Or.1992); United States v. Holby, 345 F.Supp. 639, 640 (S.D.N.Y. 1972), *rev'd on other grounds*, 477 F.2d 649 (2d Cir. 1973).

143. FED. R. CRIM. P. 10; WRIGHT, § 162.

144. FED. R. CRIM. P. 10 does not require a precise formality. WRIGHT, § 161. As long as the defendant is represented by counsel and was fully aware of what was going on at the time he enters his plea, the mandate of the rule is satisfied. *Hamilton*, 368 U.S. at 54–55; Mayes v. United States, 177 F.2d 505, 507 (8th Cir. 1949). Rule 10 does not

apply, however, to the requirements for the taking of a plea of guilty, which instead are governed by FED. R. CRIM. P. 11; these requirements are by necessity more detailed and sophisticated, enabling the court to determine whether or not the guilty plea was made knowingly, intelligently and voluntarily. WRIGHT, §§ 172–174.

145. *See* LaFAVE ET AL., § 11.2(b).

146. *See* 18 U.S.C. § 3281 *et seq.* (except in cases punishable by death, indictment or information must be filed within five years after the crime's commission.); United States v. Ewell, 383 U.S. 116, 122 (1966) (stating that statutes of limitations provide "the primary guarantee against bringing overly stale criminal charges").

147. 18 U.S.C. § 3292.

limitations period commences. If there is any argument that a statute of limitations has run, a motion to dismiss should be filed.[148]

In cases in which no arrest has been made, the statute of limitations provides the only check on the time by which the government must move forward with its case. But even where the government brings an indictment before the expiration of the statute of limitations, pre-indictment delay can result in a denial of due process where the defendant can prove actual prejudice to his or her ability to present a defense *and* that the delay was for the purpose of hampering the defense or in reckless disregard of the need to prepare a defense.[149] Motions to dismiss on due process grounds are difficult to win, however, particularly given that courts routinely reject claims of prejudice based on the deterioration of evidence or the fading of witness' memories over time.

In cases in which an arrest has been made on a complaint, the Speedy Trial Act requires that the indictment must be returned within 30 days of the arrest, subject to various excludable periods.[150] The parties may agree to extend this time and do so rather routinely in cases where a defendant arrested on a complaint has not been detained in custody pending trial. If the indictment is not returned within the requisite time period, the defendant can move for dismissal of the complaint.[151] The dismissal can be either with or without prejudice. The factors relevant to this determination are the seriousness of the offense, the facts and circumstances of the case that led to dismissal, and the impact of a reprosecution on the administration of the Speedy Trial Act and on the administration of justice.[152] As a practical matter, complaints generally will not be dismissed with prejudice unless the delay was intentional or purely to obtain a tactical advantage.[153]

If a complaint is dismissed without prejudice, a new complaint may be filed, and the time tolled on the dismissed case will be disregarded; a new 30 day period will begin. But refiling after dismissals cannot continue indefinitely to the detriment of the defendant. A judge may thus dismiss the complaint with prejudice if he believes that a prosecutor is acting in bad faith. Of course, once there is a constitutional, as opposed to a statutory, violation of the speedy trial right, a judge is compelled to dismiss with prejudice.[154] Failure of the defendant to move

---

148. Jurisdictions differ as to whether failure to raise the matter before trial or entry of a plea constitutes a waiver. Federal circuit courts are split on the matter, though most conclude that failure to raise this defense pretrial does amount to waiver. *See* LaFave et al., § 18.5(a).

149. United States v. Lovasco, 431 U.S. 783, 790 (1977). *See* LaFave et al., § 18.5(b).

150. *See* 18 U.S.C. § 3161 *et seq.* The exclusions are enumerated in § 3161(h).

151. 18 U.S.C. § 3162.

152. § 3162(a)(2).

153. *See, e.g.,* United States v. Hawthorne, 705 F.2d 258, 261 (7th Cir. 1983) (affirming lower court's dismissal of case without prejudice where delay in indictment was not intentional or designed to obtain tactical advantage and crime charged was serious).

154. *See* Strunk v. United States, 412 U.S. 434, 439–40 (1973); LaFave et al., §§ 18.1, 18.3(b).

before trial for dismissal of an indictment on statutory speedy trial grounds constitutes a waiver.[155]

§ 11.7   The Christopher Indictment

Having reviewed the basic legal ground rules and DOJ policies applicable to the indictment process, we turn to our illustrative case and the process leading up to and then following the presentation of the indictment to the grand jury.

§ 11.7(a) Deciding Who to Charge and What to Charge Them With

We noted at the end of Chapter 10 that by early April 2005, AUSA Knapp and Special Agent Martinez decided that they had completed their investigation and were now in a position to move forward with the process of selecting which of the targets of their investigation should be charged and with what federal criminal offenses. To that end, Knapp and Martinez met on April 17, 2005 and reviewed the evidence that they had gathered—including in particular the ways in which their investigation had strengthened their proof—as to each of the targets, Christopher, Van Ness and Wagner. (As this review of the evidence is in large part repetitive of the review conducted at the outset of the investigation, we suggest rereading § 10.5(a) before proceeding further, focusing in particular on the elements of each of the different offenses with which the targets could be charged.) They also considered, albeit only briefly, whether they might pursue a charge against CMS Bank based on respondeat superior liability for the illegal acts of Ernest Wagner. We now turn to the analysis as to each potential defendant.

(1) Christopher

In addition to the testimony of cooperating witness Gilbert Santiago, the government's evidence against Christopher now included: (1) surveillance and phone records showing that over the past year Christopher frequently made calls to Colombia on his cell phone and more recently called the same Colombian number from outside his office on both his cell phone and a nearby pay phone; (2) bank records showing Christopher's signature on the account-opening documents for the five accounts in which deposits in amounts less than $10,000 repeatedly were made; and (3) phony IFD invoices dated January 17, 2005 and adding up to exactly $25,000, which represented the precise amount of Christopher's anticipated deposit of proceeds from the January shipment. These facts both corroborated much of what Santiago had told the government (concerning the invoices and bank accounts in particular) and provided affirmative evidence of Christopher's involvement in the kind of suspicious behavior (being in possession of phony invoices and making calls to Colombia from a pay phone outside his own office) that circumstantially

---

155. *See* LaFave et al. §§ 18.1, 18.3(b).

would provide support for the government's view that Christopher knowingly was involved in unlawful activity. Knapp also knew she had a powerful "common sense" argument she could make to the jury—that the sophisticated and experienced suppliers of the sizable quantities of cocaine being imported through Christopher never would have entrusted their extremely valuable "merchandise" to someone who did not fully appreciate its value and importance.

Although AUSA Knapp realized that her case against Christopher still was likely to succeed or fail depending on whether the jury found Santiago's testimony credible, she was comfortable that there was more than adequate corroboration to move forward with narcotics trafficking charges, including importation, distribution, and conspiracy, as well as related charges stemming from the deposits of the illegal proceeds of the narcotics trafficking, including money laundering, money laundering conspiracy, structuring and structuring conspiracy. As to all of these charges, in other words, Knapp concluded that the case was "readily provable" and that the evidence was "probably sufficient to obtain . . . a conviction."[156]

(2) William Van Ness

With respect to Van Ness, there remained ample evidence that he actually transported the cocaine shipments in Van Ness Trucking trucks: both Santiago and Long would testify to that effect; the taped call between Long and Santiago clearly showed Van Ness was supposed to pick up the intercepted shipment; and other seized records would provide additional corroboration of this point. From its investigation, the government also had learned that: (1) Van Ness regularly drove Christopher to work; and (2) phone records showed a consistent pattern over the past year of Christopher calling a particular number in Colombia and then immediately calling Van Ness. Both of these pieces of evidence could be used to rebut Van Ness' likely defense—that he didn't know that Christopher's otherwise legitimate business had become involved in the importation and distribution of illegal narcotics—by showing quite specifically the close relationship and frequent contact and communication between the brothers-in-law. In addition, the records subpoenaed from Van Ness Trucking demonstrated that IFD paid Van Ness double the standard per pound rate for each of the shipments that contained cocaine and thus provided some circumstantial evidence of Van Ness' knowledge that there was something very different about these particular deliveries.

Knapp viewed the case against Van Ness as the most difficult of the three targets, principally because she did not have a single witness who could testify directly that Van Ness was told or knew that the shipments he was transporting contained cocaine. At best, Knapp would be able to establish that Van Ness, like Mario Long, was aware that what he was

---

156. *See supra* § 11.1(c), (d) (quoting DOJ policy).

transporting was especially valuable and was being handled with particular care, and she would have to argue to the jury that common sense strongly suggested that he must have known it was illegal drugs, either by being told directly or by drawing the only reasonable inferences.

Knapp personally believed that Van Ness was in fact guilty and, for the reasons just stated, thought a jury "probably" would agree, and she therefore decided to go forward in charging Van Ness with narcotics distribution conspiracy, multiple counts of narcotics distribution relating to the shipments between September and December 2004, and attempted possession with intent to distribute the final January 2005 cocaine shipment that was intercepted by law enforcement.

(3) Ernest Wagner

Of all of the individual targets, it was clear that Wagner was the one against whom the government had secured the most substantial additional evidence. As a result of the investigation, the government now knew that: (1) Wagner had opened the IFD accounts; (2) his initials appeared on several slips for deposits of less than $10,000; and (3) Barbara Weiss would testify that on one occasion he instructed her to subdivide into amounts less than $10,000 a large amount of cash that Santiago had brought to the bank to deposit. These additional facts together provided substantial direct evidence of Wagner's involvement in illegal structuring and also strongly suggested that he was likely to have known that the money being deposited came from some form of illegal activity. Knapp concluded that this evidence was sufficient for her to be comfortable that a conviction was extremely likely on the charge of structuring deposits in amounts of less then $10,000.

As to the money laundering charges, Knapp acknowledged that the proof was not quite as strong because she would have to prove that Wagner knew the money being deposited came from some type of unlawful activity (albeit not that Wagner specifically knew it came from narcotics distribution). Nevertheless, she felt it was appropriate to proceed with this more serious charge as well, principally because she believed, and thought a jury would believe, that there was no way Wagner could have been involved in this type of structuring and in the kind of discussion that Santiago would describe without knowing or deliberately closing his eyes to the obviously illicit nature of the funds.

(4) CMS Bank

Knapp also considered, although only briefly, whether it would be appropriate or useful to bring criminal charges against CMS Bank based on the illegal conduct of its employee, Ernest Wagner. Knapp considered that CMS Bank had fully cooperated in promptly providing documents to the United States Attorney's Office, that they had fired Wagner as soon as they learned what he had done, that they recently (and before learning of Wagner's actions) implemented more comprehensive and strict anti-money laundering policies that in all likelihood would detect such unlawful activity in the future, and that Wagner's conduct, by all accounts, was an isolated event at the bank, which had no prior history of similar problems. For all of these reasons, Knapp concluded that this was not an appropriate case for corporate prosecution.[157]

§ 11.7(b) The Indictment

Having decided who she thought should be indicted, AUSA Knapp now had to obtain the requisite approvals of her superiors. She first presented a "prosecution memo" to one of her section supervisors. That memo included a thorough review of the evidence, a draft of the proposed indictment, and an analysis of the most important charging and drafting decisions that she had made. After reviewing the memo, Knapp's supervisor raised some questions about the sufficiency of the evidence against Van Ness, but ultimately decided that it was a close call and one that Knapp was in the best position to make. Once Knapp's supervisor had signed off on the prosecution, the indictment (though not necessarily the "prosecution memo") was reviewed, approved and signed by the United States Attorney himself, Kevin O'Reilly (or one his top deputies acting on his behalf).

Set out below is the indictment that AUSA Knapp drafted.[158] Following the indictment is an explanation and analysis of the most relevant features of the various counts. Then, in the next section, we will follow Knapp to the grand jury where she will present to the grand jurors the indictment and the evidence in support of the various charges.

---

157. Knapp would not even have considered indicting IFD or Van Ness trucking, as those small, closely held corporate entities were in substance indistinguishable from their owners, Christopher and Van Ness, respectively, and thus there was no reason to think indicting the business would accomplish anything beyond what would be accomplished by indicting the principals.

158. It should be noted that while this indictment, for illustrative purposes, contains 22 separate counts, AUSA Knapp very well might have drafted a much more streamlined version containing many fewer counts but still capturing the same basic crimes and carrying the same sentencing consequences. For example, Counts 1 and 3–12 might have been eliminated, leaving only Count 2—conspiracy to distribute cocaine—to effectively capture, for evidentiary and sentencing purposes, the whole of the narcotics importation and distribution operation.

UNITED STATES DISTRICT COURT
EASTERN DISTRICT OF NEW YORK

- X

UNITED STATES OF AMERICA   I N D I C T M E N T

     - against -   Cr. No. _____

PAUL CHRISTOPHER,
WILLIAM VAN NESS and
ERNEST WAGNER,

          Defendants.
- X

THE GRAND JURY CHARGES:

COUNT ONE
(Narcotics Conspiracy: Importation)

     1.   In or about and between May 2004 and January 2005, both dates being approximate and inclusive, within the Eastern District of New York and elsewhere, the defendant PAUL CHRISTOPHER, together with others, did knowingly and intentionally conspire to import into the United States from a place outside thereof five kilograms or more of a substance containing cocaine, a Schedule II controlled substance, in violation of Title 21, United States Code, Section 952(a).

     (Title 21, United States Code, Sections 963, 960(a)(1) and 960(b)(1)(B)(ii); Title 18, United States Code, Sections 3551 et seq.)

COUNT TWO
(Narcotics Conspiracy: Distribution and Possession with Intent to Distribute)

     2.   In or about and between May 2004 and January 2005, both dates being approximate and inclusive, within the Eastern District of New York, the defendants PAUL CHRISTOPHER and WILLIAM VAN NESS, together with others, did knowingly and intentionally conspire to distribute and possess with intent to distribute five kilograms or more of a substance containing cocaine, a Schedule II controlled substance, in violation of Title 21, United States Code, Section 841(a)(1).

     (Title 21, United States Code, Sections 846 and 841(b)(1)(A)(ii)(II); Title 18, United States Code, Sections 3551 et seq.)

COUNT THREE
(Narcotics Importation)

3.   In or about September 2004, within the Eastern District of New York and elsewhere, the defendant PAUL CHRISTOPHER, together with others, did knowingly and intentionally import into the United States from a place outside thereof five kilograms or more of a substance containing cocaine, a Schedule II controlled substance.

(Title 21, United States Code, Sections 952(a), 960(a)(1) and 960(b)(1)(B)(ii); Title 18, United States Code, Sections 2 and 3551 et seq.)

(Counts 4 through 7 would be identical except for the dates; each would cover one of the monthly shipments between October 2004 and January 2005.)

COUNT EIGHT
(Narcotics Distribution and Possession with Intent to Distribute)

4.   In or about September 2004, within the Eastern District of New York, the defendants PAUL CHRISTOPHER and WILLIAM VAN NESS did knowingly and intentionally distribute and possess with intent to distribute five kilograms or more of a substance containing cocaine, a Schedule II controlled substance.

(Title 21, United States Code, Sections 841(a)(1) and 841(b)(1)(A)(ii)(II); Title 18, United States Code, Sections 2 and 3551 et seq.)

(Counts 9 through 11 would be identical except for the dates; each would cover one of the monthly shipments between October and December 2004.)

COUNT TWLEVE
(Attempted Narcotics Possession)

5.   In or about January 2005, within the Eastern District of New York, the defendants PAUL CHRISTOPHER and WILLIAM VAN NESS did knowingly and intentionally attempt to possess with intent to distribute five kilograms or more of a substance containing cocaine, a Schedule II controlled substance, in violation of Title 21, United States Code, Section 841(a)(1).

(Title 21, United States Code, Sections 846 and 841(b)(1)(A)(ii)(II); Title 18, United States Code, Sections 2 and 3551 et seq.)

Introduction to Structuring Counts Thirteen through Seventeen

6.   At all times relevant to this indictment, the currency reporting requirements provided as follows:

(a)   Transactions in currency were defined as transactions involving the physical transfer of currency from one person to another, pursuant to Title 31, Code of Federal Regulations, Section 103.11(ii)(2).

(b)　　　Domestic financial institutions were required by law and regulation to file a Currency Transaction Report (IRS Form 4789, hereinafter referred to as a "CTR") with the Internal Revenue Service ("IRS") for each transaction in currency, such as a deposit, withdrawal, exchange of currency or other payment or transfer, by, through or to a financial institution, in excess of $10,000, pursuant to Title 31, United States Code, Section 5313 and Title 31, Code of Federal Regulations, Section 103.22.

(c)　　　CTRs were filed with the IRS on forms that required, among other things, disclosure of the identity of the individual who conducted the transaction and the individual or organization for whom the transaction was completed.

(d)　　　CTRs were required to be filed to assist the United States in criminal, tax and regulatory investigations and proceedings, as stated in Title 31, Code of Federal Regulations, Section 103.20.

(e)　　　It was unlawful to "structure" a transaction in currency for the purpose of evading the requirement that a financial institution file a CTR with the IRS. "Structuring" financial transactions included, but were not limited to: (1) the practice of subdividing an amount of currency in excess of $10,000 into amounts of $10,000 or less, prior to transacting business with one or more domestic financial institutions or businesses, and then conducting separate transactions in currency with those amounts, in an attempt to evade the above-described currency reporting requirements and (2) the conduct of a transaction, or series of currency transactions, including transactions at or below $10,000, in an attempt to evade the above-described currency reporting requirements, as stated in Title 31, Code of Federal Regulations, Section 103.11(gg).

COUNT THIRTEEN
(Structuring Conspiracy)

7.　　　Paragraphs 6(a) through 6(e) are realleged and incorporated by reference as if fully set forth herein.

8.　　　On or about and between August 2004 and December 2004, both dates being approximate and inclusive, within the Eastern District of New York and elsewhere, the defendants PAUL CHRISTOPHER and ERNEST WAGNER, together with others, did knowingly and willfully conspire to defraud the United States by impeding, impairing, obstructing and defeating the lawful governmental functions of the IRS in its authorized functions of collecting information regarding transactions in United States currency in excess of Ten Thousand Dollars ($10,000).

9.　　　It was a part of this conspiracy that the defendants PAUL CHRISTOPHER and ERNEST WAGNER, together with others, for the purpose of evading the reporting requirements of Section 5313(a) of Title 31 of the United States Code, would structure financial transactions with domestic financial institutions by breaking down an amount of currency in excess of Ten Thousand Dollars ($10,000) into amounts less than Ten Thousand Dollars ($10,000) and then separately depositing these smaller amounts.

274

10.   In furtherance of the conspiracy and to effect the objects thereof, the defendants PAUL CHRISTOPHER and ERNEST WAGNER, together with others, committed and caused to be committed, within the Eastern District of New York, the following:

OVERT ACTS

a.   On or about August 15, 2004, the defendant PAUL CHRISTOPHER caused a co-conspirator whose identity is known to the grand jury to travel to the CMS Bank branch located at 1 Ferris Wheel Drive, Coney Island, New York, to open five bank accounts.

b.   On or about August 15, 2004, the defendant ERNEST WAGNER assisted this co-conspirator in opening those five bank accounts.

c.   On or about September 30, 2004, the defendant ERNEST WAGNER assisted this co-conspirator in depositing approximately $25,000 in cash into the five accounts in amounts less than $10,000.

d.   On or about October 31, 2004, the defendant ERNEST WAGNER assisted this co-conspirator in depositing approximately $25,000 in cash into the five accounts in amounts less than $10,000.

e.   On or about November 30, 2004, the defendant ERNEST WAGNER assisted this co-conspirator in depositing approximately $25,000 in cash into the five accounts in amounts less than $10,000.

f.   On or about December 30, 2004, the defendant ERNEST WAGNER assisted this co-conspirator in depositing approximately $25,000 in cash into the five accounts in amounts less than $10,000.

(Title 18, United States Code, Sections 371 and 3551 et seq.)

COUNT FOURTEEN
(Structuring)

11.   Paragraphs 6(a) through 6(e) are realleged and incorporated by reference as if fully set forth herein.

12.   On or about September 30, 2004, within the Eastern District of New York, the defendants PAUL CHRISTOPHER and ERNEST WAGNER, for the purpose of evading the reporting requirements of Title 31, United States Code, Section 5313(a) and the regulations prescribed thereunder, knowingly and intentionally structured and attempted to structure currency transactions with a domestic financial institution, to wit: CMS Bank, by causing a sum of money in excess of $10,000, to wit: $25,000, to be deposited into CMS Bank as cash in amounts less than $10,000.

(Title 31, United States Code, Sections 5324(a)(3) and 5324(c)(1); Title 18, United States Code, Sections 2 and 3551 et seq.)

(Counts 15 through 17 would be identical except for the dates; each would cover the deposits following the monthly shipments between October and December 2004.)

COUNT EIGHTEEN
(Money Laundering Conspiracy)

13.   In or about and between September 2004 and December 2004, both dates being approximate and inclusive, within the Eastern District of New York, the defendants PAUL CHRISTOPHER and ERNEST WAGNER, together with others, knowing that the property involved in financial transactions represented the proceeds of some form of unlawful activity, did knowingly and intentionally conspire to conduct financial transactions affecting interstate and foreign commerce, to wit: cash deposits made at CMS Bank in Coney Island, New York, which transactions in fact involved the proceeds of a specified unlawful activity, to wit: narcotics trafficking, (a) with intent to promote the carrying on of the specified unlawful activity, and (b) knowing that the transactions were designed to (i) conceal and disguise the nature, location, source, ownership and control of such proceeds, and (ii) avoid a transaction reporting requirement under federal law, all in violation of Title 18, United States Code, Section 1956(a)(1).

(Title 18, United States Code, Sections 1956(h) and 3551 et seq.)

COUNT NINETEEN
(Money Laundering)

14.   On or about September 30, 2004, within the Eastern District of New York, the defendants PAUL CHRISTOPHER and ERNEST WAGNER, knowing that the property involved in financial transactions represented the proceeds of some form of unlawful activity, did knowingly and intentionally conduct financial transactions affecting interstate and foreign commerce, to wit: cash deposits of $25,000 in amounts less than $10,000 made at CMS Bank in Coney Island, New York, which transactions in fact involved the proceeds of a specified unlawful activity, to wit: narcotics trafficking, (a) with intent to promote the carrying on of the specified unlawful activity, and (b) knowing that the transactions were designed to (i) conceal and disguise the nature, location, source, ownership and control of such proceeds, and (ii) avoid a transaction reporting requirement under federal law.

(Title 18, United States Code, Sections 1956(a)(1), 2 and 3551 et seq.)

(Counts 20 through 22 would be identical except for the dates; each would cover the deposits following the monthly shipments between October and December 2004.)

276

FORFEITURE ALLEGATION
FOR MONEY LAUNDERING COUNTS

15.   Pursuant to Title 18, United States Code, Section 982(a)(1), upon conviction of any of the offenses set forth above in Counts Eighteen through Twenty-Two, the defendants PAUL CHRISTOPHER and ERNEST WAGNER shall forfeit to the United States the following property:

(a)   All right, title and interest in any and all property, real and personal, involved in the offenses that are charged in Counts Eighteen through Twenty-Two, and that the aforementioned defendants are convicted of, and all property traceable to such property.

(b)   Such forfeitable property includes, but is not limited to, the following:

(i)   the sum of $25,000.00, as alleged in Count Nineteen;

(ii)   the sum of $25,000.00, as alleged in Count Twenty;

(iii)   the sum of $25,000.00, as alleged in Count Twenty-One;

(iv)   the sum of $25,000.00, as alleged in Count Twenty-Two;

16.   If more than one defendant is convicted of the offenses charged in Counts Eighteen through Twenty-Two, the defendants so convicted are jointly and severally liable for the value of all property, real or personal, involved in the offense charged in those counts, and all property traceable to such property.

17.   If, by any act or omission of the defendants, the property described in paragraph 15(b) or any portion thereof:

(a)   cannot be located upon the exercise of due diligence;

(b)   has been transferred, sold to, or deposited with a third party;

(c)   has been placed beyond the jurisdiction of the Court;

(d)   has been substantially diminished in value; or

(e)   has been commingled with other property which cannot be divided without difficulty;

the defendants shall forfeit substitute property, up to the value of the property described in subparagraphs 15(a) through 15(b) above, pursuant to Title 18, United States Code, Section 982, which incorporates Title 21, United States Code, Section 853(p).

(Title 18, United States Code, Section 982; Title 21, United States Code, Section 853(p))

FORFEITURE ALLEGATION
FOR NARCOTICS COUNTS

(This would follow the same outline as the prior forfeiture allegations for the money laundering counts, but relying entirely on 21 U.S.C. § 853(a), and would apply to Counts 1 through 12 charging Christopher and Van Ness.)

A TRUE BILL

_____

FOREPERSON

Kevin O'Reilly
_____
KEVIN O'REILLY
UNITED STATES ATTORNEY
EASTERN DISTRICT OF NEW YORK

_____

Count One: The first count charges Christopher alone with conspiring to import cocaine. Although the government might have charged Van Ness in this conspiracy as well, AUSA Knapp thought that her argument to the jury on Van Ness would be strongest if she limited the charges against him to conduct she would easily be able to prove—i.e., his actual pick-up and delivery of the cocaine shipments. In terms of dates, Knapp decided to start the importation conspiracy in May 2004, the month when Santiago would testify that he was first approached by Christopher concerning a loan and the possibility of laundering illegal narcotics proceeds. Although the only proof of actual importations of cocaine shipments prior to Santiago's direct involvement in August 2004 would be Santiago's testimony that Christopher had told him about the earlier shipments, Knapp believed that May 2004 was the logical as well as factual starting point for this conspiracy and would ensure the admissibility of all conversations between Santiago and Christopher dating that far back.

Since a conspiracy requires an agreement between two or more individuals, this charge refers to Christopher conspiring "together with others." DOJ practice usually is not to name co-conspirators who are not the subject of the same indictment; rather, the reference is, as here, a general one, with the understanding that evidence as to the identity of these co-conspirators (in this case, Gilbert Santiago, Mario Long and the individuals who were shipping the cocaine through Christopher) will be presented to the grand jury.

Notice that Count One, like most narcotics conspiracy counts, consists entirely of a simple gravamen paragraph; the means by which the conspiracy was carried out and details such as the specific dates of drug shipments are not specified (though they might later be sought by the

278

defendant through a motion for a bill of particulars), at least in part because federal narcotics conspiracy laws, unlike most general conspiracy laws, do not require proof of any overt act in furtherance of the conspiracy.[159]

Count One, like all the narcotics counts, alleges a specific narcotic—cocaine—as well as an amount—"five kilograms or more." Different quantities of different narcotics trigger different statutory mandatory minimum and maximum sentences and are therefore considered "elements" of the offense that must be alleged in the indictment and proved to a jury beyond a reasonable doubt.[160] Here, as the offense involves five kilograms or more of cocaine, the statutory mandatory minimum prison term is 10 years (for a first time offender) and the statutory maximum prison term is life. The fact that the aggregate quantities of cocaine imported here are much greater than five kilograms makes no difference at the indictment stage, as the statutory mandatory minimum and statutory maximum are the same above that five kilogram threshold. However, the total amount of cocaine involved will be taken into account in a significant way at sentencing, through the Sentencing Guidelines determination of a base offense level.

The charge also includes language to satisfy the venue requirement that the crime take place, at least in part, within the district in which it is being prosecuted. The specific phrasing—"within the Eastern District of New York and elsewhere"—reflects the fact that the crime of conspiring to import takes place both within the Eastern District of New York (where the cocaine is received and then distributed) and elsewhere (i.e., the location from where it is shipped).

Finally, Count One, like all the charges, recites the pertinent provisions of the United States Code that make conspiracy to import cocaine a federal crime (Title 21, United States Code, Sections 963, 960(a)(1) and 960(b)(1)(B)(ii)), as well as those sections that govern the sentencing for such an offense (Title 18, United States Code, Sections 3551 *et seq.*).

Count Two. Count Two charges both Christopher and Van Ness with conspiring to distribute and possess with intent to distribute cocaine. The time frame is the same as Count One—May 2004 to January 2005—notwithstanding the fact that the prosecution has no evidence to tie Van Ness to the conspiracy until August 2004 (when Santiago becomes involved)—because the prosecutor knows that the jury will be instructed that Van Ness can be held responsible for knowingly

---

159. United States v. Shabani, 513 U.S. 10, 15–16 (1994); United States v. Carillo, 229 F.3d 177, 181 (2d Cir. 2000); United States v. Bermudez, 526 F.2d 89, 95 (2d Cir. 1975).

160. *See* Apprendi v. New Jersey, 530 U.S. 466, 490 (2000) ("Other than the fact of a prior conviction, any fact that increases the penalty for a crime beyond the prescribed statutory maximum must be submitted to a jury, and proved beyond a reasonable doubt.").

joining an illegal conspiracy that may have started several months earlier.[161]

Here it should be emphasized that for Sentencing Guidelines purposes it will not matter whether Christopher or Van Ness is convicted of both importation and distribution or just one or the other. This is because the Sentencing Guidelines mandate that the range of imprisonment in a narcotics trafficking case be calculated based on the aggregate amount of narcotics involved, irrespective of how many different counts the defendant is charged with (or convicted of).

Counts Three through Eleven. These are the substantive (as opposed to conspiracy) counts of importing and distributing narcotics, with a separate count corresponding to each individual shipment between September 2004 and January 2005. AUSA Knapp chose to limit these substantive counts to correspond to those months as to which Santiago will be in a position to testify about the shipments from his personal knowledge and involvement. The importation counts charge Christopher alone, while the distribution counts charge both Christopher and Van Ness, for the reasons previously stated.

Each one of these counts cites an additional provision, 18 U.S.C. § 2, which is the federal criminal aiding and abetting statute. Although technically not required to be alleged in the indictment,[162] the citation to § 2 puts the defendants on clear notice that Knapp may argue that even if the jury finds that Christopher merely aided or assisted others in their illegal importation of cocaine, or that Van Ness merely aided or assisted Christopher in distributing the cocaine, they still are as criminally culpable as if they had been the principal persons importing and/or distributing the drugs. (The same aiding and abetting citation also is included in the substantive counts charging structuring and money laundering, for similar reasons.)

Count Twelve. Neither Christopher nor Van Ness succeeded in actually possessing or distributing the final cocaine shipment that was intercepted by federal agents in January 2005. Accordingly, as to that shipment, the appropriate substantive charge is *attempted* distribution and possession with intent to distribute, as reflected in Count Twelve. (The cocaine was successfully imported into the United States, however, and so the corresponding substantive importation charge (Count Seven) is no different than the charges corresponding to the preceding months where the deliveries were more successful (Counts Three through Six)).

---

161. *See, e.g.,* United States v. Osborne, 332 F.3d 1307, 1314 (10th Cir. 2003). *See generally* Pinkerton v. United States, 328 U.S. 640, 646–47 (1946).

162. *See generally* Williams v. United States, 168 U.S. 382, 389 (1897) (noting that a conviction may be sustained on the basis of a statute or regulation other than that cited). *See also* United States v. Armstrong, 909 F.2d 1238, 1241 (9th Cir. 1990) ("Aiding and abetting is implied in every federal indictment for a substantive offense.").

Counts Thirteen through Seventeen. The structuring charges against Christopher and Wagner—both conspiracy and substantive–require a certain amount of background to explain how and why the described activity is criminal. The introductory paragraphs—6(a) through 6(e)—accomplish this objective. Recall that the indictment, and thus this explanatory language, typically will be read to the jury at the outset of the case and also likely will be given to them at the end of the trial as an aid to their deliberations.

In addition, a structuring conspiracy, like any conspiracy charged under the general federal criminal conspiracy statute (18 U.S.C. § 371), requires at least one overt act in furtherance of the conspiracy (by any of the co-conspirators), and so Count Thirteen alleges several overt acts (paragraph 10, subparagraphs a–f), from which the jury need only find one has been proved beyond a reasonable doubt. Such overt acts provide varying degrees of detail; here, they tell a more particularized narrative story of how the crime was committed. Inclusion of these details also provides the prosecution with a much stronger position to resist any later motion from the defendants for a bill of particulars.

As with the earlier narcotics counts, the references in these overt act paragraphs to "a co-conspirator whose identity is known to the grand jury" comports with standard DOJ practice, and the grand jury will hear evidence that this unidentified person is in fact Gilbert Santiago.

Counts Eighteen through Twenty–Two. The money laundering charges identify the "specified unlawful activity"—here, narcotics trafficking—that is an essential element of the offense, as well as the particular type of transaction (i.e., cash deposits at a particular bank). While some of these details go slightly beyond what may be technically required, they serve a practical function of putting the defendant (and later a jury) on notice of at least the basic particulars of the conduct the government intends to prove. As with the narcotics conspiracy charges, the crime of money laundering conspiracy is created by a specific statute (18 U.S.C. § 1956(h)) that does not incorporate the traditional common law requirement of an overt act in furtherance of the conspiracy, and accordingly no such overt act is (or need be) alleged in the indictment.

Forfeiture Allegations. Here, the focus is on depriving the defendants of the proceeds of the unlawful activity. The allegations include specific reference to the most obvious source of such proceeds—the funds deposited in the IFD CMS Bank accounts opened by Santiago—even though such specifics are not required. Finally, the forfeiture allegations provide for joint and several liability and put the defendants on notice that if the specified proceeds from the IFD accounts are no longer there, the government will attempt to forfeit other or so-called "substitute" assets of the defendants.

§ 11.8 Grand Jury Presentation in the Christopher Case

In anticipation of presenting the Christopher case to the grand jury, AUSA Knapp reserved two hours of grand jury time for April 25, 2005.

Recall that the grand jury already heard one small part of the story from Barbara Weiss, formerly of CMS Bank; now, it would hear the rest of the relevant evidence against Christopher, Van Ness and Wagner.

Because the rules of evidence do not apply to grand jury proceedings, Knapp had broad discretion in deciding how to present her evidence. She knew that she would use Agent Martinez to summarize the documentary evidence that had been gathered during the course of the investigation—i.e., bank records, phone records, etc. The major question was whether to bring her two principal cooperating witnesses—Gilert Santiago and Mario Long—before the grand jury and present their first-hand accounts or instead to simply allow Agent Martinez to repeat for the grand jury a summary of what Santiago and Long had said during proffer sessions (i.e., to present a hearsay account of their statements).

Knapp decided to follow the general practice in the Eastern and Southern Districts of New York and have Agent Martinez simply summarize the cooperator testimony. The principal rationale for this approach was the strategic concern not to create prior sworn statements of the government's key witnesses at an early stage of the case, without the kind of comprehensive witness preparation that typically takes place before trial, where such sworn statements would later be disclosed and likely would provide fodder for cross-examination.[163] This approach in part (some would say in large part) prevented the grand jury from making an independent assessment of the strength and reliability of the government's most important proof—here, most notably, Santiago's credibility. But Knapp also knew that both the courts and Department of Justice policy clearly permitted the use of agent testimony to summarize witness statements so long as it was made clear to the grand jury when the agent was providing second-hand knowledge.[164] In accordance with office practice, she would tell the grand jury that they had the right to ask to hear directly from Santiago and Long, and she concluded that presenting a hearsay account in the first instance was proper and fair, particularly where, as here, the cooperator information was independently corroborated in significant respects.

Having made the decision to rely primarily on Agent Martinez, Knapp spent the day before the grand jury presentation preparing him for his testimony. Together they reviewed the DEA–6 reports summarizing the proffer statements that had been made by Santiago and Long, as

---

163. We note that in many other United States Attorney's Offices around the country, the standard approach is exactly the opposite; cooperators are routinely called to testify before the grand jury, with one perceived strategic advantage being that their story is then "locked in" under oath.

164. *See* United States v. Ruggiero, 934 F.2d 440, 447 (2d Cir. 1991) (indictment should be dismissed where "the government misleads the grand jury into thinking

it is receiving firsthand testimony when it is in fact receiving hearsay or (2) if there is a high probability that the defendant would not have been indicted had only nonhearsay evidence been used"); United States v. Hogan, 712 F.2d 757, 761 (2d Cir. 1983) (noting that "extensive reliance on hearsay testimony in the grand jury is disfavored ... precisely because it is not first-rate proof").

well as the bank records, invoices, phone records and other documentary evidence. Knapp had prepared an outline of the questions she would ask Agent Martinez before the grand jury, and together they went through this "Q & A," checking facts where necessary and refining the presentation so that it would be clear and crisp.

The next morning, April 25, 2005, Knapp met Martinez at the courthouse, where the grand jury was sitting. To begin her presentation Knapp went into the grand jury room alone. She introduced herself to the court reporter and handed a copy of the proposed indictment to the grand jury foreperson. She then confirmed on the record that a quorum of at least 16 grand jurors was present and that none of the grand jurors knew Paul Christopher, William Van Ness, Ernest Wagner or Agent Martinez. Knapp then said the following to the grand jury:

> I'm here to present the case of United States v. Paul Christopher, William Van Ness and Ernest Wagner. You will hear evidence this morning of a long-running conspiracy to import cocaine into this country and distribute it and to illegally launder and hide from authorities the proceeds of that drug smuggling operation.

> You will hear evidence that Paul Christopher, through a business called International Food Distributors, received the shipments of cocaine; that his brother-in-law William Van Ness, through his company, Van Ness Trucking, transported these cocaine shipments once they arrived in Christopher's Queens warehouse; and that Wagner, a banker at CMS Bank, helped Christopher set up accounts to illegally hide the proceeds of these cocaine shipments.

> You will recall that you already heard some evidence in this case— from Ms. Barbara Weiss, a CMS Bank teller, who testified about her interactions one day with Ernest Wagner and someone named Gilbert Santiago.

> Today you are going to hear from Special Agent Ralph Martinez of the DEA. Special Agent Martinez's testimony will be mostly hearsay, meaning that most of what he tells you will be based on things he has learned through interviewing other people and from reviewing reports and other records that have been gathered and generated during this investigation.

> As you have been told many times, hearsay is admissible in this proceeding and you are entitled to rely on it. However, you have the right to hear from persons with first-hand knowledge of any of the things you hear about today, and if you wish to exercise that right, just let me know and we will make our best effort to bring such persons before you.

> Also remember that I am here simply as your legal advisor. Nothing I have said and nothing I will say is evidence. The only evidence will come from the witnesses from whom you hear testimony and from any documents or other tangible material that we put before you.

We'll follow the standard order today: I will call in Agent Martinez, ask him a series of questions, and when we are finished, if any of you has any questions, I will be happy to pose them to the witness so long as they call for relevant information. I'll then read you the proposed indictment, instruct you on the law, and leave you to deliberate.

With that introduction, Knapp called Agent Martinez into the grand jury room. The foreperson administered the oath and then Knapp began her questioning. Over the next hour or so, Agent Martinez recounted all of the evidence gathered during the investigation, including statements from cooperating witnesses, bank records, phone records, etc.

When Agent Martinez finished testifying, Knapp asked the grand jurors if they had any questions. One grand juror asked if the search of the Superior Warehouse was legal. Knapp responded by saying that this was not a relevant consideration for the grand jury because this was an issue that could and likely would be taken up later, if an indictment was returned, when the case was before a district court. Another grand juror asked what Santiago and Long were receiving in exchange for providing information. Knapp thought that was an appropriate question and thus asked Agent Martinez to explain the basic terms of the cooperation agreements, which he did.

When the grand jurors finished their questions, Agent Martinez was excused and Knapp read the proposed indictment to the grand jury. Knapp then instructed the grand jurors on the law applicable to each count, setting out the elements and exactly what the government had to prove for each crime charged. Following the instructions, and with no further questions from the grand jury, Knapp left the grand jury room (along with the court reporter) to allow the grand jurors to deliberate in complete privacy behind closed doors. Within ten minutes, the grand jury room door opened and the foreperson informed Knapp that the grand jury had returned a "true bill" on all counts.

Knapp then accompanied the grand jury foreperson to the on-duty magistrate judge, where the indictment was "returned" in open court.[165] At that time, and at the prosecution's request, the magistrate judge signed arrest warrants for each of the three defendants.[166]

§ 11.9 The Arraignments of Christopher, Van Ness and Wagner

Agent Martinez and other officers arrested Christopher and Van Ness later that same day. The defendants were processed at DEA Headquarters and brought to the district court, where they were lodged in detention pens to await their arraignment. After being read their *Miranda* warnings, Christopher refused to say anything and asked for his lawyer; Van Ness at first said he would talk, and proceeded to

---

165. FED. R. CRIM. P. 6(f).   **166.** FED. R. CRIM. P. 9.

explain that he was not close to and rarely even spoke to Christopher (his brother-in-law), but then decided to wait until he had consulted with his attorney before saying anything further. Both men called their attorneys, and Richard Clark and Martin Rothman, representing Christopher and Van Ness respectively, arrived at the courthouse shortly thereafter and spoke briefly to their clients.

The case was subsequently called and counsel filed their notices of appearance. Both defendants entered pleas of not guilty. Knapp served an order obtained from the judge restraining Christopher from disposing of any of the property listed in the forfeiture count of the indictment and freezing the IFD bank accounts and Christopher's personal account. She also requested that both defendants be detained, citing the presumption in favor of detention in narcotics cases and noting the seriousness of the charges: both defendants were alleged to have participated in an extended cocaine importation scheme (which Knapp described in some detail); the wholesale value of the drugs involved was well over $1,000,000; and both defendants faced statutory mandatory minimum prison terms of 10 years if convicted. Based on these facts, plus the apparent connections that Christopher in particular apparently had in Colombia and South America, Knapp argued that the risk of flight by both Christopher and Van Ness was too great to allow pre-trial release under any circumstances.

Clark responded first, for Christopher, and objected that the restraining order would prevent Christopher from conducting his business. The court resolved that matter by requiring Christopher to put his shares of stock in the corporation and any deeds to business property in the custody of the court and to agree to have the United States Attorney's Office monitor his bank accounts. As to bail, Clark argued that Christopher had solid roots in the community (including a family), ran a successful business, had no prior criminal involvement and therefore presented no risk of flight. He requested his client's release on a $100,000 bond, and he said Christopher's wife was present in court and was prepared to co-sign the bond.

Rothman argued next, and contended that—based on the prosecutor's own description of the facts—Van Ness was at most accused of being a minor figure in the drug operation, that he also ran an established business and was a long-time member of the community. He pointed out that there was no evidence that his client had any ties to any foreign country and requested bail on terms at least as favorable as Christopher.

When counsel finished arguing the court set bail as follows: Christopher's bond would be set at $1,000,000; it would have to be co-signed by his wife and another responsible surety (each of whom could be held responsible for $1,000,000 if Christopher later failed to appear); and, he would have to post as collateral the deed to his house. Van Ness would be released on a $500,000 bond signed by one responsible surety, and he too would have to post the deed to his house as collateral. After Christopher, Van Ness and their respective sureties had signed the bonds, the judge released both defendants with the stipulation that they had 48 hours to post their houses as collateral or else they would be re-arrested and detained in prison pending trial.

Unlike Christopher and Van Ness, neither of whom had retained counsel or communicated with (or been contacted by) the government before being indicted,[167] Ernest Wagner's attorney, Isabel Johnson, had had extensive pre-indictment conversations with AUSA Knapp, as recounted in Chapter 10. In fact, just a week before Knapp took her case to the grand jury, she advised Johnson that she intended to go forward with charging Wagner with money laundering and structuring. Johnson repeated her request for a meeting with the Chief of the Criminal Division, Daniel Anon, who obliged. The next day both AUSA Knapp and Anon listened for 30 minutes as Johnson made her "pitch" as to why Wagner should not be charged at all or, if charged, why the indictment should be limited to structuring. When the meeting ended, Johnson was told that her views would be considered and that, if Wagner nevertheless was charged, he would be permitted to self-surrender at the courthouse (as opposed to being arrested by agents). After the meeting, Anon told AUSA Knapp that the decision was hers, and that if she thought she had the proof to get a conviction on both charges, she should go forward.

Accordingly, when the grand jury voted to indict Wagner, AUSA Knapp immediately called Johnson, told her what had occurred, agreed to fax her the indictment, and said that she would allow Wagner to self-surrender by the end of business that day. Johnson told Knapp that she would contact her client and they would be at the courthouse within an hour. Johnson and Wagner arrived at court shortly thereafter, Wagner surrendered, was processed, went before the duty magistrate, pleaded not guilty and was released on a $100,000 bond.

---

167. As to why AUSA Knapp had reached out to Wagner but not to Christopher or Van Ness pre-indictment, the answer is simply that she anticipated that the latter two would be charged with narcotics-related crimes potentially carrying substantial jail time, and thus she viewed them—in contrast to Wagner—as presenting too great a risk of flight if they were notified of their target status before charges were brought (and thus before a bail package could be put in place to ensure their continued presence in the jurisdiction).

Chapter 12

PLEA NEGOTIATION AND THE NON–COOPERATING DEFENDANT

Table of Sections

Sec.
12.0 Introduction.
12.1 Charge Bargaining.
12.2 Sentence Bargaining.
12.3 Plea Bargaining for Judicial Leniency: Departures and Non–Guidelines Sentences.
12.4 Additional Features of Plea Agreements.
12.5 Pleas Without an Agreement.
12.6 Counseling and Negotiating a Plea: The Defense Lawyer's Perspective.
12.7 The Wagner Plea Negotiation.
   12.7(a) The Government's Position.
   12.7(b) The Defendant's Position.
   12.7(c) The Negotiation.
12.8 The Agreement.
12.9 Wagner's Guilty Plea.

§ 12.0 Introduction

We introduced the subject of plea negotiation in Chapter 8 with a discussion of negotiation over cooperation—the award of sentencing concessions to defendants who provide "substantial assistance" to the government in the prosecution of others. We now turn to the more common type of plea negotiation, that involving a defendant who is prepared to plead guilty but will not be cooperating. This can occur for a variety of reasons: the defendant may be unwilling to cooperate; he or she may have no information about other crimes; or he or she may not be given the opportunity to cooperate because the government believes him or her to be a principal target, and therefore not an appropriate subject for the benefits that flow to cooperators.

Even in cases where cooperation is not relevant, however, avoiding the time, expense and especially the risk of losing at trial usually is important. Consequently, plea negotiation is highly likely to take place and to resolve these cases as well. And, as has always been the case, the negotiation is almost invariably about how much leniency in punishment the defendant can obtain in return for giving up the right to trial.

As we discussed in Chapter 7, before the promulgation of the Sentencing Guidelines, the backdrop for negotiations between the parties was the almost untrammeled discretion of the judge to impose any sentence up to the maximum term of imprisonment for the crime for which the defendant was convicted. Negotiations were premised on informal sentencing conventions—the predilections of particular judges and the unwritten rule that a guilty plea would be rewarded. The implementation of the Sentencing Guidelines substantially reduced this judicial discretion in sentencing. And while the power to accept or reject a negotiated plea resides in the court, as a practical matter the parties exercise substantial control over the sentencing decision on the basis of how they negotiate the charges to which the defendant will plead and the application of the Guidelines factors and underlying facts that will be considered in determining the offense level.

To be sure, the Supreme Court's *Booker* decision in 2005[1] restored some of the sentencing discretion that judges exercised prior to the advent of the Guidelines. But the Department of Justice's reaction to *Booker* was to reaffirm the Department's directive that "[f]ederal prosecutors must actively seek sentences within the range established by the Sentencing Guidelines in all but extraordinary cases,"[2] and statistics collected in the first several months of post-*Booker* sentencing indicate that judges continue to impose Guidelines sentences in the vast majority of cases.[3] The Guidelines therefore remain the focal point of virtually all plea negotiations.

This chapter will describe the typical process by which plea bargaining takes place in the federal system, focusing on the two principal types of bargains—charge bargains, where the parties agree to the particular offense to which the defendant will plead guilty, and sentence bargaining, where the parties agree on how the Guidelines should be applied in the particular case. We will then illustrate these concepts in describing the post-indictment plea negotiation for defendant Ernest Wagner.

1. *See supra* §§ 7.0 & 7.3.

2. *See* James B. Comey, Department Policies and Procedures Concerning Sentencing, p. 2, *available at* http://sentencing.typepad.com/sentencing_law_and_ policy/files/dag_jan_28_comey_memo_on_ booker.pdf (Jan. 28, booker.pdf (Jan. 28, 2005) (hereinafter "Comey Memo").

3. *See supra* § 7.3.

§ 12.1   Charge Bargaining

As we discussed in Chapter 11, federal prosecutors enjoy virtually untrammeled discretion in making a charging decision. Statutory and case law require only that there be probable cause to support a charge and that it not be brought vindictively or selectively.[4] This broad grant of discretion has important implications in terms of punishment, because under federal law it is common to find a number of statutes from which a prosecutor can choose that punish the same conduct with varying degrees of severity. For example, it may be possible to charge a defendant with either a misdemeanor or a felony for the same conduct[5] or to charge a violation of one of two felony statutes that permit vastly different punishments.[6]

The prosecutor's discretion over the charge decision impacts on plea negotiation in either of two contexts. First, in cases where negotiation precedes the filing of formal charges by indictment, the negotiations can affect what charges in fact will be filed. Second, as a practical matter the prosecutor's discretion extends to the power to drop more serious charges or substitute reduced charges for those originally brought (subject to certain policy restrictions discussed below). Accordingly, even where they follow the filing of the indictment, negotiations can affect the ultimate charge as to which the defendant will plead guilty and be sentenced.

As described in Chapter 9, Rule 11 of the Federal Rules of Criminal Procedure—which governs plea bargaining—specifically authorizes "charge bargaining," whereby the government agrees that it will "not bring, or will move to dismiss, other charges."[7] While Rule 11 prohibits the court from participating in plea negotiations,[8] the court has the power to accept or reject a "charge bargain" agreement,[9] and if it is rejected, the defendant is entitled to withdraw his plea.[10]

Rule 11 does not itself provide any guidance as to when a judge should accept or reject a charge bargain. The Sentencing Commission, however, has issued policy statements "intended to ensure that plea negotiation practices: (1) promote the statutory purposes of sentencing prescribed in 18 U.S.C. § 3553(a); and (2) do not perpetuate unwarranted sentencing disparity."[11] While these policy statements are not binding

---

4. *See* LaFave et al., § 13.4.

5. *Compare* 18 U.S.C. § 1701 (obstruction of mails generally, punishable by up to 6 months in prison) *with* 18 U.S.C. § 1703 (delay or destruction of mail or newspapers, punishable by up to 5 years in prison).

6. *Compare* 18 U.S.C. § 371 (the general conspiracy statute, providing for punishment of up to 5 years in prison) *with* 21 U.S.C. § 846 (the narcotics conspiracy statute, providing for punishment in the same way as the underlying substantive offense,

which in most cases involves a maximum penalty of at least 20 years in prison and can involve a mandatory minimum of that length).

7. Fed. R. Crim. P. 11(c)(1)(A).

8. Fed. R. Crim. P. 11(c)(1).

9. Fed. R. Crim. P. 11(c)(3)(A).

10. Fed. R. Crim. P. 11(c)(5).

11. USSG Ch. 6, Pt. B, intro. comment.

on the courts, they provide the general framework that judges typically follow.

With respect to charge bargains, the Guidelines provide that a court may accept such an agreement if the court determines that "the remaining charges adequately reflect the seriousness of the actual offense behavior" and "accepting the agreement will not undermine the statutory purposes of sentencing or the sentencing guidelines."[12] While this language gives judges wide latitude to reject charge bargains, in practice judges rarely invoke this particular power,[13] whether because of fear of intruding "upon the charging discretion of the prosecutor,"[14] concern about the added burden to their docket where rejecting a charge bargain would lead to a trial instead of a plea of guilty, or a feeling that federal sentences are too harsh in many cases and any kind of bargaining that ameliorates the Guidelines' severity should be encouraged.[15]

While a broad grant of authority under Rule 11 and a generally hands-off approach by the judiciary thus would appear to allow for broad discretion in the area of charge bargaining, Department of Justice policy is, at least in theory, much more restrictive. Under the 2003 Ashcroft Memorandum (reaffirmed in 2005 following *Booker*), discussed previously in § 11.1(d), the ability of federal prosecutors to enter into charge bargains—i.e., to decline or dismiss charges as part of a plea agreement—is limited by the general prosecutorial mandate to pursue the "most serious readily provable charge." In other words, federal prosecutors may not agree to drop or forego the "most serious readily provable charge" except in limited exceptional circumstances noted previously, namely: (1) where the sentence would be unaffected; (2) pursuant to a "fast-track" program; (3) where there has been a post-indictment change in the ability to prove the case; (4) where necessary to obtain the defendant's cooperation; (5) in the case of a "statutory enhancement;" and (6) "other exceptional circumstances," such as an exceptionally lengthy prosecution in a particularly over-burdened office.[16]

Notwithstanding this recent directive, federal prosecutors retain some flexibility in charge bargaining. The term "readily provable" is ultimately a subjective one, and a prosecutor anxious to dispose of a case without trial, or concerned about the harshness of a sentence under the

---

12. USSG § 6B1.2(a), p.s. The policy statement further directs the court to state its reasons for so finding on the record. *Id.*; *see* FED. R. CRIM. P. 11(c)(5).

13. John Gleeson, *Sentencing Bargaining Under the Guidelines*, 8 FED. SENT. REP. 314, 315 (1996) (noting that such "authority is almost never invoked").

14. USSG § 6B1.2, p.s. & comment. (backg'd).

15. *See* Paul J. Hofer & Mark H. Allenbaugh, *The Reason Behind the Rules: Finding and Using the Philosophy of the Federal*

Sentencing Guidelines, 40 AM. CRIM. L. REV. 19, 85 n.17 (2003).

16. John Ashcroft, Departmental Policy Concerning Charging Criminal Offenses, Disposition of Charges, and Sentencing, pp. 3–5, *available at* http://www.fd.org/TXW/pdf_lib/memoagcds.pdf (Sept. 23, 2003) (hereinafter "Ashcroft Memorandum"). In addition, Department policy is that "the sentencing court should be informed if a plea agreement involves a 'charge bargain.'" *Id.*

Guidelines, may not interpret the term strictly. Moreover, Department policy continues to permit the United States Attorney in each district to consider the office's caseload pressure and resources in deciding whether it is appropriate to forego a plea to the "most serious readily provable offense." While there is no hard evidence as to how broadly or narrowly these exceptions are applied, it can be expected that the answer will continue to vary from office to office depending on the policies of particular United States Attorneys and the degree of supervision and control exercised over individual prosecutors.

Prior to the Supreme Court's *Booker* decision, it seemed likely that, absent fundamental changes in the Guidelines and in statutorily prescribed mandatory minimum sentences, charge bargaining would continue to be one method used by prosecutors and defense lawyers, and tacitly if not expressly approved by judges, to ameliorate if not circumvent what many perceived to be the undue harshness and rigidity of the mandatory Sentencing Guidelines regime, particularly in drug cases. *Booker*, however, provided a new "escape hatch" from the Guidelines and may, to some degree, reduce the willingness of prosecutors and/or judges to participate in some of the more "creative" charge bargaining that took place in the pre-*Booker* era.[17]

Plea bargaining policy of the Justice Department to the side, the Sentencing Guidelines have a significant impact on charge bargaining and must be thoroughly scrutinized in each case. While a plea to a reduced charge often will carry with it a correspondingly lower sentence under the Guidelines (as we will see in § 12.6 in connection with Ernest Wagner's plea negotiation), in some situations an apparent reduction in charge may result in no reduction in the ultimate sentence because of various specific features of a particular guideline[18] or because of a

17. Studies predating *Booker* and the Ashcroft Memorandum indicate that charge bargaining in the form of dismissing or foregoing "readily provable" counts was a relatively common method used by prosecutors to "circumvent" the Guidelines. *See, e.g.,* Stephen J. Schulhofer & Ilene H. Nagel, *Plea Negotiations Under the Federal Sentencing Guidelines: Guideline Circumvention and its Dynamics in the Post-Mistretta Period*, 91 NW. U. L. REV. 1284, 1285, 1293 (1997) (concluding that the Guidelines are "circumvented in an identifiable number of cases (approximately 20–35%)" and that "charge bargaining which leads to the dismissal of readily provable counts" was "[b]y far[] the most important vehicle for Guidelines evasion"). The authors of this study suggested that the best solution to "[b]ehind-the-scenes" circumvention would be to allow "a greater number of legitimate, officially authorized opportunities for the exercise of sound judicial discretion." *Id.* at

1316. They presumably were quite pleased when *Booker* rendered the Guidelines "advisory." The Ashcroft Memorandum and recent (but pre-*Booker*) congressional legislation aimed at exercising tighter control over the federal sentencing process (discussed further *infra* at Chapter 17) suggest, however, that current policymakers hold a different view and disagree with Schulhofer and Nagel's belief that "[f]urther efforts to tighten the sentencing system in order to squeeze out opportunities for circumvention are both unwise and, in practical terms, doomed to failure." *Id.*

18. For example, a bank teller who takes $50,000 from his employer could be charged under the bank larceny statute, 18 U.S.C. § 2113(b), which carries a maximum sentence of 10 years, or the bank embezzlement statute, 18 U.S.C. § 656, which has a 30 year maximum. Although the larceny count would have a lower maximum, the

Guidelines policy that a charge bargain may not preclude the conduct underlying any dismissed or foregone charge "from being considered under the provisions of § 1B1.3 (Relevant Conduct) in connection with the count(s) of which the defendant is convicted."[19]

§ 12.2   Sentence Bargaining

Once the charge has been determined, the parties cannot negotiate over what guideline applies to a given statutory violation; the Sentencing Guidelines make that determination.[20] But virtually every other aspect of the Guidelines calculation that ultimately will determine a defendant's Guidelines advisory sentence—from determining how to set the base offense level (such as quantity of drugs or amount of money stolen), to calculating specific offense characteristics (such as whether a dangerous weapon was used in connection with a crime), to Chapter 3 adjustments (such as the defendant's role in the offense)—is, within certain constraints, open to negotiation and agreement between the parties.

Plea bargaining over how the Sentencing Guidelines will apply in a particular case—"sentence bargaining" for short[21]—is, like charge bargaining, specifically authorized by Rule 11. The most common type of such plea agreement authorized by that rule is a sentence *recommendation* bargain. Under this type of agreement, the government promises to *"recommend, or agree not to oppose* the defendant's request, that a particular sentence or sentencing range is appropriate or that a particu-

---

Guidelines range would be the same since both fall under USSG § 2B1.1 (Larceny, Embezzlement and Other Forms of Theft). Thus, in those bank theft cases in which the Sentencing Guidelines require some prison time but less than 10 years and there are no grounds for departure, the count of conviction would usually make no difference to the sentence. However, were there grounds for departure to a probationary sentence, it should be noted that a defendant convicted under the embezzlement statute, which carries the 30 year maximum, is statutorily barred from receiving probation under 18 U.S.C. § 3561(a).

19. USSG § 6B1.2, p s & comment. (backg'd). For example, even if Paul Christopher agreed to plead guilty to only one of the substantive cocaine importation counts in exchange for dismissal of the remaining drug counts, such an agreement could not prevent the sentencing court from considering the quantity of drugs associated with the dismissed counts in calculating his base offense level. The only way to ensure that Christopher received a substantially reduced sentence would require what most would characterize as an act of Guidelines circumvention: allowing him to plead to a

charge carrying a lower statutory maximum penalty that would effectively "cap" his sentence and trump the Guidelines, such as the crime of using a telephone to facilitate a drug trafficking crime (carrying a 4 year maximum prison term under 21 U.S.C. § 843(b)), or simple possession of the drugs (carrying a 1 year statutory maximum sentence under 21 U.S.C. § 844). If allowed, such a plea would appear to run afoul of both the Guidelines (directing that judges accept charge bargains only where the result adequately reflects the seriousness of the defendant's conduct) and Department of Justice policy (requiring a plea to the most serious readily provable offense unless an enumerated exception is applicable).

20. *See* USSG § 1B1.2(a); *id.,* App. A.

21. *See, e.g.,* In re Ellis, 356 F.3d 1198, 1228 (9th Cir. 2004) (en banc) (explaining that "[i]n sentence bargains, both the prosecutor and defense agree both on a guilty plea to the initial charges and on a sentence or sentence recommendation."); United States v. Pimentel, 932 F.2d 1029, 1033 (2d Cir. 1991) (explaining that "sentence bargaining" is when the government "offer[s] to recommend or agree to a particular sentence" under Rule 11).

lar provision of the Sentencing Guidelines ... or sentencing factor does or does not apply."[22] However, the rule clearly states that "such a recommendation or request does not bind the court."[23] As such, this type of agreement carries with it no enforceable guarantees as to the outcome; moreover, whatever the outcome (that is, whether the court adopts the agreement and its recommendation(s) or not), the defendant cannot retract his or her plea of guilty.

Rule 11 also authorizes a sentence *agreement*. Here, the government does not simply recommend, but actually *"agree[s]* that a specific sentence or sentencing range is the appropriate disposition of the case, or that a particular Guideline ... or sentencing factor does or does not apply."[24] Unlike a sentence recommendation, a sentence agreement entered pursuant to this section of Rule 11 "binds the court once the court accepts the plea agreement."[25] Accordingly, and as with a charge bargain, if this type of plea agreement is rejected by the court, the defendant is entitled to withdraw his plea.[26] However, unlike the rather common scenarios of charge bargaining or sentence recommendations, most United States Attorney's Offices only rarely allow prosecutors to enter into binding sentence agreements, whether because of the uncertainty that arises as a result of a defendant's ability to withdraw his or her plea if such an agreement ultimately is rejected by the court or because of a variety of other institutional concerns.[27] Finally, because the binding aspect of such sentencing agreements should be unaffected by *Booker*,[28] it may be that the Department of Justice or individual United States Attorney's Offices will attempt to use such agreements either

---

22. FED. R. CRIM. P. 11(c)(1)(B) (emphasis added).

23. *Id.*

24. FED. R. CRIM. P. 11(c)(1)(C) (emphasis added).

25. *Id.*

26. FED. R. CRIM. P. 11(c)(5).

27. *See* Gleeson, *supra* note 13, at 318 (listing a variety of reasons prosecutors rarely enter into binding sentencing agreements); *Pimentel*, 932 F.2d at 1033 (noting prosecutor's explanation that the reluctance to enter into binding sentence agreements stemmed from the government's belief that "courts will accord greater deference to agreements to reduce charges than to sentencing recommendations"). To these possible explanations we would add the fact that prosecutors often will not be aware of all of the facts relevant to sentencing at the time of the plea and thus entering into a binding sentencing agreement at that early time may be viewed as bestowing on a defendant the unjustified benefit of a sentence calculation based on incomplete information.

For a recent example of a sentence agreement that was rejected by a judge in the high-profile Enron prosecutions, see Carrie Johnson, *Lea Fastow Withdraws Plea Agreement,* WASHINGTON POST, Apr. 7, 2004. In response to the judge's rejection of the proposed sentence agreement, and to achieve its goal of ensuring a minimal sentence for the wife of a high-level cooperator in the Enron cases, the government resorted to a charge bargain—dismissing all of the felony charges against Ms. Fastow and having her agree instead to plead guilty to a single misdemeanor tax charge. This charge bargain provided a maximum penalty of one year in prison, and under the Guidelines it would have been possible for her to receive a sentence well below that. But despite the government's argument for less time, the judge ultimately imposed the maximum sentence of a year in prison. *Id.* The Lea Fastow case thus suggests that there still is considerable room for charge bargaining, at least where it furthers an interest the government deems sufficiently important.

28. United States v. Cieslowski, 410 F.3d 353, 363-64 (7th Cir. 2005).

more broadly or in particular cases to "rein in" some of the sentencing discretion that *Booker* returned to the judiciary.

The applicable non-binding policy statement of the Sentencing Guidelines instructs judges to accept a plea bargain sentence recommendation or sentence agreement so long as: (1) the recommended or agreed sentence "is within the applicable guideline range;" or (2) the recommended or agreed sentence "departs from the applicable guideline range for justifiable reasons."[29] Prior to *Booker* the courts were split on the significance to be afforded to this policy statement and what constitute "justifiable reasons," with some courts endorsing departures from the applicable Sentencing Guidelines where, e.g., the prosecution faces "proof problems"[30] or where necessary to secure a "global plea" from a large number of defendants,[31] while others construed the policy statement to limit compromises as to the applicable Guidelines to those narrow instances in which a "downward departure" otherwise would be authorized under 18 U.S.C. § 3553(b).[32] The Sentencing Commission has now weighed in on this split, squarely siding with those courts that have read "justifiable reasons" to be limited to facts that would support an authorized departure under § 3553(b).[33] Here too it remains to be seen whether the increased sentencing flexibility afforded to judges by *Booker* (and *Booker's* excision of § 3553(b))—to the extent it is not preemptively curtailed by the following strict Department of Justice plea bargaining policies—translates into a broader judicial acceptance of sentence agreements that reach a more lenient sentencing result than otherwise called for under the Guidelines through an analysis of all of the factors listed in 18 U.S.C. § 3553(a).

Department of Justice policy instructs prosecutors generally that any sentencing recommendation contained in a plea agreement "must honestly reflect the totality and seriousness of the defendant's conduct and must be fully consistent with the Guidelines and applicable statutes and with the readily provable facts about the defendant's history and conduct."[34] And as noted previously, following *Booker* federal prosecutors

---

29. USSG § 6B1.2(b), (c), p.s.

30. United States v. Goodall, 236 F.3d 700, 705 (D.C. Cir. 2001) (holding that Rule 11 "plainly countenances agreed-upon sentences falling outside the otherwise applicable Guidelines range").

31. United States v. Aguilar, 884 F.Supp. 88, 89 (E.D.N.Y. 1995) (Weinstein, J.) (360–month Guidelines sentence reduced by agreement to 188 months).

32. *See* John M. Dick, Note, *Allowing Sentence Bargains to Fall Outside of the Guidelines Without Valid Departures: It Is Time for the Commission to Act,* 48 HAS-TINGS L.J. 1017, 1046–1050 (1997); *see also* United States v. Peveler, 359 F.3d 369, 374

(6th Cir. 2004); United States v. Carrozza, 4 F.3d 70, 87 (1st Cir. 1993).

33. USSG § 6B1.2, p.s., comment. (backg'd.).

34. Ashcroft Memorandum at 5. Although only sentence "recommendation[s]" are mentioned, the memorandum presumably was intended to apply to sentence "agreements" as well. It also should be noted that the memorandum grants federal prosecutors essentially complete discretion in one more limited area, namely, freedom to enter into a plea agreement under which they recommend a particular sentence within the applicable Guidelines range. For example, if the applicable range is 70 to 87 months, the prosecutor has complete discre-

were reminded of their obligation to "actively seek sentences within the ranges established by the Sentencing Guidelines in all but extraordinary cases" and that supervisory authorization would be required "to recommend or stipulate to a sentence outside the appropriate Guidelines range."[35]

Because it is the facts that drive the application of the Sentencing Guidelines, the plea negotiation process will often focus on what facts the prosecution can and cannot prove and how the provable facts should be applied to various Guidelines considerations.[36] Such agreements can concern the entire range of Guidelines factors. The most common are those involving adjustments for "acceptance of responsibility" (affording a defendant as much as a 3–level reduction) or for the defendant's "role in the offense" (allowing as much as a 4–level reduction or a 4–level increase). Such agreements also may deal with facts relevant to determining "specific offense characteristics" enumerated in particular Guidelines (such as, for example, whether the crime caused "serious bodily injury"). And agreements dealing with the existence of "relevant conduct"—whether proven at trial or not—may be extremely important in many cases, since this factor can have a dramatic effect on the sentence.[37]

Agreements as to the relevant facts typically are incorporated into written plea agreements or in stipulations accompanying such agreements.[38] While there is evidence that overt manipulation of facts sometimes occurs in such agreements or stipulations, there are substantial barriers to agreements involving a misleading presentation of the actual facts relevant to sentencing. The Guidelines clearly forbid the practice, stating that any factual stipulation "must fully and accurately disclose all factors relevant to the determination of sentence" and that "it is not appropriate for the parties to stipulate to misleading or non-existent factors."[39] The courts too have been clear in stating that the parties cannot agree to withhold relevant facts from the sentencing judge.[40]

---

tion to agree to recommend the low end, 70 months.

35. Comey Memo at 2.

36. In this connection it is critical to remember that the sentencing judge need only find facts proven by a preponderance of the evidence—i.e., find that the facts are more likely true than not—in order to rely on them in applying the Sentencing Guidelines.

37. The court is required to calculate the sentence based on all "relevant conduct" that is proven by a preponderance of the evidence, not just the particular conduct that forms the basis for the charge(s) to which the defendant will plead guilty, and the expansive concept of "relevant conduct" includes, *inter alia*, "reasonably fore-

seeable acts . . . of others in furtherance of [] jointly undertaken criminal activity" and all acts that "were part of the same course of conduct or common scheme or plan as the offense of conviction." USSG § 1B1.3. Even conduct for which a defendant was acquitted by a jury may be factored into sentencing as "relevant conduct" if found by the sentencing judge to have been proved by a "preponderance of the evidence." *See* United States v. Watts, 519 U.S. 148, 154 (1997).

38. USSG § 6B1.4, p.s.

39. USSG § 6B1.4, p.s. & comment. (backg'd).

40. Such an agreement is unenforceable as against public policy. *See, e.g.,* United States v. Schilling, 142 F.3d 388, 395 n.11

Moreover, as we shall explain in more detail in Chapter 17, sentencing facts, whether agreed upon by the parties or not, are gathered by the Probation Department, an arm of the court, and embodied in presentence reports presented to the sentencing judge, so that any stipulations diverting from the actual facts are unlikely to remain unchallenged.

Consistent with these pronouncements and procedures governing the determination of facts relevant to sentencing, prosecutors are directed by the Department of Justice to disclose to the court and the Probation Department all "readily provable facts [that] are relevant to calculations under the Sentencing Guidelines." Prosecutors may not "fact bargain"—that is, agree with the defendant not to disclose to the court certain facts that would impact the Sentencing Guidelines calculation—and thus may not enter into a plea agreement that results in the sentencing court having "less than a full understanding of all readily provable facts relevant to sentencing."[41]

Despite these limits on what the parties can agree to and the court's power to look behind the facts and Guidelines calculations agreed upon by the parties, agreements as to the facts and the application of the Guidelines are heavily relied upon by the courts, and in many cases are not closely scrutinized. This is most likely because, just as with charge bargains, judges have strong incentives to give full force and effect to sentence agreements between the parties in order to encourage disposition of cases by guilty plea; reduce the number of sentencing appeals; and add flexibility to the comparatively restrictive scheme contained in the Guidelines.[42]

To the preceding discussion of various forms of sentencing agreements should be added those in which the prosecution agrees to tell the court that the government does not oppose a certain defense request or takes no position on a request. While not as good as an affirmative agreement, even this position can be useful to the defendant. For example, it is a common feature of plea agreements that the government will "take no position" on where, within an agreed-upon Guidelines range, a defendant should be sentenced. Although the ultimate decision of course rests with the judge, such an agreement offers some advantage by freeing the defense to argue for the lowest point in the stipulated range without opening itself up to a government response that expressly demands a more severe punishment.[43]

(7th Cir. 1998); United States v. Fagge, 101 F.3d 232, 234 n.1 (2d Cir. 1996).

41. Ashcroft Memorandum at 5.

42. *See* Schulhofer & Nagel, *supra* note 17, at 1300–1311.

43. Of course, if in making such an argument the defense states facts that the government believes are inaccurate or represent a mischaracterization of the offense, the prosecutor will feel free to "correct" the record so long as he or she continues to refrain from urging the judge to impose a sentence at a particular point in the applicable Guidelines range.

§ 12.3 Plea Bargaining for Judicial Leniency: Departures and Non–Guidelines Sentences

While in most situations the primary focus of any plea bargaining between the defendant and the government will be on the application of the Guidelines, we have previously noted two potential "escape hatches" that may allow for a lower (or higher) sentence—and that therefore must be carefully considered—in every case.

The first "escape hatch," built into the Guidelines system itself, is of course the downward (and upward) departure mechanism. To reiterate, if the defendant can show mitigating circumstances (or the government can show aggravating circumstances) that are not "adequately taken into account" by the Guidelines, the sentencing judge has the discretion to impose a lower (or higher) sentence than the Guidelines otherwise provide for.[44]

As a practical matter, however, the prosecutor has extremely limited authority to agree to—or even to agree not to oppose—a defendant's motion for a downward departure. Following passage of the so-called Feeney Amendment to the PROTECT Act in early 2003[45] and the issuance of the Ashcroft Memorandum later that year,[46] the Department's current policy is that prosecutors may seek, stipulate to, or accede to a downward departure at sentencing only for two discrete sets of defendants: those who cooperate and provide "substantial assistance" (i.e., departures under § 5K1.1) and those who enter pleas pursuant to an authorized "fast track" prosecution program.[47] Beyond these two limited categories, Department of Justice policy is that "Government acquiescence in a downward departure (i.e., departures under § 5K2.0) should be ... a 'rare occurrence.' "[48] Prosecutors are directed to "affirmatively oppose downward departures that are not supported by the facts and the law and must not agree to 'stand silent' with respect to such departures."[49]

What does all of this mean in practice? Many United States Attorney's Offices implement this strongly anti-departure Department of Justice policy by requiring that virtually all defendants, as part of a standard-form plea agreement, waive their right to even *seek* or make arguments in support of a downward departure. While such a waiver

---

44. We focus on downward departures in this context and mention upward departures only parenthetically because, as a practical matter, it is almost unheard of that a defendant, as part of a plea negotiation, would agree to an upward departure (in fact, in our experience, it is also almost unheard of for the prosecution even to ask for an upward departure as part of a plea). On the other hand, in the case of a genuinely meritorious downward departure situation, there is at least the possibility that a prosecutor will agree to, or at least agree not to oppose, such an application.

45. *See supra* § 7.2(i); Ashcroft Memorandum at 6 ("In passing the PROTECT Act, Congress has made clear its view that there have been too many downward departures from the Sentencing Guidelines.").

46. Ashcroft Memorandum at 6.

47. *Id.* at 6–7.

48. *Id.* at 7.

49. *Id.*

technically does not foreclose a judge from granting a departure, practically speaking it is only in the rarest of circumstances that a judge will *sua sponte* consider and grant a downward departure where the parties have bargained that right away. That being said, there are those "rare" cases where the argument for a departure is sufficiently meritorious that the prosecutor may be persuaded either to not oppose (or to take no position on) any such application, thereby leaving it in the judge's discretion,[50] or at least to allow the defendant to make the motion, which the government can then oppose, again leaving the ultimate decision in the hands of the judge.

The second potential "escape hatch" from the Guidelines is of more recent vintage and follows from the Supreme Court's *Booker* decision. Recall that *Booker* rendered the Sentencing Guidelines only "advisory" and authorized federal judges to impose so-called non-Guidelines sentences pursuant to an application of the factors set forth in 18 U.S.C. § 3553(a).[51]

Assessing the value of this additional Guidelines "escape hatch" in any particular case is extremely difficult, especially in these first months following the *Booker* decision. It is simply too early to attempt to describe in any comprehensive way the factual and/or legal bases on which such non-Guidelines sentences are most likely to be imposed by the district courts and upheld by the appellate courts. At this point in time, much seems to depend on the particular facts and circumstances of the defendant's case and the defendant's personal situation and whether those facts and circumstances amount to a persuasive and legally appropriate basis for a sentencing judge to impose a sentence outside the Guidelines. As noted in Chapter 7, to a large degree the value also will turn on the particular judge to whom the case is assigned and into which side of the post-*Booker* split of opinion he or she falls. If the particular judge deems the Guidelines presumptively correct and applies them in all or almost all cases, any *Booker* argument for a non-Guidelines sentence may be close to worthless. Contrarily, if the judge seems to be open to non-Guidelines sentences, viewing the Guidelines as just one factor to be given equal weight along with the many other considerations in 18 U.S.C. § 3553(a), a factually and legally strong argument for a non-Guidelines sentence may be a central consideration in any plea negotiation.

50. A commitment from the government not to oppose or to take no position on a departure motion may make it more likely that a judge will grant such a request for the additional reason that the government's agreed-to non-opposition will operate as a waiver of its right to appeal the court's decision on this issue.

51. While *Booker* of course affords the prosecution a similar independent basis to argue for a more severe non-Guidelines sentence pursuant to those same § 3553(a) factors, it is unlikely that prosecutors will seek to do so in the context of a negotiated plea. We therefore focus here on what is likely to be a much more common consideration from the defendant's point of view.

In the plea bargaining context, and as with departures, the possibility of seeking a non-Guidelines sentence is substantially impacted—and diminished—by Department of Justice policy. As noted, following *Booker* the Department reiterated that federal prosecutors *"must* actively seek sentences within the ranges established by the Sentencing Guidelines in all but extraordinary cases" and that supervisory authorization would be required "to recommend or stipulate to a sentence outside the appropriate Guidelines range."[52] Some United States Attorney's Offices have implemented this edict by demanding that defendants, as part of any plea agreement, agree not just on how the Guidelines should apply in the particular case, but also agree to (a) waive their right to seek or argue for a non-Guidelines sentence under 18 U.S.C. § 3533(a)[53] and (b) stipulate that a sentence within the agreed-upon Guidelines range would be "reasonable."[54] Early anecdotal experience suggests, however, that this type of waiver may not be as widely or insistently demanded by United States Attorney's Offices as have downward departure waivers. And of course even where such a waiver is part of a plea agreement, the court is not bound by that agreement and retains the freedom to impose a non-Guidelines sentence where the circumstances so warrant.[55]

§ 12.4 Additional Features of Plea Agreements

While the central component of most plea agreements will be the parties' agreement on the charge and/or sentencing considerations, a wide variety of additional promises—involving concessions from the defendant and the government alike—may be demanded as part of the plea negotiation process. For example, many if not most standard plea agreements require a defendant to waive his or her right to appeal the conviction or sentence, so long as the sentence handed down by the judge is within or below the Sentencing Guidelines range provided for (or estimated) in the plea agreement.[56] Other concessions commonly re-

52. Comey Memo at 2.

53. Some in the defense bar have objected to such waivers as effectively taking away something that the Supreme Court held in *Booker* is constitutionally required, namely, that the Guidelines be non-binding. Many federal prosecutors, on the other hand, appear to be of the view that the Guidelines are presumptively reasonable and that, therefore, requiring a defendant to so stipulate furthers the shared goal of the Department of Justice and Congress to promote sentencing uniformity through consistent application of the Guidelines.

54. By stipulating that any sentence within the Guidelines range would be "reasonable," a defendant effectively relinquishes his or her right to appeal that sentence. This is because, following *Booker,* "reasonableness" is the ultimate standard of review

on appeal. *See, e.g.,* United States v. Crosby, 397 F.3d 103, 110 (2d Cir. 2005).

55. While defense counsel who has signed a plea agreement waiving the right to seek either a downward departure or a non-Guidelines sentence cannot make arguments in support thereof, nothing prevents the attorney from putting before the court the facts that might warrant such leniency and from at least arguing that such facts justify a sentence at the low end of the calculated and agreed-to Guidelines range. The district judge inclined to grant leniency can do the rest without requiring the defense attorney to violate the agreement.

56. Such waivers of appeal are generally enforceable absent some constitutional error or other "miscarriage of justice." *See, e.g.,* United States v. Johnson, 347 F.3d

quired of defendants in standard form plea agreements include: waiver of the right to additional disclosure of evidence, even if favorable to the accused;[57] agreement to a certain amount of forfeiture or restitution; provision of financial disclosure to the United States Attorney's Offices; or, that a non-indigent defendant waive all rights to bring a claim under the Hyde Amendment[58] for reimbursement for attorney's fees and expenses, which would otherwise be an option where it can be shown that the government's position with respect to dropped charges had been "vexatious, frivolous or in bad faith."

Additional obligations may be assumed by prosecutors as well, including promises not to bring additional charges, not to seek an upward departure under the Sentencing Guidelines, not to appeal the sentence where it is at least as severe as the Guidelines range set forth in the agreement, or to abide by promises that proffer admissions will not be used against the defendant in connection with sentencing (in those cases where the proffer sessions have not led to successful cooperation). Plea agreements also contain other warnings and limitations, from those concerning potential collateral consequences (including loss of the right to vote or, in the case of an alien, deportation from the country) to those clearly stating that other government agencies (such as other United States Attorney's Offices, the IRS, or state authorities) will not be bound by the agreement.

Whether and to what extent any of these or other standard plea agreement provisions will be negotiable will depend on the particular United States Attorney's Offices, the individual AUSA handling the case, and the unique facts of each defendant's criminal involvement and personal circumstances.[59]

412, 414–15 (2d Cir. 2003) (discussing cases from several circuits).

57. Until 2002 it was assumed that the defendant's right to exculpatory evidence under Brady v. Maryland, 373 U.S. 83 (1963), and its progeny discussed *infra* at § 13.3, applied to the decision to plead guilty. However, in United States. v. Ruiz, 536 U.S. 622, 633 (2002), the Supreme Court held that the *Brady* rule is designed to assure a fair trial, a right that is waived by the defendant's decision to plead guilty. *Ruiz* involved the failure of the government to provide impeachment material, a category of favorable evidence within the *Brady* rule, *see* Giglio v. United States, 405 U.S. 150 (1972). Cases following *Ruiz*, however, make clear that the underlying principle is not limited to impeachment material. *See,*

e.g., United States v. Le, 306 F.Supp.2d 589, 591–92 (E.D. Va. 2004). *But see* McCann v. Mangialardi, 337 F.3d 782, 787–88 (7th Cir. 2003) (*Ruiz* does not permit government to withhold evidence of actual innocence).

58. The Hyde Amendment is codified as a statutory note to 18 U.S.C. § 3006A.

59. For a comparison of standard plea (and cooperation and proffer) agreements utilized by the United States Attorney's Offices within the Second Circuit, see Federal Bar Council, Committee on Second Circuit Courts, *Proffer, Plea and Cooperation Agreements in the Second Circuit* (June 2003); Alan Vinegrad, *Proffer, Plea and Cooperation Agreements in the Second Circuit,* N.Y.L.J., Aug. 7, 2003, at 4.

§ 12.5   Pleas Without an Agreement

In rare cases, a defendant may wish to plead guilty to the charge(s) in the indictment without a written agreement with the government. Such a plea is perfectly proper, and so long as the defendant pleads to each and every charge in the indictment, there will be no trial and no adverse impact on the 2 or 3–level Guidelines reduction for acceptance of responsibility. For example, a defendant who believes he or she has a substantial argument on a Guidelines issue (such as the scope of "relevant conduct" or the proper role adjustment), but who is unable to convince the government of their position, may wish to preserve the right to appeal the sentencing judge's decision on such an issue. In such a situation, a "straight plea," without any written agreement may be the only way for the defendant to preserve his or her right to appeal.[60] Similarly, if the prosecutor is demanding that the defendant agree not to move for a downward departure, and/or not to move for a non-Guidelines sentence pursuant to *Booker*, and the defendant has a substantial or meaningful chance of prevailing on such a motion, a guilty plea without an agreement may be warranted.[61]

§ 12.6   Counseling and Negotiating a Plea: The Defense Lawyer's Perspective

In virtually every case, the defense attorney will be required to raise with the client the possibility of entering a plea of guilty. There may, of course, be situations in which the defendant will from the outset insist upon a trial. But often, the defendant, inevitably uncertain about the result of a trial but secure in the knowledge that if convicted he or she will face a greater punishment, will consider a guilty plea. To advise the defendant competently about such a plea, the defense attorney must be intimately familiar with the Sentencing Guidelines, including the departure mechanism and the post-*Booker* possibilities for non-Guidelines

---

60. By referring to a situation where the defendant is "unable to convince the government," we focus on the somewhat extreme case where the government will not even agree to disagree on the point. For example, if the defense thinks a minor role adjustment is in order and the government disagrees, an "open plea" to preserve this issue on appeal would only be necessary if the government insists that any plea agreement include a stipulation that rules out such an adjustment. In most cases it should be possible to at least persuade the prosecutor to agree that the defendant may argue

for the adjustment and the prosecution may argue against it. The issue is then preserved for appeal on this point in the event of an unfavorable ruling for the defendant, and at the same time the parties can agree to whatever other mutual benefits might flow from a negotiated written agreement.

61. As discussed *supra* at § 9.1, Rule 11 (a)(2) also provides for a conditional plea of guilty, designed to give a defendant standing to appeal an adverse decision on a pretrial motion.

sentences (pursuant to the factors set forth in 18 U.S.C. § 3553(a)). Only a thorough understanding of these rules will put the attorney in the position to realistically propose less severe charges, alternative ways of calculating the Guidelines, or other grounds for leniency. In short, while the prosecutor typically approaches a plea bargain by thinking about what the sentence "should be" under the Guidelines, the defense lawyer's job is to imagine what the charges and the sentence "could be."

Before raising the possibility of a plea with the defendant, considerable effort must be placed on "crunching" the Guidelines numbers and weighing all of the possibilities for leniency. The discussion will begin with an assessment of the chances of a conviction and the likely sentence that would be imposed. That sentence would then be compared with what would be imposed under various "best case" and "worst case" plea scenarios. The defendant will also have to be advised about rights that he or she would have to surrender in order to obtain the benefits of the plea agreement.

Once the defendant has decided to pursue a plea bargain (and the attorney is comfortable that the client will in fact be able to allocute, i.e., admit his or her guilt), the defense lawyer can enter into the negotiation with the government. This negotiation will involve the defense lawyer trying to persuade the prosecutor to move as close to the defendant's "best case" scenario as possible by arguing that certain facts are not "readily provable," and therefore need not be charged, or by arguing that certain ameliorative Guidelines factors are applicable. Ultimately, of course, the defense attorney must persuade the sentencing court, not the prosecutor, but as a practical matter the experienced practitioner knows that obtaining the government's agreement on (or at least a promise not to oppose) a position favorable to the defendant goes a long way—often all the way—toward assuring that the defendant's view carries the day.

A final note is in order about the differing perspectives of the defense lawyer and the prosecutor within the federal sentencing framework. The defense attorney, of course, is not constrained by Department of Justice policy. While the prosecutor's obligation is to see that the Guidelines are faithfully implemented, the defense attorney's overarching responsibility is to secure as lenient a deal as possible for the defendant within the bounds of the rules of ethics. In other words, if there is a more favorable way to resolve a client's case that holds out some reasonable prospect of success, the defense attorney's obligation is to propose and press for it, notwithstanding any potential conflict with the Guidelines' stated goals and purposes.

§ 12.7　The Wagner Plea Negotiation

It will be recalled that Ernest Wagner was a vice-president at CMS Bank and was indicted for conspiring with Paul Christopher to structure financial transactions in order to avoid disclosure laws (31 U.S.C. § 5324) and for money laundering (18 U.S.C. § 1956), with four substantive counts connected with each conspiracy count. The total amount of money alleged in the indictment to have been involved was $100,000. Shortly after the arraignment on the indictment, Wagner's attorney, Isabel Johnson, called AUSA Knapp and said that her client might be interested in pleading guilty. She requested that Knapp send her a proposed plea agreement so that she could intelligently discuss the options with her client.

§ 12.7(a)　The Government's Position

On learning that Wagner might plead guilty, Knapp determined that she would require a plea to one of the money laundering counts, since money laundering carried more severe sentencing consequences than structuring and thus represented the "most serious readily provable offense" under Department of Justice policies. The applicable Guidelines section relevant to the money laundering statute, 18 U.S.C. § 1956, is § 2S1.1. Applying that section, and following the instructions for calculating the Guidelines range set forth in § 1B1.1, she determined the following:

1. Pursuant to § 2S1.1(a)(2), the Base Offense Level would be "8 plus the number of offense levels from the table in § 2B1.1 ... corresponding to the value of the laundered funds."[62] Because the value of the laundered funds was $100,000, 8 additional levels would be added under § 2B1.1(b)(1)(E). Accordingly, the Base Offense Level would be 16.

2. As to the Specific Offense Characteristics, § 2S1.1(b)(1) might apply and add an additional 6 levels, if she could prove that Wagner "knew or believed that any of the laundered funds were the proceeds of, or were intended to promote" narcotics importation or distribution. While Knapp knew this was something of a stretch, she thought she might be able to convince a judge that this was more likely true than not (i.e., by a preponderance of the evidence). Although she might be prepared to bargain this enhancement away later to reach an agreement, Knapp decided to include it in her initial offer.

3. Under § 2S1.1(b)(2)(B), 2 additional levels would be added because the conviction would be under 18 U.S.C. § 1956.

62. Knapp concluded that the higher base offense level under USSG § 2S1.1(a)(1) would not apply because she did not have proof that Wagner committed or participated in the commission of the underlying narcotics smuggling offenses "from which the laundered funds were derived."

4. The Application Notes in the Commentary to § 2S1.1(b)(2)(B) suggested that Knapp did not have sufficient proof to show that Wagner was "in the business of laundering funds" (§ 2S1.1(b)(2)(C); Application Note 4) or that the offense "involved sophisticated laundering" (§ 2S1.1(b)(3); Application Note 5), and thus she determined that neither of these additional Specific Offense Characteristics enhancements applied.

5. As to Chapter 3 Adjustments, the first question was whether Wagner would qualify for a Mitigating Role in the money laundering offense under § 3B1.2. Knapp knew that this was a particularly malleable section of the Guidelines, which provided for a 2–level reduction if Wagner's role was "minor," a 4–level reduction if it was "minimal," and a 3–level reduction if it was somewhere in between. The Application Notes of the Commentary indicated that a "minimal participant" must be "among the least culpable of those involved in the conduct of the group" and that "the defendant's lack of knowledge or understanding of the scope and structure of the enterprise and of the activities of others is indicative of a role as a minimal participant."[63] A minor participant, on the other hand, was said to be a person who was "less culpable than most other participants, but whose role could not be described as minimal."[64] Knapp's view was that while Wagner probably was "among the least culpable" of those involved in laundering the narcotics proceeds (Santiago and Christopher clearly being the most culpable), he nevertheless played a not insignificant role by facilitating the bank transactions and, given the repeat nature of the deposit activity, in all probability had some sense of the scope of the operation. While she briefly considered offering Wagner no role reduction at all, she ultimately decided that offering a 2–level reduction for minor role was an appropriate inducement for a guilty plea.

6. Finally, Knapp considered § 3E1.1, Acceptance of Responsibility. If Wagner agreed to plead guilty, he would be entitled to a 2–level reduction under § 3E1.1(a),[65] and because his combined offense level before considering the application of § 3E1.1 would be 16 or greater, Knapp also was prepared to agree to an additional 1–level reduction under § 3E1.1(b)(2), assuming Wagner entered his plea in a timely manner. In sum, then, Knapp would agree to a combined reduction of 3 levels under § 3E1.1.

---

63. USSG § 3B1.2, comment. (n.4).   **65.** *See id.,* § 3E1.1, comment. (n.3).
64. *Id.,* § 3B1.2, comment. (n.5).

Based on these calculations, Knapp drafted a plea offer to send to Johnson that provided, in pertinent part, the following Sentencing Guidelines recommendation:

Base offense level (§ 2S1.1(a); § 2B1.1(b)(1)(E))	16
Knew or believed funds related to narcotics activity (§ 2S1.1(B)(1))	+6
Conviction under 18 U.S.C. § 1956 (§ 2S1.1(b)(2)(B))	+2
Minor role (§ 3B1.2(b))	-2
Acceptance of responsibility (§ 3E1.1(a) & (b))	<u>-3</u>
Total offense level:	19

Because Wagner had no prior criminal convictions, he would have zero criminal history points and thus his Criminal History Category under Chapter 4 of the Guidelines would be I. Consulting the Sentencing Table (located in § 7.2(h), supra) for a total offense level of 19 with a Criminal History Category of I, Knapp determined that Wagner's sentencing range would be 30 to 37 months imprisonment. Knapp's plea offer to Johnson was, in sum, an agreement with a recommended sentencing range of 30 to 37 months, or 2½ to 3 years and one month imprisonment, with Knapp further agreeing, consistent with her office's standard policy, to "take no position" at the time of sentencing as to where within the 30 to 37 month range Wagner should be sentenced.

§ 12.7(b) The Defendant's Position

When Johnson received the government's plea offer, she arranged a meeting with her client but first did some Guidelines number crunching of her own. She started by calculating the worst case scenario if her client went to trial and was convicted of one or more of the "top" counts of money laundering. Her analysis was similar to AUSA Knapp's analysis, except that she knew that if there was a trial her client would not get 3 levels off for acceptance of responsibility and very well might not receive 2 levels off for "minor role." Under that scenario, her client would be at a level 24, facing 51 to 63 months, or 4 years and 3 months to 5 years and 3 months in prison, which was close to double the amount of time being offered by Knapp.[66]

---

66. If Wagner testified at trial and it was determined that he testified falsely (not an unlikely event if he were convicted), an upward adjustment of 2 levels would be possible under USSG § 3C1.1, bringing the total offense level to 26, which would raise the sentence to 63–78 months.

Johnson came up with two alternative plea scenarios under which Wagner could do much better than the 30 to 37 months sentence recommendation being offered by the government. The first approach involved trying to persuade the government to let Wagner plead to a structuring count instead of a money laundering count–in other words, to agree to a "charge bargain" to the less serious of the two different species of crimes with which Wagner had been charged (including dismissal of the more serious money laundering charge). Johnson calculated that a structuring plea realistically would look something like this:

Base offense level (§ 2S1.3(a)(2)); (§ 2B1.1(b)(1)(E))	14
Knew/believed funds were proceeds of unlawful activity (§ 2S1.3(B)(1))	+2
Minor role (§ 3B1.2(b))	-2
Acceptance of responsibility (§ 3E1.1(a))	-2
Total offense level:	12

Under this scenario, Wagner would be at a level 12, with a 10–16 month range of imprisonment. But more importantly, he would be within Zone C of the Sentencing Table, which meant that, even under the Guidelines, the sentencing judge would have the option of a "split sentence"—that is, half of the time in prison and the other half in home confinement or community confinement.[67] And if Johnson could convince Knapp or the court either (1) not to add the 2 levels for knowing or believing the funds were the proceeds of unlawful activity, or (2) to give 4 levels off for minimal role instead of just 2 for minor role, Wagner's total offense level would go down to 10. That offense level carries a range of imprisonment of 6 to 12 months, but again, more importantly, would put Wagner in Zone B of the Sentencing Table, thereby allowing the judge to sentence him within the Guidelines to probation *without any time in prison*, by substituting an equivalent period of 6 to 12 months of home confinement or community confinement during a term of probation.[68]

Alternatively, if the prosecutor could not be convinced to allow Wagner to plead only to structuring and insisted the plea had to be to money laundering, Johnson thought that, at the very least, she should be able to convince Knapp to forego the 6–level enhancement under the money laundering guideline, which applied only where the government could prove that the defendant knew or believed the money related to

---

67. USSG § 5C1.1(d).   **68.** *Id.,* § 5C1.1(c)(3).

narcotics trafficking activity. That concession alone would reduce Johnson's total offense level from 19 to 13, cutting his prison exposure by more than 50%, from 30 to 37 months down to 12 to 18 months (a result almost as good as a structuring plea). And, if Johnson additionally was able to persuade the prosecutor to agree to a "minimal" as opposed to just "minor" role adjustment, Wagner's total offense level would be reduced even further, bringing him into Zone C, again with the chance of a "split sentence" under the Guidelines that would allow him to serve up to half of his sentence in home or community confinement.

After Johnson had concluded her analysis, she called Wagner and the two of them met in Johnson's office for several hours. After discussing at length the government's proof and the likelihood of a conviction at trial, Johnson explained the different possibilities under the Sentencing Guidelines, emphasizing throughout that there were no iron-clad guarantees and that the judge ultimately would have to decide whether any agreement reached by the parties was acceptable. Johnson and Wagner also discussed in detail Wagner's personal family situation and the fact that he was the sole financial support for his wife and two young children. Johnson explained that these facts, along with the absence of any prior criminal or other regulatory history, would provide a basis for arguing for a more lenient sentence than the Guidelines otherwise would call for either as a downward departure from the Guidelines range or as a non-Guidelines sentence based on all of the § 3553(a) factors. Johnson cautioned, however, that both departures and non-Guidelines sentences were hard to come by and that there could be no guarantees or even reliable predictions as to whether this particular judge would decide to grant Wagner any leniency. Ultimately, Wagner presented his bottom line to his attorney. He would plead guilty only if he had a reasonable chance of no jail time; otherwise, he was prepared to take his chances and go to trial. He remained uninterested in cooperating, principally because he feared for his own safety and that of his family.

§ 12.7(c) The Negotiation

Armed with this information, Johnson set up an appointment to speak in person with AUSA Knapp. A few days later they met at the United States Attorney's Offices. Johnson began the meeting by telling Knapp that the only way her client was prepared to plead guilty was if he was looking at a realistic chance of a non-incarceratory sentence of probation. She then outlined for Knapp her proposal based on a plea to a structuring charge. Knapp heard her out but replied that she would not drop the top charge of money laundering as part of a charge bargain, because that was the most serious offense, she was confident she could prove it, and under those circumstances Department of Justice policy required a plea to that top count.

Johnson more or less expected this response and so moved on to her alternative proposal, a better Guidelines agreement in connection with a money laundering plea, focusing first on the 6–level enhancement applicable where a defendant knows or believes the money comes from narcotics trafficking. Johnson argued that Wagner did not know and did not believe it was drug money and that he was prepared to testify at sentencing to that effect. Johnson added that she strongly doubted any government witness would testify otherwise and that it simply did not make sense that someone in Wagner's position—no criminal record, solid job at a bank, and a family at home—would risk everything for little if any remuneration if he really believed Santiago was a drug trafficker. After some back and forth, Knapp said she might be persuaded on this point but wanted to think about it a little more and discuss it with her supervisor.

The final issue presented a more difficult problem for Johnson—that Wagner should get 4 levels off for minimal role instead of just 2 for minor role. Citing Application Note 4 to § 3B1.2, Johnson emphasized that, even if Wagner were prepared to admit that he knew (or deliberately closed his eyes to a strong suspicion) that the money came from something illegal (as he would have to for a guilty plea), he would testify that he knew virtually nothing about the "scope and structure of the enterprise and of the activities of others." Knapp responded by saying that in her view "minimal role" adjustments are generally reserved for those who play little more than a courier-type role—e.g., a drug courier who does nothing more than transport the narcotics from one location to another or a money courier who does the same. She told Johnson that she would think about this too, but thought it was unlikely the government would agree to the 4 levels off for minimal role.

Two days later, Knapp called Johnson and told her she had considered the issues and discussed them with her supervisor and that their conclusion was that the government would agree to recommend that the 6–level enhancement under § 2S1.1(b)(1) was not applicable but they could only agree to a 2–level reduction for minor role (and thus not to a 4–level reduction for minimal role). That would leave Wagner at a total offense level of 13, with a corresponding prison range of 12 to 18 months. Johnson told Knapp she appreciated the concession on the 6–level enhancement, but she at least needed to be able to argue for the 4–level minimal role adjustment, even if the government was not prepared to agree to it. Johnson suggested that the parties agree that at least a 2–level minor role adjustment was appropriate and that the government "take no position" on the defendant's expected argument that it should be a 4–level minimal role adjustment. Knapp said she was not prepared to take "no position" on this, as she viewed that as tantamount to a concession, but she would agree that Wagner was free to argue in favor of the 4–level adjustment and Knapp would be free to oppose it. Knapp said that was as good a deal as she could offer. Johnson told Wagner she was unsure if her client would accept, but she would let her know in the next few days.

After this conversation, Johnson met again with Wagner and explained where things stood. She told Wagner the worst case scenario under the government's final offer was likely to be 12 to 18 months in prison and that they also had a decent chance at convincing the judge to give him a minimal role 4–level adjustment, which could lead to a split sentence of 5 months in prison and 5 months home or community confinement. Johnson also reminded Wagner that, apart from all of this, they would move for a "downward departure" and/or a non-Guidelines sentence based principally on Wagner's family circumstances (he had a dependent wife and two young children), and while such an application would be a bit of a long shot, if the judge granted it, he might get straight probation with no jail time.[69]

Johnson also repeated what she had told Wagner when they first met to discuss a possible plea: that while Judge Sheridan had the power to reject the government's recommendations concerning the inapplicability of the 6–level enhancement or even the applicability of the modest 2–level role adjustment, her strong belief, based on both her knowledge of Judge Sheridan's sentencing practices and the particular facts of Wagner's case, was that the judge would at least go along with the parties' agreement, if not sentence Wagner less severely. Johnson explained that the decision in the end was Wagner's alone, but added that in her view the government's offer was a reasonable one.

Two days later, Wagner called Johnson and told her he would accept the deal. Johnson then called Knapp, who drafted up the plea agreement, which read as follows:

69. Johnson did not have to "bargain" to preserve Wagner's right to make a downward departure motion or to seek a non-Guidelines sentence because the Eastern District of New York, unlike some other United States Attorney's Offices, does not typically require waivers of these rights as part of its standard plea agreements.

§ 12.8   The Agreement

DC:LK
F#2005X01285

UNITED STATES DISTRICT COURT
EASTERN DISTRICT OF NEW YORK
- X

UNITED STATES OF AMERICA	PLEA AGREEMENT
- against -	05 Cr. 735 (WS)
ERNEST WAGNER,	
Defendant.	

- X

Pursuant to Rule 11 of the Federal Rules of Criminal Procedure, the United States Attorney's Office for the Eastern District of New York (the "Office") and ERNEST WAGNER (the "defendant") agree to the following:

1.   The defendant will plead guilty to Count Eighteen of the above-captioned indictment, charging a violation of 18 U.S.C. § 1956(h). The count carries the following statutory penalties:

2.   Maximum term of imprisonment: 20 years (18 U.S.C. §§ 1956(h); 1956(a)(1)(A)(i)).

2.   Minimum term of imprisonment: none (18 U.S.C. §§ 1956(h); 1956(a)(1)(A)(i)).

3.   Minimum supervised release term: none; maximum supervised release term: 3 years, to follow any term of imprisonment; if a condition of release is violated, the defendant may be sentenced to up to 2 years without credit for pre-release imprisonment or time previously served on post-release supervision (18 U.S.C. § 3583.)

4.   Maximum fine: $500,000, or twice the value of the laundered proceeds.
(18 U.S.C. §§ 1956(h);1956(a)(1)(A)(i)).

5.　　　　　Restitution: N/A
　　　　　(18 U.S.C. § 3663).

6.　　　　　$100 special assessment
　　　　　(18 U.S.C. § 3013).

7.　　　　　Other penalties: N/A

2.　　　The defendant understands that although imposition of a sentence in accordance with the United States Sentencing Guidelines (the "Guidelines") is not mandatory, the Guidelines are advisory and the Court is required to consider any applicable Guidelines provisions as well as other factors enumerated in 18 U.S.C. § 3553(a) to arrive at an appropriate sentence in this case. The Office will advise the Court and the Probation Department of all information relevant to sentencing, including criminal activity engaged in by the defendant, and such information may be used by the Court in determining the defendant's sentence. Based on information known to the Office at this time, the Office estimates the likely adjusted offense level under the Sentencing Guidelines to be level 13, which is predicated on the following Guidelines calculation:

Base Offense Level (§§ 2S1.1(a)(1); 2B1.1(b)(1)(E))	16
Conviction under § 1956(h)(§ 2S1.1(b)(2)(B))	+ 2
Minor Role (§3B1.2(b))	- 2
Less: Acceptance of Responsibility (§ 3E1.1(b))	- 3
Adjusted Offense Level	13

This level carries a range of imprisonment of 12 to 18 months, assuming that the defendant falls within Criminal History Category I. The defendant agrees to this Guidelines calculation and agrees not to dispute or seek a hearing with respect to the above-listed stipulated Guidelines, except that the defendant may argue that he is entitled to a 4-level reduction pursuant to U.S.S.G. § 3B1.2(a). The government agrees to recommend this Guidelines calculation and agrees not to dispute or seek a hearing with respect to the above-listed stipulated Guidelines, except that the government reserves the right to oppose any request by the defendant for a 4-level minimal role adjustment pursuant to § 3B1.2(a).

3.　　　The Guidelines estimate set forth in paragraph 2 is not binding on the Probation Department or the Court. If the Guidelines offense level determined by the

Probation Department or the Court is different from the estimate, the defendant will not be entitled to withdraw the plea.

    4.   The defendant will not file an appeal or otherwise challenge the conviction or sentence in the event that the Court imposes a term of imprisonment of 18 months or less, even if the Court employs a Guidelines analysis different from that set forth in paragraph 2. The defendant waives all defenses based on the statute of limitations and venue with respect to any prosecution that is not time-barred on the date that this agreement is signed in the event that (a) the defendant's conviction is later vacated for any reason, (b) the defendant violates this agreement or (c) the defendant's plea is later withdrawn. The defendant waives any right to additional disclosure from the government in connection with the guilty plea.[69] The defendant agrees that with respect to all charges referred to in paragraphs 1 and 5(a) he is not a "prevailing party" within the meaning of the "Hyde Amendment," Section 617, P.L. 105-119 (Nov. 26, 1997), and will not file any claim under that law.[70] The defendant agrees to pay the special assessment by check payable to the Clerk of the Court at or before sentencing.

    5.   The Office agrees that:

        a.   no further criminal charges will be brought against the defendant based on the defendant's alleged participation in the laundering of proceeds of unlawful activity and structuring transactions, as described in Counts Thirteen through Twenty-Two of the indictment, for the period August 2004 to December 2004, it being understood that this agreement does not bar the use of such conduct as a predicate act or as the basis for a sentencing enhancement in a subsequent prosecution including, but not limited to, a prosecution pursuant to 18 U.S.C. §§ 1961 et seq.; and, at the time of sentencing, it will move to dismiss with prejudice the open counts of the indictment;

and, based upon information now known to the Office, it will

        b.   take no position on where within the applicable Sentencing Guidelines range the defendant's sentence should fall;

        c.   and make no motion for an upward departure under the Sentencing Guidelines.

---

[69] *See supra* note 56.

[70] *See supra* § 8.3(f) n.58.

If information relevant to sentencing, as determined by the Office, becomes known to the Office after the date of this agreement, the Office will not be bound by paragraphs 5(b) and 5(c).

6.   This agreement does not bind any federal, state, or local prosecuting authority other than the Office, and does not prohibit the Office from initiating or prosecuting any civil or administrative proceedings directly or indirectly involving the defendant.

7.   No promises, agreements or conditions have been entered into by the parties other than those set forth in this agreement and none will be entered into unless memorialized in writing and signed by all parties. This agreement supersedes all prior promises, agreements or conditions between the parties. To become effective, this agreement must be signed by all signatories listed below.

Dated: Brooklyn, New York
        May 14, 2005

                                        Respectfully submitted,

                                        Kevin O'Reilly
                                        United States Attorney
                                        Eastern District of N.Y.

                                        By: _Laura Knapp_
                                             Laura Knapp
                                             Assistant U.S. Attorney

Agreed and consented to:

Ernest Wagner
Ernest Wagner
Defendant

Approved by: Approved by:

Isabel Johnson   _Nisha Bandhi_

Isabel Johnson, Esq.   Nisha Bandhi
Counsel to Defendant   Supervising Assistant U.S. Attorney

---

§ 12.9   Wagner's Guilty Plea

On May 14, 2005, Wagner, Johnson and Knapp appeared before Judge Sheridan and Wagner pleaded guilty pursuant to the agreement set forth above. Judge Sheridan explained to Wagner that, although he had entered into an agreement whereby the government would make certain recommendations about how to apply the Sentencing Guidelines, the ultimate decisions on all Guidelines issues would be entirely up to the court and even if the court disagreed with the government's recommendations and sentenced Wagner more severely, Wagner would not be able to take his plea back. Wagner stated that he understood this and then, in response to Judge Sheridan's questioning, admitted that he helped Santiago open the accounts and deposit the funds. Wagner said that he strongly suspected the money came from illegal activity, but that he had closed his eyes and deliberately avoided learning anything more. When Judge Sheridan asked if he knew or suspected the money came from illegal narcotics trafficking, Wagner said "absolutely not." At the conclusion of the allocution, Judge Sheridan accepted Wagner's plea and set a sentencing date for August 25, 2005.

Having now completed our discussion of plea negotiations and the guilty plea of Ernest Wagner, we return in the next chapter to the defendants who are on track to contest their cases at trial, Paul Christopher and William Van Ness.

Part IV

THE TRIAL PROCESS

Chapter 13

PRETRIAL DISCOVERY

Table of Sections

Sec.
13.0   Introduction.
13.1   The Law of Discovery—Policy Considerations.
13.2   The Right to Notice.
    13.2(a) The Defendant's Right to Notice.
    13.2(b) The Government's Right to Notice.
13.3   The Defendant's Right to Exculpatory Evidence.
    13.3(a) What Constitutes *Brady* Material.
    13.3(b) The Materiality Standard.
    13.3(c) The Timing of Disclosure of *Brady* Material.
13.4   Discovery of Defendant's Prior Criminal Record and Statements, and
        Witness Statements.
    13.4(a) Discovery by the Defense of the Defendant's Prior Criminal Record
          and Statements.
    13.4(b) Discovery of Government Witnesses and Their Statements by the
          Defense.
    13.4(c)   Discovery of the Statements of Defense Witnesses by the Govern-
          ment.
13.5   Discovery of Documents, Tangible Objects, Reports of Examinations, and
        Criminal Records.
    13.5(a) Discovery by the Defense.
    13.5(b) Discovery by the Prosecution.
13.6   The Pretrial Discovery Process.
    13.6(a) The Initial Discovery Request.
    13.6(b) The Discovery Conference.
    13.6(c) The Final Discovery Letter.
13.7   Informal Defense Discovery.
    13.7(a) Witness Interviews by Defense Counsel.
    13.7(b) Informal Discovery From the Government.
    13.7(c) Informal Discovery From Other Sources.
    13.7(d) Rule 17(c) Subpoenas.
13.8   United States v. Christopher.
    13.8(a) Defense Interviews.

13.8(b) The Defense Attorneys' Post–Interview Evaluation of the Christopher Case.

13.8(c) The Discovery Conference.

13.8(d) Discovery Letters.

---

§ 13.0　Introduction

The filing of an indictment not only perfects the charges against the defendant, but it also usually marks the culmination of the government's investigation of the case. As discussed in Chapter 11, while technically the indictment reflects a determination by the grand jury that there is probable cause to believe that the defendant has committed criminal acts, in fact it nearly always signifies that the prosecutor personally believes that there is sufficient evidence to sustain the government's burden of proof, i.e., that a reasonable juror could (and will) find the defendant guilty beyond a reasonable doubt.[1] Additional corroborative information certainly may be sought after the indictment is filed or may be obtained by the government through the decision of co-defendants to cooperate. In addition, the case undoubtedly will need refinement before it is ready to be presented to a jury, and, as we shall see, both formal and informal pretrial discovery devices are available to the prosecution. Nevertheless, the bulk of the prosecution's investigative work normally will be completed at this stage. This is illustrated in the Christopher case, where, by the time the indictment was filed, all of the essential government witnesses had been interviewed and supporting tangible evidence, such as the seized drugs and telephone and bank records, had been obtained and analyzed.

Typically, the defense attorney is in a very different position. While there are sources of information available to defense counsel early on in the life of the case, such as the complaint in a police-initiated arrest case or the indictment (if the government opts to include means paragraphs detailing the charges), defense counsel will need to learn a good deal more before being able to advise the defendant intelligently. The defense attorney should begin the search for more information immediately upon entering the case, invoking whatever formal and informal discovery processes are available, not only to develop and perfect the defendant's case theory, but also to discover everything possible about the government's evidence.[2]

---

1. *See supra* § 11.1(c).

2. *See* Strickland v. Washington, 466 U.S. 668, 695 (1984) ("[C]ounsel has a duty to make reasonable investigations or to make a reasonable decision that makes particular investigations unnecessary."); Johnson v. Baldwin, 114 F.3d 835, 839–40 (9th Cir. 1997) (failure to perform pretrial investigation and interview potential alibi witnesses rendered counsel ineffective); AMERICAN BAR ASSOCIATION STANDARDS FOR CRIMINAL JUSTICE § 4–4.1 (a) (3d ed. 1993) (hereinafter "ABA STANDARD") ("Defense counsel should conduct a prompt investigation of the circumstances of the case and explore all avenues leading to facts relevant to the

Consider the situation confronting Richard Clark and Martin Rothman, the attorneys for Paul Christopher and William Van Ness, respectively. As we have posited the facts, they entered the case when their clients were arraigned on the indictment.[3] At that juncture, the lawyers would not have discussed the case at length with either client. They would be aware from the indictment that their clients are alleged to have been involved in a drug importation and money laundering scheme between May 2004 and January 2005. They would know that arrests were made at Superior Warehouse, and they also could have obtained from the magistrate judge's office a copy of the complaint that the government filed against Mario Long and Gilbert Santiago, which contains information provided by Agent Martinez concerning the seizure of drugs and the search of the warehouse. Since neither Long nor Santiago is named in the indictment, the attorneys could assume with some confidence that these individuals were cooperating with the government and would testify against their clients.

However, there is much that the attorneys do not know about the charges. For example, they do not know the roles that their clients are alleged to have played or precisely what acts they are alleged to have performed. The allegations in the accusatory instruments provide the outline of the likely testimony by Santiago and Long, but the attorneys do not know the details of that testimony, nor what grounds might exist to attack it. And while defense counsel might understand in general terms how to attack the veracity of a cooperating witness, the details of the potential impeachment material for Long and Santiago remain to be discovered. In addition, the lawyers do not know the other witnesses that the government may have to support its case, the tangible evidence that may exist or the statements that may have been made by their clients. Similarly, the defense attorneys are not in a position even to determine what defenses exist to the charges or whether there are legal grounds upon which to object to the government's right to use the evidence it has obtained (or to bring the case at all).

For these reasons, the discussion that follows focuses mainly on discovery by the defense. While the government has some post-indictment discovery rights under the rules, they are relatively limited. The prosecution's efforts are primarily directed at providing information to the defense as required by the statutory rules and the Constitution so that the defense can adequately prepare its case.

Our analysis begins with a brief review of the policy considerations underlying the law of pretrial discovery in criminal cases. This is followed by an analysis of the constitutional and statutory rules governing the formal pretrial discovery rights of the defense and the prosecu-

merits of the case and the penalty in the event of conviction.... The duty to investigate exists regardless of the accused's admissions or statements to defense counsel of facts constituting guilt or the accused's stated desire to plead guilty.").

3. *See supra* § 11.9.

tion: (1) the right to notice; (2) the right to exculpatory material; (3) rules regarding the discovery of the identity and statements of witnesses; and (4) rules regarding the discovery of tangible evidence. Finally, we describe the informal means employed by the parties to supplement the formal rules. The chapter ends at the point immediately prior to litigation of unresolved discovery issues, which is the subject of Chapter 14, dealing with pretrial motion practice.

§ 13.1 The Law of Discovery—Policy Considerations

For most lawyers, the model of discovery first encountered is probably that which takes place in a civil context. Law students studying civil procedure learn that one policy consideration is dominant: nearly complete pretrial disclosure is mandated because it leads to the most expeditious disposition of cases.[4] Limits on civil pretrial discovery exist principally to protect interests reflected in common law privileges and the work product of lawyers.[5] Aside from these constraints, exhaustive responsive pleadings are required, and both sides have sweeping powers to discover documentary evidence and, most importantly, to examine opposing parties and witnesses prior to trial, obtaining sworn testimony whenever they believe it appropriate.[6]

Pretrial discovery in criminal cases is much more restricted. Efficiency is a goal, but not the dominant one. More important is the perceived need to protect prosecution witnesses from intimidation and to limit tampering or the subornation of perjury.[7] While some argue that restrictions on pretrial discovery by the defense create an unlevel playing field, others counter that the government bears a heavy burden of proof, while the defendant need do nothing in his or her own defense. Whether danger to witnesses is a sufficiently pervasive risk to justify the deference it receives in the criminal discovery process, whether witnesses and parties in criminal cases pose a greater threat to commit perjury than their civil counterparts, and whether the government with its comparatively vast investigative resources and power to compel testimony is really at a disadvantage, have been long debated.[8] Whatever the merits of either point of view, the federal law reflects a compromise between them.

§ 13.2 The Right to Notice

§ 13.2(a) The Defendant's Right to Notice

The defendant's right to notice has three dimensions:

(1) The Constitution requires that an indictment be sufficiently detailed to inform the defendant of the nature of the charges against

---

4. *See, e.g.,* Roger S. Haydock & David F. Herr, Discovery Practice § 2.01 (4th ed. 2002).

5. For discussion regarding non-discoverable materials, see *id.* §§ 4.08, 10.01–10.03.

6. *Id.* §§ 2.03(c), 16.01, 21.01.

7. *See* LaFave et al., § 20.1(b).

8. *See* Wright, § 252 and authorities cited therein.

him or her and to protect against a subsequent prosecution for the same offense.[9] We have noted, however, that this requirement can be met with limited detail and without significant disclosure of the government's evidence.[10]

(2) The Federal Rules provide that the defendant may under certain circumstances move for further amplification of the allegations in the indictment in a "bill of particulars."[11] While a bill of particulars cannot rectify an indictment that fails to state a cause of action against the accused (i.e., does not allege all of the elements of the offense), it can remedy notice deficiencies.[12] To the extent that facts are added in the bill of particulars, they become, in effect, part of the indictment, and the government's proof will be limited correspondingly by the facts so added.

The bill of particulars, therefore, can be a useful source of information to the defendant and is typically granted when necessary to ensure that the government has divulged basic facts and the means by which the crime is alleged to have been committed. However, courts uniformly hold that it is not an "investigative tool" and cannot be used to discover the evidence on which the government might rely to prove its case.[13] The line between facts that "amplify the pleadings" and those that comprise the government's "evidence" is an obscure one. The most that can be said with reasonable confidence is that courts are likely to grant bills of particulars only with respect to very basic facts missing from the indictment (e.g., date, time, place, identity of victim) and the general means by which the offense is alleged to have been committed (e.g., use of a particular kind of weapon).[14] However, since courts have broad discretion in this area,[15] defense counsel should not overlook the possibility that information beyond the basics might be obtained if requested, particularly in complex cases. A more detailed discussion of the law governing defense motions for bills of particulars will be found in the illustrative discovery motion, *infra* § 14.5.

(3) The Federal Rules also provide that the government may notify the defendant of its intention to use evidence against him or her that might be the subject of a motion to suppress, and it appears that most United States Attorney's Offices provide such notice.[16] If no such notice is given, the defendant may demand that any such evidence be identi-

---

9. *See* LaFave et al., § 19.2(b) (*citing* Hamling v. United States, 418 U.S. 87 (1974)). It should be stressed that it is the indictment alone that must provide this notice, even in cases initiated by complaint. The government is not bound by the assertions made in the complaint. It may change its theory or add or eliminate factual allegations at the grand jury stage.

10. *See supra* § 11.2(a).

11. Fed. R. Crim. P. 7(f). *See* Wright, § 129.

12. *See* LaFave et al., § 19.2(f).

13. *Id.*

14. *See* Wright, § 129.

15. LaFave et al., § 19.2(f).

16. Fed. R. Crim. P. 12(b)(4)(A). *See* Wright, § 197.

fied.[17] The purpose of the notice provisions is to provide the defendant with the facts necessary to comply with the requirement that suppression motions be made prior to trial.[18] On its face, the rule only requires disclosure of the nature of the potentially suppressible evidence to be used by the government—for example, a statement obtained from the defendant, tangible evidence seized from the defendant's custody or control, or certain identification procedures that involve the defendant.[19] The rule does not expressly require the government to disclose the circumstances surrounding the way in which the police obtained the evidence at issue. Nonetheless, because those circumstances—e.g., whether the police acted with or without a warrant—are the matters at issue in a motion to suppress, the government typically discloses these facts as well.[20]

The government also must provide the defendant with similar notice of its intent to use evidence of extrinsic or uncharged misconduct on the part of the defendant, so called "prior bad act" evidence.[21] The rule requires the government to provide "reasonable notice in advance of trial, or during trial if the court excuses pretrial notice on good cause shown.... "[22] If the government fails to satisfy this notice requirement, the evidence at issue is inadmissible.[23] Such notice gives the defendant an adequate opportunity to move *in limine* (i.e., prior to trial) to preclude the government from offering such "prior bad act" or "other act" evidence at trial.[24]

§ 13.2(b) The Government's Right to Notice

A central feature of pleading in criminal cases is, of course, that the defendant is not required to respond to allegations contained in the complaint or indictment, other than by entering an oral plea of guilty or not guilty.[25] In addition, as a general rule, the defendant has no obli-

---

17. Fed. R. Crim. P. 12(b)(4)(B); Wright, § 197.

18. Fed. R. Crim. P. 12(b)(3)(C), 12(b)(4)(A), & 12(b)(4)(B).

19. In *Watkins v. Sowders,* 449 U.S. 341, 347–49 (1981), the Supreme Court distinguished identification issues from those involving illegally obtained confessions or tangible evidence, holding that in most cases identification issues could be resolved at trial, without a pretrial hearing. Left untouched, however, was the right to a pretrial hearing where the issue is the denial of the defendant's right to counsel at a line-up. *Id.* (*distinguishing* United States v. Wade, 388 U.S. 218 (1967), and holding that right to counsel extends to post-indictment identification procedures). *See* 2 Edward J. Imwinkelried et al., Courtroom Criminal Evidence § 2826 (3d ed. 1998).

20. *See, e.g.,* United States v. Hernandez, 299 F.3d 984, 990–91 (8th Cir. 2002)

(suggesting that where party objecting to a vehicle search was part owner of vehicle, the fact that officers knew of such ownership should have been disclosed to defense); United States v. Hurse, 453 F.2d 128, 130–31 (8th Cir. 1971) (ordering identity of confidential informant disclosed to defense to adequately determine whether probable cause justified warrantless search of defendant's home).

21. Fed. R. Evid. 404(b).

22. Id.

23. Fed. R. Evid. 404(b) advisory committee's note (1991 amendments).

24. *Id.*

25. *See* Fed. R. Crim. P. 10(a)(3); Wright, § 161.

gation to inform the government of the defense that he or she will present at trial. However, three kinds of defenses do require notice: an alibi defense;[26] a defense related to mental incapacity;[27] and a defense based upon a claim of public authority.[28] The rationale behind these disclosure rules is that these defenses in most cases will require the government to offer rebuttal evidence and advance notice will prevent disruption of the trial.[29]

§ 13.3   The Defendant's Right to Exculpatory Evidence[30]

In *Brady v. Maryland*,[31] the Supreme Court held that the due process clause gives the defendant the right to obtain "favorable" evidence in the possession of the government if it is material either to guilt or punishment.[32] In a decision subsequent to *Brady*, *Giglio v. United States*,[33] the Supreme Court made clear that the government must also produce information that could be used to impeach government witnesses. The failure to provide such information may result in reversal of a conviction, regardless of whether the prosecutor acted in good faith.[34] Prosecutors, moreover, are responsible for searching for *Brady* and *Giglio* material in all the files in the possession of, or available to, the prosecution team. This includes information in the possession of investigating agencies and even local police forces if there is a joint investigation involving those offices.

§ 13.3(a) What Constitutes *Brady* Material

It is not possible to enumerate all of the kinds of information that might be considered "favorable" to the defendant because that depends to a large extent on the facts of the case.[35] The following, however, are commonly found examples of *Brady* material: a confession by another person to a charged crime; failure of an eyewitness to identify the defendant as the perpetrator of the crime; results of examinations favorable to the defense; information that tends to implicate another person in the crime or to exclude the defendant; information that tends to support the defendant's alibi; and information that tends to establish an articulated defense or an obvious defense even if not yet articulated.[36] Examples of *Giglio* (impeachment) material are: benefits provided by the government to a witness, such as the potential for a reduced sentence; a government witness' prior convictions or evidence of crimes committed

---

26. FED. R. CRIM. P. 12.1(a) (notice of alibi defense required after written demand by the government); WRIGHT, § 202.

27. FED. R. CRIM. P. 12.2; WRIGHT, §§ 206–209.

28. FED. R. CRIM. P. 12.3.

29. *See, e.g.,* FED. R. CRIM. P. 12.2 advisory committee's note.

30. *See generally* LAFAVE ET AL., § 24.3(b).

31. 373 U.S. 83 (1963).

32. *Id.* at 87; MOORE, § 616.06.

33. 405 U.S. 150 (1972).

34. *Id.* at 153–54.

35. See *infra* § 13.6 (The Pretrial Discovery Process) for a discussion of the framing of *Brady* requests.

36. *See generally* LAFAVE ET AL., § 24.3(b).

even if the witness was not convicted; a government witness' prior false statements; material differences between the witness' account and other witnesses' accounts, even uncalled witnesses; and evidence of a witness' memory or psychiatric problems.[37] We discuss below the process by which *Brady* material is obtained.[38]

§ 13.3(b) The Materiality Standard

The government's failure to turn over *Brady* material can result in the reversal of a conviction. The test is whether "there is a reasonable probability that had the evidence been disclosed to the defense, the result of the proceeding would have been different."[39] The burden of meeting this standard is a heavy one, which on occasion may induce prosecutors to withhold disclosure of evidence that is only arguably favorable. In other instances, where a prosecutor believes that the evidence need not be disclosed, but recognizes that the matter is a close call, he or she will often disclose the information or, at minimum, submit it to the judge for an *in camera* review.

§ 13.3(c) The Timing of Disclosure of *Brady* Material

The government generally is not required to disclose all exculpatory and impeachment material immediately upon a defendant's request.[40] Rather, the government "suppresses" (i.e., fails to disclose) evidence within the meaning of *Brady* only if it fails to provide the evidence to the defense in time for its effective use *at trial*.[41] The time required for the effective use of a particular item of evidence will depend on the materiality of the evidence and the circumstances of the particular case.[42] However, a prosecutor who does not produce *Brady* material significantly in advance of trial, particularly where the defendant makes a timely

---

37. *See, e.g.*, Spicer v. Roxbury Corr. Inst., Warden, 194 F.3d 547, 556–62 (4th Cir. 1999) (conviction reversed for nondisclosure of prosecution witness' prior inconsistent statement); Ouimette v. Moran, 942 F.2d 1, 12–13 (1st Cir. 1991) (conviction reversed for nondisclosure of prosecution witness' prior convictions). *See* MOORE, § 616.06.

38. *See infra* § 13.6

39. United States v. Bagley, 473 U.S. 667, 682 n.13 (1985). *Accord* Strickler v. Greene, 527 U.S. 263 (1999) (stressing that defendant must meet materiality standard); Kyles v. Whitley, 514 U.S. 419, 434 (1995) (evidence is material if it "could reasonably be taken to put the whole case in such a different light as to undermine confidence in the verdict"). *See also* MOORE, § 616.06.

40. United States v. Coppa, 267 F.3d 132, 144 (2d Cir. 2001). *See* MOORE, § 616.06.

41. *Coppa*, 267 F.3d at 142–44. As discussed in § 12.4, the Supreme Court has held that a defendant has no constitutional right to disclosure of evidence favorable to the defendant (here impeachment material) prior to pleading guilty. *See* United States v. Ruiz, 536 U.S. 622, 632–33 (2002). *See also* MOORE, § 616.06. In addition, as also discussed, some United States Attorney's Offices require as a matter of course in all plea agreements that the defendant waive any right to *Brady* material. *See generally* U.S. ATTORNEYS' MANUAL, TITLE 9, CRIMINAL RESOURCE MANUAL § 626 (1) (1997) ("[T]he Supreme Court has repeatedly held that a criminal defendant can elect to waive many important constitutional and statutory rights during the plea bargaining process." (citations omitted)).

42. *Coppa*, 267 F.3d at 143. *See also* 1 MARK J. KADISH ET AL., CRIMINAL LAW ADVOCACY § 9.02 (2004).

request, faces greater risk of reversal.[43] It also should be noted that in a number of jurisdictions, the local rules require immediate disclosure of *Brady* material.[44] The government may move to delay disclosures relating to the identity of witnesses where security concerns are implicated.

§ 13.4 Discovery of Defendant's Prior Criminal Record and Statements, and Witness Statements

§ 13.4(a) Discovery by the Defense of the Defendant's Prior Criminal Record and Statements

The Federal Rules provide that the defendant has a right to obtain a copy of his or her own prior criminal record in the possession of the government or that should, with due diligence, be known to the government,[45] as well as his or her prior bad acts.[46] These items should be requested, because it is not always the case that the defendant will understand, recall, or disclose that information to counsel.

The rules also provide that the defendant has the right to discover the substance of any statement he or she may have made to a law enforcement officer whose identity as an officer was known by the defendant at the time. This includes both written and oral statements (assuming the government intends to use the oral statement at trial or the government has a written record of the oral statement). The Rules also provide for discovery of any relevant written or recorded statement by the defendant in the possession of the government, as well as the defendant's testimony before the grand jury or in any other pretrial hearing in connection with the indictment.[47]

§ 13.4(b) Discovery of Government Witnesses and Their Statements by the Defense

The most significant limitation on defense pretrial discovery is the restriction on the defense's access to government witnesses. The Federal

---

43. United States v. Gil, 297 F.3d 93, 105–106 (2d Cir. 2002) (reversing conviction for a *Brady* violation where the government produced *Brady* material one business day prior to trial and the defendant had made numerous prior requests for such information). *See generally* MOORE, § 616.06.

44. For example, the District of Massachusetts has promulgated a local rule that requires the government to provide exculpatory information to the defense within 28 days following arraignment, *see* D. MASS. L.R. 116.1(C)(1), and impeachment material at least 21 days prior to trial, *see id.* at 116.2(B)(2).

45. FED. R. CRIM. P. 16(a)(1)(D).

46. The defendant should request evidence of prior bad acts that the government may intend to introduce in its case-in-chief.

Rule 404 of the Federal Rules of Evidence provides that "upon request, by the accused, the prosecution in a criminal case shall provide reasonable notice in advance of trial" of any such evidence. FED. R. EVID. 404(b). In such a situation the defendant may seek an *in limine* determination as to whether the government will be permitted to use such evidence at trial. *See infra* § 15.4(a) (discussing *in limine* motions). This issue can also be raised as part of an omnibus motion, which is discussed *infra* at Chapter 14.

47. FED. R. CRIM. P. 16(a)(1); WRIGHT, § 253. Note that Rule 16 does not give the defendant a right to statements made to third parties or unrecorded statements made to police officers who are not known by the defendant to be such. *See* FED. R. CRIM. P. 16(a)(1)(A) and (a)(1)(B)(ii).

Rules do not authorize pretrial discovery of the names and statements of government witnesses or prospective government witnesses.[48] Nevertheless, there are some ways to obtain this crucial information:

(1) *Discretionary discovery.* The discovery rules were expressly intended to set minimum discovery rights and do not preclude courts from ordering additional discovery beyond that minimum.[49] However, judges retain a good deal of discretion in regulating discovery, and while many judges will not go beyond the letter of the rules, others will be more open to requests for greater disclosure than the rules require. Therefore, unless the predilection of a particular judge to abide strictly by the rules is clear, it is wise for defense counsel to seek discovery aggressively, particularly in cases in which the concerns about disclosure (e.g. the security of a witness) are inapplicable or where the lack of access to witnesses or their statements impairs the defendant's ability to prepare a defense.

Under certain circumstances, the court has discretionary authority to order disclosure of government witness lists.[50] In exercising this discretion, the court will weigh the defendant's specific need for disclosure against the government's need for concealment of witness identities.[51] Conclusory assertions that disclosure is necessary are insufficient.[52] Rather, some particularized showing of need is required.[53]

These discretionary powers of the court can also be exercised by prosecutors. It is thus possible that prosecutors will provide names and even statements of witnesses, particularly in situations in which they do not fear that tampering will occur and where full disclosure is viewed as useful to securing a guilty plea.[54]

(2) *Witnesses from whom the government does not intend to present testimony.* The limitations on defense discovery of the statements of government witnesses is designed to protect those whom the government intends to call at trial. In certain circumstances, it can be argued that

---

48. FED. R. CRIM. P. 16(a)(2); WRIGHT, § 254. There is, under the Federal Rules, a right to depose witnesses in criminal cases, but it is very limited and not commonly invoked. *See* FED. R. CRIM. P. 15; WRIGHT, §§ 241–245.

49. *See* FED. R. CRIM. P. 16 advisory committee's note (1974 amendments).

50. *See Bejasa,* 904 F.2d at 139–140. *See also* MOORE, § 616.02.

51. *See* Roviaro v. United States, 353 U.S. 53, 59–61 (1957); *Broccolo,* 797 F.Supp. at 1193; United States v. Upton, 856 F.Supp. 727, 751 (E.D.N.Y. 1994). *See*

also 1 JAMES CISSELL, FEDERAL CRIMINAL TRIALS § 7–7 (6th ed. 2003).

52. United States v. Kelly, 91 F.Supp.2d 580, 586 (S.D.N.Y. 2000). *See* WRIGHT, § 437; *Court Refuses to Suppress Items Seized from Broker–Dealer's Desk at Sterling Foster and Co.,* N.Y.L.J., Feb. 16, 2001, at 17.

53. *Kelly,* 91 F.Supp.2d at 586. *See* WRIGHT, § 437; *Court Refuses to Suppress Items Seized, supra* note 52.

54. *See* Jed S. Rakoff, *How to Discover the Federal Government's Proof in Criminal Cases,* THE PRACTICAL LAWYER 13, 14 (July 15, 1983).

documents containing statements of witnesses whom the government does not intend to call are discoverable by the defense.[55]

(3) *Pretrial discovery of "3500 material."* In *Jencks v. United States*, the Supreme Court held that the confrontation clause mandates disclosure of government witnesses' prior written or recorded statements so that they can be cross-examined about any inconsistencies between those statements and their present testimony.[56] To protect against pretrial discovery of the identity of these witnesses or the contents of their statements, 18 U.S.C. § 3500 provides that the defendant does not have a right to such statements until after completion of the witness' direct examination.[57] However, the law does not prevent the government from disclosing so-called "3500 material" earlier. Doing so provides defense counsel an opportunity to study the statements fully, while avoiding unnecessary delay in the commencement of cross-examination at trial. Witness statements therefore may be provided either on the eve of trial or earlier depending upon the policy of the prosecutor, the views of the trial judge and the persuasiveness of defense counsel. In any event, most prosecutors do not wait until after a witness testifies on direct examination before producing the 3500 material for that witness because the prosecutor knows that defense counsel would have a reasonable basis to request an adjournment of the trial for a few hours or longer to review the material and prepare his or her cross-examination. Most judges do not look favorably on such avoidable delays and often expressly encourage prosecutors to produce the 3500 material well in advance of trial.[58]

---

55. *See* FED. R. CRIM. P. 16(a)(1)(E) & (F). An additional barrier is presented in the case of confidential informants who the government does not intend to call because of a qualified privilege. The government must produce such information where the informant's testimony would be "material to the defense." The defendant has the burden of establishing the need for the informer's identity and must show "the events to which a witness might testify, and the relevance of those events to the crime charged.... " United States v. Valenzuela-Bernal, 458 U.S. 858, 871 (1982) (interpreting *Roviaro*); *see Roviaro*, 353 U.S. at 60–61. Courts sometimes compromise under these circumstances and deny the application to compel disclosure of the informant's identity, but require the government to produce the informant for a private meeting with defense counsel. *See* MOORE, § 616.07.

56. Jencks v. United States, 353 U.S. 657, 668–69 (1957). *See* FED. R. CRIM. P. 26.2; WRIGHT, §§ 436–439.

57. 18 U.S.C. § 3500, *incorporated in* FED. R. CRIM. P. 26.2. *See* WRIGHT, §§ 436–

439. This statute is commonly known as the Jencks Act and the statements with which it deals as "3500 material." Section 3500(e) defines a statement for purposes of disclosure as either: (1) a written statement made by the witness and signed or otherwise adopted by him; (2) a stenographic record or mechanical or electronic recording or a transcript of such record or recording which is substantially verbatim and made contemporaneously with the oral statement; or (3) a statement of a witness made to a grand jury. *See* § 3500.

58. Although judges do not have the power to compel such early disclosure, *see* § 3500(a) (providing that "no statement or report ... shall be the subject of subpoena, discovery, or inspection until said witness has testified on direct examination in the trial of the case"); United States v. Lewis, 35 F.3d 148, 150–51 (4th Cir. 1994); United States v. Algie, 667 F.2d 569, 571–72 (6th Cir. 1982); MOORE, § 626.2.04, few prosecutors find it advisable to resist a judge's arm-twisting on this issue.

Even when the prosecutor elects to turn over 3500 material prior to trial,[59] he or she will rarely do so more than one or two weeks before trial. Indeed, in longer trials, it is not uncommon for the government to produce its 3500 material on a rolling basis throughout the trial (usually a few days prior to each witness' actual testimony).

As we note in the next section, the government has a right to discover statements of defense witnesses similar to the right of the defendant. A comment is in order here about practices that have arisen among both prosecutors and defense attorneys in attempting to limit disclosure of 3500 material. It will be recalled that only prior written or recorded statements—not oral ones—are covered by the rule. As a result, it has become a common practice for both the government and the defense to limit their note-taking while interviewing witnesses, despite the obvious importance of having such records. While little attention has been given to these sorts of maneuvers that arguably circumvent an otherwise mandated discovery obligation, such conduct certainly raises questions about the fairness and integrity of the process.

§ 13.4(c) Discovery of the Statements of Defense Witnesses by the Government

Rule 16 excludes from pretrial discovery statements made by the defendant to the defendant's attorney or statements made to the defendant or the defense attorney by an identified or prospective defense or government witness.[60] The rules do, however, provide the government with a right analogous to the defendant's right to 3500 material, i.e., to prior written or recorded statements of defense witnesses—other than the defendant—for use during cross-examination after the witness has testified.[61]

Again, this is not a pretrial discovery right. Moreover, it is not nearly as likely that the court will encourage defense attorneys, as opposed to prosecutors, to turn over such material prior to the completion of the direct examination. However, where the government has produced its 3500 material significantly prior to its witnesses' testimony, it is generally considered good form for defense counsel to produce the prior recorded statements of its witnesses at least before the defense witnesses take the stand.

§ 13.5 Discovery of Documents, Tangible Objects, Reports of Examinations, and Criminal Records

§ 13.5(a) Discovery by the Defense

In contrast to the restricted access to government witnesses and witness statements, the defense has broad access to documents, tangible

---

59. Defense counsel may be able to encourage the prosecutor to do so by agreeing to expedite the government's case, for example, by agreeing to stipulate as to certain undisputed facts or the testimony of a custodial witness.

60. Fed. R. Crim. P. 16(b)(2)(B).

61. Fed. R. Crim. P. 26.2.

evidence and scientific or other reports in the possession of the government. These items are available for inspection or copying so long as the object sought will be offered by the government in its case-in-chief or is "material" to the preparation of the defense.[62] At the initial stage of the discovery process, the government makes an assessment of the materiality of the information in its possession that must be produced. If the issue is contested, the burden is on the defendant to establish the materiality of any documents or materials sought.[63]

§ 13.5(b)   Discovery by the Prosecution

The rules give the government the right to discover documents, tangible evidence and reports of examinations and tests from the defendant where: (a) the government has complied with a similar discovery demand made by the defense; and (b) the defense intends to introduce such evidence at trial.[64] Note that government discovery in this area is reciprocal only, and that unlike the analysis for evidence of this kind applicable to the defense, the government has no right to the evidence solely because it is "material" to the preparation of its case.

As noted, the defendant's reciprocal obligations to produce documents and information to the government are triggered by the defendant's own requests (except for disclosure of expert witnesses, discussed immediately below). For this reason, there theoretically could be a case where the defendant chooses not to request documents and information from the government in order to avoid triggering the defendant's reciprocal discovery obligation. It is, however, difficult to imagine many situations in which that tactical decision would be made given the limited discovery available to the defendant and the possible importance of such information for preparing a defense.

The Rules also permit government discovery of statements by expert witnesses whom the defendant intends to call at trial. The defense must produce all statements that are incorporated in any report of an examination or test undertaken by the expert witness.[65] Such reports may include the defendant's statements to an expert during an examination.[66]

---

62. Fed. R. Crim. P. 16(a)(1)(E) & (F); Wright, §§ 254, 254.1, 254.2.

63. LaFave et al., § 20.3(g).

64. Fed. R. Crim. P. 16(b)(1)(A) & (B); Wright, § 255.

65. Fed. R. Crim. P. 16(b)(1)(B) & (b)(2). See Wright, § 255. This again is a reciprocal right that applies only if the defense has

made a discovery request pursuant to Rule 16(a)(1)(C) or (D). See supra § 13.5(a).

66. See Fed. R. Crim. P. 16(b)(2). Statements made in the course of a competency evaluation are inadmissible as evidence against the accused on the issue of guilt (as opposed to the issue of sanity or mental competence). See Fed. R. Crim. P. 12.2(c)(4);

§ 13.6   The Pretrial Discovery Process[67]

§ 13.6(a)   The Initial Discovery Request

Although the discovery process is to a large extent based upon the notion that the defense will make specific requests for information, in many instances the government will take the initiative in turning over material it believes to be covered by the rules. Even then, however, the defense attorney should draft a letter to the prosecutor to request all of the documents and information desired by the defense. This letter, an illustration of which is provided below,[68] serves several purposes. First, it provides a checklist of the requested items for reference during the discussion with the prosecutor. Second, it creates a record that the defendant has requested certain categories of information and documents in the event the government fails to produce discoverable materials. Third, it eventually may be submitted to the court, along with the prosecution's response, as part of a formal motion to compel discovery.[69] As to the contents of the letter, the defense attorney should in the first instance be guided by the requirements of the Federal Rules and case law already discussed, making sure to be as specific as possible.

Requests for *Brady* material pose a special problem in this regard. In some situations, the favorable nature of the information will be so clear that the prosecutor will turn it over to the defense without any request for it being made. In other situations, however, the evidence may not be seen as so favorable on its face that it would lead the prosecutor to disclose it, and yet it could be of great importance given the theory of the defense. In order to ensure that such evidence is identified by the prosecutor, the defense attorney should make a specific request for it. The problem that the attorney faces in making *Brady* requests, however, is often not knowing what specific evidence the government possesses. It is, therefore, necessary for defense counsel to speculate about and anticipate the proof that would support possible defense theories under consideration and then to request that the government provide specific items of evidence that would support each theory.[70] Faced with specific requests of this type, the prosecution will be forced either: (a) to indicate that it does not possess any of the specified information, which itself may be important to know; (b) risk reversal if the information is not turned over, because the defendant consequently could not perfect or was forced to abandon a particular trial theory; or (c) advise the court that it has information of the type requested and seek a judicial declaration that it does not constitute *Brady* material.

WRIGHT, § 209. *See generally* MCCORMICK, §§ 15, 134, 136.

67. For discovery techniques, see generally MARILYN J. BERGER, JOHN B. MITCHELL, & RONALD H. CLARK, PRETRIAL ADVOCACY (1988).

68. *See infra* § 13.8(d).

69. Local court rules may mandate that counsel attempt informal resolution of discovery issues before filing a formal motion. *See, e.g.,* D.AK. L. CR. R. 16.1(a); C.D.ILL. CR. R. 16.1(C); N.D.GA. L. R. APPX. IV(d).

70. *See* ABA STANDARD 4–4.1(a) (setting forth defense counsel's duty to investigate).

§ 13.6(b) The Discovery Conference

The discovery process in the federal system is designed to occur in two stages. In compliance with local rules in effect in most districts, the defense attorney and prosecutor first meet in a discovery conference, at which time the defense will present discovery requests and the prosecutor will make such reciprocal requests as the rules permit.[71] The parties will attempt to dispose of as many issues as possible. The results of the conference often will be memorialized in an exchange of letters.[72] If the conference fails to resolve all of the issues, the defense will make a formal discovery motion.[73]

A discovery conference is an opportunity for the parties to resolve a wide range of pretrial matters in an efficient manner. If conducted properly, it can avoid unnecessary litigation over plainly discoverable matters, and it can provide both parties with more discovery than the rules require. The formality of the conference and the nature of the discussions that take place vary depending on the dictates of the local rules, the established practices of the jurisdiction, the nature of the case, and the relationship between the defense counsel and the prosecutor. The conference can be as formal as a scheduled meeting at the prosecutor's offices or as informal as a telephone call or a discussion at the courthouse before or after the initial pretrial court conference.[74]

§ 13.6(c) The Final Discovery Letter

It is often advisable for defense counsel to draft a final letter after the conference or discussion with the government, memorializing the agreements reached and identifying the areas of disagreement. Recording the parties' agreement helps to ensure that there are no misunderstandings about what will be provided; recording the disagreements will specify the issues that will be the subject of a discovery motion. The prosecution may reply to that letter, but does not always do so.

§ 13.7 Informal Defense Discovery

In this section, we will consider various ways other than those embodied in the constitutional and statutory rules just discussed in which the defense attorney can obtain information about the government's case. We focus on defense discovery because we already have described most of the tools that are available to the prosecution to determine the facts, including facts about the involvement of the defen-

---

71. *See* WRIGHT, § 257.

72. *See infra* § 13.8(d).

73. The discovery motion will be part of an omnibus pretrial motion, discussed in Chapter 14.

74. Informal practices effectively may supersede those provided for in the rules. For example, in the Southern and Eastern Districts of New York, the United States Attorney's Offices in virtually every case, and before any request is made, will send the defense attorney a so-called "Rule 16 letter," providing all information that the prosecutor believes is discoverable. Defense counsel then will often make specific additional requests after receiving the letter and enclosed disclosures.

dant in criminal activity. These include interrogation of the defendant and witnesses and searches by the police, witness interviews by prosecutors, and compelling testimony and the production of documentary evidence through the grand jury process.

It cannot be overemphasized how important it is for the defense similarly to devise and implement a comprehensive investigative strategy as early as possible in all cases. The goals should include identifying all possible sources of information, documents and witnesses that can be used to challenge all the elements of the government's case and to buttress all the factual and legal aspects of the defense. Pretrial investigation is one of the most important factors in determining whether a defendant prevails at trial, particularly in complex cases where the government often spends years investigating the facts prior to indictment and very often has inside information regarding the conduct under investigation from a cooperating witness. Even in cases that do not go to trial, effective pretrial investigation often will assist defense counsel in negotiating a more favorable plea bargain if counsel is able to uncover problems with the government's case or discover facts that place the government's allegations in a more sympathetic context.

It is essential for the defense attorney to attempt to discover the government's evidence through informal means because of the limits on discovery imposed by the formal rules—especially the restrictions on access to witness statements—and because of the restrictive way in which the formal rules may be interpreted by prosecutors and judges. For example, it cannot be assumed that all evidence that might be helpful to the defense will be discovered pursuant to *Brady* because of limitations on the way *Brady* material is defined and on what is deemed to be "favorable." Similarly, a witness' prior statements—3500 material—are usually received only on the eve of trial, which often will be too late to make most effective use of the information or to investigate leads revealed in the statements.

In addition to obtaining information in the government's files, it is also important to learn what the government does not know about its case since that can be used to undermine its theory of prosecution or the truthfulness of its witnesses. Defense counsel should not assume that the government has a complete or accurate picture of the facts when it obtains an indictment. Agents and prosecutors at times become overly committed to a particular view of the case, which may cause them to focus their attention on certain facts and not others. In addition, the government's heavy reliance on cooperating witnesses and informants can be a double-edged sword—just as clients are not always completely honest and forthcoming with their counsel, cooperating witnesses also can be less than fully candid, especially when seeking to trade their information for a deal with the government.

What follows is a discussion of some of the informal means available to defense attorneys to discover the identity and statements of government witnesses and other evidence not available through formal means.

§ 13.7(a) Witness Interviews by Defense Counsel

A crucial aspect of informal discovery is to find and interview all available witnesses, whether they are friendly, hostile or neutral to the defense. Some witnesses will be known by virtue of their being named in accusatory instruments—such as in the complaint and indictment identifying Mario Long, Arthur Murphy and Gilbert Santiago, all of whom were believed to be cooperating with the government. Others will be identified by the defendant. Still others can be found through field investigations.

Unlike the prosecutor, the defense attorney has no power to compel anyone to speak with him or her prior to trial, except for a very limited right to depose witnesses pursuant to court order.[75] Nevertheless, every effort should be made to interview all potential witnesses, including government witnesses. Obtaining the cooperation of witnesses friendly to the defense will not be difficult for obvious reasons. Neutral or hostile witnesses present challenges, particularly when they do not wish to be associated with the defense or fear that they either will be embarrassed or will be forced to spend time attending court proceedings. While these witnesses cannot be compelled to be interviewed, the government cannot expressly discourage them from cooperating with or speaking to the defense.[76]

Defense counsel should consider several different approaches when attempting to interview reluctant witnesses. In some cases, an appeal to principle might be effective—the need, that is, for persons accused of a crime to be given the opportunity to defend themselves. In other cases, the process can be explained in a manner that reassures the witness that he or she will not be seriously inconvenienced; for example, by explaining that the information provided by the witness may help to resolve the case without trial. In still other circumstances, explaining the defendant's power to subpoena witnesses at trial may persuade the witness to cooperate.[77]

---

75. The exception is a limited right to depose witnesses in "exceptional circumstances." *See* FED. R. CRIM. P. 15; WRIGHT, §§ 241–245. The defendant can, of course, compel witnesses to appear at trial through the issuance of trial subpoenas. *See* FED. R. CRIM. P. 17; WRIGHT § 271. But even in these situations, the witness is not obligated to discuss his or her testimony prior to taking the stand.

76. *See* United States v. Agostino, 132 F.3d 1183, 1191–92 (7th Cir. 1997); ABA STANDARD 3–3.1(d) (1993). *See also* United States v. Black, 767 F.2d 1334, 1337–38 (9th Cir. 1985) (noting that prosecutor may inform witness that he can choose not to be interviewed by defense); Gregory v. United States, 369 F.2d 185, 188 (D.C. Cir. 1966) (holding that it is improper for the government to instruct potential witnesses not to speak with the defense outside prosecutor's presence).

77. On motivating witnesses, see DAVID F. BINDER & PAUL B. BERGMAN, FACT INVESTIGATION: FROM HYPOTHESIS TO PROOF 221–243 (1984).

Whenever possible, all witness interviews should be conducted by the defense lawyer and a trained investigator or, at least, some other third party. If the defense counsel has to testify about what the witness said, counsel would risk disqualification.[78] Having the other party familiar with the same information and available to testify instead can avoid this result. In a similar vein, if the witness' testimony at trial contradicts his interview statements, the investigator or other assisting party present during the interview can be called to impeach the witness.[79] Whenever necessary, it should be made clear to the witness that it is wholly appropriate for the witness to communicate to the defense attorney whatever the witness knows about the case, whether or not he or she has already spoken to the government or testified before the grand jury.[80]

The questioning technique to be employed during the interview obviously depends in large part upon the witness' relationship to and feelings about the case. With friendly or neutral witnesses, a "direct examination" approach combining open and closed questions can be employed. With hostile witnesses, closed questions may be appropriate when it is clear that he or she is reluctant to talk or intent on saying as little as possible. There is no reason, however, to attempt to discredit either the witness or his or her story during the interview. At best, that will simply antagonize the witness and make him or her even less willing to provide useful information. At worst, it will give the witness advance warning as to what to expect on cross-examination at trial.[81] Lastly, even recalcitrant witnesses often will speak to defense lawyers who have taken the time to determine the best manner and approach for soliciting a witness' cooperation. For example, many witnesses initially refuse to discuss what they perceive to be the disputed issues in a case, while agreeing to discuss the surrounding collateral issues. However, once the witness begins speaking and becomes comfortable, often the witness will discuss everything relevant to the case.

---

78. *See* Federal Deposit Ins. Corp. v. United States Fire Ins. Co., 50 F.3d 1304, 1317 (5th Cir. 1995) (lawyer disqualified because he likely would have to testify adversely to client); Lamborn v. Dittmer, 873 F.2d 522, 531 (2d Cir. 1989) (ordering new trial and remanding with direction to disqualify plaintiff's lawyer and permit defense to elicit testimony from him adverse to his client); Model Rules of Prof'l Conduct R. 3.7(a) (1983, as amended 2003) (hereinafter "Model Rule") ("A lawyer shall not act as advocate at a trial in which the lawyer is likely to be a necessary witness unless the testimony relates to an uncontested issue ... [or] disqualification of the lawyer would work substantial hardship on the client."); Model Code of Prof'l Responsibility DR 5–102(A) (1983 ed.).

79. Fed. R. Evid. 607 & 613.

80. Fed. R. Crim. P. 6(e)(2) (prohibiting disclosure of matters occurring before the grand jury by designated individuals; designated individuals do not include witnesses themselves); Wright, § 106.

81. On witness interviewing, see generally Berger, Mitchell & Clark, *supra* note 67, at ch. 5; Binder & Bergman, *supra* note 77, at chs. 11–15; Thomas L. Shaffer & Robert S. Redmount, Legal Interviewing and Counseling (1980).

§ 13.7(b)   Informal Discovery From the Government

It should be remembered that, with few exceptions,[82] the government is never prohibited from disclosing its evidence prior to trial; it is merely not forced to do so. In preparing for the discovery conference, therefore, it is important that the defense be prepared to ask for as much information as is necessary to prepare a defense.

Indeed, much of the discussions between defense counsel and the government often will relate to requests for information not specifically discoverable under the Federal Rules or pursuant to a *Brady* demand. The discussions regarding access to material expressly discoverable under the rules typically involve the defense counsel attempting to persuade the government as to what is material to the defense; it serves little purpose for the government to resist providing that information, particularly if the defense has adequately supported its claim of materiality. The negotiations therefore often can turn quickly to issues related to informal discovery, where the result is determined by how far the parties are willing to negotiate disclosure of material that is plainly not discoverable formally. Here, tactical decisions must be made on both sides.

We suggest considering these factors when engaging in informal discovery:

(1) It is often in the interest of the prosecution to reveal much of its evidence early in a case. While the prosecutor who has developed a case and who is persuaded by the evidence personally may prefer to present it at trial, he or she very frequently will have to defer to institutional pressures and attempt to resolve the case by obtaining a guilty plea. One very effective way to accomplish this goal is to demonstrate to the defense attorney that the likelihood of a conviction after trial, with the risk of a higher sentence, is great. Given the limitations on formal discovery available to the defense and the reluctance of government witnesses (and, at times, the defendant) to be forthcoming, the defense attorney may not be in a position to advise the defendant to accept a guilty plea unless the prosecutor supplies the information necessary to analyze properly the defendant's likelihood of success at trial.

(2) A prosecutor may be motivated to disclose the government's evidence in return for disclosures by the defense. There is no rule prohibiting an attorney from disclosing any information when doing so is in the interests of his or her client, including statements and information provided to the attorney in confidence, as long as the client consents.[83] In revealing such information, attorneys commonly assure

---

82. *See, e.g.,* Fed. R. Crim. P. 6(e) (government may not disclose grand jury testimony of witnesses other than the defendant); Wright, § 106 (same).

83. *See generally* Rakoff, *supra* note 54, at 14 (prosecutors may disclose more information than required by law in furtherance of plea negotiations); Model Rule 1.6(a) ("A lawyer shall not reveal information relating to the representation of a client unless the client gives informed consent [or] the disclosure is impliedly authorized in order to carry out the representation. . . . ").

each other that what is said will be used only to assess each other's evidence and not against the other party at trial. In determining whether or not to reveal information in order to obtain information, defense counsel should keep in mind that one advantage the defense has at trial over the government is that the government generally knows much less about the possible defense strategy. As a result, defense counsel has to balance the loss of this advantage against the potential for persuading the government about the weakness of its case when deciding whether to disclose information in pursuit of a more favorable plea or dismissal of the charges.

§ 13.7(c) Informal Discovery From Other Sources

Every defense investigation should begin with a thorough review of the court files and documents relating to all defendants and cooperating witnesses, including the complaint or indictment, the docket sheet (indicating all court activity), the magistrate judge's file containing all documents related to the initial appearance, transcripts of bail hearings, and any affidavit in support of a warrant or electronic surveillance. In addition, proceedings in other cases that have factual connections to the present one can be a treasure trove of useful material, and counsel should obtain court filings and transcripts of the testimony of informants, agents and experts in any such cases.

Defense counsel should always visit the site of important events, including the place of offense, place of arrest (where relevant) and the location at which evidence was seized. While private investigators often are helpful in assisting defense counsel's investigation, counsel will be questioning the witnesses about the events and locations at issue. Being able to visualize the physical surroundings can be crucial in eliciting helpful facts or impeaching witnesses about those events.

Pretrial discovery also can be obtained in evidentiary hearings that take place prior to trial, even when such hearings are conducted for other purposes. We have already noted that the preliminary hearing, when available, is useful to the defense principally as a discovery device.[84] Similarly, hearings on motions to suppress evidence may result in discovery of information useful at trial, as is discussed in greater detail in Chapter 14.

§ 13.7(d) Rule 17(c) Subpoenas

Rule 17(c) allows both the government and the defense to seek court approval to issue and serve trial subpoenas on third parties directing the production of documents in advance of trial.[85] Rule 17(c) subpoenas are a

---

84. *See supra* Chapter 6.

85. Rule 17(c) provides in pertinent part: "The court may direct the witness to produce the designated items in court before trial or before they are to be offered into evidence. When the items arrive, the

powerful tool available to the defense. While the government has the power of the grand jury to compel the production of documents (and testimony) to discover information helpful to its case, the defendant's first opportunity to compel the production of potentially helpful documents or other materials is through the use of Rule 17(c) subpoenas. In order to obtain such subpoenas, the defense is typically required to submit a proposed subpoena to the judge along with an affidavit explaining the reason the desired information is relevant, necessary to the preparation of the defense and needed prior to trial.[86]

After the subpoena is served on a third party, that party, or the government on its behalf, may move to quash the subpoena. Rule 17 provides that "[o]n motion made promptly, the court may quash or modify the subpoena if compliance would be unreasonable or oppressive."[87] Under Rule 17(c), the court must determine the reasonableness of a subpoena.[88] The party that served a Rule 17(c) subpoena has to meet the following conditions to defeat a motion to quash: relevance, admissibility, necessity and specificity.[89]

Rule 17(c) subpoenas provide one of the few instances where the defense is given a power nearly equal that of the prosecution—the power to compel any person or entity to produce documents prior to trial. For every factual allegation underlying the government's case, defense counsel should consider whether there is any non-governmental source that could have documents relevant to that fact. Whenever this question is answered affirmatively, subpoenas should be pursued. In addition, defense counsel should subpoena all documents and materials that might indicate that the government's witnesses are not being truthful. For example, subpoenas served on government informants have been known to uncover documents and other materials indicating that the informant has understated his own role in criminal wrongdoing or exaggerated the role of the defendant. It should be noted, however, that the case law is

court may permit the parties and their attorneys to inspect all or part of them." Note that this rule does not permit the defense to subpoena witnesses prior to trial in order to obtain testimony. Testimonial subpoenas direct the witness to appear in court at the time of trial.

86. Although the rule does not specifically provide that the application for such a subpoena can be made *ex parte*, in many jurisdictions such *ex parte* applications are permitted so that both the government and the defendant can compel the production of information and documents prior to trial without disclosing trial strategy to the other side. This issue is a controversial one, and the practice varies depending on the jurisdiction. The government often argues that since Rule 17(c) does not specifically provide that a defendant may make an *ex*

parte application to serve a subpoena compelling the production of documents pretrial, no such right exists. However, Rule 17(b) does provide that indigent defendants can make a request *ex parte* for the court to issue subpoenas for necessary trial witnesses. Defense counsel can argue that since the rule recognizes the legitimacy of indigent defendants not disclosing to the government their potential witnesses, it would be inconsistent to require that pretrial Rule 17(c) subpoenas be disclosed and thereby allow the government to learn the defendant's trial strategy.

87. Fed. R. Crim. P. 17(c)(2).

88. *See* United States v. Nixon, 418 U.S. 683, 699–700 (1974).

89. *See id.* at 699.

mixed as to whether and when Rule 17(c) subpoenas properly may be used solely to obtain impeachment material.[90] Defense counsel also should seek to subpoena documents and materials that could support any fact important to the defense. Even if the government is not necessarily contesting a given fact, offering supporting documentation for factual assertions underlying the defense case often will buttress the defendant's claims in the eyes of the jury.

§ 13.8　United States v. Christopher

§ 13.8(a)　Defense Interviews

1.　Interview of Paul Christopher

On April 27, 2005, Paul Christopher met with his attorney, Richard Clark, at Clark's office. Clark then reviewed the allegations in the indictment with Christopher and explained what had to be proven. He indicated that he did not presently have enough information to offer any advice and said that it was important that Christopher provide as much information as he had on the matter.

Christopher then explained that during 2004 he had suffered a serious decline in business due to a decline in price for the coffee that he imported and distributed. He became short of cash and attempted to obtain bank loans, but was unsuccessful.

Desperate, he decided to engage in a scheme designed to increase his income by avoiding taxes on the proceeds of coffee sales. He once had been approached by a man who he had been told had connections with organized crime and who proposed to sell coffee and other foods to retailers for cash in return for a percentage of the payments. Because these transactions would be undocumented and in cash, the people who supplied the coffee could choose not to report the proceeds to the Internal Revenue Service. Christopher had not been interested at the time, but later contacted the man (who he only knew as Frankie) and entered into the deal with him. Christopher said he deposited the cash in the bank accounts referenced in the indictment. All deposits were in amounts under $10,000 in order to avoid IRS regulations requiring banks to report cash transactions greater than that amount. Christopher said that he created five of those accounts in order to shield some money if, for some reason, the ownership of one of the accounts became known and the IRS accordingly demanded payment (plus interest) of that uncovered unreported income.

90.　*Compare* United States v. LaRouche Campaign, 841 F.2d 1176, 1180 & n.7 (1st Cir. 1988) (Rule 17(c) subpoena seeking impeachment material affirmed), *with* United States v. Hardy, 224 F.3d 752, 755–56 (8th Cir. 2000) (Rule 17(c) subpoena seeking impeachment material quashed); United States v. Cherry, 876 F.Supp. 547, 552–53 (S.D.N.Y. 1995) (Rule 17(c) cannot be used to acquire impeachment material because "documents are not evidentiary for Rule 17(c) purposes if their use is limited to impeachment").

Christopher further reported that he had been introduced to Gilbert Santiago by William Van Ness, who was his brother-in-law and for whom Santiago had been working. Christopher knew from Van Ness that Santiago was an ex-convict on supervised release. Christopher wanted to keep as low a profile as possible in this scheme, and so he hired Santiago to set up the banking arrangement and make the deposits, thinking that Santiago both would be willing to do so and, because of his supervised status, would be unlikely to disclose it once he became involved. As a cover, he made Santiago manager of Superior Warehouse and told his employees there, including Mario Long, to take directions from him.

Christopher stated that Santiago opened the accounts and that he and Santiago signed the bank signature cards. He indicated that the amounts enumerated in the indictment were the amounts received from Frankie in accordance with their agreement. He adamantly insisted that he had no knowledge of any drug trafficking. He stated that he realized that what he had done was a business crime, but that he would never be involved with drugs.

Christopher also stated that he never told Van Ness what he and Santiago were doing and that Van Ness had no knowledge of, or involvement in, the scheme.

Christopher told Clark that he had received a call from Ernest Wagner at CMS Bank shortly after the raid on the warehouse, and Wagner told him that a DEA agent had interviewed him about IFD's accounts. Christopher said that when he received that news, he immediately closed the phony accounts, hoping that somehow their existence would not be discovered by the Internal Revenue Service. He was shocked, he said, to hear that the DEA was investigating him.

2. Interview of William Van Ness

On April 28, 2005, William Van Ness met with his lawyer, Martin Rothman, at Rothman's office. Rothman began the interview by explaining everything he knew about the government's charges and allegations against Van Ness.

Van Ness said that he knew Gilbert Santiago because Santiago used to work for him, and he was aware that Santiago was an ex-convict on supervised release. Van Ness further stated he knew that Santiago had begun to work for Christopher at Christopher's warehouse, but that he never had any reason to believe that Santiago's work was anything but lawful.

Van Ness said that he was Christopher's brother-in-law. He said that he had long done business with Christopher and that he had indeed transported the shipments on the dates listed in the indictment. He stated that he did not look inside the crates and had no knowledge that they contained cocaine. He indicated that while he knew that Santiago had been involved with drugs in the past, he never had any problem with

Santiago while Santiago worked for him. He said he thought that Christopher had hired Santiago because he needed a supervisor, and since Santiago had been a good employee for Van Ness, he believed that Christopher made a good choice.

3. Joint Defense Meeting

On April 30, 2005, Clark and Rothman met to discuss the proceedings pending against their clients, Christopher and Van Ness. Prior to the meeting, the lawyers agreed that Christopher and Van Ness had common interests. The lawyers knew that Christopher and Van Ness were not only brothers-in-law, they were also very good friends and wanted their lawyers to work closely together. While both Clark and Rothman knew that circumstances might change and that their clients' interests might deviate, they agreed that it was prudent for them to enter into a joint defense agreement so that anything discussed between the lawyers and everything discussed at any joint meetings with the clients would be privileged and confidential and could not be disclosed or used against them.[91]

§ 13.8(b) The Defense Attorneys' Post–Interview Evaluation of the Christopher Case

From their review of the indictment and the interviews with Christopher and Van Ness, the attorneys reached the following tentative conclusions regarding their case theories.

(1) The Indictment

While the indictment appeared to be legally sufficient, it may be possible to obtain more information about the specifics of the charges in a bill of particulars.

(2) The Evidence Against Christopher

The lawyers concluded that since Santiago and Long were not charged as defendants, they were the principal sources of evidence against their clients. The interviews of the defendants confirmed that conclusion, and it therefore became crucial to learn what these witnesses had said and what grounds might exist for challenging their credibility. Obviously, the lawyers also needed to know whether the government had any other witnesses.

As to the tangible evidence that the government possessed, Clark knew that drugs allegedly had been seized in January, but he would need independent verification of that allegation. He also would need to learn the manner in which the seizure occurred in order to determine whether the evidence could be suppressed. Moreover, Clark could not tell from the indictment whether drugs allegedly possessed at other specified

---

91. For a discussion of the joint defense privilege, and the limitations on the protec-   tion afforded by joint defense agreements, see *supra* § 5.2.

times had been seized. Nor did he know what the IFD bank records would reveal about the alleged money laundering operation.

As to the quality of the government's evidence, it seemed that Santiago, now undoubtedly cooperating with the government in order to obtain sentencing concessions, was an impeachable witness given his prior narcotics conviction. Moreover, with his history of narcotics trafficking, it would be reasonable to argue that the activities charged reflected a rogue operation conducted without Christopher's knowledge. Christopher would have to admit to violating the tax laws to present an alternative explanation for his conduct, but such an explanation carries much less serious consequences than a narcotics conviction.

(3) The Evidence Against Van Ness

Rothman believed that it might be possible to proceed with a "reasonable doubt" defense, based on what Christopher and Van Ness both had said. If the government had no proof that Van Ness was involved in discussions about narcotics with either of the likely government witnesses, and if, as it appears, there was no direct evidence to demonstrate that he knew that the material he was transporting contained cocaine, it would seem that the government's case could be challenged successfully without having to offer any alternative explanation for Van Ness' behavior. However, Van Ness himself also would be able to testify that he did not know he was transporting drugs. Of course, this analysis ultimately would depend on what additional evidence, if any, the government possessed.

Let us now turn to the steps that Clark and Rothman took in their pursuit of additional information necessary to support their potential defense theories.

§ 13.8(c) The Discovery Conference

Clark and Rothman met with AUSA Knapp on May 20, 2005. Knapp confirmed that the principal government witness would be Santiago and that both Santiago and Long had signed cooperation agreements. She refused to provide copies of those agreements or of the cooperating witness' statements prior to trial.

Knapp also disclosed that the government had surveillance and phone records showing a consistent pattern over the past year of Christopher calling a particular number in Colombia and then immediately calling Van Ness, and she agreed to provide Clark and Rothman with those records, consistent with her Rule 16 obligations.

Knapp asked what position the defendants were taking in response to the charges, and Clark responded that he was not prepared to disclose his defense strategies unless he believed that the government was open to reconsidering the merits of its case. However, without getting into specifics, Clark did state that he believed based on what he knew that the defense would be able to present a compelling defense. Knapp said she had strong evidence that the two were willing participants. She indicated that she would be willing to discuss ways to limit their exposure at sentencing if they pleaded guilty and cooperated in making a case against the supplier. To preserve this option, Clark decided not to disclose that both defendants had insisted that they knew nothing about the narcotics trafficking. He wanted to wait until he reviewed the discovery material, including the surveillance and phone records showing calls from Christopher to Colombia and Van Ness, to evaluate the credibility of those denials. Also, until he concluded that there was a possibility that Knapp would reject the claims of her cooperating witness and reconsider the charges, he did not want to disclose what the defendants were telling their lawyers or that the defense may be able to present compelling arguments at trial that this was a rogue operation run by Santiago, since that would only serve to help the government better prepare for trial. For example, Knapp would know that the defendants might testify and affirmatively deny the allegations, and she therefore would work hard to find information and witnesses to impeach their claims.

The discussion then turned to the defendant's *Brady* requests, and one point of conflict arose: Clark wanted to obtain any statements by Long or Santiago in furtherance of the conspiracy that would tend to prove that they, and not Christopher and Van Ness, in fact committed the crimes alleged. Knapp said that if there were such statements, she believed they were 3500 material, and as such statements of government witnesses not discoverable prior to trial, and that in any case she disagreed that they would constitute *Brady* material.

With that discussion the conference ended, and the attorneys agreed to memorialize the discussion in an exchange of discovery letters.

§ 13.8(d) Discovery Letters

The following are the discovery letters exchanged by Clark and Knapp. Rather than specifically enumerating all of the matters and materials involved in the discovery process, these letters serve as examples of how to reference discovery items categorically. While the requests for Rule 16 discovery, *Brady* material and a bill of particulars appear in a single letter, they also could be the subject of two or three separate letters. Note that Rothman would engage in similar correspondence, focusing most specifically on efforts to determine what evidence, if any, the government possessed indicating that Van Ness had knowledge of the contents of the crates that he transported.

Richard C. Clark, Esq.
Attorney at Law
377 Broadway
New York, NY 10003
(212) 862–9543

May 21, 2005

Laura Knapp, Esq.
Assistant United States Attorney
U.S. Attorney's Office
225 Cadman Plaza East
Brooklyn, NY 11201

    Re: <u>United States v. Paul Christopher</u>

Dear Ms. Knapp:

    Based on our discussions at our meeting on May 20, 2005, it is our understanding that the government has agreed to copy and produce to Paul Christopher all documents that (i) the government may introduce in its case-in-chief at trial, or (ii) are material to the preparation of Mr. Christopher's defense. <u>See</u> Rule 16(a)(1)(C) of the Federal Rules of Criminal Procedure. In addition, the government has agreed to produce the following information and documents to Mr. Christopher:

(1)   The exact amount of cocaine seized at Kennedy Airport from the shipment of coffee addressed to Superior Warehouse on January 11, 2005, and the exact amount of cocaine seized from Superior Warehouse on January 12, 2005, along with any results of examinations or tests of said cocaine.

(2)   The names of any law enforcement agents involved in the seizure of drugs from Kennedy Airport on January 11, 2005 and from the Superior Warehouse on January 12, 2005.

(3)   All documents related to any electronic surveillance conducted with respect to this case, and copies of all transcripts of any conversations intercepted by that surveillance.

    In addition, you made the following representations regarding other specific discovery requests:

(1)   The government's investigation has revealed no prior criminal record for either of the defendants named in the Indictment.

(2)   Apart from the cocaine seized on January 11 and 12, 2005 from Kennedy Airport and Superior Warehouse, the government is not in possession of, nor will offer in evidence, any narcotics seized from or otherwise linked to either defendant.

(3)   No unindicted co-conspirators, nor any other person known to the government to be involved in the crimes alleged in the Indictment, was an agent, employee or otherwise associated with the government prior to January of 2005.

If our understanding as to these matters is in any way incorrect, please inform us as soon as possible.

In addition to the information and documents that the government has already agreed to produce to Mr. Christopher, we request that the government produce the following materials and information pursuant to Rules 16 and 7(f) of the Federal Rules of Criminal Procedure and *Brady v. Maryland*, 373 U.S. 83 (1963), and its progeny including *United States v. Agors*, 427 U.S. 97 (1976), and *Giglio v. United States*, 405 U.S. 150 (1972), and the Fifth and Sixth Amendments of the United States Constitution. Each request calls for all responsive items which are within the possession, custody, or control of the government, or which are either known to exist or could by the exercise of due diligence become known to the government. Each request is also of a continuing nature, and we request prompt notice in the event that responsive information comes to the government's attention at any point in the future. If the government declines to provide any information requested, please advise us of the government's objection so that we can consider bringing any dispute to the attention of the Court.

Statements of the Defendant Paul Christopher

1.   All records, reports, memoranda, notes, or other writings that contain the substance of any oral statement made by Mr. Christopher to government or law enforcement authorities, regardless of the government's intentions with respect to the statement's use at trial. See Rule 16(a)(1)(A), Fed. R. Crim. P. This request includes internal reports and memoranda prepared by law enforcement agents to the extent that statements of Mr. Christopher are related or described within. Where a statement is contained in more than one writing, please provide each such writing.

2.   All written or recorded statements made by Mr. Christopher, at any time and in any context, regardless of the government's intentions with respect to their use at trial. See Rule 16(a)(1)(B), Fed. R. Crim. P.

3.   The substance of all oral statements made by Mr. Christopher to government or law enforcement authorities that have not been disclosed pursuant to Requests 1 and 2 above and that the government may use at trial. See Rule 16(a)(1)(A), Fed. R. Crim. P. This request includes not only statements that the government intends to introduce at trial, but also statements that the government may "use" for impeachment or other purposes.

4.   All recorded testimony of Mr. Christopher or of any person authorized to legally bind Mr. Christopher or to make admissions on Mr. Christopher's behalf before any grand jury.

5.   With respect to the government's due diligence obligation, please provide the name and whereabouts of any government agent or employee who has had contact with Mr. Christopher, but who has not been interviewed to determine whether Mr. Christopher made statements in his or her presence.

Documents and Tangible Objects

6.   Copies of all books, papers, documents and photographs that are material to the preparation of the defense or are intended for use at trial. Rule 16(a)(1)(E), Fed. R. Crim. P.

7.   A description of all tangible objects, buildings or places material to the preparation of the defense, intended for use at trial or obtained from Mr. Christopher, which have not already been described or produced by the government. Rule 16(a)(1)(E), Fed. R. Crim. P.

8.   The results or reports of any examination or scientific test. Rule 16(a)(1)(F), Fed. R. Crim. P.

9.   A detailed description of any documents, objects or physical evidence relating to this case that have been destroyed or lost, or are no longer in the custody or control of the government. If the government contemplates destroying or releasing any such items in the future, we request notice and an opportunity to object prior to any such action.

10.   Details regarding any searches conducted in the course of this investigation and whether or not items seized in the search will be introduced by the government as evidence at trial, including but not limited to the premises searched, the date of the search, copies of any warrants and applications for warrants, the names of the officers who conducted the search, descriptions of any items seized, the name of any individual purporting to give consent to any such search and the purported relationship between that person and the premises searched.

Charts, Summaries, Analyses or Reports

11.   All charts, summaries or calculations reflecting the contents of writings or other documents that are either (a) material to the preparation of the defense, or (b) intended for use by the government as evidence-in-chief at trial.

12.   Copies of all handwriting exemplars or handwriting samples used to perform any handwriting analyses in connection with the investigation in this case.

Hearsay Testimony

13.   Please state whether the government intends to offer any hearsay evidence pursuant to Rules 803(24) and/or 804(5) of the Federal Rules of Evidence. If so, provide the information required by the Rules.

Other Crimes, Wrongs, or Acts

14.   Please describe any evidence of uncharged conduct of Mr. Christopher that the government intends to introduce at trial. Rule 404(b), Fed. R. Evid.

Expert Testimony

15.   Please disclose any evidence that the government may present at trial under Rules 702, 703, or 705 of the Federal Rules of Evidence by providing a written report prepared and signed by the witness that includes a complete statement of all opinions to be expressed and the basis and reasons therefor, the data or other information relied upon in forming such opinions, and the qualifications of the witness. See Rule 16(a)(1)(F), Fed. R. Crim. P.

Brady Material

16.   In addition to the above, please provide all documents, books, papers, photographs, tests or experiments, objects, statements of witnesses, and other evidence and information that (i) tends to exculpate Mr. Christopher, (ii) may be favorable or useful to the defense as to either guilt or punishment, or (iii) tends to affect the weight or credibility of evidence to be presented against Mr. Christopher. This request applies to evidence that is within the possession, custody or control of the government, known by the government or could by the exercise of due diligence become known to the government. Brady v. Maryland, 373 U.S. 83 (1963).

17.   We specifically request all statements made by any of Mr. Christopher's alleged coconspirators, or any other witness, that tend to exculpate Mr. Christopher or tend to show that the acts alleged in the Indictment were not committed in the presence of the defendants, and/or were committed by others.

18.   We specifically request all grand jury testimony by any of Mr. Christopher's alleged coconspirators, or any other witness, that tends to exculpate Mr. Christopher.

19.   We specifically request any and all information that tends to show that Gilbert Santiago engaged in any narcotics transaction without the involvement or participation of Mr. Christopher.

20.   If the government is aware of facts that would constitute Brady material but assumes that Mr. Christopher or counsel knows or should know such facts, please verify that counsel is aware of these facts.

21.   If the government possesses information responsive to any of these requests but takes the position or continues to take the position (as you did at our meeting regarding our request for statements of any cooperating witness that acts alleged in the Indictment were not committed in the presence of the defendants and/or were committed by others) that it does not fall within its Brady obligations, please inform us so that we may seek the Court's intervention.

Bill of Particulars

22.   We request that the government describe with greater particularity the charges against Mr. Christopher contained in the Indictment. See Rule 7(f) of the Federal Rules of Criminal Procedure. See also United States v. Torres, 901 F.2d 205, 234 (2d Cir. 1990), cert. denied, 498 U.S. 906 (1990); United States v. Davidoff, 845 F.2d 1151, 1154 (2d Cir. 1988); United States v. Bortnovsky, 820 F.2d 572, 574 (2d Cir. 1987); United States v. Panza, 750 F.2d

1141, 1148 (2d Cir. 1984). Specifically, we request that the government provide the following information relating to the allegations in the Indictment:

(1) Specifically identify the "others" alleged to have conspired with Mr. Christopher in violation of Title 21, United States Code, Sections 952(a), 960(a)(1), 960(b)(1)(B)(ii) and 963, referred to in Count 1, ¶ 1 of the Indictment.

(2) Specifically identify any overt acts performed by or involving any individual involved in the alleged conspiracy referred to in Count 1, ¶ 1 of the Indictment by indicating:

(a) the dates and times of such activity;

(b) the names of the individuals involved;

(c) the location of each act;

(d) the precise amounts of each alleged controlled substance involved in each alleged act, if applicable; and

(e) each alleged act itself and the specific means by which it transpired.[94]

(3) Specifically identify any instances of agreement by or among any individual or individuals involved in the alleged conspiracy referred to in Count 1, ¶ 1 of the Indictment.

(4) Specifically identify each alleged instance of Mr. Christopher or an alleged coconspirator of Mr. Christopher importing a controlled substance as alleged in Count 1, ¶ 1, Count 3, ¶ 3, Count 4, Count 5, Count 6, and Count 7, of the Indictment.

(5) Specifically identify the "others" alleged to have conspired with Mr. Christopher and/or Mr. Van Ness in violation of Title 21, United States Code, Sections 841(a), 841(b)(1)(A)(ii)(II) and 846, referred to in Count 2, ¶ 2 of the Indictment.

(6) Specifically identify each alleged instance of Mr. Christopher, Mr. Van Ness or an alleged coconspirator of Mr. Christopher and/or Mr. Van Ness

---

[94] **Note that in the requests that follow specific details such as those in (a)-(e) would be restated in the actual letter.**

distributing or possessing with intent to distribute a controlled substance as alleged in Count 2, ¶ 2 of the Indictment.

(7)   Specifically identify the "others" alleged to have collaborated with Mr. Christopher in violation of Title 21, United States Code, Sections 952(a), 960(a)(1) and 960(b)(1)(B)(ii), referred to in Count 3, ¶ 3, Count 4, ¶ 4, Count 5, Count 6, and Count 7, of the Indictment.

(8)   Specifically identify each alleged instance of Mr. Christopher, Mr. Van Ness or any alleged collaborator of Mr. Christopher and/or Mr. Van Ness distributing or possessing with intent to distribute a controlled substance in violation of Title 21, United States Code, Sections 841(a)(1) and 841(b)(1)(A)(ii)(II), referred to in Count 8, Count 9, Count 10, Count 11, and Count 12, of the Indictment.

(9)   Specifically identify the "others" alleged to have conspired with Mr. Christopher in violation of Title 18, United States Code, Section 371 referred to in Count 13, ¶¶ 7-9 of the Indictment.

(10)   Specifically identify the locations "within the Eastern District of New York and elsewhere" at which the alleged conspiracy referred to in Count 13, ¶ 8 of the Indictment occurred.

(11)   Specifically identify the "co-conspirator whose identity is known" who is alleged to have conspired with Mr. Christopher in violation of Title 18, United States Code, Section 371 referred to in Count 13, ¶¶10(a)-(f) of the Indictment.

(12)   Specifically identify each of the five bank accounts referenced in Count 13, ¶10(a) of the Indictment.

(13)   Confirm whether the five bank accounts referenced in Count 13, ¶ 10(a) of the Indictment are the same accounts referenced in Count 13, ¶¶10(b)-(f); if they are not, specifically identify any and all accounts referenced in ¶¶ 10(b)-(f).

(14)   Specifically identify any overt acts performed by or involving any individual involved in the alleged conspiracy referred to in Count 13, ¶ 10 of the Indictment that are not already delineated therein.

    (15)   Specifically identify any alleged instances of agreement by or among any individual or individuals involved in the alleged conspiracy referred to in Count 13, ¶¶ 7-10 of the Indictment.

    (16)   Specifically identify the alleged instance of structuring in violation of Title 31, United States Code, Sections 5324(a)(3) and (c)(1) referenced in Count 14, ¶ 12 , Count 15, Count 16, and Count 17, of the Indictment.

    (17)   Specifically identify the "others" alleged to have conspired with Mr. Christopher and/or Mr. Wagner in violation of Title 18, United States Code, Sections 1956(a)(1) and 1956(h), referred to in Count 18, ¶ 13 of the Indictment.

    (18)   Specifically identify any overt acts performed by or involving any individual involved in the alleged conspiracy referred to in Count 18, ¶ 13 of the Indictment.

    23.   Lastly, please produce and/or identify any and all documents that are responsive to any of Mr. Christopher's requests for particulars.

Thank you for your cooperation.

                          Very truly yours,

                          Rich Clark

                          Richard C. Clark

U.S. Department of Justice
United States Attorney
Eastern District of New York

May 25, 2005

Richard C. Clark, Esq.
377 Broadway
New York, NY 10003

     Re: <u>United States v. Paul Christopher</u>

Dear Mr. Clark:

     Pursuant to Rule 16 of the Federal Rules of Criminal Procedure, and in response to your letter of May 21, 2005, the government hereby furnishes the following discovery with respect to the above case.

     1.   Please find enclosed the following items of discovery, which I agreed to provide you at the discovery conference:

          (a)   Laboratory report on the drugs referred to in the first paragraph (unnumbered) of your letter, including the amount seized.

          (b)   Documents related to a pen register.

          (c)   Documents seized from Superior Warehouse.

          (d)   Other documents, including bank records, phone records and other records.

     2.   Please be advised that the Drug Enforcement Agency agents involved in the seizure of cocaine referred to in the first paragraph (unnumbered) of your letter are Ralph Martinez, William Foster, and Gloria Richards.

     3.   The representations made by you in the second paragraph (unnumbered) of your letter concerning the government's position on these matters are correct.

     4.   The government declines to disclose any of the additional particulars requested in ¶¶ 22-23 of your letter since the Indictment provides more than sufficient details concerning the charges to satisfy Rule 7 of the Federal Rules of Criminal Procedure.

     5.   The United States requests reciprocal discovery pursuant to Rule 16(b) of the Federal Rules of Criminal Procedure.

6.   The government is aware of its obligations under <u>Brady v. Maryland</u>, and does not accept the characterization of these obligations in ¶¶ 16-21 of your letter. The government is not presently aware of any exculpatory information with respect to your client.

7.   The government is aware of and will comply with its continuing duty to disclose such newly discovered additional information required by Rule 16(c) of the Federal Rules of Criminal Procedure, <u>Brady v. Maryland</u>, and the obligation to assure a fair trial.

Very truly yours,

Kevin O'Reilly
United States Attorney

By: *Laura Knapp*
Laura Knapp
Assistant U.S. Attorney
(718) 330-1248

The pretrial discovery process just described has framed the outstanding issues between the prosecution and the defense. In the next chapter, we will turn to the pretrial motion stage, when these and other issues that must be resolved before trial will be litigated.

Chapter 14

PRETRIAL MOTIONS

Table of Sections

Sec.
14.0 Introduction.
14.1 The Statutory Design.
14.2 Drafting the Motion.
    14.2(a) Formal Motion Practice.
    14.2(b) Motion Practice Variations.
14.3 Grounds for Motions.
    14.3(a) Motions for Discovery.
    14.3(b) Motions to Suppress Evidence.
    14.3(c) Defenses and Objections Based on Defects in the Institution of the Prosecution.
    14.3(d) Defenses and Objections Based on Defects in the Indictment.
14.4 Strategic Considerations.
14.5 The Christopher Motion Papers.
14.6 The Government's Response to the Pretrial Motion.
14.7 Hearings on Pretrial Motions—Introduction.
14.8 Commencing the Hearing—The Burden of Proof.
    14.8(a) The Burden of Going Forward.
    14.8(b) The Burden of Persuasion.
    14.8(c) The Qualitative Burden.
    14.8(d) The Quantitative Burden.
14.9 Examination of Witnesses—Tactical Considerations.
14.10 Final Argument.
14.11 The Christopher Hearing.
14.12 Appeal From an Adverse Determination.
14.13 Setting a Trial Date—Time Limitations.

§ 14.0 Introduction

After the indictment has been returned, the factual issues to be litigated at trial are generally established. Before a trial can occur, however, the Federal Rules permit, and in some instances require, the parties to raise legal issues concerning certain jurisdictional and evidentiary matters. In this chapter, we summarize the rules and practices relating to the subject matter and drafting of pretrial motions and illustrate them by a set of motion papers from the Christopher case. We also describe various less formal means used to resolve issues at the pretrial motion stage, as well as immediately prior to trial. We then discuss the hearing that can be precipitated to resolve disputes raised by the motion papers.

We must make two further points about our discussion of pretrial motion practice in this chapter. First, we focus exclusively on the defendant as the moving party. We take this approach because it is almost always the defendant who will be seeking relief from actions taken by the government either in investigating the case or formulating the charges. On rare occasions, however, the government may engage in formal motion practice—for example, if it seeks to depose a witness,[1] or to enforce its reciprocal discovery rights.[2] Second, we are concerned here with motions brought at a time well in advance of trial. There is one kind of motion—the *in limine* motion—that is almost always made on the eve of trial. The *in limine* motion is made in an attempt to obtain a ruling in advance on evidentiary issues that either the government or the defendant anticipate arising during the testimony of certain witnesses. We defer discussion of motions *in limine* to Chapter 15 dealing with pretrial preparation.

§ 14.1 The Statutory Design

Rule 12 of the Federal Rules of Criminal Procedure governs pretrial motion practice and generally provides that any issue that may affect the trial and that can be resolved prior to the commencement of the trial should be resolved then. Some issues must be raised before trial in order to avoid waiver.[3] Rule 12 requires that pretrial motions be brought at the time of arraignment or as soon thereafter as possible.[4] In felony cases, therefore, all such motions are made in the district court, rather than before the magistrate.[5] Typically, the judge sets a schedule for the filing of pretrial motions at the initial pretrial conference or, in more complex cases, after defense counsel has an adequate opportunity to review the materials disclosed by the government pursuant to its obligations under Rule 16.[6]

1. FED. R. CRIM. P. 15.

2. FED. R. CRIM. P. 16(b).

3. FED. R. CRIM. P. 12(b)(3), 12(e). *See* WRIGHT, § 193.

4. FED. R. CRIM. P. 12(b)(4)(B), 12(c). *See* WRIGHT, § 192.

5. The motions could, however, be heard by the magistrate on referral from the district court, after which the magistrate submits proposed findings and conclusions to the district court. This procedure comports with due process. United States v. Raddatz, 447 U.S. 667, 673–76 (1980).

6. FED. R. CRIM. P. 12(c).

The issues covered by Rule 12 fall into two general categories:

(1) Those motions that relate to the power of the government to bring the prosecution. These include: motions alleging lack of subject matter jurisdiction;[7] motions alleging defects in the indictment or in the prosecution of the indictment;[8] and motions for severance.[9]

(2) Those motions that relate to the evidence that will be available for use at trial. These include motions for discovery[10] and motions to suppress illegally obtained evidence.[11]

For both types of motions, there is obvious reason for a pretrial resolution of the issues. A successful challenge to the right to prosecute—for example, on the grounds that the prosecution is barred by the double jeopardy clause—may obviate the trial altogether. A successful motion to suppress evidence material to the outcome of the proceeding on the grounds that it was illegally obtained also may obviate the trial altogether or at least avoid interrupting it to deal with the issue.

To enforce the policies favoring pretrial resolution of issues, Rule 12 contains strict waiver provisions. Rule 12(b) requires that most motions be filed prior to trial, including: defenses and objections based on defects in the institution of the prosecution;[12] defenses and objections based on defects in the indictment (other than that it fails to allege jurisdiction in the court or to charge an offense, which may be raised at any time during the pendency of the proceedings);[13] motions to suppress evidence;[14] requests for discovery under Rule 16;[15] and motions for severance of charges or defendants under Rule 14.[16] In most instances, failure to make the motions specified in the rule at the required time will constitute a waiver.[17] A court, however, may grant relief from the waiver for good cause.[18]

---

7. FED. R. CRIM. P. 12(b)(3)(B). The court lacks subject matter jurisdiction if, for example, the indictment does not charge a federal crime or is based upon an unconstitutional statute. *See* WRIGHT, § 193 (noting distinction between subject matter jurisdiction and jurisdiction over the person).

8. FED. R. CRIM. P. 12(b)(3)(A), 12(b)(3)(B). This category would include, for example, defects in the drafting of the indictment resulting in misjoinder, duplicity, or multiplicity. *See infra* §§ 14.3(c) & 14.3(d).

9. FED. R. CRIM. P. 12(b)(3)(D). *See* FED. R. CRIM. P. 8, 14. *See supra* § 11.3.

10. FED. R. CRIM. P. 12(b)(3)(E).

11. FED. R. CRIM. P. 12(b)(3)(C). To implement this policy, the rule provides for disclosure of evidence that is subject to the exclusionary rule. FED. R. CRIM. P. 12(b)(4). Either the defendant may request such information from the government or the government may provide the information without awaiting a request. The rule does not mandate government disclosure. However, the advisory committee notes make it clear that it was contemplated that the government would comply. *See* FED. R. CRIM. P. 12 advisory committee's note (1974 and 2002 amendments); WRIGHT, § 197.

12. FED. R. CRIM. P. 12(b)(3)(A).

13. FED. R. CRIM. P. 12(b)(3)(B).

14. FED. R. CRIM. P. 12(b)(3)(C).

15. FED. R. CRIM. P. 12(b)(3)(E).

16. FED. R. CRIM. P. 12(b)(3)(D).

17. *See* FED. R. CRIM. P. 12(e). The only exception is a motion to dismiss for lack of subject matter jurisdiction, which can be made at any time. FED. R. CRIM. P. 12(b)(3)(B). *See* WRIGHT, § 193.

18. Courts generally have found good cause if new evidence has been discovered or the defendant lacked the opportunity to raise the issue previously. *See* WRIGHT, § 193 n.23 & n.24. *See also* Wainwright v. Sykes, 433 U.S. 72, 84 (1977) (requiring cause and actual prejudice).

§ 14.2 Drafting the Motion

§ 14.2(a) Formal Motion Practice

Rule 12 provides that pretrial motions may be made either orally or in writing.[19] However, the usual practice of the federal courts is to require that the motion be written and that all issues that can be resolved prior to trial be addressed in a single, "omnibus" motion.

Rule 12 is silent as to the contents of the motion, and we have observed significant differences in the form motions take among districts and practitioners. Unless a particular jurisdiction or judge favors more informal motion practice, the following complete form of motion papers should be used.

The four parts of a complete submission are these:

(1) *Notice of motion.* The notice of motion simply informs the opponent of the nature of the issue being raised and the date set for the submission.

(2) *The motion.* The motion itself states the specific relief requested, and, in conclusory language, the statutory or case law basis for the relief the movant is seeking.

(3) *The Averment—Affidavit or Declaration.* An averment may take the form of an affidavit or declaration. An affidavit is a sworn and notarized document and a declaration is a statutorily authorized substitute that does not need notarization.[20] The statement alleges the facts in support of the relief requested (or opposed) by the party. It may be based either on personal knowledge or on hearsay, characterized in these documents as "on information and belief." There may be one or several averments attached to an omnibus motion, depending upon what factual showing is required and who is in possession of the relevant knowledge. Averments are required in all motions except those that raise only legal issues relating to the pleadings and documents already before the court.

(4) *The memorandum of law.* The memorandum of law contains two parts: a preliminary statement and the legal argument on the point or points raised by the motion. The preliminary statement always contains a description of the procedural status of the case and either incorporates by reference the facts alleged in the affidavit or paraphrases those facts. In cases in which no affidavit is required, and the pleadings and record papers contain all the factual information necessary for the disposition of the motion, the preliminary

---

19. Fed. R. Crim. P. 12(b)(1) (importing Fed. R. Crim. P. 47).

20. Title 28, U.S.C. § 1746 permits the filing of a declaration, which is a statement made under the penalties of perjury, in any circumstance in which an affidavit is re-

quired. Examples of declarations may be found in Paul Christopher's moving papers below. Affidavits are shown in the government's papers. There is no difference between the two formats in federal court.

statement will recite the relevant facts contained in those documents to provide a factual basis for the arguments that follow.

Following the preliminary statement, each issue that is addressed by the motions is presented in a separately numbered "point." The heading of the point is framed as an assertion of the movant's claim as to the relief that should be granted.

Legal argument in the memorandum of law may be extensive when dealing with issues that will be resolved based on the moving papers, i.e., those about which there is no factual dispute and consequently will not give rise to an evidentiary hearing. Where the goal of the motion papers is to obtain an evidentiary hearing, however, the legal argument in the memorandum can be more summary in nature, limited to a brief analysis of the applicable law and leading cases. Courts commonly permit this memorandum to be supplemented by a posthearing memorandum that argues in greater detail how the testimony should be evaluated and applied to the legal issues. In such a memorandum, the preliminary statement and argument incorporate those facts proven at the hearing.

§ 14.2(b) Motion Practice Variations

The practitioner is certain to see motion papers that vary significantly from the four part format described above. For example, motion papers that combine the notice of motion and the motion are common. In this format, the notice of motion will contain a succinct yet complete statement of the relief sought and a citation to the rule, statute, or leading case authorizing the granting of the relief sought. The document entitled "motion" itself is omitted.

In some courts, two part motions are accepted as well, especially when the motion is limited to identifying legal authority in support of a request for an evidentiary hearing. The two part motion eliminates the memorandum of law and includes a simple legal argument in the last paragraphs of the attorney affidavit or declaration. While the placement of legal arguments in a sworn statement of fact is technically incorrect, it is accepted for reasons of expedience in some jurisdictions.

Another variation is the letter motion. In this format, the notice of motion, motion, affidavit or declaration, and memorandum are combined in a letter that states the relief sought and sets out the factual basis and legal argument. The response also may be in letter form. While this form is often used for motions *in limine*, it is rarely used for omnibus pretrial motions.

§ 14.3 Grounds for Motions

In virtually all cases that are not resolved pre-indictment or immediately following the return of the indictment, defense counsel should file pretrial motions. It will be a rare case in which the defendant has no legal issues to raise prior to a trial. As discussed below, there can be many strategic benefits to raising certain issues pretrial, even if those motions are unsuccessful. The pretrial motions that should be considered in every case fall into three broad categories: motions to compel discovery, motions to exclude evidence, and motions to dismiss the indictment or counts of the indictment or defendants. We summarize here the grounds for making the most common of these motions.

§ 14.3(a) Motions for Discovery

Whenever the government declines to produce documents or information responsive to any of the types of discovery requests discussed in Chapter 13, defense counsel may file a motion to compel discovery. Such motions typically address areas where reasonable minds could differ concerning the scope of the government's discovery obligation, such as requests for bills of particulars, whether documents are "material to the defense" under Rule 16, and whether documents or information constitute *Brady* or *Giglio* material that must be disclosed pretrial.

§ 14.3(b) Motions to Suppress Evidence

The exclusionary rule precludes the prosecution's use in its case-in-chief of evidence obtained illegally by law enforcement. The rule extends not only to the particular evidence discovered directly by illegal means, but subject to a number of exceptions, it also may prohibit the use of evidence that is subsequently derived from the initial illegal governmental action.[21] When defense counsel believes that evidence may have been obtained illegally, the proper legal mechanism to invoke the exclusionary rule is a motion to suppress the tainted evidence. Such motions can seek to exclude evidence obtained through a variety of means, including interrogations, searches and seizures, wiretaps and surveillance, and witness identification procedures.

While it is beyond the scope of this book to describe the vast body of law regarding the exclusionary rule,[22] defense counsel should, of course, investigate fully the facts surrounding any police activity in the case to determine whether the government's evidence was obtained in violation of the defendant's constitutional or statutory rights. Recall that Rule 12 of the Federal Rules provides for the government to notify the defendant of evidence that might be subject to a motion to suppress in order to facilitate the motion process.[23]

§ 14.3(c) Defenses and Objections Based on Defects in the Institution of the Prosecution

By and large, prosecutors have broad discretion to conduct investigations, institute criminal proceedings, determine what charges to bring,

---

21. *See supra* § 4.5(c); LaFave et al., §§ 3.1, 9.3–9.6.

22. *See generally* LaFave et al., ch. 3 (arrest, seizure), ch. 4 (wiretapping and electronic surveillance), ch. 6 (interrogations and confessions), ch. 7 (identification procedures), chs. 9 & 10 (scope and administration of the exclusionary rule).

23. *See supra* § 13.2(a)(3).

and enter into plea bargains provided they have probable cause to believe a crime has occurred.[24] There are some limitations on this authority, however, including prohibitions against double jeopardy and the right of the defendant to a timely prosecution, i.e., one within the statute of limitations and within constitutional and statutory speedy trial rules. Grounds for these motions were described in Chapter 11, describing the rules for drafting the indictment.[25]

§ 14.3(d) Defenses and Objections Based on Defects in the Indictment

The government also has broad discretion to determine the subject matter and form of its charging instrument. Nonetheless, there are a few restrictions, the violation of which can serve as grounds for narrowing the matters in dispute at trial or for amending or even dismissing the indictment. The most common of these motions allege the defects of improper venue, duplicity or multiplicity, and improper joinder of charges or defendants. Grounds for these motions were discussed in Chapter 11, dealing with drafting the indictment.[26] In addition, while not a basis to dismiss the indictment, surplusage (i.e., statements in the indictment that are not relevant to the crime charged) can be struck on motion by the defense.[27]

§ 14.4 Strategic Considerations

The preceding discussion indicates how pretrial motions can serve to protect a variety of particular rights afforded the defendant by the Constitution, statutes, and procedural and common law rules. Apart from enforcement of the defendant's rights, however, there exist a variety of strategic benefits to bringing a pretrial motion. As long as the motion can be supported by non-frivolous claims, these benefits should be weighed in formulating pretrial plans.

For example, to further the goal of obtaining information regarding the government's case and its witnesses, pretrial motions can assist the defense by raising issues to which the government must respond by providing factual information, either in a written submission or at a hearing where its witnesses would be subject to cross-examination. Evidentiary hearings are fertile sources of information about the government's case and may even provide access to government witnesses and their prior statements, depending on the matter in dispute.[28] If the

---

24. *See* Wayte v. United States, 470 U.S. 598, 608 (1985); Bordenkircher v. Hayes, 434 U.S. 357, 364 (1978); LaFave et al., §§ 13.1(a)–(e), 13.2(a).

25. *See supra* § 11.3 (double jeopardy), § 11.6 (speedy trial and statute of limitations rules).

26. *See supra* § 11.2(b) (venue), § 11.3 (multiplicity, duplicity and joinder).

27. *See* Fed. R. Crim. P. 7(d); Wright, § 127.

28. *See supra* § 13.4(b) (discussing "3500 material"); Fed. R. Crim. P. 26.2(g) (providing for the discovery of statements of witnesses at hearings on motions to suppress).

government does not respond in full to the defendant's arguments or presentation at a hearing, it risks weakening its own position and, in turn, losing the motion. The more the government is required to disclose evidence in its possession or present evidence in support of its position in response to the motion, the more the defense learns about the government's case.

There are other potential collateral benefits for the defense to be gained by filing pretrial motions. Motions can force the government to make representations and commitments regarding its case (for example, specific items of evidence that it will or will not offer) that it may come to regret at the time of trial. In addition, pretrial motions present an opportunity for the defense to educate the judge about the merits of the defense case and weaknesses in the government's case. Prior to the filing of motions, the judge's knowledge of the case is often limited to the information contained in the government's charging instrument.

§ 14.5 The Christopher Motion Papers

The moving papers submitted by Clark on Christopher's behalf and the government's response appear below. Christopher raises two issues: suppression of the drugs and other evidence seized from his warehouse and the need for a bill of particulars.

In studying the motion papers, note that where the dispute turns on facts that the attorney is as competent as anyone to recite, an attorney declaration setting forth those facts is sufficient. By contrast, where motions raise factual issues that the defendant or the case agent is in the best position to assert, a hearsay affidavit by an attorney is not considered sufficient protection against the filing of a frivolous claim.[29] Thus, in support of the motion to suppress, the defendant had to submit a declaration based upon personal knowledge, and in response Agent Martinez submitted a similar affidavit.

---

29. *See* United States v. Gillette, 383 F.2d 843, 848 (2d Cir. 1967); United States v. Shaw, 260 F.Supp.2d. 567, 570 (E.D.N.Y. 2003). Unless someone with personal knowledge assumes the risk of a perjury prosecution if the affidavit is false and misleading, courts are justified in denying a hearing. Recognizing that a defendant might, in such circumstances, be forced to make incriminating statements, in derogation of the defendant's Fifth Amendment rights, in order to meet the requirements for asserting other constitutional claims, the Court in *Simmons v. United States,* 390 U.S. 377, 394 (1968), precluded from use

"on the issue of guilt" a defendant's statement made in an affidavit or at a hearing. Thus, where the defendant is the person with knowledge, his or her allegations and not that of the lawyer are appropriate to satisfy the burden of going forward. For example, in moving to suppress tangible evidence, in order to satisfy the production burden, the defendant must allege and prove a reasonable expectation of privacy. *See* Rawlings v. Kentucky, 448 U.S. 98, 104–105 (1980); United States v. Salvucci, 448 U.S. 83, 91 (1980); Rakas v. Illinois, 439 U.S. 128, 143 (1978).

UNITED STATES DISTRICT COURT
EASTERN DISTRICT OF NEW YORK
--X
                        :

UNITED STATES OF AMERICA   :

                        :   No. 05 Cr. 735

          v.   :

                        :   **NOTICE OF**
                        :   **OMNIBUS MOTION**

PAUL CHRISTOPHER and   :
WILLIAM VAN NESS,   :

        Defendants.   :

--X

      PLEASE TAKE NOTICE that upon the annexed motion, declarations of Paul Christopher and Richard Clark, Esq., memorandum of law, and upon all prior proceedings, the defendant, PAUL CHRISTOPHER, by his attorney, Richard Clark, Esq., will move this Court before the Honorable Walter Sheridan, United States District Judge for the Eastern District of New York sitting at the United States Courthouse, Courtroom 128, Cadman Plaza, Brooklyn, New York, on the 28th day of June, 2005, at 10:00 A.M. or as soon thereafter as counsel can be heard, for an order granting suppression of certain evidence and a bill of particulars.

Dated: New York, New York
       June 23, 2005

                                    Rich Clark
                                    Richard Clark, Esq.
                                    Attorney for Paul Christopher
                                    377 Broadway
                                    New York, N.Y. 10003
                                    (212) 862–9543

                                    To: Kevin O'Reilly, Esq.
                                    United States Attorney
                                    Eastern District of New York
                                    225 Cadman Plaza East
                                    Brooklyn, NY 11201

                                    ATTN: Laura Knapp, Esq.
                                    Asst. U. S. Attorney

UNITED STATES DISTRICT COURT
EASTERN DISTRICT OF NEW YORK
---X
                                          :
UNITED STATES OF AMERICA   :
                                          :
                                          :   No. 05 Cr. 735
            v.   :
                                          :   **OMNIBUS MOTION**
                                          :
PAUL CHRISTOPHER and   :
WILLIAM VAN NESS,   :
                                          :
            Defendants.   :
                                          :
---X

        PLEASE TAKE NOTICE that upon the indictment, attached declarations, memorandum of law, and upon all prior proceedings in this case, PAUL CHRISTOPHER, by his attorney Richard Clark, Esq., moves this Court for an order:

        1.   pursuant to Fed.R.Crim.P. Rule 12(b)(3), suppressing any and all evidence seized by law enforcement officers during a search of Superior Warehouse, 149 Grand Street, Queens, New York and any and all evidence derived from the unlawful search, based on the defendant's claim that he had a reasonable expectation of privacy at the premises, and that the search was illegal because it was conducted without a warrant, exigent circumstances justifying the failure to obtain a warrant, valid consent or any other exception to the Fourth Amendment warrant requirement;

        2.   pursuant to Fed.R.Crim.P. Rule 7(f), compelling the government to provide a bill of particulars based on the defendant's claim that the indictment is vague and does not provide meaningful notice of the charges against him; and

        3.   pursuant to Fed.R.Crim.P. 12(c), granting a hearing on any of the above requests, should the Court deem it necessary, at such time as this Court directs, and any additional relief this Court deems appropriate under the circumstances.

Dated: New York, New York
        June 23, 2005

                                                Rich Clark
                                                Richard Clark, Esq.
                                                Attorney for Paul Christopher
                                                377 Broadway
                                                New York, N.Y. 10003
                                                (212) 862–9543

UNITED STATES DISTRICT COURT
EASTERN DISTRICT OF NEW YORK
---X

UNITED STATES OF AMERICA   :

                            :   No. 05 Cr. 735

          v.   :

                            :   **DECLARATION IN SUPPORT OF**
                            :   **OMNIBUS MOTION**

PAUL CHRISTOPHER and   :
WILLIAM VAN NESS,

                            :

          Defendants.   :

                            :

---X

I, Richard Clark, hereby declare under the penalties of perjury, pursuant to 28 U.S.C. § 1746, that:

1.   I am the attorney of record for the defendant, Paul Christopher, and am familiar with all the facts and prior proceedings in this case. I make this declaration in support of the defendant's motions for suppression of certain illegally seized evidence, and a bill of particulars.

2.   This declaration is made on personal knowledge and information and belief. I have reviewed the official court papers, had conversations with Assistant United States Attorney Laura Knapp, and made an independent investigation into the facts and circumstances of this case.

3.   The defendant Paul Christopher was arrested on April 25, 2005 and charged, in a multi-count indictment, with conspiracy to distribute in excess of five kilograms of cocaine, distribution of more than five kilograms of cocaine and money laundering.

SUPPRESSION OF PHYSICAL EVIDENCE

4.   On January 12, 2005, agents of the Drug Enforcement Administration entered and searched the premises of Superior Warehouse, 149 Grand Street, Queens, N.Y. The agents had not secured arrest warrants for any persons believed to be at that location or a search warrant for the warehouse.

5.   Paul Christopher, the owner of that warehouse and the business operating from it, indicates in an attached declaration that he did not give the agents permission to enter the warehouse, nor did he authorize any of the employees present at that time to permit anyone to enter or search those premises.

6.   I have been informed by Assistant United States Attorney Laura Knapp that the agents claim to have seized several packages of a mixture containing a detectable amount of cocaine from a locked storage area in that warehouse. She also informs me that one of the agents inspected and removed certain documents from another area of the warehouse. The government has indicated its intent to offer the items seized from the warehouse as evidence against my client, Paul Christopher.

THE BILL OF PARTICULARS ISSUE

7.   I have had several discussions with AUSA Knapp about the discovery in this case. Based on those discussions and my own investigation, I believe that the government has in its possession many boxes of documents relating to business dealings and financial transactions involving Superior Warehouse, 149 Grand Street in Queens, and Paul Christopher.

8.   Based on conversations with AUSA Knapp, I understand that some of these documents were seized during a search of Superior Warehouse, and other documents were obtained from various financial institutions by a government subpoena. It is my understanding that the government intends to use some or all of these documents against Mr. Christopher at trial.

9.   The referenced documents relate to substantial business activities and financial transactions over a period spanning nine months in 2004 and 2005. The documents encompass hundreds of business transactions.

10.   The government has not identified the particular documents or, more specifically, the particular underlying transactions that are the subject of Counts One, Two, Eighteen and Nineteen of the Indictment. As a result, Paul Christopher lacks meaningful notice of the charges against him.

I declare under the penalty of perjury that the foregoing is true and correct.

WHEREFORE, it is respectfully submitted that this Court should enter an order suppressing the evidence seized in the aforementioned search because it violated the protections of the Fourth Amendment, directing the government to provide meaningful notice by supplementing the information set forth in the Indictment with a bill of particulars, granting a hearing on this motion, and granting such other relief as this Court deems just and proper.

Dated: New York, New York
      June 23, 2005

Rich Clark

Richard Clark
Attorney for Paul Christopher
377 Broadway
New York, N.Y. 10003
(212) 862–9543

UNITED STATES DISTRICT COURT
EASTERN DISTRICT OF NEW YORK
--X

UNITED STATES OF AMERICA   :

                        :   No. 05 Cr. 735

          v.   :

                        :   **DECLARATION IN SUPPORT OF**
                        :   **OMNIBUS MOTION**

PAUL CHRISTOPHER and   :
WILLIAM VAN NESS,   :

        Defendants.   :
--X

I, Paul Christopher, hereby declare under the penalties of perjury, pursuant to 28 U.S.C. § 1746, that:

1.   I am the defendant in this case, and am familiar with all the facts and prior proceedings of this case. I make this declaration in support of a motion for suppression of certain illegally seized evidence and for a bill of particulars.

2.   I was arrested on April 25, 2005 and charged in a multi-count indictment with conspiracy to distribute in excess of five kilograms of cocaine, distribution of more than five kilograms of cocaine and money laundering.

3.   This declaration is made on personal knowledge and information and belief. I am the owner of Superior Warehouse, Inc., 149 Grand Street, Queens, N.Y. ("Superior") and have had conversations with Mario Long, the foreman of the warehouse.

4.   On January 12, 2005, agents of the Drug Enforcement Administration entered and searched the premises of Superior. The agents did not have warrants authorizing their actions.

5.   Superior is a wholly owned subsidiary of International Food Distributors, Inc. I am the sole shareholder of both corporations.

6.   In September, 1990, I hired Mario Long to be the foreman of Superior. At that time, I instructed him that he was not authorized to permit any person not employed by me to enter the warehouse unless I specifically authorized him to permit entry on a particular occasion. I told him to contact me if anyone not otherwise authorized to enter the premises sought permission to enter. I gave those instructions because I regularly store valuable merchandise at that location and am concerned about being robbed. After I hired Gilbert Santiago as the manager of Superior, I repeated that instruction to Mr. Long and told him that Mr. Santiago was also authorized to permit him, Long, to allow entry to others. I repeated my instruction to contact me, or Mr. Santiago, before permitting entry to anyone not otherwise authorized to enter the warehouse.

7.   On January 12, 2005, persons identifying themselves as agents of the Drug Enforcement Administration spoke to Mario Long at Superior. The agents asked Long if he would permit them to enter and search the warehouse. Upon information and belief, Mr. Long told the agents that he did not have authority to consent without first obtaining permission from the manager of the warehouse. The agents told Long that his consent was immaterial because they would obtain a warrant and enter forcefully. At that point, Long did not prevent their entry.

8.   Neither Mr. Santiago nor I ever gave Long authorization to admit agents of the Drug Enforcement Administration to Superior on January 12, 2005 or any other day. Long had explicit instructions to deny such permission and I had set up specific procedures to ensure that a person with authority would respond to a situation such as the one presented on the day in question. Had the agents acted reasonably and not coerced Long to permit them entry, I, or my authorized representative, would have been summoned to the scene and denied the agents permission to enter.

I declare under the penalty of perjury that the foregoing is true and correct.

WHEREFORE, it is respectfully submitted that this Court should enter an order suppressing the evidence seized in that search because it violated the protections of the Fourth Amendment, directing the government to provide a bill of particulars, granting a hearing on this motion and granting such other relief as this Court deems just and proper.

Dated: New York, New York
       June 23, 2005

                                          Paul Christopher
                                          Paul Christopher

UNITED STATES DISTRICT COURT
EASTERN DISTRICT OF NEW YORK
--X
                       :

UNITED STATES OF AMERICA   :

                       :   No. 05 Cr. 735

          v.   :   **MEMORANDUM IN SUPPORT OF**
                       :   **OMNIBUS MOTION**

PAUL CHRISTOPHER and   :
WILLIAM VAN NESS,   :

        Defendants.   :

--X

MEMORANDUM OF LAW IN SUPPORT OF DEFENDANT'S OMNIBUS MOTION FOR
SUPPRESSION OF EVIDENCE AND FOR A BILL OF PARTICULARS

                                    Richard Clark
                                    Attorney for Defendant Paul Christopher
                                    377 Broadway
                                    New York, New York 10003
                                    (212) 862–9543

PRELIMINARY STATEMENT

Paul Christopher was indicted with William Van Ness for violation of 21 U.S.C. §§ 841, 846, 952, 960 and 963 (Distribution and Importation of Cocaine and Conspiracy to Commit Those Offenses) and 18 U.S.C. § 1956 (Money Laundering).

Agents of the Drug Enforcement Administration searched a warehouse owned by Mr. Christopher after coercing consent to enter and search from an employee who lacked both actual authority and any objective indicia of authority to consent to their entry, as more fully detailed in the declaration of Paul Christopher attached to the annexed motion.

The government also has produced a large volume of documents reflecting business transactions far broader in scope than the incidents of unlawful activity specifically identified by the government, as is more fully detailed in the declaration of Richard Clark attached to the annexed motion. Nevertheless, the government refuses to identify which of those business dealings and transactions constitute the basis for its allegations in Counts One, Two, Eighteen and Nineteen of the Indictment.

POINT I

ITEMS SEIZED FROM THE DEFENDANT'S WAREHOUSE MUST BE SUPPRESSED BECAUSE THE SEARCH WAS CONDUCTED WITHOUT A WARRANT OR VALID CONSENT

A.　　*The Agents Unreasonably Relied Upon a Person Clearly Lacking Actual or Apparent Authority to Permit the Agents to Enter or Search the Warehouse.*

Every warrantless search of a private premises is per se unreasonable and presumptively invalid under the Fourth Amendment. *Horton v. California,* 496 U.S. 128, 133 (2002); *Katz v. United States,* 389 U.S. 347, 357-58 (1967). All warrantless searches must fall under one of the "specifically established and well-delineated exceptions" to the warrant requirement. *Horton,* 496 U.S. at 134; *Katz,* 389 U.S. at 357. In this case, law enforcement agents transparently attempted to bring this case under the consent exception by pressuring the first employee they met at the premises to permit them to enter and search the location. They made no attempt to determine who was in charge or who might be authorized to permit access to third parties. The agents' reliance on the alleged third party consent was unreasonable. As a result, the search and resulting seizure of certain items was illegal and must be suppressed. *Illinois v. Rodriguez,* 497 U.S. 177, 182-83 (2002).

When consent is given by someone other than the individual who holds the expectation of privacy in the location, the person authorizing the entry must have the requisite authority. *United States v. Matlock*, 415 U.S. 164, 171-72 (1974). Although the third party need not have a property interest in the location to have sufficient authority to permit a search, he or she must have been given sufficient control over the premises so that the person conferring that control could be said to have assumed the risk that the third party might "permit the common area to be searched." *Id.*

The Supreme Court has recently reaffirmed *Matlock*, holding that when the government relies upon the authority of a third party to consent to a search, the government must show that reliance to have been reasonable under all the circumstances of the case. *Rodriguez*, 497 U.S. at 182-83. In the instant case, the agents' reliance upon Long's authority was patently unreasonable and merely a pretext to gain entry. The agents made no attempt to ascertain who owned or managed the premises. Long told them he was only an employee and should not let them in the warehouse. They did not question Long about his position or authority. Instead, they simply told him they would secure a warrant and force entry if he did not admit them.

Had the agents made any reasonable effort to learn whether or not the first individual they met possessed actual authority, or even claimed to have authority, to permit their entry, the agents would have learned that Long was a low level employee who had been instructed not to permit entry to anyone.

Permitting the government to circumvent the warrant requirement by relying on anyone they happen to meet for consent to enter and search would completely eviscerate the Fourth Amendment protections. Because the agents unreasonably relied upon third party consent in this case and had no other justification for their warrantless search, the fruits of their illegal conduct, including all the items seized from the warehouse after that entry, must be suppressed. *Wong Sun v. United States*, 371 U.S. 471, 487-88 (1963).

B.   *Long's Consent was Involuntary.*

Any consent to waive the protections of the Fourth Amendment must be voluntary. Words of consent offered in the face of coercion are a nullity. *Bumper v. North Carolina*, 391 U.S. 543, 550 (1968). Government agents may not force citizens to legitimize their otherwise illegal actions by lying to them about their authority. For example, the Supreme Court has held that when a police officer stated falsely that he had a warrant, and the defendant believed, incorrectly, that he had no choice but to submit, that submission was coerced and not a valid waiver. *Id.* In this case the agents misled Long and coerced him into speaking words of consent.

The agents informed Mario Long that if he did not consent the agents *would get a warrant* and enter by force, rather than informing him that they would *apply for a warrant* and only enter if they obtained it. In other words, Long was told in effect that his consent was a mere formality, and that his real choice was either to permit the agents to enter or be subjected to their use of force to gain entry. *Cf. United States v. Faruolo*, 506 F.2d 490, 497 (2d Cir. 1974) (discussing distinction between situations where an agent says he would apply for warrant and where he adds that he *believes* he would get one).

Government agents must not be permitted to bully citizens into surrendering their substantial rights by falsely claiming greater power and authority than our laws give them. Long's illusory consent was invalid because it was coerced. Since the agents had no justification for their warrantless search, the fruits of their illegal conduct, including all the items seized from the warehouse after that entry, must be suppressed. *Wong Sun*, 371 U.S. at 487-88.

POINT II

THE GOVERNMENT SHOULD BE REQUIRED TO PROVIDE A BILL OF PARTICULARS

By letter dated May 21, 2005, Mr. Christopher requested that the government describe with greater particularity the charges against Mr. Christopher contained in Indictment No. 05 Cr. 735 (WS). The government denied this request by letter dated May 25, 2005. As a result of the vague and skeletal manner in which the charges are described in the Indictment and the lack of details revealed by the discovery materials provided, Mr. Christopher is unable to determine the factual predicate of the charges against him. These failings significantly impair Mr. Christopher's ability to defend against the charges and, thus, offend due process. Accordingly, the government should be compelled to provide more detailed information regarding the charges against Mr. Christopher.

Rule 7(f) of the Federal Rules of Criminal Procedure:

> permits a defendant to seek a bill of particulars in order to
> identify with sufficient particularity the nature of the
> charge pending against him, thereby enabling defendant to
> prepare for trial, to prevent surprise, and to interpose a
> plea of double jeopardy should he be prosecuted a second
> time for the same offense.

United States v. Bortnovsky, 820 F.2d 572, 574 (2d Cir. 1987). The decision of whether to grant or deny a motion for a bill of particulars rests within the district court's sound discretion. *United States v. Davidoff*, 845 F.2d 1151, 1154 (2d Cir. 1988); *United States v. Panza*, 750 F.2d 1141, 1148 (2d Cir. 1984). A bill of particulars is required where the charges are "so general that they do not advise the defendant of the specific acts of which he is accused." *United States v. Torres*, 901 F.2d 205, 234 (2d Cir. 1990),

Counts One and Two charge Mr. Christopher with conspiracy to import and to possess and distribute a controlled substance. Counts Eighteen and Nineteen of the Indictment charge Mr. Christopher with money laundering and conspiring to commit money laundering by manipulating financial transactions in furtherance of specified criminal activity.

Counts One and Two include a timeframe for the specified activity spanning nine months. Discovery materials and conversations with the government indicate that the alleged offense conduct involved shipments to Superior Warehouse, a business operation owned by Mr. Christopher. This warehouse receives numerous shipments and deliveries and stores hundreds of containers daily. The Indictment does not identify which of these deliveries and storage arrangements are alleged to constitute criminal activity.

Count Eighteen of the Indictment charges Mr. Christopher with conspiracy to commit money laundering, and Count Nineteen charges actual money laundering. While Count Nineteen identifies a specific date on which the alleged illegal financial transactions occurred, Count Eighteen does not. In fact, Count Eighteen identifies a time period spanning four months. Additionally, while Count Nineteen identifies the amount of money and the subdivided sums, Count Eighteen does not. Finally, neither count identifies the bank accounts utilized in furtherance of the alleged criminal activity.

Because of the limited information provided by the government with regard to these counts, Mr. Christopher does not know which shipments or storage contracts or which bank transactions are alleged by the government to have been illegal. Stated differently, Mr. Christopher does not know the basis for the charges in Counts One, Two, Eighteen, and Nineteen of the Indictment. As a result, the government must be required to provide particulars regarding these charges.

In *Bortnovsky*, the defendants were indicted for allegedly engaging in a scheme to defraud the Federal Emergency Management Administration and the New York Property Insurance Underwriting Association through the submission of false and inflated insurance claims for, *inter alia*, burglary losses. 820 F.2d at 573. The Second Circuit reversed their convictions on the basis that the district court abused its discretion when it denied the defendants' motion for a bill of particulars. *Id.* The trial court should have required the government to identify "which of appellants' insurance claims for burglary losses were fraudulent and which of the many invoices submitted to substantiate these claims were falsified." *Id.* at 573-74. As a result of the court's failure to do so, the defendants were forced, at trial, to explain the circumstances of eight actual robberies and to confront numerous documents unrelated to the charges, thus effectively and impermissibly shifting the burden of proof from the government to the defendant. *Id.* at 574-75.

Similarly, in the instant case, absent a bill of particulars, Mr. Christopher will be in the position of having to explain the circumstances surrounding all shipments, deliveries, storage arrangements, and financial transactions occurring during periods spanning many months and totaling in the hundreds. Documents and records seized by the government as potential evidence reflect the breadth of these activities and transactions. Such burden-shifting is impermissible.

Moreover, the fact that the government has provided documents pursuant to its discovery obligations does nothing to relieve the heavy burden placed on Mr. Christopher by the lack of particularity in the Indictment. The government has provided copies of those documents that it presently intends to introduce at trial. In addition, the government has provided access to the documents and materials seized from the search of Superior Warehouse and subpoenaed from various financial institutions. These documents are comprised of delivery schedules, shipment invoices, bank records, and other records that fill several large boxes. Having access to these documents does little to relieve the burden on Mr. Christopher of having to speculate as to which of those business records the government may rely on at trial in its direct case or as rebuttal evidence.

In *United States v. Davidoff*, 845 F.2d 1151 (2d Cir. 1988), the Second Circuit again reversed convictions based on the trial court's denial of a motion for a bill of particulars. In that case, the defendants requested a bill of particulars concerning unspecified RICO violations alleged in the indictment. *Id.* at 1153. The district court denied the motion, suggesting that the bill of particulars would reveal the government's proof and that some of the information requested was already contained in documents provided to the defendants. *Id.* At trial, the government was permitted to introduce evidence concerning certain alleged extortions of three companies which were not identified in the indictment. *Id.*

The Second Circuit reversed, stating that "it is simply unrealistic to think that a defendant preparing to meet charges of extorting funds from one company had a fair opportunity to defend against allegations of extortions against unrelated companies." *Id.* at 1154. Furthermore, the Court concluded that the government was not excused from its obligation to inform the defendants of the charges against them merely because it turned over some 6,000 pages of *Jencks* material. The volume of material was so great and the references in the materials were too oblique to provide notice of one of the extortions; further, the materials completely failed to mention the other two alleged extortion victims altogether. Thus, the Court concluded that a bill of particulars should have been granted, and reversed the convictions.

Here too, the fact that the government has provided substantial discovery does not cure the Indictment's lack of specificity:

> While the practice of voluntary discovery is to be encouraged, and in any event is required by Local Rule 18(b), it may not substitute for straightforward identification in a bill of essentials matters that the defendant needs to avoid surprise at trial, to interpose a pleas of double jeopardy and to know "with sufficient particularity the nature of the charges against him."

United States v. DeGroote, 122 F.R.D. 131, 143 (W.D.N.Y. 1988) (quoting *Bortnovsky*, 820 F.2d at 574).

Just as the defendant in *Bortnovsky* had a right to know which of his insurance claims for burglary losses were alleged by the government to be fraudulent, Mr. Christopher has a right to know which business and bank records seized from Superior Warehouse and subpoenaed from various financial institutions are alleged by the government to reflect narcotics trafficking and money laundering. This is clearly a situation in which a bill of particulars is "vital to [defendant's] understanding of the charges pending and to the preparation of a defense," and is absolutely necessary in order to "prevent[] the Government in its attempt to proceed furtively." *Bortnovsky*, 820 F.2d at 575. Moreover, it is difficult to fathom what prejudice the government will suffer by providing the desired information.

Accordingly, the Court should grant the motion and direct the government to provide information responsive to the requests for particulars made by Mr. Christopher.

CONCLUSION

For all of the aforementioned reasons, it is respectfully submitted that the Court should order the suppression of all evidence seized as a result of the warrantless search, order the production of a bill of particulars, and grant such other relief as the Court deems warranted.

Respectfully submitted,

Rich Clark

Richard Clark
Attorney for Paul Christopher
377 Broadway
New York, New York 10003
(212) 862–9543

§ 14.6   The Government's Response to the Pretrial Motion

Upon being served by the movant, the respondent will have a specified period of time to file a response.[30] The response typically consists of an affidavit (or declaration) in opposition to defendant's motion which, as with the movant's affidavit, must also be based on personal knowledge—i.e., that of Agent Martinez, who has such knowledge of the facts surrounding the search of Superior Warehouse. As we have noted, no affidavit would be required if the respondent accepted the movant's statement of the facts, disagreeing only with the legal conclusions to be drawn from them. The government would also file a memorandum in opposition to the motion, which is similar in form to the movant's memorandum of law.[31]

---

30. *See* FED. R. CRIM. P. 12, 45; WRIGHT, § 754.

31. In certain jurisdictions, it is common for the government to submit a letter, rather than a formal memorandum of law, opposing the defendant's motion and consenting to a hearing to resolve the factual disputes.

UNITED STATES DISTRICT COURT
EASTERN DISTRICT OF NEW YORK
--X
                                            :
UNITED STATES OF AMERICA   :
                                            :
                                            :   No. 05 Cr. 735
              v.   :
                                            :   **AFFIDAVIT IN OPPOSITION TO**
                                            :   **OMNIBUS MOTION**
PAUL CHRISTOPHER and   :
WILLIAM VAN NESS,   :
                                            :
              Defendants.   :
                                            :
--X

STATE OF NEW YORK
                              ss.:
COUNTY OF KINGS

RALPH MARTINEZ, being duly sworn, deposes and states:

1.   I am an Agent of the Drug Enforcement Administration, and in that capacity conducted an investigation into possible narcotics violations at Superior Warehouse, 149 Grand Street, in Queens County. I make this affidavit on personal knowledge and information and belief, the latter arising from my role as the case agent in the instant indictment, in opposition to the defendant's omnibus motion. I have included only the facts pertinent to the lawfulness of the search of the warehouse.

2.   The investigation commenced when cocaine was discovered by Customs officials in an inspection of crates of coffee which were part of a shipment from Colombia which arrived at Kennedy Airport on January 11, 2005. The crates were addressed to Superior Warehouse.

3.   On January 12, the crates, including a crate containing a small trace amount of the cocaine, were delivered to Superior Warehouse by a DEA agent posing as a delivery truck driver. He observed all of the crates being taken from the truck and carried into the warehouse.

4.   Within thirty minutes of the delivery of the crates to the warehouse, I, along with other agents of the DEA, went to the warehouse and spoke with Mario Long, the foreman. We identified ourselves as DEA agents investigating narcotics shipments. Thereafter, I requested that

Long permit us to enter the warehouse to search it for narcotics. I informed Long of the government's authority to obtain a search warrant for the premises. Long gave us permission to enter the warehouse.

      5.   After I entered the warehouse, a homing device detected the presence of the beeper installed in the crates at Kennedy Airport. The signal came from behind a locked steel door. I requested that Long unlock the door. When I again informed Long of the government's authority to obtain a search warrant, Long obtained a key, and I opened the door.

      6.   At no time did I threaten Long or pressure him in any fashion.

      Wherefore, it is respectfully submitted that the defendant's motion to suppress any and all tangible evidence seized from Superior Warehouse should be denied in all respects.

Ralph Martinez
Ralph Martinez

Sworn to before me this 3rd day of July, 2005

Robert Bogski
Notary Public

UNITED STATES DISTRICT COURT
EASTERN DISTRICT OF NEW YORK
--X
                                     :

UNITED STATES OF AMERICA   :
                                       :

                                     :   No. 05 Cr. 735

            v.   :

                                     :   **MEMORANDUM IN OPPOSITION TO**
                                   :   **OMNIBUS MOTION**

PAUL CHRISTOPHER and   :
WILLIAM VAN NESS,
                                     :

           Defendants.   :
                                     :

--X

MEMORANDUM OF LAW IN OPPOSITION TO DEFENDANT'S OMNIBUS MOTION

                                       Kevin O'Reilly, Esq.
                                         United States Attorney
                                         Eastern District of New York
                                         225 Cadman Plaza East
                                         Brooklyn, NY 11201

                                         By: LAURA KNAPP, ESQ.
                                                 ASST. U.S. ATTORNEY

                                         TO: RICHARD CLARK, ESQ.
                                                 377 Broadway
                                                 New York, NY 10003

PRELIMINARY STATEMENT

Paul Christopher and William Van Ness are jointly charged in a twenty-four count indictment with importing and distributing cocaine and money laundering. Christopher asks this Court to suppress the narcotics and other evidence legally seized from his warehouse and to compel the production of a bill of particulars. Both of those claims should be rejected.

I. THE MOTION TO SUPPRESS MUST BE DENIED

A.   *The Agents' Reliance on Mario Long's Consent Was Reasonable.*

The defense admits, as it must, that third party consent, reasonably relied upon by government agents, meets one of the specific exceptions to the warrant requirement. *Illinois v. Rodriguez,* 497 U.S. 177, 182-83 (1990); *United States v. Matlock,* 415 U.S. 164, 171-72 (1974). They do not contend that Long did not consent, but rather that the DEA agents did not act reasonably when they relied upon a man who identified himself as the foreman of the warehouse when they accepted his consent and searched the warehouse. Under the law, if they acted reasonably, their search was valid.

Rodriguez makes it clear that the inquiry is fact-specific based upon the reasonableness of the agents' action, under the circumstances presented at the time the consent was given. In this case, the agents announced their presence and waited for someone to come to the door. It is reasonable to assume that the person who answers the door at a warehouse has the authority to permit or deny entry.

Mario Long came to the door and identified himself as the foreman of the warehouse. The agents reasonably understood a foreman to have the power to permit entry. In addition, after they advised Long of their identity and purpose, he clearly considered their request and communicated to them that he had considered his position, and having considered it, would permit their entry. The law does not require agents pursuing an active narcotics investigation to engage in a separate detailed investigation of the corporate structure of an organization to determine if the man who answers the door and identifies himself as an employee of the company has authority to let them in. Under all the circumstances, the agents acted reasonably.

B.   *Long's Consent Was Freely Given.*

The voluntariness of an individual's consent to search is a question of fact to be answered by considering all the circumstances of a given incident. *United States v. Puglisi,* 702 F.2d 240, 243 (2d Cir. 1986). In this case, Agent Martinez's explanation that the agents could obtain a warrant is conduct that has been repeatedly accepted by the Second Circuit as noncoercive. *United States v.*

Tutino, 883 F.2d 1125, 1137 (2d Cir. 1989); *United States v. Calvente,* 722 F.2d 1019, 1023 (2d Cir. 1983); *United States v. Faruolo,* 506 F.2d 490, 497 (2d Cir. 1974). It is well-settled that government agents are permitted to explain their legal options to a citizen, and that individual's choice in the face of those options is a free, informed exercise of will. The defendant's characterization of *Faruolo* as distinguishing between a statement that the agents can apply for a warrant and a statement that they believe they will obtain one is simply incorrect; the *Faruolo* Court expressly held that "the well founded advice of a law enforcement agent that, absent a consent to search, a warrant can be obtained does not constitute coercion." *Faruolo,* 506 F.2d at 495. *Faruolo* only requires that the statement be a "fair and sensible appraisal of the realities facing the defendant" based on the totality of the circumstances. *Id.* In this case, not only did Agent Martinez indicate that Long's permission was necessary, which in turn indicates that Long was free to refuse it, but the question of probable cause to satisfy a warrant application was all but foregone in light of the evidence already obtained as of the time Agent Martinez's statement occurred. Such evidence included the discovery at Kennedy Airport of the cocaine inside a shipment of crates addressed to Superior Warehouse, the controlled delivery to Superior Warehouse of the subject crate by an undercover agent posing as a delivery truck driver, and the mere thirty minutes of elapsed time between the controlled delivery and Agent Martinez's statement. That this statement was "well-founded" cannot seriously be disputed.

Moreover, the defendant's reliance on *Bumper v. North Carolina,* 391 U.S. 543, 550 (1968), is similarly misplaced as *Bumper* turns on completely different facts and a wholly separate legal principle. In that case, the police officer lied to the defendant, saying he already had a warrant. Clearly, a defendant does not make a knowing choice when it is based upon false information from the police. *Cf. Calvente,* 722 F.2d at 1023 ("Defendant's argument that it was coercive for [the a]gent [ ] to advise [the defendant] that agents were in the process of obtaining a search warrant for her home is meritless.").

This case involved no false information or misstatement of the legal situation. Although the defense argues that Agent Martinez misrepresented his authority by saying that the government could get a warrant, that statement was an accurate evaluation of the situation because the agents had ample probable cause. Agent Martinez simply explained the legal process to Mario Long and explained to him his options. Long made a free and voluntary choice in the face of those options. Consent is not coerced when it is the product of free will, with knowledge of the government's legitimate options. The suppression motion must be denied.

II.   THE DEFENSE IS NOT ENTITLED TO A BILL OF PARTICULARS
BECAUSE THE INDICTMENT PROVIDES ADEQUATE NOTICE OF
THE CHARGES

The defendant's motion to compel production of a bill of particulars to amplify the notice set forth in Counts One, Two, Eighteen and Nineteen of the Indictment is without merit. The law of this Circuit governing this matter is clear. The function of a bill of particulars is to:

> provide [the] defendant with information about the details of the charge against him if this is necessary to the preparation of his defense, and to avoid prejudicial surprise at the trial. . . . A bill of particulars should be required only where the charges of the indictment are so general that they do not advise the defendant of the specific acts of which he is accused. . . . Whether to grant a bill of particulars rests within the sound discretion of the district court. . . . Acquisition of evidentiary detail is not the function of the bill of particulars. . . . So long as the defendant was adequately informed of the charges against him and was not unfairly surprised at trial as a consequence of the denial of the bill of particulars, the trial court has not abused its discretion.

United States v. Torres, 901 F.2d 205, 234 (2d Cir. 1990) (citations omitted; internal quotations omitted). Furthermore, according to the Second Circuit:

> an indictment is adequate so long as it contains the elements of the offense, sufficiently apprises the defendant of what he must be prepared to meet, and is detailed enough to assure against double jeopardy. . . . Under this test we have consistently sustained indictments which track the language of a statute and, in addition, do little more than state time and place in approximate terms.

United States v. Salazar, 485 F.2d 1272, 1277 (2d Cir. 1973) (citations omitted).

In essence, the defendant is asking the government to identify with particularity the overt acts in furtherance of the conspiracies charged in the Indictment that the government intends to prove at trial. It is well-settled, however, that "there is no general requirement that the government disclose in a bill of particulars all the overt acts it will prove in establishing a conspiracy charge." *United States v. Carroll*, 510 F.2d 507, 509 (2d Cir. 1975); *accord United States v. Anton*, No. 99 Cr. 1019, 2000 WL 134328, at *3 (S.D.N.Y. Feb. 3, 2000).

Moreover, regarding both the conspiracies and the substantive offenses, the information contained in the Indictment, especially when taken with the discovery supplied to the defense, presents a situation in which "the type of conduct [charged in the Indictment] is sufficiently concrete and particular as to permit a reasonably focused investigation." *See United States v. Sattar*, 272 F. Supp. 2d 348, 369 (S.D.N.Y. 2003) (citation omitted; internal quotations omitted); *accord United States v. Bortnovsky*, 820 F.2d 572, 574 (2d Cir. 1987) (explaining the purpose of a bill of particulars is "to identify with sufficient particularity the nature of the charge pending against him, thereby enabling defendant to prepare for trial, to prevent surprise, and to interpose a plea of double jeopardy should he be prosecuted a second time for the same offense"). Based on the Indictment and discovery already provided, the defendant knows what offenses are alleged, most of the other individuals who participated, the location of the narcotics deliveries and the names of certain financial institutions conducting the criminal monetary transactions, the general time frame for these events, and the general amount of narcotics involved. This information certainly permits a "reasonably focused investigation."

It is not the proper function of a bill of particulars to serve as an investigative tool for discovering the government's evidence in advance of trial. *See Torres*, 901 F.2d at 234; *United States v. Patterson*, No. 02 Cr. 283, 2002 WL 31890950, at *9-10 (S.D.N.Y. Dec. 27, 2002). A bill of particulars in this case would be just that, given the ample notice of the charges and underlying activities otherwise available to the defendant through the Indictment and proper discovery.

III. CONCLUSION

For the foregoing reasons, the defendant's omnibus motion should be denied in its entirety.

Respectfully submitted,
Kevin O'Reilly
United States Attorney for the Eastern
District of New York

By: *Laura Knapp*
Laura Knapp
Assistant U.S. Attorney
225 Cadman Pl. East
Brooklyn, NY 11201
(718) 330–2118

---

§ 14.7   Hearings on Pretrial Motions—Introduction[32]

Where there is a mixed question of law and fact in a pretrial motion, the relief requested will always include a request for a hearing to resolve the factual issue. Whether a hearing will be granted depends upon several factors. First, the movant will have to meet the burden of going forward, i.e., make out a *prima facie* case on the moving papers. Failure to make such a showing will result in summary denial of the motion. Second, the respondent must dispute some or all of the facts asserted. If the respondent does not do so, the facts will be deemed to have been established, and therefore no hearing will be required.[33]

Assuming that a factual dispute is properly framed, a hearing will be held. It can be viewed as a type of trial, with the issue not being the guilt

---

32. *See generally supra* Chapter 3; Fed. R. Crim. P. 12; Wright, § 194; Marilyn J. Berger, John B. Mitchell, & Ronald H. Clark, Pretrial Advocacy 261–311 (1988).

33. *See* United States v. Chavez-Marquez, 66 F.3d 259, 261 (10th Cir. 1995);

United States v. Pedroni, 958 F.2d 262, 267 (9th Cir. 1992); LaFave, Search § 11.2(d) & n.128.

or innocence of the defendant, but rather a preliminary issue, such as the admissibility or suppression of a piece of evidence.

§ 14.8 Commencing the Hearing—The Burden of Proof

§ 14.8(a) The Burden of Going Forward

Meeting the burden of going forward in the moving papers only permits the movant to reach the hearing stage. At the hearing, the movant still bears the burden of persuasion.[34] The factual allegations in the affidavit or declaration can be viewed as having the same relation to the hearing as the complaint has to the preliminary examination or the indictment to the trial: neither can be relied upon at the later stage, at which the party with the burden must meet it anew through testimony elicited under oath.[35]

§ 14.8(b) The Burden of Persuasion

Courts have propounded different theories as to who should bear the burden of persuasion on issues litigated in pretrial hearings. We will not attempt here to indicate how the burden is allocated on all pretrial issues, but we can offer the following guidelines.

The general rule is that the movant—usually the defendant—bears the entire burden of proof, i.e. the burden of persuasion as well as the burden of going forward.[36] Whether this is justified on the grounds that the movant usually has the relevant information or is seeking a change in his or her legal status or that there is a "presumption of regularity" of judicially approved governmental action, most issues of burden allocation are resolved this way.

There are, however, certain instances when the burden shifts to the government after the defendant has met the burden of going forward. The most important of these are motions to suppress statements allegedly taken in violation of the *Miranda* rule and motions to suppress illegally seized evidence. In the former situation, if a defendant establishes that he or she has been subject to custodial interrogation, made a statement and asserts that the *Miranda* warnings were not given and/or the rights accorded the defendant not waived, the burden of persuasion shifts to the government to prove that the warnings were given and adequately waived.[37] In the Fourth Amendment context, if a defendant establishes that a place in which he or she has a legitimate expectation of privacy was searched without a warrant (and the government con-

---

34. A court is not required, as a matter of law, to hold an evidentiary hearing unless the movant's affidavit contains sufficient factual allegation, which, if proven, would require granting of the relief requested. Wright, § 675. *See, e.g. Chavez–Marquez*, 66 F.3d at 261; *Pedroni*, 958 F.2d at 262.

35. Subject to the approval of the parties and the court, it may be appropriate to

meet this burden, at least in part, by stipulation or proffer. *See supra* § 3.2(c).

36. *See* LaFave, Search § 11.2(b).

37. North Carolina v. Butler, 441 U.S. 369, 372–73 (1979); Miranda v. Arizona, 384 U.S. 436, 475 (1966). *See* LaFave et al., § 10.3(c).

cedes that fact), the burden of persuasion shifts to the government to justify the search as falling within one of the exceptions to the warrant requirement.[38]

§ 14.8(c) The Qualitative Burden

In order to meet the qualitative burden at a hearing, live witness testimony subject to cross-examination is usually required. The rules of evidence do not apply at such hearings, however, and therefore hearsay testimony is admissible, as it is at the preliminary hearing.[39]

While live witness testimony is the rule at pretrial hearings, in certain circumstances, witnesses may not be required to appear, with the burden of proof being met by proffer. A proffer may be permitted, for example, in situations in which a defendant seeking discovery must establish the materiality of some potential evidence—for example, if the defendant is making a *Brady* request, he or she must show how the document is material to some theory of defense.[40] Rather than being required to call witnesses to demonstrate materiality, the attorney will be permitted simply to explain how the information sought is material to the defense theory. Similarly, while the defendant has a right to subpoena witnesses at a pretrial hearing,[41] it is not as broad as that at trial, and a preliminary showing of relevance—also by proffer—may be required.[42]

§ 14.8(d) The Quantitative Burden

As to the quantitative burden, with one exception, due process requirements are satisfied at the pretrial stage by proof by a preponderance of the credible evidence.[43] A preponderance is generally defined in terms of the comparative weight of the credible evidence adduced by the two sides.[44]

§ 14.9 Examination of Witnesses—Tactical Considerations

The techniques for examination of witnesses at a hearing depend upon its goals. In some cases, the hearing is used more as an opportunity

---

38. *See* LaFave et al., § 10.3(b).

39. United States v. Matlock, 415 U.S. 164, 172–73 (1974). *See* Fed. R. Crim. P. 5.1(e), 41; Wright, § 675.

40. Fed. R. Crim. P. 16(a)(1)(E). *See supra* Chapter 13; Wright, § 254.

41. *See* Fed. R. Crim. P. 17; Wright, § 271 n.9.

42. This might occur, for example, if the defendant were challenging the veracity of an affidavit in support of a search warrant, and wanted to call the source of an agent's information. After an appropriate proffer, the defendant will be permitted to satisfy the burden of going forward by subpoenaing a witness who was the source of the police officer's allegations. The proffer would indicate that the witness would contradict the officer's allegations regarding the information claimed to have been provided by the witness. *See, e.g.,* United States v. Bowe, 698 F.2d 560, 564–65 (2d Cir. 1983).

43. Lego v. Twomey, 404 U.S. 477, 488–89 (1972). *See* LaFave et al., § 10.4(b). There is only one pretrial motion issue on which a higher burden of persuasion is required: the waiver of the right to counsel at a lineup. In *United States v. Wade,* 388 U.S. 218, 250–51 (1967), the Court said that such a waiver must be shown by clear and convincing evidence. *See* LaFave et al., § 10.4(d).

44. *See supra* § 3.1(a)(2).

for discovery of evidence useful for trial than it is to prove facts already known to the defense attorney.[45] In that situation, direct and cross-examination will be similar to that found at the preliminary examination: the direct examination by the prosecutor will be as limited in scope as possible, and the cross-examination will be conducted along the lines of a thorough direct examination, designed to elicit testimony from the witness rather than to lead the witness to the lawyer's conclusions.[46]

In other cases, the attorney will be at least as interested in winning the argument as in using the hearing to obtain information for use at trial. If information obtained in witness interviews or formal discovery reveals police misconduct, for example, the cross-examination will be a hybrid of that conducted at trial—using leading questions to develop a theory of suppression, while using open questions to discover additional facts. Thus in the Christopher case, for example, the defense attorney would, prior to the cross-examination of Agent Martinez, be in possession of the minutes of his preliminary hearing testimony, his grand jury testimony, and police reports prepared by him, insofar as they referred to the entry and search of Superior Warehouse.[47] If the attorney had also interviewed Mario Long, he would be in a good position to develop the theory advanced in his moving papers, i.e., that the search was a product of Long's "submission to authority" and lack of consent.[48] If Agent Martinez were to deny having told Long that the search was inevitable with or without his consent, the prior written and recorded statements and Long's testimony would serve to impeach the agent. As a result, cross-examination in the Christopher pretrial motion hearing will more likely resemble trial cross-examination in terms of the form of questions used than discovery cross at a preliminary examination: its principal purpose will be to further the cross-examiner's theory of suppression.[49]

The defense typically will not call the defendant at a suppression hearing, unless required to do so in order to satisfy the burden of going forward. Even in these circumstances, however, if a witness like Mario Long is available by subpoena to contradict the testimony offered by the government's witness, he or she may be called rather than the defendant.

The overall tone of a pretrial hearing usually will be less formal than one would find at a trial. The attorneys are less concerned with the appearance that they are conveying than they would be if a jury were present. In addition, there is not the same concern with committing prejudicial error in the examination of witnesses. Finally, with the trier of fact typically experienced in dealing with the issues involved, familiar with the facts in contention through the papers, and interested in a

45. *See supra* § 14.4.

46. See the discussion of discovery cross-examination *supra* at § 3.3(f).

47. *See* Fed. R. Crim. P. 26.2, discussed *supra* in § 13.4(b).

48. *See supra* § 2.2.

49. For an illustration of that type of cross-examination, see *supra* § 6.3(b).

prompt determination, the hearing typically will be conducted in a more expeditious manner than a jury trial.

§ 14.10　Final Argument

The hearing often concludes with closing argument by the parties. However, unlike at trial, the judge is not obligated to permit argument and may end the hearing when the parties rest. Because of this possibility, and because the court will be more likely to base its legal analysis on the parties' memoranda of law than on their oral arguments, special care should be taken in the preparation of that document.

The attorneys should, of course, be prepared to make their legal arguments orally. In doing so, they should again keep in mind that the fact-finder is a judge and not a jury, and that the judge will likely be less impressed with linguistic style than with an argument that cogently analyzes the facts and applies them to the applicable law. Making a convincing showing as to what facts the judge should find is, at times, even more important than persuading the judge on the applicable legal standard. A mistake by the court on that matter can be corrected on appeal. An adverse conclusion by the court as to the facts is likely to be fatal, since appellate courts will rarely second guess findings of facts by the trier of those facts.

Following the arguments, the judge may decide the case from the bench. When the law or the application of the law to the particular facts of the case is in dispute, however, the judge will often reserve decision until the submission of posthearing memoranda by the parties.[50]

§ 14.11　The Christopher Hearing

On July 20, 2005, the parties appeared before Judge Sheridan for a hearing on the omnibus motions. The judge began with the motion for bill of particulars because it involved only a question of law and no factual disputes and therefore required no hearing. He denied the motion, agreeing with the government that the defense had sufficient notice.

The hearing then moved to the suppression issue, and the judge ruled that testimony would be required to determine whether the consent exception to the warrant requirement would be applied. He stated that since the government had not disputed either Christopher's assertion of ownership of the warehouse or that the DEA entry had been warrantless, Christopher had met his burden of going forward in establishing a privacy interest and a facial violation of the Constitution. Therefore, he concluded, the testimony should deal exclusively with the issue of consent, on which the burden of persuasion would fall on the government.

---

50. *See* FED. R. CRIM. P. 12(d); WRIGHT, § 194. Sometimes, though, the court may defer decision until the trial. *See* FED. R. CRIM. P. 12 (d); WRIGHT, § 194.

AUSA Knapp then called Agent Ralph Martinez to the stand. Martinez testified about the discovery of the cocaine at Kennedy Airport, the controlled delivery to the warehouse, and his arrival there with the other agents. The following testimony relates to the consent issue, and illustrates the form of direct examination at a motion to suppress. The reader will note the use of closed questions to direct the witness to the issues in dispute, followed by open questions that permit the witness to elaborate on his answers.

AUSA Knapp:	Agent Martinez, directing your attention to approximately 2 p.m. on the afternoon of January 12, 2005, tell the judge where you were and what you did at that time?
Martinez:	I was with Special Agents Richards and Foster in a van across from the Superior Warehouse. At that time we left the van and proceeded to the warehouse.
Knapp:	Agent, what was the first thing that you did when you arrived at the warehouse?
Martinez:	We knocked at the office door, and a person wearing overalls with the name "Mario" on them opened it. I asked that person if the foreman or manager was present. He said that he was the foreman and he asked us what we wanted.
Knapp:	And what did you say?
Martinez:	I told him that we were agents of the Drug Enforcement Administration, and that we were investigating the importation and distribution of cocaine at Superior Warehouse. I told him that we had reason to believe that cocaine was present in the warehouse and we wanted his permission to enter and search it.
Knapp:	And how did he respond?
Martinez:	He said that he was uncertain what to do because the manager was not present.
Knapp:	Did he mention the name of the manager?
Martinez:	Yes, he said that the manager's name was Gil.
Knapp:	What did you say after the foreman said that he was uncertain whether to let you in?

Martinez:	I told him that the decision was up to him, but that we would have to secure the warehouse anyway to see that nothing was destroyed, and that we also would obtain a search warrant authorizing us to conduct a search.
Knapp:	And what did the foreman say to that?
Martinez:	He hesitated for a moment, and then said something to the effect that he didn't want to have any trouble with the authorities, and that he would permit us to enter and search.

The balance of the direct examination sought to elicit testimony concerning the events occurring inside the warehouse, using the same mix of closed and open questions. Martinez testified that once he was inside the warehouse, he used the homing device that had been installed in the crate containing cocaine at Kennedy Airport to detect the presence of the container. Martinez said that the beeper indicated that the crate was behind a locked steel door and that he asked Long to unlock the door. Long again said he was not sure that he should open the door and that he thought he should wait for Gil. The agent said that he again advised Long that the warehouse would be secured while the agents obtained a warrant to enter and search the area behind the locked door. He said Long then obtained a key and gave it to him to open the door and that the crate containing the beeper and the cocaine was then found. After Martinez testified that he opened the crate and confirmed the contents, the direct examination ended.

Richard Clark then cross-examined Agent Martinez. Using leading questions typical of trial cross-examination,[51] Clark attempted to develop Christopher's theory of suppression, i.e., that Long's consent was involuntary and that, in any event, he lacked the necessary authority, either actual or apparent, to permit the agent to enter and search the premises.

Clark:	Now, Agent Martinez, you testified on direct examination that on January 12, 2005 at about 2 p.m. you approached someone who identified himself as the foreman of the warehouse. Is that correct?
Martinez:	Yes.
Clark:	You had never met this person before, is that right?

---

51. *See supra* § 3.3(f). *See, e.g., infra* § 16.5(g).

Martinez: Yes.

Clark: And although you had been in radio contact with Agent Sobel after he delivered the crates to the warehouse, all that you knew leading up to your arrival was that the delivery had occurred and that the crates had been taken into the warehouse?

Martinez: Yes. And we also knew that Sobel had already left the premises.

Clark: You hadn't read Sobel's report providing a description of the person who signed for the crates, had you?

Martinez: No, we didn't have his report at that time, but we did know that someone by the name of Mario had signed for the crates.

Clark: Now you assumed that the person you spoke to when you arrived was the same person who had signed for the crates?

Martinez: Yes, because he had the name Mario on his overalls.

Clark: This person told you, after you identified yourself, that he was the foreman of the warehouse?

Martinez: Yes.

Clark: You didn't ask him, did you, whether his authority extended to permitting people, other than authorized personnel, to enter Superior Warehouse?

Martinez: No. I accepted his statement that he was the foreman.

Clark: And after you requested permission to search, this person told you that that he had been instructed to first obtain permission from the manager of the warehouse, Gil, before letting anyone other than authorized personnel enter?

Martinez: Well he said that he was unsure what to do because as I understood it, he was supposed to consult with Gil.

Clark: He didn't tell you that if Gil wasn't around he had the authority to decide what to do in a situation such as this, did he?

Martinez: No. He simply said that he was unsure.

Clark:	You then immediately responded in an effort to eliminate his uncertainty, didn't you?
Martinez:	I don't know what you mean.
Clark:	Well, the next thing you told him was that you would get a warrant and search the premises anyway, so that he might as well consent.
Martinez:	I didn't tell him he might as well consent, I just told him we'd get a warrant.
Clark:	You also told him that pending getting the warrant, you'd enter and secure the premises anyway to ensure that nothing was destroyed, didn't you?
Martinez:	Well, I don't know if I used the word enter, but I did say we would secure the premises against destruction of evidence.
Clark:	You never told the foreman, did you, that your authority to obtain a search warrant would depend on a magistrate's review of what you knew about Superior Warehouse, did you?
Martinez:	No, I didn't say what the process was.
Clark:	And the reason you told him about getting a warrant was to persuade him to consent to your searching the building, right?
Martinez:	That is correct.
Clark:	And after you told the foreman that you'd get a search warrant and meanwhile secure the premises, he said okay, or words to that effect; that he didn't wish to have any trouble with the DEA, isn't that right?
Martinez:	He said he didn't want to have any trouble with the authorities, and so he agreed that we could enter and search.
Clark:	Well, when you say he agreed, he didn't use the word "agree" did he?
Martinez:	I don't believe that was his word.
Clark:	He said that to avoid any trouble he would let you enter and search, isn't that right?
Martinez:	In substance yes.

In the balance of the cross-examination, Clark questioned Martinez, regarding the physical security measures at the warehouse. He had Martinez confirm that there were "no trespassing" signs posted and that there were exterior and interior locks in the second security area to which Long provided the key. Those questions were designed to suggest that the agents acted unreasonably, given the concern over the heightened expectation of privacy suggested by the physical setting. He then developed the final exchanges between Martinez and Long to highlight Martinez's "assurances" to Long that the agents would obtain a warrant and forcefully search behind the locked door if Long did not consent.

The government had no redirect of Agent Martinez and he was excused. The government then rested.

Clark then called Mario Long, whom he had served with a subpoena. Knapp objected to the defendant calling a potential trial witness for the government at a pretrial hearing. She argued that the examination was solely for the purpose of discovery and not relevant to the suppression issue. Clark responded by proffering the testimony he hoped to elicit from Long. Clark stated that Long's testimony would be limited to the events about which Martinez testified in which he was involved. Judge Sheridan ruled that Long's testimony was sufficiently material to the consent issue and permitted the defense to call him. Long then testified that he had been told by Christopher and Santiago not to permit anyone into the warehouse without their prior approval. He further testified that he chose to disregard this instruction when Martinez informed him that the agents would secure the premises and obtain a search warrant if he failed to cooperate. On cross-examination Knapp established the fact that Long's decision was a judgment call he made as foreman and was based upon his desire not to obstruct the DEA agents. Following Long's testimony, the defense rested.

Clark and Knapp both made legal arguments, analyzed the facts developed at the hearing, and sought to apply those facts to the law governing allegedly consensual searches. Following the argument, Judge Sheridan deferred ruling on the motion and requested posthearing memoranda concerning the actual or apparent authority of Mario Long to authorize a search of Superior Warehouse.[52] The judge said he thought the parties' original memoranda adequately briefed the issue of coercion, but that if the parties believed that the testimony at the hearing added something on this issue, they could address that in their supplemental memoranda as well.

On August 1, 2005, Judge Sheridan issued a written opinion denying the suppression motion. He ruled that under all the circumstances, the

---

52. *See* Illinois v. Rodriguez, 497 U.S. 177, 188–89 (1990); LaFave et al., § 3.10(d).

agents acted reasonably in relying on the permission of the foreman to enter and search the warehouse.

§ 14.12   Appeal From an Adverse Determination[53]

In general, a defendant may not take an interlocutory appeal from an adverse determination of a pretrial motion.[54] Such a ruling does not constitute a final judgment, and an appeal would interrupt the normal progress of a criminal case prior to completion, without any certainty that the error being appealed would contribute to an unjust result.[55]

The government's right to an immediate appeal from an adverse determination of a pretrial motion is not similarly limited.[56] The government is permitted to appeal any decision, judgment, or order of a district court dismissing an indictment or information as to any one or more counts, except when the double jeopardy clause would preclude further prosecution.[57] Government appeals also are permitted from pretrial motions suppressing or excluding evidence, so long as the decision on the motion is rendered prior to the commencement of the trial, i.e., before jeopardy has "attached."[58]

§ 14.13   Setting a Trial Date—Time Limitations[59]

The Sixth Amendment guarantees that "[i]n all criminal prosecutions, the accused shall enjoy the right to a speedy and public trial...."[60] Its focus is on the harm caused by pretrial detention or restraint and related disruptions resulting from outstanding criminal charges. The Sixth Amendment requires that an indictment be dismissed only if the delay is deemed excessive and unnecessary, and courts balance the length of the delay, the reasons for the delay, and the prejudice to the defendant when deciding motions to dismiss on this basis.[61] While impermissible delay requires dismissal of the indictment, courts have set an extremely high standard for a defendant to meet to obtain this relief.[62]

---

53. *See* Wright, §§ 195, 678.

54. 28 U.S.C. § 1291; DiBella v. United States, 369 U.S. 121, 129–132 (1962). *See* LaFave, Search § 11.7(a). An exception to this rule is found in the Bail Reform Act of 1984, 18 U.S.C. §§ 3141 *et seq.*, which permits an interlocutory appeal of a denial of pretrial release. *See* 18 U.S.C. § 3145(c).

55. An exception to this rule exists to enable the defendant to appeal a denial of a motion to dismiss based on double jeopardy grounds without having first to submit to a trial of the general issue. *See* Abney v. United States, 431 U.S. 651, 661–62 (1977).

56. 18 U.S.C. § 3731. *See* LaFave, Search § 11.7(b).

57. § 3731.

58. *Id.* In a jury trial, jeopardy attaches when the full jury is empanelled and sworn. *See* Downum v. United States, 372 U.S. 734, 737 (1963). In a bench trial, jeopardy attaches when the court begins to hear evidence. *See* Serfass v. United States, 420 U.S. 377, 388 (1975).

59. LaFave et al., §§ 18.1–18.4.

60. U.S. const. amend. VI; *see* Smith v. Hooey, 393 U.S. 374, 377–378 (1969).

61. *See* Barker v. Wingo, 407 U.S. 514, 530–33 (1972).

62. Strunk v. United States, 412 U.S. 434, 440 (1973) (rejecting credit for time served as remedy for undue delay and reaffirming dismissal as the "only possible remedy"). Additionally as to waiver, the

Relief from delay also can be obtained under the Speedy Trial Act of 1974.[63] It establishes outer time limits for key stages of a criminal prosecution—including indictment and trial—and provides for exclusions of time on various grounds. Violation of any of these provisions provides a basis for dismissal on motion by the defense.[64] Also, Rule 48(b) of the Federal Rules of Criminal Procedure grants the district court some discretion to dismiss an indictment for "unnecessary delay."[65]

On the day Judge Sheridan announced his opinion on the pretrial motions, he also discussed with counsel setting a trial date in compliance with the Speedy Trial Act, which requires a trial to begin not more than 70 days from indictment or from the date of the defendant's initial appearance, whichever comes first, after certain periods are excluded.[66] One such excluded period is the time between the filing of pretrial motions and the conclusion of the hearing or other disposition.[67] Another is any period up to 30 days in which the court had a pretrial motion under advisement.[68]

The Christopher indictment was returned on April 25, 2005 and the decision on the motions filed on August 1, for an elapsed time of 98 days. From that period, the time between the filing of the omnibus motion on June 23, and the conclusion of the hearing on July 20, a total of 27 days, would be subtracted. An additional 12 days would be excluded for the period between the conclusion of the hearing and Judge Sheridan's decision on the motion to suppress on August 1. Hence a total of 39 days would be subtracted, making the relevant elapsed time under the statute 59 days as of the court's August 1 ruling on the omnibus motion. To comply with the statute, the judge would have to have set the trial no later than 11 days after his decision. However, another provision of the Speedy Trial Act permits the court to exclude time if it determines that "the ends of justice served by taking such action outweigh the best interest of the public and the defendant in a speedy trial."[69] This provision regularly applies to account for time elapsed during negotiations, discovery proceedings, and trial preparation so that if both parties consent, the judge can set a trial date that gives both sides sufficient time to prepare.

Supreme Court has held: "We reject, therefore, the rule that a defendant who fails to demand a speedy trial forever waives his right. This does not mean, however, that the defendant has no responsibility to assert his right. We think the better rule is that the defendant's assertion of or failure to assert his right to a speedy trial is one of the factors to be considered in an inquiry into the deprivation of the right." *Barker*, 407 U.S. at 528.

63. 18 U.S.C. §§ 3161 *et seq.*

64. 18 U.S.C. § 3162(a)(2). Dismissal can be with or without prejudice depending on the circumstances and the interests of justice. *Id.* Failure to make a motion prior to trial or entry of a plea constitutes waiver. *Id.*

65. Fed. R. Crim. P. 48(b).

66. § 3161(c)(1).

67. § 3161(h)(1)(F).

68. § 3161(h)(1)(J).

69. § 3161(h)(8)(A).

Since it was clear in the Christopher case that neither the judge nor the attorneys would be ready and adequately prepared for trial within the allotted time period, all agreed on a trial date of September 12, 2005. The defense attorneys waived any objection to excluding the time up to that date and Judge Sheridan entered an order finding the exclusion served the "ends of justice".[70]

70. *Id.*

Chapter 15

PREPARATION FOR TRIAL

Table of Sections

Sec.
15.0 Introduction.
15.1 Constructing a Trial Theory.
  15.1(a) The Burden of Proof at Trial.
  15.1(b) Trial Theories.
15.2 Articulating the Trial Theory—Formulating the Closing Argument.
15.3 Proving the Trial Theory—Marshalling the Evidence.
15.4 Addressing Legal Issues Prior to Trial.
  15.4(a) *In Limine* Motions.
  15.4(b) Proposed Voir Dire Questions.
  15.4(c) Requests to Charge.
15.5 Preparation of Evidence for Use at Trial.
  15.5(a) Witness Preparation.
  15.5(b) Preparation of Tangible Evidence and Exhibits.
  15.5(c) Preparation of Stipulations.
15.6 United States v. Christopher—Preparation for Trial by the Prosecution and Defense.
  15.6(a) Trial Theories.
  15.6(b) Proving the Trial Theory—Marshalling the Evidence.
  15.6(c) Addressing Legal Issues Prior to Trial.
  15.6(d) Preparation of Tangible Evidence, Exhibits and Stipulations.

§ 15.0 Introduction

In our illustrative case, successful plea negotiations do not appear to be likely. The government believes it has a strong case against Christopher, who it believes is the most culpable of all of those involved, and the government has not received any indication that Christopher can provide information that will be useful in prosecuting those who imported the narcotics. For his part, Christopher has maintained his innocence and is facing such a long prison sentence that he believes it worth the risk of trial. Van Ness also has denied any involvement in the charged criminal activity and believes the government's case against him is somewhat weaker, which has further persuaded him to take the risk of trial as well.

A trial, therefore, appears inevitable, and in this chapter we will describe the many steps that must be taken to prepare for it. We will first discuss pretrial preparation in general and then describe how the attorneys prepared for trial in the Christopher case.

§ 15.1 Constructing a Trial Theory

With the completion of pretrial motions, both parties should finalize their theories as to how the case will be tried. The prosecution's evidence typically will be complete and the government will usually know at least the general outlines of the defendant's likely position. The defense still may be unsure about precisely what the government's witnesses will say, but will have a fairly clear idea of their identity and the thrust of their testimony. While events at trial may cause either party—and particularly the defense—to adjust its theory, in most cases the positions both parties adopt at trial will be those decided upon well before the trial begins. We will describe here the types of trial theories that may be presented. First, however, we will discuss the burden of proof at trial because it is applicable to all these theories.

§ 15.1(a) The Burden of Proof at Trial

While the criminal trial may be popularly characterized as a "search for truth," it is more precisely a contest over whether the prosecution has proven beyond a reasonable doubt all of the elements of the crimes charged. Putting exhortations of juries by attorneys to the side, a trial is not about abstract notions of moral "guilt" or "innocence," but rather about the more mundane issue of applying rules governing how to admit, present, test, and weigh evidence in order to resolve whether the government has met its burden of proof.

Proof at trial, as at any other hearing, requires that both the burden of going forward and the burden of persuasion be met. To meet the former burden at trial, sufficient evidence must be adduced by the government to make out a *prima facie* case, i.e., one in which a rational trier of fact, considering the evidence in the light most favorable to the government, *could* find guilt beyond a reasonable doubt.[1] Failure to do so will result in the entry of a judgment of acquittal by the court.[2] If the burden of going forward is met, the government will then have the burden of persuading a unanimous jury[3] (or a judge if the jury is waived)[4] that it *has* proven every element beyond a reasonable doubt.[5]

---

1. Jackson v. Virginia, 443 U.S. 307, 318–19 (1979).

2. Fed. R. Crim. P. 29; Wright, § 462.

3. Federal law requires a unanimous verdict of guilt. *See* Fed. R. Crim. P. 31(a); Wright, § 511.

4. Fed. R. Crim. P. 23(a).

5. We have defined the standard in terms of probability. *See supra* § 3.1(a). Reasonable doubt also has been defined in a variety of other ways, such as: a doubt based upon reason and common sense, the

The defense bears no burden with respect to proof of any element of a criminal statute.[6] Moreover, while the prosecution must prove every element contained in the statute beyond a reasonable doubt, in most cases the defense usually will either focus on demonstrating such doubt as to a single element, or in effect concede that the government may have proven beyond a reasonable doubt that the crime was committed but not that the defendant committed it.[7] In either case, the defense may choose to suggest to the trier of fact its explanation of what happened, but this will be done as a means of demonstrating that the government has not sustained *its* burden of proof rather than as an assumption of that burden by the defense.

§ 15.1(b) Trial Theories

The government's "general" trial theory is always that the defendant did the proscribed acts with the requisite intent. Its specific theory in a given case will relate to its arguments of how the evidence proves its general theory, including contextual arguments that do not necessarily relate to a specific element that must be proven, such as the defendant's motive or opportunity to commit the crime.

A further note is in order about the role of motive. As a matter of law, the government never has to prove *why* a person committed criminal acts, but only that he *did* so with the requisite *mens rea*. What drove the person to do it is irrelevant, unless it constitutes a defense recognized by law. At the same time, in most situations the parties will attempt to adduce evidence about the defendant's motive because it bears directly on the defendant's intent. If the government is not able to offer a credible explanation for why the defendant may have committed the crime, or if the defendant is able to show that he or she had no such motive, a jury may be more inclined to find that the government's theory of prosecution is lacking and determine that there is reasonable doubt as to one or more of the elements that the government must prove.

We believe that it is possible to group all available trial theories into the following three categories:

1. "Pure" Reasonable Doubt. As we have just noted, the government has the burden of proving each essential element of a statute

---

kind of doubt that would make a reasonable person hesitate to act on an important matter; or proof of such a convincing character that a reasonable person would not hesitate to rely upon it in the most important of his or her affairs. 1A KEVIN F. O'MALLEY ET AL., FEDERAL JURY PRACTICE AND INSTRUCTIONS § 12.10 (5th ed. 2000 & Supp. 2004); 1 LEONARD B. SAND ET AL., MODERN FEDERAL JURY INSTRUCTIONS § 4.01, Instruction 4–2 (2005).

6. *See* In re Winship, 397 U.S. 358, 362–63 (1970). There are, however, certain "defenses" for which the defendant bears a burden of going forward, e.g., self-defense, *see* United States v. Perry, 223 F.3d 431, 433 (7th Cir. 2000), and "affirmative defenses" for which he or she also bears the burden of persuasion, e.g., the insanity defense, *see* 18 U.S.C. § 17(b).

7. *See supra* § 3.1(a).

beyond a reasonable doubt, and in every criminal case the ultimate question posed to the trier of fact will be whether that burden has been met. By the term "pure" reasonable doubt, however, we mean to suggest a more specific theory about the adequacy of the government's proof. As we use the term, it applies to a defense focusing solely on the strength of the government's case, without offering any kind of alternative explanation of the facts.

2. Conflicting Evidence. In this instance, the defense offers its own evidence to negate the government's proof of one or more of the essential elements. While the ultimate question will remain whether the conflicting evidence is sufficient to raise a reasonable doubt, the approach to raising such a doubt is different than that described in the "pure" reasonable doubt case. In fact, the defense may implicitly concede that the evidence adduced by the government would be sufficient if not countered by different facts or an alternative explanation for the facts offered by the government. Examples include cases in which a defendant offers alibi witnesses or other witnesses who describe events in question differently than those testifying for the government and cases in which the defendant testifies in order to demonstrate that his *mens rea* was different than that alleged by the government.

3. Justification or Excuse. Federal statutory and common law provide various specific defenses to charges of crimes, most categorized as either justifications or excuses.

Justification defenses are those in which the defendant concedes having done the acts enumerated in the statute, with the requisite intent, but argues that some higher good recognized by the law was served by so doing.[8] Self-defense and defense of others are the most common examples of these defenses, which also include enforcing the law and necessity.[9]

Excuse defenses can best be understood as specific qualifications of the general principle of *mens rea,* i.e., that all persons have the capacity to choose, and are responsible for choosing, to do that which is prohibited by law.[10] The most commonly offered excuses are insanity[11] and duress.[12]

§ 15.2 Articulating the Trial Theory—Formulating the Closing Argument

Once the trial theory is formulated, the next step in trial preparation is for the attorney to think through how to persuade the jury during

---

8. Wayne R. LaFave & Austin M. Scott, Jr., Substantive Criminal Law §§ 9.4–9.10 (2d ed. 1986 & Supp. 2003).

9. The entrapment defense, by which the defense argues that the defendant committed the proscribed act only because he or she was induced to do so by the government, is related to justification defenses in the sense that the defendant's culpability is outweighed by society's interest in supporting some greater good, here, deterring police misconduct. LaFave & Scott, *supra* note 8, § 9.8.

10. *Id.,* § 9.1–9.3.

11. *Id.,* § 9.1.

12. *Id.,* § 9.3.

closing argument to find in favor of his or her side. This should occur early on in trial preparation because knowing what the attorney will want to argue in the closing will help to ensure that he or she will elicit the evidence needed to support the argument since the attorney will only be permitted to base an argument on facts, and inferences drawn from those facts, which have been adduced at trial. It is therefore crucial for the attorney to focus attention on this goal: the decision about which witnesses to present and how witnesses will be cross-examined must be informed by the attorney's view of what needs to be proven and how that proof can be elicited in the most compelling manner.

Our emphasis on planning the closing argument early is not meant to suggest that one should actually write it out, word for word, or that one needs at this stage to practice delivering it.[13] Rather, the concept of the argument should be framed: what are the issues in dispute; what facts will each witness establish or fail to establish; and how will the various pieces of testimony support the attorney's trial theory. Moreover, attorneys should keep in mind that while they may be aware of every factual and legal nuance in the case, and may be persuaded of the correctness of their position, the jury is at the outset of the case completely ignorant of the evidence and uncommitted to either side. The attorney therefore should consider how to respond to the questions that the jury is likely to have as the evidence is being presented as well as at the conclusion of the case:

— What is the significance of the testimony of various witnesses with respect to the theory of the party, and what inferences should be drawn from it?

— Why should the witness be believed or disbelieved?

— How can the flaws in the theory of each side—and without question there will be flaws—be explained?

§ 15.3   Proving the Trial Theory—Marshalling the Evidence

After determining the facts that need to be proven, the lawyer must turn to the question of how to elicit or confront this proof during the course of the trial. What competent witnesses—i.e., those with personal knowledge of the facts—are available to testify? What are their strengths and weaknesses? What tangible evidence is available, and how must it be introduced?

In considering all of these questions, the attorney will have to confront the rules of evidence governing a wide variety of issues, including: hearsay rules;[14] rules relating to authenticating tangible evidence;[15] rules governing expert testimony;[16] and rules regarding impeach-

---

13. Techniques for delivering the closing argument are discussed *infra* at § 16.11.

14. Fed. R. Evid. 801–803. *See* Weinstein & Berger, §§ 801–803.

15. Fed. R. Evid. 901 & 902. *See* Weinstein & Berger, §§ 901 & 902.

ment.[17] The attorney should be clear as to the legal basis for offering each item of evidence and attempt to anticipate any objections that might be made to its admission.

Note should be made of an especially complex problem faced by the defense: whether to have the defendant testify. Calling the defendant to the stand is a high risk, high reward proposition. Many lawyers believe that jurors want to hear from the defendant, despite the fact that they will be instructed to draw no inferences from his or her failure to testify. And, if the defendant does well, it can mean his or her acquittal. On the other hand, jurors may, despite the court's instructions to the contrary, interpret the defendant's decision to testify as an assumption of the burden of proof so that if the defendant is less than credible, the likelihood of conviction is greatly enhanced. The ultimate decision of whether the defendant testifies need not be made until after the close of the government's case. Nevertheless, given the extensive preparation necessary and the fact that the decision may be the most important made by the defense, a tentative decision should be made early on, subject to change depending on any subsequent anticipation of whether the jury is likely to find that the government met its burden. Of course, there are some trials where the defendant will not be able to testify, either because he or she would admit guilt or confirm a fact unrelated to guilt or innocence that would significantly damage his or her credibility and therefore obviate any helpful testimony.[18]

§ 15.4 Addressing Legal Issues Prior to Trial

Determining what facts are at issue and how the evidence on that issue will be elicited is the first phase of trial preparation. The second is to deal with the legal issues that will arise at trial. These issues consist of: (a) evidentiary questions unresolved prior to this time, which are addressed by *in limine* motions; (b) rules related to jury selection, which are addressed in proposed voir dire questions; and (c) the judge's final instructions to the jury on the law, which are addressed in requests to charge.

§ 15.4(a) *In Limine* Motions

Motions *in limine* are generally made shortly before the commencement of trial.[19] They are designed to resolve evidentiary issues that could not be dealt with at the pretrial stage and that would otherwise have to be considered during the trial. By addressing such matters in advance of trial, motions *in limine* (and any attendant evidentiary hearing the court may wish to conduct) allow the issues to be resolved before the jury is

---

16. FED. R. EVID. 702. *See* WEINSTEIN & BERGER, § 702.

17. FED. R. EVID. 607–609. *See* WEINSTEIN & BERGER, §§ 608 & 609.

18. *See, e.g.,* FED. R. EVID. 404(b) (admissibility of other crimes, wrongs or acts) & 609 (admissibility of prior convictions).

19. *See generally* FED. R. EVID. 103(a) (authorizing rulings on admissibility of evidence "either at or before trial").

empanelled, thus avoiding unnecessary delay, and reducing the chance that prejudicial or otherwise improper evidence might be presented to the jury before the opposing side has an opportunity to voice an objection.[20] Such rulings also allow the parties to make strategic decisions that may be dependent on whether or not the disputed evidence is admitted.

Common examples of *in limine* motions include requests for a ruling on the use of a diagram or other piece of demonstrative evidence as an aid to the jury or a ruling on whether a testifying defendant can be impeached on the basis of a prior criminal record or bad acts.

In limine motions can be made formally. They are also commonly made in letter form as we will illustrate in § 15.6(c).

§ 15.4(b) Proposed Voir Dire Questions

As we shall explain in more detail in Chapter 16,[21] the initial stage of the trial is devoted to the questioning of prospective jurors—the voir dire—prior to their selection. The voir dire is conducted for two purposes: first, to determine whether jurors should be excused for cause, either by the judge *sua sponte* or after a challenge by either attorney; and second, whether they should be excused after "peremptory" challenges by one of the attorneys. Challenges for cause are granted whenever the judge finds that because of some bias, prejudice or interest, the juror cannot be fair and impartial to one side or the other. Peremptory challenges are limited in number but are granted without requiring the party to give a reason for not wanting the person to serve.[22]

As we also will explain in Chapter 16, the prevailing practice in federal court is to have the judge, and not the attorneys, conduct the examination of prospective jurors. Nevertheless, counsel have the right to offer proposed voir dire questions relevant to a juror's ability to serve fairly and impartially.[23] These questions should be prepared and submitted to the court prior to the time that the jurors are assembled. Counsel need not draft questions that the court uniformly asks. These include questions regarding the juror's understanding of general principles of criminal procedure, such as the presumption of innocence, and the prospective juror's familiarity with any of the people, events, or places involved in the case. Uniform questioning also addresses the prospective jurors' knowledge of general principles of law and their basic demograph-

---

20. *See* Palmieri v. Defaria, 88 F.3d 136, 141 (2d Cir. 1996) ("The purpose of an *in limine* motion is to aid the trial process by enabling the Court to rule in advance of trial on the relevance of certain forecasted evidence, as to issues that are definitely set for trial, without lengthy argument at, or interruption of, the trial." (citation omitted; internal quotations omitted)); United States v. Downing, 753 F.2d 1224, 1241 (3d Cir. 1985) ("It would appear that the most efficient procedure that the district court can

use in making the reliability determination is an *in limine* hearing.").

21. *See infra* § 16.1(a)

22. Limitations on this rule are discussed *infra* at § 16.1(a).

23. In certain types of cases in federal court that involve particularly controversial issues, defense counsel may request limited attorney-led voir dire, although such requests are rarely granted.

ic information. But there invariably will be subjects specific to every case that the attorney would like to have explored. In conceptualizing what those subjects might be in each case, it is again essential to link the inquiry to the theory upon which the case will be argued by the party, i.e., given that theory, what kind of person with what kind of attitudes would most likely be open to—or biased against—the attorney's argument. In drafting proposed voir dire questions, the attorney must keep in mind that he or she is requesting the court to ask them, and that they therefore will have to be balanced in tone, rather than in terms overly favorable to the party's position.

§ 15.4(c) Requests to Charge

At the close of the testimony, generally after (or occasionally before) closing arguments, the judge will instruct the jury on the applicable principles of law involved in the case.[24] The charge to the jury is an extremely important moment in the trial because the jurors will rely heavily on the judge's explanation of the law in applying the facts that they find. An instruction cast in language favorable to the attorney's theory is therefore of great value, and the attorney should do as much as possible to persuade the court to give such a favorable charge. The attorney should submit a favorable standard instruction,[25] or adapt a standard instruction, or write an original instruction tailored to the specific issues raised by the case. The instruction must be supported by, and correctly state, the governing law. Because legal principles may be expressed in different ways, however, either party will benefit if it can persuade the court to frame the legal issues for the jury in a manner favorable to its own trial theory. Once again, however, a request that is excessively slanted is not likely to be accepted by the court.

Under the rules, the court has the discretion to require submission of written requests for jury instruction "[a]t the close of the evidence or at any earlier time that the court reasonably sets."[26] It is common for judges to order that proposed charges be submitted as early as a week before the start of trial. But even if the attorney is not required to file requests for jury instructions prior to trial, it is important to have drafts of the more important instructions completed at this stage. Preparing the drafts will ensure that counsel is clear on the precise legal standards the jury will apply to the evidence.

§ 15.5 Preparation of Evidence for Use at Trial

Having planned how the case will be presented, and having addressed the legal issues just described, there remains one final step in

---

24. FED. R. CRIM. P. 30(c); WRIGHT, § 483.

25. There are widely used compilations of standard instructions, and most requests for charges are drawn from these sources, which are themselves derived from instruc-

tions approved of in reported cases. *See, e.g.,* O'MALLEY ET AL., *supra* note 5; SAND ET AL., *supra* note 5.

26. FED. R. CRIM. P. 30(a).

the process of pretrial preparation: readying the witnesses and tangible evidence.

§ 15.5(a) Witness Preparation

The attorney should make contact with each person whom he or she expects to call. Where necessary, subpoenas should be prepared and served.[27] Once contacted, it is essential to go over the witness's direct testimony in as much detail as possible to assure that the witness presents his or her story in a coherent way. Needless to say, it is impermissible for the attorney to suggest what the witness' testimony should be, but rehearsing the testimony by repeating it and giving structure to its flow is appropriate.[28]

In addition to preparing the witness' direct testimony, the attorney should conduct what he or she believes will be the cross-examination as well since that will help the witness to respond effectively. Although, as with direct testimony, the attorney must avoid telling the witness what to say, the attorney may explain to the witness how to respond appropriately to questions on cross-examination. In this regard, it is important to impress upon the witness that whatever his or her sympathies, it is not the witness' role to argue with the cross-examiner or to volunteer information in an effort to help the party calling the witness. Not only could this lead the witness to stray from the facts as he or she knows them, but it can cause the proponent's side more harm than good. The witness should be made to understand that it is the lawyer's role to argue the views of the side represented and that the lawyer can best do that if the witness simply responds without attempting to put a particular gloss on the facts.

It is also important to try to attune the witness to the rhythm of testifying. On direct examination, the witness should be told that he or she will have an opportunity to respond fully to the question, which will typically be non-leading, but should answer the precise question that the lawyer asks. On cross-examination, of course, the witness will be asked leading questions and must listen carefully to make sure that the cross-examiner does not put words in the witness' mouth that the witness would not otherwise accept. The attorney also should explain to the witness that his or her testimony most probably will be interrupted by objections, during both direct and cross-examination, and that when an objection is made, the witness should stop speaking until told to continue. This advice is of special tactical importance during cross-examination, when the attorney's objections may be designed to prevent harmful testimony from being heard by the jury.

---

27. The right to subpoena witnesses is set forth in FED. R. CRIM. P. 17. The clerk of court provides blank and endorsed subpoenas, which then are filled in and served by the party. *See* WRIGHT, § 273.

28. For a discussion of the ethical considerations involved in witness preparation, see CHARLES W. WOLFRAM, MODERN LEGAL ETHICS § 12.4.3 (1986).

In preparing a witness, it is important for the lawyer to be aware that, for most people, testifying is an anxiety-producing event. The lawyer can help to ease that anxiety by explaining to the witness that all that is required is for the witness to respond as truthfully and accurately as possible to the questions put by the lawyers or the judge and to react to any confusion that may be experienced as one would if questioned in a less stylized and stressful atmosphere. The witness also should be put at ease about the possibility that he or she might not recall a fact, or become confused about a question. These are common events in a courtroom, and the witness need only say that he or she does not recall or does not understand. It is the lawyer's job to refresh the witness' recollection or clarify the situation.

Proper preparation of the testimony and of the witness for the courtroom experience can be of immense value to the attorney, not only because it offers the best chance that the witness will be effective, but also because it reflects favorably in the eyes of the jury on the professionalism and competence of the attorney. That too may be important to the ultimate outcome of the case.

The discussion of witness preparation thus far has focused on the witness who is friendly to the side that calls him or her, or is at least neutral. On some occasions, however, the attorney may be required to call a hostile witness, one who might not even be willing to speak with the attorney before trial. Under these circumstances, the kind of witness preparation discussed here obviously cannot be accomplished. Such witnesses should be approached as one would approach a witness to be cross-examined.[29]

§ 15.5(b) Preparation of Tangible Evidence and Exhibits

Nearly every criminal trial will involve the use of one or more kinds of physical evidence. It is very important that the attorney make the necessary arrangements to have such material available and ready when needed. The following steps are essential:

(1) Retrieving Evidence of Criminality in Police Custody

The prosecutor obviously must assure that this evidence is produced for the trial. Typically, this will be done by the case agent or other police official who will testify with respect to the evidence and who will be authorized to retrieve it from the property clerk's office where it is held.

(2) Producing Prior Statements of Witnesses

As we have noted, prior written and recorded statements of witnesses (other than the defendant), or 3500 material, must be made available to the opposing side for possible use in cross-examination. Copies of these statements should be prepared by the party that possess-

---

29. *See supra* §§ 3.3(d)-(f); Fed. R. Evid. 607.

es them and delivered at the appropriate time. To avoid disclosing work product, the attorney should be guided by the rule that the attorney must produce documents that attempt to memorialize the statement of the witness and not documents that contain only the thoughts or trial theory of the attorney.[30]

(3) Premarking Evidence

All documents and other tangible materials that a party will seek to have introduced as evidence must be appropriately marked for identification. It is common practice for such material to be premarked, i.e., identified prior to the time that it is actually offered. Typically, evidence to be offered by the government is marked with successive numbers, while defense evidence is marked with successive letters. However, the government's 3500 material is often marked differently, with the statements of each witness given a separate number (e.g., 3501).

§ 15.5(c)   Preparation of Stipulations

In many cases, the parties will not contest certain facts asserted by the opposing side. This is commonly true of authentication testimony, e.g., where a witness is called simply to verify that a certain document is kept in the regular course of business,[31] or to identify the nature of a particular substance (such as narcotics). In such cases, each side may want to enter into a stipulation. This is a binding, written agreement reciting what the witness' testimony would have been if called, which is read to the jury by the party having the burden of production on the particular issue. Stipulations on uncontested facts are useful in saving time and avoiding tedium, and the parties should consider entering into them whenever doing so will not weaken the case. Stipulations can also serve a strategic purpose in communicating to the jury that the attorney is not overly concerned with that stipulated fact and therefore has no need to try to challenge it. An example is provided in § 15.6(d).

§ 15.6   United States v. Christopher—Preparation for Trial by the Prosecution and Defense

§ 15.6(a)   Trial Theories

Considering first the prosecution's burden of proof, there would appear to be sufficient evidence of intent to satisfy the government's burden of going forward. Santiago's testimony alone would suffice for this purpose against Christopher: a reasonable trier of fact *could,* if he or she believed Santiago, find beyond a reasonable doubt that Christopher was a knowing participant in the drug operation. Santiago's testimony alone might not, however, be sufficient to meet the burden of going forward on the issue of Van Ness' intent since Santiago could not testify

---

30. *See* Fed. R. Crim. P. 16; Wright,   **31.** Fed. R. Evid. 803(6).
§ 254. *See also* 18 U.S.C. § 3500.

that Van Ness knew that there were narcotics in the crates. But a *prima facie* case would be made out when that testimony was augmented by the phone records showing that Van Ness regularly spoke to Christopher following Christopher's calls to Colombia and by the billing records showing that Van Ness was paid by IFD twice the standard per pound rate for shipments that contained cocaine.[32]

Whether the government will be able to sustain its burden of persuading a jury of the defendants' guilt is another matter. There is, to be sure, no real dispute about many of the facts that the government will adduce. There is ample evidence that a narcotics operation took place at Superior Warehouse and that proceeds from it were laundered in fictitious bank accounts. Christopher cannot contest that he owned the warehouse and IFD or that he was a signatory on the bank accounts. Similarly, Van Ness is not likely to claim that he never transported crates for IFD. The real dispute, therefore, is whether the defendants can be shown to have had the requisite knowledge and intent to engage in narcotics trafficking and, in Christopher's case, financial crimes related to narcotics profits. That issue is what the lawyers' trial theories will focus upon.

Recall that in § 15.1(b) we described three types of trial theories, two of which are relevant here: "pure" reasonable doubt and conflicting evidence.[33]

1. Christopher—Case Theory

Christopher will employ both of these theories. First, he will attempt to create a reasonable doubt simply by undermining Santiago's testimony. Santiago's knowledge of the narcotics trade, as evidenced by his prior conviction and his central operational role in both the distribution of cocaine and money laundering, point to *his* involvement, not Christopher's participation. Santiago's motive to implicate Christopher in order to obtain the sentencing leniency benefits from his cooperation agreement could be used by Christopher to raise a reasonable doubt regarding the truth of Santiago's allegation that Christopher was involved.

Second, Christopher will offer a different explanation of the most directly damning evidence against him—the banking transactions. His involvement in them is irrefutable, but it could be explained as a tax avoidance scheme rather than one involving narcotics. Richard Clark, Christopher's lawyer, will attempt to deal with this issue by admitting Christopher's responsibility for opening the accounts but presenting this alternative explanation having nothing to do with the crimes charged in the indictment.

To meet the likely position that Christopher will take, AUSA Knapp must confront the fact that the government's only direct evidence of

---

32. *See supra* § 11.7(a).   **33.** There is nothing in the case that raises justification or excuse defenses.

Christopher's knowledge comes from Santiago's testimony, and Santiago's credibility is questionable. Knapp must address this problem with her proof by introducing strong corroborating evidence. One example of such evidence is the fact that Christopher was a signatory to the fictitious business accounts in which he made cash deposits. Another is the very fact that he was the sole owner of a relatively small business over which he exercised day-to-day supervision, from which it can be inferred that Santiago would not be able to engage in drug dealings without Christopher's knowledge. She could call Christopher's bookkeeper or other employees to support the position that it is implausible that two employees could have run this drug conspiracy without his knowledge and direction.

It seemed to Clark and Christopher that the evidence against Christopher was strong enough to require an alternative explanation of the incontrovertible facts. Christopher also appeared to be a credible witness. He had a respectable background, no prior convictions upon which he could be impeached, and the ability to present an innocent explanation of the facts relied upon by the government. As a result, Clark and Christopher determined that the risk of Christopher testifying was worth taking.

2. Van Ness—Case Theory

Martin Rothman strongly considered invoking a pure reasonable doubt defense, focusing on the weakness of the government's evidence of Van Ness' knowledge of the narcotics enterprise. As he learned through pretrial discovery, nothing in Santiago's testimony would prove that Van Ness had any knowledge of the presence of cocaine in the crates or that he participated in money laundering. In addition, neither the evidence that he had telephone conversations with Christopher nor his company's records prove involvement in narcotics. The fact that he was paid a higher price for certain shipments, while suspicious, does not in and of itself prove that narcotics were involved, even if he offers no explanation for these transactions. However, because Rothman believes that Van Ness would be a good witness and would affirmatively provide an innocent explanation for the government's evidence, Van Ness and he are leaning towards presenting a defense case consisting primarily of Van Ness' testimony.

Knapp understands that the proof of Van Ness' knowledge of the cocaine operation is weaker, since Santiago cannot testify to it. Knapp can show, however, that Van Ness knew that Santiago was a convicted narcotics trafficker and was close to Christopher personally. She will also show that Van Ness was the trucker who always transported the cocaine and that he was regularly contacted by Christopher after Christopher had placed a call to Colombia; and she will argue that Christopher would only trust his valuable cargo to someone who knew its nature and would protect it. The fact that Van Ness was paid nearly twice his usual rate for such shipments is further evidence that he knew he was transporting narcotics.

§ 15.6(b) Proving the Trial Theory—Marshalling the Evidence

Let us now describe how the prosecutor and two defense attorneys would plan for the testimony through which they will attempt to prove their contentions. We will reserve for Chapter 16 the description of the actual testimony elicited on direct and cross-examination.

Knapp's proof on the drug distribution charges would be based upon Santiago's testimony, corroborated by Mario Long and the seizure of narcotics at the airport and from the IFD warehouse. To prove the drug seizure, she would call the agents involved in the placement of the beeper inside the crate at the airport and in the delivery of this crate and the search of the warehouse. Unless the parties entered into a stipulation as to the drugs, she would also call a chemist to establish that the substance was cocaine and how much it weighed.

The proof on the money laundering counts would be based on Santiago's testimony about opening the accounts at CMS Bank and making the deposits after the drugs were sold. The government can corroborate the banking transactions through bank documents, which may be admissible through stipulations or the testimony of bank employees. Knapp might call a banker or some other qualified individual to testify as an expert regarding money laundering to explain why the pattern of transactions is consistent with a scheme to launder money. Knapp also may choose to corroborate Santiago's testimony that Christopher signed bank documents by calling a handwriting expert.

In addition, Knapp would want to develop testimony about the limited size of Christopher's business in order to argue that it is implausible that two employees (Santiago and Long) could have run this drug conspiracy without Christopher's knowledge and direction. As noted above, she might call Christopher's bookkeeper or some other employee.

As for the defense attorneys, the basic issue would be whether either of the defendants would testify—no other witnesses or tangible evidence appear to be available—or whether it would be sufficient to attack the government's witnesses.

§ 15.6(c) Addressing Legal Issues Prior to Trial

1. In Limine Motions

The following is an *in limine* motion, in letter form, from AUSA Knapp to the court requesting a ruling on whether testimony about statements by Christopher made prior to the date of the conspiracy alleged in the indictment will be permitted. Attorney Clark's response follows.

U.S. Department of Justice
United States Attorney
Eastern District of New York

September 5, 2005

Honorable Walter Sheridan
United States District Judge
United States District Court
Eastern District of New York
225 Cadman Plaza East
Brooklyn, NY 11201

Re: <u>United States v. Christopher and Van Ness</u> - 05 Cr. 735 (WS)

Your Honor:

        This case is scheduled for trial starting next week and an evidentiary matter has come to my attention during the preparation of one of the government's witnesses. Accordingly, the government respectfully submits this letter seeking an *in limine* ruling on the admissibility of certain evidence in the government's case-in-chief.

        As the Court may recall from prior submissions in this case, Gilbert Santiago, a former employee of the defendant Paul Christopher, is a cooperating witness. The government expects that Santiago would testify, in relevant part, that in May of last year he had a conversation with defendant Christopher in which Santiago was promised money if he put defendant Christopher in touch with a narcotics trafficker who could lend or otherwise make money available to Christopher. About three or four months later, Santiago went to Christopher to inquire about whether the connection had been successful and whether Santiago would be getting any money from Christopher.

        Christopher told Santiago, in substance, that the connection had been made and Christopher had distributed cocaine on prior occasions. Christopher invited Santiago to join in the ongoing narcotics dealing and Santiago entered into the conspiracy with Christopher, which is charged in the indictment now pending before this Court. That indictment charges Christopher with being a member of the conspiracy which began in August of last year.

        The government submits that Santiago's testimony about Christopher's admission to trafficking in narcotics prior to August of last year is admissible to prove a conspiracy. Such testimony about the background of a conspiracy has been approved by the Second Circuit, even when the evidence "does not directly establish an element of the offense charges, in order to provide background for the events charged in the indictment." <u>United States v. Coonan</u>, 938 F.2d 1553, 1561 (2d Cir. 2003) (quoting <u>United States v. Daly</u>, 842 F.2d 1380, 1388 (2d Cir. 1988)).

     Should the Court analyze this issue under Fed.R.Evid. 404(b), Other Crimes, Wrongs or Acts, the government submits that the statement would be admissible to prove defendant Christopher's knowledge and intent. <u>United States v. Aguirre</u>, 716 F.2d 293 (5th Cir. 1983). The pretrial motions in this case indicated that defendant Christopher intends to rely on the defense that he did not know about, or participate in, the narcotics trafficking operation run through the business he owns, International Food Distributors. Thus, the proffered testimony would certainly be relevant and probative on that issue.

     Thank you for your attention to this matter.

                         Respectfully submitted,

                         Laura Knapp

                         Laura Knapp
                         Assistant United States Attorney

cc: Richard Clark, Esq.
     Charles Berman, Esq.

Richard Clark, Esq.
377 Broadway
New York, New York 10003
(212) 862–9543

September 9, 2005

Honorable Walter Sheridan
United States District Judge
United States District Court
Eastern District of New York
225 Cadman Plaza East
Brooklyn, NY 11201

Re: <u>United States v. Christopher and Van Ness</u> - 05 Cr. 735 (WS)

Dear Judge Sheridan:

    I write in response to the government's application for an *in limine* ruling on the admissibility of testimony of a cooperating witness who would assert that my client, Paul Christopher, made statements admitting prior, uncharged instances of narcotics trafficking. I urge the Court to preclude that testimony. It is inadmissible because its prejudicial value outweighs its probativeness, and, in any event, it is beyond the scope of the conspiracy.

    The government makes two arguments in support of the admissibility of this testimony. The first is that such testimony is admissible as appropriate proof in a conspiracy trial. That argument rests upon a misreading of <u>United States v. Coonan</u>, 938 F.2d 1553 (2d Cir. 2003). In that case, evidence of uncharged crimes committed by other defendants was admitted as "background" evidence to prove the existence of a conspiracy. It did not purport to prove intent or knowledge of the defendant. Thus <u>Coonan</u> does not stand for the proposition that the government may circumvent Fed.R.Evid. 403 and 404 by labeling the evidence as background to the conspiracy. Moreover, in this instance, Christopher's alleged prior statements do not constitute proof of the existence of the charged conspiracy as was the case in <u>Coonan</u>.

    The government's other contention is that the evidence meets the requirements of Fed.R.Evid. 404(b) because it establishes knowledge and intent. It is improper for the government to anticipate a potential defense. <u>United States v. Aguirre</u>, 716 F.2d 293 (5th Cir. 1983). However, should the defendant place that issue in dispute at trial, Christopher's statements to Santiago would still be inadmissible because their minimal probative value is outweighed by the danger of unfair prejudice.   Fed.R.Evid. 403.   The government expects to elicit many statements from its cooperating witness, which, if credited, would be probative of Christopher's intent and knowledge. Christopher's statement to Santiago regarding prior drug dealings is therefore merely cumulative. However, its prejudicial impact would be great; it would require a trial within a trial likelihood of jury confusion would be enhanced.

The issues of motive, intent and opportunity raised by the government are merely illusory notions that seek instead to improperly show Mr. Christopher's actions in this case are in conformity with his prior conduct. See United States v. Gordon, 987 F.2d 902, 908 (2d Cir. 1993) ("Rule 404(b) does not authorize the admission of any and every sort of other-act evidence simply because a defendant proffers an innocent explanation for the charged conduct."); United States v. Oppon, 863 F.2d 141, 149 (1st Cir. 1988) (Coffin, J., concurring) (noting that if disputed intent alone is sufficient justification for admission of prior bad act evidence, "the general bar against propensity evidence would be swallowed up").

We respectfully urge the Court to preclude this testimony.

Respectfully submitted,

Rich Clark

Richard Clark, Esq.

cc: Laura Knapp, Esq.
        Martin Rothman, Esq.

---

2. Proposed Voir Dire Questions

Martin Rothman submitted the following proposed voir dire questions to Judge Sheridan on behalf of Van Ness. They reflect his trial theory by introducing, albeit in necessarily neutral terms, that there are cooperating witnesses in the case and that it is the juror's responsibility to determine credibility, the inference being that there is a special task involved in determining the credibility of such witnesses. The questions also raise the issue of narcotics. Most jurors are aware of the government's "war" on drugs and may have strong attitudes toward anyone charged with a narcotics offense. Others who have had personal experiences with drugs, or who have family members with drug related problems, may have such negative views about narcotics offenses that they would not be able to serve as fair and impartial jurors. Still others may believe that it is wrong for the government to criminalize the use and sale of narcotics. Rothman also includes questions aimed at eliciting details regarding the jurors' background that he does not believe the judge would otherwise ask.

UNITED STATES DISTRICT COURT
SOUTHERN DISTRICT OF NEW YORK

UNITED STATES OF AMERICA	)
	)
–v–	) 05 Cr. 735 (WS)
	)
PAUL CHRISTOPHER and	)
WILLIAM VAN NESS,	)
	)
Defendants.	)

DEFENDANT WILLIAM VAN NESS'
PROPOSED VOIR DIRE QUESTIONS

The defendant, WILLIAM VAN NESS, respectfully requests that, in addition to its customary questions, the Court cover the following areas in its voir dire. The Court is requested to pursue more detailed questioning if a particular juror's answer reveals that further inquiry is appropriate, concluding in such instance with an inquiry as to whether the juror is certain that the particular fact or circumstances would not influence the juror in favor of or against the government or the defendant.

1.   This case involves allegations of cocaine distribution. Given the publicity surrounding the government's "war on drugs" and the problems society faces with narcotics addiction, do any of you believe that you could not be a fair and impartial juror in a case in which the charge is narcotics distribution? Has any juror had any personal experiences with cocaine or does any juror have any close relatives or friends who may have been involved in some way with cocaine; if so, as a result of that experience, would you be unable to serve as a fair and impartial juror?

2.   In this case you will hear testimony of witnesses who have pleaded guilty and agreed to testify in return for sentencing considerations. In deciding what weight to give a cooperating witness' testimony, will you consider whether the witness has anything to gain from testifying on behalf of the government? Will any juror believe such a witness merely because he or she has been called to testify on behalf of the government?

3.   Do you belong to any associations, organizations or civic clubs? If yes, which ones?

4.   What are your hobbies or interests outside of work and family?

5.   Which specific magazines or other periodicals do you subscribe to or read?

Dated: New York, New York
       September 10, 2005

Respectfully submitted,

Martin Rothman

Martin Rothman, Esq.
Attorney for William Van Ness

TO: Kevin O'Reilly, Esq.
       United States Attorney
       Eastern District of New York
       225 Cadman Plaza East
       Brooklyn, New York 11201

Attn.:   Laura Knapp, Esq.
       Assistant United States Attorney

AUSA Knapp also submitted proposed voir dire questions. She first offered a brief summary of the charges to determine whether their nature would preclude the juror from sitting on the case. She then identified the likely witnesses and the locations involved in the case and asked the court to inquire whether any juror has prior knowledge of those people or places that would interfere with his or her ability to consider only the evidence introduced at trial. She proposed questions related to the juror's prior experience with law enforcement to expose any hostility that the juror might harbor against the government. She also offered a question about cooperating witnesses to determine whether the testimony of such a witness would be considered, and not discounted solely because of the cooperation agreement.

3. Requests to Charge

Judge Sheridan ordered each attorney to submit requests to charge prior to the date set for trial. In all, the attorneys would submit proposed instructions on twenty to thirty subjects, almost all of them standard charges from a form book or prior cases. Following is an example of two different charges on accomplice testimony, the first by the defense and the second by the government. Both of the instructions correctly state the law but each attempts to incorporate the essence of the parties' different trial theories.

* * * * *

411

Defense Request No. 11

Weighing the Credibility of a Cooperating Witness

In this case there has been testimony from two government witnesses who pled guilty after entering into agreements with the government to testify. There is evidence that the government agreed to dismiss some charges against the witnesses and agreed not to prosecute them on other charges in exchange for their guilty pleas and testimony at this trial. The government also promised to bring the witnesses' cooperation to the attention of the sentencing court.

You should consider with caution whether the informer received any benefits or promises from the government that would motivate the informer to testify falsely against the defendant, or to exaggerate the conduct of the defendant. For example, the informer may believe that he or she will only continue to receive these benefits if he or she produces evidence of criminal conduct. You also should scrutinize the informer's testimony closely to determine whether or not it is colored in such a way as to place guilt upon the defendant in order to further the informant's own interests. Such a witness, confronted with the realization that he can win his own freedom or reduce his period of incarceration by helping to convict another, has a motive to falsify his testimony.

Therefore, you should examine such testimony with caution and weigh it with great care. If, after scrutinizing his testimony, you decide to accept it, you may give it whatever weight, if any, you find it deserves.

Adapted from 1 Leonard B. Sand et al., Modern Federal Jury Instructions § 7.01, Instruction 7–11 (2005); 1A Kevin F. O'Malley et al., Federal Jury Practice and Instructions § 15.02 (5th ed. 2000 & Supp. 2004).

Government Request No. 11

Accomplice Testimony

The government's position is that Gilbert Santiago was involved in the crimes charged in the indictment. The proof is that he pleaded guilty as part of a cooperation agreement in which he hopes to receive a sentencing concession in return for his truthful testimony. While the testimony of a cooperating witness must be considered with some suspicion because of the person's interest in the outcome of the proceedings, the fact of cooperation is not in and of itself reason to discount the witness' testimony. You are to consider the witness' testimony along with whatever corroborative evidence the government has offered in determining the reliability of the statements made by the witness.

Adapted from 1 Josephine R. Potuto et al., Federal Criminal Jury Instructions § 3.11 (2d ed. 1991).

---

§ 15.6(d) Preparation of Tangible Evidence, Exhibits and Stipulations

AUSA Knapp premarked the documents she intended to introduce and, on the Friday preceding the trial, gave the defense attorneys copies of all 3500 material.[34] Knapp also drafted a stipulation covering the testimony of the DEA chemist with respect to the identity and quantity of drugs seized at Kennedy Airport and at the warehouse. She also drafted a stipulation covering the testimony of the custodian of the telephone records, to enable records of those calls to be introduced in evidence and to establish that the calls were made from Christopher's office and from the public telephone outside his office during the DEA surveillance. Following is the stipulation drafted by Knapp with regard to the testimony of the DEA chemist.

34. The defense had no statements or tangible evidence to provide under reciprocal discovery rules. *See supra* § 13.5(b).

UNITED STATES DISTRICT COURT
EASTERN DISTRICT OF NEW YORK

	)	
UNITED STATES OF AMERICA	)	
	)	
v.	)	**STIPULATION**
	)	
	)	05 Cr. 735 (WS)
PAUL CHRISTOPHER and	)	
WILLIAM VAN NESS, Defendants	)	
	)	

IT IS AGREED by Richard Clark, Esq., counsel for the defendant PAUL CHRISTOPHER, Martin Rothman, Esq., counsel for the defendant WILLIAM VAN NESS and the UNITED STATES OF AMERICA, by Laura Knapp, Assistant United States Attorney, that if Randolph Johnson were called as a witness he would testify that he is a chemist employed by the Drug Enforcement Administration, and that on January 17, 2005 he examined the contents of Government's Exhibit 1 herein, a plastic bag containing a quantity of white powder, and determined that it consisted of approximately 9.8 kilograms of a mixture of substances containing cocaine.

Rich Clark
Richard Clark
Counsel to Paul Christopher

Martin Rothman
Martin Rothman
Counsel to William Van Ness

Laura Knapp
Laura Knapp
Assistant United States Attorney

_____

The parties in the Christopher case would next meet in the district court on September 15, 2005 for the commencement of the trial.

Chapter 16

THE TRIAL

Table of Sections

Sec.
16.0   Introduction.
16.1   Jury Selection.
    16.1(a) The Voir Dire.
    16.1(b) Strategic Considerations in Selecting Juries.
    16.1(c) The Selection Process.
16.2   Preliminary Instructions to the Jury.
16.3   Opening Statements.
    16.3(a) Rules Related to the Opening Statement.
    16.3(b) Strategic Considerations—Prosecution and Defense Openings.
    16.3(c) United States v. Christopher and Van Ness—Opening Statements.
16.4   The Government's Case-in-Chief—Rules Related to Eliciting Testimony.
    16.4(a) Establishing Competence—Laying the Foundation for the Witness' Testimony.
    16.4(b) Establishing the Reliability of the Witness' Testimony.
    16.4(c) Establishing the Relevance of the Witness' Testimony.
    16.4(d) The Government's Case-in-Chief—Strategic Considerations.
    16.4(e) Eliciting Direct Testimony—Forms of Questions.
    16.4(f) United States v. Christopher—The Government's Case-in-Chief.
    16.4(g) Conducting a Direct Examination—The Testimony of Gilbert Santiago.
16.5   Challenging the Government's Case-in-Chief—Cross-examination.
    16.5(a) The Scope of Cross-examination.
    16.5(b) Types of Cross-examination.
    16.5(c) Preparing for Cross-examination.
    16.5(d) The Decision Whether to Cross-examine.
    16.5(e) Eliciting Testimony on Cross-examination—The Structure of the Examination.
    16.5(f) Eliciting Testimony on Cross-examination.
    16.5(g) United States v. Christopher—The Cross-examination of Gilbert Santiago.
16.6   Re-examination.
    16.6(a) Re-direct Examination.
    16.6(b) Re-cross Examination.

16.7   Motion for Judgment of Acquittal.
16.8   The Defense Case.
16.9   The Rebuttal Case.
16.10   Concluding the Trial—Requests to Charge.
16.11   Closing Argument.
        16.11(a) Rules Regarding Closing Argument.
        16.11(b) The Focus of the Closing—The Primacy of Facts.
        16.11(c) Stylistic Considerations.
        16.11(d) The Prosecution Closing.
        16.11(e) The Defense Closing.
        16.11(f) United States v. Christopher—Closing Arguments.
16.12   Jury Instructions.
16.13   Jury Deliberations.
16.14   Verdict.
16.15   United States v. Christopher—The Verdict.

---

§ 16.0   Introduction

This chapter will describe each stage of the trial, from the selection of the jury through the verdict. At each stage, we will illustrate certain important features of the process of examining witnesses, handling evidence and argument with excerpts from the trial of Paul Christopher and William Van Ness in our model case.

§ 16.1   Jury Selection

The defendant has a constitutional right to a trial by jury, except in trials of petty offenses.[1] The right can be waived, but only with the consent of the government and the court.[2] Under federal law, the right is to a jury of 12, although the parties can, with the court's permission, stipulate to a smaller jury.[3] Even without a stipulation, the court can allow a jury of 11 to return a verdict if there is good cause to excuse a juror after deliberations have begun.[4]

Selection initially will be from a list of jurors compiled in accordance with a statutory (and constitutional) requirement that juries be composed of a "fair cross-section" of the community.[5] The Jury Selection Act of 1968[6] sets certain basic criteria for jury service,[7] which are to be

---

1. U.S. Const. Amend. VI. A petty offense is a Class B misdemeanor, a Class C misdemeanor, or an infraction, for which the maximum fine is no greater than $5,000 for an individual and $10,000 for an organization. *See* 18 U.S.C. § 19; Fed. R. Crim. P. 58 advisory committee's note (1990 addition). *See also* Fed. R. Crim. P. 58(a); Rules of Procedure for the Trial of Misdemeanors Before United States Magistrates R 1 (1980). *See generally* Wright, § 371.

2. Fed. R. Crim. P. 23(a).

3. Fed. R. Crim. P. 23(b)(2)(A).

4. Fed. R. Crim. P. 23(b)(3).

5. 28 U.S.C. § 1861. Taylor v. Louisiana, 419 U.S. 522, 528–29 (1975).

6. 28 U.S.C. §§ 1861–1869.

7. The statute provides that jurors must be 18 years old, citizens of the United States, English-speaking, not under indictment, not convicted of a felony unless the juror's civil rights have been restored, and not impaired in a manner that would pre-supplemented by plans adopted in each federal district.[8] The local rules will also determine methods by which persons are to be identified for jury service.[9]

§ 16.1(a) The Voir Dire

From the jury list, a number of prospective jurors are called to the courtroom in which the trial is to take place. This group will form the "panel" or "venire" from which the ultimate trial or "petit" jury will be chosen, after the "voir dire" or examination of the jurors. The voir dire is conducted for the purpose of determining whether the jurors are qualified to sit or are to be excused either for "cause" or after a "peremptory" challenge as discussed in § 15.4(b). Any juror will be excused for cause either by the court *sua sponte* or after challenge by one of the parties if the court concludes that the juror cannot render a fair and impartial verdict.[10] Peremptory challenges are premised on the belief that the parties should have at least some right to eliminate jurors whom they believe will be hostile to their side, even if not excludable for cause.[11] Unlike cause challenges, however, peremptory challenges are limited in number: in most cases, the government has 6 peremptory challenges and the defense 10.[12]

Typically, questions will be addressed to the panel as a whole.[13] The judge will always conduct a preliminary round and usually will conduct the entire voir dire. The judge may, however, allow the attorneys to conduct additional questioning. The attorneys will be permitted to submit proposed voir dire questions.[14] In some cases, particularly those raising sensitive issues, jurors may also be questioned individually.[15]

Prior to oral questioning—and typically some time before the jury selection process begins—written questionnaires may be given to the jury panel. The questionnaire will request general background information about the prospective juror and include questions specifically related

---

vent them from functioning as jurors. *See* § 1865(b).

8. Thus, local rules may exempt on request certain persons on the basis of extreme inconvenience or undue hardship. *See e.g.,* Amended Plan for Random Selection of Grand and Petit Jurors in the United States District Court for the Southern District of New York, art. VI, *available at* http://www.nysd.uscourts.gov/juryplanapr02.pdf (last visited July 8, 2005) (exempting upon request, inter alia, persons over 70 and volunteer firefighters and ambulance technicians).

9. *Id.*, art III.

10. *See* LaFave et al., § 22.3(a).

11. *Id.* The party exercising a peremptory challenge need not give a reason for

doing so in most situations. However, the Supreme Court has held, however, that the equal protection clause prohibits the use of peremptory challenges to strike jurors solely because of race. Batson v. Kentucky, 476 U.S. 79, 84 (1986); Powers v. Ohio, 499 U.S. 400, 412 (1991). Similarly, challenges based solely on gender are also prohibited. J.E.B. v. Alabama ex rel. T.B., 511 U.S. 127, 146 (1994). *See* LaFave et al., § 22.3(d).

12. Fed. R. Crim. P. 24(b). If there is more than one defendant, all will share the 10 challenges, although the judge may grant additional peremptories in such cases. *Id.* In capital cases, each side has 20 peremptory challenges. *Id. See* Wright, § 385.

13. Wright, § 381.

14. Fed. R. Crim. P. 24(a).

15. Wright, § 381.

to the case, including those approved by the judge after a request by one of the parties. While these questionnaires are most commonly used in very complex or widely publicized cases, they also may be useful in cases in which a particular issue is controversial or in cases in which lengthy trials (longer than 1–2 weeks) are expected. We suggest that counsel should consider requesting a written questionnaire in all cases because, through the use of questionnaires, it is possible to learn more about the prospective jurors than is typically learned during a federal voir dire.

While the trial judge has broad discretion to decide what questions to ask, the failure to ask a question proposed by a party or to inquire extensively enough about an issue relevant to the juror's fitness to serve may be reversible error.[16] In order to preserve the issue for appeal, however, the attorney must make specific objections to any question asked by the court or to the court's failure to ask a question and, upon the court's refusal to ask the specific question, must exercise a peremptory challenge.[17]

Finally, it should be noted that in some districts, jury selection is conducted by magistrate judges on behalf of the district court judge.

§ 16.1(b) Strategic Considerations in Selecting Juries

In the federal system, the circumscribed role played by the attorneys in the voir dire significantly limits the amount of potentially relevant information that can be obtained about prospective jurors. Judicial control of the voir dire also limits the lawyer's ability to "educate" the jury during the questioning—i.e., by posing questions designed to acquaint the jurors with the attorney's trial theory. Moreover, judges are for the most part reluctant to make searching inquiries into the backgrounds or attitudes of jurors and are commonly content with the jurors' representations that they have no personal stake or interest in the outcome, no knowledge of the issues or the parties that would affect their neutrality, and no other reason why they might not be able to render a fair and impartial verdict. In most cases, therefore, the lawyers should be prepared for juries to be selected rapidly and on the basis of relatively little information about the jurors.

§ 16.1(c) The Selection Process

Two common methods of selecting the jury are the "struck panel" method, in which the judge will question the entire panel at the outset, and the "twelve in the box" system, in which the judge randomly selects twelve jurors and questions only those actually sitting in the jury box.

16. Rosales–Lopez v. United States, 451 U.S. 182, 188 (1981). *See* United States v. Barnes, 604 F.2d 121, 137 (2d Cir. 1979) (containing a useful description of the types of questions asked in a very extensive voir dire, as well as a review of cases discussing when specific inquiries are, or are not, required).

17. FED. R. CRIM. P. 51. *See* United States v. Urian, 858 F.2d 124, 126 (3d Cir. 1988).

418

(1) The Struck Panel Method

In this method, the judge begins by addressing the entire panel of jurors called to the courtroom. He or she makes general introductory remarks and then asks questions that are designed to determine whether there is a basis for a challenge for cause, i.e., whether the jurors harbor any views or know of any facts or information that would disable them from sitting fairly or impartially in the case. If jurors respond affirmatively, they are questioned in greater detail, either in open court, at the bench, or in the judge's robing room. At the end of this questioning process, the court may itself excuse a prospective juror for cause and will rule on challenges for cause made by either of the parties.

At the conclusion of the challenge for cause phase of the selection process, the judge will then have the clerk randomly call 32 jurors from among those remaining on the panel. Those 32 jurors will then be asked to provide basic demographic information—e.g., community of residence, employment, educational background and family situation. The parties will then exercise their peremptory challenges. Usually, the peremptory challenges are exercised in rounds, with the defense striking two and the prosecution one in each of the first four rounds. In the last two rounds, each side strikes one juror in each round. However, at this level of detail, there is wide variety in practice.[18]

As the jurors are struck, those next in line fill in the places of the excused juror. Once all the peremptory challenges have been exercised (including challenges to alternate jurors),[19] there should be 12 jurors and 2 alternates remaining in the jury box, assuming that no new challenges for cause emerge. The remaining panel members will then be excused.

(2) The Twelve in the Box Method

In this method, the judge seats 12 jurors in the jury box and questions them as to possible challenges for cause. As the 12 are winnowed down by cause challenges, they are replaced by others, randomly selected, until 12 jurors against whom there are no cause challenges remain. The first round of peremptory strikes takes place and then jurors are selected at random from the panel to replace those struck. The new jurors in the jury box are first questioned to discover

---

18. The Federal Rules do not themselves prescribe the selection process further. Local practices vary with respect to whether jurors are moved from seat to seat as others preceding them in the jury box are excused or remain in the seat to which they were first called, with others filling in the empty spaces; whether the strikes are attributed to each side in open court; and whether the parties may save a strike for the next round or must exercise a certain number of peremptory challenges per round or lose the strike. These are just a few examples of the differences in practice.

19. Rule 24 provides for the seating of up to six alternate jurors, who are examined in the same manner as the regular jurors and who will replace any juror who is unable to continue to serve. FED. R. CRIM. P. 24(c). Additional peremptory challenges are provided for when alternate jurors are selected, the number depending upon the number of alternates. WRIGHT, § 388.

challenges for cause, and replaced if any are excused, and then the next round of peremptory challenges is conducted.

The key difference between the two systems is that in the struck panel method, one may strike from the entire panel after having learned something about all the prospective jurors. In the last round or two of the 12 in the box system, the lawyers are striking jurors they know something about, to be replaced with jurors they know nothing about. Thus in the latter system lawyers frequently "pass" in the last round or two, lest they find themselves with no challenges left and even less appealing jurors than those whom they struck.

§ 16.2 Preliminary Instructions to the Jury

When the jury selection process is completed, the jurors will be sworn, and the judge will give them a set of preliminary instructions. These will relate to the presumption of innocence and the government's burden of proof and to the duty of the jurors to consider only evidence adduced in the courtroom, to read nothing about the case and not to discuss the case among themselves until it is submitted. The judge also may describe the nature of witness testimony and announce rules of conduct for jurors during the trial, such as whether the jurors may take notes and whether they may submit questions during the trial. These matters are either the subject of local rules or the policies of individual judges. It is also common practice for judges to describe the indictment to the jury, either by reading it to them (if it is brief) or characterizing it in general terms. If the judge does not do this, it may be done by the prosecutor.

§ 16.3 Opening Statements

After the jury is sworn, the parties will have the opportunity to give opening statements. In deference to its production burden, the prosecution will be called upon first and will always give an opening statement that explains to the jury its proof. Prosecutors will summarize the charges contained in the indictment to the jury, explaining the evidence that the government will adduce to prove the charges.[20]

In deference to the fact that the defense has no burden of proof, it will be given a choice whether to open or not and also may be given the option of following the prosecution or deferring the opening until it begins its own case. Defense attorneys virtually always will exercise the right to give an opening statement at the outset of the case. Otherwise, the jury hears the evidence with only the government's theory of the case in mind.

20. The Federal Rules are silent as to whether the prosecution must give an opening statement. Case law suggests that the prosecution "can skip" it. United States v. Welch, 97 F.3d 142, 148 (6th Cir. 1996).

§ 16.3(a) Rules Related to the Opening Statement

Both the prosecution and defense must observe certain limitations on what can be said in an opening statement. Improper statements may result in an admonition by the judge and a curative instruction to the jury. In extreme cases, improper statements can be grounds for reversal: if made by the prosecutor, when it deprives the defendant of a fair trial;[21] if made by the defense attorney, when it constitutes ineffective assistance of counsel.[22]

The most common ground for judicial intervention in opening statements is when counsel engages in argument.[23] Attorneys are also prohibited from giving their personal opinions as to the guilt or innocence of the defendant[24] or asserting facts that the attorney has no reasonable grounds to believe can be proven.[25]

In addition to rules about the opening statement relevant to both sides, some rules are directed specifically to the conduct of either the prosecution or the defense. Prosecutors must, under most circumstances, avoid making statements predicting the likely defense case, since the defendant has the right not to put on a case and such statements may impinge upon the defendant's right to remain silent.[26] Similarly, the prosecution should avoid comments related to the pretrial procedures—arrest or indictment by grand jury—through which the defendant was brought to trial, since it is always improper for a prosecutor to suggest that a defendant is guilty merely because he or she is being prosecuted or has been indicted.[27] Defense counsel must be aware of the fact that statements made by them during the defense opening may "open the door" to the admission of evidence on that subject, even if it would not have been admissible otherwise.[28]

§ 16.3(b) Strategic Considerations—Prosecution and Defense Openings

Listed below are some guidelines about the opening statements that may be useful:

21. United States v. Johnson, 968 F.2d 768, 769–770 (8th Cir. 1992).

22. Ouber v. Guarino, 293 F.3d 19, 28 (1st Cir. 2002) (failure to fulfill promise made in the opening statement to call witnesses or present evidence).

23. United States v. Zielie, 734 F.2d 1447, 1455 (11th Cir. 1984).

24. *See* MODEL RULES OF PROF'L CONDUCT R. 3.4(e) (1983, as amended 2003); MODEL CODE OF PROF'L RESPONSIBILITY DR 7–106(C)(4) (1983 ed.).

25. United States v. Taren–Palma, 997 F.2d 525, 532 (9th Cir. 1993).

26. In United States v. Gentile, 525 F.2d 252, 255–56 (2d Cir. 1975), the district court dismissed the indictment after the prosecution had stated in its opening that the defense would be entrapment. The appeals court, assuming the propriety of that action, held that the double jeopardy clause did not prevent reindictment.

27. United States v. Bess, 593 F.2d 749, 754 (6th Cir. 1979) (the prosecutor in closing argument stated that if the United States did not believe that the defendant was guilty the case would never have been presented to the jury).

28. United States v. Croft, 124 F.3d 1109, 1120 (9th Cir. 1997).

1. We have noted that argument—by which we mean drawing inferences in support of a party's case theory from the facts in evidence—is objectionable as a matter of law in the opening statement and can lead to an interruption in the lawyer's presentation and an admonition from the court. This does not mean, however, that the lawyer must limit his or her statements to a dispassionate summary of the anticipated evidence. Rather, each side has to be persuasive in suggesting in the opening statement that there is substantial support for the side's case theory. While both sides should couch their statements in terms of what they expect the evidence will (or will not) reveal, they should do so in a way that emphasizes their trial theory and stresses the most important evidence supporting it. Both sides should also use the opening statement as a way to "pull the teeth" on unfavorable evidence that is sure to be adduced.

2. To say that the purpose of the opening statement is to explain what the attorney believes the evidence will reveal is not to say that it is necessary to describe all of the evidence in the case. The jury cannot possibly assimilate that much detail. More importantly, if such detail is imposed upon them, their attention will be deflected from the crucial task of becoming focused on each party's trial theory. The opening should focus on narrowing the issues for the jury. By the time the openings are given, the attorneys will have identified precisely the real issues in contention, and explaining this to the jury will help it to focus its attention on the proof related to these issues.

3. We have noted that the parties may allude to the law in their opening statements. This should be done with care, however, in order to avoid the vices both of argument and of invasion of the province of the judge. The attorney can refer to basic concepts concerning the burden of proof or the elements of a crime or a defense, so long as he or she does not launch into a jury instruction on these matters.

4. Some strategic considerations in opening statements are different for prosecutors and defense attorneys. The prosecutor should describe the evidence that will support a finding of proof beyond a reasonable doubt for each element of the charge. The opening should, that is, tell the story of the prosecution's case so that when the jurors are presented with a piece of evidence they will understand where in the prosecution's story it fits. Every statement of the prosecutor should be in support of its trial theory of why the defendant is guilty of the charged offense, and the jury should understand how the evidence that is being discussed provides such support. One commonly hears prosecutors telling juries that their opening is a "roadmap" of the case. While the cliche is a bit tired, it does describe in essence what the prosecution opening is about.

As for the defense, although there is no obligation to make an opening statement, it is generally poor practice for the defense to waive this opportunity. Because in the federal system the attorney is not likely to have had much—or indeed any—direct contact with the jury during the voir dire, the opening gives the defense attorney the opportunity to present himself or herself to the jury, to begin to establish rapport with it, and remind the jury of the government's burden of proof and the presumption of innocence. Even more important, the jury, having heard the presentation of damning evidence by the prosecution, should be provided with reasons to doubt that evidence and support the conclusion that the defendant is not guilty.

Because the defense has no burden to meet in most cases, the defense opening will usually be more narrowly focused than the government's opening. As with the prosecution, the defense must explain its theory of the case. It is generally not effective to limit the opening simply to highlighting the failings of the government proof, without offering the defense's own explanation of the evidence. This alternative explanation does not have to explain exactly what happened, but it must offer facts that will demonstrate the weaknesses of the government's case. While openings are not summations and should be pared down for the reasons discussed above, defense openings must be a substantive rebuttal to the government's preview and should introduce the defense themes, even if the level of detail given is far less than in the government's opening.

Accomplishing this presents several challenges. Because the defense case might consist in large part, or entirely, of fragments of a story established in piecemeal fashion during cross-examination of the government's witnesses, the defense must find some way to present its theory so that the jury will understand the import of the cross-examinations. Defense counsel must often do this, moreover, without alerting the government to the particular means that will be used to impeach the government witnesses or the identity of the defense witnesses. One of the best weapons the defense may have is the element of surprise, enhanced by the limits on government access to the defense case in pretrial discovery and the fact that the government must go first. Similarly, defense counsel should be cautious about making promises in the opening as to what evidence it will adduce, since it is often unclear how the case may evolve. The defense may decide to present fewer witnesses than planned or no witnesses at all if counsel believes at the end of the government's case that the government has not met its burden.

§ 16.3(c) United States v. Christopher and Van Ness—Opening Statements

(1) The Court's Ruling on the Motion in Limine

Prior to the opening statements, Judge Sheridan ruled on the government's motion in limine to introduce evidence of prior instances of Mr. Christopher's alleged drug trafficking. He issued his ruling then so that the parties would know what could and could not be stated in their openings. The judge ruled that the government may not introduce any evidence that Paul Christopher had engaged in drug trafficking prior to the course of conduct alleged in the indictment. The judge found that such evidence would require a trial within a trial and that, since the government's proof of such other acts consisted entirely of the testimony of Gilbert Santiago, the probative value of such evidence was substantially outweighed by the risk of unfair prejudice.[29]

(2) Knapp's Opening Statement

Good afternoon members of the jury. As Judge Sheridan told you this morning, my name is Laura Knapp and I am an Assistant United States Attorney, representing the United States in this case. Seated with me at counsel table and assisting me is Special Agent Ralph Martinez of the Drug Enforcement Administration.

This case is about how the defendants, Paul Christopher and William Van Ness, along with two other men you will meet, Gilbert Santiago and Mario Long, turned a legitimate business into a cocaine importation and distribution enterprise. You will learn that Paul Christopher is a businessman who owns International Food Distributors, a once legitimate business that, under his leadership, branched out into cocaine importation and distribution and money laundering. You will also learn that William Van Ness played a key role in that organization, picking up and delivering those cocaine shipments for his brother-in-law, Paul Christopher. You will learn about the activities of these two men from a number of sources, including two men who worked in that corrupt organization, Gilbert Santiago and Mario Long, who are both intimately familiar with its day to day functioning.

(Knapp then describes the gist of the structuring and money laundering counts in the same way, giving approximate dates and amounts.)

The government will prove all of these charges by presenting you with three kinds of evidence. You will hear from several witnesses who will tell you what they saw, heard, did or learned about the events of this case. You will see physical evidence, including the cocaine and bank and business records. You will also be presented with stipulations, which are agreements between the parties, about

---

29. *See* FED. R. EVID. 403 (relevant evidence may be excluded if its probative value is substantially outweighed by the danger of unfair prejudice).

certain facts that are uncontested and that you may accept, in your role as the judges of the facts in this case.

The government's evidence will begin with the testimony of Gilbert Santiago. Mr. Santiago was the manager of Superior Warehouse, a company owned by Paul Christopher, and part of the operation of his food importing business, International Food Distributors. Mr. Santiago will tell you that he was hired by Mr. Christopher, on the recommendation of William Van Ness, who knew that Santiago had been convicted of narcotics trafficking. Thereafter, Christopher solicited Mr. Santiago to handle the receipt and distribution of crates of coffee each containing nearly ten kilograms, or 22 pounds of cocaine. He will tell you that he agreed to do that, and that he received about one-third of the profits from the drug activity, with Christopher receiving the other two-thirds. Mr. Santiago will tell you how the shipments of cocaine were received at Superior Warehouse on behalf of Paul Christopher and later shipped by William Van Ness to cash paying customers. We will have other witnesses who will describe how those drugs were discovered by the Drug Enforcement Administration. And we will show you the drugs that were seized at the warehouse.

Mr. Santiago will also tell you that at Christopher's behest he opened bank accounts in fictitious names, in order to hide, or launder, the proceeds from the drug operation. We will produce records proving that large amounts of cash were deposited in those accounts, and we will prove that, when Paul Christopher learned that his banking activities were being investigated by the Drug Enforcement Administration, he abruptly closed them.

Knapp would go on to summarize the testimony of each of the other witnesses. She would also bring out Santiago's and Long's cooperation agreements and guilty pleas. This tactic is a common one, useful because it demonstrates to the jury that the party offering the witness is forthright and not trying to hide the facts that might adversely affect the witness' credibility.

Now, you will also learn that after Gilbert Santiago was arrested in connection with the drug seizure at Superior Warehouse, he entered into a cooperation agreement with the government and pleaded guilty to conspiracy to distribute cocaine. He also has a prior conviction for narcotics distribution. Mr. Santiago has agreed to cooperate and testify because he hopes that by doing so he will spend less time in jail when his punishment is ultimately determined by the judge. Mr. Santiago may not be a person you like, or a person whose criminal acts you would ever endorse. But at the end of the trial the issue for you is *not* going to be whether you like Mr. Santiago or approve of what he has done. The questions in the end will be did his testimony make sense, did it ring true, and was it corroborated by and consistent with all of the other evidence you

will hear and see in this case, and the answers to all of these
questions, we submit, will be yes.

The evidence you will hear over the next several days will establish
that these two defendants are guilty of the crimes charged in this
indictment. I want to talk with you now about the indictment. It
contains 22 counts, and additional provisions providing for forfeiture
of property. It may be helpful to think of those counts in two
categories.

The first category concerns narcotics, and is the subject of
Counts 1–12. They charge Paul Christopher and William Van Ness
with both conspiring or agreeing with others to import multiple
shipments of cocaine, with participating in the actual importation of
those shipments, and with possession and attempted possession of
the cocaine with intent to distribute it. The second category concerns financial transactions related to the narcotics activities. These
transactions are the subject of Counts 13–22. They charge Paul
Christopher with conspiring to launder money and laundering it,
that is to conceal its source as proceeds of narcotics activities, and
with conspiring to structure financial transactions and with structuring, that is to break bank deposits into small sums in order to
avoid reporting requirements.

In addition to these Counts the indictment contains forfeiture
allegations, charging that property that has been used in the illegal
activities charged in the indictment should be forfeited to the
government. There are two forfeiture allegations, one charging that
the property of Paul Christopher and William Van Ness used in
their narcotics activities should be forfeited and the other charging
that the property of Paul Christopher used in the money laundering
activities should be forfeited.

Knapp would end her opening by asking the jurors to pay attention
to the evidence and keep an open mind. Her last words would be:

At the end of all the evidence, I will have the opportunity to
present a closing argument to you. At that time I will ask you to
return the only verdict consistent with all of the evidence you will
have heard—a verdict that both defendants are guilty, beyond a
reasonable doubt, of each and every one of the crimes charged in the
indictment.

(3) The Defense Openings

(a) Clark's Opening for Christopher. Clark's opening statement would present Christopher's theory of defense—that Santiago engaged in a rogue operation unbeknownst to him and that he was an unwitting participant in Santiago's narcotics scheme. In addition, Clark would provide an explanation to the jury for certain facts that he expected the government to elicit and that on their face appeared damaging to Christopher. Thus, he would state that the evidence would establish that the bank accounts were set up not to launder the proceeds of illegal narcotics activities, but to skim cash from Christopher's legitimate operations and avoid reporting the income to the Internal Revenue Service. In making this statement, Clark would obviously be taking a calculated risk, because he is admitting that Christopher has committed another federal offense. The risk would be a prudent one, however, because the existence of the bank accounts must be explained. Even if he could be prosecuted for tax evasion, that is a much less serious crime.

(b) Rothman's Opening for Van Ness. Rothman's opening would emphasize that Van Ness ran a legitimate trucking business and that he was unaware of any of the illegal activities in which Santiago and/or Christopher might have been engaged. It also would stress the government's burden of proof, and the absence of evidence of Van Ness' guilty knowledge.

> Members of the jury, my name is Martin Rothman and I have the pleasure of representing William Van Ness in this case. The government is going to prove to you that William Van Ness drove a truck and did some business with his brother-in-law, Paul Christopher. Mr. Van Ness doesn't dispute these facts. He embraces them— doing legitimate business with his brother-in-law was exactly what he thought he was engaged in. As you'll see, the government's entire case will be that William Van Ness' trucking company picked up shipments from Superior Warehouse that its witnesses say included crates containing cocaine and that's it. There will be no evidence that Mr. Van Ness knew about the cocaine or intended to do anything other than to deliver crates containing food. As Judge Sheridan will tell you in his instructions on the law applicable to this case, William Van Ness is not guilty of the crimes charged in the indictment if he simply delivered crates that he did not know contained cocaine.

> Ms. Knapp has described several different witnesses and other sources of evidence, but in the course of the government's case you will learn that neither Gilbert Santiago, the person who was in charge of the cocaine distribution scheme and the government's star witness, nor any other individual, even so much as spoke with William Van Ness about narcotics, intimated that the crates might contain cocaine, or suggested that by distributing the crates, Mr.

Van Ness would be furthering the objects of an illegal conspiracy. The government's evidence in this case will fail to prove beyond a reasonable doubt that Mr. Van Ness acted knowingly and willfully, as those words will be explained to you by Judge Sheridan,—in other words, with knowledge that the shipment contained cocaine, and thus, your job will be easy at the end of this case because the government simply has no evidence that Mr. Van Ness knew the shipment contained cocaine.

As you will hear from Judge Sheridan, your role is made easier by the safeguards we have in our system that require that Mr. Van Ness be presumed innocent as he sits here throughout this trial and the government must prove their theory beyond a reasonable doubt. In addition, Mr. Van Ness has no obligation whatsoever to present evidence of any kind or prove anything.

As Judge Sheridan told you, there are two defendants on trial in this case. You must consider the evidence the government presents separately as to each of the defendants, as if there were two separate trials being conducted in this courtroom. Please give each case the separate consideration it deserves, by keeping an open mind, listening to and considering both the direct and cross-examination, not forming any opinions until you have heard all the evidence and the judge's instructions on the law. If you follow that course, I am certain that after you have heard all the evidence and lack of evidence, you will find that the government has not proven beyond a reasonable doubt that William Van Ness committed any of the crimes charged in the indictment and that you will find him not guilty.

---

§ 16.4 The Government's Case-in-Chief—Rules Related to Eliciting Testimony

After opening statements are completed, the testimonial stage of the trial begins. The process starts with the government's case-in-chief, during which it will put on whatever evidence it has to meet both its burden of production and burden of persuasion with respect to each element of the crimes charged.[30]

All evidence must be elicited through the testimony of witnesses,[31] each of whom must be shown to be *competent* to testify about the

30. Theoretically, there are circumstances in which the government would not have to adduce in its direct case evidence to counter a defense asserted by the defendant, since the defendant will not yet have put the issue into the case. In such circumstances, the government would have a right to meet the defense in a rebuttal case. As a practical matter, however, where it is conceded by defense counsel that the defense will be offered, the court will permit the prosecution to anticipate it, rather than have to reopen the case and recall witnesses already called for other purposes.

31. Or the functional equivalent of that testimony, i.e. stipulation.

matters that will be asked of them; to have testimony that is *relevant;* and to meet standards of *reliability* required of trial witnesses by the rules of evidence. Let us review these principles, introduced in Chapter 3.[32]

§ 16.4(a) Establishing Competence—Laying the Foundation for the Witness' Testimony

The initial task in any direct examination is to establish that the witness is competent to testify about that which he or she is being questioned. Unless this "foundation" is laid, the testimony will not be permitted. The type of foundation that will be required depends upon the type of witness being examined. Occurrence witnesses must be shown to have been in a position to perceive the events in question. Authentication witnesses must be shown to be familiar with the item to be identified. Opinion witnesses must be shown either to have personal knowledge of the matter they will appraise, or, if they are experts, a basis for reaching the conclusions that they will announce.[33]

Specific questioning litanies designed to establish competence of the various witness types have developed over time. We will not recite these protocols here.[34] However, the process of demonstrating competence can be fully understood as involving two tasks: establishing the *personal qualifications* of the witness to give testimony; and establishing the witness' *basis of knowledge* of the facts in question.

(1) Personal Qualifications

For most witnesses, the qualifications necessary to testify are demonstrated simply by the witness' appearance on the witness stand. That is, most witnesses must be shown to be in possession of the mental and physical characteristics required to observe, recall, and communicate about the events in question. The attorney usually does not need to be concerned with making an extensive showing of these qualifications, although on occasion it may be important to address a particular physical impairment that might raise questions in this regard.

The one special case with respect to personal qualifications is the expert witness. Usually called to give an opinion with respect to some scientific fact, the person's expertise—education, experience, special training—is elicited prior to the time that his or her opinion can be given.[35]

(2) Basis of Knowledge

The means for establishing the basis of knowledge of the most common type of witness is to elicit testimony as to what he or she

32. *See supra* § 3.3(b).

33. For a discussion of types of witnesses, see *supra* § 3.3(c).

34. A useful compilation is found in MAUET, at 319–327 (introducing expert testimony), 155–157 (introducing character testimony), 168–175 (introducing exhibits).

35. FED. R. EVID. 703.

experienced about an event or scene through the use of his or her senses.[36] Beyond being *competent* to observe, therefore, the witness must be asked questions that will establish the witness' opportunity to see, hear, etc., by placing the witness at the scene, demonstrating his or her familiarity with the place and/or people in it, and having the witness describe the conditions there in a way that will demonstrate the likelihood that the witness' observation was accurate.

While first-hand perception of the subject matter of the testimony is most commonly the basis of knowledge, there are circumstances in which the witness can testify as to what the witness learned from others. Thus, occurrence witnesses can testify about that which others told them concerning events relevant to the case, if that testimony falls within an exception to the hearsay rule.[37] Similarly, authentication witnesses can rely on documentary entries made by others,[38] expert witnesses can testify to scientific investigations not conducted personally,[39] and opinion witnesses can testify to the reputation of another witness or the defendant.[40]

§ 16.4(b) Establishing the Reliability of the Witness' Testimony

Testimony designed to demonstrate competence by proving the witness' personal qualifications and basis of knowledge must meet the standards established for trial testimony by the rules of evidence. If they do, the testimony will be deemed to be reliable enough to be considered by the trier of fact. Rules regulating the testimony at trial of occurrence witness,[41] expert witnesses,[42] and authentication witnesses[43] must be studied in detail prior to the time that testimony is offered. Again, the proponent of the testimony should either seek an *in limine* ruling if admissibility is in doubt or be prepared to proffer the basis for admissibility in response to an objection at the time the testimony is offered.

---

36. FED. R. EVID. 602.

37. *See* McCORMICK, § 10. A recent ruling by the Supreme Court regarding the admissibility of hearsay statements of unavailable witnesses requires caution insofar as texts rely on the standard announced in *Ohio v. Roberts*, 448 U.S. 56, 65–66 (1980) (admissibility linked to a judicial determination of sufficient "indicia of reliability"). In *Crawford v. Washington*, 541 U.S. 36 (2004), the Court held that the *Roberts* test is not applicable to "testimonial" statements, i.e., statements made under circumstances which would lead an objective witness reasonably to believe that the statement would be available for use at a later proceeding. The Court ruled that the Sixth Amendment confrontation clause would be violated unless that statement was subject to cross-examination at the time it was made. *Id.* at 59.

38. *See* McCORMICK, § 219.

39. *See id.*, § 15.

40. *See id.*, § 191.

41. FED. R. EVID. 801–807 (defining hearsay and exceptions to the hearsay rule).

42. FED. R. EVID. 702–706.

43. FED. R. EVID. 901–902.

§ 16.4(c) Establishing the Relevance of the Witness' Testimony

To be relevant, testimony must be shown to have some tendency to make the existence of a fact of consequence more probable or less probable than it would be without that testimony.[44] Evidence that does not meet that test is inadmissible.[45]

Challenges to the relevance of testimony can be made either to the propriety of calling a witness at all or to the propriety of a particular question propounded to a witness whose testimony is otherwise relevant. In either case, the most common response by the party seeking to elicit the testimony is to make a proffer, or offer of proof of the proposed testimony. Judges may reserve ruling on relevance issues by accepting testimony subject to connection or to a motion to strike.

§ 16.4(d) The Government's Case-in-Chief—Strategic Considerations

1. Structuring a Believable Narrative

Whether the events in question are to be related by several witnesses or by a single witness, the direct examiner is faced with the tactical decision of how to order the narrative: What facts should be elicited first? Should the attorney begin with the event itself or build to it? Should he or she lead with the strongest witness or end with that witness?

Questions of this sort cannot be fully answered in the abstract, since each case will have its own unique characteristics. In planning the narrative, however, the following considerations should be kept in mind.

(a) It is normally best to put the critical events before the jury as succinctly and quickly as possible: to restate, in the form of evidence, the ultimate facts at issue and then to turn to whatever corroborative evidence of those facts that the witness, or other witnesses, can provide. Put in the terms of the three kinds of testimony that were discussed in the last section, occurrence testimony should normally precede opinion and authentication testimony.

(b) As to presenting the occurrence, it is necessary to provide an orderly chronology in order to enable the trier of fact to comprehend the testimony and to appreciate its significance. People are accustomed to having a scene set for them first, hearing the preliminary events next, and then being brought to the occurrence itself. In preparing for a trial, the prosecutor may try explaining the facts of the case to a person

---

44. FED. R. EVID. 401. *See* WEINSTEIN & BERGER, §§ 401.02–401.08.

45. FED. R. EVID. 402. A court also may exclude testimony, even if it is deemed to be relevant, if its probative value is substan-tially outweighed by the danger of unfair prejudice, or if it would confuse the jury, or be duplicative, or otherwise a waste of time. FED. R. EVID. 403. *See* WEINSTEIN & BERGER, §§ 403.02–403.06.

unfamiliar with them to determine whether the narrative naturally falls into that sequence.

2. Establishing the Credibility of the Witness

A second component of presenting a believable narrative on direct examination is to establish that the witness, as distinct from his or her story, is credible. This task is complicated by the rules limiting the extent to which evidence of the witness' character can be offered or his or her testimony "bolstered" by showing that it is consistent with what the witness has said in the past about the events in question. We must examine these rules before suggesting means by which personal credibility can be established.

(a) Evidence of the Witness' Good Character

"Character evidence," as used in the rules of evidence, refers to evidence in the form of testimony either as to the witness' opinion of a person's character or trait of character; or the witness' opinion as to a person's reputation for a particular character trait.[46] It is generally impermissible under the rules to introduce evidence of a witness' good character on direct examination unless the witness' character previously has been challenged, in which case evidence of good character can be offered.[47]

The one exception to the rule concerns the character of a defendant in a criminal case. It is permissible to introduce character evidence in the defense case,[48] although doing so provides the government with an opportunity it might otherwise not have to attack the defendant's character. It is because such evidence "opens the door" to potentially harmful evidence by the prosecution—e.g., introduction of a defendant's prior criminal record through cross-examination of a character witness— that defense counsel generally refrains from eliciting character evidence unless the defendant's history is free of prior bad conduct.[49]

Despite the general rule prohibiting character evidence, there are informal practices in all courts that give the direct examiner some leeway in establishing the character of the witness during the development of the narrative. "Background" evidence is permitted that provides demographic information about the witness: employment status (nature of job, length of employment) is always allowed, even when it has

---

46. FED. R. EVID. 608(a).

47. FED. R. EVID. 608(b). WEINSTEIN & BERGER, § 608.11. If the witness' character is attacked on cross, evidence of good character and truthfulness is admissible on redirect. FED. R. EVID. 608(a); WEINSTEIN & BERGER, §§ 608.11, 608.13. The rationale behind this limitation is that evidence of this sort is not sufficiently relevant to risk the prejudice and confusion it might cause until credibility is attacked.

The rules also allow the defendant to introduce opinion evidence that goes to the victim's character. FED. R. EVID. 404(a)(2); WEINSTEIN & BERGER, §§ 404.10–404.12. *See also* WEINSTEIN & BERGER, § 608.13.

48. FED. R. EVID. 404(a)(1); MCCORMICK, § 191.

49. FED. R. EVID. 404(a)(1); MCCORMICK, § 191.

nothing whatever to do with the case, other than to enable the jury to assess the witness' credibility. Similarly, defendants will be permitted to testify and bolster their credibility without putting their character in issue by testifying that they were in the military and received medals or at least an honorable discharge; and even that they had never been arrested or convicted of a crime. Marital status and place and length of residence are offered less frequently, but when colorably relevant to the credibility of the witness may be elicited. Of course, if the direct examiner pushes too far, it is likely that he or she will be stopped or warned that he or she is opening the door on the issue of character and to rebuttal testimony on negative character traits or behavior.

The rules prohibiting the proponent from eliciting character evidence do not apply to establishing *negative* character traits. As we noted above with respect to gaps or inconsistencies in the witness' versions of the events, it is generally helpful—or at least less harmful—to the witness' credibility to bring such evidence out on direct examination. Obviously, we do not mean to suggest that the direct examiner should call opinion witnesses to denounce the witness in question. We do suggest, however, that evidence of misconduct that is very likely to be brought out on cross-examination, be brought out on direct. This is a useful way of defusing the issue and avoiding the impression that the witness and/or the party presenting the witness is not being completely forthcoming.

(b) Evidence That the Witness' Testimony Is Consistent With Earlier Accounts Given by the Witness

With one exception, it is impermissible to "bolster" a witness' testimony by showing that the witness made prior consistent statements in the past. The exception to the rule is that such testimony is permitted if the statement is "one of identification of a person made after perceiving the person."[50]

The general prohibitions against bolstering should not be confused with the rules regarding eliciting prior statements either when the witness' present testimony has been attacked on cross-examination as a recent fabrication;[51] or when a witness has a present failure of recollection.[52] Prior statements may be elicited in those circumstances.

§ 16.4(e) Eliciting Direct Testimony—Forms of Questions

We have previously suggested that direct examination should take the form of a combination of open and closed questions, avoiding both

---

50. FED. R. EVID. 801(d)(1)(C); WEINSTEIN & BERGER, § 801.23. The rationale behind the exceptions is that earlier identifications are likely to be less suggestive than those made in court. *See* FED. R. EVID. 801 advisory committee's note.

51. *See* FED. R. EVID. 801(d)(1)(B); WEINSTEIN & BERGER, § 801.22.

52. FED. R. EVID. 803(5); WEINSTEIN & BERGER, § 803.07.

narrative and leading questions.[53] This is because the open and closed forms are best adapted to facilitate the witness' effort to relate his or her story, which, of course, is the purpose of direct examination. Narrative questions are inappropriate because they provide too little assistance to the witness and increase the danger that inadmissible, irrelevant and prejudicial testimony will be introduced. Leading questions are inappropriate because they undermine the purpose of direct examination in that they effectively shift the testimonial function to the lawyer. It is for these reasons that neither narrative or leading questions should *normally* be used on direct and are, under the rules, objectionable if they are used.[54]

The "art" of direct examination is in developing an effective blend of open and closed questions, so that the narrative flows well.

§ 16.4(f) United States v. Christopher—The Government's Case-in-Chief

The government's first witness was Gilbert Santiago. He was followed by three other witnesses. Santiago was called first because he alone could provide a complete chronological overview of the events that occurred during the course of the conspiracy and could describe the roles of Christopher and Van Ness in it. Santiago's entire direct testimony will not be recounted here; it would essentially track his written proffer.[55] In the next section, however, we will present excerpts of the testimony in order to demonstrate the principles of direct examination that we have discussed above. After a discussion of the principles of cross-examination, we will again present excerpts of the cross of Santiago by Clark and Rothman.

The government's other witnesses were essentially called to corroborate and explain Santiago's testimony. Mario Long testified about the warehouse operations, the role played by Santiago and Van Ness in handling the drugs, and Christopher's instructions to take orders from Santiago.

Agent Martinez testified to the detection and seizure of the drugs on October 12. The drugs were introduced into evidence through him, after he authenticated them by establishing a reliable chain of custody.[56] The stipulation of the parties regarding the testimony of the chemist as to the weight and nature of the drugs was read at that point. Martinez also provided expert testimony as to the manner in which drugs are smuggled into the country and distributed. He testified to the records seized in the

---

53. *See supra* § 3.3(e).

54. There are exceptions to these rules. A narrative question may be appropriate in the case of a thoroughly prepared and experienced witness, e.g., a police officer. Similarly, leading questions are not objectionable when the issue is not in dispute, and asking it in a leading form saves time.

FED. R. EVID. 611(c) also allows a party to use leading questions in examining a hostile witness or one identified with the adverse party. WEINSTEIN & BERGER, § 611.06.

55. *See supra* § 8.3(e).

56. MAUET, at 179–183.

search at Superior Warehouse, although they had been introduced through Santiago. He also testified regarding Superior records produced by the company in response to a subpoena. He described Christopher's movements during the DEA surveillance of him, and the telephone records were introduced by stipulation.

Finally, a handwriting expert was called to identify Christopher's signature on the signature cards used to open the bank accounts in fictitious company names; a stipulation was read into the record concerning the testimony of an official from the New York Department of State, to prove Christopher's ownership interest in IFD and Superior Warehouse; and bank records showing cash deposits of less than ten thousand dollars were introduced by stipulation.

§ 16.4(g) Conducting a Direct Examination—The Testimony of Gilbert Santiago

As we have noted, the ultimate goal of direct examination is to structure a believable narrative and establish the witness as a credible person. The starting point for this task is to lay a foundation for the narrative by establishing the witness' competence to testify—his basis of knowledge—and, to the extent relevant, his credibility. In eliciting this or any other testimony, the attorney must be prepared to defend each question asked against challenge by opposing counsel or the judge on both substantive grounds and as to the form of the question.[57]

After the witness is sworn and states his or her name and address, some biographical information will commonly be elicited, such as employment history and educational background. The testimony would begin with a series of questions designed to establish when and how Santiago came to meet Van Ness and how he was hired and became a manager there. Knapp also would introduce at this point the fact that Santiago had recently been released from prison and was on supervised release for a narcotics violation and that Van Ness knew that. This would be relevant to the government's theory that Santiago was later hired by Christopher after Van Ness learned of Santiago's experience in drug trafficking.

The foundation testimony would be completed by eliciting testimony regarding the beginning of Santiago's involvement in the conspiracy. The substance of the conversation between Christopher and Santiago and Santiago's later involvement in the drug operation would then be adduced. Note throughout the examination the use of open questions that allow the witness to describe the events in his own way, comple-

---

57. *See supra* § 3.3. We described substantive objections as those related to the competency of the witness to testify, the relevance of the testimony, or its admissibility under the rules of evidence. Objections as to form include leading (on direct examination), compound questions, argumentative questions and questions likely to confuse the witness.

mented by closed questions to keep him on track and assure that all relevant points are covered:

AUSA Knapp: Did there come a time in May, 2004, when you had a conversation with William Van Ness?

Santiago: Yes.

Knapp: Where did the conversation take place?

Santiago: In his office at the trucking company.

Knapp: Was anyone else present during this conversation?

Santiago: Yes, Paul Christopher.

Knapp: What if anything did Van Ness say during this conversation?

Knapp would be prepared at this point for an objection by Christopher's attorney on the grounds of hearsay. Her response would be that the statement was admissible against Van Ness as an admission and against Christopher because it was a statement made in furtherance of a conspiracy, and therefore an admissible form of hearsay.[58] The court would permit the question, although conditionally, i.e., subject to connection or to a motion to strike, if the conspiracy were not established and Van Ness and Christopher were not shown to have been members of that conspiracy.[59]

Santiago: He told me that he wanted to introduce me to Paul Christopher, who he said was his brother-in-law.

Knapp: What if anything happened after Van Ness introduced you to Paul Christopher?

Santiago: Van Ness then left the office.

58. Fed. R. Evid. 801(d)(2)(E). Weinstein & Berger, § 801.34.

59. Bourjaily v. United States, 483 U.S. 171, 175 (1987); United States v. Vinson, 606 F.2d 149, 153 (6th Cir. 1979) (existence of conspiracy as basis for introduction of co-conspirator's statements is a preliminary question for the trial judge; court may, within its discretion under Rule 611(a), admit the statements subject to later proof of conspiracy).

Knapp:	Did a conversation ensue between you and Christopher thereafter?
Santiago:	Yes.
Knapp:	Tell the jury what Christopher said to you and what you said to him.
Santiago:	Mr. Christopher told me that he understood that I had been in prison for cocaine trafficking. He said that his company, International Food Distributors, which imported coffee and other food products from South America, was in trouble and needed a sizeable loan to survive.
Knapp:	What if anything did Christopher suggest with regard to obtaining a loan?
Santiago:	Christopher said that because the banks had turned him down he thought he might turn to another source who had surplus cash that he wanted to replace with legitimate money. Christopher told me that he knew I had been involved in narcotics trafficking, and he asked me if I could help him get in touch with people I knew who would be in possession of cash and who would want to clean the money through making a loan to him.
Knapp:	How did you respond?
Santiago:	I told him I would think about it and that he should get back to me within about a week.
Knapp:	What if anything did you do with regard to Christopher's proposal?
Santiago:	Later that week I spoke with someone named Frankie who I used to know when I was in the drug business.
Knapp:	What did you tell Frankie and what did he say to you?
Santiago:	I told him that I knew someone in need of money who was in a legitimate business and who could launder drug money.
Knapp:	What was Frankie's response?
Santiago:	He told me to stay out of it because I was under supervision after my release from prison and that he would deal with it without involving me. He said he knew someone who he thought would be interested in the situation I had proposed.

Knapp:	How did you respond?
Santiago:	I told Frankie that the person who would contact him was named Paul Christopher, that he ran a large warehouse business, and that I would give him Frankie's name and explain to him how to contact Frankie.

The testimony would then turn to the next phase of the conspiracy, when Santiago came to work for Christopher.

Santiago:	I received a call from Mr. Christopher in early August 2004 while I was working at Van Ness Trucking as the day foreman. Christopher told me that he had received a loan through the contact that I had made for him. He said he had paid off the loan by accepting delivery of three drug shipments. He said that the man who had loaned him the money had called him and told him that he wanted to continue the relationship with him to import cocaine in food shipments.
Knapp:	Did Christopher tell you what the amount of the loan that he received was?
Santiago:	I think that he did, but I don't remember what he said.
Knapp:	Let me show you what has been premarked Government's exhibit 3501A for identification, and ask you to look at paragraph 7.[60] Does that refresh your recollection as to what Mr. Christopher told you he had been loaned?
Santiago:	Yes it does.
Knapp:	May I have 3501(A) back?
Santiago:	Yes.
Knapp:	And what is your present recollection as to what Christopher said?
Santiago:	He said that he had been loaned $50,000.

---

60. The document used to refresh the witness' recollection is the DEA6 report of Santiago's statement written by Agent Martinez at the time of Santiago's proffer agreement. *See supra* § 8.3(e).

This is the technique for responding to a frequent event at a trial, a memory lapse on the part of the witness. Note that any document can be used for this purpose; it need not be admitted into evidence or even admissible. It should not be read aloud or characterized, but merely given to the witness to read after showing it to opposing counsel.[61] After the detour caused by the need to refresh the witness' recollection, the attorney then asks what might be called a "bridge" question, i.e., one which includes within it the substance of the witness' answer prior to the interruption. This assures that both the witness and the jury keep the chronology of the testimony in mind.

Knapp: Now, when Christopher told you that the person who lent him the money wanted him to continue to import cocaine, did he say how he had responded to the man?

Santiago: Christopher said he was afraid to say no, and that the lender had offered him a percentage of the proceeds for each shipment. He said that he decided to accept the shipments provided he could figure out how to run the operation and deal with the cash while still operating his warehouses.

Knapp: Did you learn from Christopher why he was telling you about this?

Santiago: He asked me to run the operation for him and said that he would make me the manager of Superior Warehouse. He told me that Mario Long would serve as my foreman and that he could be trusted.

Knapp: Did Christopher inform you what your responsibilities would involve?

Santiago: I was to set up bank accounts, supervise the receipt and delivery of crates containing drugs, and make deposits in various bank accounts that we would set up.

The government would elicit additional details about the money laundering scheme. Then the questioning would turn to the details of

61. For illustrations of the technique for refreshing recollection, see MAUET, at 145–147.

the cocaine distribution scheme and Van Ness' role in transporting the crates containing narcotics.

Knapp: Did there come a time in September, 2004, that you had a conversation with Paul Christopher regarding a narcotics shipment?

Santiago: Yes.

Knapp: Where did that conversation take place?

Santiago: At my office in Superior Warehouse.

Knapp: Could you tell the jury what you said to Christopher and what he said to you at that time?

Santiago: Christopher told me that another shipment was coming in and that Mario Long, the foreman, would help me with it because he was loyal and could be trusted.

Knapp: Did Christopher subsequently have a conversation with Long in your presence?

Santiago: Yes. He told Long that he had made a special deal for a very high priced shipment and that he wanted Long to take special care to place some specially marked crates as I directed him.

Knapp: Did any further discussion occur?

Santiago: Yes. Long, Christopher and I spoke and we agreed that Long would place the crates in the locked security area where they would remain until I would check them out. Christopher said that after I cleared the shipment for delivery, his brother-in-law's trucking firm would pick up the crates.

Knapp: Did Christopher mention anything else about his brother in-laws trucking firm at that time?

Santiago: Yes. He said he had always used his brother-in-law's firm for special shipments and that he wanted to do so now.

Knapp: Did there come a time in September, 2004, when you were involved with a shipment at the warehouse?

440

Santiago: Yes. I was called by Long and told that a shipment had arrived. I inspected the crate in the security area and saw ten sealed packages that were wrapped in burlap. I poked a hole in one of the packages and tasted the powder which I recognized as cocaine. I taped the hole over and then called Van Ness Trucking.

Knapp: Did there come a time when Mr. Van Ness arrived?

Santiago: Yes. He came in his truck within fifteen minutes and I loaded the crate onto the truck myself.

Knapp: Did you have an opportunity to speak with Christopher on the following day?

Santiago: Yes. I spoke with him in my office where he gave me a briefcase that contained $25,000 in cash. He told me to deposit the cash in three different accounts using relatively equal amounts. He also gave me $12,500 for myself from the shipment.

Knapp: Did you subsequently carry out Mr. Christopher's instructions?

Santiago: Yes. Later that day I deposited the money in the accounts that we had opened at a nearby branch of CMS Bank.

While the direct examination of Gilbert Santiago establishes his competence to prove the elements of a conspiracy and that Van Ness and Christopher participated in this conspiracy, Santiago's credibility as a witness is in doubt because of his motive to lie. AUSA Knapp chose to confront this issue directly by first revealing the impeaching information herself through questions that focus on the nature of Santiago's plea agreement with the government, followed by questions that suggest that the agreement itself is a safeguard against unreliable testimony because of Santiago's belief that if he violated the obligation under the agreement to testify truthfully he would lose any chance for leniency and could and would be prosecuted for perjury and obstruction.

Knapp: Mr. Santiago, did there come a time on February 25, 2005 when you pleaded guilty to federal drug charges?

Santiago: Yes.

Knapp: In connection with that guilty plea, did you sign a written cooperation agreement with the government?

Santiago: Yes.

Knapp: What charge did you plead guilty to in connection with this cooperation agreement?

Santiago: Conspiracy to distribute cocaine.

Knapp: Have you been sentenced yet on that charge?

Santiago: No.

Knapp: What's your understanding of the maximum sentence you could receive for pleading guilty to that charge?

Santiago: Life in prison.

Knapp: What did you agree to do by signing the cooperation agreement?

Santiago: I agreed to cooperate, tell the government what I know, and testify when they ask me to.

Knapp: What's your understanding of what the government agreed to do if you hold up your end of the bargain?

Santiago: They will write a letter to the judge who is going to sentence me, so I can get a lower sentence.

Knapp: What's your understanding of what happens if you violate your cooperation agreement with the government?

Santiago: There will be no letter to the judge. I go to jail for at least 10 years. Maybe a lot more, because the government could then file a piece of paper that means I have to go to jail for at least 20 years.

Knapp: Anything else?

Santiago: I can be prosecuted for perjury and obstruction of justice.

Knapp: As you understand it, if the government writes a letter to the judge on your behalf, is the judge required to give you a lower sentence?

Santiago: No.

442

Knapp:	As you understand it, if the government writes a letter to the judge, who decides how much time you have to spend in prison—the government or the judge?
Santiago:	The judge.
Knapp:	Have you been promised any particular sentence?
Santiago:	No.
Knapp:	As you sit here today, do you know what sentence you will receive?
Santiago:	No.

§ 16.5 Challenging the Government's Case-in-Chief—Cross-examination

We have described the government's goal on direct examination as producing competent, relevant and reliable evidence with respect to each element of the crimes charged. We can describe the goal of the defense on cross-examination in the same way: either to produce reliable evidence on an issue favorable to the defense, but not emphasized by the prosecution, or to undermine the direct examination by demonstrating that the testimony offered to prove an element was either not competent (i.e., the witness did not have personal knowledge of that about which he or she testified); of limited relevance (because the witness omitted aspects of the story that when taken in context minimize the importance of that to which the witness testified); and/or not reliable (because, for example, the witness had some bias, prejudice or interest in the outcome). Cross-examination is designed to persuade the jury that there is a different reality with regard to the issue in dispute than that suggested by the direct examination.

While this section discusses cross-examination by the defense, the same rules and techniques apply, of course, to cross-examination conducted by the prosecution. Our focus on the defense is in recognition of the fact that most cross-examination is conducted by defense counsel since most testimony at trial is by government witnesses. It is not uncommon for the defense to offer no testimony at all, and in almost every case it will present far fewer witnesses than the government.

§ 16.5(a) The Scope of Cross-examination

The cross-examiner may inquire into any matter that relates to the credibility of the witness or any aspect of the facts mentioned by the witness. The cross-examiner may not, however, seek to elicit facts from the witness that are not part of the subject-matter about which the witness testified on direct examination, even if they are relevant to the case and the witness is competent to testify about them.[62] Many judges, however, take a practical approach in defining the scope of the cross-examination and adopt a broad definition of the "subject matter" of the direct examination, particularly if the area that is the subject of the cross-examination is intended to undermine the other side's purpose for calling the witness. In cases in which the cross-examiner wishes to explore with the witness a subject that was not even arguably raised on direct, the proper procedure takes one of two forms. The attorney can await the presentation of his or her case (e.g., in the defense case where the witness is testifying for the government or in the government's rebuttal case where the direct is of a defense witness) and call the witness on direct. Alternatively, the attorney, as provided by the rules, may ask the court to allow the cross-examiner to engage in a direct examination of the witness at that point.[63] Such an examination, which occurs when cross-examination would normally occur, is supposed to be conducted in the same manner as if the witness had been called by the defense and examined on direct examination, i.e., through the use of nonleading questions unless the witness is clearly hostile. Many judges, however, will not hold lawyers to the strict letter of the rule and will simply permit a more expansive cross-examination.

The restrictive rule limiting the scope of cross-examination to the subject matter of the direct does not mean that the inquiry is restricted only to the specific *facts* so elicited. A "rule of completeness" permits the cross-examiner to elicit omitted facts so long as they are pertinent to the matter testified to on direct.[64] The obvious purpose of this rule is to insure that the cross-examiner will have a full opportunity to establish facts in support of the examiner's trial theory and to challenge the truthfulness and accuracy of the direct testimony.

§ 16.5(b) Types of Cross-examination

We noted in Chapter 3 that cross-examination could be either accrediting or discrediting.[65] Both types of cross-examination may be employed in the examination of the same witness. In the discussion that follows, we will examine these concepts more closely and illustrate them with the cross-examinations of Gilbert Santiago by Christopher's and Van Ness' lawyers. Let us first review the principles of cross-examination previously enumerated.

(1) Accrediting Cross-examination

An accrediting cross-examination is one in which the purpose is to adduce facts from the witness that support the cross-examiner's theory of the case or, at least, demonstrate that the witness has not testified on

---

62. FED. R. EVID. 611(b). *See* WEINSTEIN & BERGER, § 611.03.

63. FED. R. EVID. 611(b).

64. *See* MCCORMICK, § 21.

65. *See supra* § 3.3(f).

direct in a manner inconsistent with that theory. An accrediting cross-examination is not directed at demonstrating that the witness' story is false but, rather, is directed at demonstrating that the direct examination did not tell the full story or emphasizing the important facts related to the opponent's trial theory that shed a different light on the events in question. Similarly, an accrediting cross-examination is not intended to show that the witness is not worthy of belief. Instead, this type of examination portrays the witness as credible with respect to the additional facts elicited on cross-examination that support the examiner's trial theory. It is important to stress that putting aside the popular treatment of the trial in books, movies and television, accrediting cross-examination is the most common tool used by the defense to support the defendant's trial theory.

(2) Discrediting Cross-examination

Discrediting cross-examination is designed to demonstrate that the witness' story is not worthy of belief or that the witness is not a person who should be believed, even if the witness' story seems superficially credible. Discrediting the narrative of a witness is accomplished by demonstrating that it is illogical or otherwise at odds with common experience. Discrediting the witness directly can be done in a variety of ways. The witness' competence, i.e., his or her ability to perceive, recall and communicate about the matter in question, can be challenged. Cross-examination demonstrating incompetence can go to the physical conditions under which an observation was made or the condition of the witness at the time. The witness also can be attacked on the grounds of bias or that he or she has a motive to lie. This would include cross-examination designed to reveal preexisting prejudices that are related to the subject matter of the litigation or to one of the litigants, or some personal gain that the witness may obtain by testifying untruthfully.[66] Reliability also can be attacked on the grounds that the witness cannot be trusted, either because of prior bad acts, including prior convictions involving dishonesty;[67] or because he or she has made inconsistent statements about the events in question.[68]

§ 16.5(c) Preparing for Cross-examination

A major and obvious difference between direct examination and cross-examination is that the former can in most cases be meticulously planned in advance. Although the attorney must be equipped to handle the unexpected, for the most part the direct examination should be completely predictable. Cross-examination is by its nature more spontaneous and less predictable, since the lawyer must react to testimony, the

---

66. *See* FED. R. EVID. 404(b) (allowing a party to introduce evidence of other acts to show, inter alia, motive, knowledge and intent); WEINSTEIN & BERGER, §§ 404.20–404.22.

67. FED. R. EVID. 609(a). *See* WEINSTEIN & BERGER, §§ 609.02–609.08.

68. FED. R. EVID. 613. *See* WEINSTEIN & BERGER, §§ 613.02–613.05.

specifics of which are often not entirely known, particularly where the lawyer has had no access to the witness prior to the trial. Notwithstanding this inherent uncertainty, it is rare that the lawyer will be faced with the problem of confronting wholly unanticipated testimony. Consider these sources of knowledge as to the identity of the witnesses and to what they will testify:

1. *The opponent's case theory.* Through examination of the pleadings, formal and informal discovery processes, proposed voir dire questions, and opening statements, both parties will have a clear understanding of the nature of the opponent's case theory. That, in turn, provides important insights into what the testimony of that party's witnesses will *have* to be in order to make out its case. Obviously, this would only apply to the prosecutor to the extent that it can be predicted from the defendant's opening statement that the defendant will introduce testimony as part of the defense case.

2. *Prior statements of witnesses.* The most important source of information for the cross-examiner is the witness' prior statements about the case. These statements can come in many forms: the complaint, affidavits accompanying warrants; grand jury testimony, testimony at pretrial hearings, statements made by (or to) law enforcement officers and embodied in 3500 material and statements of government witnesses made to defense attorneys or their investigators. Such statements provide a "safety net" for the attorney, because they will either be a guide to how the witness will testify on direct or can be used to impeach the witness. That is, during the direct examination the witness either will testify consistently with the prior statement, in which case the attorney can plan in advance how to adduce accrediting information from the witness or how to meet the damaging material contained in the statement; or the witness will testify inconsistently with the statement, in which case the cross-examination will employ established procedures for impeaching the witness' credibility.[69] Thus, counsel should study with great care every document related in any way to the witness and the anticipated subject area of the direct-examination.

§ 16.5(d) The Decision Whether to Cross-examine

The fact that a party has a right to cross-examine does not necessarily mean that counsel should take advantage of it. In almost every instance, opposing witnesses will be cross-examined because most opposing witnesses either have evidence that is favorable to the cross-examiner and can be used for accrediting purposes or testify in a way that is damaging to the cross-examiner's theory of the case, requiring a discred-

---

69. For illustrations of techniques for impeachment with prior inconsistent statements, see MAUET, at 280–293.

iting cross. Even if the cross-examination consists of nothing more than emphasizing a helpful fact that was part of the direct, that can be an effective reminder to the jury of the importance of that fact to the party's theory.

Some witnesses, however, may provide testimony relevant to proving an essential element of a crime or a defense, but the existence of the element may not be in dispute. In such situations, it may be appropriate to waive cross-examination altogether and thereby emphasize to the jury the questioner's view that the testimony was insignificant. While one of the hardest things for many lawyers to say is "I have no questions," that can send an extremely effective message to the jury. Needless to say, this rationale should not be used as an excuse for counsel to forego cross-examination of a difficult witness or a witness for whom there is limited impeachment material. The test is whether the potential areas of cross-examination would be more or less effective than sending the message that the witness need not be cross-examined because he or she did not undermine the party's theory of the case.

§ 16.5(e) Eliciting Testimony on Cross-examination—The Structure of the Examination

When we discussed the structure of direct testimony we indicated that usually it followed a predictable linear format, i.e., one that established the witness' competence and then related a narrative in a way that would make sense to the jury, i.e., with a beginning, a middle, and an end.

Structural considerations for cross-examination are quite different. There are no external constraints on the cross-examiner such as those faced by the direct examiner. For example, the cross-examiner obviously is not concerned with the requirements for demonstrating competence, other than to explain the basis for accrediting the witness' testimony as to an issue in dispute. Nor is the cross-examiner concerned about eliciting a sequential narrative. Rather, on cross-examination, counsel has the freedom to select any topic on which to question the witness and any order in which to cover those topics that seems appropriate.

In deciding upon the structure of the cross-examination, we find it useful to think of each area to be covered as a chapter in a book, the object of which is either to have the witness accredit the cross-examiner's theory or to demonstrate that the witness' account is not worthy of belief, or both. The title of each chapter should be the ultimate conclusion one wishes the jury to draw (e.g., Santiago Is Lying to Save Himself). The chapter title is the argument the lawyer wants to make to the jury; it is *not* the final question—the "one too many" question—to ask the witness. Thinking in terms of chapters may help the attorney to focus on both the sequence of the subjects to be raised and the organization of the questions within each subject. Here are some possible considerations:

447

1. As a general rule, if the cross-examination will contain both accrediting and discrediting chapters, it is best to deal with the accrediting ones first. This is because the cross-examiner wishes to have the witness cooperate on these topics to validate the cross-examiner's trial theory. If the cross-examination begins with questions designed to impeach the witness on one aspect of his or her testimony, the witness' attitude is likely to be hostile by the time the accrediting topics are covered. In addition, it generally sends the wrong message to the jury to discredit the witness before eliciting testimony from the witness that you will argue to the jury was truthful.

2. The order of the remaining chapters should honor the primacy-recency rule. That is, jurors are most apt to recall what they hear first and last. Counsel should select the two strongest areas and generally save to the end of the examination the stronger of the two and use the other to begin this portion of the cross-examination. Ending the cross-examination on a high note with the most important area of cross-examination is important to leave the desired impression with the jury of the witness and his or her credibility. After selecting the first and last chapters for the cross-examination, the remaining chapters then can be organized in a manner that will make the most effective use of the cross-examination material, such as prior inconsistent statements, and de-emphasize those chapters that may fall flat.

3. Another advantage of the chapter approach is that it allows counsel to be flexible. If the direct appears to end on a particularly damning fact, it may make sense to begin the cross-examination with the chapter directed to impeaching the testimony regarding that fact. Shifting from subject to subject can also be used to keep the witness off-balance. Similarly, if the witness introduces a subject during cross-examination, it often can be effective to turn to that chapter immediately.

4. Most cross-examinations will not use all the chapters that have been prepared. Counsel has to distinguish between those cross-examination areas that support the party's theory and therefore will impress the jury and those areas that will be less effective. The chapter approach allows you to make decisions about whether or not to use a particular chapter following the direct and even while in the midst of the cross-examination.

5. However the cross-examination is structured, it is important to note that it need not, and should not, attempt to deal with all of the areas covered on direct examination. For the most part, the direct testimony will be damaging, and it is best not to emphasize that by repeating it. Rather, cross-examination is a targeted approach driven by the available evidence. The attorney should avoid cross-examination on inconsequential points, even where there

is a demonstrable discrepancy. Dwelling on such topics may be viewed by the jury as an act of desperation or nitpicking, and could also create sympathy for the witness. Rather, the cross-examination must be specifically targeted at the parts of the direct testimony (or the characteristics of the witness) that persuasively support the examiner's theory and/or discredit the witness.

§ 16.5(f) Eliciting Testimony on Cross-examination

As with direct examination, the form of questions used on cross-examination is directly related to the purpose of the examination. On direct, the focus is on the witness, and the purpose is to have the witness relate a story. The open-closed questioning process is designed to facilitate that, by allowing the witness freedom to respond. On cross-examination, the focus is on the examiner, who will be telling the story by making short declarative statements interrupted only by the witness' affirmation. The purpose is *never* to have the witness relate again the testimony given on direct examination. Instead, it is to have the witness confirm the cross-examiner's trial theory or to demonstrate why the witness' direct examination should not be believed. Open questions should therefore be avoided altogether, as they are likely to result simply in a confirmation of the direct examination. Closed questions, however, do have a role, and can be effectively used in two situations. First, they can be used to set the stage for the point that the cross-examiner will ultimately make with a leading question. Building to the point by having the witness establish its premises through his or her own words will help to dramatize it. Second, closed questions may be used when it is necessary for the cross-examiner to explore an area in an effort to obtain additional accrediting or discrediting facts that have not been elicited on direct or provided through the discovery process. This is a potentially dangerous practice because the cross-examiner is exploring a new area without knowing whether a harmful response will be given. The danger can be reduced if closed questions are used and the witness is asked first about neutral facts. With this information obtained, the lawyer may be in a position to assess the risk of a harmful answer to a pointed leading question.

The leading question, however, is best suited for cross-examination, because it contains the cross-examiner's desired response and gives the attorney the maximum degree of control over the witness. Much of what occurs on cross-examination is the witness' yes or no response to a declaration made by the lawyer. While witnesses have the right to explain that they cannot answer with a simple yes or no, even then the witness is responding to the suggestion made by the lawyer. However, it is often the case that when a witness does not give a simple yes or no answer, it is because the questions are too long or not sufficiently leading to make clear to everyone, including the witness, what the answer should be to the question. In other situations, however, an answer other than yes or no will be an obvious evasion. If that occurs, there are ways in which the witness can be conditioned to answer directly. For example, the lawyer can respond to a lengthy, unresponsive answer by simply asking the identical question again. By the third time, the witness is usually conditioned.

While leading questions are the rule on cross-examination, they do present a danger for the attorney. Because leading questions are by their nature argumentative in tone, they are frequently misused to engage in argument with the witness. It is perfectly proper, of course, to persist in a line of questions until the witness provides the facts that the attorney is seeking. It is improper, and often harmful to the attorney's case, to persist until the witness draws the *inference* from those facts that the lawyer wants drawn. It should be kept in mind that the goal of the trial is not to persuade the *witness* of the attorney's trial theory, but the jury or judge.

As to the sequence of questions within each of the topics or "chapters" of the cross-examination discussed above, we find the metaphor of a "box" useful. The walls of the box are composed of preliminary or set-up questions, the purpose of which is to insure that there will be only one possible response to the final question—the lid of the box—that the examiner asks. At the outset, counsel should ask the preliminary or set-up questions necessary to establish the four walls of the box in which the witness will be confined prior to tipping the witness off as to the purpose of the set-up questions. Every question should be broken down so that it conveys only one new fact. By the time the key question to the cross-examination is asked—i.e., the one that the witness may dispute—the four walls of the box should be in place so that witness is boxed in and the witness must answer the key question affirmatively (which serves as the lid to the figurative box). Finally, counsel should pause for the jury to get the point before turning to the next chapter. It is almost always the case that the cross-examination should proceed in this way. Asking the key question without first creating the box is usually a strategic mistake, because it allows the witness to provide an answer other than the desired one or invites a narrative response from the witness that destroys the effect of the examination. The same is even more true of the cross-examination that asks one question too many. This is the question that draws the inference created by the earlier questions. It is the point that the attorney wants to make in his or her closing argument, and it should be reserved for that stage, when it cannot be explained away by the witness' response.

We will illustrate below these principles just discussed through two simple cross-examinations.

1. Assume that the witness is Santiago who the defense is arguing is lying to lessen his own criminal exposure or sentence pursuant to his plea agreement. The title of this chapter should be "The Witness Will Lie to Obtain a Benefit for Himself." Assume that Santiago admitted on

direct examination that he had used drugs while on supervised release for his prior offense. The questioning would then be as follows:

Q: You would lie to obtain an important benefit for yourself, wouldn't you?

A: No.

Q: When you were on supervised release two years ago in an unrelated case, you wanted to complete that successfully so that you wouldn't go back to jail, right?

A: I guess.

Q: And you viewed that as a benefit that you desperately wanted– to avoid going back to jail?

A: Yes.

Q: And you knew that if you violated the terms of your supervised release you'd go back to jail?

A: That's right.

Q: You admitted on direct that you used drugs while on supervised release, didn't you?

A: Yes.

Q: You never told your probation officer about your drug use, did you?

A: Of course not.

Q: In fact, you lied to your probation officer to avoid going back to jail?

A: Yea.

Q: In other words, you lied in order to obtain a benefit for yourself?

A: Yes.

In this way, the defense counsel can take what is a helpful, but somewhat extraneous fact—that the defendant used drugs while on supervised release—and turn it into an admission that is the centerpiece of the cross-examination: that the witness will lie to obtain a benefit for himself. Having thus established this fact for the jury, the next chapter would be focused on showing the benefits that the witness hopes to obtain by testifying against the defendant.

Note the exclusive use of leading questions and the building of the walls through a series of questions that the attorney knew that the witness would have to answer in the way suggested by the attorney, either because the witness would not be credible if he answered any other way (e.g., that he wanted to avoid going back to jail) or because the attorney had a "safety net" (e.g., the witness' admission on direct that he used drugs while on supervised release).

2. Consider another example. To establish that it was dark out at the time that the agents were surveilling Superior Warehouse so that it would not have been possible for them to identify the people outside the warehouse as the testifying agent claimed, the box would be set up as follows:

Q: Agent, you are careful in maintaining notes of your undercover operations, correct? (Wall 1)

A: Yes.

Q: You are equally careful in typing up the summary of the investigation in a DEA Form 6? (Wall 2)

A: Yes.

Q: You keep a record of the start time and duration of undercover operations because those could be important facts in your investigation? (Wall 3)

A: Correct.

Q: The undercover operation at issue took place approximately three weeks after clocks were set back an hour at the end of daylight savings time? (If necessary, the witness is shown a copy of the New York Times giving such a reminder to refresh the witness' recollection.) (Wall 4)

A: Yes.

Q: Agent, comparing your handwritten log, which indicated that you completed your review of the undercover procedures with your team prior to the operation at 6:08 p.m., with your DEA Form 6, which indicates that you were conducting surveillance of the location for 1 hour and 50 minutes prior to observing people outside the warehouse, isn't it the case that the actual transaction could not have taken place prior to 7:58 p.m. (The "key" question and lid to the box).

A: Apparently so.

This cross-examination illustrates the point that in examining an uncooperative witness (as most will be on cross) the further away questions are from the issue that the witness is expected to dispute, the more likely it will be that the witness will give counsel the desired answers. In other words, the questioner must disguise that he or she is asking the specific questions to set up the witness for the key question so that the witness will not fight the questions. For example, if it was necessary to begin the above cross-examination by establishing that the area was not well lit, counsel could present a poster board of the location of the transaction and have the witness identify everything he recalls being present at that location, while counsel draws the objects described by the witness. Since the witness is not focused on the fact that he is about to be cross-examined about his inability to see the defendant, he presumably would not strain to recall lights being present (this of course assumes that the outside of the warehouse was not well lit).

Counsel also can try to create a safety net or backstop by using statements by third parties or something else to establish a needed fact for a cross-examination. Using the above example, counsel should have visited the location of the transaction prior to trial and would know whether lights were present at the location at the time of the visit. Counsel could show the witness a photograph of the location and establish that the location appears identical to the way it appeared on the night of the transaction to show that there were no lights. Similarly, counsel could use a copy of the National Weather Service report for that day showing it to have been a dark night, in case the witness were to testify that there may have been bright moonlight.

It again should be noted that the "key" question is different from the "ultimate" question, the proverbial "one question too many" that should not be asked. For example, in the above example, the "ultimate" question is "so it was dark at the time of the transaction preventing you from seeing if the participant was the defendant." That should be the title of the cross-examination chapter, but asking that last question would prompt the witness to recover and give some explanation for why he could see the defendant notwithstanding that it was pitch black at the time. Again, having established the lighting conditions, the attorney has all that he or she needs to argue to the jury the inference that it should draw. It is neither necessary nor productive to argue that point with the witness.

§ 16.5(g) United States v. Christopher—The Cross-examination of Gilbert Santiago

The attorneys for Christopher and Van Ness approached the cross-examination of Santiago differently. Rothman, Van Ness' attorney, seeks to engage in an accrediting cross-examination, i.e., to use him to support Van Ness' trial theory that Van Ness was an unwitting participant in the distribution scheme. Van Ness' cross-examination thus does not challenge the logic of Santiago's direct examination, nor his veracity as a witness. By contrast, Christopher's trial theory is that Santiago conducted a 'rogue' operation while acting as the manager of Superior Warehouse, and that once Santiago was caught, he sought to frame Christopher and Van Ness in order to avoid charges carrying a mandatory minimum of twenty years. Thus, Clark's cross-examination is discrediting—it impeaches Santiago as someone with a motive to lie and therefore someone whom the jury should not trust.

Santiago's cross-examination is one of those that can for the most part be prepared in advance of trial, because the attorneys will have received the 3500 material, which includes Santiago's post-arrest statements, handwritten notes and a report of his statements at a proffer session, his subsequent plea agreement and the minutes of Santiago's guilty plea. Santiago cannot vary much from these statements without subjecting himself to damaging impeachment. Both defense attorneys, therefore, can develop their trial theories through questions to Santiago with a good deal of safety.

In the cross-examination that follows, note the attorneys' reliance on leading questions and the effectiveness of this form of question in controlling the witness' answers and validating the statements of fact contained in the questions.

These examinations also illustrate certain other basic points that we have made about cross-examination. First, there is no attempt made by these attorneys to take Santiago through his direct testimony again—only those portions of it that relate to the defendant's theory are discussed. Second, the cross-examiner moves from point to point without regard to the sequence of events to which the witness testified on direct examination. Third, the attorneys do not attempt to argue with the witness or try to push the witness to draw the conclusion from the testimony that the attorney has in mind. Argument and conclusion-drawing are best left to the closing argument.

Finally, note the way in which each point in the examination is approached by asking a series of questions, as opposed to going to the critical area at once. This technique is effective for several reasons: first, it permits the attorney to tell the story in his or her own way; second, it reduces the likelihood of a damaging response, or if such a response appears likely to be forthcoming, it enables an attorney to discontinue a line of questioning without excessive damage. Finally, this multiple question technique, because of its crescendo effect, is also useful in capturing the jury's attention.

1. Cross-examination on behalf of Van Ness

The following illustrates the accrediting cross-examination of Santiago. Note that at no point is Santiago's truth or credibility attacked. The entire thrust of the examination is to demonstrate that the witness never discussed drugs with Van Ness or, for that matter, any intention on Christopher's part to engage in a money laundering scheme using the profits from narcotics distribution. The cross-examination employs the "chapter" approach discussed above.[70] The first concerns Santiago's employment by Van Ness, and it consists of an accrediting line of questions directed at showing that there was nothing sinister about that employment, despite Santiago's narcotics conviction. The point is made by eliciting from Santiago that Van Ness was sincerely interested in his rehabilitation and in helping him satisfy his supervised release commitments and that Van Ness dealt regularly with Santiago's probation officer, who made regular visits to the company and with whom Van Ness discussed Santiago's duties. The second chapter deals with Santia-

70. *See supra* § 16.5(e).

go's employment with Christopher and is designed to demonstrate Van Ness' lack of knowledge of what transpired between Santiago and Christopher.

———————

Rothman:	Now, Mr. Santiago you indicated on direct examination that you were promoted from assistant night foreman to the position of day foreman, correct?
Santiago:	Yes.
Rothman:	And it was Mr. Van Ness who gave you that promotion, correct?
Santiago:	Yes.
Rothman:	Mr. Van Ness told you, didn't he, that the basis of promotion was your hard work and the fact that he believed you could be trusted to see that the shipments got out on time, correct?
Santiago:	Yes.
Rothman:	Mr. Van Ness told you that the recommendation for your promotion was made by the night foreman based upon his evaluation of you, correct?
Santiago:	Yes.
Rothman:	And indeed you had worked very hard as the assistant night foreman, right?
Santiago:	Yes.
Rothman:	You had been very punctual in your attendance and in seeing that shipments got out on time, true?
Santiago:	Yes.
Rothman:	Would it be fair to say, Mr. Santiago, that at the time of your promotion you had never spoken to the night foreman about money laundering or distributing cocaine?
Santiago:	Yes.
Rothman:	At the time of your promotion you had not talked to Mr. Van Ness about any interest in laundering money or distributing cocaine?

Santiago: Correct.

Rothman: And as far as you knew, Mr. Van Ness continued to prepare reports for your probation officer, Mr. Rogers.

Santiago: Yes.

Rothman: And you knew that those reports certified your employment and your promotion, correct?

Santiago: Yes.

Rothman: Now I believe you said, on direct examination, that after having been promoted to day foreman, you had some social contact with William Van Ness, is that right?

Santiago: Yes.

Rothman: And on these occasions Mr. Van Ness and you would have a greater opportunity to speak with one another, isn't that correct?

Santiago: Yes.

Rothman: Would it be fair to say Mr. Santiago, that Mr. Van Ness never, on any of these occasions, raised any question about whether you continued to have contacts with people in the narcotics trade?

Santiago: That's correct.

Rothman: Mr. Van Ness never discussed narcotics or any criminal activity with you did he?

Santiago: No.

Rothman: And you never discussed any such activity with him during the period of your employment at Van Ness Trucking, right?

Santiago: Right.

Rothman: Now, Mr. Van Ness told you that he did business with Superior Warehouse?

Santiago: Yes.

Rothman: And you knew from your work that Superior Warehouse was owned by Mr. Van Ness' brother-in-law, Mr. Christopher, right?

Santiago: Yes.

Rothman: You also knew that Superior Warehouse was a regular customer of Van Ness Trucking, correct?

Santiago: Yes.

Rothman: Superior Warehouse shipped coffee and other food goods that International Food Distributors imported from Colombia, correct?

Santiago: That was my understanding.

Rothman: In fact, the person you later learned was Paul Christopher was someone you had previously seen at Van Ness Trucking speaking with Mr. Van Ness.

Santiago: Yes.

Rothman: And you had also heard Mr. Christopher speak with the foreman at Van Ness about details related to some of the shipping contracts.

Santiago: Yes.

Rothman: On some of these occasions you saw Mr. Christopher and the foreman speaking alone, correct?

Santiago: Yes.

Rothman: On other occasions, Mr. Van Ness may have been present as well, isn't that correct?

Santiago: Yes.

Rothman: And you learned of the substance of these conversations when you spoke with the foreman, didn't you?

Santiago: Yes. He told me who he was speaking to and what arrangements Christopher wanted to make with regard to shipping.

Rothman: I take it then that after you became the day foreman, you didn't see anything unusual in speaking to Christopher with Mr. Van Ness out of the office, isn't that correct?

Santiago: If you mean did I think it was suspicious?

Rothman: Yes. That's what I mean.

Santiago: No, I didn't think it was suspicious at all.

Rothman: And it didn't make you suspicious, did it, that after Mr. Van Ness introduced you to Paul Christopher he left the office leaving Christopher to deal with you?

Santiago: No. I didn't think that was suspicious either at that time.

Rothman: After all, you were the day foreman and it was your responsibility to deal with customers regarding shipping details wasn't it?

Santiago: Yes.

Rothman: Before Mr. Van Ness left his office, after having introduced you to Paul Christopher, there was no conversation about cocaine trafficking or Mr. Christopher's financial problems, was there?

Santiago: No.

Rothman: And after the conversation that you claim you had with Mr. Christopher, you didn't speak with Mr. Van Ness about the subject matter that you and he discussed, did you?

Santiago: No.

Rothman: In fact, you never had a conversation with Mr. Van Ness about Mr. Christopher's financial condition, did you?

Santiago: I assumed he knew.

Rothman: My question, however, was whether you and Mr. Van Ness spoke about the fact that Mr. Christopher was in a serious financial condition and needed a loan. And you never did have such a conversation, did you?

Santiago: I didn't tell Van Ness that Christopher was in debt and needed a loan.

Rothman: And you didn't tell Mr. Van Ness that Mr. Christopher had inquired about raising some money by borrowing it from some drug dealer?

Santiago: No.

Rothman: In fact, you never told Mr. Van Ness that you were thinking of contacting an old acquaintance from the narcotics trade who had excess cash and might be interested in laundering some money through a legitimate business, like either Van Ness Trucking or Superior Warehouse, did you?

Santiago: Like I said, I didn't discuss with Mr. Van Ness any of the negotiations with Mr. Christopher because I assumed he knew about it and didn't want to be directly involved.

Rothman: When you say you assumed Mr. Van Ness knew about it, did he ever ask you whether you were able to make the contact that you had told Mr. Christopher you would attempt to arrange?

Santiago: No.

Rothman: Do you recall when you were arrested, you were asked questions and gave answers to the arresting agents?

Santiago: Yes.

Rothman: And didn't you tell those agents following your arrest that when you spoke with Christopher about his financial problems, you did not share that information with Mr. Van Ness and didn't know whether he was aware of it or not?

Santiago: Yea.

Rothman: Now you testified on direct examination that in the beginning of September, 2004, you were told by Mr. Christopher that a cocaine shipment was arriving, isn't that correct?

Santiago: Yes.

Rothman: At that time you were the manager of Superior Warehouse and a vice president of International Food Distributors, correct?

Santiago: Yes.

Rothman: You had left Mr. Van Ness' employment and had begun employment with Mr. Christopher, isn't that right?

Santiago: Yes.

Rothman: And when you had left Mr. Van Ness' employ, you had told him that Mr. Christopher had offered you a position as manager of Superior Warehouse, and that this would pay a better salary, didn't you?

Santiago: Yes, and he congratulated me and wished me well.

Rothman: I take it that at no time prior to your leaving, did you mention that Christopher wanted you to run a cocaine distribution operation out of Superior?

Santiago: No.

Rothman: Or that Christopher wanted you to set up phony bank accounts to deposit the proceeds from this scheme?

Santiago: No.

Rothman: You also claim that Christopher said that he would use his brother-in-law's trucking company to deliver the shipments, didn't he?

Santiago: Yes.

Rothman: He didn't say that his brother-in-law knew that there was cocaine in the crates, did he?

Santiago: No.

---

2. Cross-examination on behalf of Christopher

Clark did not have the luxury of conducting an accrediting cross-examination that assumes the truthfulness of the witness, as did Rothman. Clark must discredit Santiago by attacking both the logic of his testimony and by demonstrating that he has a motive to lie. It is Christopher's theory that Santiago was conducting a rogue operation unbeknownst to Christopher or Van Ness, that Santiago was loyal to Van Ness, and therefore when he plea bargained with the government he did not directly implicate him in the operation. No such loyalty, he would argue, prevented Santiago from falsely accusing Christopher of direct involvement in narcotics distribution.

Note the use of the "chapter" approach in this discrediting cross-examination. There is no attempt on Clark's part to follow a chronological order, and certainly he had no interest in having Santiago repeat all of his direct testimony. Instead, Clark began by asking Santiago about Frankie, the man who he had identified as the contact between Christopher and the drug dealer who made the loan. The purpose of the examination was to try to demonstrate the illogical nature of the entire story about Frankie and, in the process, to bring out discrediting facts about Santiago's involvement with people engaged in narcotics trafficking.

Note also the use of the "box" approach, described above,[71] and repeated in each chapter of this cross examination: Clark asks a series of leading questions that he knew the witness would have to answer in the way suggested by the attorney, either because the witness would not be credible if he answered any other way or because the attorney had a "safety net," e.g., Santiago's proffer statement, that established the relationship of Santiago with Frankie in violation of the conditions of Santiago's release from prison and his failure to inform his probation officer of that. When Santiago responds that he did not think that violated the rules, the box is closed, and the point of the examination—that Santiago does not tell the truth—is made.

Clark: In May, 2004, you claim you contacted an old acquaintance of yours named Frankie, isn't that right?

Santiago: Yes.

Clark: You knew Frankie from your days as a cocaine dealer, didn't you?

Santiago: I knew him at the time I had been convicted in 1998.

Clark: And it would be fair to say, wouldn't it, that Frankie and you maintained contact, even after you had been released from jail?

Santiago: We had some common social acquaintances.

Clark: You knew at the time that it was violation of the conditions of your release for you to continue to associate with known drug dealers?

Santiago: Yes, but I didn't consider what I did to violate the rules.

Clark: You spoke with Frankie on several occasions after you had been released from jail and before May, 2004, and that was a violation itself, wasn't it?

Santiago: I don't know whether it was.

Clark: Well you didn't tell Mr. Rogers, your probation officer, that you had been in touch with Frankie, did you?

Santiago: No.

---

71. *See supra* § 16.5(f).

Clark: And that is because you thought you might get in trouble, correct?

Santiago: I didn't think it was any of his business.

Clark: Mr. Santiago, is it your testimony that you believed your probation officer would think it was ok for you to be spending time with a drug dealer?

Santiago: No.

Clark: You knew that was a violation of your probation, didn't you?

Santiago: I guess so.

Clark: So when you said a minute ago that you didn't think speaking with Frankie violates the rules, that was a lie, wasn't it?

Santiago: I don't know.

Clark: Now this man by the name of Frankie, can you tell the jury how to find him?

Santiago: He works out at Kennedy Airport.

Clark: Doing what?

Santiago: He hangs out there and hustles.

Clark: When you say he hustles, you mean he engages in illegal activities, like narcotics.

Santiago: Not only narcotics, loan sharking too.

Clark: Can you tell the jury his last name?

Santiago: I don't know it.

Clark: Do you have an address for him, where he resides?

Santiago: I don't.

Clark: I take it that you can't reach this man by telephone, then, can you?

Santiago: Yes, you can call him, he has a car phone and he is usually in his car.

Clark:	Did you give AUSA Knapp the phone number for Frankie after you were arrested?
Santiago:	Yes, but the number had been disconnected.
Clark:	Subsequent to your arrest, did you make any effort to introduce one of the DEA agents to your friend Frankie?
Santiago:	I couldn't find him.
Clark:	Well, did you go with agent Martinez or one of his associates to Kennedy Airport to see if you could find him?
Santiago:	He wouldn't speak with them if we could locate him.
Clark:	Well, you could have introduced them to Frankie as other friends of yours who were interested in laundering money?
Santiago:	That would be difficult, he doesn't trust strangers particularly when he is introduced to them face to face.
Clark;	Why doesn't he trust strangers?
Santiago:	They could turn him in.
Clark:	Didn't you testify on direct examination that after speaking with Frankie, you told Mr. Christopher how to contact him to set up the money laundering scheme?
Santiago:	Yes, but Christopher would not meet Frankie on a face to face basis before Frankie would decide whether he wished to deal with him.
Clark:	Yes, but you say you gave Mr. Christopher information about how to contact Frankie, did that include his phone number?
Santiago:	That was the only information I gave him.
Clark:	So you gave a phone number of a person you knew to be suspicious of strangers to another stranger who could, if he chose, trace that number and Frankie himself, didn't you?
Santiago:	Yes, but I didn't think that Christopher would report him.
Clark:	But Frankie didn't know that did he?

Santiago: No.

The cross-examination then shifted from discrediting Santiago's testimony that Christopher was a partner of his in drug dealing to an attack against Santiago's credibility based on his being a person whom the jury should not trust to tell the truth. The testimony regarding Christopher's involvement focused on Santiago's attempts to cover up after his arrest; his naming of Christopher in return for leniency; and the substantial reduction in sentence that he expected to receive.

Clark: Now, you were arrested on January 13, 2005, after the DEA seized the drugs at the airport and at the warehouse, weren't you?

Santiago: Yes.

Clark: And the previous day you had a conversation with Mario Long, didn't you?

Santiago: Long called me and told me that the drugs were at the warehouse.

Clark: You told Long not to worry about a thing, didn't you?

Santiago: Something like that.

Clark: And you told Long to lie and claim he and Murphy knew nothing about the cocaine.

Santiago: Basically yes.

Clark: Now, on the day you were arrested you met Agent Martinez, the agent in charge of the investigation, didn't you?

Santiago: I met him when I was taken to DEA headquarters.

Clark: Agent Martinez read you your rights at which time you told him you wanted to speak with a lawyer, didn't you?

Santiago: Well, I said I wanted to speak with a lawyer before I said anything.

Clark: And then you met Mr. Berman at the initial appearance before Magistrate Roger Brown, didn't you?

Santiago: Well, I was permitted a phone call and I called him.

Clark: And when Mr. Berman came down you had an opportunity to speak with him, didn't you?

Santiago: Yes, we spoke.

Clark: After that conversation you didn't speak with AUSA Knapp or Agent Martinez regarding what you knew of the drug scheme, nor of Christopher's participation, did you?

Santiago: No. We proceeded to the bail hearing.

Clark: And at the bail hearing, Mr. Berman represented that you were a bona fide employee and manager of Superior Warehouse and that your employment was legitimate there, not that you had engaged in any illegal activity?

Santiago: Yes. My defense was that I was innocent and didn't know anything other than that Superior distributed coffee and other food products.

Clark: After the bail hearing, and after hearing your lawyer's argument the magistrate agreed to release you, didn't he?

Santiago: Provided I sign a bond, and give them the deed to my house.

Clark: The government said it was going to appeal this decision, and AUSA Knapp asked the magistrate to keep you in jail until another judge could review the decision, isn't that correct?

Santiago: Yes.

Clark: And you learned subsequently, the reviewing judge had decided to detain you and keep you in jail reversing the decision of the magistrate, didn't you?

Santiago: Yes.

Clark: And would it be fair to say, Mr. Santiago, that you didn't say anything about Mr. Christopher's being your drug partner until after you learned that you would not be released on bail, isn't that correct?

Santiago: Well, after that I met with Mr. Berman and we discussed what would be in my best interest.

Clark: At that time when you met with Mr. Berman you knew that you faced a possible mandatory minimum of 20 years in a federal penitentiary if you were convicted of the charges against you, didn't you?

Santiago: If the Government sought to charge me as a previously convicted felon.

Clark: And you were a previously convicted felon, weren't you, stemming from a 1998 narcotics conviction right here in the Eastern District?

Santiago: Yes.

Clark: You also learned that the maximum term you could be sentenced to was life in prison, isn't that right?

Santiago: Yes.

Clark: So you knew that you faced spending at least the best years of your life behind bars?

Santiago: Yes.

Clark: And you didn't want to do that, did you?

Santiago: Of course not.

Clark: And you knew that if you told the government that Christopher and Van Ness had nothing to do with drug trafficking that you would not be able to get a deal, isn't that right?

Santiago: That's right.

Clark: In addition you knew, because Mr. Berman and you reviewed the complaint, that the DEA had overheard your conversation with Mario Long in which you told Long to deny knowledge of the cocaine and to tell the other worker arrested to keep his mouth shut, didn't you?

Santiago: We suspected that the conversation had been taped.

Clark: And so the situation looked pretty grim for you, didn't it?

Santiago: Well I don't know what you mean by pretty grim.

Clark: Well, the government had a pretty good case against you, given that they had found the drugs, obtained Mario Long's cooperation, and taped a conversation between you and he in which you admitted your involvement.

Santiago: Well, that's why my lawyer and I believed that it would be in my best interest to cooperate with the Government.

Clark: But you understood, did you not, that in cooperating, Agent Martinez and AUSA Knapp wanted information from you that would link other people to the scheme, particularly Mr. Christopher, because he was the owner of the warehouse?

Santiago: Well, I knew that if I could help them with their case I would benefit from that.

Clark: And you knew that Mario Long had already benefited by providing information against you?

Santiago: Yes, we suspected that.

Clark: So the only other people available for you to provide information against were Christopher and Van Ness, because Long had already committed himself to providing information against you, isn't that right?

Santiago: Well, if you mean that I had to provide additional information, I thought I did.

Clark: Now Mr. Santiago, after speaking with the government, you came back to court and pleaded guilty to a one count information that did not charge you with being a previously convicted felon, isn't that correct?

Santiago: That's right.

Clark: In other words, in exchange for your cooperation, the Government agreed not to pursue a charge that would require a mandatory minimum of 20 years in a federal penitentiary, isn't that right?

Santiago:	They charged me only with one count of conspiracy, but it covered all the drug shipments I knew about.
Clark:	Yes. And by not charging you with having been previously convicted, you now faced only a mandatory minimum of 10 years, isn't that correct?
Santiago:	That was my understanding.
Clark:	And it was part of your agreement with the Government that the Government would file a letter with the court detailing your cooperation that would allow you to spend even less than 10 years in prison?
Santiago:	Well, I didn't know what sentence I would get.
Clark:	But you knew that the Government would tell the judge about your cooperation, and that Mr. Berman, your attorney, would ask the judge to go below the mandatory minimum of ten years, didn't you?
Santiago:	I knew that my lawyer would make that request.
Clark:	And you knew from speaking with your lawyer that the judge had the authority to sentence you to below the minimum of 10 years only if you cooperated, didn't you?
Santiago:	My lawyer said it was possible under the law.
Clark:	And you hoped, did you not, that by providing information about Mr. Christopher and Mr. Van Ness that you would serve substantially less than 10 years?
Santiago:	Well, I hope to do as well as I might on sentence.
Clark:	And to you that means getting a sentence of less than ten years, doesn't it?
Santiago:	Yes. I would hope for less.
Clark:	Perhaps even as little as two to four years or no years in jail, isn't that correct?
Santiago:	Maybe.
Clark:	Mr. Santiago, you have not yet been sentenced, have you?
Santiago:	No.

Clark: In fact Mr. Santiago, it is your hope that your testimony here will help you to reduce your sentence from that mandatory minimum 10 year sentence, which you desperately hope to avoid, to as little as two or no years in jail, isn't that right?

Santiago: Yes.

---

§ 16.6   Re-examination

§ 16.6(a)   Re-direct Examination

At the conclusion of the cross-examination, the party presenting the witness will be given the opportunity to conduct a re-direct examination of that witness. The purpose of the re-direct is to rehabilitate the witness insofar as the witness' testimony was undermined or challenged on cross-examination. For this reason, re-direct examination is limited to what was raised on cross-examination. It is not properly employed to adduce testimony as to matters that should have been adduced on direct, but were either forgotten or developed in a less than adequate way. An objection to re-direct that is beyond the scope of the cross will be sustained, and the opposing counsel should monitor the re-direct carefully in order to prevent abuse.

Re-direct examination is governed by the rules of direct examination, not cross-examination. It is therefore not permissible to lead one's witness on re-direct. However, in view of the fact that the witness will already have testified on both direct and cross-examination about the subject of the re-direct testimony, more latitude in asking closed questions can be expected.

Since the purpose of re-direct is to control or repair the damage done to a witness on cross, the right to conduct a re-direct should be exercised only when it appears that such action is essential. Where there was no appreciable damage, or where there is nothing on re-direct that can repair it, the right should be waived or the re-direct significantly limited for several reasons. First, conducting a re-direct is a tacit admission that the witness in fact was damaged and, therefore, it can be more useful to convey the impression that there was no damage to the extent that is believable. Second, a juror's attention span and interest in a particular witness may often be limited; prolonging the examination may in this regard be counter-productive. Third, an ill-advised re-direct can have the effect of magnifying the damage done, rather than minimizing it. It should in this regard be recognized that the decision to conduct a re-direct will often be made on very short notice, without the attorney having time to think through the implications of the action. Finally, exercising the right to conduct a re-direct can give rise to the right of the opposing party to conduct a re-cross examination, in which it is possible that additional damage might occur.

Consider AUSA Knapp's choices on re-direct examination of Santiago in light of this discussion. Rothman's accrediting cross-examination on behalf of Van Ness effectively demonstrated the limits of Santiago's testimony in proving the defendant's knowledge. Nothing additional could be elicited on re-direct, however, and a rephrasing of points already made would simply permit Rothman to make his points again on re-cross. Knapp therefore asked no additional questions regarding Van Ness.

As to Christopher, however, there were certain avenues available. First, Knapp developed additional facts about the cooperation agreement, since Clark's cross-examination had left the impression that Santiago had expected a sentence of 2–4 years, when he had been facing a mandatory 20 years. She therefore elicited the fact that no sentence had been promised, that in fact Santiago was told that that decision would be the judge's, and that the judge was not a party to any agreement between them. For all Santiago knew, then, he could receive a mandatory minimum of ten years or a much longer sentence. Similarly, she used the re-direct to stress the point that if it were discovered that Santiago had lied in any respect, he believed that the agreement would be dissolved and he would be subject to the original mandatory 20 year sentence.

§ 16.6(b)   Re-cross Examination

There is little to add here to what has been said about both re-direct examination and cross-examination generally. The scope of re-cross is limited to what is raised on re-direct—it is not an occasion for embellishment upon the original cross-examination. Similarly, re-cross is a right that need not be asserted and should not be if there was nothing in the re-direct that undermined the points made during the original cross-examination. Finally, there is no right to have a second cross-examination, and judges often discourage it.

§ 16.7   Motion for Judgment of Acquittal

When all of the witnesses in the government's case-in-chief have been examined and re-examined, the government will rest. At that point, the defense will move for a judgment of acquittal on the grounds that the government has not sustained its burden of going forward, either on the indictment as a whole or on one or more counts.[72] The motion is made at the close of the government's case because the defendant, protected by the presumption of innocence, cannot be required to rebut a substantively deficient prosecution case.

---

72. FED. R. CRIM. P. 29(a). *See* WRIGHT §§ 461-470.

The test on the motion is this: viewing the evidence in the light most favorable to the government, and giving full deference to the right of the jury to determine credibility, weigh the evidence, and draw justifiable inferences, the motion should be granted if no reasonable juror could fairly find that the government had proven the defendant's guilt beyond a reasonable doubt.[73] If the court concludes that a juror could reasonably find the defendant guilty by the requisite burden of proof, it must deny the motion and submit the case to the jury. It can, however, reserve decision on the motion until after the defense case.[74] Moreover, the court ultimately has the power to overrule the jury's finding of guilt and direct a judgment of acquittal.[75] It cannot, of course, direct a verdict of guilty, since that would be inconsistent with the defendant's constitutional right to a trial by jury.[76]

§ 16.8 The Defense Case

It is the constitutional right of the defendant under the Fifth Amendment not to present any evidence at all or, even if evidence is presented, to remain personally silent. In furtherance of that right, it has been held that it is impermissible for the prosecution or the court to comment on the defendant's failure to testify.[77] The defendant also has a right to have an instruction given to the jury that it may not draw any inferences from the defendant's failure to testify.[78]

While the defense may rest without offering any evidence, it may at times be necessary to call the defendant and/or witnesses either to establish an alternative explanation for conduct that irrefutably occurred or to present some affirmative defense to the charges. Should the

---

73. Jackson v. Virginia, 443 U.S. 307, 315 (1979).

74. FED. R. CRIM. P. 29(b). If the judge reserves decision on the motion, he or she still may only consider the evidence that the prosecution offered in its case-in-chief.

75. FED. R. CRIM. P. 29(c). *See* WRIGHT § 465. Similarly, the court can direct a judgment of acquittal if the jury "hangs,", i.e., fails to reach a verdict on one or more counts.

76. The government's right to appeal a judgment of acquittal depends upon when it was made. The double jeopardy clause prohibits a "further prosecution" once jeopardy has attached. United States v. Scott, 437 U.S. 82, 87 (1978). Therefore, if the motion is granted prior to the time that the jury has returned a guilty verdict, there can be no appeal, since further prosecution would be required. If, however, the motion were granted after the jury had reached a guilty verdict, all that would be required would be to reinstate the guilty verdict, and therefore

an appeal could be taken. United States v. Steed, 646 F.2d 136 (4th Cir. 1981). *See* WRIGHT, § 469; LaFAVE ET AL., §§ 24.3, 24.4, 26.3(a). When it appears that the trial court is seriously considering granting a Rule 29 motion, the government's argument often will be that the court should wait until the jury reaches its verdict, so that the government's right to appeal is preserved. The Advisory Committee Notes to the 1994 amendment of Rule 29 specifically state that reserving the decision until after the verdict is a way to balance the interests of the parties.

77. Griffin v. California, 380 U.S. 609, 614 (1965).

78. Carter v. Kentucky, 450 U.S. 288, 301 (1981). Although a court cannot refuse to give the instruction once requested, in *Lakeside v. Oregon,* 435 U.S. 333, 341 (1978), the Court rejected defendant's argument that it is constitutionally impermissible to give the instruction over a defendant's objection. *See also* LaFAVE ET AL., § 23.4(c).

defendant choose to take the stand, he or she will be treated the same as any other witness and be subject to cross-examination within the normal rules. Of particular importance is the fact that the defendant can be impeached on the basis of prior convictions or bad acts. This evidence may be offered because it tends to show that the defendant is not credible or worthy of belief and is generally not admissible for that purpose if the defendant does not testify.[79] Similarly, prior statements and tangible evidence excluded from the government's case-in-chief under the exclusionary rule may be used to impeach the defendant if he or she testifies to the contrary.[80]

Van Ness and his attorney decided that Van Ness would testify even though from the outset they viewed the government's evidence of Van Ness' knowledge as weak, and nothing in the testimony of Santiago changed that view. Van Ness and his counsel seriously considered resting without Van Ness testifying in which case they would have to stress the failure of the government's proof on the key *mens rea* issue—knowledge and intent. However, they decided that Van Ness should testify and assert his innocence to "seal the deal," particularly since Van Ness had no other witnesses to put on to prove the negative proposition of his ignorance, except Christopher himself, and obviously Christopher could not be called by Van Ness without violating Christopher's privilege against self-incrimination.[81] In his testimony, Van Ness denied any knowledge that drugs were being shipped and explained that he was paid more for valuable cargo that required special care without being told the nature of the merchandise.

Christopher's plan at the outset had been to offer an alternative explanation of the damaging facts against him—drugs were received and delivered by his company and his employees, and he was clearly linked to the banking transactions. It would have been a possible strategy for Christopher to rest as well and rely on Clark's closing to raise a reasonable doubt as to whether Santiago, who on cross-examination had admitted both to experience in narcotics and to developing his own drug customers, had conducted the drug operation on his own. It was concluded, however, that the argument would be much more credible to the jury if Christopher would testify and provide an alternative explanation for opening the bank accounts and depositing cash in them. Without Christopher's explanation, his plan to evade taxes would not be sufficiently established from the cross-examination of Santiago to argue to the jury on summation. He would have to explain that he made cash deposits of legitimate funds and then failed to report them in order to avoid taxes.

---

79. *See* FED. R. EVID. 609(a); WEINSTEIN & BERGER, § 609.02.

80. *See* Harris v. New York, 401 U.S. 222, 226 (1971); United States v. Havens, 446 U.S. 620, 627–28 (1980). *See also* LA-FAVE ET AL., § 9.6(a).

81. If Christopher took the stand in his own defense, however, he would be subject to cross-examination by Van Ness.

Christopher, therefore, testified to the facts as he originally told them to his lawyer.

The defense then rested.

§ 16.9   The Rebuttal Case

In some circumstances, the government will have the right to put on evidence at the close of the defense case to rebut matters raised for the first time in the defense case. That is the limited purpose of the rebuttal case, just as the re-direct examination is limited to matters raised on cross-examination. The government cannot use the rebuttal case to adduce evidence that it should have brought out in its case-in-chief.

In some situations in which a rebuttal case would otherwise be appropriate, it can be obviated if the defense indicates, in response to a discovery demand, or in its opening statement, that it will rely on some defense. Then the government will be permitted to counter it in its case-in-chief, which is often a more efficient way to proceed. A typical example of such a case is when the defense is committed to an insanity plea. The government will receive notice of that[82] and be permitted to put on evidence to prove the defendant's sanity in the first instance as part of its case-in-chief.[83]

§ 16.10   Concluding the Trial—Requests to Charge

After the defense rests, and any rebuttal case on the part of the government is completed, the testimonial phase of the trial is over. Several steps remain to be taken, however, before the trial itself is completed.

First, requests to charge that have been submitted to the court must be ruled upon by the judge. We discussed the submission of proposed jury instructions, their purpose, and the style of drafting them in Chapter 15, where we emphasized the need to focus on this important matter at the outset of trial preparation. We noted there as well that the rules permit the court to order the submission of requests at any time prior to closing argument.[84] The final review of the charges by the court will occur at the close of the evidence, in a "charging conference," at which the court will hear argument as to disputed instructions. The judge will then advise counsel as to how he will instruct the jury with respect to the relevant principles of law. The reason for the rule requiring this to be done before closing argument is to avoid being "charged out," which occurs when an attorney in closing argument makes statements concerning the law that are refuted by the judge's charge.

---

82. *See* Fed. R. Crim. P. 12.2(a); Wright, §§ 206–209. *See also* Fed. R. Crim. P. 12.1(a) (requiring notice of an alibi defense); Wright, §§ 201–203.

83. *See* Wright, § 207.

84. Fed. R. Crim. P. 30(a). *See* Wright, § 482.

§ 16.11   Closing Argument

§ 16.11(a)   Rules Regarding Closing Argument

The rules govern the order of closing argument, providing for an initial argument by the prosecution, to be followed by the defense closing, with the prosecution having the right to rebut the defense closing.[85] While cases dealing with trials that occurred before the rule was adopted held that the prosecution could waive its initial argument and rely solely on its rebuttal,[86] it is doubtful that this is permissible now, since the purpose of the rule is to give the defendant notice of the prosecutor's argument.[87] In any event, it is inconceivable as a practical matter that the prosecution would waive its opportunity to argue its case affirmatively, rather than simply attempting to rebut the defense argument. Similarly, while the defense may be entitled to waive closing argument, it is difficult to imagine a situation in which it would be reasonably competent for the defense to do so.

Rules regarding proper argument mirror to some degree those regarding opening statements, such as those prohibiting inflammatory remarks or statements of personal belief.[88] Argument, of course, while not proper in an opening statement, is the very purpose of the closing. What is not permitted are assertions not based on facts established during the trial, statements designed to mislead the jury as to the law, and appeals to emotion or prejudice.[89] Such tactics may lead to disruption of the closing argument by objection, damaging admonitions by the judge, and, albeit rarely, the declaration of a mistrial or reversal of a conviction on appeal.[90]

§ 16.11(b)   The Focus of the Closing—The Primacy of Facts

We have emphasized throughout this book that the trial lawyer's principal concern is with ascertaining and presenting facts. It is the purpose of the closing to present to the jury the attorney's argument as to how these facts, and the inferences that can be drawn from them, support his or her party's position. This is the lawyer's opportunity to pull together all that has been elicited at trial—to solve the case. In doing so, it will not only be necessary to demonstrate the strength of his

---

85. FED. R. CRIM. P. 29.1. *See* WRIGHT, § 471.

86. United States v. Yaughn, 493 F.2d 441, 445 (5th Cir. 1974).

87. *See* FED. R. CRIM. P. 29.1 advisory committee's note (1974 addition). The Advisory Committee Notes suggest that the issue is not necessarily foreclosed and states the Committee's view that if the prosecution waives its initial argument, it also waives its right to rebut. *Id.* (1975 enactment).

88. *See supra* § 16.3(a); MAUET, at 401–461.

89. *See* LAFAVE ET AL., § 24.7(d).

90. *Id.,* § 24.7(e) As the authors observe, the danger of reversal is a small one, even, it appears, when the appellate court is outraged by the conduct of the prosecutor. *See, e.g.,* Darden v. Wainwright, 477 U.S. 168, 185–86 (1986).

or her side's position, but to provide a credible explanation for the weaknesses that will inevitably have been brought out by the other side.

Note should be made of the place of legal argument in the closing—in a word, it is largely inappropriate. At the trial level, in contrast to the appellate, the law of the case is settled; it is what the judge has advised counsel will be contained in his or her forthcoming instructions. The lawyer can allude to those instructions, but should resist the urge to interpret the law too extensively. This is the province of the court, and the overactive lawyer will probably hear from the bench.

§ 16.11(c) Stylistic Considerations

The fact that the closing argument is a very important aspect of the lawyer's task does not mean that it is all that matters or that there is a single way to do it. A case that has been poorly presented is unlikely to be saved by the closing argument, no matter how dazzling it may be. The ability to move an audience through one's oratory may give an attorney an edge and it is extremely important to prepare and deliver a summation that will hold the jury's attention. Nevertheless, a thorough and orderly presentation, even if low-key, has as good a chance to persuade as one that may play better on the stage.

While each lawyer will have to develop his or her own style of argument, a few suggestions might be in order. First, the use of metaphor can be extremely effective in providing the jury with an understanding of the attorney's case theory. It is worthwhile trying to identify some well known story or concept with which the story of the trial can be compared and even using the opening statement to introduce it. Second, it is extremely important to convey to the jury that one is sincere about the argument he or she is making. Again, histrionics are not called for, but direct engagement with the jury is a necessity. The closing argument should not be a prepared speech, read from the lectern. What the lawyer needs is a carefully organized outline of the points he or she needs to make, delivered extemporaneously.

§ 16.11(d) The Prosecution Closing

The prosecution, as we noted, has the right to give both the first closing argument and a rebuttal to the defense closing. The purposes of the two are different.

The principal closing should be approached as if it were the only opportunity that the prosecutor has to address the jury: nothing that needs to be said in closing argument should be reserved for the rebuttal. It may be tempting to do that because of the dramatic effect it might have on the jury, but it is dangerous since if the defense does not argue in the manner anticipated, the prosecutor may be foreclosed. Thus, since the prosecutor must prove the defendant's guilt on each element of the crime charged in the principal closing argument, the prosecutor must show the jury what evidence has been elicited as to each element. For reasons we have explained, however, in most cases not all elements will be in dispute and so the prosecutor's attention will be quickly directed to those facts, and the inferences that can be drawn from them, that relate to the issues in dispute.

A word of caution is in order in this regard. In characterizing the dispute between the government and the defendant, the prosecutor must take care not to improperly anticipate the defense argument, since that could constitute error. If it is obvious from the defense opening statement, cross-examination or direct case that certain issues will be put in dispute, it is perfectly appropriate for the prosecutor to refer to them. But if that is not the case, an anticipatory argument might violate the defendant's right to remain silent by unfairly suggesting to the jury that the defense has failed to establish that which it had no obligation to establish.

As to the rebuttal argument of the prosecution, again it is important to remember that it is just that: a rebuttal to the defense argument. The rebuttal should deal exclusively with what the defense attorney has said. It should be (and may be required to be) relatively brief. It need not deal with every point and, indeed, need not be given at all if the defense did no particular harm in its closing, although such instances will be rare.

§ 16.11(e)   The Defense Closing

Three principal tactical considerations seem to us to form the basis of defense strategy in the closing argument:

(1) The prosecution has the burden of proving guilt beyond a reasonable doubt, and with the exception of a few affirmative defenses, the defendant has no obligation to prove anything. This is a point that will have been emphasized to the jury by the judge and counsel at the outset of the case, and it should be restated in the final instructions. Juries repeatedly demonstrate—sometimes to the amazement of lawyers—their ability to understand and implement this rule. It is crucial for the defense attorney to press the point in closing argument and to explain to the jury how the rule is related to the presumption of innocence. This is particularly true when, as is often the case, the defendant does not testify or put on evidence.

(2) The fact that the defense closing follows the prosecution's gives the defense attorney the opportunity to narrow the issues for the jury. As we have noted, the prosecutor perforce will have to address at least to some extent all of the issues in the case. The defense attorney need not and will do well to focus only on that which is in dispute.

Following the prosecution closing also necessarily makes the defense closing at least in part a rebuttal. While all of the important points in support of the defense theory should be prepared in advance, it is also important that the defense attorney listen with care to the prosecutor's arguments, since it is certain that the jury will be waiting to hear how they are answered.

(3) To the extent possible, the closing argument should attempt to humanize the defendant. Of course, if he or she has testified, there may be facts on the record with respect to the character or background of the defendant, and argument as to these matters can be based on those facts. But even if the defendant has not testified, there are ways in which to express to the jury the fact that it is being asked to sit in judgment of an individual, who has a life outside the courtroom and is facing what for most would be an unthinkable event.

§ 16.11(f)   United States v. Christopher—Closing Arguments

We offer two excerpts from the closings in the Christopher case to illustrate our central theme about closing arguments, the primacy of arguing about the facts and what they establish. The arguments in this case would be lengthy and detailed, requiring perhaps three to five hours or longer for the three attorneys. Of course, different advocates may take more or less time, depending on the complexity of the trial and the styles of the lawyers.

(1) The Government's Closing

What follows are the sections of AUSA Knapp's summation and Clark's argument on the five bank accounts. Having already discussed, among other things, Santiago's credibility and his version of the events, AUSA Knapp continues:

* * *

... You don't just have to take Gilbert Santiago's word for all this, although you certainly could. A host of undisputed facts supports his testimony and leads to only one conclusion, the guilt of these defendants. I want to talk now about the bank accounts. You heard the testimony about the bank accounts and there is no dispute that five different accounts were set up. You have seen the records.

There is no dispute that Paul Christopher knew about these accounts, had Gilbert Santiago set them up and signed these signature cards. Christopher told you that himself when he testified. He says that he had these accounts set up in order to evade taxes. Well, Gilbert Santiago tells you that's not true, but you don't have to just take his word for that. Examination of these records and the undisputed facts also tells you that Paul Christopher had these accounts set up for the purpose of laundering drug money and he used these accounts for the purpose of laundering drug money.

First, consider the fact that these accounts were set up in August, soon after Gilbert Santiago came to work for Paul Christopher. Now Gilbert Santiago is not a tax accountant or a tax expert.

He is a man who was involved in drugs and who came to Paul Christopher's attention as a man who used to have connections to drug dealers. Does it make sense that Paul Christopher, who is an experienced businessman, who has run a business for years, would suddenly start using multiple bank accounts in August of 2004 and ask Gilbert Santiago to oversee that operation, unless his purpose was to launder drug money? Nothing else makes sense. The suddenness of this decision, the involvement of Gilbert Santiago, his responsibility for this operation, all point to the drug connection. After all, if only tax evasion was involved, why wouldn't Paul Christopher simply make the deposits himself? For that kind of common, though illegal and wrongful conduct, why does he need to pay Gilbert Santiago one third of the cash proceeds? Ladies and gentlemen, Gilbert Santiago's involvement as the overseer of those accounts and his receipt of one third of the money are proof beyond a reasonable doubt, by themselves, of Paul Christopher's guilt on the money laundering charges in this indictment.

But as you know, there is more evidence that proves that these accounts were set up and used only to launder drug profits and were never intended, or used, solely to evade taxes on legitimate income. First, you will recall that Mr. Clark brought out on cross-examination that Christopher never took cash directly out of the business but always deposited all the cash in the bank. If he wanted to evade taxes, why didn't he take some cash out of the business rather than create a paper trail?

And of course, the records themselves support that conclusion. Please examine these records. You will note that the deposits are made once a month, just like the drug shipments. You will note that the total amounts deposited add up to just two thirds of the amount of money Gilbert Santiago tells you he and Christopher were paid for the shipments.

These records are undisputed. The amounts of money deposited, the dates, the patterns, all of these things lead to only one conclusion, these accounts were set up by Paul Christopher to launder the drug profits. His version, of simple tax evasion, is contradicted by these records, which I urge you to examine during your deliberations, as well as all the other evidence in this case.

(2) Christopher's Closing

Having already talked about Santiago's lack of credibility and his being the key to the government's case, Clark presents an alternative explanation of what the bank records demonstrate:

* * *

As Judge Sheridan will instruct you shortly, the government at all times must prove its theory beyond a reasonable doubt, and Mr.

Christopher does not have to prove anything or present any evidence whatsoever. In fact, I could sit down right now because it is so clear that the government has failed to meet its burden of proving the charges beyond a reasonable doubt, and the government has not even come close to overcoming the presumption of Mr. Christopher's innocence. But, I am not going to sit down because in addition to the failing of the government's own proof, Mr. Christopher did present evidence, including his own testimony, which highlights even further why the government's evidence does not amount to proof beyond a reasonable doubt.

In fact, although Mr. Christopher need not prove anything, it is clear that the only reasonable inferences that can be drawn from the facts the government has introduced in evidence and from Mr. Christopher's own testimony is that Mr. Christopher was in no way a knowing participant in Gilbert Santiago's scheme to traffic in drugs. Rather, the evidence showed that Paul Christopher decided that he needed someone trustworthy to help him in a scheme he knew was wrong, his plan to evade taxes. He asked Gilbert Santiago because he knew Santiago would not be shocked by such garden variety illegality as tax evasion and Santiago had been a good worker for his brother-in-law. He asked Santiago to help him with the tax evasion scheme and paid him well enough to ensure that he could trust the man not to reveal the scheme or skim off the cash for himself. Santiago, of course, saw a way to profit from the tax scheme and also make a lot more money by getting back into the drug business.

The facts that the government argues prove, at best, only that Paul Christopher engaged in this tax evasion scheme. Only Santiago and Long can be linked directly to drugs. Only Santiago had any experience with narcotics trafficking. He controlled the drug distribution scheme and the bank accounts. He saw a chance to get back into making money through drugs and set up a little insurance policy. As an experienced drug dealer, he knew that if he were caught, he needed someone to turn in, someone to testify against so that he could save himself from spending the rest of his life in prison. Someone whose freedom he could trade for his own.

Since he was in control of the cash, the invoices and the story he eventually would tell the government if he got caught, is it any surprise that the major outlines of his story fit together? Does the fact that all the deposits were made at one time of the month mean anything besides the fact that Santiago held all the cash for the month and deposited it at once, possibly even so that he could attribute all of it to the drug deals if he was caught? The money in those CMS Bank accounts has nothing to do with Gilbert Santiago's drug dealing. However much money he made from those deals, and you can draw your own conclusions from Agent Martinez's testimony about the prices of cocaine, that is money he kept somewhere else, for himself and Mario Long. The relatively small amount of money, for drug dealers, he claims he and Christopher split for the cocaine scheme just happens to match the money in the accounts because that is how his story fit together. The real money Santiago made as a dealer is money I submit the government will never find. The money in the CMS Bank accounts is from Mr. Christopher's tax evasion.

Let me again stress that your job is made easier by the protections of our great system. Because your job is not to ask yourself, as you might in your everyday life, what do I think is more likely—the government's theory that Mr. Christopher was directing Gilbert Santiago's drug dealing or that Gilbert Santiago took advantage of a situation to resume his career as a drug dealer without the knowledge of Mr. Christopher. Rather, the only question you must answer is whether the substantial and persuasive evidence of Mr. Christopher's attempt to reduce his tax liability—which explains all of the evidence that the government claims corroborates the testimony of Mr. Santiago, the admitted liar who you wouldn't rely on for any important decision in your life–raises a reasonable doubt in your mind. In other words, the question is the same now as it was at the beginning of the trial: Has the government proven the charges beyond a reasonable doubt?

---

§ 16.12 Jury Instructions

The rules permit the judge to charge the jury on the law of the case before or after closing argument, or on both occasions.[91] The most common practice is to give the charge after the arguments. The judge may also "marshall the evidence", i.e., give his or her version of what each side has attempted to prove, although in our experience this is rarely done.

The judges' instructions to the jury cover a wide range of matters, each falling within the following categories: (a) general instructions on the jury's function; (b) instructions concerning the elements of the offenses charged in the indictment and of any legal defenses made by the defendant; and (c) instructions concerning particular evidentiary matters relevant to the trial.

If counsel believes that the judge has erred in giving the charge, he or she must object before the jury retires to deliberate or else the objection is waived.[92]

---

91. FED. R. CRIM. P. 30(c). *See* WRIGHT, § 483.

92. FED. R. CRIM. P. 30(d). *See* WRIGHT, § 484. *But see* FED. R. CRIM. P. 52(b) (plain error review).

§ 16.13 Jury Deliberations

When the jury instructions are given and any objections by counsel dealt with, the judge dismisses any alternate jurors who may have been selected and the jury retires to deliberate. They take with them into the jury room the indictment and upon request or as a matter of course (depending on the judge) any documentary or tangible material that has been admitted into evidence.[93] The jurors also may request that the court repeat or explain instructions on the law or have testimony read back to them. Whenever such a request is made, counsel for both sides will be called and along with the defendant will be present when the judge rules on the request or provides the jury with the information it seeks.[94]

§ 16.14 Verdict

In federal cases, the verdict of the jury must be unanimous.[95] A defendant convicted or acquitted by a jury may not be tried again for the same offense, but when the jury fails to reach a verdict (a "hung" jury), the defendant may be retried.[96]

§ 16.15 United States v. Christopher—The Verdict

The Christopher case was submitted to the jury on September 20, 2005 after five days of testimony. On September 22 the foreperson of the jury sent word that a verdict had been reached. The parties assembled in the courtroom and the foreperson announced that Paul Christopher had been found guilty on all counts. A special verdict was announced on the forfeiture count, with the jury finding that the assets listed in the indictment were subject to forfeiture. The foreperson then announced that William Van Ness had been found not guilty on all counts.

Judge Sheridan then thanked the jury and dismissed it. He advised Van Ness that he was free to go. He then revoked Christopher's bail and remanded him to the Metropolitan Detention Center. He set October 18, 2005 for sentencing and adjourned the court.

93. Some judges will not send exhibits to the jury room unless they are requested.

94. *See* LaFave et al., § 24.9(b).

95. Fed. R. Crim. P. 31(a). *See* Wright, § 511.

96. United States v. Perez, 22 U.S. (9 Wheat.) 579, 579–580 (1824). *See* LaFave et al., § 24.3(b).

*

Part V

SENTENCING

Chapter 17

SENTENCING

Table of Sections

Sec.
17.0   Introduction.
17.1   Determining Sentencing Facts.
    17.1(a) The Presentence Investigation.
    17.1(b) The Presentence Report.
17.2   Negotiating Challenges to the Presentence Report.
17.3   Litigating Disputed Facts in the Presentence Report.
    17.3(a) The Presentence Memorandum.
    17.3(b) The Sentencing Hearing—Burden of Proof.
17.4   The Sentencing Decision.
17.5   Strategic and Policy Considerations in Connection with Sentencing.
    17.5(a) The Defense Perspective.
    17.5(b) The Prosecution Perspective.
17.6   The Sentencing of Paul Christopher.
    17.6(a) Calculating Christopher's Sentence.
    17.6(b) The Objections Stage.
    17.6(c) Resolving Contested Issues.
    17.6(d) The Sentencing Hearing.
    17.6(e) The Imposition of Christopher's Sentence.
17.7   The Sentencing of Ernest Wagner.
17.8   The Sentencing of Gilbert Santiago and Mario Long.

---

§ 17.0   Introduction

We introduced in Chapters 7 and 12 the substantive law of sentencing in the federal system under the Sentencing Guidelines and the Supreme Court's landmark *Booker* decision in 2005. In this chapter we turn to the procedural aspects of the sentencing process: how relevant facts are determined and litigated. We then conclude with a description of the sentencing process as applied to the various defendants in the Christopher case.

484

§ 17.1   Determining Sentencing Facts

Following a conviction, the case will be adjourned for sentencing, which will occur after completion of a presentence investigation and report prepared by the United States Probation Department.[1] Both the government and the defense are entitled to review this report, and they may object to any assertions contained in it. To resolve such objections the court will convene a sentencing hearing in which the parties may proceed either by proffer or through testimony. What follows is a description of the fact-finding process, including an analysis of the burden of proof at the sentence hearing.

§ 17.1(a)   The Presentence Investigation

Primary responsibility for collecting facts relevant to sentencing and for calculating the sentence under the Guidelines lies with the Probation Department, an investigatory arm of the court.[2] The presentence report contains information about the defendant's criminal record and the circumstances of the crime, as well as other information that the Probation Department believes may be relevant to the judge's sentence determination. This may include the defendant's work and education history, family life, substance abuse history and personal data. A confidential sentence recommendation may also be included.[3]

In writing the presentence report, the probation officer will often choose among competing factual claims. The probation officer is generally unrestricted in his or her use of the sources available to the Department and has the discretion to accord greater weight to some sources over others.[4] Although the ultimate factual and legal determinations are the responsibility of the judge, the presentence report is crucial in framing the issues.

The presentence investigation will always include the following steps:

(1)   Presentence Interview of the Defendant

The defendant will be asked to appear for a presentence interview with the probation officer and will be asked about personal and family history, past substance abuse, prior criminal record, current financial situation and facts related to the offense of conviction. Since there are potential hazards for the defendant in the interview, he or she should be prepared for it by defense counsel, who also should be present.[5]

---

1. *See* USSG § 6A1.1, p.s. The agency is sometimes referred to as the United States Probation Service, but we shall use the name by which it is commonly known.

2. *See* FED. R. CRIM. P. 32(c).

3. *See* FED. R. CRIM. P. 32(d).

4. *See* KATE SMITH & JOSE CABRANES, FEAR OF JUDGING: SENTENCING GUIDELINES IN THE FEDERAL COURTS 85–91 (1998).

5. The defendant does not have a Sixth Amendment right to counsel at the presentence interview. United States v. Tyler, 281 F.3d 84, 96 (3d Cir. 2002). Thus there is no requirement of an explicit waiver, nor can

All defendants should be counseled to be cooperative at the interview and to give truthful responses to any questions that, in accordance with counsel's advice, are to be answered at all. The defendant should neither exaggerate nor minimize his or her role in the offense. Moreover, it should be made clear to the defendant that if unsure of an answer, he or she should say so rather than risk giving one that might be interpreted as a deliberate falsehood; under the Guidelines, a two point upward adjustment for obstruction of justice may be made for a material misstatement to the probation officer.[6]

While false or misleading answers should not be counseled, defendants should be advised to decline to answer certain questions.[7] In considering the kinds of questions that should not be answered, a distinction should be drawn between defendants who have pleaded guilty and defendants who have been convicted at trial. With respect to the former, care should be taken to respond only to questions relating specifically to the conduct underlying the count of conviction, since admissions with respect to other activities could reveal relevant conduct and raise the offense level.[8] To reduce or minimize the possibility of such harmful admissions, counsel for a defendant who has pleaded guilty often will prepare a written statement in advance, describing the defendant's admissions with respect to the count(s) to which a guilty plea was entered. Alternatively, and preferably from the defendant's point of view, the probation officer may be prepared to rely on the defendant's allocution at the guilty plea and nothing more.

As to the defendant who has been convicted after a trial, discussion of acts beyond those revealed at trial should be avoided for the same reasons. Moreover, any discussion of the offense of conviction itself is problematic. Exculpatory statements that contradict trial testimony or appear to undermine the jury's verdict could be considered obstructive. Inculpatory statements, if inconsistent with the defendant's testimony at trial, could lead to the conclusion that the defendant committed perjury at trial, which can also lead to a two point upward adjustment. Even if the defendant did not testify, such statements could be used against him or her in the event of a successful appeal and retrial. In any event, the defendant convicted at trial is almost certain to be denied the adjustment for acceptance of responsibility, which is the major incentive for

statements be suppressed because counsel was not present. However, counsel cannot be barred from the interview. United States v. Herrera–Figueroa, 918 F.2d 1430, 1433 (9th Cir. 1990).

6. *See* USSG § 3C1.1 (Obstructing or Impeding the Administration of Justice).

7. The Guidelines make clear that a refusal to answer—as opposed to an affirmative misrepresentation—will not constitute an obstruction of justice. *See* USSG § 3C1.1, comment. (n.2). Moreover, the de-

fendant retains a Fifth Amendment privilege with respect both to conduct beyond the offense of conviction, *see* USSG § 3E1.1, comment. (n.1a); United States v. Austin, 17 F.3d 27, 30 (2d Cir. 1994), as well as with respect to the offense of conviction prior to being sentenced. *See* United States v. Brown, 52 Fed.Appx. 612, 614 (4th Cir. 2002).

8. For a discussion of relevant conduct under the Guidelines, see *infra* Chapter 7 and USSG § 1B1.3.

making a statement regarding the offense conduct. Absent very unusual circumstances, therefore, the defendant convicted after trial is best advised to remain silent with respect to this topic.

(2) Interview of the Assistant United States Attorney

In almost every case, the probation officer will obtain the government's version of the pertinent facts by interviewing the prosecuting attorney. It also is common for the probation officer to talk with the agents who investigated the case or other law enforcement personnel. In cases involving relevant conduct that is not readily apparent, or in which the defendant's prior record may not be clear, the prosecutor may write a memorandum detailing what the investigation revealed about relevant conduct, applicable adjustments and the defendant's criminal history.

In most police-initiated cases, such as the Santiago case, the discussions with the prosecutor and agents may be brief and straightforward. In more complex cases, the probation officer may need several sessions with the prosecutor and agents to get a full picture of the case and the roles of the defendants.

It also should be noted that, while it is not the norm, in certain cases defense counsel may decide to make a submission to the probation officer prior to issuance of the presentence report, in order to present the defendant's view of a particularly important disputed sentencing factor (such as drug quantity or loss amount) earlier rather than later in the process.

§ 17.1(b) The Presentence Report

Once the investigation is complete, the probation officer prepares a presentence report detailing the facts relevant to sentencing. Also included are the Probation Department's Guidelines calculations. The presentence report includes an analysis of the factors used to calculate the Guidelines range and the probation officer's reasons for either applying or not applying the various mitigating and aggravating factors that go into determining the offense level (e.g., whether the defendant should receive a 2 or 3 level reduction for acceptance of responsibility).[9] A model presentence report for Gilbert Santiago is included below in § 17.8.

§ 17.2 Negotiating Challenges to the Presentence Report

The presentence report must be disclosed to counsel for both the defendant and the government before the sentencing hearing occurs.[10]

---

9. Following *Booker* the probation officer's responsibility continues to be to ensure that the sentencing judge is presented with all information relevant to sentencing. To the extent *Booker* makes additional considerations relevant (or more relevant than before), *see* 18 U.S.C. § 3553(a), the presentence report no doubt will expand to reflect those facts as well.

10. In many jurisdictions, practice or local rules dictate specific timetables for earlier disclosure. *See, e.g.,* D.Conn. L. Cr. R. 32(a) ("Unless otherwise ordered by the Court, the Probation Officer shall, not more

Upon receiving the report, both parties must identify any issues in dispute and inform the Probation Department of those issues.[11]

The Guidelines require the probation officer to give disputed issues further consideration and either revise the presentence report or explain a decision not to revise it.[12]

§ 17.3   Litigating Disputed Facts in the Presentence Report

§ 17.3(a)   The Presentence Memorandum

Both parties may submit a letter or memorandum to the court that presents the sentencing issues in dispute and argues the party's view with respect to the Guidelines range the court should adopt. Further, a presentence memorandum may be submitted even where no factual dispute exists, in an effort to advance the party's position with regard to the severity of the sentence the court should impose and the propriety of any departures and/or a non-Guidelines sentence.

§ 17.3(b)   The Sentencing Hearing—Burden of Proof

The government always carries the burden of persuasion with respect to facts in issue that establish the offense level.[13] The party seeking an adjustment, however, has the burden of persuasion with regard to establishing the facts that form the basis for the adjustment. The defendant carries the burden of proof when seeking to establish facts at the hearing that will decrease the sentence; the government carries the burden when it seeks to establish facts that will increase the sentence. This allocation of burdens follows the general principle that the party seeking the relief carries the burden.[14]

In most cases, presentence reports reflect the government's version of events. Therefore, most evidentiary hearings arise on the defendant's motion objecting to facts and calculations contained in the report, which typically is defended by the prosecution, not the Probation Department

---

than 6 weeks after the verdict or finding of guilt, disclose the presentence investigation report, including the worksheets utilized to calculate sentencing guideline ranges, to the defendant and to counsel for the defendant and the government.").

11. See FED. R. CRIM. P. 32(f). The courts must provide an opportunity for the submission of oral or written objections to the report at this stage, prior to the sentencing hearing. *See,* USSG § 6A1.3, p.s. (Resolution of Disputed Factors); *see also* United States v. Markin, 263 F.3d 491, 498 (6th Cir. 2001).

12. Although the defendant does not waive an objection to the presentence report by ignoring the pre-hearing objections process, he or she will have missed an op-

portunity to attempt to frame the issues and change the report. Moreover, it is best not to wait too long to identify the issues in dispute. *See, e.g.,* United States v. Zuleta–Alvarez, 922 F.2d 33, 36 (1st Cir. 1990) (defendants waived right to introduce rebuttal evidence when they raised only general objections to the presentence reports and waited until the day of the sentencing hearing to request production of a witness).

13. United States v. Howard, 894 F.2d 1085, 1090 (9th Cir. 1990).

14. *See, e.g.,* United States v. McDowell, 888 F.2d 285 (3d Cir. 1989); United States v. Valladares–Helguera, 78 Fed.Appx. 232 (4th Cir. 2003); United States v. Rodriguez, 896 F.2d 1031 (6th Cir. 1990); United States v. Rice, 52 F.3d 843 (10th Cir. 1995).

(except in those relatively infrequent situations where the prosecution and defense are in agreement with each other but the Probation Department sees things differently). While judges may rely on it, neither the courts nor the Guidelines accord any special presumption to the conclusions found in the presentence report.

Defendants have a due process right to accurate and fair determinations of sentencing facts.[15] The Guidelines leave it to the court's discretion to determine whether an evidentiary hearing is necessary or whether proffers, written statements of counsel or affidavits of witnesses may satisfy the burden of persuasion. The Guidelines do state, however, that depending upon the nature of the dispute, its relevance to the sentencing determination, and applicable case law, an evidentiary hearing may be the only reliable way to resolve a dispute.[16] A majority of courts today decline to apply the confrontation clause to such evidentiary hearings.[17]

As recently reaffirmed following the Supreme Court's *Booker* decision, the quantitative burden in factual disputes at the sentencing stage is generally by a preponderance of the evidence.[18] As to the qualitative burden, the court may consider relevant information, as long as the information has "sufficient indicia of reliability to support its probable accuracy."[19]

§ 17.4   The Sentencing Decision

After the hearing, the court must make factual determinations regarding the issues in dispute[20] or rule that the sentence would be the same regardless of the determination of the particular fact at issue.[21] Even after *Booker* rendered the Guidelines calculation advisory only, sentencing courts must "consider" the Guidelines and thus will continue, in all or almost all cases, to make a legal determination of the

---

15. United States v. Fatico, 603 F.2d 1053, 1054 (2d Cir. 1979).

16. Defense counsel should consider the impact of failure to request an evidentiary hearing upon an appeal of a Guidelines determination involving a disputed fact. While failure to make a request may not be dispositive, it does carry some weight with the appellate court because the defendant is in the best position to inform the court of the value of such a hearing. *See* United States v. Rios–Ramirez, 929 F.2d 563, 566 n.2 (10th Cir. 1991). Because a fact may have a quantifiable effect on the Guidelines range, the defendant will have a strong due process argument for having a hearing to resolve a dispute that clearly would affect the range. Some courts have held that, where defense counsel voices an objection to facts in the Presentence Report and the dispute is "reasonable," the defendant must be given an opportunity to present evidence in support of the objection. *See,*

e.g., United States v. Palta, 880 F.2d 636 (2d Cir. 1989).

17. *See, e.g.,* United States v. Wise, 976 F.2d 393, 401 (8th Cir. 1992).

18. See § 7.3, n. 100 supra.

19. USSG § 6A1.3, p.s. (Resolution of Disputed Factors).

20. *Id.*; United States v. Burch, 873 F.2d 765, 767 (5th Cir. 1989).

21. United States v. Willard, 909 F.2d 780, 780 (4th Cir. 1990); United States v. Bermingham, 855 F.2d 925, 931 (2d Cir. 1988). This principle appears to have survived *Booker. See, e.g.,* United States v. Crosby, 397 F.3d 103, 112 (2d Cir. 2005) (explaining that resolution of a factually or legally complex Guidelines issue can be avoided so long as the judge fairly determines to impose a non-Guidelines sentence that would be the same irrespective of how the issue was resolved).

applicable Sentencing Guidelines range under the particular facts of the case.[22]

After hearing from all counsel and offering the defendant the opportunity to speak, the court must then impose sentence. As described in §§ 7.2(i) and 7.3, the court has essentially three options following its consideration of the Guidelines and the other considerations set forth in 18 U.S.C. § 3553(a): impose a sentence within the Guidelines range; depart up or down from the Guidelines range under the Guidelines departure mechanisms set forth in Chapter 5, Part K of the Guidelines; or impose a non-Guidelines sentence. If the court grants an upward or downward departure or imposes a non-Guidelines sentence, it must state on the record the bases for its decision.[23] The court has seven days to correct a mathematical or other clear error.[24] Other challenges to the sentence must be addressed on appeal.[25] In the post-Booker regime, a party may appeal a sentence on the ground that it is not "reasonable," i.e., not reasonable in its length and/or not reasonable because it was improperly calculated or otherwise improperly decided as a matter of fact or law.[26]

§ 17.5 Strategic and Policy Considerations in Connection with Sentencing

§ 17.5(a) The Defense Perspective

The defense lawyer's obligations in connection with sentencing are effectively the same as they are in connection with plea bargaining: do whatever is legally and ethically permissible to achieve for the client the most lenient sentence possible. The defense lawyer has three relevant audiences for these efforts: the prosecutor, the probation officer and the judge. In non-trial cases, the process of negotiating with the prosecutor typically will have begun, and sometimes will have been exhausted, at the plea negotiation stage. The presentence interview process presents an opportunity to highlight particularly helpful facts and make legal arguments to the probation officer, with the hope of influencing his or her sentencing calculations and recommendations in the presentence report. A failure to persuade the probation officer may require further discussion with the prosecutor, who sometimes can be persuaded to agree with defense counsel that the probation officer's analysis is in error. Of course, failure to convince the prosecutor and/or probation

22. *See, e.g., Crosby,* 397 F.3d at 111 (explaining that "a sentencing judge normally will have to determine the applicable Guidelines range"). See § 7.3, supra.

23. 18 U.S.C. § 3553(c); *Crosby,* 397 F.3d at 116.

24. FED. R. CRIM. P. 35(a) (as amended 2002). Before the amendment, many courts recognized an inherent power to correct clear error within a short period after sen-

tence. *See, e.g.,* United States v. Cook, 890 F.2d 672, 675 (4th Cir. 1989).

25. 18 U.S.C. § 3742.

26. *Booker,* 125 S. Ct. at 755–56. *See, e.g.* United States v. Selioutsky, 409 F.3d 114, 119 (2d Cir. 2005); United States v. Hadash, 408 F.3d 1080 (8th Cir. 2005); *Crosby,* 397 F.3d at 114–16.

officer never represents a final defeat, as the ultimate decision on all issues relating to sentencing and the application (or non-application) of the Sentencing Guidelines rests exclusively with the sentencing judge.

Whoever the audience, the defense lawyer's focus in the sentencing process can be divided into two principal areas. The first requires the defense attorney to think carefully and comprehensively about the facts of the crime of conviction and whether any components of the Guidelines calculation could be analyzed or re-calculated in a way that would be more favorable to the defendant. The second requires the defense lawyer to focus creatively on the unique and individual circumstances of both the case and the defendant's personal history to determine whether there are any bases to persuade the court that the case is so atypical in one or more ways that the court should grant leniency by either departing from the sentencing range called for by the Guidelines or imposing a non-Guidelines sentence.

As should be apparent, to properly carry out these dual analyses, defense counsel must be thoroughly and intimately familiar with the Guidelines, how sentencing ranges are calculated, and the full range of possible bases for leniency in the form of both downward departure applications and arguments for non-Guidelines sentences under the factors set forth in 18 U.S.C. § 3553(a).[27]

§ 17.5(b) The Prosecution Perspective

The prosecutor's job at sentencing is less clear. It plainly is not to seek the maximum sentence in every case, although in some cases that may be the appropriate position for the prosecution to take. As at the plea bargaining stage, the prosecutor's overriding obligations at the time of sentencing are to see that the defendant is sentenced in conformity with the actual facts of the case and with what the Sentencing Guidelines call for. But it is equally true that in many if not most cases, the prosecutor will confront discretionary choices that can have a tremendous impact on the defendant's ultimate sentence. Bedrock principles such as "equity, fairness and uniformity"[28] may inform the prosecutor's approach to making such choices, but rarely will they provide a clear answer.

For example, on issues of Guidelines calculations, will the government challenge a close call resolved in favor of the defendant in the presentence report? Where the defendant has made a downward departure motion or seeks a non-Guidelines sentence, will the government

---

27. Such factors under 18 U.S.C. § 3553(a) include the history and characteristics of the defendant, the nature of the offense, the need for deterrence, the likelihood of recidivism, the public's need for protection, and avoiding unwarranted sentencing disparities among similarly situated defendants.

28. John Ashcroft, Departmental Policy Concerning Charging Criminal Offenses, Disposition of Charges, and Sentencing, p. 1, *available at* http://www.fd.org/TXW/ pdf_lib/memoagcds.pdf (Sept. 23, 2003).

oppose, and if so, how strongly? Once a sentencing range has been determined, should the prosecutor urge the judge to impose the maximum time in prison or should he or she take no position in response to the defendant's request for the minimum? More subtly, and throughout the sentencing process, on which facts and arguments will the government focus the court's attention, which facts and arguments will it choose not to highlight, which of the defendant's assertions will it challenge, and with how much zeal?

To some degree these questions are answered by Department of Justice policies and the policies of individual United States Attorney's Offices. But ultimately the prosecutorial compass can be no more or less clear than the inexorable prosecutorial command to see that "justice is done"[29] in each and every case.

§ 17.6   The Sentencing of Paul Christopher

About ten days after Christopher was convicted, he and his attorney met with the probation officer, Joan Rich, at the Metropolitan Detention Center, where Christopher was being held following his conviction. Rich had already met with AUSA Knapp and Agent Martinez and therefore knew the government's version of the case.

Officer Rich asked Christopher about his family and personal background. She interviewed him about his work history, his educational history and his military service. They discussed his health, including any history of use and abuse of alcohol and controlled substances. Upon the advice of his counsel, he declined to make any statement about the incidents leading to his conviction. The interview was then concluded.

§ 17.6(a)   Calculating Christopher's Sentence

(1) Determining the Offense Level

Christopher was convicted of conspiracy to import cocaine (Count One); conspiracy to distribute and possess with intent to distribute cocaine (Count Two); multiple counts of importation, distribution, and possession and attempted possession with intent to distribute cocaine (Counts Three–Twelve); structuring conspiracy (Count Thirteen); multiple counts of illegal structuring (Counts Fourteen—Seventeen); money laundering conspiracy (Count Eighteen); and four counts of substantive money laundering (Counts Nineteen—Twenty-Two). What follows is the offense level calculation the probation officer must make with respect to each violation, taking into account the Base Offense Level, Specific Offense Characteristics, and appropriate adjustments.[30]

---

29. United States v. Reynolds, 345 U.S. 1, 12 (1953).

30. *See* USSG § 1B1.1(d) (explaining how to proceed where there are multiple counts of conviction).

(a) Narcotics Importation, Distribution and Possession Conspiracy, Narcotics Distribution and Possession, and Attempted Narcotics Possession. As discussed in detail in § 7.2(e), the Guidelines provide that where, as here, there are multiple counts of conviction, "all counts involving substantially the same harm shall be grouped together."[31] Because each of the nine different narcotics counts on which Christopher was convicted involves "substantially the same harm" (i.e., the unlawful importation and distribution of cocaine),[32] the Guidelines instruct that his sentence be calculated as if he were convicted of only one count that includes the aggregate quantity of the cocaine encompassed by all twelve.[33] (The same type of calculation, based on aggregate dollars involved, will be required for the separately grouped money laundering and structuring counts.)

The probation officer had been told by AUSA Knapp that the proof at trial established the following on the issue of drug quantity: first, the shipment intercepted in January 2005 contained 9.8 kilos of cocaine; second, Santiago specifically testified that Christopher had informed him that each of the shipments beginning in September 2004 would involve between 9 and 10 kilograms; third, Santiago further testified that Christopher had informed him that, prior to September 2004, he had received three additional shipments for which he was effectively paid $50,000; and fourth, there had been no testimony as to the quantities of cocaine that were imported during the three pre-September shipments. Based on this evidence, the probation officer determined that the five shipments between September and January corresponded to at least 45 kilograms of cocaine (that is, five times at least 9 kilograms per shipment), and that, in light of the $50,000 compensation, the three prior shipments must have added up to at least 5 additional kilograms. The probation officer therefore determined that there was sufficient evidence to find that the aggregate quantity of cocaine for which Christopher should be held responsible was at least 50 kilograms, which put Christo-

---

31. *Id.* § 3D1.2.

32. The "grouping" provisions of the Guidelines provide that counts involve "substantially the same harm" where, among other things, "the offense level is determined largely on the basis of the total amount of harm or loss, the quantity of a substance involved, or some other measure of aggregate harm.... " USSG § 3D1.2(d). Narcotics counts fall within this definition because the offense level is determined largely based on the aggregate quantity of illegal drugs involved; money laundering and structuring counts fall within this definition because the offense levels for those crimes are determined largely based on the aggregate dollar amount involved.

33. *See* USSG Ch. 3, Pt. D, intro. comment. (Multiple Counts) ("In order to limit the significance of the formal charging decision and to prevent multiple punishment for substantially identical offense conduct, this Part provides rules for grouping offenses together. Convictions on multiple counts do not result in a sentence enhancement unless they represent additional conduct that is not otherwise accounted for by the guidelines. In essence, counts that are grouped together are treated as constituting a single offense for purposes of the guidelines.").

pher's Base Offense Level at 36 (which applies to any amount of cocaine between 50 and 150 kilograms).[34]

While no Specific Offense Characteristics applied,[35] there was one applicable Chapter 3 adjustment for Christopher's management role in the scheme. Probation Officer Rich believed that an upward adjustment was appropriate because Christopher was a leader or supervisor of a group of criminals that included Santiago, Long and Wagner, and accordingly she assigned a 2–level upward adjustment,[36] bringing the offense level for the narcotics counts as a group to 38.

(b) Money Laundering. The money laundering guideline made the calculation of the Base Offense Level for Christopher's group of "closely related" money laundering counts simple, setting it at the offense level "for the underlying offense from which the laundered funds were derived."[37] Here the underlying offenses are the narcotics counts just discussed, and so the Base Offense Level is the same, 36. To this must be added one Specific Offense Characteristic enhancement: 2 additional levels because Christopher was convicted under 18 U.S.C. § 1956.[38] With respect to Christopher's role in the money laundering offense, the probation officer viewed him as a supervisor (of Santiago), and so she added the same 2 additional levels under § 3B1.1. The total offense level for the group of money laundering counts was therefore 40, 2 levels higher than for the group of narcotics counts.

(c) Structuring. The Base Offense Level under the structuring guideline is 6,[39] plus additional offense levels related to the amount of money involved.[40] Christopher was convicted of four substantive counts of structuring, involving a total of $100,000 based on the four deposits of $25,000 each between September and December 2004. But he also was convicted of a structuring conspiracy that continued through and included the failed January 2005 shipment, from which was expected an additional $25,000 in cash to be deposited. Because Rich viewed this last anticipated deposit as an "intended loss" within the scope of the conspiracy for which Santiago was convicted, it too was added to the total dollar figure used to set the Base Offense Level for the group of structuring counts, for a total of $125,000.[41] This added 10 levels.[42] An additional 2 levels were added as a Specific Offense Characteristic, because Christopher knew that the funds were proceeds of and/or intended to promote

---

34. *See id.* § 2D1.1(c)(2) (Drug Quantity Table).

35. *See id.* § 2D1.1(b)(1)-(6).

36. *See id.* § 3B1.1(c).

37. *Id.* § 2S1.1(a)(1).

38. *See id.* § 2S1.1(b)(2).

39. The base offense level for structuring in violation of 31 U.S.C. § 5324 is found in USSG § 2S1.3.

40. *See id.* § 2S1.3(a)(2) (referencing § 2B1.1).

41. *See id.* § 2B1.1, comment. (n.3A) (explaining that "loss is the greater of actual loss or intended loss"), comment. (n.3Aii) (defining "intended loss" to include even harm that was "impossible or unlikely to occur," such as "in a government sting operation").

42. *See id.* § 2B1.1(b)(1)(F).

an unlawful activity—narcotics trafficking.[43] And as with the money laundering counts, 2 additional levels were added for Christopher's role in supervising Santiago and Wagner. The combined level was therefore 20 for the group of structuring counts.

(d) Determining the Combined Offense Level. With an offense level corresponding to each of the three closely related groups of charges just reviewed, the question then becomes how to arrive at a single "Combined Offense Level" that incorporates all three. While this type of calculation can be among the most complicated of all Guidelines analyses, in Christopher's case it was relatively easy. First, application note 6 to the money laundering guideline[44] mandates that the money laundering group be treated as "closely related" to the narcotics group and therefore combined into one group. The Guidelines further provide that the offense level for this combined group is the higher of the two separate groups,[45] and so here, where the narcotics group is at a level 38 and the money laundering group is at a level 40, 40 is the offense level for the combined group.

That leaves one last issue: determining whether the separate group of structuring counts has any impact on the offense level for the combined narcotics/money laundering group. Here, the answer is no, because the Guidelines provide that any group "9 or more levels less serious than the Group with the highest offense level" be "disregard[ed]."[46] Since the group with the highest offense level is 40 and the structuring group is at an offense level of 20, the latter is simply disregarded, although the Guidelines further provide that the disregarding of the lower group "may provide a reason for sentencing at the higher end" of the ultimate sentencing range.[47]

(e) Acceptance of Responsibility. The final adjustment in determining the Total Offense Level—which comes only after the "grouping" analysis has been completed—requires consideration of whether the defendant has demonstrated that he has accepted responsibility for the crime.[48] Because Christopher went to trial and, on the advice of counsel, did not make any statement about his conduct at the presentence interview, Rich concluded that no adjustment was appropriate.

(2) Determining the Criminal History Category

Because Christopher has no prior record, he was assigned no criminal history points and was placed in Criminal History Category I.[49]

---

43.   *See id.* § 2S1.3(b)(1)(A).

44.   *See id.* § 2S1.1.

45.   Application note 6 to USSG § 2S1.1 specifically mandates grouping under "subsection (c) of § 3D1.2," and § 3D1.3(a) in turn provides that for counts grouped un-der § 3D1.2(c), the offense level is the highest number in the group.

46.   USSG § 3D1.4(c).

47.   *Id.*

48.   *See id.* § 3E1.1.

49.   *See generally id.* § 4A1.1.

(3) Christopher's Guidelines Range

Paul Christopher's Total Offense Level is therefore 40 and his Criminal History Category is I, yielding a Sentencing Guidelines range of 292–365 months (24.3 years to 30.4 years) in prison. Because Christopher was convicted of a statute carrying a 10 year mandatory minimum, even a downward departure or a non-Guidelines sentence could not reduce his sentence below 10 years, unless he cooperated.[50] In addition to the sentence of imprisonment, the court will be required by the narcotics laws to impose a 5–year term of supervised release to begin upon Christopher's release from prison.[51] The Guidelines also require the imposition of a fine between $25,000 and $250,000 in this case[52] and the imposition of a special assessment of $100 on each count of conviction.[53]

§ 17.6(b) The Objections Stage

(1) Defense Objections

Christopher's attorney, Richard Clark, felt that the probation officer's recommendation of a sentencing range of 292–365 months was excessive. Although convicted of a serious offense, his client had been a legitimate businessman who regrettably became associated with an international narcotics smuggling organization led by individuals who certainly were much more culpable than he. Clark believed, moreover, that any judge would find it difficult to impose a sentence longer than 20 years on a first time narcotics offender in a case like this. The first line of attack for Clark, accordingly, was to come up with arguments he could present to reduce the severity of the Probation Department's proposed Guidelines calculation.

Clark knew that he could not seek a downward adjustment for acceptance of responsibility without having his client make damaging admissions. In addition, Christopher was either unwilling or unable to cooperate by disclosing the identities of the individuals in Colombia who supplied him with the cocaine, and the government typically is not interested in a defendant's cooperation after a conviction at trial, ruling out a downward departure on that ground. Clark also considered seeking a downward departure on the grounds that Christopher was coerced into committing the crime,[54] but this too would require admissions, and it was a weak argument in any case. And Clark concluded that there was

---

50. *See* 21 U.S.C. § 841. Cooperation need not occur prior to conviction. Rule 35 permits the government to return to the sentencing court within one year of the imposition of sentence to move for a reduction of sentence based on cooperation. FED. R. CRIM. P. 35(b)(1).

51. *See* 21 U.S.C. §§ 960(b)(1) & 841(b)(1)(A).

52. *See* USSG § 5E1.2 (Fines for Individual Defendants).

53. *See* 18 U.S.C. § 3013; *see also* USSG § 5E1.2, comment. (n.2).

54. *See* USSG § 5K2.12, p.s. (Coercion and Duress).

nothing about Christopher's personal situation that could support a departure on grounds of "extraordinary family circumstances."[55]

Clark therefore decided to focus on two calculations that the probation officer had made: the quantity of cocaine that was used to set the Base Offense Level for the group of narcotics counts and the assessment of upward adjustments for Christopher's alleged supervisory or "aggravating role" in the offenses. Clark decided to challenge these calculations as being incorrect applications of the Guidelines under the facts of Christopher's case.

Clark's first step was to draft a letter to the probation officer, in which he noted his objections to the report and suggested his own Guidelines calculation. Clark's letter, which suggests a Guideline range of 121 to 151 months, follows.

55. *See id.* § 5H1.6, p.s. (Family Ties and Responsibilities).

Richard Clark, Esq.
377 Broadway
New York, N.Y. 10003
(212) 862–9543

October 5, 2005

Ms. Joan Rich
United States Probation Officer
United States Probation Department
Eastern District of New York
225 Cadman Plaza East
Brooklyn, NY 11201

Re: <u>United States v. Paul Christopher</u>

Dear Ms. Rich:

    In conformance with our local rules and practice, I am writing to note my objections to the Presentence Report prepared in the case of *United States v. Paul Christopher* and to request that you review and reconsider your Guidelines calculation. I believe that your report overstates the amount of cocaine for which Mr. Christopher should be held liable under the Guidelines and that his role in the offense was much less significant than your report suggests. I believe that Mr. Christopher's overall offense level should be 32, and his Guidelines range should be adjusted downward to 121-151 months.

    Turning first to the amount of cocaine used to set Mr. Christopher's base offense level, the simple fact is that the government seized only one cocaine shipment of 9.8 kilograms in January 2005. While two-time convicted narcotics felon Gilbert Santiago did testify at trial that Mr. Christopher told him in August 2004 that the shipments that would follow would each be between 9 and 10 kilograms, and while Santiago further testified that four additional shipments did in fact arrive between September and December, there was not a scintilla of evidence presented at trial as to the actual quantities of cocaine contained in these alleged shipments. Based on this flimsy evidentiary record, we do not believe Mr. Christopher appropriately may be sentenced based on speculation about the quantities involved in these alleged additional shipments. *See United States v. McLean,* 287 F.3d 127, 133 (2d Cir. 2002) (reiterating the Second Circuit's requirement of "specific evidence" before a court may consider, for purposes of sentencing, quantities of drugs relating to prior transactions where no narcotics were actually seized) (citing *United States v. Shonubi,* 103 F.3d 1085, 1087 (2d Cir. 1997)).

    Even more insupportable is the inclusion of an additional quantity of cocaine of at least 5 kilograms based on three other alleged shipments that Santiago suggested may have taken place prior to his direct involvement. Santiago did not claim to have personal knowledge about these alleged earlier transactions. He only said that Mr. Christopher said something about earlier deals. Moreover, his testimony did not offer any specifics about these purported transactions -- and certainly no specifics about the quantities of cocaine involved -- and there was no independent corroboration whatever of Christopher's alleged statement. We submit that this bald assertion by a two-time narcotics felon cooperating witness is not a reliable basis for this part of your recommendation and certainly will not provide an adequate basis for Judge Sheridan to make the factual findings of "specific evidence" of drug quantity that will be required at the time of sentencing.

       Accordingly, Mr. Christopher's base offense level should be calculated based on the approximately 9.8 kilograms of cocaine that actually were seized, which corresponds to a base offense level of 32.

       The upward adjustment for leader or organizer is also unwarranted in this case. Although Mr. Christopher was the leader of his own legitimate business, the government's evidence at trial was that Mr. Christopher was merely a deliveryman for major international narcotics traffickers who plainly ran a large operation both outside and inside the United States. The government's proof showed that Mr. Christopher only held the cocaine for a short time before delivering it and receiving a regular payment each time. Although he has been found legally responsible for the importation as a co-conspirator and aider and abetter, there was no evidence that Mr. Christopher played any role in importing the cocaine or in later selling it. And although not coerced as a matter of law, the government's evidence showed that Mr. Christopher was clearly a person who succumbed to unusual financial pressure and, eventually, to pressure from the international traffickers with whom he is alleged to have been involved.

       Under the circumstances of this case, the two level upward adjustment under § 3B1.1(c) is unsupported by the facts. We instead urge that you consider Mr. Christopher in the light of the larger and much more culpable organization in which he played only a very small role. On the facts of this case as they developed at trial, we urge you to revisit this issue and assign Mr. Christopher a downward adjustment of two levels, under § 3B1.2(b), *Minor role.* And because you have calculated the offense level for the money laundering counts by borrowing the Guidelines from the underlying narcotics convictions, Mr. Christopher's role in the money laundering offenses must as a matter of logic be analyzed through the same lens of considering his relatively minor part in the overall narcotics importation and distribution organization.

       Based on these revised calculations, Mr. Christopher's total offense level for the narcotics group should be 30 (32 less 2 for minor role), and for the money laundering group 32 (32 plus 2 for § 1956 and minus 2 for minor role). As the higher offense level governs under the grouping rules, Mr. Christopher's Guidelines range should be no greater than a level 32, corresponding to 121 to 151 months in prison.

       Thank you for your attention to this matter.

                              Sincerely,

                              Rich Clark

                              Richard Clark
                              Attorney for Paul Christopher

cc: The Honorable Walter Sheridan
       United States District Judge

       Laura Knapp, Esq.
       Assistant United States Attorney

---

(2) The Government's Position

AUSA Knapp found that the presentence report's factual assertions and Guidelines analysis were consistent with the views she expressed to Probation Officer Rich. Although she was uncertain whether Judge

Sheridan would accept all of the calculations, she believed that there was a factually and legally adequate basis for them in the record. When she received her copy of Clark's letter to the Probation Department, she did nothing in response. For now the dispute was between Clark and the Probation Department.

(3) The Probation Department Response

About ten days before the scheduled sentence date, Clark received an addendum to the presentence report from Rich. In the addendum, Rich noted that she had received Clark's letter and reviewed it along with her report. Rich reported that she disagreed with counsel's position on both issues and that these points remain in dispute and must be resolved by the sentencing judge.

§ 17.6(c)   Resolving Contested Issues

About a week before the Christopher sentencing, Clark called Knapp to attempt to reach a compromise on the Guidelines calculations. Knapp acknowledged that the Guidelines range was harsh, but believed that the Probation Department's position was legally correct. She said that she would agree with Clark that no additional levels should be added or subtracted for his role in the offense if he would agree to drop his other contentions concerning drug quantity (i.e., agree to a Base Offense Level of 36). She noted that Christopher would then have a range of 235–293 months under the controlling money laundering group (36 plus 2 for a conviction under § 1956) and stood a very good chance of getting the bottom of that range (or even less, if a non-Guidelines sentence were imposed).

Clark adhered to the position he took in his letter and so the attorneys concluded that the court would have to resolve the dispute. Clark said that he would seek an evidentiary hearing and wrote a letter to Judge Sheridan to that effect.

In preparation for the hearing, Clark also wrote a sentencing letter, which took the form of a brief in support of his positions on the quantity of cocaine that should be used to set the Base Offense Level and on the proper adjustment for Christopher's role in the offense.[56] The letter closed with an argument in mitigation and for a non-Guidelines sentence, stating, in essence, that Christopher had led a blameless life before becoming involved in this matter, that he and his family already were devastated by his conviction and that a sentence of over 20 years

---

56. In our experience, the sentencing letter and the more formal sentencing memorandum formats may be used interchangeably. While stylistically the former might more often be used to set forth shorter, more straight-forward matters and the latter longer more complex ones there is no controlling rule or etiquette as between them. We have seen, and written, very lengthy letters containing legal arguments, factual submissions, and arguments in mitigation. Conversely, the more formal memorandum format may be used to offer a short argument in mitigation.

was wildly in excess of what was "necessary" to achieve the sentencing purposes set forth in 18 U.S.C. § 3553(a).

The government responded to the legal arguments in Clark's letter in a letter submitted shortly before the sentencing hearing, including emphasizing the Department of Justice's position that a "reasonable" sentence under *Booker* is—as in virtually all cases—the sentence called for by the Guidelines.

§ 17.6(d) The Sentencing Hearing

On October 18, 2005 the parties assembled for the last time in Judge Sheridan's courtroom. Clark and Christopher each stated that they had reviewed the presentence report. Clark then detailed several minor factual errors in the personal background section and noted the objections to the drug quantity/Base Offense Level determination and the role in the offense adjustment. Judge Sheridan asked the government to proceed with its proof on the disputed issues.

Knapp began her presentation by proffering to the court a brief summary of Gilbert Santiago's testimony about Paul Christopher's role in the offense and the drug shipments that had preceded the January 2005 shipment that was intercepted by law enforcement agents. Judge Sheridan said he recalled the testimony and would not require Knapp to conduct another complete direct examination, but that he would permit her to elicit testimony from Santiago on the specific issues in dispute.

Santiago was called to the stand and sworn. Knapp asked him if he recalled his first conversation with Christopher about the cocaine dealings. Santiago said he did and testified:

> Christopher told me he had done three previous shipments and paid off a debt of some kind, I believe it was $50,000. He said he wanted to keep doing the deals and needed someone to help him handle the money he would now be making. I can't say for sure how many other deals he was involved in, but I know that while I was with him he did a shipment each month and I had given him my friend Frankie's name about three months before our first shipment arrived.

Knapp also asked Santiago whether he knew the quantity of narcotics involved in the shipments between September and December 2004, and Santiago reiterated his trial testimony that Christopher had told him each shipment would be between 9 and 10 kilograms, that each shipment in fact arrived in a box that appeared, at least from the outside, to be identical to the previous shipments and that the amounts of money Christopher had given Santiago to keep for himself and to deposit into the phony accounts had been the same for each shipment: $12,500 and $25,000, respectively.

Clark then cross-examined Santiago, beginning with his first conversation with Christopher. He established that Santiago never saw any documents or receipts relating to any loan or prior deals, that Santiago took no notes of the conversation and never again talked with Christopher about earlier deals and that Santiago had absolutely no idea how much if any cocaine or other controlled substance had been involved.

With respect to the shipments that Santiago had been involved in, Clark got Santiago to confirm that he had neither weighed nor opened the boxes in which he believed the cocaine had been shipped and that he could not say for sure whether or how much cocaine was contained inside.

Clark then turned to Christopher's role in the offense and established that Santiago had observed Christopher to be very nervous about dealing with his Colombian "bosses," had conversations during which Christopher appeared to be concerned with following the "bosses'" instructions exactly and on more than one occasion spoke about his desire not to anger the "bosses" in any way. He also established that as far as Santiago knew, Christopher was not aware of how the cocaine came into the country or where it went after it was delivered.

Neither side called any other witnesses on the disputed sentencing issues. The court then heard argument from both attorneys.

Knapp began by laying out her argument with respect to drug quantity. The 9.8 kilograms of seized cocaine were not in dispute. She urged the Court to credit Santiago's testimony that Christopher had told him that each of the shipments beginning in September 2004 would be between 9 and 10 kilograms each, pointing out that this statement was corroborated both by the cocaine seized in January 2005 and by the fact that each shipment generated proceeds of $25,000 cash that Santiago deposited in the phony accounts. As to the shipments that pre-dated Santiago's direct involvement, Knapp argued that while Santiago was never told specific quantities, it was enough that Christopher had specified how much he had been compensated–$50,000. Knapp argued that as a matter of simple logic, if Christopher later had at least $25,000 in profits from each shipment of between 9 and 10 kilograms of cocaine, the $50,000 in earlier compensation must have corresponded to at least 5 kilograms of cocaine. She further noted that the wholesale value of one kilogram of cocaine was at most $20,000, and argued that if the earlier shipments had totaled less than 5 kilograms, Christopher's $50,000 in compensation (or loan forgiveness) would have represented more than 50% of the wholesale value of the drugs, an amount no major trafficking organization ever would pay to someone like Christopher.

As to Christopher's role in the offense, Knapp argued that it was clear that Christopher was a supervisor of at least Santiago and Wagner and that the case fell under the plain words of the Guidelines section assigning an upward adjustment to anyone who exercised a managing or supervising position in the offense.

Clark went next, arguing that even if Santiago could be believed—which he contended he could not—his testimony didn't measure up to the well-established requirement of "specific evidence," as set forth in the *Shonubi* line of cases decided by the Second Circuit. Santiago simply could not say with any degree of certainty, much less that it was more likely than not, that any particular shipment actually contained cocaine or, if it did, how much.

Clark further argued that Christopher's role in the offense had to be measured against the larger cocaine importation organization of which he was just one member. In the context of that larger organization, Christopher was a minor participant. He suggested that to hold Christopher responsible as a supervisor or manager would mean there was no meaningful distinction between him and his much more culpable Colombian bosses.

After listening to counsels' arguments, Judge Sheridan stated that he found Santiago's testimony credible at the hearing, as he felt it had been at the trial. He noted that under the Second Circuit's decision in *McClean*, which the defendant had cited in his letter, it was perfectly appropriate for him to base his finding as to overall drug quantity on the uncorroborated testimony of a convicted drug dealer, so long as he found that testimony credible. The judge explained that he believed there was more than enough "specific evidence" to hold Christopher responsible for the five shipments between September and January. But as to the shipments before Santiago's direct involvement, Judge Sheridan found that, while it was a close call, Santiago's single conversation with Christopher was too slender a reed to satisfy the "specific evidence" requirement. The judge accordingly found that Christopher was culpably involved in five shipments of cocaine, not just the one as the defense had argued, but also not all eight as the prosecution had advocated, and assigned a Base Offense Level of 34 (corresponding to the aggregate amount from five shipments multiplied by between 9 and 10 kilograms each).

As to the role in the offense, Judge Sheridan agreed with Clark's argument that Christopher worked for the cocaine importers and distributors and exercised no authority to run the illegal enterprise, and that his Colombian counterparts determined when the shipments came in and where they went from Christopher's warehouse. On these facts, the judge ruled that Christopher was not a leader or supervisor of this criminal conduct and that his role in handling the shipment was no greater than Santiago's. However, he rejected Clark's suggestion that Christopher get a reduction for playing a minor role in the offense, since he played too big a role, for too a long a time, for that downward adjustment. Accordingly, there would be no upward or downward adjustment for Christopher's role in the offense.

503

§ 17.6(e)   The Imposition of Christopher's Sentence

Based on those factual findings and rulings of law, Judge Sheridan found that Christopher's Total Offense Level was 36 and his Criminal History Category was I. This made the sentencing range 188–235 months in prison. The judge then asked the parties to address the court on the appropriate sentence for Christopher.

AUSA Knapp reminded Judge Sheridan that the evidence had demonstrated that Christopher played a critical role in a major cocaine importation and distribution ring and never admitted his responsibility for this very serious crime. For these reasons, she said, he appropriately was facing a severe sentence under the Guidelines, and (consistent with Department of Justice policy) she advocated for imposition of a sentence consistent with the determined Guidelines range, although she took no position on where within the Guidelines range Christopher should be sentenced.

Clark went next, imploring the Court to consider a non-Guidelines sentence pursuant to the considerations of 18 U.S.C. § 3553(a). He argued that the sentence suggested by the Guidelines—of almost 16 years in prison—was extremely, even unimaginably harsh for a man like Christopher, who had otherwise led a productive and law-abiding life. Clark supported his plea for a non-Guidelines sentence by describing Christopher's long business career, his family and his personal background.

Judge Sheridan asked Christopher if he wished to address the court and the defendant said that he did not. Judge Sheridan then announced that he would impose a Guidelines sentence of 188 months, to be followed by 5 years of supervised release. He explained that in this case he believed the Guidelines sentence was "reasonable" and necessary for deterrence and punishment and to send a strong message that those who facilitated large-scale drug-trafficking under the guise of legitimate business would be punished severely. Judge Sheridan stated that he had considered the § 3553(a) factors and found nothing particularly compelling or unique in Christopher's background to justify a less severe non-Guidelines sentence. In view of the forfeiture of Christopher's interests in IFD and Superior Warehouse, Judge Sheridan declined to impose a fine. Christopher would, however, be required to pay a $100 special assessment for each count on which he had been convicted. The judge closed the proceedings by reminding Christopher of his right to appeal.

Christopher, who had been remanded into federal custody following the jury's verdict, would remain in custody, and the next morning Clark filed a notice of appeal of both his conviction and his sentence.

§ 17.7   The Sentencing of Ernest Wagner

It will be recalled from Chapter 11 that Ernest Wagner's plea agreement left only one Guidelines calculation issue open for the court to decide: whether he should receive a 2 level downward adjustment for "minor role," as the government stipulated, or a 4 level downward adjustment for "minimal role," as his counsel had attempted to persuade the government during plea negotiations. The remainder of his Guidelines calculation—Base Offense Level of 16, 2 additional levels because the plea was for violation of 18 U.S.C. § 1956, and 3 levels off for Acceptance of Responsibility—was stipulated by the parties.

Like Christopher, Wagner was interviewed by the Probation Department (in fact, by the same probation officer, who was assigned to all the defendants in this case) shortly after his guilty plea and a full history of Wagner's background and the circumstances of his involvement in the money laundering aspect of the conspiracy was set forth in his presentence report. After consulting with some colleagues in her office, Probation Officer Rich ended up agreeing with the government's position on role, i.e., Wagner should only receive 2 levels off as a "minor participant," and accordingly recommended that the government's overall estimate of a total offense level of 13 and a sentencing range of 12–18 months be adopted by the court.

Much like in Christopher's case, Wagner's attorney, Inga Porter, filed an objection letter, arguing that Christopher was entitled to a 4–level downward adjustment for minimal role, and not just 2 levels off for minor role. Porter's letter emphasized (as she had during plea negotiations) Wagner's "lack of knowledge or understanding of the scope and structure of the enterprise and of the activities of others," quoting from the pertinent Guidelines application note providing that such evidence is "indicative of a role as minimal participant."

After Probation Officer Rich declined to revise her recommendation as to the "mitigating role" adjustment, Porter prepared Wagner's sentencing letter for the court. In addition to repeating his arguments about role in the offense, Porter included in her letter a motion for a downward departure and a request for a non-Guidelines sentence based primarily on what she described as Wagner's "extraordinary" family commitments. An excerpt from the defendant's letter addressing the pleas for a downward departure and a non-Guidelines sentence is set forth below:

Inga Porter, Esq.
1465 Broadway
New York, NY 10015

Honorable Walter Sheridan   August 17, 2005
United States District Court
Eastern District of New York
225 Cadman Plaza East
Brooklyn, NY 11201

Your Honor:

In connection with the upcoming sentencing of Ernest Wagner, I write: (1) to challenge the Probation Department's decision to accord Mr. Wagner only a 2-level reduction for minor role, and to urge the Court to instead accord him a 4-level reduction for minimal role, and (2) to move for a downward departure and a non-Guidelines sentence based on his otherwise laudable personal history and, most importantly, the devastating consequences that an incarceratory sentence would have on Mr. Wagner's family, including his two young children.

Role in the Offense

. . . .

Personal Background/Circumstances of the Offense/Family Issues

Mr. Wagner lives in a modest Brooklyn rental apartment with his wife, Johanna, and their two small children, Ernest, Jr., 4 years old, and Emily, 15 months. Since the birth of Ernest, Jr., Johanna has remained at home to care for their children, and Mr. Wagner has been his family's sole provider. The family is struggling to make ends meet. Mr. Wagner, while employed at CMS Bank, earned up to $40,500 a year, which constituted his family's entire income. As a result of this case, he recently was laid off. However, he has since landed a job as a supermarket manager, and while the pay is significantly less, it enables him and his family to make ends meet. Neither Mr. Wagner's nor Johanna's parents are still alive and the young couple has no other sources of financial support.

As reflected in the presentence report, Mr. Wagner has no prior criminal record. He has an impressive work history for a young man of his age. Mr. Wagner began working as a bank teller after high school graduation and attended evening classes for the next five years at the City University of New York (CUNY), where he ultimately earned a bachelor's degree in economics. Mr. Wagner received consistently excellent work performance reviews at the bank, and, following his graduation from CUNY, he was promoted to a management position. During this time, Johanna gave birth to their two children.

Mr. Wagner's offense arose in a particular and unique set of circumstances. The bank had set ambitious goals for the opening of new accounts and Mr. Wagner understood that the opening of several new accounts for Mr. Santiago would help him achieve this difficult and, in some ways, unrealistic expectation. Moreover, Mr. Wagner was keenly aware of his family's economic difficulties, as well as his own struggles to break into a professional banking career, and as a new manager he felt great pressure to succeed. None of this is an excuse for Mr. Wagner's serious mistakes, which he has admitted and for which he takes full responsibility, but I do believe it is relevant to place his conduct in context.

If Mr. Wagner receives a sentence of incarceration, Johanna, Ernest, Jr., and Emily inevitably will suffer greatly in his absence. Johanna, 26, is currently a full-time homemaker and did not finish high school. Given her youth and limited work experience, it is doubtful that, even if she were to find a job, she would earn enough to afford rent, daily living expenses and childcare for their children.

Mr. Wagner's young children in particular would be devastated by his absence. Each morning, Mr. Wagner feeds his children breakfast and spends time with them, and he returns from work most nights in time to help his wife put them to bed. Mr. Wagner also spends every weekend with his children, taking them to the park, museums, and to play-dates with friends. He is, in short, an integral and essential part of their lives.

If Your Honor incarcerates Mr. Wagner, his family will likely lose their apartment and will have difficulty locating an affordable place of their own. More importantly, given her relative youth, absence of any meaningful employment history, and lack of financial resources, Johanna faces at best an almost impossible struggle to raise and support these two young children on her own. She has no one other than Mr. Wagner to turn to for support.

It is exactly these types of concerns that authorize the Court to depart downward on the basis of family circumstances. *See United States v. Alba*, 9333 F.2d 1117, 1122 (2d Cir. 1991) (affirming departure where incarceration "might well result in the destruction of an otherwise strong family unit" including wife, daughters age 4 and 11, grandmother, and wheelchair-bound father, all of whom defendant supported).

Moreover, the facts here, and Mr. Wagner's request for a departure to a non-incarceratory sentence, fit squarely within the criteria for departures based on the loss of caretaking or financial support set forth in the Sentencing Guidelines. *See* § 5H1.6, Application Note 1(B), requiring: (i) "substantial, direct, and specific loss of essential caretaking, or essential financial support, to the defendant's family"; (ii) loss of caretaking or financial support substantially in excess of "harm ordinarily incident to incarceration for a similarly situated defendant"; (iii) defendant's caretaking or financial support is irreplaceable to the defendant's family; and (iv) departure "effectively will address the loss of caretaking or financial support." Indeed, the situation of Mr. Wagner and his family is even more dire than these criteria require, as his absence will deprive his wife and children of *both* essential caretaking and essential financial support, not just one or the other.

In addition, under 18 U.S.C. § 3553(a), which after *Booker* provides this Court with greater flexibility to render "individualized justice," *United States v. Crosby*, 397 F.3d 103, 112 (2d Cir. 2005), I urge Your Honor to consider both Mr. Wagner's otherwise laudable life story and his family's desperate need for his continuing presence and support. Together these considerations demonstrate that the need for punishment and deterrence and to protect the public can adequately be served here by imposition of a non-incarceratory sentence such as house arrest with strict limitations.

In sum, Your Honor, Mr. Wagner has accepted full responsibility for the crimes in which he participated. In order to ensure that Johanna, Ernest, Jr., and Emily are not unnecessarily deprived of Mr. Wagner's essential material and emotional support, we respectfully request that Your Honor downwardly depart and/or to impose a non-Guidelines sentence that would adequately punish Mr. Wagner but spare his family by not sending him to prison.

Respectfully submitted,

Inga Porter

Inga Porter, Esq.

cc: Laura Knapp, Esq.
        Assistant United States Attorney

_____

AUSA Knapp decided that with respect to Wagner's role in the offense, she would adhere to the position she had taken at the time of the plea–i.e., that Wagner was a "minor" but not a "minimal" participant. On the downward departure/non-Guidelines issue, while Knapp was sympathetic to Wagner's family circumstances, and did not doubt that his wife and two young children were financially dependent on him, she believed the situation was unfortunately fairly standard, and certainly not "extraordinary" for a white collar defendant such as Wagner. In addition, Knapp knew that Department of Justice policy on downward departure motions and requests for non-Guidelines sentences was quite strict: they were to be opposed except in the rarest of circumstances. An excerpt from Knapp's letter, opposing the requests for a more lenient sentence, follows:

U.S. Department of Justice
United States Attorney
Eastern District of New York

August 23, 2005

Honorable Walter Sheridan
United States District Court
Eastern District of New York
225 Cadman Plaza East
Brooklyn, NY 11201

      Re: U.S. v. Ernest Wagner, 05-Cr-735 (WS)

Dear Judge Sheridan:

          The Government respectfully submits this letter in response to the defendant's sentencing letter dated August 17, 2005. In his letter, the defendant seeks a 4-level downward adjustment for "minimal role" and also moves for a downward departure or a non-Guidelines sentence based on alleged extraordinary family circumstances. For the reasons stated herein, both of the defendant's applications should be denied.

I.   Role in the Offense

    . . . .

II.   Extraordinary Family Circumstances

          The defendant argues that the Court should depart downward because he is the sole provider for his wife and their children. While we do not doubt that a sentence of incarceration regrettably will have a negative impact on Mr. Wagner's wife and children, we do not think that impact is so out of the ordinary in this case that it warrants a departure.

          Family circumstances have been deemed generally irrelevant by the Sentencing Commission and are therefore discouraged as a basis for downward departures. *See United States v. Galante*, 111 F.3d 1029, 1034 (2d Cir. 1997), *citing Koon v. United States*, 518 U.S. 81, 116 S.Ct. 2035, 2045 (1996). However, a sentencing court may consider family circumstances as a basis for downward departure pursuant to U.S.S.G. § 5H1.6 when said circumstances are "extraordinary." *See Galante*, 111 F.3d at 1033 (citations omitted).

          Under U.S.S.G. § 5H1.6, which was specifically amended in 2003 to substantially reduce the circumstances under which so-called "family circumstances" departures would be granted,[57] the defendant must show that the harm to his family "substantially exceeds the harm ordinarily incident to incarceration for a similarly situated defendant." Application Note 1(B)(ii). Moreover, the court must find that there are "no remedial or ameliorative programs reasonably . . . available." *Id.,* Note 1(B)(iii).

These Amendments are consistent with long-standing Second Circuit law strictly circumscribing such departures. Thus, prior to the 2003 Amendments, the Second Circuit had explained that hardships to a defendant's family resulting from incarceration generally do not warrant a downward departure. *Galante,* 111 F.3d at 1034; *see also United States v. Johnson,* 964 F.2d 124, 128 (2d Cir. 1992) (disruption of defendant's life and difficulties for those who depend on defendant are inherent in the punishment of incarceration). To warrant a downward departure, the Circuit had held, the defendant's family must be "uniquely dependent on the defendant's ability to maintain existing financial and emotional commitments." *United States v. Faria,* 161 F.3d 761, 762 (2d Cir. 1998) (quoting *United States v. Sprei,* 145 F.3d 528, 535 (2d Cir. 1998)). This standard was held to have been met only in cases where the defendant was the *sole* caretaker for a young or disabled relative. *United States v. Ayala,* 75 F. Supp. 2d 126 (S.D.N.Y. 1999)(emphasis added); *United States v. Alba,* 933 F.2d 1117 (2d. Cir. 1991). Accordingly, when the defendant's family had some other means of support -- however imperfect -- courts have always been reluctant to find that "exceptional circumstances" exist. *See e.g. Faria,* 161 F.3d at 762 (reversing downward departure based on extraordinary family circumstances in part because defendant was not sole source of financial support); *United States v. Maurer,* 76 F. Supp. 2d 353 (S.D.N.Y. 1999) (denying downward departure when defendant was not sole source of financial support and defendant's children received emotional support from other members of defendant's extended family).

The 2003 Amendments to § 5H1.6 reaffirm these basic principles and weigh heavily against any departure here. Although the defendant claims to be the sole support for his wife and children in his letter motion, the record reflects that his wife was at one time employed full-time as a cashier, and there is no reason to believe that she would be unable to find employment now. In addition, while the parents of the defendant and his wife are deceased, the presentence report indicates that Mrs. Wagner has a sister who regularly spends time with the children, and presumably would be available to help her sister with childcare responsibilities for the relatively short time that Mr. Wagner may spend in prison. *See United States v. Smith,* 331 F.3d 292 (2d Cir. 2003) (reversing family circumstances downward departure where defendant faced 10 to 16 months in jail and relatives were available to assist with childcare, and concluding that "[t]he hardship caused in this case will neither be of long duration nor particularly severe").

For all of these reasons, we respectfully submit that the defendant has not met the stringent criteria for a downward departure under § 5H1.6 of the Guidelines.

---

[57] *See* PROTECT Act, Pub. L. 108-21, 117 Stat 650, 68 Fed. Reg. 60154 (Oct. 21, 2003), discussed *supra* at § 7.2(i)(1).

III.   Request for a Non-Guidelines Sentence

Although no longer binding on this Court following *Booker*, the Sentencing Guidelines represent the considered judgment of the Sentencing Commission, an expert body comprising members from all areas of the legal profession and tasked with determining appropriate sentences in particular types of cases. Both *Booker* and *United States v. Crosby*, 397 F.3d 103, 113-14 (2d Cir. 2005), stress the continuing importance and relevance of the Guidelines in determining an appropriate sentence. As the *Crosby* court explained:

> [I]t is important to bear in mind that *Booker/Fanfan* and section 3553(a) do more than render the Guidelines a body of casual advice, to be consulted or overlooked at the whim of a sentencing judge. Thus, it would be a mistake to think that, after *Booker/Fanfan*, district judges may return to the sentencing regime that existed before 1987 and exercise unfettered discretion to select any sentence within the applicable statutory maximum and minimum. On the contrary, the Supreme Court expects sentencing judges faithfully to discharge their statutory obligation to "consider" the Guidelines and all of the other factors listed in section 3553(a). We have every confidence that the judges of this Circuit will do so, and that the resulting sentences will continue to substantially reduce unwarranted disparities while now achieving somewhat more individualized justice.

The government submits that here, the sentence called for by the Guidelines is eminently "reasonable." The defendant's lack of criminal history is reflected in his criminal history category of I; his comparatively minor role is reflected in an appropriate reduction in his offense level; and his plea of guilty and acceptance of responsibility are similarly recognized and rewarded in his Guidelines calculation. In addition, the defendant appears to have been an educated, successful and motivated banker making a decent salary and thus his attempt to offer a mitigating explanation for his criminal conduct falls flat. There is, in short, nothing so unique or extraordinary about the defendant's "history and characteristics" or about his decision to participate in serious criminal activity that suggests a non-Guidelines sentence would be appropriate here. Moreover, as noted above, while the defendant's family – like all families of individuals who choose to commit crimes – no doubt will suffer some hardship from the defendant's absence, he is *not* the sole caretaker and his children have an able-bodied mother and some other family support capable of providing for the defendant's children.

*   *   *

For all of these reasons, we urge the Court to reject the defendant's applications for a lower sentence based on his role in the offense, his family circumstances and/or other § 3553(a) considerations. We thus ask that the Court sentence the defendant within the range called for by the Guidelines and recommended in the presentence report: 12 to 18 months in prison.

Respectfully submitted,

Laura Knapp
Assistant United States Attorney

cc: Inga Porter, Esq.

Wagner's case had come before Judge Sheridan for sentencing on August 25, 2005 (prior to the trial of Christopher and Van Ness). The judge indicated that he had reviewed the presentence report and the letters from counsel and was prepared to hear any additional arguments. Wagner's attorney, Inga Porter, argued first, emphasizing the key points on the role issue and pleading with the judge to show mercy and to impose a non-incarceratory sentence, either under his power to depart downwardly or to impose a non-Guidelines sentence, all to avoid unduly and unnecessarily punishing Wagner's wife and two young children, who he explained were totally dependent on him for their financial and emotional support.

When Porter finished, Judge Sheridan asked Wagner if he wished to say anything. Wagner then stated as follows:

> First I want to say that what I did was wrong and stupid and I freely admit and accept that. I have taken responsibility for the crime I committed by pleading guilty. I know that I played a part in allowing drug traffickers to carry on their dirty and destructive business, and for that I am ashamed and deeply sorry. What I beg of the Court more than anything is that you allow me to continue to take responsibility for the most important thing in my life–my family. I really don't know how my wife and kids will make it without me, and I can promise Your Honor that you will never regret giving me a second chance.

The judge thanked Mr. Wagner for his statement and then called on the government, at which point AUSA Knapp briefly restated that the government thought 2 levels off for minor role was the proper adjustment based on Wagner's role in the offense and that the government opposed the requests for a downward departure and for a non-Guidelines sentence because the situation facing Wagner's family, while extremely unfortunate, was a fairly common and certainly not "extraordinary" byproduct of criminal activity by those with familial financial responsibilities.

Following the arguments, Judge Sheridan announced his rulings. He first addressed the issue of "Role in the Offense," explaining that he thought that both sides had made compelling points. He said he thought it was a close call but that his best judgment was that "minimal" role is really reserved for mere courier-type defendants and here, Wagner had played a more significant role. He therefore adopted the Probation Department's recommendation of a 2–level reduction for "minor" role, leaving Wagner's Total Offense Level at 13, carrying a range of imprisonment of 12–18 months.

Judge Sheridan went on to explain that while he too was sympathetic to the argument that Wagner's family needed him for financial and other support, he did not think this was a case of such utter and total dependence that a § 5H1.6 departure was warranted. Judge Sheridan noted that since Wagner's Total Offense Level was now 13, if he imposed a Guidelines sentence, 12 months in prison would be the minimum.

Judge Sheridan went on to observe that, in his opinion, a year in jail no doubt would cause substantial disruption to Wagner's wife and children. He noted that if the offense level was reduced by just one, from 13 down to 12 (reflecting a Guidelines range of 10–16 months), Wagner would then be within Zone C, where under the Guidelines he would be eligible for a split sentence of 5 months in prison and 5 months of home confinement.[58] Judge Sheridan explained that based on how close Wagner's Guidelines sentence was to Zone C, and the very substantial (even if not "extraordinary") family hardships that any significant period of incarceration would cause, he was going to impose a non-Guidelines sentence of 6 months imprisonment and 6 months home confinement during which Santiago could work to support his family. He also imposed a term of 3 years supervised release to follow the home confinement, a fine of $15,000 to be paid over the 3 years of supervised release,[59] and a special assessment of $100 corresponding to the one count to which Wagner pled guilty. As promised in the plea agreement, the government then moved to dismiss all the open counts of the indictment. Judge Sheridan granted the government's motion and, to conclude the sentencing, permitted Wagner to self-surrender within 60 days to the federal prison to which he would be designated by the Bureau of Prisons.

§ 17.8   The Sentencing of Gilbert Santiago and Mario Long

As is typically the case in prosecutions involving cooperating witnesses, the government postponed the sentencings of Gilbert Santiago and Mario Long until all the non-cooperating defendants (i.e., Christopher and Wagner) had been sentenced. The reason for this–well demonstrated in this case–is that the cooperating witnesses may be needed to testify as to disputed issues at the sentencings of co-defendants or at their trials. The interests of the government and the cooperator are usually aligned in this regard. The government typically feels that, if further testimony may be needed, it is better off with a yet-to-be sentenced cooperator who still has every incentive to remain cooperative. And the cooperator usually is happy to have as much opportunity as possible to assist the government in tangible ways. In our case, with the sentencings of Christopher and Wagner completed, those of Santiago and Long could now proceed.

(1) Gilbert Santiago. Like Paul Christopher, Gilbert Santiago was interviewed by the Probation Department in the presence of his counsel. Unlike Christopher, Santiago chose to discuss the offense and provide answers to all the probation officer's questions. About a month before the sentence, Berman received the following presentence report:

---

58. *See* USSG § 5C1.1(d).

59. *Id.* § 5E1.2(c)(3) (setting out a minimum fine of $3,000 and a maximum fine of $30,000 for offense level 12–13).

UNITED STATES DISTRICT COURT
EASTERN DISTRICT OF NEW YORK PRESENTENCE REPORT

United States of America

vs.   05 Cr. 735 (WS)

Gilbert Santiago

Offense: 21 USC §§ 846, 841(a) and 841(b)(1)(A), Conspiracy to Possess Five Kilograms or More of Cocaine with Intent to Distribute.

Date of arrest: 1/13/05

Custodial Status: Detained since arrest

Legal Residence: 1401 37th St., Astoria, NY

DoB: 10/25/50

Race: White

Sex: M

Citizenship: US

Place of Birth: Philadelphia, PA

Dependents: Three

Education: Some college

Soc. Sec: 062–11–3320

FBI #: N322322703–053

U.S. Marshal #: 88456-111

Detainers or other pending charges: None

Other Defendants: Mario Long, Paul Christopher, Ernest Wagner—related cases

AUSA: Laura Knapp

Defense Counsel: Charles Berman

Sentencing Judge: Honorable Walter Sheridan

Sentencing Date: 10/28/05

Part A. The Offense

Charge(s) and Conviction(s)

1. On February 25, 2005 the defendant pleaded guilty to a one-count information charging him with conspiracy to possess more than 5 kilograms of cocaine with intent to distribute.

2. There is a plea agreement in this case. If the defendant's cooperation is satisfactory, the government will file a motion on his behalf at the time of sentencing.

3. Since the offense occurred after November 1, 1987, the Sentencing Reform Act of 1984 is applicable.

The Offense Conduct

4. On January 11, 2005, Agents of the DEA discovered just under ten kilograms of cocaine in crates of foodstuff imported into the United States from Colombia. On January 12, 2005, the crates were delivered to Superior Warehouse. The defendant, Gilbert Santiago, directed the shipment of the cocaine in and out of the warehouse and helped launder the proceeds. Santiago was arrested after a controlled delivery to the warehouse. Co-defendant Mario Long accepted the controlled delivery.

5. Subsequent investigation revealed that similar amounts of cocaine had been shipped through Superior Warehouse on seven prior occasions. Gilbert Santiago only conspired to distribute the final four shipments. On those occasions, Gilbert Santiago came to the warehouse after the shipments were accepted by others, examined the shipments and arranged for further distribution of the cocaine. He worked with Paul Christopher, the owner of the warehouse. On each occasion the cocaine was picked up by William Van Ness, Christopher's brother-in-law.

6. Gilbert Santiago set up a number of bank accounts at the Coney Island Avenue branch of CMS Bank. After each shipment, he laundered the proceeds of the transactions by making

structured deposits to avoid currency reporting requirements. A total of $125,000 was either laundered or was part of the conspiracy to launder.

Adjustment for Role in the Offense

7. In the view of the Probation Department, no adjustment for role in the offense is appropriate in this case.

Acceptance of Responsibility

8. The defendant admitted his guilt during the presentence interview. He said that he knew he was involved in distributing cocaine and laundering money. Through his admission and his cooperation (which included testifying at the trial and sentencing of Paul Christopher), the Probation Department believes that this defendant has accepted responsibility for his actions.

Offense Level Computation

9. Base Offense Level: The base offense level under § 2D1.1 is determined by the quantity of cocaine. Here there were just under 40 kilograms, yielding a base offense level of   34.

10. Specific offense characteristic: none.   0

11. Adjustment for Role in the Offense: none   0

12. Adjustment for Obstruction of Justice: none.   0

13. Adjusted offense level: 34

14. Adjustment for Acceptance of Responsibility: -3

15. Total Offense Level: 31

Part B. The Defendant's Criminal History

16.   Date: 9/15/98

        Court: USDC EDNY

        Charge: Poss. Coc. w/intent to Dist.

        Sentence: 5 years

       On September 15, 1998, the defendant was convicted on a plea of guilty before the Honorable Chester Murphy, U.S. District Judge, EDNY, of possession of cocaine with intent to distribute. According to court records, the defendant sold one kilogram of cocaine to an undercover agent of the Drug Enforcement Administration. Accordingly, three criminal history points are added pursuant to § 4A1.1(a).

       17. At the time of this offense the defendant was on supervised release from his 1998 conviction. Two additional criminal history points are added pursuant to § 4A1.1(d).

       18. Since this offense occurred less than two years after the defendant's release from prison and two points were added under § 4A1.1(d), one additional criminal history point is added under § 4A1.1(e).

Criminal History Computation

       19. Since the defendant has six criminal history points, his criminal history category is III.

Part C. Sentencing Options

Custody

       20. Statutory Provisions: The maximum term of imprisonment is life. 21 USC § 841(b)(1)(A).

       21. Mandatory Minimum: The mandatory minimum term of imprisonment is ten years. 21 USC § 841(b)(1)(A).

       22. Guideline Provisions: Based on a total offense level of 31 and a criminal history category of III, the Guidelines imprisonment range is 135–168 months.

Supervised Release

       23. Statutory provisions: The statute requires a five year term of supervised release. 21 USC § 841(b)(1)(A).

Probation

       24. Statutory Provisions: Probation is not authorized for a class B felony. 18 USC § 3561.

Part D. Offender Characteristics

Family Ties, Family Responsibilities, and Community Ties

25 & 26. (This section describes the defendant's personal history and family background in two or three paragraphs.)

Mental and Emotional Health

27. This defendant reports no mental or emotional problems, nor any history of treatment for such problems. He impressed this officer as alert, oriented and of normal intelligence.

Physical Condition, Including Drug Dependence and Alcohol Abuse

28. The defendant had his appendix removed in 1996 and suffers from food allergies. He is currently under the care of a physician for that allergic condition. He has a scar on his stomach from the surgery noted above. He has no tattoos or other scars. He has no history of drug abuse and reports that he drinks a beer or two once or twice a week.

Education and Vocational Skills

29. (This paragraph details the defendant's educational background.)

Employment Record

30. (This paragraph sets out the defendant's work history, including information about what verification was received for each claimed period of employment.)

Part E. Fines and Restitution

Statutory Provisions:

31. The maximum fine is $4,000,000. 21 USC § 841(b)(1)(A).

32. A special assessment of $100 is mandatory. 18 USC § 3013(a)(2)(A).

Guidelines Provisions:

33. The fine range for this offense is $15,000 to $150,000. § 5E1.2(c)(3).

34. Subject to the defendant's ability to pay, the court shall impose an additional fine amount that is at least sufficient to pay the costs to the government of any imprisonment, probation, or supervised release ordered. The most recent advisory from the Administrative Office of the United States Courts suggests that a monthly cost of $1933.80 be used for imprisonment, a monthly cost of $287.73 be used for supervision, and a monthly cost of $1675.23 for community confinement.

Defendant's Ability to Pay

35. The defendant has no assets and his salary is used to meet his monthly expenses.

36. Based on the defendant's financial disclosure forms, he appears unable to pay a fine.

Part F. Factors That May Warrant Departure

37. Pursuant to guideline § 5K1.1, upon motion of the government, the Court may consider a downward departure in the light of the defendant's cooperation.

Impact of Plea Agreement

38. This defendant pled guilty pursuant to an agreement in which the government accepted his plea to a single narcotics count in satisfaction of all charges, including potential money laundering charges. Under the multiple count rules, § 3D1.4, any money laundering counts likely would have increased the defendant's Guidelines score by two levels. *See* USSG §§ 2S1.1(a)(1) (providing that where defendant is found guilty of money laundering, and is also guilty of the underlying offense from which the laundered funds were derived, base offense level is to be that corresponding to the underlying offense) and 2S1.1(b)(2)(B) (adding an additional two levels where the money laundering conviction is under 18 U.S.C. § 1956). The plea agreement thus had an impact on the Guidelines range.

Respectfully submitted,

Bernice Thompson
Chief U.S. Probation Officer

Prepared by: _____
               Joan Rich, US Probation Officer

Approved by: _____
              Shelly Alvérnez, Supervising USPO

Santiago and his counsel reviewed the presentence report, which recommended a Guidelines range of 135–168 months, a term consistent with the government's Guidelines estimate at the time of Santiago's cooperation agreement. Two weeks before Santiago's scheduled sentencing, AUSA Knapp wrote the following 5K1.1 letter motion on behalf of Santiago, outlining his cooperation and triggering the court's power to downwardly depart under the Guidelines.

U.S. Department of Justice
United States Attorney
Eastern District of New York

October 12, 2005

Honorable Walter Sheridan
United States District Judge
United States District Court
Eastern District of New York
225 Cadman Plaza East
Brooklyn, NY 11201

       Re: <u>U.S. v. Gilbert Santiago, 05-Cr-735 (WS)</u>

Your Honor:

      The Government respectfully submits this letter on behalf of Gilbert Santiago, who will come before this Court for sentencing, having pled guilty to one count of conspiracy to possess 5 or more kilograms of cocaine with intent to distribute. We respectfully ask this Court to accept this letter as a motion under 18 USC § 3553(e) and United States Sentencing Guidelines § 5K1.1, asking that this Court impose a sentence which reflects Santiago's very substantial assistance in the investigation and prosecution of others who have committed offenses against the United States.

      As Your Honor knows from the trial of co-defendant Paul Christopher, Santiago assisted Christopher and others in accepting delivery of a substantial quantity of cocaine in four shipments during the fall of 2004. Santiago assisted in storing the shipments, sending them to their local distributor and laundering the $25,000 a month generated by these activities. Santiago was arrested in mid-January 2005 and began to cooperate with the Government about a week later.

      This Court is aware of Santiago's substantial and valuable assistance in the prosecution of Paul Christopher, having heard Santiago's testimony at the trial and the sentencing hearing. Santiago's trial testimony was clear, straightforward and found credible by the jury. In our estimation, the Government could not have proven its case against Paul Christopher without Gilbert Santiago's assistance.

      Santiago also played the key role in initiating the investigation against Christopher. Although the Government had information suggesting Christopher's involvement, Santiago's early and complete cooperation allowed the Government to move quickly and decisively, denying Christopher the opportunity to destroy evidence or otherwise hinder the investigation.

Santiago played an active role in the investigation of Paul Christopher, providing information about the distribution scheme, including the number, size, and frequency of deliveries, and providing Christopher's cell phone number. This information enabled the government to acquire additional evidence against Christopher that was central to his conviction. While Santiago's assistance did not include any direct communication or contact with Christopher, the information and subsequent evidence acquired by the Government, some of which was disclosed to Christopher in the course of the proceedings, would have brought Santiago to Christopher's attention as the likely source of that information. In this way, Santiago's assistance involved a certain amount of risk to himself.

Santiago also rendered substantial assistance that led to the conviction of Ernest Wagner, who pled guilty in connection with his role as a CMS Bank employee in facilitating the laundering of the narcotics proceeds generated by the activities of Paul Christopher and others. During his initial proffer session, Santiago forthrightly disclosed his role in depositing approximately $100,000 in drug proceeds in several phony accounts in amounts less than $10,000, with the help of Wagner. The government did not previously know about this money laundering and structuring activity and, as a result of Santiago's disclosures, was able to secure the testimony of another CMS Bank employee who significantly corroborated Santiago's statements. We have little doubt that it was the knowledge that both Santiago and this corroborative witness would testify against Wagner that ultimately led him to decide to plead guilty.

In sum, Santiago's cooperation was substantial, significant and fruitful, leading to the conviction of Paul Christopher, who was sentenced to over 15 years in prison, and Ernest Wagner, who was sentenced to 6 months in prison. His cooperation was timely, coming a week after his arrest, and we believe it was complete and truthful. In the estimation of the DEA agents who worked with him he revealed all he knew about the illegal activities with which he had been involved. I share that evaluation. We respectfully ask the Court to accord his substantial assistance due consideration in imposing sentence.

Respectfully submitted,

Laura Knapp

Laura Knapp
Assistant United States Attorney

cc: Charles Berman, Esq.

Note that the prosecutor's letter tracks the cooperation factors set out in the Guidelines.[60] It addresses: the significance and usefulness of the cooperation; its truthfulness and reliability; the nature and extent of the assistance; any risk of danger; and the timeliness of the cooperation.[61] The letter also recites the offense conduct, fulfilling the prosecutor's obligation to make a complete presentation to the court.

60. *See id.* § 5K1.1, p.s.

61. In our experience, cooperation letters range from the positive to the very positive. Judges often try to discern how strongly the government feels about a particular case, since this is an area in which the government is obligated to say positive things about a criminal defendant it has both prosecuted and, in a manner of speaking, befriended. Thus, cooperation letters can be rife with pat phrases and clichés and any negative information, other than the recitation of the admitted offense conduct, stands out.

On October 28, 2005, Gilbert Santiago appeared in front of Judge Sheridan for the imposition of sentence. AUSA Knapp repeated the statements regarding cooperation made in her letter to the court. Berman noted that any sentence imposed by Judge Sheridan would be in addition to (and would run consecutively with) the sentence imposed against Santiago for violating the conditions of his supervised release stemming from his 1998 conviction. Santiago apologized and then pleaded for leniency.

Judge Sheridan told Santiago that he had observed his testimony and listened to AUSA Knapp and believed that his cooperation was the key to the successful prosecution of Paul Christopher and the guilty plea of Ernest Wagner. Balancing Santiago's past criminal record and the present conviction against his cooperation and the additional time he faced on the violation of the conditions of his supervised release, Judge Sheridan departed downward from the 135 month low end of Santiago's Guidelines range, and from the 120 month (or ten year) statutory mandatory minimum, to impose a sentence of 60 months in prison, to be followed by five years of supervised release. Judge Sheridan noted that his reduction was slightly better than the typical "50% off" he gave to cooperators, explaining that this was because Santiago's cooperation led to multiple convictions, because it was his impression that Santiago, unlike many cooperators he had seen, had been particularly careful in his testimony to make clear not just what he did know but also what he didn't know, and because 60 months was one-half of the statutory mandatory minimum prison term. He also cautioned Santiago, a now two-time felon narcotics offender, that if he ever committed a third drug offense he would almost certainly spend the rest of his life in prison.[62] The judge waived any fine because Santiago was without financial means to pay a fine, but imposed the mandatory $100 special assessment.[63] After the sentencing hearing, Judge Sheridan prepared the following Judgment and Commitment order.

---

62. *See, e.g.*, USSG § 4B1.1 (Career Offender).

63. Because Santiago was already incarcerated, there was no need to address a surrender date. Santiago would receive full credit toward his 60 month prison sentence for the time in prison he had served since his arrest.

UNITED STATES DISTRICT COURT
EASTERN DISTRICT OF NEW YORK

UNITED STATES OF AMERICA **JUDGMENT IN A CRIMINAL CASE**

v.

Case Number: 05-CR-735-(WS)

Laura Knapp, Assistant U.S. Attorney

GILBERT SANTIAGO Charles Berman, Defendant's Attorney

The defendant pleaded guilty to count 1 of the above-captioned one count information. Accordingly, he is adjudged guilty of such count, which involves the following offense:

Title & Section	Nature of Offense	Date Offense Concluded	Count Number(s)
21 U.S.C. § 846	Conspiracy to possess with intent to distribute cocaine	January 12, 2005	1

The defendant is sentenced as provided in pages 2 through 4 of this judgment. The sentence is imposed pursuant to the Sentencing Reform Act of 1984.

The remaining counts of the prior twenty-four-count Indictment are dismissed on the motion of the United States as to this defendant only.

It is ordered that the defendant pay a special assessment of $100 for count 1 of the information, which shall be due immediately.

It is further ordered that the defendant shall notify the United States Attorney for this district within thirty (30) days of any change of name, residence, or mailing address until all fines, restitution, costs, and special assessments imposed by this judgment are fully paid.

Defendant's Soc. Sec. No.: 062–11–3320
Defendant's U.S. Marshall No.: 88456-111
Defendant's Date of Birth: December 25, 1950 October 28, 2005
Date of Imposition of Sentence

Defendant's Legal Address: 1401 37th St.
Astoria, New York

Defendant's Current Address: Same

Walter Sheridan
WALTER SHERIDAN
U.S. DISTRICT JUDGE

SIGNED October 28, 2005

IMPRISONMENT

The defendant is hereby committed to the custody of the United States Bureau of Prisons to be imprisoned for a term of 60 months on count 1 of the one count information.

The Court recommends that the defendant be incarcerated at an institution in New York.

SUPERVISED RELEASE

Upon release from imprisonment, the defendant shall be placed on supervised release for a term of 5 years on count 1 of the one count information.

While on supervised release, the defendant shall comply with the standard conditions of supervision adopted by this Court (set forth below). In addition, the defendant shall:

not commit another federal, state, or local crime;

not possess illegal controlled substances;

not possess a firearm, destructive device, or other dangerous weapon;

report in person to the probation office in the district to which the defendant is released within seventy-two (72) hours of release from the custody of the Bureau of Prisons;

provide to the probation officer any requested financial information.

STANDARD CONDITIONS OF SUPERVISION

While the defendant is on supervised release pursuant to this judgment, the defendant shall:

(1)   not leave the judicial district without the permission of the Court or probation officer;

(2)   report to the probation officer as directed by the Court or probation officer and submit a truthful and complete written report within the first five (5) days of each month;

(3)   answer truthfully all inquiries by the probation officer and follow the instructions of the probation officer;

(4)   support his or her dependents and meet other family responsibilities;

(5)   work regularly at a lawful occupation unless excused by the probation officer for schooling, training, or other acceptable reasons;

(6) notify the probation officer within seventy-two (72) hours of any change in residence or employment;

(7) refrain from excessive use of alcohol and shall not purchase, possess, use, distribute, or administer any narcotic or other controlled substance, or any parapharnelia related to such substances, except as prescribed by a physician;

(8) not frequent places where controlled substances are illegally sold, used, distributed, or administered;

(9) not associate with any persons engaged in criminal activity, and shall not associate with any person convicted of a felony unless granted permission to do so by the probation officer;

(10) permit a probation officer to visit him or her at any time at home or elsewhere and shall permit confiscation of any contraband observed in plain view by the probation officer;

(11) notify the probation officer within seventy-two (72) hours of being arrested or questioned by a law enforcement officer;

(12) not enter into any agreement to act as an informer or a special agent of a law enforcement agency without the permission of the Court; and

(13) notify third parties of risks that may be occasioned by the defendant's criminal record or personal history or characteristics, and permit the probation officer to make such notification and to confirm the defendant's compliance with such notification requirement, as directed by the probation.

FINE/RESTITUTION

No fine is ordered based on the Court's assessment of the defendant's inability to pay.

Restitution is not applicable in this case.

STATEMENT OF REASONS

The Court adopts as its findings of fact the statements and the guideline applications in the presentence report, paragraphs 1 through 38, subject to and including any findings made by the Court at the defendant's sentencing hearing.

Guideline Range Determined by the Court

Total Offense Level:	31
Criminal History Category:	III
Imprisonment Range:	135 to 168 months

Supervised Release Range:	5 years
Fine Range:	$15,000 to $150,000 (plus cost of imprisonment/supervision)

The sentence is below the guidelines range on the basis of the defendant's substantial assistance to the government in the prosecution of other persons and/or crimes pursuant to §5K1.1.

525

(2) Mario Long. Mario Long's case was then called. Like Clark and Berman, his attorney, Candace Jones, attended the presentence interview, reviewed the report and prepared for the sentencing. AUSA Knapp wrote a 5K1.1 letter indicating Long's cooperation and spoke on his behalf at sentencing. Based on his Guidelines range of 70 to 87 months,[64] and his standard 50% reduction, Judge Sheridan sentenced Long to 35 months in prison, followed by 5 years of supervised release, with a $100 special assessment and no fine. Long was given 30 days to surrender.

Court was then adjourned.

64. *See supra* § 8.5 (describing the Guidelines calculation in Long's case).

Appendix A

SELECTED PROVISIONS OF THE UNITED STATES CONSTITUTION

AMENDMENT IV [1791]

The right of the people to be secure in their persons, houses, papers, and effects, against unreasonable searches and seizures, shall not be violated, and no Warrants shall issue, but upon probable cause, supported by Oath or affirmation, and particularly describing the place to be searched, and the persons or things to be seized.

AMENDMENT V [1791]

No person shall be held to answer for a capital, or otherwise infamous crime, unless on a presentment or indictment of a Grand Jury, except in cases arising in the land or naval forces, or in the Militia, when in actual service in time of War or public danger; nor shall any person be subject for the same offence to be twice put in jeopardy of life or limb; nor shall be compelled in any criminal case to be a witness against himself, nor be deprived of life, liberty, or property, without due process of law; nor shall private property be taken for public use, without just compensation.

AMENDMENT VI [1791]

In all criminal prosecutions, the accused shall enjoy the right to a speedy and public trial, by an impartial jury of the State and district wherein the crime shall have been committed, which district shall have been previously ascertained by law, and to be informed of the nature and cause of the accusation; to be confronted with the witnesses against him; to have compulsory process for obtaining witnesses in his favor, and to have the Assistance of Counsel for his defence.

Amendment VIII [1791]

Excessive bail shall not be required, nor excessive fines imposed, nor cruel and unusual punishments inflicted.

Amendment XIV [1868]

Section 1. All persons born or naturalized in the United States, and subject to the jurisdiction thereof, are citizens of the United States and of the State wherein they reside. No State shall make or enforce any law which shall abridge the privileges or immunities of citizens of the United States; nor shall any State deprive any person of life, liberty, or property, without due process of law; nor deny to any person within its jurisdiction the equal protection of the laws.

Section 5. The Congress shall have power to enforce, by appropriate legislation, the provisions of this article.

Appendix B

SELECTED RULES OF FEDERAL CRIMINAL PROCEDURE

II. PRELIMINARY PROCEEDINGS

Rule 3. The Complaint

The complaint is a written statement of the essential facts constituting the offense charged. It must be made under oath before a magistrate judge or, if none is reasonably available, before a state or local judicial officer.

(As amended Apr. 24, 1972, eff. Oct. 1, 1972; Apr. 22, 1993, eff. Dec. 1, 1993; Apr. 29, 2002, eff. Dec. 1, 2002.)

Rule 4. Arrest Warrant or Summons on a Complaint

(a) Issuance. If the complaint or one or more affidavits filed with the complaint establish probable cause to believe that an offense has been committed and that the defendant committed it, the judge must issue an arrest warrant to an officer authorized to execute it. At the request of an attorney for the government, the judge must issue a summons, instead of a warrant, to a person authorized to serve it. A judge may issue more than one warrant or summons on the same complaint. If a defendant fails to appear in response to a summons, a judge may, and upon request of an attorney for the government must, issue a warrant.

(b) Form.

(1) Warrant. A warrant must:

(A) contain the defendant's name or, if it is unknown, a name or description by which the defendant can be identified with reasonable certainty;

(B) describe the offense charged in the complaint;

(C) command that the defendant be arrested and brought without unnecessary delay before a magistrate judge or, if none is reasonably available, before a state or local judicial officer; and

(D) be signed by a judge.

(2) Summons. A summons must be in the same form as a warrant except that it must require the defendant to appear before a magistrate judge at a stated time and place.

(c) Execution or Service, and Return.

(1) By Whom. Only a marshal or other authorized officer may execute a warrant. Any person authorized to serve a summons in a federal civil action may serve a summons.

(2) Location. A warrant may be executed, or a summons served, within the jurisdiction of the United States or anywhere else a federal statute authorizes an arrest.

(3) Manner.

(A) A warrant is executed by arresting the defendant. Upon arrest, an officer possessing the warrant must show it to the defendant. If the officer does not possess the warrant, the officer must inform the defendant of the warrant's existence and of the offense charged and, at the defendant's request, must show the warrant to the defendant as soon as possible.

(B) A summons is served on an individual defendant:

    (i) by delivering a copy to the defendant personally; or

    (ii) by leaving a copy at the defendant's residence or usual place of abode with a person of suitable age and discretion residing at that location and by mailing a copy to the defendant's last known address.

(C) A summons is served on an organization by delivering a copy to an officer, to a managing or general agent, or to another agent appointed or legally authorized to receive service of process. A copy must also be mailed to the organization's last known address within the district or to its principal place of business elsewhere in the United States.

(4) Return.

(A) After executing a warrant, the officer must return it to the judge before whom the defendant is brought in accordance with Rule 5. At the request of an attorney for the government, an unexecuted warrant must be brought back to and canceled by a magistrate judge or, if none is reasonably available, by a state or local judicial officer.

(B) The person to whom a summons was delivered for service must return it on or before the return day.

(C) At the request of an attorney for the government, a judge may deliver an unexecuted warrant, an unserved summons, or a copy of the warrant or summons to the marshal or other authorized person for execution or service.

(As amended Feb. 28, 1966, eff. July 1, 1966; Apr. 24, 1972, eff. Oct. 1, 1972; Apr. 22, 1974, eff. Dec. 1, 1975; July 31, 1975, Pub.L. 94–64, § 3(1)–(3), 89 Stat. 370; Mar. 9, 1987, eff. Aug. 1, 1987; Apr. 22, 1993, eff. Dec. 1, 1993; Apr. 29, 2002, eff. Dec. 1, 2002.)

Rule 5. Initial Appearance

(a) In General.

(1) Appearance Upon an Arrest.

(A) A person making an arrest within the United States must take the defendant without unnecessary delay before a magistrate judge, or before a state or local judicial officer as Rule 5(c) provides, unless a statute provides otherwise.

(B) A person making an arrest outside the United States must take the defendant without unnecessary delay before a magistrate judge, unless a statute provides otherwise.

(2) Exceptions.

(A) An officer making an arrest under a warrant issued upon a complaint charging solely a violation of 18 U.S.C. § 1073 need not comply with this rule if:

(i) the person arrested is transferred without unnecessary delay to the custody of appropriate state or local authorities in the district of arrest; and

(ii) an attorney for the government moves promptly, in the district where the warrant was issued, to dismiss the complaint.

(B) If a defendant is arrested for violating probation or supervised release, Rule 32.1 applies.

(C) If a defendant is arrested for failing to appear in another district, Rule 40 applies.

(3) Appearance Upon a Summons. When a defendant appears in response to a summons under Rule 4, a magistrate judge must proceed under Rule 5(d) or (e), as applicable.

(b) Arrest Without a Warrant. If a defendant is arrested without a warrant, a complaint meeting Rule 4(a)'s requirement of probable cause must be promptly filed in the district where the offense was allegedly committed.

(c) Place of Initial Appearance; Transfer to Another District.

(1) Arrest in the District Where the Offense Was Allegedly Committed. If the defendant is arrested in the district where the offense was allegedly committed:

> **(A)** the initial appearance must be in that district; and

> **(B)** if a magistrate judge is not reasonably available, the initial appearance may be before a state or local judicial officer.

(2) Arrest in a District Other Than Where the Offense Was Allegedly Committed. If the defendant was arrested in a district other than where the offense was allegedly committed, the initial appearance must be:

> **(A)** in the district of arrest; or

> **(B)** in an adjacent district if:

>> **(i)** the appearance can occur more promptly there; or

>> **(ii)** the offense was allegedly committed there and the initial appearance will occur on the day of arrest.

(3) Procedures in a District Other Than Where the Offense Was Allegedly Committed. If the initial appearance occurs in a district other than where the offense was allegedly committed, the following procedures apply:

> **(A)** the magistrate judge must inform the defendant about the provisions of Rule 20;

> **(B)** if the defendant was arrested without a warrant, the district court where the offense was allegedly committed must first issue a warrant before the magistrate judge transfers the defendant to that district;

> **(C)** the magistrate judge must conduct a preliminary hearing if required by Rule 5.1 or Rule 58(b)(2)(G);

> **(D)** the magistrate judge must transfer the defendant to the district where the offense was allegedly committed if:

>> **(i)** the government produces the warrant, a certified copy of the warrant, a facsimile of either, or other appropriate form of either; and

>> **(ii)** the judge finds that the defendant is the same person named in the indictment, information, or warrant; and

> **(E)** when a defendant is transferred and discharged, the clerk must promptly transmit the papers and any bail to the clerk in the district where the offense was allegedly committed.

(d) Procedure in a Felony Case.

(1) Advice. If the defendant is charged with a felony, the judge must inform the defendant of the following:

(A) the complaint against the defendant, and any affidavit filed with it;

(B) the defendant's right to retain counsel or to request that counsel be appointed if the defendant cannot obtain counsel;

(C) the circumstances, if any, under which the defendant may secure pretrial release;

(D) any right to a preliminary hearing; and

(E) the defendant's right not to make a statement, and that any statement made may be used against the defendant.

(2) Consulting with Counsel. The judge must allow the defendant reasonable opportunity to consult with counsel.

(3) Detention or Release. The judge must detain or release the defendant as provided by statute or these rules.

(4) Plea. A defendant may be asked to plead only under Rule 10.

(e) Procedure in a Misdemeanor Case. If the defendant is charged with a misdemeanor only, the judge must inform the defendant in accordance with Rule 58(b)(2).

(f) Video Teleconferencing. Video teleconferencing may be used to conduct an appearance under this rule if the defendant consents.

(As amended Feb. 28, 1966, eff. July 1, 1966; Apr. 24, 1972, eff. Oct. 1, 1972; Apr. 28, 1982, eff. Aug. 1, 1982; Oct. 12, 1984, Pub.L. 98–473, Title II, § 209(a), 98 Stat. 1986; Mar. 9, 1987, eff. Aug. 1, 1987; May 1, 1990, eff. Dec. 1, 1990; Apr. 22, 1993, eff. Dec. 1, 1993; Apr. 27, 1995, eff. Dec. 1, 1995; Apr. 29, 2002, eff. Dec. 1, 2002.)

Rule 5.1. Preliminary Hearing

(a) In General. If a defendant is charged with an offense other than a petty offense, a magistrate judge must conduct a preliminary hearing unless:

(1) the defendant waives the hearing;

(2) the defendant is indicted;

(3) the government files an information under Rule 7(b) charging the defendant with a felony;

(4) the government files an information charging the defendant with a misdemeanor; or

(5) the defendant is charged with a misdemeanor and consents to trial before a magistrate judge.

(b) Selecting a District. A defendant arrested in a district other than where the offense was allegedly committed may elect to have the preliminary hearing conducted in the district where the prosecution is pending.

(c) Scheduling. The magistrate judge must hold the preliminary hearing within a reasonable time, but no later than 10 days after the initial appearance if the defendant is in custody and no later than 20 days if not in custody.

(d) Extending the Time. With the defendant's consent and upon a showing of good cause—taking into account the public interest in the prompt disposition of criminal cases—a magistrate judge may extend the time limits in Rule 5.1(c) one or more times. If the defendant does not consent, the magistrate judge may extend the time limits only on a showing that extraordinary circumstances exist and justice requires the delay.

(e) Hearing and Finding. At the preliminary hearing, the defendant may cross-examine adverse witnesses and may introduce evidence but may not object to evidence on the ground that it was unlawfully acquired. If the magistrate judge finds probable cause to believe an offense has been committed and the defendant committed it, the magistrate judge must promptly require the defendant to appear for further proceedings.

(f) Discharging the Defendant. If the magistrate judge finds no probable cause to believe an offense has been committed or the defendant committed it, the magistrate judge must dismiss the complaint and discharge the defendant. A discharge does not preclude the government from later prosecuting the defendant for the same offense.

(g) Recording the Proceedings. The preliminary hearing must be recorded by a court reporter or by a suitable recording device. A recording of the proceeding may be made available to any party upon request. A copy of the recording and a transcript may be provided to any party upon request and upon any payment required by applicable Judicial Conference regulations.

(h) Producing a Statement.

(1) In General. Rule 26.2(a)–(d) and (f) applies at any hearing under this rule, unless the magistrate judge for good cause rules otherwise in a particular case.

(2) Sanctions for Not Producing a Statement. If a party disobeys a Rule 26.2 order to deliver a statement to the moving party, the magistrate judge must not consider the testimony of a witness whose statement is withheld.

(Added Apr. 24, 1972, eff. Oct. 1, 1972, and amended Mar. 9, 1987, eff. Aug. 1, 1987; Apr. 22, 1993, eff. Dec. 1, 1993; Apr. 24, 1998, eff. Dec. 1, 1998; Apr. 29, 2002, eff. Dec. 1, 2002.)

III. THE GRAND JURY, THE INDICTMENT, AND THE INFORMATION

Rule 6. The Grand Jury

(a) Summoning a Grand Jury.

(1) In General. When the public interest so requires, the court must order that one or more grand juries be summoned. A grand jury must have 16 to 23 members, and the court must order that enough legally qualified persons be summoned to meet this requirement.

(2) Alternate Jurors. When a grand jury is selected, the court may also select alternate jurors. Alternate jurors must have the same qualifications and be selected in the same manner as any other juror. Alternate jurors replace jurors in the same sequence in which the alternates were selected. An alternate juror who replaces a juror is subject to the same challenges, takes the same oath, and has the same authority as the other jurors.

(b) Objection to the Grand Jury or to a Grand Juror.

(1) Challenges. Either the government or a defendant may challenge the grand jury on the ground that it was not lawfully drawn, summoned, or selected, and may challenge an individual juror on the ground that the juror is not legally qualified.

(2) Motion to Dismiss an Indictment. A party may move to dismiss the indictment based on an objection to the grand jury or on an individual juror's lack of legal qualification, unless the court has previously ruled on the same objection under Rule 6(b)(1). The motion to dismiss is governed by 28 U.S.C. § 1867(e). The court must not dismiss the indictment on the ground that a grand juror was not legally qualified if the record shows that at least 12 qualified jurors concurred in the indictment.

(c) Foreperson and Deputy Foreperson.
The court will appoint one juror as the foreperson and another as the deputy foreperson. In the foreperson's absence, the deputy foreperson will act as the foreperson. The foreperson may administer oaths and affirmations and will sign all indictments. The foreperson—or another juror designated by the foreperson—will record the number of jurors concurring in every indictment and will file the record with the clerk, but the record may not be made public unless the court so orders.

(d) Who May Be Present.

(1) While the Grand Jury Is in Session. The following persons may be present while the grand jury is in session: attorneys for the government, the witness being questioned, interpreters when needed, and a court reporter or an operator of a recording device.

(2) During Deliberations and Voting. No person other than the jurors, and any interpreter needed to assist a hearing-impaired or speech-impaired juror, may be present while the grand jury is deliberating or voting.

(e) Recording and Disclosing the Proceedings.

(1) Recording the Proceedings. Except while the grand jury is deliberating or voting, all proceedings must be recorded by a court reporter or by a suitable recording device. But the validity of a prosecution is not affected by the unintentional failure to make a recording. Unless the court orders otherwise, an attorney for the government will retain control of the recording, the reporter's notes, and any transcript prepared from those notes.

(2) Secrecy.

(A) No obligation of secrecy may be imposed on any person except in accordance with Rule 6(e)(2)(B).

(B) Unless these rules provide otherwise, the following persons must not disclose a matter occurring before the grand jury:

    (i) a grand juror;

    (ii) an interpreter;

    (iii) a court reporter;

    (iv) an operator of a recording device;

    (v) a person who transcribes recorded testimony;

    (vi) an attorney for the government; or

    (vii) a person to whom disclosure is made under Rule 6(e)(3)(A)(ii) or (iii).

(3) Exceptions.

(A) Disclosure of a grand-jury matter—other than the grand jury's deliberations or any grand juror's vote—may be made to:

    (i) an attorney for the government for use in performing that attorney's duty;

    (ii) any government personnel—including those of a state, state subdivision, Indian tribe, or foreign government—that an attorney for the government considers necessary to assist in performing that attorney's duty to enforce federal criminal law; or

    (iii) a person authorized by 18 U.S.C. § 3322.

(B) A person to whom information is disclosed under Rule 6(e)(3)(A)(ii) may use that information only to assist an attorney for the government in performing that attorney's duty to enforce federal criminal law. An attorney for the government must promptly provide the court that impaneled the grand jury with the names of all persons to whom a disclosure has been made, and must certify that the attorney has advised those persons of their obligation of secrecy under this rule.

(C) An attorney for the government may disclose any grand-jury matter to another federal grand jury.

(D) An attorney for the government may disclose any grand-jury matter involving foreign intelligence, counterintelligence (as defined in 50 U.S.C. § 401a), or foreign intelligence information (as defined in Rule 6(e)(3)(D)(iii)) to any federal law enforcement, intelligence, protective, immigration, national defense, or national security official to assist the official receiving the information in the performance of that official's duties. An attorney for the government may also disclose any grand jury matter involving, within the United States or elsewhere, a threat of attack or other grave hostile acts of a foreign power or its agent, a threat of domestic or international sabotage or terrorism, or clandestine intelligence gathering activities by an intelligence service or network of a foreign power or by its agent, to any appropriate Federal, State, State subdivision, Indian tribal, or foreign government official, for the purpose of preventing or responding to such threat or activities.

(i) Any official who receives information under Rule 6(e)(3)(D) may use the information only as necessary in the conduct of that person's official duties subject to any limitations on the unauthorized disclosure of such information. Any State, State subdivision, Indian tribal, or foreign government official who receives information under Rule 6(e)(3)(D) may use the information only consistent with such guidelines as the Attorney General and the Director of National Intelligence shall jointly issue.

(ii) Within a reasonable time after disclosure is made under Rule 6(e)(3)(D), an attorney for the government must file, under seal, a notice with the court in the district where the grand jury convened stating that such information was disclosed and the departments, agencies, or entities to which the disclosure was made.

(iii) As used in Rule 6(e)(3)(D), the term "foreign intelligence information" means:

(a) information, whether or not it concerns a United States person, that relates to the ability of the United States to protect against—

• actual or potential attack or other grave hostile acts of a foreign power or its agent;

- sabotage or international terrorism by a foreign power or its agent; or

- clandestine intelligence activities by an intelligence service or network of a foreign power or by its agent; or

(b) information, whether or not it concerns a United States person, with respect to a foreign power or foreign territory that relates to—

- the national defense or the security of the United States; or

- the conduct of the foreign affairs of the United States.

(E) The court may authorize disclosure—at a time, in a manner, and subject to any other conditions that it directs—of a grand-jury matter:

(i) preliminarily to or in connection with a judicial proceeding;

(ii) at the request of a defendant who shows that a ground may exist to dismiss the indictment because of a matter that occurred before the grand jury;

(iii) at the request of the government, when sought by a foreign court or prosecutor for use in an official criminal investigation;

(iv) at the request of the government if it shows that the matter may disclose a violation of State, Indian tribal, or foreign criminal law, as long as the disclosure is to an appropriate state, state-subdivision, Indian tribal, or foreign government official for the purpose of enforcing that law; or

(v) at the request of the government if it shows that the matter may disclose a violation of military criminal law under the Uniform Code of Military Justice, as long as the disclosure is to an appropriate military official for the purpose of enforcing that law.

(F) A petition to disclose a grand-jury matter under Rule 6(e)(3)(E)(i) must be filed in the district where the grand jury convened. Unless the hearing is ex parte—as it may be when the government is the petitioner—the petitioner must serve the petition on, and the court must afford a reasonable opportunity to appear and be heard to:

(i) an attorney for the government;

(ii) the parties to the judicial proceeding; and

(iii) any other person whom the court may designate.

(G) If the petition to disclose arises out of a judicial proceeding in another district, the petitioned court must transfer the petition to the other court unless the petitioned court can reasonably determine whether disclosure is proper. If the petitioned court decides to transfer, it must send to the transferee court the material sought to be disclosed, if feasible, and a written evaluation of the need for continued grand-jury secrecy. The transferee court must afford those persons identified in Rule 6(e)(3)(F) a reasonable opportunity to appear and be heard.

(4) Sealed Indictment. The magistrate judge to whom an indictment is returned may direct that the indictment be kept secret until the defendant is in custody or has been released pending trial. The clerk must then seal the indictment, and no person may disclose the indictment's existence except as necessary to issue or execute a warrant or summons.

(5) Closed Hearing. Subject to any right to an open hearing in a contempt proceeding, the court must close any hearing to the extent necessary to prevent disclosure of a matter occurring before a grand jury.

(6) Sealed Records. Records, orders, and subpoenas relating to grand-jury proceedings must be kept under seal to the extent and as long as necessary to prevent the unauthorized disclosure of a matter occurring before a grand jury.

(7) Contempt. A knowing violation of Rule 6, or of guidelines jointly issued by the Attorney General and the Director of National Intelligence pursuant to Rule 6, may be punished as a contempt of court.

(f) Indictment and Return. A grand jury may indict only if at least 12 jurors concur. The grand jury—or its foreperson or deputy foreperson—must return the indictment to a magistrate judge in open court. If a complaint or information is pending against the defendant and 12 jurors do not concur in the indictment, the foreperson must promptly and in writing report the lack of concurrence to the magistrate judge.

(g) Discharging the Grand Jury. A grand jury must serve until the court discharges it, but it may serve more than 18 months only if the court, having determined that an extension is in the public interest, extends the grand jury's service. An extension may be granted for no more than 6 months, except as otherwise provided by statute.

(h) Excusing a Juror. At any time, for good cause, the court may excuse a juror either temporarily or permanently, and if permanently, the court may impanel an alternate juror in place of the excused juror.

(i) "Indian Tribe" Defined. "Indian tribe" means an Indian tribe recognized by the Secretary of the Interior on a list published in the Federal Register under 25 U.S.C. § 479a–1.

(As amended Feb. 28, 1966, eff. July 1, 1966; Apr. 24, 1972, eff. Oct. 1, 1972; Apr. 26, 1976, eff. Aug. 1, 1976; July 30, 1977, Pub.L. 95–78, § 2(a), 91 Stat. 319; Apr. 30, 1979, eff. Aug. 1, 1979; Apr. 28, 1983, eff. Aug. 1, 1983; Apr. 29, 1985, eff. Aug. 1, 1985; Oct. 12, 1984, Pub.L. 98–473, Title II, § 215(f), 98 Stat. 2016; Apr. 29, 1985, eff. Aug. 1, 1985; Mar. 9, 1987, eff. Aug. 1, 1987; Apr. 22, 1993, eff. Dec. 1, 1993; Apr. 29, 1999, eff. Dec. 1, 1999; Oct. 26, 2001, Pub.L. 107–56, Title II, § 203(a), 115 Stat. 278; Apr. 29, 2002; eff. Dec. 1, 2002; Nov. 25, 2002, Pub.L. 107–296, Title VIII, § 895, 116 Stat. 2256; Dec. 17, 2004, Pub.L. 108–458, Title VI, § 6501(a), 118 Stat. 3760.)

Rule 7. The Indictment and the Information

(a) When Used.

(1) Felony. An offense (other than criminal contempt) must be prosecuted by an indictment if it is punishable:

(A) by death; or

(B) by imprisonment for more than one year.

(2) Misdemeanor. An offense punishable by imprisonment for one year or less may be prosecuted in accordance with Rule 58(b)(1).

(b) Waiving Indictment. An offense punishable by imprisonment for more than one year may be prosecuted by information if the defendant—in open court and after being advised of the nature of the charge and of the defendant's rights—waives prosecution by indictment.

(c) Nature and Contents.

(1) In General. The indictment or information must be a plain, concise, and definite written statement of the essential facts constituting the offense charged and must be signed by an attorney for the government. It need not contain a formal introduction or conclusion. A count may incorporate by reference an allegation made in another count. A count may allege that the means by which the defendant committed the offense are unknown or that the defendant committed it by one or more specified means. For each count, the indictment or information must give the official or customary citation of the statute, rule, regulation, or other provision of law that the defendant is alleged to have violated. For purposes of an indictment referred to in section 3282 of title 18, United States Code, for which the identity of the defendant is unknown, it shall be sufficient for the indictment to describe the defendant as an individual whose name is unknown, but who has a particular DNA profile, as that term is defined in that section 3282.

(2) Criminal Forfeiture. No judgment of forfeiture may be entered in a criminal proceeding unless the indictment or the information provides notice that the defendant has an interest in property that is subject to forfeiture in accordance with the applicable statute.

(3) Citation Error. Unless the defendant was misled and thereby prejudiced, neither an error in a citation nor a citation's omission is a ground to dismiss the indictment or information or to reverse a conviction.

(d) Surplusage. Upon the defendant's motion, the court may strike surplusage from the indictment or information.

(e) Amending an Information. Unless an additional or different offense is charged or a substantial right of the defendant is prejudiced, the court may permit an information to be amended at any time before the verdict or finding.

(f) Bill of Particulars. The court may direct the government to file a bill of particulars. The defendant may move for a bill of particulars before or within 10 days after arraignment or at a later time if the court permits. The government may amend a bill of particulars subject to such conditions as justice requires.

(As amended Feb. 28, 1966, eff. July 1, 1966; Apr. 24, 1972, eff. Oct. 1, 1972; Apr. 30, 1979, eff. Aug. 1, 1979; Mar. 9, 1987, eff. Aug. 1, 1987; Apr. 17, 2000, eff. Dec. 1, 2000; Apr. 29, 2002, eff. Dec. 1, 2002; Apr. 30, 2003, Pub.L. 108–21, Title VI, § 610(b), 117 Stat. 692.)

Rule 8.   Joinder of Offenses or Defendants

(a) Joinder of Offenses. The indictment or information may charge a defendant in separate counts with 2 or more offenses if the offenses charged—whether felonies or misdemeanors or both—are of the same or similar character, or are based on the same act or transaction, or are connected with or constitute parts of a common scheme or plan.

(b) Joinder of Defendants. The indictment or information may charge 2 or more defendants if they are alleged to have participated in the same act or transaction, or in the same series of acts or transactions, constituting an offense or offenses. The defendants may be charged in one or more counts together or separately. All defendants need not be charged in each count.

(As amended Apr. 29, 2002, eff. Dec. 1, 2002.)

Rule 9.   Arrest Warrant or Summons on an Indictment or Information

(a) Issuance. The court must issue a warrant—or at the government's request, a summons—for each defendant named in an indictment or named in an information if one or more affidavits accompanying the information establish probable cause to believe that an offense has been committed and that the defendant committed it. The court may issue more than one warrant or summons for the same defendant. If a defendant fails to appear in response to a summons, the court may, and upon request of an attorney for the government must, issue a warrant. The court must issue the arrest warrant to an officer authorized to execute it or the summons to a person authorized to serve it.

(b) Form.

(1) Warrant. The warrant must conform to Rule 4(b)(1) except that it must be signed by the clerk and must describe the offense charged in the indictment or information.

(2) Summons. The summons must be in the same form as a warrant except that it must require the defendant to appear before the court at a stated time and place.

(c) Execution or Service; Return; Initial Appearance.

(1) Execution or Service.

(A) The warrant must be executed or the summons served as provided in Rule 4(c)(1), (2), and (3).

(B) The officer executing the warrant must proceed in accordance with Rule 5(a)(1).

(2) Return. A warrant or summons must be returned in accordance with Rule 4(c)(4).

(3) Initial Appearance. When an arrested or summoned defendant first appears before the court, the judge must proceed under Rule 5.

(As amended Apr. 24, 1972, eff. Oct. 1, 1972; Apr. 22, 1974, eff. Dec. 1, 1975; July 31, 1975, Pub.L. 94–64, § 3(4), 89 Stat. 370; Dec. 12, 1975, Pub.L. 94–149, § 5, 89 Stat. 806; Apr. 30, 1979, eff. Aug. 1, 1979; Apr. 28, 1982, eff. Aug. 1, 1982; Apr. 22, 1993, eff. Dec. 1, 1993; Apr. 29, 2002, eff. Dec. 1, 2002.)

IV. ARRAIGNMENT AND PREPARATION FOR TRIAL

Rule 10. Arraignment

(a) In General. An arraignment must be conducted in open court and must consist of:

(1) ensuring that the defendant has a copy of the indictment or information;

(2) reading the indictment or information to the defendant or stating to the defendant the substance of the charge; and then

(3) asking the defendant to plead to the indictment or information.

(b) Waiving Appearance. A defendant need not be present for the arraignment if:

(1) the defendant has been charged by indictment or misdemeanor information;

(2) the defendant, in a written waiver signed by both the defendant and defense counsel, has waived appearance and has affirmed that the defendant received a copy of the indictment or information and that the plea is not guilty; and

(3) the court accepts the waiver.

(c) Video Teleconferencing. Video teleconferencing may be used to arraign a defendant if the defendant consents.

(As amended Mar. 9, 1987, eff. Aug. 1, 1987; Apr. 29, 2002, eff. Dec. 1, 2002.)

Rule 11.   Pleas

(a) Entering a Plea.

(1) In General. A defendant may plead not guilty, guilty, or (with the court's consent) nolo contendere.

(2) Conditional Plea. With the consent of the court and the government, a defendant may enter a conditional plea of guilty or nolo contendere, reserving in writing the right to have an appellate court review an adverse determination of a specified pretrial motion. A defendant who prevails on appeal may then withdraw the plea.

(3) Nolo Contendere Plea. Before accepting a plea of nolo contendere, the court must consider the parties' views and the public interest in the effective administration of justice.

(4) Failure to Enter a Plea. If a defendant refuses to enter a plea or if a defendant organization fails to appear, the court must enter a plea of not guilty.

(b) Considering and Accepting a Guilty or Nolo Contendere Plea.

(1) Advising and Questioning the Defendant. Before the court accepts a plea of guilty or nolo contendere, the defendant may be placed under oath, and the court must address the defendant personally in open court. During this address, the court must inform the defendant of, and determine that the defendant understands, the following:

(A) the government's right, in a prosecution for perjury or false statement, to use against the defendant any statement that the defendant gives under oath;

(B) the right to plead not guilty, or having already so pleaded, to persist in that plea;

(C) the right to a jury trial;

(D) the right to be represented by counsel—and if necessary have the court appoint counsel—at trial and at every other stage of the proceeding;

(E) the right at trial to confront and cross-examine adverse witnesses, to be protected from compelled self-incrimination, to testify and present evidence, and to compel the attendance of witnesses;

(F) the defendant's waiver of these trial rights if the court accepts a plea of guilty or nolo contendere;

(G) the nature of each charge to which the defendant is pleading;

(H) any maximum possible penalty, including imprisonment, fine, and term of supervised release;

(I) any mandatory minimum penalty;

(J) any applicable forfeiture;

(K) the court's authority to order restitution;

(L) the court's obligation to impose a special assessment;

(M) the court's obligation to apply the Sentencing Guidelines, and the court's discretion to depart from those guidelines under some circumstances; and

(N) the terms of any plea-agreement provision waiving the right to appeal or to collaterally attack the sentence.

(2) Ensuring That a Plea Is Voluntary. Before accepting a plea of guilty or nolo contendere, the court must address the defendant personally in open court and determine that the plea is voluntary and did not result from force, threats, or promises (other than promises in a plea agreement).

(3) Determining the Factual Basis for a Plea. Before entering judgment on a guilty plea, the court must determine that there is a factual basis for the plea.

(c) Plea Agreement Procedure.

(1) In General. An attorney for the government and the defendant's attorney, or the defendant when proceeding pro se, may discuss and reach a plea agreement. The court must not participate in these discussions. If the defendant pleads guilty or nolo contendere to either a charged offense or a lesser or related offense, the plea agreement may specify that an attorney for the government will:

(A) not bring, or will move to dismiss, other charges;

(B) recommend, or agree not to oppose the defendant's request, that a particular sentence or sentencing range is appropriate or that a particular provision of the Sentencing Guidelines, or policy statement, or sentencing factor does or does not apply (such a recommendation or request does not bind the court); or

(C) agree that a specific sentence or sentencing range is the appropriate disposition of the case, or that a particular provision of the Sentencing Guidelines, or policy statement, or sentencing factor does or does not apply (such a recommendation or request binds the court once the court accepts the plea agreement).

(2) Disclosing a Plea Agreement. The parties must disclose the plea agreement in open court when the plea is offered, unless the court for good cause allows the parties to disclose the plea agreement in camera.

(3) Judicial Consideration of a Plea Agreement.

(A) To the extent the plea agreement is of the type specified in Rule 11(c)(1)(A) or (C), the court may accept the agreement, reject it, or defer a decision until the court has reviewed the presentence report.

(B) To the extent the plea agreement is of the type specified in Rule 11(c)(1)(B), the court must advise the defendant that the defendant has no right to withdraw the plea if the court does not follow the recommendation or request.

(4) Accepting a Plea Agreement. If the court accepts the plea agreement, it must inform the defendant that to the extent the plea agreement is of the type specified in Rule 11(c)(1)(A) or (C), the agreed disposition will be included in the judgment.

(5) Rejecting a Plea Agreement. If the court rejects a plea agreement containing provisions of the type specified in Rule 11(c)(1)(A) or (C), the court must do the following on the record and in open court (or, for good cause, in camera):

(A) inform the parties that the court rejects the plea agreement;

(B) advise the defendant personally that the court is not required to follow the plea agreement and give the defendant an opportunity to withdraw the plea; and

(C) advise the defendant personally that if the plea is not withdrawn, the court may dispose of the case less favorably toward the defendant than the plea agreement contemplated.

(d) Withdrawing a Guilty or Nolo Contendere Plea. A defendant may withdraw a plea of guilty or nolo contendere:

(1) before the court accepts the plea, for any reason or no reason; or

(2) after the court accepts the plea, but before it imposes sentence if:

(A) the court rejects a plea agreement under Rule 11(c)(5); or

(B) the defendant can show a fair and just reason for requesting the withdrawal.

(e) Finality of a Guilty or Nolo Contendere Plea. After the court imposes sentence, the defendant may not withdraw a plea of guilty or nolo contendere, and the plea may be set aside only on direct appeal or collateral attack.

(f) Admissibility or Inadmissibility of a Plea, Plea Discussions, and Related Statements. The admissibility or inadmissibility of a plea, a plea discussion, and any related statement is governed by Federal Rule of Evidence 410.

(g) Recording the Proceedings. The proceedings during which the defendant enters a plea must be recorded by a court reporter or by a suitable recording device. If there is a guilty plea or a nolo contendere plea, the record must include the inquiries and advice to the defendant required under Rule 11(b) and (c).

(h) Harmless Error. A variance from the requirements of this rule is harmless error if it does not affect substantial rights.

(As amended Feb. 28, 1966, eff. July 1, 1966; Apr. 22, 1974, eff. Dec. 1, 1975; July 31, 1975, Pub.L. 94–64, § 3(5)–(10), 89 Stat. 371, 372; Apr. 30, 1979, eff. Aug. 1, 1979, and Dec. 1, 1980; Apr. 28, 1982, eff. Aug. 1, 1982; Apr. 28, 1983, eff. Aug. 1, 1983; Apr. 29, 1985, eff. Aug. 1, 1985; Mar. 9, 1987, eff. Aug. 1, 1987; Nov. 18, 1988, Pub.L. 100–690, Title VII, § 7076, 102 Stat. 4406; Apr. 25, 1989, eff. Dec. 1, 1989; Apr. 29, 1999, eff. Dec. 1, 1999; Apr. 29, 2002, eff. Dec. 1, 2002.)

FEDERAL RULES OF CRIMINAL PROCEDURE FOR THE UNITED STATES DISTRICT COURTS

Rule 12. Pleadings and Pretrial Motions

(a) Pleadings. The pleadings in a criminal proceeding are the indictment, the information, and the pleas of not guilty, guilty, and nolo contendere.

(b) Pretrial Motions.

(1) **In General.** Rule 47 applies to a pretrial motion.

(2) **Motions That May Be Made Before Trial.** A party may raise by pretrial motion any defense, objection, or request that the court can determine without a trial of the general issue.

(3) **Motions That Must Be Made Before Trial.** The following must be raised before trial:

(A) a motion alleging a defect in instituting the prosecution;

(B) a motion alleging a defect in the indictment or information—but at any time while the case is pending, the court may hear a claim that the indictment or information fails to invoke the court's jurisdiction or to state an offense;

(C) a motion to suppress evidence;

(D) a Rule 14 motion to sever charges or defendants; and

(E) a Rule 16 motion for discovery.

(4) Notice of the Government's Intent to Use Evidence.

(A) At the Government's Discretion. At the arraignment or as soon afterward as practicable, the government may notify the defendant of its intent to use specified evidence at trial in order to afford the defendant an opportunity to object before trial under Rule 12(b)(3)(C).

(B) At the Defendant's Request. At the arraignment or as soon afterward as practicable, the defendant may, in order to have an opportunity to move to suppress evidence under Rule 12(b)(3)(C), request notice of the government's intent to use (in its evidence-in-chief at trial) any evidence that the defendant may be entitled to discover under Rule 16.

(c) Motion Deadline. The court may, at the arraignment or as soon afterward as practicable, set a deadline for the parties to make pretrial motions and may also schedule a motion hearing.

(d) Ruling on a Motion. The court must decide every pretrial motion before trial unless it finds good cause to defer a ruling. The court must not defer ruling on a pretrial motion if the deferral will adversely affect a party's right to appeal. When factual issues are involved in deciding a motion, the court must state its essential findings on the record.

(e) Waiver of a Defense, Objection, or Request. A party waives any Rule 12(b)(3) defense, objection, or request not raised by the deadline the court sets under Rule 12(c) or by any extension the court provides. For good cause, the court may grant relief from the waiver.

(f) Recording the Proceedings. All proceedings at a motion hearing, including any findings of fact and conclusions of law made orally by the court, must be recorded by a court reporter or a suitable recording device.

(g) Defendant's Continued Custody or Release Status. If the court grants a motion to dismiss based on a defect in instituting the prosecution, in the indictment, or in the information, it may order the defendant to be released or detained under 18 U.S.C. § 3142 for a specified time until a new indictment or information is filed. This rule does not affect any federal statutory period of limitations.

(h) Producing Statements at a Suppression Hearing. Rule 26.2 applies at a suppression hearing under Rule 12(b)(3)(C). At a suppression hearing, a law enforcement officer is considered a government witness.

(As amended Apr. 22, 1974, eff. Dec. 1, 1975; July 31, 1975, Pub.L. 94–64, § 3(11), (12), 89 Stat. 372; Apr. 28, 1983, eff. Aug. 1, 1983; Mar. 9, 1987, eff. Aug. 1, 1987; Apr. 22, 1993, eff. Dec. 1, 1993; Apr. 29, 2002, eff. Dec. 1, 2002.)

Rule 12.1. Notice of an Alibi Defense

(a) Government's Request for Notice and Defendant's Response.

(1) Government's Request. An attorney for the government may request in writing that the defendant notify an attorney for the government of any intended alibi defense. The request must state the time, date, and place of the alleged offense.

(2) Defendant's Response. Within 10 days after the request, or at some other time the court sets, the defendant must serve written notice on an attorney for the government of any intended alibi defense. The defendant's notice must state:

(A) each specific place where the defendant claims to have been at the time of the alleged offense; and

(B) the name, address, and telephone number of each alibi witness on whom the defendant intends to rely.

(b) Disclosing Government Witnesses.

(1) Disclosure. If the defendant serves a Rule 12.1(a)(2) notice, an attorney for the government must disclose in writing to the defendant or the defendant's attorney:

(A) the name, address, and telephone number of each witness the government intends to rely on to establish the defendant's presence at the scene of the alleged offense; and

(B) each government rebuttal witness to the defendant's alibi defense.

(2) Time to Disclose. Unless the court directs otherwise, an attorney for the government must give its Rule 12.1(b)(1) disclosure within 10 days after the defendant serves notice of an intended alibi defense under Rule 12.1(a)(2), but no later than 10 days before trial.

(c) Continuing Duty to Disclose. Both an attorney for the government and the defendant must promptly disclose in writing to the other party the name, address, and telephone number of each additional witness if:

(1) the disclosing party learns of the witness before or during trial; and

(2) the witness should have been disclosed under Rule 12.1(a) or (b) if the disclosing party had known of the witness earlier.

(d) Exceptions. For good cause, the court may grant an exception to any requirement of Rule 12.1(a)—(c).

(e) Failure to Comply. If a party fails to comply with this rule, the court may exclude the testimony of any undisclosed witness regarding the defendant's alibi. This rule does not limit the defendant's right to testify.

(f) Inadmissibility of Withdrawn Intention. Evidence of an intention to rely on an alibi defense, later withdrawn, or of a statement made in connection with that intention, is not, in any civil or criminal proceeding, admissible against the person who gave notice of the intention.

(Added Apr. 22, 1974, eff. Dec. 1, 1975, and amended July 31, 1975, Pub.L. 94–64, § 3(13), 89 Stat. 372; Apr. 29, 1985, eff. Aug. 1, 1985; Mar. 9, 1987, eff. Aug. 1, 1987; Apr. 29, 2002, eff. Dec. 1, 2002.)

Rule 12.2.   Notice of an Insanity Defense; Mental Examination

(a) Notice of an Insanity Defense. A defendant who intends to assert a defense of insanity at the time of the alleged offense must so notify an attorney for the government in writing within the time provided for filing a pretrial motion, or at any later time the court sets, and file a copy of the notice with the clerk. A defendant who fails to do so cannot rely on an insanity defense. The court may, for good cause, allow the defendant to file the notice late, grant additional trial-preparation time, or make other appropriate orders.

(b) Notice of Expert Evidence of a Mental Condition. If a defendant intends to introduce expert evidence relating to a mental disease or defect or any other mental condition of the defendant bearing on either (1) the issue of guilt or (2) the issue of punishment in a capital case, the defendant must—within the time provided for filing a pretrial motion or at any later time the court sets—notify an attorney for the government in writing of this intention and file a copy of the notice with the clerk. The court may, for good cause, allow the defendant to file the notice late, grant the parties additional trial-preparation time, or make other appropriate orders.

(c) Mental Examination.

(1) Authority to Order an Examination; Procedures.

(A) The court may order the defendant to submit to a competency examination under 18 U.S.C. § 4241.

(B) If the defendant provides notice under Rule 12.2(a), the court must, upon the government's motion, order the defendant to be examined under 18 U.S.C. § 4242. If the defendant provides notice under Rule 12.2(b) the court may, upon the government's motion, order the defendant to be examined under procedures ordered by the court.

(2) Disclosing Results and Reports of Capital Sentencing Examination. The results and reports of any examination conducted solely under Rule 12.2(c)(1) after notice under Rule 12.2(b)(2) must be sealed and must not be disclosed to any attorney for the government or the defendant unless the defendant is found guilty of one or more capital crimes and the defendant confirms an intent to offer during sentencing proceedings expert evidence on mental condition.

(3) Disclosing Results and Reports of the Defendant's Expert Examination. After disclosure under Rule 12.2(c)(2) of the results and reports of the government's examination, the defendant must disclose to the government the results and reports of any examination on mental condition conducted by the defendant's expert about which the defendant intends to introduce expert evidence.

(4) Inadmissibility of a Defendant's Statements. No statement made by a defendant in the course of any examination conducted under this rule (whether conducted with or without the defendant's consent), no testimony by the expert based on the statement, and no other fruits of the statement may be admitted into evidence against the defendant in any criminal proceeding except on an issue regarding mental condition on which the defendant:

(A) has introduced evidence of incompetency or evidence requiring notice under Rule 12.2(a) or (b)(1), or

(B) has introduced expert evidence in a capital sentencing proceeding requiring notice under Rule 12.2(b)(2).

(d) Failure to Comply. If the defendant fails to give notice under Rule 12.2(b) or does not submit to an examination when ordered under Rule 12.2(c), the court may exclude any expert evidence from the defendant on the issue of the defendant's mental disease, mental defect, or any other mental condition bearing on the defendant's guilt or the issue of punishment in a capital case.

(e) Inadmissibility of Withdrawn Intention. Evidence of an intention as to which notice was given under Rule 12.2(a) or (b), later withdrawn, is not, in any civil or criminal proceeding, admissible against the person who gave notice of the intention.

(Added Apr. 22, 1974, eff. Dec. 1, 1975, and amended July 31, 1975, Pub.L. 94–64, § 3(14), 89 Stat. 373; Apr. 28, 1983, eff. Aug. 1, 1983; Oct. 12, 1984, Pub.L. 98–473, Title II, § 404, 98 Stat. 2067; Oct. 30, 1984, Pub.L. 98–596, § 11(a), (b), 98 Stat. 3138; Apr. 29, 1985, eff. Aug. 1, 1985; Nov. 10, 1986, Pub.L. 99–646, § 24, 100 Stat. 3597; Mar. 9, 1987, eff. Aug. 1, 1987; Apr. 29, 2002, eff. Dec. 1, 2002.)

Rule 12.3. Notice of a Public–Authority Defense

(a) Notice of the Defense and Disclosure of Witnesses.

(1) Notice in General. If a defendant intends to assert a defense of actual or believed exercise of public authority on behalf of a law enforcement agency or federal intelligence agency at the time of the alleged offense, the defendant must so notify an attorney for the government in writing and must file a copy of the notice with the clerk within the time provided for filing a pretrial motion, or at any later time the court sets. The notice filed with the clerk must be under seal if the notice identifies a federal intelligence agency as the source of public authority.

(2) Contents of Notice. The notice must contain the following information:

(A) the law enforcement agency or federal intelligence agency involved;

(B) the agency member on whose behalf the defendant claims to have acted; and

(C) the time during which the defendant claims to have acted with public authority.

(3) Response to the Notice. An attorney for the government must serve a written response on the defendant or the defendant's attorney within 10 days after receiving the defendant's notice, but no later than 20 days before trial. The response must admit or deny that the defendant exercised the public authority identified in the defendant's notice.

(4) Disclosing Witnesses.

(A) Government's Request. An attorney for the government may request in writing that the defendant disclose the name, address, and telephone number of each witness the defendant intends to rely on to establish a public-authority defense. An attorney for the government may serve the request when the government serves its response to the defendant's notice under Rule 12.3(a)(3), or later, but must serve the request no later than 20 days before trial.

(B) Defendant's Response. Within 7 days after receiving the government's request, the defendant must serve on an attorney for the government a written statement of the name, address, and telephone number of each witness.

(C) Government's Reply. Within 7 days after receiving the defendant's statement, an attorney for the government must serve on the defendant or the defendant's attorney a written statement of the name, address, and telephone number of each witness the government intends to rely on to oppose the defendant's public-authority defense.

(5) Additional Time. The court may, for good cause, allow a party additional time to comply with this rule.

(b) Continuing Duty to Disclose. Both an attorney for the government and the defendant must promptly disclose in writing to the other party the name, address, and telephone number of any additional witness if:

(1) the disclosing party learns of the witness before or during trial; and

(2) the witness should have been disclosed under Rule 12.3(a)(4) if the disclosing party had known of the witness earlier.

(c) Failure to Comply. If a party fails to comply with this rule, the court may exclude the testimony of any undisclosed witness regarding the public-authority defense. This rule does not limit the defendant's right to testify.

(d) Protective Procedures Unaffected. This rule does not limit the court's authority to issue appropriate protective orders or to order that any filings be under seal.

(e) Inadmissibility of Withdrawn Intention. Evidence of an intention as to which notice was given under Rule 12.3(a), later withdrawn, is not, in any civil or criminal proceeding, admissible against the person who gave notice of the intention.

(Added Pub.L. 100–690, Title VI, § 6483,
Nov. 18, 1988, 102 Stat. 4382; Apr. 29,
2002, eff. Dec. 1, 2002.)

Rule 12.4. Disclosure Statement

(a) Who Must File.

(1) Nongovernmental Corporate Party. Any nongovernmental corporate party to a proceeding in a district court must file a statement that identifies any parent corporation and any publicly held corporation that owns 10% or more of its stock or states that there is no such corporation.

(2) Organizational Victim. If an organization is a victim of the alleged criminal activity, the government must file a statement identifying the victim. If the organizational victim is a corporation, the statement must also disclose the information required by Rule 12.4(a)(1) to the extent it can be obtained through due diligence.

(b) Time for Filing; Supplemental Filing. A party must:

(1) file the Rule 12.4(a) statement upon the defendant's initial appearance; and

(2) promptly file a supplemental statement upon any change in the information that the statement requires.

(Added Apr. 29, 2002, eff. Dec. 1, 2002.)

Rule 13.   Joint Trial of Separate Cases

The court may order that separate cases be tried together as though brought in a single indictment or information if all offenses and all defendants could have been joined in a single indictment or information.

(As amended Apr. 29, 2002, eff. Dec. 1, 2002.)

Rule 14.   Relief from Prejudicial Joinder

(a) Relief. If the joinder of offenses or defendants in an indictment, an information, or a consolidation for trial appears to prejudice a defendant or the government, the court may order separate trials of counts, sever the defendants' trials, or provide any other relief that justice requires.

(b) Defendant's Statements. Before ruling on a defendant's motion to sever, the court may order an attorney for the government to deliver to the court for in camera inspection any defendant's statement that the government intends to use as evidence.

(As amended Feb. 28, 1966, eff. July 1, 1966; Apr. 29, 2002, eff. Dec. 1, 2002.)

Rule 15.   Depositions

(a) When Taken.

(1) In General. A party may move that a prospective witness be deposed in order to preserve testimony for trial. The court may grant the motion because of exceptional circumstances and in the interest of justice. If the court orders the deposition to be taken, it may also require the deponent to produce at the deposition any designated material that is not privileged, including any book, paper, document, record, recording, or data.

(2) Detained Material Witness. A witness who is detained under 18 U.S.C. § 3144 may request to be deposed by filing a written motion and giving notice to the parties. The court may then order that the deposition be taken and may discharge the witness after the witness has signed under oath the deposition transcript.

(b) Notice.

(1) In General. A party seeking to take a deposition must give every other party reasonable written notice of the deposition's date and location. The notice must state the name and address of each deponent. If requested by a party receiving the notice, the court may, for good cause, change the deposition's date or location.

(2) To the Custodial Officer. A party seeking to take the deposition must also notify the officer who has custody of the defendant of the scheduled date and location.

(c) Defendant's Presence.

(1) Defendant in Custody. The officer who has custody of the defendant must produce the defendant at the deposition and keep the defendant in the witness's presence during the examination, unless the defendant:

(A) waives in writing the right to be present; or

(B) persists in disruptive conduct justifying exclusion after being warned by the court that disruptive conduct will result in the defendant's exclusion.

(2) Defendant Not in Custody. A defendant who is not in custody has the right upon request to be present at the deposition, subject to any conditions imposed by the court. If the government tenders the defendant's expenses as provided in Rule 15(d) but the defendant still fails to appear, the defendant—absent good cause—waives both the right to appear and any objection to the taking and use of the deposition based on that right.

(d) Expenses. If the deposition was requested by the government, the court may—or if the defendant is unable to bear the deposition expenses, the court must—order the government to pay:

(1) any reasonable travel and subsistence expenses of the defendant and the defendant's attorney to attend the deposition; and

(2) the costs of the deposition transcript.

(e) Manner of Taking. Unless these rules or a court order provides otherwise, a deposition must be taken and filed in the same manner as a deposition in a civil action, except that:

(1) A defendant may not be deposed without that defendant's consent.

(2) The scope and manner of the deposition examination and cross-examination must be the same as would be allowed during trial.

(3) The government must provide to the defendant or the defendant's attorney, for use at the deposition, any statement of the deponent in the government's possession to which the defendant would be entitled at trial.

(f) Use as Evidence. A party may use all or part of a deposition as provided by the Federal Rules of Evidence.

(g) Objections. A party objecting to deposition testimony or evidence must state the grounds for the objection during the deposition.

(h) Depositions by Agreement Permitted. The parties may by agreement take and use a deposition with the court's consent.

(As amended Apr. 22, 1974, eff. Dec. 1, 1975; July 31, 1975, Pub.L. 94–64, § 3(15)–(19), 89 Stat. 373, 374; Oct. 12, 1984, Pub.L. 98–473, Title II, § 209(b), 98 Stat. 1986; Mar. 9, 1987, eff. Aug. 1, 1987; Apr. 29, 2002, eff Dec. 1, 2002.)

Rule 16.   Discovery and Inspection

(a) Government's Disclosure.

(1) Information Subject to Disclosure.

(A) Defendant's Oral Statement. Upon a defendant's request, the government must disclose to the defendant the substance of any relevant oral statement made by the defendant, before or after arrest, in response to interrogation by a person the defendant knew was a government agent if the government intends to use the statement at trial.

(B) Defendant's Written or Recorded Statement. Upon a defendant's request, the government must disclose to the defendant, and make available for inspection, copying, or photographing, all of the following:

(i) any relevant written or recorded statement by the defendant if:

- the statement is within the government's possession, custody, or control; and

- the attorney for the government knows—or through due diligence could know—that the statement exists;

(ii) the portion of any written record containing the substance of any relevant oral statement made before or after arrest if the defendant made the statement in response to interrogation by a person the defendant knew was a government agent; and

(iii) the defendant's recorded testimony before a grand jury relating to the charged offense.

(C) Organizational Defendant. Upon a defendant's request, if the defendant is an organization, the government must disclose to the defendant any statement described in Rule 16(a)(1)(A) and (B) if the government contends that the person making the statement:

(i) was legally able to bind the defendant regarding the subject of the statement because of that person's position as the defendant's director, officer, employee, or agent; or

(ii) was personally involved in the alleged conduct constituting the offense and was legally able to bind the

555

defendant regarding that conduct because of that person's position as the defendant's director, officer, employee, or agent.

(D) Defendant's Prior Record. Upon a defendant's request, the government must furnish the defendant with a copy of the defendant's prior criminal record that is within the government's possession, custody, or control if the attorney for the government knows—or through due diligence could know—that the record exists.

(E) Documents and Objects. Upon a defendant's request, the government must permit the defendant to inspect and to copy or photograph books, papers, documents, data, photographs, tangible objects, buildings or places, or copies or portions of any of these items, if the item is within the government's possession, custody, or control and:

    (i) the item is material to preparing the defense;

    (ii) the government intends to use the item in its case-in-chief at trial; or

    (iii) the item was obtained from or belongs to the defendant.

(F) Reports of Examinations and Tests. Upon a defendant's request, the government must permit a defendant to inspect and to copy or photograph the results or reports of any physical or mental examination and of any scientific test or experiment if:

    (i) the item is within the government's possession, custody, or control;

    (ii) the attorney for the government knows—or through due diligence could know—that the item exists; and

    (iii) the item is material to preparing the defense or the government intends to use the item in its case-in-chief at trial.

(G) Expert witnesses.—At the defendant's request, the government must give to the defendant a written summary of any testimony that the government intends to use under Rules 702, 703, or 705 of the Federal Rules of Evidence during its case-in-chief at trial. If the government requests discovery under subdivision (b)(1)(C)(ii) and the defendant complies, the government must, at the defendant's request, give to the defendant a written summary of testimony that the government intends to use under Rules 702, 703, or 705 of the Federal Rules of Evidence as evidence at trial on the issue of the defendant's mental condition. The summary provided under this subparagraph must describe the witness's opinions, the bases and reasons for those opinions, and the witness's qualifications.

(2) Information Not Subject to Disclosure. Except as Rule 16(a)(1) provides otherwise, this rule does not authorize the discovery or inspection of reports, memoranda, or other internal government documents made by an attorney for the government or other government agent in connection with investigating or prosecuting the case. Nor does this rule authorize the discovery or inspection of statements made by prospective government witnesses except as provided in 18 U.S.C. § 3500.

(3) Grand Jury Transcripts. This rule does not apply to the discovery or inspection of a grand jury's recorded proceedings, except as provided in Rules 6, 12(h), 16(a)(1), and 26.2.

(b) Defendant's Disclosure.

(1) Information Subject to Disclosure.

(A) Documents and Objects. If a defendant requests disclosure under Rule 16(a)(1)(E) and the government complies, then the defendant must permit the government, upon request, to inspect and to copy or photograph books, papers, documents, data, photographs, tangible objects, buildings or places, or copies or portions of any of these items if:

 (i) the item is within the defendant's possession, custody, or control; and

 (ii) the defendant intends to use the item in the defendant's case-in-chief at trial.

(B) Reports of Examinations and Tests. If a defendant requests disclosure under Rule 16(a)(1)(F) and the government complies, the defendant must permit the government, upon request, to inspect and to copy or photograph the results or reports of any physical or mental examination and of any scientific test or experiment if:

 (i) the item is within the defendant's possession, custody, or control; and

 (ii) the defendant intends to use the item in the defendant's case-in-chief at trial, or intends to call the witness who prepared the report and the report relates to the witness's testimony.

(C) Expert witnesses.—The defendant must, at the government's request, give to the government a written summary of any testimony that the defendant intends to use under Rules 702, 703, or 705 of the Federal Rules of Evidence as evidence at trial, if—

(i) the defendant requests disclosure under subdivision (a)(1)(G) and the government complies; or

(ii) the defendant has given notice under Rule 12.2(b) of an intent to present expert testimony on the defendant's mental condition.

This summary must describe the witness's opinions, the bases and reasons for those opinions, and the witness's qualifications.

(2) Information Not Subject to Disclosure. Except for scientific or medical reports, Rule 16(b)(1) does not authorize discovery or inspection of:

(A) reports, memoranda, or other documents made by the defendant, or the defendant's attorney or agent, during the case's investigation or defense; or

(B) a statement made to the defendant, or the defendant's attorney or agent, by:

(i) the defendant;

(ii) a government or defense witness; or

(iii) a prospective government or defense witness.

(c) Continuing Duty to Disclose. A party who discovers additional evidence or material before or during trial must promptly disclose its existence to the other party or the court if:

(1) the evidence or material is subject to discovery or inspection under this rule; and

(2) the other party previously requested, or the court ordered, its production.

(d) Regulating Discovery.

(1) Protective and Modifying Orders. At any time the court may, for good cause, deny, restrict, or defer discovery or inspection, or grant other appropriate relief. The court may permit a party to show good cause by a written statement that the court will inspect ex parte. If relief is granted, the court must preserve the entire text of the party's statement under seal.

(2) Failure to Comply. If a party fails to comply with this rule, the court may:

(A) order that party to permit the discovery or inspection; specify its time, place, and manner; and prescribe other just terms and conditions;

(B) grant a continuance;

(C) prohibit that party from introducing the undisclosed evidence; or

(D) enter any other order that is just under the circumstances.

(As amended Feb. 28, 1966, eff. July 1, 1966; Apr. 22, 1974, eff. Dec. 1, 1975; July 31, 1975, Pub.L. 94–64, § 3(20)–(28), 89 Stat. 374, 375; Dec. 12, 1975, Pub.L. 94–149, § 5, 89 Stat. 806; Apr. 28, 1983, eff. Aug. 1, 1983; Mar. 9, 1987, eff. Aug. 1, 1987; Apr. 30, 1991, eff. Dec. 1, 1991; Apr. 22, 1993, eff. Dec. 1, 1993; Apr. 29, 1994, eff. Dec. 1, 1994; Apr. 29, 2002, eff. Dec. 1, 2002; Nov. 2, 2002, eff. Dec. 1, 2002; Pub.L. 107–273, Div. C, Title I, § 11019(b), Nov. 2, 2002, 116 Stat. 1825.)

Rule 17. Subpoena

(a) **Content.** A subpoena must state the court's name and the title of the proceeding, include the seal of the court, and command the witness to attend and testify at the time and place the subpoena specifies. The clerk must issue a blank subpoena—signed and sealed—to the party requesting it, and that party must fill in the blanks before the subpoena is served.

(b) **Defendant Unable to Pay.** Upon a defendant's ex parte application, the court must order that a subpoena be issued for a named witness if the defendant shows an inability to pay the witness's fees and the necessity of the witness's presence for an adequate defense. If the court orders a subpoena to be issued, the process costs and witness fees will be paid in the same manner as those paid for witnesses the government subpoenas.

(c) **Producing Documents and Objects.**

(1) **In General.** A subpoena may order the witness to produce any books, papers, documents, data, or other objects the subpoena designates. The court may direct the witness to produce the designated items in court before trial or before they are to be offered in evidence. When the items arrive, the court may permit the parties and their attorneys to inspect all or part of them.

(2) **Quashing or Modifying the Subpoena.** On motion made promptly, the court may quash or modify the subpoena if compliance would be unreasonable or oppressive.

(d) **Service.** A marshal, a deputy marshal, or any nonparty who is at least 18 years old may serve a subpoena. The server must deliver a copy of the subpoena to the witness and must tender to the witness one day's witness-attendance fee and the legal mileage allowance. The server need not tender the attendance fee or mileage allowance when the United States, a federal officer, or a federal agency has requested the subpoena.

(e) **Place of Service.**

(1) **In the United States.** A subpoena requiring a witness to attend a hearing or trial may be served at any place within the United States.

(2) In a Foreign Country. If the witness is in a foreign country, 28 U.S.C. § 1783 governs the subpoena's service.

(f) Issuing a Deposition Subpoena.

(1) Issuance. A court order to take a deposition authorizes the clerk in the district where the deposition is to be taken to issue a subpoena for any witness named or described in the order.

(2) Place. After considering the convenience of the witness and the parties, the court may order—and the subpoena may require— the witness to appear anywhere the court designates.

(g) Contempt. The court (other than a magistrate judge) may hold in contempt a witness who, without adequate excuse, disobeys a subpoena issued by a federal court in that district. A magistrate judge may hold in contempt a witness who, without adequate excuse, disobeys a subpoena issued by that magistrate judge as provided in 28 U.S.C. § 636(e).

(h) Information Not Subject to a Subpoena. No party may subpoena a statement of a witness or of a prospective witness under this rule. Rule 26.2 governs the production of the statement.

(As amended Dec. 27, 1948, eff. Oct. 20, 1949; Feb. 28, 1966, eff. July 1, 1966; Apr. 24, 1972, eff. Oct. 1, 1972; Apr. 22, 1974, eff. Dec. 1, 1975; July 31, 1975, Pub.L. 94– 64, § 3(29), 89 Stat. 375; Apr. 30, 1979, eff. Dec. 1, 1980; Mar. 9, 1987, eff. Aug. 1, 1987; Apr. 22, 1993, eff. Dec. 1, 1993; Apr. 29, 2002, eff. Dec. 1, 2002.)

Rule 17.1.   Pretrial Conference

On its own, or on a party's motion, the court may hold one or more pretrial conferences to promote a fair and expeditious trial. When a conference ends, the court must prepare and file a memorandum of any matters agreed to during the conference. The government may not use any statement made during the conference by the defendant or the defendant's attorney unless it is in writing and is signed by the defendant and the defendant's attorney.

(Added Feb. 28, 1966, eff. July 1, 1966, and amended Mar. 9, 1987, eff Aug. 1, 1987; Apr. 29, 2002, eff. Dec. 1, 2002.)

V. VENUE

Rule 18.   Place of Prosecution and Trial

Unless a statute or these rules permit otherwise, the government must prosecute an offense in a district where the offense was committed.

The court must set the place of trial within the district with due regard for the convenience of the defendant and the witnesses, and the prompt administration of justice.

(As amended Feb. 28, 1966, eff. July 1, 1966; Apr. 30, 1979, eff. Aug. 1, 1979; Apr. 29, 2002, eff. Dec. 1, 2002.)

VI. TRIAL

Rule 23. Jury or Nonjury Trial

(a) **Jury Trial.** If the defendant is entitled to a jury trial, the trial must be by jury unless:

(1) the defendant waives a jury trial in writing;

(2) the government consents; and

(3) the court approves.

(b) **Jury Size.**

(1) **In General.** A jury consists of 12 persons unless this rule provides otherwise.

(2) **Stipulation for a Smaller Jury.** At any time before the verdict, the parties may, with the court's approval, stipulate in writing that:

(A) the jury may consist of fewer than 12 persons; or

(B) a jury of fewer than 12 persons may return a verdict if the court finds it necessary to excuse a juror for good cause after the trial begins.

(3) **Court Order for a Jury of 11.** After the jury has retired to deliberate, the court may permit a jury of 11 persons to return a verdict, even without a stipulation by the parties, if the court finds good cause to excuse a juror.

(c) **Nonjury Trial.** In a case tried without a jury, the court must find the defendant guilty or not guilty. If a party requests before the finding of guilty or not guilty, the court must state its specific findings of fact in open court or in a written decision or opinion.

(As amended Feb. 28, 1966, eff. July 1, 1966; Apr. 26, 1976, eff. Oct. 1, 1977; Pub.L. 95–78, § 2(b), July 30, 1977, 91 Stat. 320; Apr. 28, 1983, eff. Aug. 1, 1983; Apr. 29, 2002, eff. Dec. 1, 2002.)

Rule 24. Trial Jurors

(a) **Examination.**

(1) **In General.** The court may examine prospective jurors or may permit the attorneys for the parties to do so.

(2) **Court Examination.** If the court examines the jurors, it must permit the attorneys for the parties to:

            (A) ask further questions that the court considers proper; or

            (B) submit further questions that the court may ask if it considers them proper.

(b) Peremptory Challenges. Each side is entitled to the number of peremptory challenges to prospective jurors specified below. The court may allow additional peremptory challenges to multiple defendants, and may allow the defendants to exercise those challenges separately or jointly.

     (1) Capital Case. Each side has 20 peremptory challenges when the government seeks the death penalty.

     (2) Other Felony Case. The government has 6 peremptory challenges and the defendant or defendants jointly have 10 peremptory challenges when the defendant is charged with a crime punishable by imprisonment of more than one year.

     (3) Misdemeanor Case. Each side has 3 peremptory challenges when the defendant is charged with a crime punishable by fine, imprisonment of one year or less, or both.

(c) Alternate Jurors.

     (1) In General. The court may impanel up to 6 alternate jurors to replace any jurors who are unable to perform or who are disqualified from performing their duties.

     (2) Procedure.

         (A) Alternate jurors must have the same qualifications and be selected and sworn in the same manner as any other juror.

         (B) Alternate jurors replace jurors in the same sequence in which the alternates were selected. An alternate juror who replaces a juror has the same authority as the other jurors.

     (3) Retaining Alternate Jurors. The court may retain alternate jurors after the jury retires to deliberate. The court must ensure that a retained alternate does not discuss the case with anyone until that alternate replaces a juror or is discharged. If an alternate replaces a juror after deliberations have begun, the court must instruct the jury to begin its deliberations anew.

     (4) Peremptory Challenges. Each side is entitled to the number of additional peremptory challenges to prospective alternate jurors specified below. These additional challenges may be used only to remove alternate jurors.

         (A) One or Two Alternates. One additional peremptory challenge is permitted when one or two alternates are impaneled.

(B) Three or Four Alternates. Two additional peremptory challenges are permitted when three or four alternates are impaneled.

(C) Five or Six Alternates. Three additional peremptory challenges are permitted when five or six alternates are impaneled.

(As amended Feb. 28, 1966, eff. July 1, 1966; Mar. 9, 1987, eff. Aug. 1, 1987; Apr. 29, 1999, eff. Dec. 1, 1999; Apr. 29, 2002, eff. Dec. 1, 2002.)

Rule 26.2. Producing a Witness's Statement

(a) Motion to Produce. After a witness other than the defendant has testified on direct examination, the court, on motion of a party who did not call the witness, must order an attorney for the government or the defendant and the defendant's attorney to produce, for the examination and use of the moving party, any statement of the witness that is in their possession and that relates to the subject matter of the witness's testimony.

(b) Producing the Entire Statement. If the entire statement relates to the subject matter of the witness's testimony, the court must order that the statement be delivered to the moving party.

(c) Producing a Redacted Statement. If the party who called the witness claims that the statement contains information that is privileged or does not relate to the subject matter of the witness's testimony, the court must inspect the statement in camera. After excising any privileged or unrelated portions, the court must order delivery of the redacted statement to the moving party. If the defendant objects to an excision, the court must preserve the entire statement with the excised portion indicated, under seal, as part of the record.

(d) Recess to Examine a Statement. The court may recess the proceedings to allow time for a party to examine the statement and prepare for its use.

(e) Sanction for Failure to Produce or Deliver a Statement. If the party who called the witness disobeys an order to produce or deliver a statement, the court must strike the witness's testimony from the record. If an attorney for the government disobeys the order, the court must declare a mistrial if justice so requires.

(f) "Statement" Defined. As used in this rule, a witness's "statement" means:

(1) a written statement that the witness makes and signs, or otherwise adopts or approves;

(2) a substantially verbatim, contemporaneously recorded recital of the witness's oral statement that is contained in any recording or any transcription of a recording; or

(3) the witness's statement to a grand jury, however taken or recorded, or a transcription of such a statement.

(g) Scope. This rule applies at trial, at a suppression hearing under Rule 12, and to the extent specified in the following rules:

(1) Rule 5.1(h) (preliminary hearing);

(2) Rule 32(i)(2) (sentencing);

(3) Rule 32.1(e) (hearing to revoke or modify probation or supervised release);

(4) Rule 46(j) (detention hearing); and

(5) Rule 8 of the Rules Governing Proceedings under 28 U.S.C. § 2255.

(Added Apr. 30, 1979, eff. Dec. 1, 1980, and amended Mar. 9, 1987, eff. Aug. 1, 1987; Apr. 22, 1993, eff. Dec. 1, 1993 Apr. 24, 1998, eff. Dec. 1, 1998; Apr. 29, 2002, eff. Dec. 1, 2002.)

Rule 29. Motion for a Judgment of Acquittal

(a) Before Submission to the Jury. After the government closes its evidence or after the close of all the evidence, the court on the defendant's motion must enter a judgment of acquittal of any offense for which the evidence is insufficient to sustain a conviction. The court may on its own consider whether the evidence is insufficient to sustain a conviction. If the court denies a motion for a judgment of acquittal at the close of the government's evidence, the defendant may offer evidence without having reserved the right to do so.

(b) Reserving Decision. The court may reserve decision on the motion, proceed with the trial (where the motion is made before the close of all the evidence), submit the case to the jury, and decide the motion either before the jury returns a verdict or after it returns a verdict of guilty or is discharged without having returned a verdict. If the court reserves decision, it must decide the motion on the basis of the evidence at the time the ruling was reserved.

(c) After Jury Verdict or Discharge.

(1) Time for a Motion. A defendant may move for a judgment of acquittal, or renew such a motion, within 7 days after a guilty verdict or after the court discharges the jury, whichever is later, or within any other time the court sets during the 7–day period.

(2) Ruling on the Motion. If the jury has returned a guilty verdict, the court may set aside the verdict and enter an acquittal. If the jury has failed to return a verdict, the court may enter a judgment of acquittal.

(3) No Prior Motion Required. A defendant is not required to move for a judgment of acquittal before the court submits the case to the jury as a prerequisite for making such a motion after jury discharge.

(d) Conditional Ruling on a Motion for a New Trial.

(1) Motion for a New Trial. If the court enters a judgment of acquittal after a guilty verdict, the court must also conditionally determine whether any motion for a new trial should be granted if the judgment of acquittal is later vacated or reversed. The court must specify the reasons for that determination.

(2) Finality. The court's order conditionally granting a motion for a new trial does not affect the finality of the judgment of acquittal.

(3) Appeal.

(A) Grant of a Motion for a New Trial. If the court conditionally grants a motion for a new trial and an appellate court later reverses the judgment of acquittal, the trial court must proceed with the new trial unless the appellate court orders otherwise.

(B) Denial of a Motion for a New Trial. If the court conditionally denies a motion for a new trial, an appellee may assert that the denial was erroneous. If the appellate court later reverses the judgment of acquittal, the trial court must proceed as the appellate court directs.

(As amended Feb. 28, 1966, eff. July 1, 1966; Nov. 10, 1986, Pub.L. 99–646, § 54(a), 100 Stat. 3607; Apr. 29, 1994, eff. Dec. 1, 1994; Apr. 29, 2002, eff. Dec. 1, 2002.)

Rule 30. Jury Instructions

(a) In General. Any party may request in writing that the court instruct the jury on the law as specified in the request. The request must be made at the close of the evidence or at any earlier time that the court reasonably sets. When the request is made, the requesting party must furnish a copy to every other party.

(b) Ruling on a Request. The court must inform the parties before closing arguments how it intends to rule on the requested instructions.

(c) Time for Giving Instructions. The court may instruct the jury before or after the arguments are completed, or at both times.

(d) Objections to Instructions. A party who objects to any portion of the instructions or to a failure to give a requested instruction must inform the court of the specific objection and the grounds for the objection before the jury retires to deliberate. An opportunity must be given to object out of the jury's hearing and, on request, out of the jury's presence. Failure to object in accordance with this rule precludes appellate review, except as permitted under Rule 52(b).

(As amended Feb. 28, 1966, eff. July 1,   25, 1988, eff. Aug. 1, 1988; Apr. 29, 2002,
1966; Mar. 9, 1987, eff. Aug. 1, 1987; Apr.   eff. Dec. 1, 2002.)

Rule 31.   Jury Verdict

(a) Return. The jury must return its verdict to a judge in open court. The verdict must be unanimous.

(b) Partial Verdicts, Mistrial, and Retrial.

(1) Multiple Defendants. If there are multiple defendants, the jury may return a verdict at any time during its deliberations as to any defendant about whom it has agreed.

(2) Multiple Counts. If the jury cannot agree on all counts as to any defendant, the jury may return a verdict on those counts on which it has agreed.

(3) Mistrial and Retrial. If the jury cannot agree on a verdict on one or more counts, the court may declare a mistrial on those counts. The government may retry any defendant on any count on which the jury could not agree.

(c) Lesser Offense or Attempt. A defendant may be found guilty of any of the following:

(1) an offense necessarily included in the offense charged;

(2) an attempt to commit the offense charged; or

(3) an attempt to commit an offense necessarily included in the offense charged, if the attempt is an offense in its own right.

(d) Jury Poll. After a verdict is returned but before the jury is discharged, the court must on a party's request, or may on its own, poll the jurors individually. If the poll reveals a lack of unanimity, the court may direct the jury to deliberate further or may declare a mistrial and discharge the jury.

(As amended Apr. 24, 1972, eff. Oct. 1,   17, 2000, eff. Dec. 1, 2000; Apr. 29, 2002,
1972; Apr. 24, 1998, eff. Dec. 1, 1998; Apr.   eff. Dec. 1, 2002.)

VII.   POST–CONVICTION PROCEDURES

Rule 32.   Sentencing and Judgment

(a) Definitions. The following definitions apply under this rule:

(1) "Crime of violence or sexual abuse" means:

(A) a crime that involves the use, attempted use, or threatened use of physical force against another's person or property; or

(B) a crime under 18 U.S.C. §§ 2241–2248 or §§ 2251–2257.

(2) "Victim" means an individual against whom the defendant committed an offense for which the court will impose sentence.

(b) Time of Sentencing.

(1) In General. The court must impose sentence without unnecessary delay.

(2) Changing Time Limits. The court may, for good cause, change any time limits prescribed in this rule.

(c) Presentence Investigation.

(1) Required Investigation.

(A) In General. The probation officer must conduct a presentence investigation and submit a report to the court before it imposes sentence unless:

(i) 18 U.S.C. § 3593(c) or another statute requires otherwise; or

(ii) the court finds that the information in the record enables it to meaningfully exercise its sentencing authority under 18 U.S.C. § 3553, and the court explains its finding on the record.

(B) Restitution. If the law requires restitution, the probation officer must conduct an investigation and submit a report that contains sufficient information for the court to order restitution.

(2) Interviewing the Defendant. The probation officer who interviews a defendant as part of a presentence investigation must, on request, give the defendant's attorney notice and a reasonable opportunity to attend the interview.

(d) Presentence Report.

(1) Applying the Sentencing Guidelines. The presentence report must:

(A) identify all applicable guidelines and policy statements of the Sentencing Commission;

(B) calculate the defendant's offense level and criminal history category;

(C) state the resulting sentencing range and kinds of sentences available;

(D) identify any factor relevant to:

(i) the appropriate kind of sentence, or

(ii) the appropriate sentence within the applicable sentencing range; and

(**E**) identify any basis for departing from the applicable sentencing range.

(**2**) **Additional Information.** The presentence report must also contain the following information:

(**A**) the defendant's history and characteristics, including:

(**i**) any prior criminal record;

(**ii**) the defendant's financial condition; and

(**iii**) any circumstances affecting the defendant's behavior that may be helpful in imposing sentence or in correctional treatment;

(**B**) verified information, stated in a nonargumentative style, that assesses the financial, social, psychological, and medical impact on any individual against whom the offense has been committed;

(**C**) when appropriate, the nature and extent of nonprison programs and resources available to the defendant;

(**D**) when the law provides for restitution, information sufficient for a restitution order;

(**E**) if the court orders a study under 18 U.S.C. § 3552(b), any resulting report and recommendation; and

(**F**) any other information that the court requires.

(**3**) **Exclusions.** The presentence report must exclude the following:

(**A**) any diagnoses that, if disclosed, might seriously disrupt a rehabilitation program;

(**B**) any sources of information obtained upon a promise of confidentiality; and

(**C**) any other information that, if disclosed, might result in physical or other harm to the defendant or others.

(**e**) **Disclosing the Report and Recommendation.**

(**1**) **Time to Disclose.** Unless the defendant has consented in writing, the probation officer must not submit a presentence report to the court or disclose its contents to anyone until the defendant has pleaded guilty or nolo contendere, or has been found guilty.

(**2**) **Minimum Required Notice.** The probation officer must give the presentence report to the defendant, the defendant's attorney, and an attorney for the government at least 35 days before sentencing unless the defendant waives this minimum period.

(**3**) **Sentence Recommendation.** By local rule or by order in a case, the court may direct the probation officer not to disclose to anyone other than the court the officer's recommendation on the sentence.

(f) Objecting to the Report.

(1) **Time to Object.** Within 14 days after receiving the presentence report, the parties must state in writing any objections, including objections to material information, sentencing guideline ranges, and policy statements contained in or omitted from the report.

(2) **Serving Objections.** An objecting party must provide a copy of its objections to the opposing party and to the probation officer.

(3) **Action on Objections.** After receiving objections, the probation officer may meet with the parties to discuss the objections. The probation officer may then investigate further and revise the presentence report as appropriate.

(g) Submitting the Report. At least 7 days before sentencing, the probation officer must submit to the court and to the parties the presentence report and an addendum containing any unresolved objections, the grounds for those objections, and the probation officer's comments on them.

(h) Notice of Possible Departure from Sentencing Guidelines. Before the court may depart from the applicable sentencing range on a ground not identified for departure either in the presentence report or in a party's prehearing submission, the court must give the parties reasonable notice that it is contemplating such a departure. The notice must specify any ground on which the court is contemplating a departure.

(i) Sentencing.

(1) **In General.** At sentencing, the court:

(A) must verify that the defendant and the defendant's attorney have read and discussed the presentence report and any addendum to the report;

(B) must give to the defendant and an attorney for the government a written summary of—or summarize in camera— any information excluded from the presentence report under Rule 32(d)(3) on which the court will rely in sentencing, and give them a reasonable opportunity to comment on that information;

(C) must allow the parties' attorneys to comment on the probation officer's determinations and other matters relating to an appropriate sentence; and

(D) may, for good cause, allow a party to make a new objection at any time before sentence is imposed.

(2) Introducing Evidence; Producing a Statement. The court may permit the parties to introduce evidence on the objections. If a witness testifies at sentencing, Rule 26.2(a)–(d) and (f) applies. If a party fails to comply with a Rule 26.2 order to produce a witness's statement, the court must not consider that witness's testimony.

(3) Court Determinations. At sentencing, the court:

(A) may accept any undisputed portion of the presentence report as a finding of fact;

(B) must—for any disputed portion of the presentence report or other controverted matter—rule on the dispute or determine that a ruling is unnecessary either because the matter will not affect sentencing, or because the court will not consider the matter in sentencing; and

(C) must append a copy of the court's determinations under this rule to any copy of the presentence report made available to the Bureau of Prisons.

(4) Opportunity to Speak.

(A) By a Party. Before imposing sentence, the court must:

(i) provide the defendant's attorney an opportunity to speak on the defendant's behalf;

(ii) address the defendant personally in order to permit the defendant to speak or present any information to mitigate the sentence; and

(iii) provide an attorney for the government an opportunity to speak equivalent to that of the defendant's attorney.

(B) By a Victim. Before imposing sentence, the court must address any victim of a crime of violence or sexual abuse who is present at sentencing and must permit the victim to speak or submit any information about the sentence. Whether or not the victim is present, a victim's right to address the court may be exercised by the following persons if present:

(i) a parent or legal guardian, if the victim is younger than 18 years or is incompetent; or

(ii) one or more family members or relatives the court designates, if the victim is deceased or incapacitated.

(C) In Camera Proceedings. Upon a party's motion and for good cause, the court may hear in camera any statement made under Rule 32(i)(4).

(j) Defendant's Right to Appeal.

(1) Advice of a Right to Appeal.

(A) Appealing a Conviction. If the defendant pleaded not guilty and was convicted, after sentencing the court must advise the defendant of the right to appeal the conviction.

(B) Appealing a Sentence. After sentencing—regardless of the defendant's plea—the court must advise the defendant of any right to appeal the sentence.

(C) Appeal Costs. The court must advise a defendant who is unable to pay appeal costs of the right to ask for permission to appeal in forma pauperis.

(2) Clerk's Filing of Notice. If the defendant so requests, the clerk must immediately prepare and file a notice of appeal on the defendant's behalf.

(k) Judgment.

(1) In General. In the judgment of conviction, the court must set forth the plea, the jury verdict or the court's findings, the adjudication, and the sentence. If the defendant is found not guilty or is otherwise entitled to be discharged, the court must so order. The judge must sign the judgment, and the clerk must enter it.

(2) Criminal Forfeiture. Forfeiture procedures are governed by Rule 32.2.

(As amended Feb. 28, 1966, eff. July 1, 1966; Apr. 24, 1972, eff. Oct. 1, 1972; Apr. 22, 1974, eff. Dec. 1, 1975; July 31, 1975, Pub.L. 94–64, § 3(31)–(34), 89 Stat. 376; Apr. 30, 1979, eff. Aug. 1, 1979, Dec. 1, 1980; Oct. 12, 1982, Pub.L. 97–291, § 3, 96 Stat. 1249; Apr. 28, 1983, eff. Aug. 1, 1983; Oct. 12, 1984, Pub.L. 98–473, Title II, § 215(a), 98 Stat. 2014; Nov. 10, 1986, Pub.L. 99–646, § 25(a), 100 Stat. 3597; Mar. 9, 1987, eff. Aug. 1, 1987; Apr. 25, 1989, eff. Dec. 1, 1989; Apr. 30, 1991, eff. Dec. 1, 1991; Apr. 22, 1993, eff. Dec. 1, 1993; Apr. 29, 1994, eff. Dec. 1, 1994; Sept. 13, 1994, Pub.L. 103–322, Title XXIII, § 230101(b), 108 Stat. 2078; Apr. 23, 1996, eff. Dec. 1, 1996; Apr. 24, 1996, Pub.L. 104–132, Title II, § 207(a), 110 Stat. 1236; Apr. 17, 2000, eff. Dec. 1, 2000; Apr. 29, 2002, eff. Dec. 1, 2002.)

Rule 32.2. Criminal Forfeiture

(a) Notice to the Defendant. A court must not enter a judgment of forfeiture in a criminal proceeding unless the indictment or information contains notice to the defendant that the government will seek the forfeiture of property as part of any sentence in accordance with the applicable statute.

(b) Entering a Preliminary Order of Forfeiture.

(1) In General. As soon as practicable after a verdict or finding of guilty, or after a plea of guilty or nolo contendere is accepted, on any count in an indictment or information regarding which criminal forfeiture is sought, the court must determine what property is subject to forfeiture under the applicable statute. If the government seeks forfeiture of specific property, the court must determine whether the government has established the requisite nexus between the property and the offense. If the government seeks a personal money judgment, the court must determine the amount of money that the defendant will be ordered to pay. The court's determination may be based on evidence already in the record, including any written plea agreement or, if the forfeiture is contested, on evidence or information presented by the parties at a hearing after the verdict or finding of guilt.

(2) Preliminary Order. If the court finds that property is subject to forfeiture, it must promptly enter a preliminary order of forfeiture setting forth the amount of any money judgment or directing the forfeiture of specific property without regard to any third party's interest in all or part of it. Determining whether a third party has such an interest must be deferred until any third party files a claim in an ancillary proceeding under Rule 32.2(c).

(3) Seizing Property. The entry of a preliminary order of forfeiture authorizes the Attorney General (or a designee) to seize the specific property subject to forfeiture; to conduct any discovery the court considers proper in identifying, locating, or disposing of the property; and to commence proceedings that comply with any statutes governing third-party rights. At sentencing—or at any time before sentencing if the defendant consents—the order of forfeiture becomes final as to the defendant and must be made a part of the sentence and be included in the judgment. The court may include in the order of forfeiture conditions reasonably necessary to preserve the property's value pending any appeal.

(4) Jury Determination. Upon a party's request in a case in which a jury returns a verdict of guilty, the jury must determine whether the government has established the requisite nexus between the property and the offense committed by the defendant.

(c) Ancillary Proceeding; Entering a Final Order of Forfeiture.

(1) In General. If, as prescribed by statute, a third party files a petition asserting an interest in the property to be forfeited, the court must conduct an ancillary proceeding, but no ancillary proceeding is required to the extent that the forfeiture consists of a money judgment.

(A) In the ancillary proceeding, the court may, on motion, dismiss the petition for lack of standing, for failure to state a claim, or for any other lawful reason. For purposes of the motion, the facts set forth in the petition are assumed to be true.

(B) After disposing of any motion filed under Rule 32.2(c)(1)(A) and before conducting a hearing on the petition, the court may permit the parties to conduct discovery in accordance with the Federal Rules of Civil Procedure if the court determines that discovery is necessary or desirable to resolve factual issues. When discovery ends, a party may move for summary judgment under Federal Rule of Civil Procedure 56.

(2) Entering a Final Order. When the ancillary proceeding ends, the court must enter a final order of forfeiture by amending the preliminary order as necessary to account for any third-party rights. If no third party files a timely petition, the preliminary order becomes the final order of forfeiture if the court finds that the defendant (or any combination of defendants convicted in the case) had an interest in the property that is forfeitable under the applicable statute. The defendant may not object to the entry of the final order on the ground that the property belongs, in whole or in part, to a codefendant or third party; nor may a third party object to the final order on the ground that the third party had an interest in the property.

(3) Multiple Petitions. If multiple third-party petitions are filed in the same case, an order dismissing or granting one petition is not appealable until rulings are made on all the petitions, unless the court determines that there is no just reason for delay.

(4) Ancillary Proceeding Not Part of Sentencing. An ancillary proceeding is not part of sentencing.

(d) Stay Pending Appeal. If a defendant appeals from a conviction or an order of forfeiture, the court may stay the order of forfeiture on terms appropriate to ensure that the property remains available pending appellate review. A stay does not delay the ancillary proceeding or the determination of a third party's rights or interests. If the court rules in favor of any third party while an appeal is pending, the court may amend the order of forfeiture but must not transfer any property interest to a third party until the decision on appeal becomes final, unless the defendant consents in writing or on the record.

(e) Subsequently Located Property; Substitute Property.

(1) In General. On the government's motion, the court may at any time enter an order of forfeiture or amend an existing order of forfeiture to include property that:

(A) is subject to forfeiture under an existing order of forfeiture but was located and identified after that order was entered; or

(B) is substitute property that qualifies for forfeiture under an applicable statute.

(2) Procedure. If the government shows that the property is subject to forfeiture under Rule 32.2(e)(1), the court must:

(A) enter an order forfeiting that property, or amend an existing preliminary or final order to include it; and

(B) if a third party files a petition claiming an interest in the property, conduct an ancillary proceeding under Rule 32.2(c).

(3) Jury Trial Limited. There is no right to a jury trial under Rule 32.2(e).

(Added Apr. 17, 2000, eff. Dec. 1, 2000, and amended Apr. 29, 2002, eff. Dec. 1, 2002.)

Rule 35. Correcting or Reducing a Sentence

(a) Correcting Clear Error. Within 7 days after sentencing, the court may correct a sentence that resulted from arithmetical, technical, or other clear error.

(b) Reducing a Sentence for Substantial Assistance.

(1) In General. Upon the government's motion made within one year of sentencing, the court may reduce a sentence if:

(A) the defendant, after sentencing, provided substantial assistance in investigating or prosecuting another person; and

(B) reducing the sentence accords with the Sentencing Commission's guidelines and policy statements.

(2) Later Motion. Upon the government's motion made more than one year after sentencing, the court may reduce a sentence if the defendant's substantial assistance involved:

(A) information not known to the defendant until one year or more after sentencing;

(B) information provided by the defendant to the government within one year of sentencing, but which did not become useful to the government until more than one year after sentencing; or

(C) information the usefulness of which could not reasonably have been anticipated by the defendant until more than one year after sentencing and which was promptly provided to the government after its usefulness was reasonably apparent to the defendant.

(3) Evaluating Substantial Assistance. In evaluating whether the defendant has provided substantial assistance, the court may consider the defendant's presentence assistance.

(4) Below Statutory Minimum. When acting under Rule 35(b), the court may reduce the sentence to a level below the minimum sentence established by statute.

(c) "Sentencing" Defined. As used in this rule, "sentencing" means the oral announcement of the sentence.

(As amended Feb. 28, 1966, eff. July 1, 1966; Apr. 30, 1979, eff. Aug. 1, 1979; Apr. 28, 1983, eff. Aug. 1, 1983; Oct. 12, 1984, Pub.L. 98–473, Title II, § 215(b), 98 Stat. 2015; Apr. 29, 1985, eff. Aug. 1, 1985; Oct. 27, 1986, Pub.L. 99–570, Title X, § 1009, 100 Stat. 3207–8; Apr. 30, 1991, eff. Dec. 1, 1991; Apr. 24, 1998, eff. Dec. 1, 1998; Apr. 29, 2002, eff. Dec. 1, 2002; Apr. 26, 2004, eff. Dec. 1, 2004.)

Rule 41. Search and Seizure

(a) Scope and Definitions.

(1) Scope. This rule does not modify any statute regulating search or seizure, or the issuance and execution of a search warrant in special circumstances.

(2) Definitions. The following definitions apply under this rule:

(A) "Property" includes documents, books, papers, any other tangible objects, and information.

(B) "Daytime" means the hours between 6:00 a.m. and 10:00 p.m. according to local time.

(C) "Federal law enforcement officer" means a government agent (other than an attorney for the government) who is engaged in enforcing the criminal laws and is within any category of officers authorized by the Attorney General to request a search warrant.

(b) Authority to Issue a Warrant. At the request of a federal law enforcement officer or an attorney for the government:

(1) a magistrate judge with authority in the district—or if none is reasonably available, a judge of a state court of record in the district—has authority to issue a warrant to search for and seize a person or property located within the district;

(2) a magistrate judge with authority in the district has authority to issue a warrant for a person or property outside the district if the person or property is located within the district when the warrant is issued but might move or be moved outside the district before the warrant is executed; and

(3) a magistrate judge—in an investigation of domestic terrorism or international terrorism (as defined in 18 U.S.C. § 2331)—having authority in any district in which activities related to the terrorism may have occurred, may issue a warrant for a person or property within or outside that district.

(c) Persons or Property Subject to Search or Seizure. A warrant may be issued for any of the following:

(1) evidence of a crime;

(2) contraband, fruits of crime, or other items illegally possessed;

(3) property designed for use, intended for use, or used in committing a crime; or

(4) a person to be arrested or a person who is unlawfully restrained.

(d) Obtaining a Warrant.

(1) Probable Cause. After receiving an affidavit or other information, a magistrate judge or a judge of a state court of record must issue the warrant if there is probable cause to search for and seize a person or property under Rule 41(c).

(2) Requesting a Warrant in the Presence of a Judge.

(A) Warrant on an Affidavit. When a federal law enforcement officer or an attorney for the government presents an affidavit in support of a warrant, the judge may require the affiant to appear personally and may examine under oath the affiant and any witness the affiant produces.

(B) Warrant on Sworn Testimony. The judge may wholly or partially dispense with a written affidavit and base a warrant on sworn testimony if doing so is reasonable under the circumstances.

(C) Recording Testimony. Testimony taken in support of a warrant must be recorded by a court reporter or by a suitable recording device, and the judge must file the transcript or recording with the clerk, along with any affidavit.

(3) Requesting a Warrant by Telephonic or Other Means.

(A) In General. A magistrate judge may issue a warrant based on information communicated by telephone or other appropriate means, including facsimile transmission.

(B) Recording Testimony. Upon learning that an applicant is requesting a warrant, a magistrate judge must:

    (i) place under oath the applicant and any person on whose testimony the application is based; and

    (ii) make a verbatim record of the conversation with a suitable recording device, if available, or by a court reporter, or in writing.

(C) Certifying Testimony. The magistrate judge must have any recording or court reporter's notes transcribed, certify the transcription's accuracy, and file a copy of the record and the transcription with the clerk. Any written verbatim record must be signed by the magistrate judge and filed with the clerk.

(D) Suppression Limited. Absent a finding of bad faith, evidence obtained from a warrant issued under Rule 41(d)(3)(A) is not subject to suppression on the ground that issuing the warrant in that manner was unreasonable under the circumstances.

(e) Issuing the Warrant.

(1) In General. The magistrate judge or a judge of a state court of record must issue the warrant to an officer authorized to execute it.

(2) Contents of the Warrant. The warrant must identify the person or property to be searched, identify any person or property to be seized, and designate the magistrate judge to whom it must be returned. The warrant must command the officer to:

(A) execute the warrant within a specified time no longer than 10 days;

(B) execute the warrant during the daytime, unless the judge for good cause expressly authorizes execution at another time; and

(C) return the warrant to the magistrate judge designated in the warrant.

(3) Warrant by Telephonic or Other Means. If a magistrate judge decides to proceed under Rule 41(d)(3)(A), the following additional procedures apply:

(A) Preparing a Proposed Duplicate Original Warrant. The applicant must prepare a "proposed duplicate original warrant" and must read or otherwise transmit the contents of that document verbatim to the magistrate judge.

(B) Preparing an Original Warrant. The magistrate judge must enter the contents of the proposed duplicate original warrant into an original warrant.

(C) Modifications. The magistrate judge may direct the applicant to modify the proposed duplicate original warrant. In that case, the judge must also modify the original warrant.

(D) Signing the Original Warrant and the Duplicate Original Warrant. Upon determining to issue the warrant, the magistrate judge must immediately sign the original warrant, enter on its face the exact time it is issued, and direct the applicant to sign the judge's name on the duplicate original warrant.

(f) Executing and Returning the Warrant.

(1) Noting the Time. The officer executing the warrant must enter on its face the exact date and time it is executed.

(2) Inventory. An officer present during the execution of the warrant must prepare and verify an inventory of any property seized. The officer must do so in the presence of another officer and the person from whom, or from whose premises, the property was taken. If either one is not present, the officer must prepare and verify the inventory in the presence of at least one other credible person.

(3) Receipt. The officer executing the warrant must:

> **(A)** give a copy of the warrant and a receipt for the property taken to the person from whom, or from whose premises, the property was taken; or

> **(B)** leave a copy of the warrant and receipt at the place where the officer took the property.

(4) Return. The officer executing the warrant must promptly return it—together with a copy of the inventory—to the magistrate judge designated on the warrant. The judge must, on request, give a copy of the inventory to the person from whom, or from whose premises, the property was taken and to the applicant for the warrant.

(g) Motion to Return Property. A person aggrieved by an unlawful search and seizure of property or by the deprivation of property may move for the property's return. The motion must be filed in the district where the property was seized. The court must receive evidence on any factual issue necessary to decide the motion. If it grants the motion, the court must return the property to the movant, but may impose reasonable conditions to protect access to the property and its use in later proceedings.

(h) Motion to Suppress. A defendant may move to suppress evidence in the court where the trial will occur, as Rule 12 provides.

(i) Forwarding Papers to the Clerk. The magistrate judge to whom the warrant is returned must attach to the warrant a copy of the return, of the inventory, and of all other related papers and must deliver them to the clerk in the district where the property was seized.

(As amended Dec. 27, 1948, eff. Oct. 20, 1949; Apr. 9, 1956, eff. July 8, 1956; Apr. 24, 1972, eff. Oct. 1, 1972; Mar. 18, 1974, eff. July 1, 1974; Apr. 26, 1976, eff. Aug. 1, 1976; July 30, 1977, Pub.L. 95–78, § 2(e), 91 Stat. 320; Apr. 30, 1979, eff. Aug. 1, 1979; Mar. 9, 1987, eff. Aug. 1, 1987; Apr. 25, 1989, eff. Dec. 1, 1989, May 1, 1990, eff. Dec. 1, 1990; Apr. 22, 1993, eff. Dec. 1, 1993; Oct. 26, 2001, Pub.L. 107–56, Title II, § 219, 115 Stat. 291; Apr. 29, 2002, eff. Dec. 1, 2002.)

IX. GENERAL PROVISIONS

Rule 43. Defendant's Presence

(a) When Required. Unless this rule, Rule 5, or Rule 10 provides otherwise, the defendant must be present at:

(1) the initial appearance, the initial arraignment, and the plea;

(2) every trial stage, including jury impanelment and the return of the verdict; and

(3) sentencing.

(b) When Not Required. A defendant need not be present under any of the following circumstances:

(1) Organizational Defendant. The defendant is an organization represented by counsel who is present.

(2) Misdemeanor Offense. The offense is punishable by fine or by imprisonment for not more than one year, or both, and with the defendant's written consent, the court permits arraignment, plea, trial, and sentencing to occur in the defendant's absence.

(3) Conference or Hearing on a Legal Question. The proceeding involves only a conference or hearing on a question of law.

(4) Sentence Correction. The proceeding involves the correction or reduction of sentence under Rule 35 or 18 U.S.C. § 3582(c).

(c) Waiving Continued Presence.

(1) In General. A defendant who was initially present at trial, or who had pleaded guilty or nolo contendere, waives the right to be present under the following circumstances:

(A) when the defendant is voluntarily absent after the trial has begun, regardless of whether the court informed the defendant of an obligation to remain during trial;

(B) in a noncapital case, when the defendant is voluntarily absent during sentencing; or

(C) when the court warns the defendant that it will remove the defendant from the courtroom for disruptive behavior, but the defendant persists in conduct that justifies removal from the courtroom.

(2) Waiver's Effect. If the defendant waives the right to be present, the trial may proceed to completion, including the verdict's return and sentencing, during the defendant's absence.

(As amended Apr. 22, 1974, eff. Dec. 1, 1975; July 31, 1975, Pub.L. 94–64, § 3(35), 89 Stat. 376; Mar. 9, 1987, eff. Aug. 1, 1987; Apr. 27, 1995, eff. Dec. 1, 1995; Apr. 24, 1998, eff. Dec. 1, 1998; Apr. 29, 2002, eff. Dec. 1, 2002.)

Rule 44.   Right to and Appointment of Counsel

(a) Right to Appointed Counsel. A defendant who is unable to obtain counsel is entitled to have counsel appointed to represent the defendant at every stage of the proceeding from initial appearance through appeal, unless the defendant waives this right.

(b) Appointment Procedure. Federal law and local court rules govern the procedure for implementing the right to counsel.

(c) Inquiry Into Joint Representation.

(1) Joint Representation. Joint representation occurs when:

(A) two or more defendants have been charged jointly under Rule 8(b) or have been joined for trial under Rule 13; and

(B) the defendants are represented by the same counsel, or counsel who are associated in law practice.

(2) Court's Responsibilities in Cases of Joint Representation. The court must promptly inquire about the propriety of joint representation and must personally advise each defendant of the right to the effective assistance of counsel, including separate representation. Unless there is good cause to believe that no conflict of interest is likely to arise, the court must take appropriate measures to protect each defendant's right to counsel.

(As amended Feb. 28, 1966, eff. July 1, 1966; Apr. 24, 1972, eff. Oct. 1, 1972; Apr. 30, 1979, eff. Dec. 1, 1980; Mar. 9, 1987, eff. Aug. 1, 1987; Apr. 22, 1993, eff. Dec. 1, 1993; Apr. 29, 2002, eff. Dec. 1, 2002.)

Rule 45.   Computing and Extending Time

(a) Computing Time. The following rules apply in computing any period of time specified in these rules, any local rule, or any court order:

(1) Day of the Event Excluded. Exclude the day of the act, event, or default that begins the period.

(2) Exclusion from Brief Periods. Exclude intermediate Saturdays, Sundays, and legal holidays when the period is less than 11 days.

(3) Last Day. Include the last day of the period unless it is a Saturday, Sunday, legal holiday, or day on which weather or other conditions make the clerk's office inaccessible. When the last day is excluded, the period runs until the end of the next day that is not a

Saturday, Sunday, legal holiday, or day when the clerk's office is inaccessible.

(4) "Legal Holiday" Defined. As used in this rule, "legal holiday" means:

(A) the day set aside by statute for observing:

(i) New Year's Day;

(ii) Martin Luther King, Jr.'s Birthday;

(iii) Washington's Birthday;

(iv) Memorial Day;

(v) Independence Day;

(vi) Labor Day;

(vii) Columbus Day;

(viii) Veterans' Day;

(ix) Thanksgiving Day;

(x) Christmas Day; and

(B) any other day declared a holiday by the President, the Congress, or the state where the district court is held.

(b) Extending Time.

(1) In General. When an act must or may be done within a specified period, the court on its own may extend the time, or for good cause may do so on a party's motion made:

(A) before the originally prescribed or previously extended time expires; or

(B) after the time expires if the party failed to act because of excusable neglect.

(2) Exceptions. The court may not extend the time to take any action under Rules 29, 33, 34, and 35, except as stated in those rules.

(c) Additional Time After Service. When these rules permit or require a party to act within a specified period after a notice or a paper has been served on that party, 3 days are added to the period if service occurs in the manner provided under Federal Rule of Civil Procedure 5(b)(2)(B), (C), or (D).

(As amended Feb. 28, 1966, eff. July 1, 1966; Dec. 4, 1967, eff. July 1, 1968; Mar. 1, 1971, eff. July 1, 1971; Apr. 28, 1982, eff. Aug. 1, 1982; Apr. 29, 1985, eff. Aug. 1, 1985; Mar. 9, 1987, eff. Aug. 1, 1987; Apr. 29, 2002, eff. Dec. 1, 2002.)

Rule 46.   Release from Custody; Supervising Detention

(a) Before Trial. The provisions of 18 U.S.C. §§ 3142 and 3144 govern pretrial release.

(b) During Trial. A person released before trial continues on release during trial under the same terms and conditions. But the court may order different terms and conditions or terminate the release if necessary to ensure that the person will be present during trial or that the person's conduct will not obstruct the orderly and expeditious progress of the trial.

(c) Pending Sentencing or Appeal. The provisions of 18 U.S.C. § 3143 govern release pending sentencing or appeal. The burden of establishing that the defendant will not flee or pose a danger to any other person or to the community rests with the defendant.

(d) Pending Hearing on a Violation of Probation or Supervised Release. Rule 32.1(a)(6) governs release pending a hearing on a violation of probation or supervised release.

(e) Surety. The court must not approve a bond unless any surety appears to be qualified. Every surety, except a legally approved corporate surety, must demonstrate by affidavit that its assets are adequate. The court may require the affidavit to describe the following:

    (1) the property that the surety proposes to use as security;

    (2) any encumbrance on that property;

    (3) the number and amount of any other undischarged bonds and bail undertakings the surety has issued; and

    (4) any other liability of the surety.

(f) Bail Forfeiture.

    (1) Declaration. The court must declare the bail forfeited if a condition of the bond is breached.

    (2) Setting Aside. The court may set aside in whole or in part a bail forfeiture upon any condition the court may impose if:

        (A) the surety later surrenders into custody the person released on the surety's appearance bond; or

        (B) it appears that justice does not require bail forfeiture.

    (3) Enforcement.

        (A) Default Judgment and Execution. If it does not set aside a bail forfeiture, the court must, upon the government's motion, enter a default judgment.

        (B) Jurisdiction and Service. By entering into a bond, each surety submits to the district court's jurisdiction and irrevocably appoints the district clerk as its agent to receive service of any filings affecting its liability.

        (C) Motion to Enforce. The court may, upon the government's motion, enforce the surety's liability without an independent action. The government must serve any motion, and notice as the court prescribes, on the district clerk. If so served, the clerk must promptly mail a copy to the surety at its last known address.

(4) Remission. After entering a judgment under Rule 46(f)(3), the court may remit in whole or in part the judgment under the same conditions specified in Rule 46(f)(2).

(g) Exoneration. The court must exonerate the surety and release any bail when a bond condition has been satisfied or when the court has set aside or remitted the forfeiture. The court must exonerate a surety who deposits cash in the amount of the bond or timely surrenders the defendant into custody.

(h) Supervising Detention Pending Trial.

(1) In General. To eliminate unnecessary detention, the court must supervise the detention within the district of any defendants awaiting trial and of any persons held as material witnesses.

(2) Reports. An attorney for the government must report biweekly to the court, listing each material witness held in custody for more than 10 days pending indictment, arraignment, or trial. For each material witness listed in the report, an attorney for the government must state why the witness should not be released with or without a deposition being taken under Rule 15(a).

(i) Forfeiture of Property. The court may dispose of a charged offense by ordering the forfeiture of 18 U.S.C. § 3142(c)(1)(B)(xi) property under 18 U.S.C. § 3146(d), if a fine in the amount of the property's value would be an appropriate sentence for the charged offense.

(j) Producing a Statement.

(1) In General. Rule 26.2(a)–(d) and (f) applies at a detention hearing under 18 U.S.C. § 3142, unless the court for good cause rules otherwise.

(2) Sanctions for Not Producing a Statement. If a party disobeys a Rule 26.2 order to produce a witness's statement, the court must not consider that witness's testimony at the detention hearing.

(As amended Apr. 9, 1956, eff. July 8, 1956; Feb. 28, 1966, eff. July 1, 1966; Apr. 24, 1972, eff. Oct. 1, 1972; Oct. 12, 1984, Pub.L. 98–473, Title II, § 209(d), 98 Stat. 1987; Mar. 9, 1987, eff. Aug. 1, 1987; Apr. 30, 1991, eff. Dec. 1, 1991; Apr. 22, 1993, eff. Dec. 1, 1993; Sept. 13, 1994, Pub.L. 103–322, Title XXXIII, § 330003(h), 108 Stat. 2141; Apr. 29, 2002, eff. Dec. 1, 2002.)

Rule 47. Motions and Supporting Affidavits

(a) In General. A party applying to the court for an order must do so by motion.

(b) Form and Content of a Motion. A motion—except when made during a trial or hearing—must be in writing, unless the court permits the party to make the motion by other means. A motion must state the grounds on which it is based and the relief or order sought. A motion may be supported by affidavit.

(c) Timing of a Motion. A party must serve a written motion—other than one that the court may hear ex parte—and any hearing notice at least 5 days before the hearing date, unless a rule or court order sets a different period. For good cause, the court may set a different period upon ex parte application.

(d) Affidavit Supporting a Motion. The moving party must serve any supporting affidavit with the motion. A responding party must serve any opposing affidavit at least one day before the hearing, unless the court permits later service.

(As amended Apr. 29, 2002, eff. Dec. 1, 2002.)

Rule 48. Dismissal

(a) By the Government. The government may, with leave of court, dismiss an indictment, information, or complaint. The government may not dismiss the prosecution during trial without the defendant's consent.

(b) By the Court. The court may dismiss an indictment, information, or complaint if unnecessary delay occurs in:

(1) presenting a charge to a grand jury;

(2) filing an information against a defendant; or

(3) bringing a defendant to trial.

(As amended Apr. 29, 2002, eff. Dec. 1, 2002.)

Rule 58. Petty Offenses and Other Misdemeanors

(a) Scope.

(1) In General. These rules apply in petty offense and other misdemeanor cases and on appeal to a district judge in a case tried by a magistrate judge, unless this rule provides otherwise.

(2) Petty Offense Case Without Imprisonment. In a case involving a petty offense for which no sentence of imprisonment will be imposed, the court may follow any provision of these rules that is not inconsistent with this rule and that the court considers appropriate.

(3) Definition. As used in this rule, the term "petty offense for which no sentence of imprisonment will be imposed" means a petty offense for which the court determines that, in the event of conviction, no sentence of imprisonment will be imposed.

(b) Pretrial Procedure.

(1) Charging Document. The trial of a misdemeanor may proceed on an indictment, information, or complaint. The trial of a petty offense may also proceed on a citation or violation notice.

(2) Initial Appearance. At the defendant's initial appearance on a petty offense or other misdemeanor charge, the magistrate judge must inform the defendant of the following:

(A) the charge, and the minimum and maximum penalties, including imprisonment, fines, any special assessment under 18 U.S.C. § 3013, and restitution under 18 U.S.C. § 3556;

(B) the right to retain counsel;

(C) the right to request the appointment of counsel if the defendant is unable to retain counsel—unless the charge is a petty offense for which the appointment of counsel is not required;

(D) the defendant's right not to make a statement, and that any statement made may be used against the defendant;

(E) the right to trial, judgment, and sentencing before a district judge—unless:

(i) the charge is a petty offense; or

(ii) the defendant consents to trial, judgment, and sentencing before a magistrate judge;

(F) the right to a jury trial before either a magistrate judge or a district judge—unless the charge is a petty offense; and

(G) if the defendant is held in custody and charged with a misdemeanor other than a petty offense, the right to a preliminary hearing under Rule 5.1, and the general circumstances, if any, under which the defendant may secure pretrial release.

(3) Arraignment.

(A) Plea Before a Magistrate Judge. A magistrate judge may take the defendant's plea in a petty offense case. In every other misdemeanor case, a magistrate judge may take the plea only if the defendant consents either in writing or on the record to be tried before a magistrate judge and specifically waives trial before a district judge. The defendant may plead not guilty, guilty, or (with the consent of the magistrate judge) nolo contendere.

(B) Failure to Consent. Except in a petty offense case, the magistrate judge must order a defendant who does not consent to trial before a magistrate judge to appear before a district judge for further proceedings.

(c) Additional Procedures in Certain Petty Offense Cases. The following procedures also apply in a case involving a petty offense for which no sentence of imprisonment will be imposed:

(1) Guilty or Nolo Contendere Plea. The court must not accept a guilty or nolo contendere plea unless satisfied that the defendant understands the nature of the charge and the maximum possible penalty.

(2) Waiving Venue.

(A) Conditions of Waiving Venue. If a defendant is arrested, held, or present in a district different from the one where the indictment, information, complaint, citation, or violation notice is pending, the defendant may state in writing a desire to plead guilty or nolo contendere; to waive venue and trial in the district where the proceeding is pending; and to consent to the court's disposing of the case in the district where the defendant was arrested, is held, or is present.

(B) Effect of Waiving Venue. Unless the defendant later pleads not guilty, the prosecution will proceed in the district where the defendant was arrested, is held, or is present. The district clerk must notify the clerk in the original district of the defendant's waiver of venue. The defendant's statement of a desire to plead guilty or nolo contendere is not admissible against the defendant.

(3) Sentencing. The court must give the defendant an opportunity to be heard in mitigation and then proceed immediately to sentencing. The court may, however, postpone sentencing to allow the probation service to investigate or to permit either party to submit additional information.

(4) Notice of a Right to Appeal. After imposing sentence in a case tried on a not-guilty plea, the court must advise the defendant of a right to appeal the conviction and of any right to appeal the sentence. If the defendant was convicted on a plea of guilty or nolo contendere, the court must advise the defendant of any right to appeal the sentence.

(d) Paying a Fixed Sum in Lieu of Appearance.

(1) In General. If the court has a local rule governing forfeiture of collateral, the court may accept a fixed-sum payment in lieu of the defendant's appearance and end the case, but the fixed sum may not exceed the maximum fine allowed by law.

(2) Notice to Appear. If the defendant fails to pay a fixed sum, request a hearing, or appear in response to a citation or violation notice, the district clerk or a magistrate judge may issue a notice for the defendant to appear before the court on a date certain. The notice may give the defendant an additional opportunity to pay a fixed sum in lieu of appearance. The district clerk must serve the notice on the defendant by mailing a copy to the defendant's last known address.

(3) **Summons or Warrant.** Upon an indictment, or upon a showing by one of the other charging documents specified in Rule 58(b)(1) of probable cause to believe that an offense has been committed and that the defendant has committed it, the court may issue an arrest warrant or, if no warrant is requested by an attorney for the government, a summons. The showing of probable cause must be made under oath or under penalty of perjury, but the affiant need not appear before the court. If the defendant fails to appear before the court in response to a summons, the court may summarily issue a warrant for the defendant's arrest.

(e) Recording the Proceedings. The court must record any proceedings under this rule by using a court reporter or a suitable recording device.

(f) New Trial. Rule 33 applies to a motion for a new trial.

(g) Appeal.

(1) From a District Judge's Order or Judgment. The Federal Rules of Appellate Procedure govern an appeal from a district judge's order or a judgment of conviction or sentence.

(2) From a Magistrate Judge's Order or Judgment.

(A) Interlocutory Appeal. Either party may appeal an order of a magistrate judge to a district judge within 10 days of its entry if a district judge's order could similarly be appealed. The party appealing must file a notice with the clerk specifying the order being appealed and must serve a copy on the adverse party.

(B) Appeal from a Conviction or Sentence. A defendant may appeal a magistrate judge's judgment of conviction or sentence to a district judge within 10 days of its entry. To appeal, the defendant must file a notice with the clerk specifying the judgment being appealed and must serve a copy on an attorney for the government.

(C) Record. The record consists of the original papers and exhibits in the case; any transcript, tape, or other recording of the proceedings; and a certified copy of the docket entries. For purposes of the appeal, a copy of the record of the proceedings must be made available to a defendant who establishes by affidavit an inability to pay or give security for the record. The Director of the Administrative Office of the United States Courts must pay for those copies.

(D) Scope of Appeal. The defendant is not entitled to a trial de novo by a district judge. The scope of the appeal is the same as in an appeal to the court of appeals from a judgment entered by a district judge.

(3) Stay of Execution and Release Pending Appeal. Rule 38 applies to a stay of a judgment of conviction or sentence. The court may release the defendant pending appeal under the law relating to release pending appeal from a district court to a court of appeals.

(Added May 1, 1990, eff. Dec. 1, 1990, and   Apr. 22, 1993, eff. Dec. 1, 1993; Apr. 29,
amended Apr. 30, 1991, eff. Dec. 1, 1991;   2002, eff. Dec. 1, 2002.)

Appendix C

CHRONOLOGY OF U.S.
v. CHRISTOPHER

The following is a chronology of the important events in the investigation and disposition of the model case, referenced to the sections of the book that describe the events.

2005

January 5

Confidential informant reports cocaine arriving at JFK Airport in coffee shipment to International Food Distributors c/o Superior Warehouse, Queens, New York, owned by Paul Christopher. (§ 2.1)

January 11

DEA Agent Martinez and Customs agents at JFK discover cocaine in coffee crate, remove all but a small trace and install homing device. (§ 2.1)

January 12

DEA Agents Martinez, Foster and Richards conduct surveillance at Superior Warehouse. Agent Sobel makes a controlled delivery of the coffee crates. Delivery received by Mario Long, assisted by Arthur Murphy. Warehouse searched. Gilbert Santiago identified as superintendent of warehouse. Records indicate that goods are distributed from warehouse by Van Ness Trucking Co., owned by William Van Ness. Long and Murphy arrested. (§ 2.2–3)

Long and Murphy booked, and interrogated. Long makes recorded call to Santiago. (§ 2.4)

January 13–17

Agent Martinez presents case to Assistant United States Attorney Laura KnappKnapp prepares and files complaint, arrest and search warrants. Gilbert Santiago arrested. Records seized from Superior Warehouse. (§ 4.6–4.11)

Initial appearances, Long, Murphy, and Santiago. Long represented by Inga Porter; Murphy by Stephen Colletti; Santiago by Charles Berman. Long and Murphy released on bail. Long waives preliminary hearing. Santiago detained pending detention hearing. (§§ 5.11–5.13)

Preventive detention hearing, Santiago. Detention ordered. Santiago appeals.District Court reverses magistrate judge's decision to release Long, ordering detention. (§ 5.14)

January 23

Santiago preliminary hearing. (§ 6.3)

January 24–5

Berman and Knapp meet to discuss cooperation by Santiago. Santiago proffer session. (§ 8.3)

January 25

Santiago proffer session. (§ 8.3(e))

January 27

Long proffer session. (§ 8.5)

January 26–29

Surveillance of International Food Distributors—Christopher and Van Ness seen together. Christopher uses pay phone. (§ 10.5(c))

February 4

Subpoenas *duces tecum* to CMS Bank, Verizon and Van Ness Trucking. (§ 10.5(c))

February 15

Santiago waiver of indictment; information filed. (§ 8.4)

February 22

Application to install pen register. (§ 10.5(d))

February 25

Santiago enters guilty plea (§ 9.4)

Murphy complaint dismissed (§ 8.6)

February 26

Long enters guilty plea. (§ 9.5)

March 2

Agent Martinez interviews Barbara Weiss, serves grand jury subpoena. (§ 10.5(e))

March 4, 10

Weiss meets with attorney Alex Wells. Weiss proffer session. (§ 10.5(f))

March 24

Application for immunity for Weiss (§ 10.5(f))

March 27

Weiss appears before grand jury. (§ 10.5(g))

March 29

Agent Martinez interviews Ernest Wagner, vice-president at CMS Bank; Wagner retains Isabel Johnson. (§ 10.5(h) and (i))

April 25

Indictment drafted for Christopher, Van Ness and Wagner. (§ 11.7(b))

Christopher case presented to grand jury. (§ 11.8)

Christopher and Van Ness arrested; Wagner surrenders. (§ 11.9)

April 27–April 30

Christopher and Van Ness meet with attorneys Richard Clark and Martin Rothman; joint defense meeting. (§ 13.8(a))

May 8

Wagner plea agreement. (§§ 12.7–12.8)

May 14

Wagner guilty plea. (§ 12.9)

May 20

Christopher and Van Ness discovery conference. (§ 13.8(c))

May 21

Defense discovery letter. (§ 13.8(d))

May 25

Government discovery letter. (§ 13.8(d))

June 23

Defense omnibus motion filed (§ 14.5)

July 3

Government's response to motion (§ 14.6)

July 20

Hearing on motion. (§ 14.11)

August 1

Rulings on motions. (§ 14.11)

August 25

Wagner sentenced (§ 17.7)

September 5–10

In limine motion and response; proposed voir dire questions; requests to charge. (§ 15.6(a)-(c))

September 12

Trial begins (§ 16.3(c))

September 20

Trial ends (§§ 16.11(f)–16.12)

September 22

Verdict (§ 16.15)

October 2

Christopher meets with probation officer (§ 17.6)

October 18

Sentencing hearing; Christopher sentenced. (§ 17.6(d))

October 28

Santiago and Long sentenced (§ 17.8)

Index

References are to Pages

ACQUITTAL, JUDGMENT OF
Motions, § 16.7

AD TESTIFICANDUM, SUBPOENAS
Grand jury, § 10.3

ADJUSTED OFFENSE LEVEL
Sentencing guidelines, § 7.2

ALLOCUTION
Guilty pleas, § 9.2

ANCILLARY PROCEEDINGS
Initial appearance, § 5.9

APPEAL AND REVIEW
Generally, § 1.1
Complaint, review of sufficiency of, § 5.4
Investigations, review of evidence by government, § 10.5
Pretrial motions, § 14.11
Pretrial release or detention, review of decisions, §§ 5.7, 5.11

APPEARANCE
Initial Appearance, this index

APPROVAL
Post-arrest investigations, tape recording, § 2.4

ARGUMENTS
Closing Arguments, this index
Evidence, § 3.3

ARRAIGNMENT
Indictments, §§ 11.5, 11.9

ARREST
Indictments, § 11.5
Investigations, § 2.2
Warrants, §§ 4.10, 4.11

ATTORNEYS
Conflicts of interest, § 5.2
Entry of defense counsel, § 5.1
Grand Jury, this index
Guilty Pleas, this index
Initial defense interview, § 5.1
Investigations, representation of witnesses and targets, §§ 10.4, 10.5
Joint defense agreements, conflicts of interest, § 5.2

ATTORNEYS—Cont'd
Joint representation, conflicts of interest, § 5.2
Other clients, conflicts of interest, § 5.2
Preliminary hearings, strategic considerations, § 6.2
Right to counsel, § 5.1

AUTHENTICATION WITNESSES
Generally, § 3.3

BASE LEVEL OFFENSE
Sentencing guidelines, § 7.2

BOOKING PROCEDURE
Investigations, § 2.3

BRADY MATERIAL
Discovery, § 13.3

BURDEN OF PROOF
Generally, § 3.1
Allocation of burden, §§ 3.1, 4.2
Clear and convincing evidence, quantitative burden, § 3.1
Decision to charge, §§ 4.2, 4.9
Going forward, burden of, §§ 3.1, 14.8
Indictment stage, § 11.1
Persuasion, burden of, §§ 3.1, 14.8
Preliminary hearings, § 6.1
Preponderance of evidence, quantitative burden, § 3.1
Pretrial motions, § 14.8
Pretrial release or detention, § 5.7
Probable cause, quantitative burden, § 3.1
Qualitative proof, §§ 3.1, 4.2, 4.9, 5.7, 14.8
Quantitative proof, §§ 3.1, 4.2, 4.9, 5.7, 14.8
Reasonable doubt, quantitative burden, § 3.1
Sentencing, § 17.3
Trial preparation, § 15.1

CHALLENGES
Grand jury, subpoenas, § 10.3

CHARACTER
Credibility of witnesses, § 16.4

CHARGE BARGAINING
Guilty pleas, § 12.1

CIVIL CONTEMPT
Grand jury, § 10.3

CLEAR AND CONVINCING EVIDENCE
Burden of proof, § 3.1

CLOSED QUESTIONS
Evidence, § 3.3

CLOSING ARGUMENTS
Generally, §§ 15.2, 16.11
Defense closing, § 16.11
Facts, primacy of, § 16.11
Focus of argument, § 16.11
Prosecution closing, § 16.11
Rules, § 16.11
Stylistic considerations, § 16.11

COMPETENCE OF WITNESSES
Generally, §§ 3.3, 16.4

COMPLAINTS
Generally, §§ 1.1, 4.9
Drafting of complaint, § 4.8
Review of sufficiency of complaint, § 5.4
Role of complaint, § 4.1
Sufficiency of complaint, review of, § 5.4
Time constraints on filing, § 4.7

CONFERENCES
Discovery, §§ 13.6, 13.8

CONFLICTS OF INTEREST
Attorneys, § 5.2

CONSENT
Post-arrest investigations, tape recording, § 2.4

CONSISTENCY OF TESTIMONY
Credibility of witnesses, § 16.4

CONSTITUTIONAL LAW
Multi-count and multi-defendant indictments, § 11.3

CONTEMPT
Grand jury, § 10.3

COOPERATING DEFENDANTS
Guilty Pleas, this index

CORPORATIONS
Indictments, § 11.1

COUNSEL
Attorneys, this index

CREDIBILITY OF WITNESSES
Generally, § 16.4

CRIMINAL CONTEMPT
Grand jury, § 10.3

CRIMINAL HISTORY
Sentencing guidelines, § 7.2

CRIMINAL RECORD
Discovery, §§ 13.4, 13.5

CROSS-EXAMINATION
Generally, §§ 3.3, 16.5

DATE
Time and Date, this index

DECISION TO CHARGE
Generally, §§ 1.1, 4.0-4.11
Allocation of burdens of going forward and persuasion, § 4.2
Arrest warrants, §§ 4.10, 4.11
Assessment of case, § 4.6
Burden of proof, §§ 4.2, 4.9
Complaints
Generally, § 4.9
Drafting of complaint, § 4.8
Role of complaint, § 4.1
Time constraints on filing, § 4.7
Drafting of complaint, § 4.8
Filing complaint, time constraints on, § 4.7
Interviewing case agent, § 4.5
Jurisdiction, § 4.3
Learning facts of case, § 4.5
Prosecutorial policy, § 4.4
Qualitative burden of proof, §§ 4.2, 4.9
Quantitative burden of proof, §§ 4.2, 4.9
Search warrants, §§ 4.10, 4.11
Time constraints on filing complaint, § 4.7
Warrants, §§ 4.10, 4.11

DELIBERATIONS OF JURY
Generally, § 16.13

DIRECT EXAMINATION
Generally, §§ 3.3, 16.4

DISCOVERY
Generally, §§ 13.0-13.8
Brady material, § 13.3
Conferences, §§ 13.6, 13.8
Criminal record and statements of defendant, §§ 13.4, 13.5
Cross-examination, § 3.3
Defendant's right to notice, § 13.2
Defense witnesses, § 13.4
Documents, § 13.5
Examinations, reports of, § 13.5
Exculpatory evidence, right to, § 13.3
Final discovery letter, §§ 13.6, 13.8
Government, discovery by
Defense witnesses, § 13.4
Documents, tangible objects, reports of examinations and criminal records, § 13.5
Right to notice, § 13.2
Government witnesses, § 13.4
Informal defense discovery, § 13.7
Initial discovery request, § 13.6
Interviews of witnesses, §§ 13.7, 13.8
Materiality standard, exculpatory evidence, § 13.3
Notice, right to, § 13.2
Policy considerations, § 13.1

DISCOVERY—Cont'd
Pretrial motions, § 14.4
Reports of examinations, § 13.5
Rule 17(c) subpoenas, § 13.8
Subpoenas, § 13.7
Tangible objects, § 13.5
Timing of disclosure of exculpatory evidence, § 13.3

DOCUMENTS
Discovery, § 13.5

DRUG ENFORCEMENT ADMINISTRATION
Investigations, § 2.1

DUCES TECUM, SUBPOENAS
Grand jury, § 10.3

EVIDENCE AND WITNESSES
Generally, §§ 3.0-3.3, 16.4-16.6
Accrediting cross-examination, §§ 3.3, 16.5
Argument, § 3.3
Authentication witnesses, § 3.3
Believable narrative, structuring, § 16.4
Burden of Proof, this index
Charging defendant with crime, written allegations of fact, § 3.2
Closed questions, § 3.3
Competence of witnesses, §§ 3.3, 16.4
Consistency of testimony, credibility of witnesses, § 16.4
Control of testimony, § 3.3
Credibility of witnesses, § 16.4
Cross-examination, §§ 3.3, 16.5
Decision whether to cross-examine, § 16.5
Direct examination, §§ 3.3, 16.4
Discovery cross-examination, § 3.3
Discrediting cross-examination, §§ 3.3, 16.5
Eliciting testimony, § 16.4
Examination of witnesses, §§ 3.3, 14.9
Form of questions, §§ 3.3, 16.4
Good character of witnesses, credibility, § 16.4
Hearings, § 3.3
Leading questions, § 3.3
Methods of proof, § 3.2
Narrative questions, § 3.3
Objections to testimony, § 3.3
Occurrence witnesses, § 3.3
Open questions, § 3.3
Opinion witnesses, § 3.3
Persons who can be witnesses, § 3.3
Preparation for cross-examination, § 16.5
Pretrial Motions, this index
Proffers of evidence, § 3.2
Rebuttal evidence, §§ 3.3, 16.9
Re-cross examination, § 16.6
Redirect examination, § 16.6
Relevance of evidence, §§ 3.3, 16.4
Reliability of witnesses, §§ 3.3, 16.4
Scope of cross-examination, § 16.5
Strategic considerations, § 16.4
Structure of cross-examination, §§ 3.3, 16.5
Structure of direct examination, § 3.3
Suppression of evidence, motion for, § 14.4

EVIDENCE AND WITNESSES—Cont'd
Tangible evidence, §§ 15.5, 15.6
Testimony, § 3.2
Trial preparation, §§ 15.1, 15.3, 15.5, 15.6
Types of cross-examination, § 16.5
Types of witnesses, § 3.3
Written allegations of fact, § 3.2

EXAMINATION OF WITNESSES
Generally, §§ 3.3, 14.9

EXAMINATIONS
Discovery, § 13.5

EXCULPATORY EVIDENCE
Discovery, § 13.3

EXCUSE OR JUSTIFICATION
Trial theories, § 15.1

EXHIBITS
Trial preparation, §§ 15.5, 15.6

EXPERT WITNESSES
Generally, § 3.3

FILING
Complaint, time constraints on filing, § 4.7

FORFEITURE
Indictments, § 11.4

GOING FORWARD, BURDEN OF
Generally, §§ 3.1, 14.8

GOOD CHARACTER
Credibility of witnesses, § 16.4

GRAND JURY
Generally, § 10.3
Ad testificandum, subpoenas, § 10.3
Advising witnesses during testimony, § 10.3
Attorneys
Representation of putative defendants and witnesses, § 10.3
Witness, attorney as, § 10.3
Challenges to subpoenas, § 10.3
Civil contempt, § 10.3
Compelling attendance, § 10.3
Contempt, § 10.3
Criminal contempt, § 10.3
Duces tecum, subpoenas, § 10.3
Immunity for witness, § 10.3
Indictment, review of, § 11.1
Investigative powers, § 10.3
Presentation to grand jury, § 10.5
Raising legal challenges to subpoenas, § 10.3
Subpoenas, § 10.3
United States Attorney, role of, § 10.3

GUILTY PLEAS
Generally, §§ 1.2, 8.0-8.6, 9.0-9.5, 12.1-12.9
Additional features of plea agreements, § 12.4
Allocution, § 9.2
Alternatives under Rule 11, § 9.1

GUILTY PLEAS—Cont'd
Attorneys
Effective assistance, § 9.3
Plea process, counsel in, §§ 9.3, 12.6
Charge bargaining, § 12.1
Consideration of plea agreement by court, § 9.2
Cooperating defendants
Generally, §§ 8.0-8.6
Commencement of cooperation process, § 8.3
Cooperation process, § 8.3
Cooperation-plea agreement, §§ 8.2, 8.3, 8.5
Decision to cooperate, § 8.1
Preparation for proffer session, § 8.3
Proffer session, § 8.2
Waiver of indictment and information, § 8.4
Departures and non-guidelines sentences, § 12.3
Judicial leniency, § 12.3
Negotiation of plea, §§ 9.2, 12.6
Non-cooperating defendants, §§ 12.0-12.9
Plea agreements, §§ 9.2, 12.8
Pleas without agreements, § 12.5
Proffer session, cooperating defendants, § 8.2
Rule 11, § 9.1
Sentence bargaining, § 12.2
Waiver of indictment and information, cooperating defendants, § 8.4

HEARINGS
Evidence, § 3.3
Preliminary Hearings, this index
Pretrial motions, §§ 14.7-14.10
Pretrial release or detention, §§ 5.6, 5.11
Sentencing, §§ 17.3, 17.6

IDENTIFICATION
Investigations, § 2.3

IMMUNITY
Grand jury, witnesses, § 10.3

IN LIMINE MOTIONS
Generally, §§ 15.4, 15.6

INDICTMENTS
Generally, §§ 1.1, 11.0-11.9
Arraignment on indictment, §§ 11.5, 11.9
Arrest of defendant, § 11.5
Burden of proof at indictment stage, § 11.1
Constitutional limitations, multi-count and multi-defendant indictments, § 11.3
Corporations, § 11.1
Drafting of indictment, § 11.2
Factors involved in prosecutor's decision to seek indictment, § 11.1
Forfeiture, § 11.4
Grand jury review, § 11.1
Joinder of offenses, § 11.3
Multi-count and multi-defendant indictments

INDICTMENTS—Cont'd
Multi-count and multi-defendant indictments—Cont'd
Generally, § 11.3
Constitutional limitations, § 11.3
Joinder of offenses, § 11.3
Permissive joinder of defendants, § 11.3
Permissive joinder of offenses, § 11.3
Permissive joinder of defendants, § 11.3
Permissive joinder of offenses, § 11.3
Pretrial motions, defenses and objections based on defects, § 14.4
Proceedings on indictment, § 11.5
Selection of charges, § 11.1
Surrender of defendant, § 11.5
Time limits on return of indictment, § 11.6

INITIAL APPEARANCE
Generally, §§ 5.3, 5.910
Ancillary proceedings, § 5.9
Removal proceedings, § 5.9
Temporary detention, § 5.9
Time considerations, § 5.8

INSTRUCTIONS TO JURY
Generally, § 16.12
Preliminary instructions, § 16.2
Requests for instructions, §§ 15.4, 15.6, 16.10

INTERROGATIONS
Post-arrest investigations, § 2.4

INVESTIGATIONS
Generally, §§ 2.0-2.6, 10.1-10.5
Approaching and defending witnesses and targets, §§ 10.4, 10.5
Arrests, § 2.2
Booking procedure, § 2.3
Consent to tape recording, post-arrest investigations, § 2.4
Court authorization for police investigation, § 10.2
Court orders, § 10.5
Devising investigative strategy, § 10.5
Drug Enforcement Administration, investigations by, § 2.1
Follow-up investigation by law enforcement agents, § 10.1
Grand Jury, this index
Identification procedure, § 2.3
Interrogations, post-arrest investigations, § 2.4
Post-arrest investigations, § 2.4
Preliminary investigative steps, § 10.5
Presentation of case to United States attorney's Office, § 2.6
Presentence investigation, § 17.1
Report of investigation, § 2.5
Representation of witnesses and targets, §§ 10.4, 10.5
Review of evidence by government, § 10.5
Searches, § 2.2

JOINDER OF OFFENSES
Indictments, § 11.3

JOINT DEFENSE AGREEMENTS
Attorneys, conflicts of interest, § 5.2

JOINT REPRESENTATION
Attorneys, conflicts of interest, § 5.2

JUDGMENT OF ACQUITTAL
Motions, § 16.7

JURISDICTION
Decision to charge, § 4.3

JURY AND JURY TRIAL
Deliberations of jury, § 16.13
Grand Jury, this index
Instructions to Jury, this index
Selection of jury, § 16.1
Voir dire, §§ 15.4, 15.6, 16.1

JUSTIFICATION OR EXCUSE
Trial theories, § 15.1

LAWYERS
Attorneys, this index

LEADING QUESTIONS
Generally, § 3.3

MARSHALLING OF EVIDENCE
Trial preparation, §§ 15.3, 15.6

MATERIALITY
Exculpatory evidence, discovery, § 13.3

MULTIPLE COUNTS
Indictments, this index
Sentencing guidelines, special rules, § 7.2

NARCOTICS
Drug Enforcement Administration, investigations, § 2.1

NARRATIVE QUESTIONS
Generally, § 3.3

NOTICE
Discovery, § 13.2

OBJECTIONS
Evidence, § 3.3

OCCURRENCE WITNESSES
Generally, § 3.3

OPEN QUESTIONS
Generally, § 3.3

OPENING STATEMENTS
Generally, § 16.3

OPINION WITNESSES
Generally, § 3.3

PERSUASION, BURDEN OF
Generally, §§ 3.1, 14.8

POST-ARREST INVESTIGATIONS
Generally, § 2.4

PRELIMINARY HEARINGS
Generally, §§ 6.0-6.3
Burden of proof, § 6.1
Defense counsel, strategic considerations, § 6.2
Prosecutor, strategic considerations, § 6.2
Strategic considerations, § 6.2

PRELIMINARY INSTRUCTIONS TO JURY
Generally, § 16.2

PREPONDERANCE OF EVIDENCE
Burden of proof, § 3.1

PRESENTENCE INVESTIGATION
Generally, § 17.1

PRESENTENCE MEMORANDUM
Generally, § 17.3

PRESENTENCE REPORT
Generally, §§ 17.1-17.3

PRETRIAL MOTIONS
Generally, §§ 14.1-14.13
Appeal from adverse determination, § 14.11
Burden of proof, § 14.8
Commencement of hearing, § 14.8
Date for trial, setting of, § 14.12
Discovery, motion for, § 14.4
Drafting of motion, § 14.3
Evidence
    Motion for suppression, § 14.4
    Written allegations of fact, § 3.2
Examination of witnesses, § 14.9
Final argument, § 14.10
Formal motion practice, § 14.3
Going forward, burden of, § 14.8
Grounds for motions, § 14.4
Hearings, §§ 14.7-14.10
Indictment, defenses and objections based on defects in, § 14.4
Institution of prosecution, defenses and objections based on, § 14.4
Persuasion, burden of, § 14.8
Qualitative burden of proof, § 14.8
Quantitative burden of proof, § 14.8
Response by government, § 14.6
Setting trial date, § 14.12
Statutory design, § 14.2
Strategic considerations, § 14.5
Suppression of evidence, motion for, § 14.4
Trial date, setting of, § 14.12
Variations on motion practice, § 14.3

PRETRIAL PROCEEDINGS
Generally, § 1.1
Detention. Pretrial Release or Detention, this index
Motions. Pretrial Motions, this index
Release. Pretrial Release or Detention, this index

PRETRIAL RELEASE OR DETENTION
Generally, §§ 5.5-5.7
Burden of proof, § 5.7
Hearing on pretrial release, § 5.6
Hearings, § 5.11
Litigation of issue, § 5.11
Persons who may be detained, § 5.7
Preventive detention proceedings, § 5.7
Qualitative burden of proof, § 5.7
Quantitative burden of proof, § 5.7
Review of detention decisions, §§ 5.7, 5.11
Standards for release, § 5.6

PREVENTIVE DETENTION
Pretrial Release or Detention, this index

PROBABLE CAUSE
Burden of proof, § 3.1

PROFFERS
Evidence, § 3.2
Guilty pleas, cooperating defendants, § 8.2

PURE REASONABLE DOUBT
Trial theories, § 15.1

QUALITATIVE PROOF
Burden of proof, §§ 3.1, 4.2, 4.9, 5.7, 14.8

QUANTITATIVE PROOF
Burden of proof, §§ 3.1, 4.2, 4.9, 5.7, 14.8

REASONABLE DOUBT
Burden of proof, § 3.1

REBUTTAL EVIDENCE
Generally, §§ 3.3, 16.9

RE-CROSS EXAMINATION
Generally, § 16.6

REDIRECT EXAMINATION
Generally, § 16.6

RELEVANCE OF EVIDENCE
Generally, §§ 3.3, 16.4

RELIABILITY
Witnesses, §§ 3.3, 16.4

REMOVAL PROCEEDINGS
Initial appearance, § 5.9

REPORTS
Discovery, examinations, § 13.5
Investigations, § 2.5
Presentence reports, §§ 17.1-17.3

REQUESTS FOR INSTRUCTIONS TO JURY
Generally, §§ 15.4, 15.6, 16.10

REVIEW
Appeal and Review, this index

RULE 11
Guilty pleas, § 9.1

RULE 17(C)
Discovery, subpoenas, § 13.8

SEARCH AND SEIZURE
Investigations, § 2.2
Warrants, §§ 4.10, 4.11

SELECTION OF JURY
Generally, § 16.1

SENTENCING
Generally, §§ 1.1, 17.0-17.8
Burden of proof at hearing, § 17.3
Challenges to presentence report, § 17.2
Decision, § 17.4
Guidelines. Sentencing Guidelines, this index
Guilty pleas, § 12.2
Hearings, §§ 17.3, 17.6
Litigation of disputed facts in presentence report, § 17.3
Negotiation of challenges to presentence report, § 17.2
Policy considerations, § 17.5
Presentence investigation, § 17.1
Presentence memorandum, § 17.3
Presentence report, §§ 17.1-17.3
Strategic considerations, § 17.5

SENTENCING GUIDELINES
Generally, §§ 7.0-7.3
Adjusted offense level, calculation of, § 7.2
Adjustments, application of, § 7.2
Base level offense, § 7.2
Computation of sentence, § 7.2
Criminal history of defendant, determination of, § 7.2
Departures from guidelines, § 7.2
Multiple counts, special rules for convictions on, § 7.2
Non-guideline sentences, § 7.2
Range, calculation of, § 7.2
Relevant conduct, § 7.2
Specific offense characteristics, § 7.2
Substantive law of sentencing, § 7.1

SPECIFIC OFFENSE CHARACTERISTICS
Sentencing guidelines, § 7.2

STAGES OF FEDERAL CRIMINAL PROCESS
Generally, § 1.1

STATEMENTS OF DEFENDANT
Discovery, §§ 13.4, 13.5

STIPULATIONS
Trial preparation, § 15.6

SUBPOENAS
Discovery, § 13.7
Grand jury, § 10.3

SUPPRESSION OF EVIDENCE
Pretrial motions, § 14.4

SURRENDER OF DEFENDANT
Indictments, § 11.5

TANGIBLE EVIDENCE
Trial preparation, §§ 15.5, 15.6

TANGIBLE OBJECTS
Discovery, § 13.5

TEMPORARY DETENTION
Initial appearance, § 5.9

TIME AND DATE
Complaint, filing of, § 4.7
Discovery, exculpatory evidence, § 13.3
Indictment, return of, § 11.6
Initial appearance, § 5.8
Pretrial motions, setting of date for trial,
§ 14.12

TRIAL
Generally, §§ 1.1, 16.0-16.15
Acquittal, motion for judgment of, § 16.7
Closing Arguments, this index
Defense case, § 16.8
Deliberations of jury, § 16.13
Evidence, this index
Instructions to Jury, this index
Judgment of acquittal, motion for, § 16.7
Motion for judgment of acquittal, § 16.7
Opening statements, § 16.3
Preparation for trial. Trial Preparation,
this index
Rebuttal case, § 16.9
Selection of jury, § 16.1
Strategic considerations
Opening statements, § 16.3
Selection of jury, § 16.1
Verdicts, §§ 16.14, 16.15
Voir dire, selection of jury, § 16.1

TRIAL PREPARATION
Generally, §§ 15.0-15.6
Articulation of trial theory, § 15.2
Burden of proof at trial, § 15.1
Closing argument, formulation of, § 15.2
Conflicting evidence, trial theories, § 15.1
Construction of trial theory, § 15.1
Evidence, §§ 15.1, 15.3, 15.5, 15.6
Excuse or justification, trial theories, § 15.1
Exhibits, §§ 15.5, 15.6
In limine motions, §§ 15.4, 15.6
Instructions to jury, requests for, §§ 15.4,
15.6
Justification or excuse, trial theories, § 15.1
Marshalling of evidence, §§ 15.3, 15.6
Pure reasonable doubt, trial theories, § 15.1
Stipulations, § 15.6
Tangible evidence, §§ 15.5, 15.6
Theory of trial, §§ 15.1-15.3, 15.6
Voir dire questions, proposal of, §§ 15.4,
15.6
Witnesses, § 15.5

UNITED STATES ATTORNEY
Grand jury, § 10.3

VERDICTS
Generally, §§ 16.14, 16.15

VOIR DIRE
Selection of jury, § 16.1

WAIVER
Guilty pleas, waiver of indictment and information, § 8.4

WARRANTS
Decision to charge, §§ 4.10, 4.11

WITNESSES
Discovery, § 13.4

†